A Historical and Realistic Analysis:
New Research on Stalin's Socialism Thought

edited by Gu Hailiang

CANUT INTERNATIONAL PUBLISHERS

Istanbul - Berlin - London - Santiago

A Historical and Realistic Analysis:
New Research on Stalin's Socialism Thought

Edited by Gu Hailiang

The English version is published in cooperation with China Renmin University Press

Chinese Title: 斯大林社会主义思想研究, ISBN: 9787300089621

Copyright © CRUP China, 2007

Canut International Publishers

Canut Intl. Turkey, Teraziler Cad. No.29. Sancaktepe, Istanbul, Turkey

Canut Intl. Germany, Heerstr. 266, D-47053, Duisburg, Germany

Canut Intl. United Kingdom, 12a Guernsay Road, London E11 4BJ, England

Copyright © Canut International Publishers, 2017

ISBN: 978-605-4923-38-0

www.canutbooks.com

About the Editor

Gu Hailiang was born in Shanghai in 1951. He is a full professor with a Master's Degree in Economics from the Chinese Academy of Social Sciences. From 1984 to 1996, he taught Marxist Theory in Marxism-Leninism Institute at the China Renmin University and became its director. Prof. Gu was promoted to associate professor in June 1991, and a full professor in 1994, and became doctorate supervisor in 1995. Since 1996, he served in the State Department and the Department of Education. In December 2001, he became the vice president of Wuhan University. From 2008 to 2010, he served as the president of Wuhan University. Since 2010 he is a member of Leading Group of Ministry of Education (vice-ministerial rank) and President of National Academy of Education Administration.

Contents

Foreword

Chapter I
THE COURSE OF STALIN'S LIFE AND SOCIALISM THOUGHT 7

I. Stalin's revolutionary career and theoretical explorations
before the October Revolution   8

II. Stalin's theory and practice of socialist revolution and construction
from 1917 to 1924   17

III. Stalin's theory and practice of socialist construction
from 1924 to 1936   22

IV. Stalin's theory and practice of socialist construction after 1936   30

Chapter II
STALIN'S PHILOSOPHICAL THOUGHT   37

I. Stalin's philosophical thought at the early stage   38

II. The critique of the Deborin school   41

III. The philosophical thought in Dialectical and Historical Materialism   47

IV. Stalin's philosophical thought in his later years   61

Chapter III
STALIN'S OUTLOOK OF SOCIALISM   73

I. Stalin's discussions on the future of socialism   73

II. Stalin's discussions on the issue of transition of capitalism into socialism   83

III. Stalin's discussions on the basic features of socialism   93

IV. Stalin's discussions on the issue of socialist construction   104

Chapter IV
STALIN'S MODEL AND SYSTEM OF SOCIALIST ECONOMY 115

I. The historical conditions and theoretical background
of the emergence of Stalin's economic model 115

II. The impacts of the theory and practice of Soviet socialist economy 122

III. The development stages of Stalin's economic model and
economic system 133

IV. The basic features of Stalin's economic model and economic system 135

V. The evaluation of Stalin's economic model 147

Chapter V
STALIN'S THEORY AND PRACTICE ON
SOCIALIST PLANNING AND MARKET 159

I. Stalin's theory on socialist planning 159

II. Stalin's theory on market 166

III. Stalin's treatment of the relationship between planning and market 173

Chapter VI
STALIN'S THEORY AND PRACTICE ON
SOCIALIST ECONOMIC DEVELOPMENT 183

I. Stalin's thought and practice on socialist industrialization 183

II. Stalin's thought on agricultural collectivization and
agricultural development 197

III. Continuously raising and continuously improving socialist
production on the basis of high degree of technology 210

Chapter VII
STALIN'S THEORY AND PRACTICE
ON SOCIALIST POLITICAL SYSTEM   223

I. The initial establishment of Soviet socialist political system and
Lenin's reform in his later years   224

II. The formation of the highly centralized Soviet political system
in the Stalin period and its features   235

III. The reasons for the formation of the highly centralized political
system in the Stalin period   254

IV. Stalin's contributions and defects in the theory of socialist political system 263

V. Rational rethinking on Stalin's political system   279

Chapter VIII
STALIN'S THEORY ON CLASS AND CLASS STRUGGLE
IN THE SOCIALIST PERIOD   289

I. The formation and development of Stalin's theory of class struggle 289

II. Stalin's major contributions to the theory of class struggle
and its errors   304

III. The practice of Stalin's theory of class struggle and
its serious consequences   318

Chapter IX
STALIN'S THEORY ON BUILDING OF A PROLETARIAN PARTY 327

I. Stalin's struggle to defend Lenin's theory of building
a ruling proletarian party   328

II. Stalin's new contributions to the theory of building a ruling party 334

III. The party should be good at selecting and training its cadres 341

IV. The party must have close ties with the masses   345

V. The summary of Stalin's experiences in building
a ruling party and its lessons   349

Chapter X
STALIN'S THOUGHTS ON SOCIALIST CULTURAL
EDUCATION AND IDEOLOGICAL WORK   359

I. Stalin's thought on the construction of socialist culture   359
II. Stalin's thought on the cause of developing socialist education   372
III. Stalin's thought on socialist ideological work   376
IV. Stalin's lessons in the ideological work   395

Chapter XI
STALIN'S THOUGHTS ON
WORLD ECONOMIC AND POLITICAL RELATIONS   403

I. "Center" and "periphery" in world economic and political relations 404
II. Capitalism and socialism in world economic and political relations 409

Chapter XII
STALIN'S THEORY AND PRACTICE ON
THE INTERNATIONAL COMMUNIST MOVEMENT   423

I. Erroneous judgment of the revolutionary situation and the
implementation of the "left"-leaning road of rushing ahead   424
II. The implementation of a high level of centralization and the
suppression the independent autonomy and creativity of various
countries' parties   431
III. Erroneous understanding of the united front policy and
implementation of the "left"-leaning closeddoorism and sectarianism 443

Chapter XIII
FOREIGN SCHOLARS STUDIES OF STALIN'S THOUGHTS   451

I. On "Stalinism"   452
II. The relationship of "Stalinism" with Marxism and with Leninism   456
III. On "Stalin Model"   463
IV. On "Second Revolution"   468
V. Brief commentary   473

Appendix
CHINESE ACADEMIC CIRCLE'S STUDIES OF
STALIN'S THOUGHT 477

I. Study on Stalin's thoughts from the late 70s to the late 80s 477

II. Studies on Stalin's thoughts from the late 80s to the late 90s 495

III. The new progress in the studies of Stalin's thought in the new century 505

Postscript 517

Foreword

New Research on Stalin's Socialism Thought is the final product of the national social science funds project - Study of the Theory and Practice of Stalin Socialism Construction. (Approval No. 96AKS 006) When the study was approved in 1996, I was the director of the Center of Marxism-Leninism Development History Study at the China Renmin University; and the key members in this study were the researchers of the study center back then, which is now known as the Institute of Marxism Studies attached to China Renmin University.

Theoretically or practically, it is very important to objectively study and evaluate Stalin's socialism thought. The theoretical and practical signifi-cance is not only for a scientific conclusion on the experience and lessons of construction of socialism in the 20th century, or an objective appraisal of the historical statue of socialism in the 20th century; it also extends to the development of today's socialism development in the world and the unders-tanding of historical destiny of socialism in the 21st century.

Since the late 1980s and early 1990s, almost all the theoretical opinions on the experience and lessons of international socialist movements invol-ved Stalin's merits and faults. They all referred about the theory and prac-tice of the construction of Stalin's socialism, especially the problems of the "Stalin Model", which was established and promoted mainly by Stalin. In his book *Stalin: Man of History* published in 1979, the British scholar Ian Grey had pointed out that when Westerners talked about Stalin, they "so loathe, curse him unceasingly and regard him as a tyrant with evil in-tentions and as 'the guiltiest sinner ever in history.'"[1] Like an icon standing in front of an oil lamp, with face blurred by the surrounding smokes, his image has paled into insignificance and became hard to identify. Ten years later, with the drastic changes in Eastern Europe and the disintegration of

1

---

1   Grey: Stalin: Man of History, p.1, Beijing, Xinhua Publishing House, 1981.

the Soviet Union in late 1980s and early 1990s, the phenomenon described by Grey made a great clamor and spread to a greater extent. Of course, the actual conditions were not worse than Grey's description years before: "there are plenty of books and studies on Stalin, some exaggerating, some over-academic. There are also many works that are out of evil and hatred, focusing on his dark side. They set barriers one after the other in the way of people getting to know this person and his importance by deliberately defaming and distorting him. On the contrary, there are very few studies on the achievements he had made". After entering the new century, opinions against Stalinism have become a fixed way of thinking, getting popular in the western academic world and also partly affecting the academic circles in China. Of course, in the overseas academic world, including some scholars from both the western and the ex-Soviet Union countries, studies on Stalin's socialism are pretty extensive. Among those studies, many of them touched upon very complicated theories and came up with some very valuable, objective theories and academic opinions.

Almost at the same time when the ideological trend of anti-Stalinism was popular, the Chinese Communist Party started a new exploration on developing socialism with Chinese characteristics, mainly by means of reform and opening-up. Deng Xiaoping Theory, formed under socialism in the process of reform and opening up that has been unprecedented in history, together with the Party's basic line, program and experience at the primary stage of socialism, have a bearing on re-examining China's experience and lessons on the way of developing socialism. Also to a great extent, directly or indirectly, they have a connection with the new understanding of the theory and practice on Stalin's socialism thought, especially the "Stalin Model" and how to make a breakthrough of its disadvantages. Just as how we deeply felt when studying on this topic, Stalin has a very important position in the historical development of the world socialist movement and Marxism, not only as a great proletarian revolutionary and a devout Marxist, but also as a main leader of both the party and the nation of Soviet Union for 30 years. If socialism movements are the most influential, yet the most controversial historical event in 20th century, Stalin is the most influential yet the most controversial person of 20th century. The scholars from different countries in the world, out of different motivations and purposes, study Stalin from different aspects and draw very different theoretical conclusions. However, in any case, the theory and practice on Stalin's socialism thought is still one of the research subjects that attract most attention.

During the last ten years, Chinese academics have had some new researches on Stalin socialism thought. However, these researches are still scattering, obviously not systematic. Especially on some important theories, the studies are not deep-going enough, for example, the relations between theory and practice of Stalin's socialism thought, Marx & Engels' socialism thought and Lenin socialism thought, the formation of economic and political system under the "Stalin Model", their nature and relations, the relations between the influence of the "Stalin Model" and the reform of national economic and political systems. With the new release of some historical data about Stalin, there is the trend that these studies will go further. What should be pointed out is that due to the different political backgrounds and positions of the foreign researchers, some of the studies are very limited. Some of the so-called "academic researches" have become the "grounds" of acting against scientific socialism and Marxism. All of these place the need for us to seriously and carefully deal with. Particularly, we need to have scientific researches and evaluations on Stalin's socialism thought.

New Research on Stalin's Socialism Thought has made a special effort to make an objective and practical analysis on the formation, development, basic characteristics and historical status of Stalin's socialism thought by earnestly studying on the previous and newly released data about Stalin while striving to maintain the basic position, opinions and methods of Marxism. It also contains a comprehensive and systematic discussion on the construction and system evolution of economy, politics and culture that have formed this model, and made a historical materialistic appraisal on this model's affection on the after-war development of theory and practice in socialist countries and the results of those countries' reform. At the same time, this book has also scientifically expounded the theoretical basis of the "Stalin Model" and its relations with Marxism and Leninism; it has scientifically commented on the main opinions and basic tendencies on Stalin-related studies done by foreign researchers in recent years; combined with the reality of China's socialism reform and modernization development, it has made a comparative study on the "Stalin Model" and the way of developing socialism with Chinese characteristics.

As for the main contents and opinions, this book has formed a relatively reasonable structure and frame of Stalin's socialism thought studies.

Firstly, in the beginning chapter of this book, the development of Stalin's thought on socialism was divided into four stages according to great historical events and the evolution of Stalin's socialism thought. The first stage is the 20 years before the October Revolution, during which Stalin as a professional revolutionary, had researched on and thought about the theories of Russian proletarian revolution and Marxism. Although at this stage, the socialism thought had not been really formed, his basic values on Marxist that were formed in this stage had an important influence on the formation and development of his socialism thought later. The second stage is from the victory of the October Revolution to the year of 1924 when Lenin died and Stalin became the leader of both the party and the nation of Soviet Union, which is the period of tentative exploration of Stalin's socialism thought. The third stage is from 1924 to 1936 when Stalin announced that he had completed the socialist transformation and the Soviet Union had entered into the era of socialist society. This is the stage that Stalin's socialism thought wasformed. The fourth stage is from 1936 to 1953 when Stalin died, which is also the period when the Soviet Union went through the Second World War and the post-war reconstruction. This is the developing stage of Stalin's socialism thought. The latter two stages are the main periods for the evolution of Stalin's socialism thought, which are also the focal point of the study in this book.

Secondly, on the basis of generally summarizing Stalin's socialism thought, in the second and third chapters, this book has made a special effort to study on the philosophy grounds of Stalin's socialism thought and his general idea of socialism. Stalin's philosophic thinking is an important part of Stalin's socialism thought and the grounds of its world view and methodology. Understanding of Stalin's philosophic thinking and his general idea of socialism should be the logical starting point of the study on Stalin's socialism thought.

Furthermore, in this book, the study of Stalin's socialism thought has mainly focused on his though of the economic, political and cultural development. With an emphasis on the mode and system of socialist economy, plan and market, economic growth and development, political system, class and class struggle, construction of the party, development of nations, cultural education and ideology, this book has drafted the basic contents and the main features of Stalin's socialism thought, which are also the contents from Chapter 4 to Chapter 11, the main part of this book.

Lastly, this book has also spent some effortsabout Stalin's theories on the relations between the world economy and politics, international communist movements and practice, which are the contents of Chapter 12 and 13 in this book.

It has to be pointed out that Stalin's socialist thought is part of the study of Stalin's thought, even the most important part, but it does not cover all. As a result, other Stalin's important thoughts are not included in the final product of this study.

For the further academic research, the last two appendixes are the comments on the studies on Stalin's thought (mainly his socialism thought) done by scholars both home and abroad.

The study conducted in this book is still at the primary stage. In fact, the study on Stalin's socialism thought has been a very important subject in the long-term studies of the history of Marxism theories and socialism. In the period between late 1980s and early 1990s, this subject was once a very hot topic when people were thinking about the huge setbacks suffered in the process of socialist movements around the world. However, the various studies on this major subject, most of which severely criticized, even ruthlessly condemned Stalin and his theory and practice on socialism, were biased for the most part. In recent years, the popularity of studying on this subject seems to have decreased. *New Research on Stalin's Socialism Thought* made some new efforts on the study of this subject and therefore came to some new theoretical conclusions, which could have some academic values.

Firstly, this book talks about Stalin's thoughts on the development of socialist economy, politics and culture and tries to have a comprehensive discussion on the relations between these thoughts which has the academic value on appraising Stalin's socialism thought from various aspects.

Secondly, using a huge amount of references of studies on Stalin's socialist thought over the last decade, even those with obvious hostility, in an effort to make scientific evaluation on Stalin, who is a great Marxist, and with the expectation of bringing objective academic effect, this book has absorbed their achievements and at the same time pointed out their shortage in order to make an objective evaluation on Stalin, a great Marxist.

Thirdly, this book hopes to recall attention to this major study subject. Especially after a decade's new development of socialist movements around the world and the new exploration of socialist economic and political revolution, people have had a more objective understanding on Stalin and the influence of his socialism thought. More and more depressed and resentful feelings now have been replaced by calm thinking and evaluation, which makes people having a more scientific understanding on Stalin's achievements and mistakes in Soviet Union's practice of socialism construction and his success and failure in the development of the socialism thought and therefore draw a conclusion that is more closer to the essence.

Gu Hailiang

2009, Beijing

5

Chapter I

The Course of Stalin's Life and Socialism Thought

Stalin's real name was Dzhugashvili. His full name was Iosif Vissarionovich Dzhugashvili, which was later changed into Joseph Vissarionovich Stalin. Stalin was a great proletarian revolutionary and a firm Marxist. He was the main leader of both the party and the nation of Soviet Union for as long as 30 years, which made him holding a very important position in the historical development of socialist movements and Marxism in the world. Scholars from different countries, out of different motives and purposes, studied on Stalin from different aspects and reached various theoretical conclusions, among which, Stalin's theories and practice of socialism are the ones that have received most attention.

To have a correct and scientific evaluation on Stalin's socialist thought, we firstly have to deeply understand the features and the historical background of Stalin's theories and practice on socialism and discuss the course and development of his thought by understanding his life and experience. Based on major historical events and the development of Stalin's socialist thought, we can divide the course of his thought into four stages. The data of Stalin's life and career stated in this chapter mainly come from the chronologies in every volume of the *Collected Works of Stalin* and the related content from *Stalin Chronology* (Edited by Liu Yan, etc, Beijing, People's Publishing House, 2003).

The first stage is the 20 years before the October Revolution, Stalin as a professional revolutionary, had researched and put thoughts on the theories of both Russian proletarian revolution and Marxism. Although in this stage, his socialist thought had not been formed in a real sense, the basic values on Marxism he achieved at this stage had important influence on the form and development of his socialist thought later.

The second stage is from the victory of October Revolution to 1924 when Lenin died and Stalin became both the party and state leader of the Soviet Union, during which Stalin made a tentative exploration of his socialist thought.

The third stage is from 1924 to 1936 when Stalin claimed that the completion of socialism transformation and the Soviet Union had become a socialist country. This was the period when Stalin's socialist thought was formed.

The fourth stage was from 1936 to 1953 when Stalin died, during which Soviet Union underwent the Second World War and the post-war reconstruction. This was the period when Stalin's socialist thought developed.

I. Stalin's revolutionary career and theoretical explorations before the October Revolution

On 9TH December, 1879, Russian calendar (21st December on the Gregorian calendar), Stalin was born in Gori, a town of Tiflis Province, Georgia. He was born poor. His father is a cobbler and his mother is the daughter of a surf. Stalin started his education in Gori Orthodox Primary School in 1888 and graduated cum laude in June, 1894. In September, he
went to the Georgian Orthodox Seminary in Tilflis, which was the capital of Georgia and also the place where the Governor appointed by the Tsar stayed. It already had a population of over 150,000 at that time. In the senior years in the seminary, Stalin started to read the works of Marx and Engels such as *Communist Manifesto* and *Capital*. He had also started to read the early works of Lenin.

Early 1898, Stalin had started his leadership in the Tilflis railway workers' Marxist group. In August of the year, Stalin joined the Mesame Dasi (the third group), the first social democratic party in Georgia. At that time, Georgia also had Pirveli Dasi (the first group), which was an organization of the nobility with radical ideas and Meori Dasi (the second group), another organization of intellectuals who studied the theories of Western Europe's Utopian Socialism society. In 1899, Stalin was expelled from the seminary for practicing Marxist propaganda. Since then, he started his career as a revolutionary.

In 1901, Stalin co-founded the newspaper Brdzola (or the Struggle)secretly published by Tilflis' social democratic party to promote the ideas from Iskra (or the Spark), a newspaper founded and edited by Lenin. In the first issue of Brdzola, the unsigned article From the Editors clearly stated that Brdzola is to spread the policies of the Central Committee of Russian Social-Democratic Labor Party (RSDLP). It pointed out that "the primary duty of the newspaper is to be as close to the masses of the workers as possible, to be able constantly to influence them and serve as their conscious and guiding centre". It also clearly put forward that the newspaper has to "explain theoretically the role the working class plays in the struggle, and throw the light of scientific socialism upon every phenomenon the workers encounter". This article was later put in Stalin's *Collected Works* as the opening article. In the same year, in the No.2 and No.3 combined issues of Brdzola, Stalin published the article The Russian Social-Democratic Party and Its Immediate Tasks, elaborating on the topic that "human thought was obliged to undergo considerable trial, suffering and change before it reached scientifically elaborated and substantiated socialism". Most importantly, the article discussed issues like that scientific socialism must combine with unpromoted workers movements, that working class has to take the leadership in the democratic liberation movements and that the primary task for revolutionary Social-Democrats is to establish an independent proletarian party.

In November 1901, Stalin went to Batumi for revolutionary activities. Batumi at that time was an important industrial city along the coast of the Black Sea. In 1902, Stalin was arrested for leading the workers movements in the factories in Batumi. In 1903, Stalin was elected in absence as the member of Caucasus United Committee of RSDLP. Also in this year, the Russian Social-Democratic Party split into two groups: Bolsheviks and Mensheviks. Stalin stood on the side of Bolsheviks. In early 1904, Stalin escaped from exile and returned to Tilflis for revolution. In September of the same year, he published the unsigned article "The Social-Democratic View on National Question" in the No.7 issue of *Proletariatis Brdzola* (or The Proletarian Struggle), which was the official newspaper of the Caucasus United Committee of Russian Social-Democratic Party. It was also Stalin's first article on national issues. The article pointed out that "if the proletariat is to achieve victory, all the workers, irrespective of nationality, must be united. Clearly, the demolition of national barriers and close unity between the Russian, Georgian, Armenian, Polish, Jewish and other proletarians is a necessary condition for the victory of the proletariat of all Russia". Based on the basic idea that everything depends on time and place, Stalin pointed out that according to their own views, every class has a different understanding of nation and that national issues serve different class interests in different periods of time. Since then, Stalin went back to Batumi, where he engaged in the Russian Revolution in 1905 and led the workers movements there.

In May 1905, in the pamphlet Briefly About Disagreements in the Party, Stalin indicated that "working-class movements and socialism must be combined, practice and theory must be integrated so that the spontaneous working-class movements will be given the nature of social democracy… therefore, the social democracy that has been combined with working-class movements will not be just mere phrases, but should become the huge power of workers". He emphasized that "our duty is to imbue the consciousness of socialism with this movement and separate advanced detachments of the proletariat to unite them in one party".These theories and propositions of Stalin were greatly influenced by Lenin. In August 1905, in the No.11 *Proletariatis Brdzola*, Stalin published the article A Reply to Social-Democrat, refuting the view that the consciousness of socialism is not introduced to the proletarians but something that the proletarians have by themselves. Stalin thought that it is a few Social-Democratic intellectuals that may establish the consciousness of socialism, and it is the whole Social-Democratic Party that imbued the consciousness into the working-class movements, making the proletarian spontaneous movements more conscious. He emphasized that "if the consciousness of socialism cannot spread among the proletarians, what is the point of it. It is just an empty phrase."[1] Lenin highly complemented on Stalin's article, saying that "in A Reply to Social-Democrat, we can see his wonderful description of the famous question 'imbuing consciousness from outside."[2]

In December 1905, on behalf of Caucasus United Committee of Russian Social-Democratic Party, Stalin attended the RSDLP First Congress held by Bolsheviks. In this congress, he was elected to the Political Commission that was in charge of reviewing the congress' resolution and made the work report of the Caucasus Bolsheviks organization. Also on this congress, Stalin met Lenin for the first time. From 1906 to 1917 before the October Revolution broke out, Stalin was standing in front of the Russian proletarian revolution as one of the major leaders. During this period, Stalin was also working hard on theories of Russian Marxism, making great efforts on combining Marxism and the concrete reality of Russia. Following are the revolution practice he was doing and the theories he was focusing on during that period:

First is the revolutionary road of Russian proletarian revolution. From 1905 to 1907 when the Russian revolution was at its hard times, the situation faced by the Russian Bolsheviks was very serious. Domestically, Stolypin had started his reactionary rule, with many revolutionaries being suppressed and imprisoned; the Czar sharpened the class differentiation through the "land reform" and stepped up the compromise and cooperation policy with the capital class in urban areas. Internationally, in addition to more and more relying on foreign countries and focusing on carving up interests, the opportunists in the labor movements had an increasingly great

---

1   Collected Works of Stalin, 1st Chinese edition, Volume 1, p.145
2   Collected Works of Lenin, second Chinese version, volume 11, p. 389, Beijing, People's Publishing House, 1987

impact on Russian working-class parties. Due to the rapid shrinking and differentiation of revolutionaries caused by the failure of the revolution, there came the "liquidators or liquidationists", who advocated for giving up the party's underground activities and setting up lawful reformist party, and the "recallists", who demanded to recall the RSDLP representatives from the state Duma and stop all revolutionary activities in lawful institutions.

In June 1907, the Czar's government dismissed the second Duma and arrested the Social-Democrats in it, which was regarded as an important signal of the Czar targeting at proletarian revolutionaries. Under this situation, Stalin was dispatched to work in Baku. From June to July in 1907, he published The London Congress of the Russian Social-Democratic Labor Party (A Delegate Note) in the first and second issue of *Bakinsky Proletary*, explaining Bolsheviks' ideological line and strategies on Russian proletarian revolution. In terms of the ideological line, he thought that "proletarians, as the only leader of our revolution, are not only concerned with Russian revolutions, but also the power that leads the Russian revolutionaries to fight against the Czar's dictatorship; that only the proletarians can unite the revolutionaries around the country and carry the revolution through to the end; that the RSDLP's task is to foster the proletarians to take the leading role of the revolution in every possible way." In terms of tactics, he pointed out that "the tactics of Bolsheviks are the tactics of proletarians in big industry, the tactics of those areas where the class contradictions and class struggle are especially clear and acute". Therefore, "Bolshevism is the real tactics of proletarians."[3] Stalin's ideas showed that he is a firm advocator of Lenin's thought and lines.

From January to February 1908, Stalin led many strikes of Baku workers. In July the same year, in No. 5 supplement of *Bakinsky Proletary*, Stalin published The Conference and the Workers, in which he looked back on the history of workers participating the conference and pointed out that under the new circumstances, the tactics and tasks of trade unions and RSDLP ranks are: unite proletarian class by fully participating in the strikes held by companies, "strengthen these commissions, imbue them with the spirit of socialism and unite them according to the respective firms. To achieve this, our works and oil field Party units must systematically come out at the head of these commissions and, in their turn, unite on an inter-district basis through their representatives also according to the respective firms. By carrying out these immediate tasks, and thereby strengthening the unions and our organization, we shall be able to weld into one the masses of the oil industry workers numbering many thousands for the forthcoming battle against oil capital."[4]

3   Colleted Works of Stalin, 1st Chinese version, volume 2, p. 62, 64, Beijing, People's Publishing House, 1953.
4   Ibid., p.140, Retrieved from Marxists Internet Archive.

In March 1912, Stalin wrote For the Party, which, together with Lenin's The Election Platform of the RSDLP, was nationwide published in the form of leaflet. Ordzhonikidze wrote to Lenin from Kiev, saying that the two leaflets "both have good effect and everyone welcomes them". In early October, Stalin wrote Mandate of the St. Petersburg Workers to Their Labor Deputy, in which he analyzed the situation and pointed out that Russian was on the eve of mass movement that is about to come. This movement could be more deep-going than the one in 1905 as working class being the leader and pioneer and peasants being the allies. This mandate also attracted much attention from Lenin. On 18 October, Stalin wrote the editorial about the result of The Elections for the Worker Curia in Petersburg for *Pravda* No.146, summing up the results of the re-election by workers. He thought that the targets, such as explaining to workers the basic task of class movement, have not been achieved and the election to some degree is still kind of spontaneous. Later, the editor of Pravda received a letter from Lenin, in which he said, "I cannot but express to you my congratulations on the leading article in No. 146. At a moment of defeat, inflicted not by the Social-Democrats…the editorial board at once look the appropriate, firm and dignified tone in pointing out the significance of a protest in principle against 'belittling.'"[5]

Second is the development of the party. From the end of 1905 to the beginning of 1906, flaunting the banner of socialism, Georgian anarchists started the movement of assaulting Social-Democrats and distorting Marxism. To fight against anarchism and protect Marxism and socialism, Stalin wrote the article Anarchism or Socialism, in which he pointed out that every class has its own ideological system as its guideline. The bourgeoisie's ideological system is liberalism; the proletariat's is socialism. Anarchism is the true enemy of Marxism, because it is built on the principle that is completely different from that of Marxism. On the basis of individual, anarchism considers the liberation of individuals as the main condition of the liberation of the masses. Therefore, their slogan is "all for individuals". Marxism is on the basis of the mass, thinking that the liberation of the mass is the main condition of the liberation of individuals. Therefore, its slogan is "all for the masses".

In July 1909, Stalin secretly went back to Baku again. At that time, the party members in Baku had seen a sharp decrease. Depression and desperation had spread all over the party. In August, Stalin wrote the editorial The Party Crisis and Our Tasks for *Bakinsky Proletary* that had resumed publication. In the editorial, he analyzed the crisis faced by the party and the basic tactics to get rid of the crisis. Stalin pointed out that the symptoms

5 Collected Works of Lenin, second Chinese version, volume 46, p. 163, Beijing, People's Publishing House, 1990, retrieved from Marxists Internet Archive.

of party's severe crisis are "the party's loss of members, the shrinking and weakness of the organizations, the latter's isolation from one another, and the absence of coordinated party work"[6] etc. He thought that the way to get rid of the party's crisis and improve the party was to link up the isolated organizations of the party to a single organism by keeping in touch with the masses. He particularly mentioned the means by which the party organizations will be able to rally the broad masses around themselves: "1) intensified agitation around daily needs linked with the general class needs of the proletariat, 2) organization and consolidation of the committees in the factories and works as the Party's most important district centers, 3) the "transfer" of the most important Party functions to the advanced workers and 4) the organization of "discussion groups" for the advanced workers."[7] This was a profound elaboration on the issue of organization construction of the party when the revolution was at low ebb.

In October 1911, Stalin drafted in detention The Declaration of RSDLP Tilflis Leader's Group (leaflet), pointing out that the victory of the counterrevolution has made many people separate themselves from revolution, given up the previous slogan and belief. In terms of the status in the modern society, working class must be revolutionary. They must fight, and during the fight "they have nothing but their chains to lose. They have a world to win." To become the leader of the masses in the future revolution, working class must have their own united and strong proletarian organization.[8] In January 1912, in the plenum of the Central Committee held after the party's congress in Prague, Stalin was by-elected in absence as the member of both the Central Committee and the Central Committee Russian bureau.

The third is the agrarian problem. The agrarian problem was one of the important focus of the social contradictions in Russia. Stalin had made extensive comments on this issue. In March 1906, Stalin published The Agrarian Question in No.5, No.9 and No.10 *Elva* (The Lightening). Later, in the No.14 issue of Elva, he published the article Concerning the Agrarian Question, commenting on the agrarian issue again. In April, Stalin gave the speech Concerning the Revision of the Agrarian Program, elaborating on the issue of agrarian program that is suitable and practicable for most areas in Russia. These articles and speech consist of the basic theoretical proposition on the agrarian issue.

In Stalin's opinion, there are two conditions that are the basis of resolving Russia's agrarian problem. The first is that "we should never forget that everything is changing and everything hinges on time an place. Therefore,

---

6 Collected Works of Stalin, first Chinese version, volume 2, p. 141, retrieved from Marxists Internet Archive.
7 ibid., p. 146, retrieved from Marxists Internet Archive.
8 For further reference, see The Chronology of Stalin edited by Liu Yanzhang, etc, p. 52-53, Beijing, People's Publishing House, 2003.

we should raise questions according to each particular case." The second is that we also should never forget that the Russian Social-Democrats today put the agrarian issue on the basis of practice. Those who want to solve this issue should also stand on this basis."[9] Stalin closely connected solving the agrarian issue with the needs of the practical development of Russian revolution.

At that time, the different political parties in Russia put up many proposals to the question how peasants can take back the land from the lords. By analyzing these proposals, Stalin had some basic propositions on this issue. Firstly, he was against "buyout with low prices", because in this way "the peasants can never be saved". This method would only "make the peasants drop in the trap of the agents." For peasants, "the only way is to take the lords' land, which means confiscating the land."[10] Secondly, he is against the method of "only taking part of the land to make peasants satisfied", advocating for taking all of the land from the lords" because "today's movements in villages are peasants' democratic movements, whose purpose is to eliminate the survivals of serfdom. To do so, the land of the lords and of the emperor must be confiscated."[11] Thirdly, he is against immediately implementing "socialization of land", "average use of land" and "municipalization of land". In Stalin's view, the "socialization of land" in essence is the attempt to start socialism from rural areas, which is impossible. "Urban areas are more developed than rural areas; the former is the leader of the latter. Therefore, any socialist process should start from unban areas."[12] The "average use of land" is also some empty word. The reason is that "the average use of land requires the equality of assets, but the assets of peasants are not equal and this situation cannot be eliminated by the current democratic revolution."[13] The "municipalization of land" (the municipal bureau owns the land and peasants can only rent the land from the municipal bureau) is also unacceptable, because peasants would "consider the land as their own property even in dreams." If the "municipalization of land" would be implemented, it would not only affect peasants, making them no longer fight as hard as before, but also extremely harm the current revolution", even make the peasants "leave the party, give up the party, have dispute with the party and finally enormously weaken the power of the revolution."[14]

9 Collected Works of Stalin, first Chinese version, volume 1, p. 211-212, 212.
10 ibid., pp.196,197.
11 ibid., pp.197,198.
12 ibid., p.199
13 ibid., p. 200.
14 Collected Works of Stalin, first Chinese version, volume 1, p. 201, 201-202.

As to the understanding of the allocation of the land, Stalin thinks that "the method of allocating land comes naturally from the current economic development."[15] He advocated that "the land taken by peasants should belong to them and be allocated by them."[16] "Allocation of the land will cause huge change of property rights. Petty bourgeoisie will step on the road of proletariat by selling the land; the rich will buy new land and start improving the cultivation skills. There will be different classes in rural areas and acute class struggle will be brought in, which will lay the foundation for the further development of capitalism."[17] Stalin generalized the basis of agrarian program as: "to eliminate the survivals of serfdom, the land of lords must all be confiscated and given to peasants to be allocated according to their own interests."[18]

The fourth is the national question. The National issue has always been an important theoretical and practical issue in Russian revolution. It is also a theoretical issue that has attracted most attention from Stalin, who made good achievements on the topic. Stalin's concentrated comments on the national issue are mainly in the article Marxism and the National Question he wrote between the end of 1912 and early 1913. In this article, Stalin criticized the wrong opinions of some Social-Democrats on the national issue, elaborated on the national theories of Marxism and explained the proletarian parties' guideline, policy and basic principles on solving national issues. For further reference, see Chapter 10 of this book "Stalin's national theory". This article is the most important work of Stalin on Marxism's national theory. It had also got Lenin's high praises too.

In February 1913, Stalin was arrested and exiled to a place in Siberia. That was his last arrest and exile. From 1902 to 1913, Stalin was arrested 7 times and exiled 6 times, and in 5 cases he had managed to escape. In February 1917, the bourgeois democratic revolution broke out in Russia and the Czar's dictatorship was overthrown. Lenin wrote: "Currently out of all the countries that are in a war, Russia is the freest one."[19] There were two regimes at that time. However, in the working class regime- the Soviets of Workers' and Soldiers' Deputies-Mensheviks and the Socialist Revolutionaries Party members held the majority. Bolsheviks, the minority, were lower in numbers of people and influence since they were doing underground activities for a long time. On the other side in the temporary government set up after the February Revolution, the Constitutional Democratic Party that represented the interests of the big bourgeoisie was

15   ibid., p. 203.
16   ibid., p. 202.
17   ibid., p. 203.
18   ibid., p. 204.
19   Collected Works of Lenin, second Chinese version, volume 29, p. 105, Beijing, People's Publishing House, 1985.

in a predominant position. Under these circumstances, the question of how to deal with the Social Revolutionaries Party, especially the Mensheviks and the bourgeois temporary government, was put on the agenda again. In March 1917, Stalin returned to Petersburg from exile and joined RSDLP (Bolshevik) Central Committee Standing Bureau and Pravda, to lead the revolutionary activities in the new situation. At the party's 7th conference (in April 24-29, 1917) Stalin gave a report on the national question and was elected to Central Committee membership (he had always been a member of Central Committee since then). He advocated Lenin's policy about transforming the bourgeois democratic revolution to socialist revolution. During July and August, at the party's 6th congress (July 26-August 3, 1917) Stalin made the Central Committee's concluding report and a report on the political situation, elaborating on Lenin's policy on the victory of the socialist revolution. In October that year, the party's Central Committee passed Lenin's proposal of armed revolt. Lenin was elected as the leader of the Central Committee's Politburo to lead the revolt. Stalin was first elected as the member of the Politburo, besides as the member of the headquarter of military operations of the revolution in this armed revolt. He was also the member of Petrograd Soviet Military Committee, taking part in the preparation of the armed revolt in October. Petrograd was later named as Leningrad.

On November 6, 1917 (October 24 in Russian calendar), the eve of the October armed revolt, Stalin published What Do We Need? in Rabochy Put. With strong passion for the revolution, he pointed out in all seriousness, "after the victory of the February revolution, power has remained in the hands of the landlords and capitalists, the bankers and speculators, the profiteers and marauders. Therein lay the fatal mistake of the workers and soldiers; that is the cause of the present disasters in the rear areas and the war front."[20]

He called on workers and soldiers that "the present government of landlords and capitalists must be replaced by a new government, a government of workers and peasants"; that "the present impostor government, which was not elected by the people and which is not accountable to the people, must be replaced by a government recognized by the people, elected by the representatives of the workers, soldiers and peasants, and accountable to these representatives." "The power must pass into the hands of the Soviets of Workers', Soldiers' and Peasants' Deputies."[21] This was the powerful voice that Stalin made on the eve of the October Revolution which was also the true reflection of his leading role in that critical time.

20 Collected Works of Stalin, first Chinese version, volume 3, p. 372, Beijing, People's Publishing House, 1955.
21 ibid., pp. 372, 373, retrieved from Marxists Internet Archive.

II. Stalin's theory and practice of socialist revolution and construction from 1917 to 1924

The period between 1917 and 1924 is not only an important turning period of Stalin's revolutionary career, but also an important period of the formation of his socialist thought. During this period, the newborn Soviet regime was faced with very complicated domestic and international situations. Led by Lenin, with correct consideration of the situation, the leaders of the party and the Soviet regime adjusted the economic, political and military policies accordingly. In rhe economic sphere after the period of wartime communism practice and secondly the nNew Economic Policy practice ies, socialist revolution and socialist construction had greatly developed. During this period, Stalin had grown up from a "student" of the revolution to a "master" of it, from an executive leader in charge of local party work to a leader of a working class party led by Lenin and finally become the highest party and state leader of the USSR.

Our study in this book on Stalin's socialist thought mainly startsfrom the development of Stalin's thought after the victory of the October Revolution. During this period, Stalin was involved in building up the Soviet regime though led by Lenin. It was during this period of time when he gradually formed his thought on socialist revolution and construction. During this period, Stalin's ideas on important theoretical questions and his practice had mainly included in the following aspects:

The first, October Revolution and its great significance: On November 7, 1917 (October 25 in Russian calendar), led by the Bolshevik Party headed by Lenin, by way of armed uprisings in urban areas, Russian proletariat and working people achieved a great victory and established the first socialist country, the dictatorship of proletariat.

Since then, socialism was transformed from an ideal to reality and from a scientific theory to a brand new social system. This was a great historic leap in the history of socialist movements in the world. In November 1918, in the article The October Revolution and the National Question, Stalin had analyzed the great significance of the October Revolution. He pointed out that "the October Revolution, having put an end to the old, bourgeois movement for national emancipation, inaugurated the era of a new, socialist movement of the workers and peasants of the oppressed nationalities, directed against all oppression—including, therefore, national oppression—against the power of the bourgeoisie, "their own" and foreign, and against imperialism in general."[22] Stalin put the emphasis on the "world-wide significance" of the October Revolution. He thought that the world-wide significance of

---

22 Collected Works of Stalin, volume 4, p. 146, retrieved from Marxists Internet Archive.

the October Revolution was mainly reflected in three aspects. The first is that "it has widened the scope of the national question and converted it from the particular question of combating national oppression in Europe into the general question of emancipating the oppressed peoples, colonies and semi-colonies from imperialism."[23] The second is that "it has opened up wide possibilities for their emancipation and the right pathtowards it, has thereby greatly facilitated the cause of the emancipation of the oppressed peoples of the West and the East, and has drawn them into the common current of the victorious struggle against imperialism".The third is that "it has thereby erected a bridge between the socialist West and the enslaved East, having created a new front of revolutions against world imperialism, extending from the proletarians of the West, through the Russian revolution, to the oppressed peoples of the East."[24]

In February 1919, Stalin published Two Camps, putting up the inference that "the world has definitely and irrevocably split into two camps: The camp of imperialism and the camp of socialism". Stalin referred to the struggle between "the camp of imperialism" and "the camp of socialism" as "the hub of the present-day affairs", which "determines the whole substance of the present domestic and foreign policies of the leaders of the old and the new worlds". The prospect must be "the tide of socialist revolution is irresistibly rising" and "imperialism is doomed to inevitable destruction."[25] Among Stalin's thought on socialism, the inference of the "two camps" later became the important theoretical basis for his understanding of the development of the international political and international economic relations.

The second, on the structure of the new Soviet regime: Stalin was elected the member of the All-Russian Central Executive Committee (ARCEC) and appointed as the commissar of the National Affairs Committee of the first Soviet Government. From 1918 to 1920, in the period of international armed interference and civil war, Stalin was the member of the Revolutionary Military Commission of the Republic and the deputy of ARCEC to the Workers and Peasants National Defense Committee. From 1919-1922, Stalin also held a concurrent position as the State Control Commissariat. In 1919, he was elected to the newly established Central Organization Bureau. Stalin, entrusted by the Party Central Committee and the National Defense Committee, he fought in different battle lines in the civil war.

---

23   ibid p.148
24   ibid., p.149, retrieved from Marxists Internet Archive.
25   Collected Works of Stalin, first Chinese version, volume 4, pp. 206, 209, retrieved from Marxists Internet Archive.

After the civil war, the Soviet nations had entered into a new era of development, the period of peaceful construction. In March 1921, the Russian Communist Party (Bolshevik) Tenth Congress was held, which decided Soviet Russia should leave back the wartime communism policy and enter into the New Economic Policy (NEP). Stalin advocated Lenin's NEP which adapted to the new situation and gave a report on The Immediate Tasks of the Party in the National Question to the congress, asking for the complete elimination of the old de facto inequality of the oppressed nations and he denounced Russian great-power chauvinism and local nationalism erroneous tendencies on the national question. In April 1922, Stalin was elected as the general secretary of the Party's Central Committee in the first plenum of the Central Committee.

When it came to how to complete the task of establishing the Union of the Soviet Socialist Republics,

Stalin, in September 1922 had proposed that the non-Russian Soviet republics become self-governing areas within the Russian republic. The Georgian communists objected to this "autonomisation" plan, seeing it as a restoration of Russian domination over their country. On this issue he had an argument with Lenin.

Stalin had denounced Georgian communists as "nationalist-socialists" and he sent an emissary, Grigory Ordzhonikidze, to persuade them. During his meeting with the Georgian leaders, Ordzhonikidze physically assaulted one of them. Upon reading Stalin's plan, Lenin sent a letter to the Political Bureau criticizing it and counterposing a union of equal republics, with the right of any of them to secede.

When—on December 30, 1922—Lenin, who was gravely ill at the time, learned of this above incident involving Ordzhonikidze he dictated a note accusing Stalin and his supporters of adopting the outlook of the Russian bureaucracy:

It is said that a united apparatus was needed. Where did that assurance come from? Did it not come from that same Russian apparatus which, as I pointed out in one of the preceding sections of my diary, we took over from tsarism and slightly anointed with Soviet oil? ...

It is quite natural that in such circumstances the "freedom to secede from the union" by which we justify ourselves will be a mere scrap of paper, unable to defend the non-Russians from the onslaught of that really Russian man, the Great Russian chauvinist, in substance a rascal and a tyrant, such as the typical Russian bureaucrat is. There is no doubt that the infinitesimal percentage of Soviet and sovietised workers will drown in that tide of chauvinistic Great Russian riff raff like a fly in milk.

In a note dictated a day later, on December 31, Lenin accused Stalin of being a Great Russian chauvinist:

The Georgian who is neglectful of this aspect of the question, or who carelessly flings about accusations of "nationalist-socialism" (whereas he himself is a real and true "nationalist-socialist", and even a vulgar Great Russian bully), violates, in substance, the interests of proletarian class solidarity, for nothing holds up the development and strengthening of proletarian class solidarity so much as national injustice .

And in a further note Lenin concluded that the "political responsibility for all this truly Great Russian nationalist campaign must, of course, be laid on Stalin and Dzherzhinsky" and argued that "the Union of Soviet Socialist Republics [be retained] only for military and diplomatic affairs, and in all other respects restore full independence to the individual people's commissariats [ministries]" of the Soviet republics.[26]

Faced by Lenin's critics, Stalin gave up his above proposition and accepted Lenin's policy of establishing a united union of nations in the way that national republics will voluntarily form an alliance of nations. In December 1922, he gave a report on the proposal of establishing the Union of Soviet Socialist Republics on the First Congress of the Soviets. Stalin also had disputes with Lenin on the matter of foreign trade monopoly and Georgia issues. Lenin in his letters wrote to the congress at the end of 1922 and the beginning of 1923, he pointed out that Stalin's style of work was too rude; and that he was seriously worried, Stalin as the general secretary, might had unlimited power in his hands and might probably cannot always be able to use this power very carefully. Therefore, Lenin had suggested the party to find another person for this position.

The third is on Lenin's role and Leninism. On April 23, 1920, Stalin published the article Lenin as the Organizer and Leader of the Russian Communist Party and gave a speech on the same day at Lenin's 50th birthday celebration banquet. In the published article Stalin elaborated on two aspects: "Lenin is the organizer of the Russian Communist Party" and "Lenin is the leader of the Russian Communist Party". Stalin pointed out that as a matter of fact, there are two groups of Marxists. The first group "usually confines itself to an outward acceptance." They are "unable or unwilling to grasp the essence of Marxism"; "unable or unwilling to put it into practice." "This converts the living, revolutionary principles of Marxism into lifeless, meaningless formulas." The second group is those Marxists represented by Lenin. They attach "prime importance not to the outward acceptance of Marxism, but to its realization, its application in practice". They also determine "the ways and means of realizing Marxism

26 Collected Works of Lenin, second Chinese version, volume 43, p. 350, Beijing, People's Publishing House, 1987.

in a way that best fits the current situation" and change "these ways and means as the situation changes."[27] After reviewing the experiences and lessons from the Russian Bourgeois Democratic Revolution in 1905 and the October Socialist Revolution in 1917, Stalin pointed out, "to retain the post of leader of the proletarian revolution and of the proletarian party, one must combine strength in theory with experience in the practical organization of the proletarian movement" and "Lenin has fully retained this old quality." Therefore, "it is Lenin, and no one else, who is today the leader of the strongest and most steeled proletarian party in the world."[28] In his speech on the celebration meeting, Stalin also elaborated on one "feature" of Lenin that no one else had talked about. That is "his modesty and his courage in acknowledging mistakes."[29]

On January, 21, 1924, Lenin passed away. On January 26, Stalin made a speech on the first session of the Third All-Union Congress of the Soviets, which was also Lenin's memorial meeting. He vowed to "fulfill his behest with honor" from aspects such as "hold high and guard the purity of the title of member of the party" "guard the unity of the party" "guard and strengthen the dictatorship of the proletariat" "strengthen with all might the alliance of the workers and the peasants" "strengthen and extend the union of republics" and "remain faithful to the principles of the Communist International". On January 28, Stalin gave the speech titled "Lenin" at the Kremlin Military School Evening, explaining "Lenin's certain characteristics as a man and a leader". He had described Lenin's characteristics as "the mountain eagle" "modesty" "force of logic" "no whining" "no boasting" "fidelity to principle" "faith in the masses" and "the genius of revolution."[30]

In April 1924, Stalin made the speech The Foundations of Leninism at Sverdlov University. He said: "Leninism is the further development of Marxism." "Leninism is Marxism of the era of imperialism and the proletarian revolution. To be more exact, Leninism is the theory and tactics of the proletarian revolution in general, the theory and tactics of the dictatorship of the proletariat in particular."[31] He also pointed out that Leninism is the school of theory and practice; that "the combination of Russian revolutionary sweep with American efficiency is the essence of Leninism in Party and state work."[32] After Lenin's death, Stalin had became one of the leaders who made the most and the most authoritative elaborations within the party.

27 Collected Works of Stalin, first Chinese version, volume 4, p. 272, retrieved from Marxists Internet Archive.
28 ibid., p. 279.
29 ibid., p. 280, retrieved from Marxists Internet Archive.
30 Retrieved from Marxists Internet Archive
31 Collected Works of Stalin, first Chinese version, volume 6, p. 63-64, Beijing, People's Publishing House, 1956, retrieved from Marxists Internet Archive.
32 Collected Works of Stalin, first Chinese version, volume 6, p. 164-165, retrieved from Marxists Internet Archive.

On the Thirteenth Congress of the Party in May 1924, Stalin was re-elected as the general secretary of the Central Committee of the Party. From then on until he passed away in 1953, he held this position.

III. Stalin's theory and practice of socialist construction from 1924 to 1936

After Lenin passed away, in order to recall Lenin's great achievement and and give their opinions on Soviet Union's socialism practice and theory after Lenin, the main leaders of the Communist Party of the USSR had made several generalizations on f Lenin's thought and his theoretical contributions. After Lenin passed away, Trotsky also published a series of articles on Lenin and these articles were collected and published in the book Lenin in—April 1924. In September 1924, Trotsky collected all his early articles and speeches and published another book of his. He also wrote a preface for his readers titled as *The Lessons of October*. Due to the important leading position he was holding in the party, the government and the army, he had a long-term contact and working relations with Lenin. He also had had disputes and arguments with Lenin. The above mentioned book had immediately aroused a heated discussion in the Party. In October 1924, at the session held by Moscow Party Committee, Kamenev made the report titled Trotskyism or Leninism?, making a detailed list of Trotsky's disputes with Lenin from 1903 to the October Revolution. He thought that the Trotsky phenomenon was definitely not personal or occasional, but "a classic historical trend" and Trotsky was "a servant of Mensheviks". In November the same year, with the same title Leninism or Trotskyism?, Stalin made a speech at the plenum of the Communist Group in the All-Union Central Council of Trade Unions, criticizing Trotsky "regarding to his absurd and preposterous argument on the October uprising, on the party and on the preparations of the October Revolution." He pointed out that Trotskyism was a special ideological system that is in "irreconcilable contradiction with Leninism"; it is the duty of the party "to bury Trotskyism as an ideological trend."[33]

This theoretical struggle lifted the curtain on the argument on the different theories of Soviet Union's transition to socialism and the mode of socialist construction to be followed in SU. The period from 1924 to 1936 was the time in which Soviet Union encountered huge social changes. It was also a period that all its socialist undertakings had rapidly developed. Corresponding to this rapid change, there came one after another various theories on the transition and construction of socialism, causing heated

---

33   ibid, pp. 281, 309, retrieved from Marxists Internet Archive.

ideological struggles in the Communist Party of the USSR. In this ideological struggle, Stalin's thought on socialist transformation and construction had gradually become mature. In the following chapters we review these thoughts of Stalin in detail. Here below is just a concise overview of some of his important thoughts.

The first, on the question of NEP. After Lenin's death, the Russian Communist Party (Bolshevik) was faced with a serious problem: Whether or not to continue implementing the "NEP". This was a huge issue that was in relation to the system and the path the socialist construction was going to take. On that matter, there were different opinions in the Russian Communist Party (Bolshevik). Stalin gave a talk, and had reduced the argument in the party before the Thirteenth Congress of the Russian Communist Party (Bolshevik) into two issues, one whether the NEP is basically correct or whether it needs to be revised. For this question, Stalin gave a clear answer, "The Central Committee and most members of the party think that the party should be a united on the idea that the NEP needs no revision."[34] In April 1925, the Central Committee of the Communist Party of the USSR (Bolshevik) (CPSU(B)) held a plenum to study on the problems during the past implementation of the NEP. The party leaders reached an agreement on adjusting the current economic policies and put forward the adjustment policy as: Leaving back "last year's limitations on circulation and pass to a more flexible national economy".

In early 1926, Stalin had taken charge of the work at the plenum of the CPSU(B). He was reelected the member of the Central Politburo, the member of the Central Organization Bureau, and the secretary of the Secretariat of the Central Committee. He was also ratified as the general secretary of the CPSU(B) and reappointed as the plenipotentiary delegate of the CPSU(B) to the Executive Committee of the Communist International. In January of that year, Stalin delivered the speech The Fight against Rights and the "Ultra-Left Deviations" at the presidium meeting of the Executive Committee of the Communist International. In his speech, Stalin pointed out that in the ideological struggle in the party, "the question of the fight against the Rights and 'Ultra-Lefts' should be concrete depending on the current political situation."

Stalin emphasized, "idea of equity: simply striking at the Rights and 'Ultra-Lefts' with equal intensity, is childish."[35]

---

34 Collected Works of Stalin, first Chinese version, volume 6, p. 4.
35 Collected Works of Stalin, first Chinese version, volume 8, p. 5, Beijing, People's Publishing House, 1954, retrieved from the Marxists Internet Archive.

In April, in the work report of the plenum of CPSU(B) The Economic Situation of the USSR and the Policy of the Party speaking to the activists of the party in Leningrad, Stalin pointed out that the NEP had two periods. "In the first period, the whole national economy was mainly dependent on agriculture. Now we have entered into the second period, which is a new period of the NEP. That is to say, our economic development has entered into the second era of the NEP and the direct industrialization."[36] During this period, we should "continue building the socialist foundation for our economy" "To promote the whole economy, what we need to do is to put focus on industry."[37] Industrialization and socialist accumulation "have great significance for us". Stalin comprehensively elaborated on the several key links of transformation from domestic accumulation to actual socialist accumulation. At the same time, he also explained his ideas on the questions such as: The right way of accumulation during industrialization, strict economy, training cadres for the construction of industry, increasing the initiative of working class, strengthening the alliance of workers and peasants, democracy within the party and maintaining the unity of the party, etc.[38]

The second, on the question whether a single country could build socialism. After the October Revolution, whether or not a single country can build socialism was an important and unavoidable question faced by the CPSU(B). Before 1924, Stalin had advocated that Russia n by itself could not build socialism. In January 1926, in his article Concerning Questions of Leninism, Stalin had pointed out, "the overthrow of the power of the bourgeoisie and establishment of the power of the proletariat in a single country does not yet mean that the complete victory of socialism has been ensured. The principal task of socialism-the organization of socialist production-has still to be fulfilled. He asked: Can this task be fulfilled; can the final victory of socialism be achieved in a single country, without the joint efforts of proletarians in several advanced countries? No, it cannot. To overthrow the bourgeoisie the efforts of a single country can be sufficient; this is proved by the history of our revolution. For the final victory of a peasant country like Russia, they are all insufficient; for that objective the efforts of the proletarians of several advanced countries are required."[39] In December 1924, Stalin gave new explanation of "complete victory of socialism" and "on the necessity of support by the Western-European proletariat" in his article The October Revolution and the Tactics of Russian Communists. He advocated that the "complete victory" means "a complete guarantee against the restoration of the old order"; that the "support by the Western-European proletariat" means "the sympathy of the European workers for our revolution,

24

36 ibid., p.110.
37 ibid., p.111.
38 Collected Works of Stalin, Volume 8, pp. 119-132.
39 ibid, pp. 60-61, retrieved from Marxists Internet Archive

their readiness to thwart the imperialists' plans of intervention."[40] In January 1925, Stalin redefined the meaning of "complete victory" and "victory in general" in his A Letter to Comrade D-ov. Stalin pointed out, "the victory of socialism in general" means "driving away the landlords and capitalists, taking power, repelling the attacks of imperialism and beginning to build a socialist economy. In all this, the proletariat in a single country can be fully successful; but a complete guarantee against restoration can be ensured only by the 'joint efforts of the proletarians in several countries.'"[41] In May 1925, in The Results of the Fourteenth Conference of the RCP (B), Stalin had publicly underlined the theory of "the victory socialism in a single country".

He analyzed two contradictions in Russia: the internal contradiction (contradiction between the proletariat and peasants) and the external contradiction (the contradiction between Russia and the main capitalist countries). In Concerning Questions of Leninism, Stalin pointed out, "what is meant by the possibility of the victory of socialism in a single country? It means the possibility of solving the contradictions between the proletariat and the peasantry by the capacity of internal forces of our country.

It means the possibility of the proletariat seizing power and using that power to build a complete socialist society in our country, with the sympathy and the support of the proletarians of other countries, although without the preliminary victory of the proletarian revolution in other countries."[42]

25

Trotsky and some other leaders were explicitly against Stalin's theory of "socialism in a single country", criticizing Stalin as completely betraying the principles on Marxism and Leninism, and following ultra nationalism. During the next two years, Stalin wrote Concerning Questions of Leninism, The Social-Democratic Deviation in Our Party, Reply to the Discussion on the Report on "The Social-Democratic Deviation in Our Party", etc, systematically criticizing Trotsky and some other leaders' opinion and finally established his theory of "socialism in a single country".

The third, on socialist industrialization. In December 1925, at the Fourteenth Congress of the CPSU(B), Stalin presented the political report of the Central Committee, putting forward the party policy on socialist industrialization. At that time, as the first socialist country, the Soviet Union was surrounded by capitalist countries. Under such circumstances, the peoples of the USSR, led by Stalin, achieved industrialization of the country, developing the USSR from an underdeveloped agricultural country to

---

40　Selected Works of Stalin, volume 1, p. 288, retrieved from Marxists Internet Archive.
41　Collected Works of Stalin, volume 7, p. 17, retrieved from Marxists Internet Archive.
42　Collected Works of Stalin, first Chinese version, volume 8, p. 64, retrieved from Marxists Internet Archive.

an advanced industrial country. Material foundation of socialism was laid and national defense capacity was also strengthened. But at the same time, Stalin's one-sided emphasis on the priority of development of heavy industry had caused the serious disproportions in the USSR's national economy in the long term. The highly centralized economic management system established in this period had later severely affected the further development of socialist productive forces.

After the struggle against Trotsky, this time Zinoviev and Kamenev had teamed up a new opposition faction. Their contradictions with Stalin became more and more violent. The Fourteenth Congress of the CPSU(B) had completely criticized Zinoviev and Kamenev's propositions, and affirmed Stalin's report with 556 votesin favor and 65 against. The Congress also passed several resolutions which denounced their opposition and disciplined them in the party. Later, the new opposition above and Trotsky gradually reached consensus on many issues and formed the Trotsky-Zinoviev Bloc. After that, they had started fighting against the majority in the Central Committee represented by Stalin. In November 1927, the Central Committee and the Central Control Commission of the CPSU(B) expelled Trotsky and Zinoviev from the Party. Later, the struggle against the Trotsky-Zinoviev was completely won by Stalin, and his leading position in the Party was consolidated.

The fourth, on the collectivization of agriculture. In December 1927, the Fifteenth Congress of the CPSU(B) was held. On behalf of Central Committee, Stalin presented the political report, putting forward the plans of gradually transforming the small individual peasants into large kolkhozes and reforming agriculture with new technology in order to overcome the contradiction between large scale industry and small peasant economy.

In the fall of 1929, there occurred the commodity shortage in the cities. Goods for everyday consumption were in short supply; long queues waiting to buy food and everyday-use goods were rampant. As a result, various opinions were held how to interpret and solve the problem of the grain crisis, which had later evolved into a fierce ideological struggle. From December 1927 to July 1928 was the first stage of the struggle between Stalin and Bukharin. At this stage, Bukharin had chosen to wage his offensive on a theoretical basis. However, the implementation of the grain collection policies was in Stalin's hand. Stalin also personally went to Siberia to check the work of grain collection in the region. During the implementation of the grain collection plan in the shortest period of time, violent practices such as searching, arresting, and confiscating was prevalent in rural areas. On the session of the politburo in February 1928, Stalin made a compromise in his discussion against Bukharin. He instructed the party organizations to cease the radical practices in the grain collection and called the party to persist in the NEP practices. After July 1928, the argument between Stalin and Bukharin entered into the second stage. Stalin came up with the theory of "tribute" as the basis to fight against Bukharin's theories. Bukharin in turn published his Notes of an Economist, Political Testament of Lenin, etc to elaborate his theory and policy suggestions. In April 1929, the Central Committee held the plenum, on which Stalin made the report The Right Deviation in the CPSU(B). When criticizing Bukharin's opinions, Stalin pointed out that the essence of this struggle was the "struggle of lines". One line is the line of the Party, the line of revolution and the line of Lenin; the other line is the line of the Bukharin bloc, which is a line against the Party. Buharin's line was accused as issuing an anti-party manifesto, resignation, slandering the Party, subverting the Party and negotiating with the Trotskyist activists to form an anti-party bloc. This line was the line of opportunism.[43]

The plenum decided to dismiss Bukharin from his post as the chief editor of Pravda. In July the same year, the Executive Committee of the Communist International dismissed Bukharin from all his posts. In November, Bukharin was expelled from the Politburo of the Central Committee, which marked the end of this struggle.

In April 1929, the Sixteenth National Congress of the Party set the task of greatly supporting the overall collectivization of agriculture. In May of that year, the Fifth Congress of the USSR officially passed the resolution on supporting the overall collectivization of towns and villages. In the second half year of 1929, the overall collectivization firstly started in three important grain-producing areas: North Caucasia, midstream and downstream of Volga River. In November 1929, Stalin published A Year of Great Change, which marked that the overall collectivization as a political movement to transform the agricultural relation of production which was fully carried out around the nation. Stalin pointed out, "the new and decisive feature of the present collective-farm moment is that the peasants are joining the collective farms not in separate groups, as it was formerly the case, but by whole villages, volosts, districts, and even okrugs. And what does that mean? It means that the medium size peasant is joining the collective farm."[44] In December 1929, Stalin made the speech with the title of Concerning Questions of Agrarian Policy in USSR, making an acute change of the policy on kulaks. He suggested connecting the collectivization with the fight against kulaks, which could also be used as the driving force to promote the overall collectivization, changing the Party's policy of limiting kulaks' exploitation into the policy of eliminating the kulak class.

43 Collected works of Stalin, volume 2, p. 11.
44 ibid., p. 118, retrieved from Marxists Internet Archive

To speed up the overall collectivization of agriculture, the government dispatched large amount of industrial workers to rural areas to help carrying out the movement. Collaborating with the local Soviets, with administrative measures, they required peasants collectively to join the farm. In January 1931, the highest Soviet of the USSR asked the local soviets to play a new role in the overall collectivization. To purse a more centralized formulation, some places even collected the houses and self-consumed milk to the kolkhozes; some places even called off the village fair. These radical activities aroused strong dissatisfaction of peasants, who expressed their grievances by killing large amount of livestock. To deal with it, Stalin wrote Dizzy with Success, focusing on these radical activities, to correct the errors in the collectivization movement. However, since the Central Committee did not change the established policy of the overall collectivization, the effect of the rectification and error-correcting was very limited. By the year of 1934, the USSR had basically completed the collectivization of agriculture, during which Stalin changed the policy of limiting rich peasants into eliminating them. Moreover, he actually supported the radical activities such as violating the interests of middle peasants, resorting to coercion, advancing impatiently and impetuously, etc. In the rural areas, due to the long-term implementation of compulsory sale to the country, the further development of agriculture was hampered, and the materialistic interests of peasants were damaged. As a result, the agricultural production could not meet the highest level existing before the First World War for a long time.

From January 7 to 12, 1933, Stalin presided over the Joint Plenum of the Central Committee and the Central Control Commission of CPSU(B). On January 7, he pointed out in *The Results of the First Five-Year Plan* that the task for five years was completed within four years; that the USSR had changed from a weak agricultural country that was manipulated by capitalist countries into a completely independent and strong industrial country that would not be manipulated by the capitalist countries, completely pushing out the capitalist activists and enlarging the front of socialist economic form. When talking about the class struggle, Stalin pointed out: elimination of classes is not achieved by weakening the class struggle but by intensifying it; elimination of countries is not achieved by weakening the regime of the country but intensifying it to the maximum. On January 11, he gave the speech Work in the Countryside, mainly talking about the weaknesses of the Party as to the work in the countryside: the negative aspects of grain trade in kolkhozes was overlooked and many mistakes were made; many party organizations disconnected with the kolkhozes and bended to the spontaneous force; the new environment was ignored and the class enemy's new tactics were not furtively disrupted; the influence and responsibility of the members of Communist Party were underestimated.

In January 1934, the Seventeenth Congress of CPSU(B) was held, on which Stalin made the work report of the Central Committee of CPSU(B). He analyzed the unprecedented economic crisis in the capitalist world, suggesting that as much as the internal contradictions in these capitalist countries are getting acuter, so will the contradictions between these countries; that they are preparing for a new World War. In December, when meeting with the representatives of metal producers, Stalin came out with the slogan "In the period of reconstruction, technique decides everything." This slogan does not only refer to naked techniques, but to technique in the service of people who master the technique. He also emphasized that the Party is mainly in charge of organizing the masses, judging the matter carefully and giving correct instruction. In February 1935, Stalin gave a speech at the Examination Committee of Kolkhozes Demonstration Regulation (Draft) under the Commission of the All-Union Second Congress of Kolkhozes, criticizing some wrong opinions and doings of some Kolkhozes' people who disregarded other people's private interests, emphasizing that under the circumstances that the Kolkhozes have not yet had abundant products and been able to provide all the Kolkhoz people and their families with everything they need, there is need to have not only the public, large-scale and decisive Kolkhoz economy which is indispensable for the satisfaction of the social needs, but also the small-scale individual economy that is inevitable for the satisfaction of private needs.

In March 1936, Stalin met and talked with Roy Howard, the general manager of Scripps-Howard Newspapers Allied Company of America. He analyzed the crisis of war, suggesting that America's democracy and the Soviet's system can peacefully coexist or have a contest. In November 1936, Stalin was present at the Extraordinary Eighth Congress of Soviets of the USSR and gave the report on the draft constitution of the USSR. Stalin talked about the changes in economy from 1921 to 1936. In 1924, no less than 20% of industry was controlled by capitalist sector; in trade 40%-50% was represented by merchants and profiteers. By 1936, capitalism was entirely banished from the industry of the USSR; trade was completely in control of the nation, artels and collective farms; the complete victory of the socialist system in every sector of the national economy had become a fact; the socialist ownership of the means of production was implemented. In terms of the class structure, the class of exploitation was eliminated, with only working class, peasant class and intelligentsia remained. Every nation had established the real cooperative relations. For all the above reasons, Stalin announced: "Our Soviet society has already, in the main, succeeded in achieving Socialism; it has created a Socialist system, i.e., it has brought about what Marxists in other words call the first, or lower, phase of Communism. Hence, in the main, we have already achieved the first phase of Communism."[45]

---

45   Retrieved from Marxists Internet Archive

In general, Stalin had led the people of the USSR to great achievement in the construction of socialism. Therefore he got great authority and reputation among the masses. At the same time, the personality cult of Stalin had gradually formed nationwide. To fight against those with different opinions, serious struggles were on and on in the Party. Stalin failed in carrying on Lenin's thought of inner-party democracy. He carried the struggles too far away within the party, regarding many inner-party disputes that were supposed to be ideological as class struggle, considering the people with whom he argued as the class enemy. With arbitrary decisions, Stalin had seriously violated the principle of democratic centralism both in the party and in the nation.

IV. Stalin's theory and practice of socialist construction after 1936

During the socialist industrialization and the overall collectivization of agriculture, Stalin had carried on a political "Great Purge". In January 1934, at the Seventeenth Congress of CPSU(B), Stalin announced that the hostile class no longer existed in the nation, which was also confirmed in the 1936 Constitution. However, at while Stalin confirmed that there was no hostile class in the nation, he still emphasized that the class struggle had become more and more intense. The Kirov's assassination in December 1934 made Stalin a lot more sure about his opinion. In February 1937, when Stalin was presiding over the plenum of the Central Committee of CPSU(B), he pointed out that we need to add the new slogan, which is "eradicate the credulous attitude on politics with political education", to the old slogan of "master techniques"; that we should abandon the theory that as we take one step further, the class struggle would gradually stop and the class enemy would gradually give in. He reiterated, "the greater our progress and the more our victories, the more ferocious the survivals of the exploiting class that was broken down, the acuter struggle form they would take, the more they would want to damage the soviet nations and the more they would struggle with in the most desperate way."[46]

As early as November 1934, the Central Executive Committee of USSR and the People's Committee had passed the resolution of the special meeting under the People's Committee of Internal Affairs, authorizing the special meeting with the right to sent those who are deemed as dangerous to society into exile for five years. In the summer of 1936, the Central Committee of CPSU(B) gave the Internal Affairs Department the full authority of one year in order to completely break down "people's enemy". In 1937, this

46 Selected Works of Stalin, volume 1, p. 129, Beijing, People's Publishing House, 1962.

right was extended indefinitely. According to these resolutions, the functions and power of the Internal Affair Department was greatly enlarged. Not following the proceedings or supervised or restricted by the party, the soviets or the judicial authority, the national security organs had caused many cases that were unjustly charged or falsely sentenced.

On the one hand, Stalin had announced the beginning of the socialist society; on the other hand, he was the leader of the Great Purge. These are the distinct reflections of the contradictions of his socialist thought.

From 1936 to the time Stalin passed away, his socialist thought had had new development during the more than ten years. Here we only make some general introduction on several major problems of the development of Stalin's thought on socialist construction in this period.

The first is the spread of Marxism and Leninism. The year of 1938 was the end of the USSR's second five-year plan and the beginning of the third one. As stipulated in the new five-year plan, industrial products should increase 92%; means of production should at least double; consumer goods increase 72%; achievement of comprehensive mechanization of agriculture; agricultural products should increase 50%; basic construction investment to reach 92 billion rubles, which is equal to the total basic construction investment of the previous two five-year plans. To achieve such great goal, the key was the leaders at every level. For this reason, the Central Committee of the CPSU(B) emphasized, "Without the knowledge of Marxism and Leninism, not knowing Bolshevism, not overcoming the backward tendency of theories, it would be very difficult for our cadres to move any single step." To help the cadres at every level and the Party members systematically to understand the theoretical basis of Marxist party, Stalin led to write the book History of the Communist Party of the USSR (Bolsheviks) and wrote in person the second part of the Chapter Four ofDialectical and Historical Materialism, which was firstly published in Pravda on September 12, 1938 and later published as a separate edition. Dialectical and Historical Materialism once was translated into over ten languages and reprinted for hundreds of times, having an extensive influence in the USSR and other socialist countries. In this book, Stalin talked about the four basic features of Marxism dialectics and their internal logic and the three basic features of materialism. Starting from the materialistic living conditions in society, he emphasized the effect of relations of production in social development and elaborated on the important reaction of social awareness. When analyzing the productive forces and socialist relations of production, he reached the conclusion that the socialist relations of production are "completely compatible" with the nature of productive forces and therefore excluded the contradiction between the two.

In October 1938, Stalin gave a speech when he was present at the Propagandists Meeting in Moscow and Leningrad, pointing out the guiding ideology and task of the History of the Communist Party of the USSR (Bolsheviks) is to provide party members and activists with a uniform textbook that has been reviewed by the Central Committee; to eliminate the disconnection between Marxism and Leninism in recent years; to introduce the lively Marxism and Leninism in CPSU(B)'s history; to demonstrate the power and effect of Marxism's theory and the rules of social development; to get rid of methods that simplified and vulgarized theoretical questions; to publish a uniform textbook that collected almost all the principles of Marxism and Leninism.

The second is the treatment of the socio-economic issues and diplomacy during the pre-World War II period. In March 1939, Stalin presided over the Eighteenth Congress of CPSU(B) and made the conclusive work report of the Central Committee. He talked about the seven pillars of the diplomatic policy that was proposed in order to strengthen Soviet Union's international status. Out of the seven pillars, the gradually increasing economic, political and cultural power was put in the first place. On the basis of modern technical equipment, the USSR completed the transformation of industry and agriculture. The new technical equipment used in industry was the No. 1 in the world. Private industry was eliminated. In terms of politics, the main achievement was the complete elimination of the survivals of the exploiting class. Stalin also put forward five suggestions, one of which was to continue developing industry, increase the productive forces of labor and improve technical equipment so that the technical equipment in industry and its speed of development can surpass that of the capitalist countries and finally surpass their economy in the next 10 to 15 years. The Great Purge lasted until 1938, which had seriously damaged the socialist democracy and suppressed the creativity and activity of cadres and the masses. At this meeting, Stalin declared that there were mistakes in this "purge", but it had come with good effect.

In August 1939, the USSR and Germany signed the Treaty of Mutual Non-Aggression. In September 1939, Stalin took part in the negotiation on the German-Soviet Boundary and Friendship Treaty and attended the signing ceremony. During this period of time, headed by Stalin, the Communist Party of Soviet Union and the government carried out the tactics of dual diplomacy. Stalin thought that "the policy of peace keeping and strengthening connection with all countries still needs to be implemented in the future"; that we should keep a cautious attitude, keeping our country from getting involved in conflicts by those who are won to reaping unfair gains by provoking the war."[47] In order to get rid of the isolated state, prevent brining

47 The Works of Stalin (1934-1952), p. 246, Beijing, People's Publishing House, 1985.

the war to the USSR and avoid getting involved in the war, at the same time of making efforts to establish the united front of anti-fascism, the USSR also increased contact with fascist Germany.

At 4:00 am on June 22, 1941, from the Baltic Sea to the Black Sea, fascist Germany made a large-scale sudden onslaught like a lightning along the USSR's western frontier, which was over 2000 kilometers from north to south. In May 1941, Stalin was appointed the chairman of the People's Committee of the USSR and speeded up the preparation for the violation of fascist Germany, but failed in theaccurate estimate the time of attack. At the end of June, Stalin was appointed the chairman of the National Defense Committee and held the concurrent position as the national defense commissar in July. In August, he took the position as the supreme commander of the USSR's armed force. When the German-Soviet War broke out, making use of Britain and America's intent to ally, the USSR took a series of practical steps to promote the establishment of the alliance of Soviet Union, America and Britain and the World Anti-Fascism Alliance. With Soviet Union's efforts and support, the United Nations Declaration was born in January 1942, which marked the official establishment of the World Anti-Fascism Alliance centering on Soviet Union, the United States, Britain and China. After that, the USSR was working actively on strengthening and consolidating the alliance. As the only socialist country, the USSR paid a lot of attention to taking flexible policies, seeking common ground while reserving differences. The USSR also put emphasis on solidarity and co-operation, seeking for solidarity with struggle, keeping the four countries as the stable core of the World Anti-Fascism Alliance. By doing this, the confidence on victory of the people from the anti-fascism countries was boosted and the positive impact was also brought to the victory of the anti-fascist war.

Soviet Union was the main force to fight against Germany. From the breakout of the German-Soviet War to the end of the European War, most forces of the German fascist army were put into the battlefield of the German-Soviet war. By 1944, the battlefield of Soviet Union had pinned down 153 to 201 of the most elite German divisions, which took up over half of the German forces' total number. During the war, Germany totally lost the force of 13.6 million, 73% of which were lost in Soviet Union. Also during the war, Soviet Union was the powerful backing and reliable rear of the anti-fascist fights by people from a series of Asian and European countries that was invaded. After the breakout of the German-Soviet War, Stalin declared in his speech on July 3, 1941, "The aim of this national patriotic war in defense of our country against the fascist oppressors is not only to eliminate the danger hanging over our country, but also to aid all the

European peoples groaning under the yoke of German fascism."[48] During the War of National Defense from 1941 to 1945, the USSR's army and its people fought with great difficulties, achieved a great victory of the anti-fascist war and assisted in defeating Japanese militarism. This was the biggest contribution of Stalin to the people of Soviet Union and the whole world. It was also the most outstanding contribution he had ever made in his whole life to the development of human civilization.

The third is the consolidation of the highly centralized socialist economic system. After the victory of the War of National Defense, Soviet Union entered into the period of economic recovery and peaceful development. In February 1946, Stalin made a speech at the Voters' Meeting of his district in Moscow, indicating that the victory of the War of National Defense had proved that the Soviet socialist system was "full of vitality."[49] As for the materialist conditions for the victory of the War of National Defense, "the first relied on the industrialization policy of the Soviet nations". The Soviet nations took a different path of industrialization, staring from heavy industry. "The second relied on the policy of collectivization." If there were not the policy of collectivization, the USSR would not be able to eliminate the backwardness of agriculture. In Stalin's opinion, the current system and policies were not taken under certain conditions to deal with certain special situations, but were the only correct path for the socialist development in the USSR.

After the Second World War, the policy of excessively taking from peasants was still in use in the Russian agriculture. The price at which the government bought grain from peasants remained the same, but the prices of industrial products had increased 20 times comparing with the same period. By ways of compulsory sale, services paid in kind at the machine-tractor station, etc, the government managed to take over half of the peasants' harvest yield. The resolution made in September 1946 and the one made at the plenum in February 1947 both emphasized on the limiting of the peasants' private plots and intensifying the management system of the kolkhozes, causing very difficult situation in rural areas. Since 1948, the phenomenon that peasants escaped to cities in large scale had constantly come up. Faced with such situations, the reform experiment of fixing the output quotas to every group started in some rural areas and was promoted in large scale in Ukraine. Andreyev, who was the member of Politburo in charge of agriculture and the chairman of the All-Union Kolkhoz Affairs Committee, actively supported the reform experiment of fixing production quotas on every group. In April 1949, the USSR Ministers' Conference passed the resolution

48   Selected Works of Stalin, volume 2, p. 480, Beijing, People's Publishing House, 1979, retrieved from Marxists Internet Archive.
49   ibid., p.49.

Measures on Improving kolkhozes, Increasing Productivity and Adjusting Payment of Labors, which further approved this method. However, this attempt of reform was in conflict with Stalin's thought. In February 1950, the editorial Against the Erroneous Tendency in the Kolkhozes was published in Pravda, criticizing Andreyev of damaging the kolkhoz ownership. Later, Andreyev was dismissed from his post and the method of fixing the farm output quotas on each individual group was abolished. Voznesensky was the member of Politburo, the vice chairman of the Ministers' Conference and the chairman of the National Planning Commission. He thought the over centralization of the government would inevitably lead to bureaucracy and economic waste, suggesting to attach great importance to the law of value and its regulation function and promote economic development by using some of the NEP of the 1920s. He also advocated for giving more decision-making power to local governments and enterprises, improving economic accounting and emphasizing on material gain. He especially laid stress on the comprehensive and balanced development of national economy, maintaining to adjust the planning work. For the reason that Voznesensky pointed out the defects of the post-war economic strategy, that heavy industry was still given priority of development and of the over-centralized administrative system, plus that the personality cult of Stalin was prevailing and the modern system was idealized, his opinions were not accepted, but severely criticized as an example of restoration of capitalism. 35

The fourth is about the theoretical and practical issues of socialist economy. As early as January 1941, Stalin had a talk with Molotov and Voznesensky, etc. Stalin thought that there should be a clear definition on political economics, which is the science of development on people's social relations of production, also known as economic relations. The kolkhoz people, workers and intellectuals all get paid by the labor expended, with the difference among people with different skills. There were also spheres such as price and cost in the Soviet Union. According to Stalin they were very far from controlling the price on the market, which requires large amount of material preparation. Planned economy cannot be used by capitalism because its production units are individuals, but the enterprises in Soviet Union were jointed by the government. Therefore, planned economy to Soviet Union is what bread to human beings, which is inevitable. In February 1950, Stalin met with the scholars who wrote The Textbook of Political Economy, deciding to set up a committee that would take charge of merging the two textbooks that had not been finalized into one. In April that year, he met with them again, asking them to finish writing the textbook within one year and submit it for discussion.

In April 1951, the draft of The Textbook of Political Economy was submitted to Stalin, who instructed to prepare for extensive discussion. From

November to December, according to Stalin's advice, CPSU(B) had many discussions on the draft of The Textbook of Political Economy. After reading the related materials about the discussions, in February 1952, Stalin published his last work Economic Problems of Socialism in the USSR, making conclusions of the historical experience on the construction of socialism. In this book, Stalin elaborated on the character of economic laws, commodity production and the law of value, basic economic laws and the balanced, proportionate law of development under socialism, admitting that under socialism the relations of production could also be not suited to the development of the productive forces. As a matter of fact, the overall collectivized relations of production were not suitable to Soviet Union's agricultural productivity at that time. Stalin may have realized that in his later years. However, he hadn't realized the contradiction between relations of production and productive forces; he also had not realized that the contradiction between the superstructure and the economic base which is the basic contradiction that has been promoting the socialist society to develop forward.

The fifth is the problem of linguistics. From May to July in 1950, Pravda organized the discussion on the problem of linguistics. Focused on the questions put up in the discussion, Stalin wrote the pamphlet Marxism and Problems of Linguistics. In the form of answering questions, Stalin criticized the linguist Marr's linguistic theories and elaborated on his own opinions. He pointed out that language is not the superstructure, which will be changed or eliminated with the change or elimination of the economic base and established with the production of the new base. However, language is different. It does not have any class nature. As a tool of communication for people in the society, it is uniform and mutual to the society. It serves every member in the society, regardless of heir social status. Language was formed at the beginning when human society was formed, not born after the birth of class.

On March 1, 1953, Stalin got a sudden attack of cerebral hemorrhage. On March 5, he passed away in his residence in the suburb out of Moscow.

Looking back on Stalin's life, it is fair to say that he is the leader of the proletariat revolution, an explorer and practitioner of socialism in the 20th century. At the same time, out of the various mistakes Stalin made in the revolution and construction practice of socialism, some are very serious. A scientific and comprehensive evaluation on Stalin and his socialist thought will have great significance in understanding the history of development of Marxism in the 20th century and the contemporary value of the scientific principles and spirits. It also has great significance in concluding the experiences and lessons of socialism in the 20th century and its laws of development.

Chapter II

Stalin's Philosophical Thought

Stalin's philosophical thought was not only an important part of his socialist thought, but also the basis of his world view and has guided the methodology in his socialist thought. Therefore, understanding of Stalin's philosophical thought is an important precondition and basis of the study on Stalin's socialist thought.

In the philosophical world abroad, the studies and evaluations on Stalin's philosophical thoughts has always been a controversial issue, some giving compliments but more disparaging it. Especially with the disintegration of the USSR at the beginning of the 1990s, the second tide of completely denying Stalin's philosophical thought has emerged again following the one at the Twentieth Congress of CPSU(B) in 1956. Some scholars at home and abroad have suggested that Stalin's philosophical thought has completely misunderstood Marxist philosophy and thereby completely deny the significance of Stalin's philosophical thought in the history of Marxism. As a result, how to evaluate Stalin's philosophical thought has become an extremely urgent and complicated research subject. We think that to correctly evaluate Stalin's philosophical thought, the research on the historical background of its origin and development, and the research of the practice of socialist construction under his leadership must be combined. Based on this view, we shall make a historical and case-by-case analysis on his important philosophical works and opinions. Only in this way, can we have a fair conclusion based on facts.

I. Stalin's philosophical thought at the early stage

According to our periodization of Stalin's philosophical thoughts, his early thoughts on philosophy refer to the period before the October Revolution. During this period, the most outstanding feature of his philosophical thought is that he had used Marxist philosophy to solve the major problems of the revolutionary practice of the Russian proletariat. Also in this period, we can observe that there are quite a few immaturities, even serious drawbacks in his philosophical thought. In general, he had adhered to the basic principles of Marxism.

Stalin's philosophical thought was gradually formed under the influence of Marxism and in the practice of proletarian revolution. The article titled Anarchism or Socialism published between 1906 and 1907 marked the formation of Stalin's world view of dialectical materialism and historical materialism. During the development of Stalin's early philosophical thought, this work marks an important stage. Today, there are still a lot of heated discussions on this article. Some think that in this work, Stalin barely had any unique understanding on Marx's philosophical theories but had simply repeated the general principles of Marxist philosophy; moreover in this work, Stalin had demonstrated the tendency of metaphysical thinking, which was the origin of his extremely serious later metaphysical thoughts. However, on this important work marking Stalin's early philosophical thought, the comments mentioned above obviously have some impropriety. We think that under the historical conditions at that time, the basic viewpoints in this book did not severely contradictwith Marxist philosophy but had quite a positive impact on the spread of it. In this book, Stalin's incisive and powerful criticism on the Russian anarchist Varlam Cherkezishvili's absurd arguments distorting and attacking Marxist philosophy had defended and scientifically commented on the basic principles of Marxist philosophy.

First, Stalin had exposed anarchists' attempt of separating and dissembling Marxism, and defended and demonstrated the integrity and unity of the scientific system of Marxism. Stalin pointed out, "Marxism is not only the theory of socialism. It is an integral world outlook, a philosophical system, from which Marx's proletarian socialism logically follows."[1] This was a sound advocate to claim that Marxist philosophy is the basis of the world outlook of scientific socialism; that Marxism is an integrated and inseparable scientific theoretical system. Stalin had pointed out that scientific socialism is the great achievement of Marx and Engels' research of social life and exploration of social development laws by making use of the materialist world outlook. The internal relations between Marxist philosophy and

1 Collected Works of Stalin, first Chinese version, volume 1, p. 274, retrieved from Marxists Internet Archive.

scientific socialism have fully displayed the unity between proletarian parties and their revolutionary activities, the struggle to eliminate capitalism and the practice of establishing socialism. It is fair to say that this particular viewpoint of Stalin is not only correct, but also profound. It also indicates that we must comprehensively and correctly grasp the scientific theoretical system of Marxism while paying attention to the internal relations between each part of it. Only in this way can it be scientifically used to solve various problems in the proletarian revolution and distinguish the essence of the attacks on Marxism by different bourgeoisie ideologies.

Second, Stalin had indicated that Marxist philosophy is a thorough materialistic monism that is united with dialectical materialism and historical materialism. Stalin had also pointed out that Marxist philosophy is never a dualistic philosophy as the anarchists had argued but the most thorough dialectical materialistic monism. To defend that, Stalin had explained the basic viewpoints of Marxist philosophy: the relation between matter and consciousness. He pointed out that from the viewpoints of dialectical materialism, consciousness and existence, concept and matter are two different forms of the same phenomenon that is usually called nature or society; that consciousness is just the reflection of the existence of matter, which has an essential difference from the original dualism that takes matter and spirit as two opposites and independent. Therefore, Stalin had insisted on the basic viewpoint that matter is primary and consciousness is secondary and that the unity of the world lies in its substantial dialectical materialistic monism.

Stalin had also especially criticized the anarchists' ridiculous attempt to reduce Marxist philosophy to vulgar materialism. Directing against the anarchists fallacy that: "Marxists philosophy advocates that eating determines ideology"; Stalin pointed out that these "anarchists did not understand at all that there are various materialistic theories in science; and that there are huge differences between different forms of materialism; and that Marxist philosophy has a substantial difference from the vulgar materialism that confuses matter and consciousness. It is a huge slander on Marxist philosophy to distort the notion emphasized by it as "man's economic status determines their consciousness".

When refuting the anarchists' distortion of Marxist philosophy, Stalin had demonstrated the basic viewpoints of historical materialism: "if the economic conditions change first and the consciousness of men undergoes a corresponding change later, it is clear that we must seek the grounds for a given ideal not in the minds of men, not in their imaginations, but in the development of their economic conditions."[2] This opinion is completely consistent with the basic viewpoints of historical dialectics and also

2 Collected Works of Stalin, first Chinese version, volume 1, p. 293, retrieved from Marxists Internet Archive.

persistent with the organic unity of dialectical and historical materialism. Stalin thought that the relation between matter and consciousness is the same as that between content and form; that matter is content and consciousness is form, which is decided by the content. Judging from the aspect of their development, content is before form, which is behind content. However, when the content is changed, the form will ultimately change accordingly. Stalin had explained his opinion with a common reality in social life. He had pointed out that the material conditions in the society are the foundation of people's consciousness and even their world view. The latter changes with the change of the former. Similarly, economy is the material foundation of the social life while the forms such as politics and law are the superstructure that is decided by the content: the economic foundation. Therefore, in a society the transformation of productive forces and relations of production can be promoted through efforts that make complete changes in the political and legal system.

Furthermore, Stalin had also criticized the anarchist distortion and attack on materialist dialectics and explained its basic viewpoints. Focusing on anarchist confusion of Marxist materialist dialectics and Hegel's metaphysical dialectics, Stalin had revealed the essential difference between Marx's materialist dialectics and Hegel's metaphysical dialectics. Stalin's explanation on the basic viewpoints of the materialistic dialectics was comparatively complete and revealed its scientific character. Stalin pointed out that everything in the world is in an eternal change and development; that both the nature and the human society also follow the same law.

Therefore, we have to observe the world and social life through the law of movement and development in materialistic dialectics. The essence of development is the extinction of the old and the emergence of the new and nothing can defeat it. "That which in life is born and grows day by day is invincible; its progress cannot be checked."[3] Proletariat, as a new born class that is growing, developing and progressing, is invincible. Evolution and revolution are the two forms basic forms of movement and change. According the law of quantitative and qualitative change, evolution prepares and lays foundation for revolution, which completes the evolution and promotes the development of it. Here Stalin's demonstration of the basic laws and viewpoints of materialistic dialectics are profound and correct; his criticism on anarchists is also sound.

Some scholars have argued that Stalin had revealed his metaphysical way of thinking when he was explaining the basic viewpoints of materialistic dialectics; as he claimed "all that which really exists, i.e. all that which grows day by day is rational; and all that which decays day by day

3 Collected Works of Stalin, first Chinese version, volume 1, p. 275, retrieved from Marxist Internet Archive.

is irrational and, consequently, cannot avoid defeat."[4] Actually, above argument is a bit too farfetched, because obviously, Stalin's opinion is nothing but the development of the related viewpoints of Engels in his book *Ludwig Feuerbach and the End of Classic German Philosophy*, and his opinion is generally consistent with that of Engels. There are also some critics arguing that Stalin had simplified the complicated historical process and the real world with the above-mentioned formulations and viewpoints; that he simply divided the world into two camps-capitalists and proletarians and that he had also pessimistically argued that establishing socialism would be impossible when proletariat class only forms a small minority in the society. We think that this censure also has no real foundation, because the basic viewpoint of materialistic dialectics advocating that the newborn things cannot be defeated was the very basis for Stalin when he argued with confidence that the bourgeoisie is already a declining class though it is still strong and whereas the proletarian class, as a newborn one, will definitely grow and finally achieve victory. For the Russian proletariat whose revolutionary activity was at a low tide, this remark by Stalin was a great boost of their confidence for the victory of the revolution.

Certainly we do not intend to argue that Stalin's this early book was highly mature, but we can easily suggest that among many works, criticizing or denouncing it, only few could reveal its real defects. Regretfully some have criticized it only to criticize it and therefore could not offer an objective and fair evaluation on it. In fact, just as Stalin himself had commented, his works at this stage were just the works of a young Marxist, a Marxist-Leninist who was not so mature. The main defect in this work was that, it had separated the theory and methodology of dialectic materialism, arguing that its methods are dialectical but its theories were materialistic. Later, this defect in his understanding of dialectic materialism was further developed in his *Dialectical and Historical Materialism*. All in all, even though there were some immaturities and defects, in that book generally its understanding on basic principles of Marxist philosophy was correct. Also the demonstration and development of some basic viewpoints were scientific, which also had a positive effect at that time. Therefore it should not be denied so easily.

II. The critique of the Deborin school

In the 1920s, in the philosophical circles of the USSR, there emerged a long-lasting debate between the school of dialectic theory and the school of mechanistic theory. At the end of the 1920s, when the debate was won with a decisive victory by the school of dialectic theory headed by Deborin,

---

4   Retrieved from Marxist Internet Archive.

they were seriously criticized by Stalin. Therefore, a combat of criticizing Deborin was started in Soviet Union's philosophical circles. This struggle had also made a significant world-wide effect.Even today, there are still a lot of scholars studying on it. There have been many different opinions on this struggle, especially on Stalin's role in it and his critique of the Deborin School. For a complete study and evaluation on Stalin's philosophical thought, it is necessary to discuss Stalin's critique of the Deborin School.

In the mid-1920s, there emerged the ideological trend of mechanistic theory, which denied the value of materialistic dialectics, its independent existence as a scientific theory. This trend had advocated that the science itself is philosophy; therefore philosophy itself should be abandoned. Mechanists applied the viewpoint of mechanical motion to explain the phenomena in nature and society. They had denied the quantitative changes or leaps in nature and society, only admitting the change of quantity. They argued that even though there were high motions and medium motions, the complicated advanced form of motion could be included in the low form of motion, which means it could be reduced to the simple mechanical motion.

As the mechanistic theory got popular, Marxist philosophy's influence and guidance on natural science studies was seriously affected, which also had negative influence on the spread and study of Marxist and Leninist philosophy. Headed by Deborin, the dialecticians had criticized the ideological trend of mechanistic theory, emphasizing that Marxist philosophy's guidance on natural sciences can never be denied. As a result, the first great debate in Soviet Union's philosophical history was formed.

In 1925, Engels' important work *Dialectics of Nature* was published in the USSR for the first time, evoking great repercussions both in philosophy and science circles. The mechanists described Engels as a mechanist to prove that their viewpoints were right. Targeting at mechanists' viewpoints, Deborin wrote his work titled "Engels and Dialectics in Biology", refuting the mechanists' distortion of Engels' opinions.

As the debate developed and deepened, the two parties held heated arguments on a series of major theoretical problems such as whether materialistic dialectics could lead science, what the exact relations between philosophy and natural science were, and whether basic laws of motion in the nature were mechanical or dialectic, and on the relationships between quality and quantity, necessity and accidentalism, etc. But later the debate started to gain political colors. On May 18, 1926, Deborin in his closing speech during an important conference described the mechanistic school as a group with the qualities of revisionism and defended his position as the revolutionary and orthodox Marxism, which had increased the conflict to a new height and confrontation between the two parties. In 1929, this long-lasting debate was completed with the thorough victory of Deborin's group. But their victory had only lasted nearly a year.

When Deborin and his school had achieved the victory in the debate and got the leading position in Soviet Union's philosophical circles, Stalin gave a speech on December 27, 1929 at the All-Union Conference of Marxist Students of Agrarian Questions, incisively criticizing that theoreticians had seriously cut off themselves from the practice of socialist construction. The All-Union Conference of Marxist Students of Agrarian Questions, convened by the Communist Academy of the CEC, USSR included 302 delegates representing scientific research institutions, agricultural and economic colleges, and newspapers and magazines. Stalin had pointed out that "the theoretical thought was not keeping pace with the development of practical successes; and that there was a certain gap between practical successes and the development of theoretical thought." He had argued: "the unfortunate thing is that precisely in this sphere, in the sphere of the theoretical treatment of questions of our economy, we are beginning to lag behind."[5] Stalin had also suggested that theorists should study in depth a series of major practical problems such as the NEP, classes, speed of construction, the Party's policy, etc, and come up with creative understanding on them and therefore overcome the situation in which theory was being separated from practice.

Stalin's speech had evoked a strong reaction in Soviet Union's theoretical circles. Represented by Mitin, a group of young theorists gave an active support to the spirit of Stalin's speech, strongly criticized Deborin and other leaders in the philosophical circles. They denounced the Deborin school as: "just focusing on the abstract study of the history of philosophy but turning a cold shoulder to the practical problems in the socialist construction and therefore causing a huge gap with the reality." Faced with the criticism and blames by Mitin and other people, Deborin School firmly refuted, thus another long-lasting debate had emerged.

On June 7, 1930, Mitin and other people published the article titled "The New Aims of Marxist-Leninst Philosophy" in *Pravda* (the central organ of the Party). The article argued that the concentrated reflection of the philosophical circles lagging behind the practice wastheir inactive participation in criticizing Rubin faction's viewpoints on political economics. They also criticized that the board of the journal *Under the Banner of Marxism* whose chief editor was Deborin actually had agreed with I.I. Rubin's opinions since Rubin's article was published without the journal's critical note. Deborin School immediately refuted this criticism and blame and pointed out at the same time that Mitin and other people's elaboration on the

5 Collected Works of Stalin, first Chinese version, volume 12, p. 127, retrieved from Marxists Internet Archive.

present situation of philosophical circles and their ideas on the tasks faced by Marxist-Leninist philosophy were correct. Since after, Mitin published other articles in *Pravda* and other newspapers or journals with a stronger critique of the Deborin School. In August and October of 1930, the Red Professor's Institute where Mitin worked passed two resolutions, criticizing Deborin School's "tendency of formalism".

Mitin faction's criticism on Deborin School had caught Stalin's attention. On December 9, 1930 when he held the talk with the members of party branch of the Red Professor's Institute, Stalin made a praise and commented:"it is a school and professor's style to refer Deborin bloc's mistake as the tendency of formalism." In Stalin's opinion, the essence of Deborin bloc's mistake was the Menshevik idealism, which meant spreading idealism from the stand point of Menshevism and making idealistic revision of Marxism. Stalin also listed Deborin school's major mistakes in detail: first, divorcement of theory from practice, meaning that Deborin school's philosophical study had highly estranged from politics and the practice of socialist construction; second, Deborin bloc stealthily substituted materialistic dialectics of Marxism with Hegel's distorted idealism; third, putting a higher value on Plekhanov's works while underrating Lenin's status and his contribution to Marxist philosophy. According to Stalin, the reason behind their attitudes was that they were critizing Marxism from the perspective of Menshevism. Based on the above analysis and misjudgment, Stalin had ordered to completely investigate everything the mechanists, Deborin activists and other revisionists did, to check all of their works and criticize everything they had written, done or said.[6] Stalin also commented: "from Deborin, one can see the most harmful political group; that it is the agent of Menshevism thought that is extremely hostile to Marxism and therefore, should be completely eliminated".

Right after Stalin's above speech, the movement, criticizing Deborin School was immediately launched in Soviet Union's philosophical circles. On January 25, 1931, the Central Committee of CPSU(B) made a resolution related to the journal Under the Banner of Marxism, pointing out that the journal was completely standing on a wrong perspective; that it "revived one of the extremely harmful traditions and doctrines-making the theory divorce from the practice and therefore defended the position of Menshevik idealism". At the same time, the resolution also dismissed Deborin from his position as the chief editor of the journal and rearranged its editorial board. Under great political pressure, Deborin was forced to make self-criticism, admitting that his previous philosophical stand was Menshevik idealism.

---

6   For further reference, see Commemorating onThe Tenth Anniversary of the Resolution of the Central Committee of CPSU(B) on "Under the Banner of Marxism" and The Collected Documents of Deborin School, p. 167, Changchun, Jilin People's Publishing House, 1982.

However, the criticism on Deborin School had not ceased but was futher escalated, thus the debate of theories was elevated to a fierce political struggle. Later, critique against Menshevik idealism of Deborin School was defined as a struggle against the "direct counter-revolutionary and fascist trend". In the *Great Soviet Encyclopedia* published in 1938, the philosophical viewpoints of Deborin School were even regarded as the distortion of Marxist philosophy, "defending the victory of class enemy over socialism, which reflected the all-offensive and vigorous resistance against socialism, the ideological shield of Trotskyite two-faced activists, spies, traitors and Trotsky proxies". At the same time, there were also some people who completely denied the significance of Deborin School's fight against the mechanistic theory, labeling it as the struggle between "two counter-revolutionary groups"; and most people of the Deborin School were blamed as Trotskyite activists.

Judging by the facts mentioned above, scholars from both home and abroad think that the criticism on Deborin School under the leadership of Stalin created a precedent of disrupting academic democracy by confusing academic and political issues and a malign tradition of resolving academic disputes with administrative measures and even elevating academic differences to struggles over matter of principles. However, this opinion alone misses any positive significance of the criticism against Deborin School. On the other hand, there are some other views which do not agree with the denial of the criticism at all. They argue that Deborin's philosophical viewpoints were idealistic in essence. Stalin criticized them only because they refused to admit their mistake. Stalin had done nothing wrong since he had intended to defend Leninism and Lenin's philosophy. Since the elimination of the negative impact of the Deborin School was an achievement urging philosophical circles to overcome the mistake of separating theory from practice, and improved the study style on Marxist philosophy the significance of this struggle cannot be denied.

45

I think we should not simply approve or deny the criticism on Deborin School led by Stalin but give it an objective and fair evaluation. It is fair to say that the debate between Deborin and his school and mechanists had certain significance in defending Marxist philosophy, but its main effect was mainly witnessed in theoretical circles, not too much on society or political sphere. In the beginning years of the Soviet Union, Bolsheviks were faced with several enormous practical social issues that were extremely complicated and which needed urgent solution, such as the socialist transformation of national economy, how to handle the class conflicts and the dictatorship of the Proletariat in a new era, how to achieve the transition to socialism, etc. However, Deborin and his school spent its main efforts on scholarly debates with the "mechanists" and focused on the issue of relations between philosophy and natural science, thus studies on philosophy were divorced from social practice and the needs of this social practice, which was more urgent. Separation from practice was one major defect of Deborin and his school in the debate and study of philosophy. In this historical context Stalin's criticism on Deborin and his school did cause certain positive impacts. However, on the other hand, Stalin's criticism on Deborin School was flawed with one-sidedness, and especially his mistakenevaluation on Deborin and his school, had caused serious negative results.

First, the criticism on Deborin and his school was one-sided. Particularly, the complete denial of Deborin School's critique of mechanistic theories was wrong. One cannot deny that Deborin and his school did have defects in their philosophical viewpoints, such as the tendency of exaggerating the value of Hegel's idealistic dialectics and Plekhanov's philosophical works in the history of Marxist philosophy, besides several inaccurate ideas related to some basic viewpoints of Marxist philosophy, etc. But, all in all, Deborin's basic philosophical viewpoints were still on the same ground with Marxist philosophy. As a famous Marxist philosopher, Deborin had made a significant contribution to the study, elaboration and defense of Marxist philosophy no matter before or after the October Revolution. However, Stalin had failed to make a complete and objective analysis on Deborin and his school's philosophical viewpoints but arbitrarily concluded that their opinions propagated idealism from the ground of Menshevism. That is to say, he thought Deborin's philosophical thought was in the main idealistic, but it is obvious that this judgment was not well-founded. The criticism of Deborin and his School led by Stalin which argued that their critique against mechanism and defending Marxist philosophy was a struggle between two counterrevolutionary groups was a serious distortion of the facts and misjudgment on the nature of this struggle.

Second, academic and political issues were confused, consequently an academic debate was turned into a kind of political struggle. Stalin evaluated Deborin and his school as Menshevik idealism, the spokesman of Menshevik ideology that was hostile to Marxism and Leninism. Thus he had mistakenly confused philosophical and political groupings, as well as philosophical and political issues. Deborin's tendency of separating theory from practice and several mistakes in his philosophical viewpoints were not political mistakes in their nature and by no means in relation with Menshevism. Deborin School was just a philosophical group that was formed in the debate against mechanistic theories, but Stalin had obviously regarded them as a hostile political group. It was under the influence of Stalin's will that the political criticism on Deborin and his school was escalated to extremes and finally defined as "direct counter-revolutionary and fascist". Stalin's mistake of treating an academic debate as a reflection of intensifying class struggle had seriously confused the contradictions consisting of two different natures and as well started the malign tradition of crudelytreating academic issues as political problems in the world socialist movement and socialist countries.

Third, the Party and its leaders had seriously intervenedintheoretical studies and interrupted academic democracy and tried to lead academic debates with administrative measures and political resolutions. The leaders' opinions were taken as the basic standard of judging the right and wrong. Stalin's instructions and the resolution of the Central Committee of CPSU(B) in January 1931 had determined the keynote of the criticism on Deborin. Therefore the debate was predominated by the Mark Mitin's side, making the arguments of Deborin and his school useless. Especially when the debate had further escalated, Mark Mitin and his group representing the party position had completely followed Stalin's instructions, thus Mitin had gained a prominent status in the history of Marxist philosophy. He and his colleagues had praised every instruction and speech Stalin's as the only standard of the truth. What they did was to set a precedent for the study style that was featured with personality cult lasting over 20 years in Soviet Union's academic circles, seriously damaging the healthy development of philosophy and sciences in the Soviet Union.

III. The philosophical thought in
Dialectical and Historical Materialism

As the second part of the fourth chapter of the book *History of the All-Union Communist Party (Bolsheviks), Short Course*, Stalin wrote in person *Dialectical and Historical Materialism*, which was published in 1938. This work was the foundation of Stalin's philosophical thought, having huge influence on the international communist movement for the next more than 20 years. During a certain historical period, due to the personality cult of Stalin, this work was regarded as "the top of the development of Marxist-Leninist philosophy". However, after Stalin's death, especially when the CPSU(B) had started the movement of criticizing Stalin's philosophical thought, many people targeted and strongly belittled it. It was also used as the evidence to prove that Stalin was just a shabby philosopher. By doing so, Stalin's status in the course of history of Marxist philosophy was completely denied. We think that this book should be neither over evaluated, nor just completely denied. Only with scientific and detailed analysis on its content and influence we can make an objective and fair evaluation of it.

By the end of the 1930s, the USSR had generally completed the social-ist industrialization and the collectivization, established socialist system and the leading position of Marxism and Leninism in ideology. In order to promote further the development of socialism in the new historical pe-riod, Stalin and the Central Committee of CPSU(B) decided to write *The History of CPSU(B)* in order to profoundly conclude the Party's historical experience and educate the cadres and party members with the theories of Marxism and Leninism. The purpose of Stalin writing *Dialectical and Historical Materialism* as the second part of the fourth chapter of the book *History of the All-Union Communist Party (Bolsheviks), Short Course* was to help the party leaders and members to understand and grasp the dialectic and historical materialistic world outlook of Marxism and Leninism. There are scholars at home and abroad who think that Stalin wrote the article only to establish his authority on philosophy, but this criticism is too one-sided.

There are a lot of critics at home and abroad, especially the western Stalinism critics have a completely negative attitude on the main viewpoints of Stalin's Dialectic Materialism and Materialism. They think that the main viewpoints in this work are either the simple repeat of Marx, Engels and Lenin's philosophical opinions without any innovation, or the wanton dis-tortion of the classic philosophers' thought with his "private goods". We think that Stalin's philosophical viewpoints in this work should not be sim-ply denied like this. To have a correct evaluation on Stalin's thought, it is necessary to make some brief comments on Stalin's major philosophical points in this work with the reference from the critics' point of view.

1. The very nature of Marxist philosophy

According to Stalin, dialectic materialism is the world view of Marxism and Leninism. He clearly revealed that the nature of Marxist philosophy is dialectic materialism. Stalin's thesis is correct and consistent with Lenin's comment on the nature of Marxist philosophy in Materialism and Empirio-Criticism. However, as some scholars have pointed out, Stalin also thought that dialectic materialism is the basic view of natural phenomena; that its method of studying and knowing that the nature is dialectic, but its explana-tion and understanding, namely its theories, on the natural phenomena are materialistic. As a result, the theories and methods of dialectic materialism were deviated and the dialectic materialism was set as the view of nature. Some western scholars think that Stalin's understanding on dialectic ma-terialism includesmainly the nature he referred toand does not include the humanized nature. It is just the pure nature that has been deviated from the humanized nature. Therefore, the human society was excluded too. Stalin equated dialectic materialism and dialectics of nature but differen-tiated dialectic materialism and historical materialism. Therefore, Stalin's philosophical system is actually a creed of the dialectics of nature consisted of two parts, one being dialectics of nature and the other being historical materialism. It is fair to say that the criticism makes some sense. Stalin's explanation on dialectic materialism, especially his understanding of the relations between dialectic materialism and historical materialism, are not in line with the original meaning of Marxist philosophy, which, on the basis of science, materialistically and dialectically resolves the relations between thinking and existence and therefore achieves the dynamic integration of materialism and dialectics. Therefore, Marxist philosophy was called modern materialism by Engels. Modern materialism is dialectic in essence, which means it is materialism. Dialectic materialism is a whole piece consisted of the material and dialectic views of nature and history, not just the material and dialectic view of nature as understood by Stalin. Judging by the course of Marxist philosophy's thought, historical materialism is not as Stalin said, but the result of Marx and Engels' application of dialectic materialism on the history of society. It is not that dialectic materialism comes earlier than historical materialism. It is until the establishment of historical materialism when materialism finally became complete and dialectic materialism.

It is only because historical materialism as the unique concept of Marxist philosophy is one of the two major theoretical foundations of scientific socialism and has therefore especially important significance in the scientific system of Marxism that is called dialectic materialism and historical materialism. The way it is called never means that historical materialism is another philosophical system which is independent from dialectic materialism. Therefore, Stalin's understanding on dialectic materialism was not comprehensive. However, Stalin's philosophical system is also not a creed of dialectics of nature like the western scholars claim, because he did not consciously conclude Marxist philosophy or dialectic materialism into dialectics of nature or dialectic materialistic view of nature. This can be told from his work *Dialectic and Historical Materialism*. Obviously, he regarded Marxist philosophy as the unity of dialectic and historical materialism, but his comments on that were unclear and self-contradicting.

2. The source of Marxist philosophy

Stalin's comments on this topic are generally in line with Lenin's explanation in *Three Sources and Three Component Parts of Marxism*. Stalin thought that when Marx and Engels were explaining their dialectics, they always quoted Hegel, who in his mind, was a philosopher that described the basic characters of dialectics, but Marx and Engels' dialectics was different because they absorbed the "rational core" of Hegel's dialectics but abandoned the idealistic shell and therefore further developed dialectics and gave it a modern and scientific form. Stalin pointed out that Feuerbach's materialistic philosophy is another important source of Marxist philosophy, but it is different from Marxist philosophy. Marx and Engels absorbed the "basic core" of Feuerbach's materialism, developed it further into scientific theories of materialism and abandoned its impure substance such as idealism, religion and ethics. In this way, Stalin had briefly revealed the relation and difference between Marxist philosophy, Hegel's philosophy and Feuerbach's philosophy. However, one thing which needs to be noticed is that Stalin only indicated the direct source of Marxism, but he said it was the source of Marxist philosophy, which made people feel that Hegel and Feuerbach's philosophy are the only sources of Marxist philosophy. Actually, the sources of Marxist philosophy are not only these two. Marx and Engels did not only critically absorb the essence of German classical philosophy, but also the rational components of modern British and French philosophy. At the same time, when establishing the materialist conception of history, they also critically absorbed the valuable theoretical assessments of British classical political economy and British and French utopian socialism. To a greater extent, Marxist philosophy is the result of comprehensive innovation of all the outstanding ideologies and cultures that were critically absorbed by Marx and Engels. Therefore, Stalin's elaboration on the source of Marxist philosophy had some defects.

3. On the basic features of materialistic dialectics

Stalin highly valued materialistic dialectics. From the perspective that is opposite to metaphysics, he generalized four basic characteristics of materialistic dialectics:

First, just opposite to metaphysics, instead of taking nature as an accidental accumulation of objects or phenomena that are segregated, isolated, independent from each other, dialectics regards them as a unified and coherent whole, out of which every object or phenomenon is organically connected, dependent on and restricted to each other. Stalin regarded universal connection as the most basic feature of materialistic dialectics, which carried on the viewpoint of Lenin and Engels that objects are universally connected.

Second, as opposite to metaphysics, instead of taking nature as being static and invariant, dialectics regards nature's state as it is in constant motion, change, renewal and development. In nature, there are always some things emerging and developing while some other things are damaging and declining. Stalin regarded the viewpoint of development as another basic feature of dialectic materialism, which again is consistent with Engels' and Lenin's comment on the theory of development.

Third, as opposite to metaphysics, instead of taking the process of development as a simple process of growing with only quantitative but no qualitative change, dialectics regards the development as a process from subtle, potential quantitative change to significant and essential change and finally to the qualitative change. During this development process, the qualitative change does not come step by step, but comes quickly and suddenly, with the stages leaping from one to another. The qualitative change also does not come on occasion but in order. It is the accumulation of many subtle and gradual quantitative changes. Obviously, what Stalin meant here was the law of quantitative and qualitative change in materialistic dialectics.

Fourth, as opposite to metaphysics, the origin of dialectics is that: the objects and phenomena in nature all have internal contradictions because they all have their front and reverse side, their past and future and their weakening and developing parts; the struggles between the two opposite sides, between the old and new and between the weakening and developing parts, thus they are the internal content of the process of development and the internal content of the change from quantity to quality. Stalin emphasized here that the essence of development is the struggle between the old and the new. This struggle is the one between the opposites in a contradiction.

The academic world at home and abroad has different understanding and evaluation on Stalin's generalization of dialectics' four features. Some critics think that there are major defects in Stalin's generalization of dialectics basic features. Since Stalin only regarded dialectics as something that is opposite to metaphysics, he had a very negative and simple understanding on dialectics and generalized the four invariant features. Therefore, dialectics was turned into something that is one-sided and metaphysical. Stalin ignored that unity of opposites is the essence and core of dialectics. He just very briefly mentioned the content of unity of the opposites when he referred to the fourth feature, which was greatly different from Lenin's related comments in *Philosophical Notebooks*.

We think that among the criticism above, some are correct, but others need some discussions. Especially the criticism which completely denies Stalin's thought on dialectics for the reason that Stalin supposedly had turned dialectics into Hegel's idealistic dialectics by separating dialectics from materialism, we do not think it is right.

Stalin did not separate dialectics from materialism when he demonstrated the basic features of dialectics. From his related comments we can clearly tell that the dialectics he mentioned is the dialectics of the nature, which is in line with the basic ground of materialism. When explaining dialectic methodology, Stalin had pointed out that "this method regards the phenomena in the nature being in constant motion and change, the development of the nature as the results of the development of contradictions and the influence of the power of the opposites in the nature."[7] However, there are some defects on Stalin's way of expression, which is a sign that his understanding of dialectics is comparatively superficial. In his explanation of dialectics, he firstly mentioned the origin of dialectics, demonstrating that the original meaning of dialectics was the art of pursuing truth by revealing and overcoming the contradictions of the demonstration from the other side. He then explained that this dialectic way of thinking was later introduced to the phenomena of the nature and became the dialectics of the nature. His way of explanation neither scientifically explained the essence of the revolutionary reform on the way and method of thinking, brought by Marx and Engels' materialistic dialectics, nor demonstrated the essence of dialectics. According to Marx and Engels, dialectics essentially is the science about the universal law of nature, society and mind. Subjective dialectics as the way of thinking is just the reflection of objective dialectics in the mind. Therefore Stalin failed at understanding in depth the relations between subjective and objective dialectics but only simply regarded dialectics as the development of dialectic way of thinking in the nature. Although there were major defects in Stalin's way of explaining, his basic viewpoint was right that the dialectic way of thinking is a scientific way to know the nature. And he was still on the ground of materialism when he was demonstrating the basic features of dialectics. It doesn't tally with his actual thoughts that he separated dialectics and materialism and thereby drifted to idealism only due to his defects on the way of demonstrating. To be exact, it is the result of Stalin's insistence to regard materialism as theory and dialectics, as methods, but it is not sufficient to say that Stalin's understanding on dialectics is idealistic.

52

As to the question whether or not Stalin's generalization of dialectics' four basic features and his basic viewpoints of demonstrating dialectics from the perspective that it is opposite to metaphysics have led to one-sidedness and metaphysics, we think that there is no doubt that Stalin's demonstration had major defects and one-sidedness of metaphysics, but it should not be completely denied.

Stalin's demonstration of dialectics' basic features from the perspective that is opposite to metaphysics highlighted the essential difference between the two, emphasized on the critical essence of dialectic revolution, which should be regarded as one merit of his dialectic thought. It is definitely not the sign that he had made dialectics one-sided and metaphysical. Stalin's generalization of dialectics' four basic features is his new attempt to establish the theoretical system of dialectics. With the combination of Marx, Engels and Lenin's rich dialectical thought, Stalin systematically

7   Selected Works of Stalin, volume 2, p. 452

demonstrated the basic viewpoints of materialistic dialectics and tried to reveal their internal relations, which is one of Stalin's important contributions to Marxist philosophy. As regards to some people who completely denied Stalin's contribution based on his defects on the generalization of the four basic features of dialectics, we do not think it is right either.

However, Stalin's generalization of the four basic features of dialectics does have major defects and drawbacks.

First, Stalin's understanding of dialectics is one-sided, ignoring the essential status of unity of opposites in dialectics. In his generalization of the four features of dialectics, although he tried to explain the important position about the unity of opposites in dialectics, admitting the existence of contradictions in objects and phenomena in the nature and while he thought that contradiction is the drive for the development of the nature, he failed at clearly considering unity of opposites as the essence and core of materialistic dialectics like Lenin did, which is a major mistake and also an important ideological root-cause that led to the metaphysical one-sidedness of his theories. The understanding of Stalin on the law of unity of opposites had serious defects because when he commented related to the content of this law, he only laid the stress on the struggle between the opposites and its effect, but not on the unity of the opposites and its effect. Based on that, some people think that Stalin only focused on the effect of struggle between the opposites and completely denied the effect of unity of the opposites, which led to his ideological root-cause of the major mistakes such as overstressing the contradiction's nature of struggle which therefore led to the magnification of the need for the elimination of counterrevolutionaries. This idea does make some sense, but we should also notice that Stalin sometimes did not deny the unity of the opposites, he even unilaterally exaggerated it. For example, he thought that the driving force of Soviet Union's social development is the consistence (harmony) of morality and politics. So, Stalin's understanding of dialectics was usually connected with his political needs, showing a tendency of pragmatism.

53

Second is the understanding of the law of quantitative and qualitative change is one-sided. When Stalin was demonstrating the third feature of dialectics, he only emphasized on the aspect that quantitative change leads to qualitative change, thus quantity turns into quality, but not that the qualitative changes will lead to new quantitative changesand by this that quality will turn into quantity. This understanding is obviously one-sided. It is undoubtedly correct that Stalin did not agree to regard development as a circular motion, but as a progressive ascending motion. However, from his comments, we can clearly feel that different understanding was implied. That the progressive ascending motion is only the change from quantitative to qualitative, from quantity to quality; the change from quality to quantity is a downward descending movement; recognition of the transform from quantity to quality and from quality to quantity both would lead to the understanding that development is a circular motion. Therefore, he only quoted Engels' view of the transform from quantity to quality, but not that from quality to quantity as elaborated in Engels' *Anti-Dühring*. As a matter of fact, while Engels stressed out the transform from quantity to quality, he also emphasized on the transform from quality to quantity. When Engels explained the universality of the transform between quality and quantity in *Anti-Dühring*, he firstly pointed out that the related thought of Marx in *Capital*, "the whole of Part IV of Marx's *Capital*—production of relative surplus-value"—deals, in the field of co-operation, division of labor and manufacture, machinery and modern industry, with innumerable cases in which quantitative change alters the quality, and also qualitative change alters the quantity of the things under consideration, in which therefore, to use the expression so hated by Herr Dühring, quantity is transformed into quality and vice versa."[8] Therefore, it is one-sided when Stalin only emphasizes on the change from quantity to quality, but not from quality to quantity. His understanding on the law of the transform between quantity and quality in dialectics is neither complete nor in line with Engels' thought on it.

54

Third, the law of the negation of the negation was abandoned as Hegel's dialectics. The law of the negation of the negation was one of the three basic laws that were firstly systematically revealed by Hegel. It is also the basic method for him to construct his philosophical system of idealism. While approving its rational content, Marx and Engels reformed it critically and revealed in depth the objectivity and universality of the negation of the negation as one of the basic laws in dialectics. Lenin in *Philosophical Notebooks* and other works also made new assessments on the law, elaborating on the essential difference between Marxist and Hegel's philosophy about the understandings of the law of the negation of the negation. However, Stalin did not include the most fundamental law of dialectics when he was generalizing the four basic features of dialectics. This is a major defect.

Some scholars think that Stalin did not deny the law of the negation of the negation. Instead, he explained it with the law of unity of the opposites and the transform between quantity and quality. He had made it clear that development is not a circular but a progressive ascending motion. However, we do not think the explanation is sufficient. According to Engels' comments in *Anti-Dühring*, as one of the three basic laws in materialistic dialectics, the law of the negation of the negation's most essential content is the spiral development of objects under the effect of the internal

---

8   Collected Works of Mars and Engels, second edition, volume 3, p. 469, Beijing, People's Publishing House, 1995, Retrieved from Marxists Internet Archive.

contradictions. Lenin also had pointed out in *Philosophical Notebooks* that the most outstanding feature of the law of the negation of the negation is the repetition of some features or natures of the lower stage at the higher stage of development as if it is a reversion to the old. From these comments we can clearly tell that Engels and Lenin both regarded the law of the negation of the negation as one of the basic laws, together with the law of unity of the opposites and the law of the transform between quantity and quality. The law of the negation of the negation is the universal law that plays a role in nature, society and mind. Its unique position in the scientific system of materialistic dialectics cannot be replaced by the other two laws. According to Rosenthal's *Handbook of Philosophy*, the reason why Stalin consciously excluded the law of the negation of the negation as the basic feature of dialectics is that in his mind, the law of the negation of negation is the remains of Hegel's idealistic philosophy and therefore should be abandoned. It is fair to say that Rosenthal's explanations were consistent with Stalin's actual thought. The aim of Stalin's comment that development should not be regarded as a circular but a progressive ascending motion was only to demonstrate that the development of objects is the transform from an old quality to a new one, namely that quantitative change leads to qualitative change. It is definitely not an explanation for the law of the negation of the negation.

To sum up, Stalin's generalization of the four basic features of dialectics have both new contributions to Marxist philosophy and major defects. Therefore, it should not be simply and completely denied but analyzed case by case.

4. The basic features of materialism of Marxist philosophy

About consciousness and being, which is the basic question of philosophy, Stalin generalized three basic features of materialism of Marxist philosophy while revealing the essence and basic viewpoints of idealism.

First, as opposite to idealism which regards the world as the reflection of "absolute spirit" and consciousness, materialism of Marxist philosophy insists that the essence of the world is materialistic; that the various phenomena in the world exist in the different forms that are in the motion under objective laws.

Second, as opposite to idealism that regards consciousness as the primary real existence and holds the view that objective nature only exists in consciousness, materialism of Marxist philosophy insists that matter and nature are the objective reality that are existing outside and independent from consciousness; that matter is primary and consciousness is secondary and that consciousness in essence is the reflection of matter.

Third, as opposite to idealism that denies the possibility of knowing the world and its laws, materialism of Marxist philosophy insists that the world and its laws can be cognized; that our knowledge about the nature, examined by experience and practice, has the significance of objective truth.

Stalin's generalization of the basic features of materialism of Marxist philosophy is the conclusion of the explanation in Engels' *Ludwig Feuerbach and the End of Classical German Philosophy* and Lenin's *Materialism and Empirio-Criticism*. Therefore, in general, his basic viewpoints are correct, insisting on the basic ground of dialectic materialism. Some people who advocate the practical materialism view and attempting to establish the "ontology" of practice, try to replace the materialist ontology with their practical ontology, which make them totally silent on the essential difference between materialism of Marxist philosophy on the one hand and vulgar materialism and mechanistic materialism on the other, in fact these "practical materialists" confuse materialism and dialectics. They have argued that Stalin regarded dialectics as method, materialism as theory, and they add that Stalin has explained the features of dialectics and materialism separately which means a deviation both from dialectics and materialism and caused some other defects in understanding Marxist philosophy. However, just based on that, can we draw the conclusion that Stalin has confused materialism of Marxist philosophy, with vulgar materialism and mechanistic materialism? We do not think that this conclusion tallies with Stalin's actual thought and doesn't have enough grounds. If we deny Stalin's thought on the three features of materialism of Marxist philosophy, we would also, to some degree, deny Engels' and Lenin's thoughts on this issue. As we have mentioned before, Stalin's viewpoints were basically the generalization of Engels' and Lenin's thoughts. In addition, when Stalin was demonstrating the first feature of materialism, he had clearly pointed out: Marxist materialist philosophy does not only regard the world as matter in essence, but also regards that the various phenomena in the world are the different forms of matter in motion: "interconnection and interdependence of phenomena as established by the dialectical method, are a law of the development of moving matter, and that the world develops in accordance with the laws of movement of matter and stands in no need of a "universal spirit".

The above comments indicated that Stalin had answered the question "how" the world's state is, while he was demonstrating "what" the essence of the world is in dialectic materialism, which explained the opposite positions of materialism and idealism on the basic philosophical question of thinking and being and the essential difference between Marxist materialism and mechanistic materialism. As for the question why Stalin did not mention vulgar materialism, we think it is related to the question he focused to explain. What he tried to point out above is the totally opposite positions of materialism of Marxist philosophy and idealism, but not the difference between materialism of Marxist philosophy and other groups of materialism. Therefore, we cannot simply consider that he confused materialism of Marxist philosophy with vulgar materialism and mechanistic materialism just because he did not mention it. Actually, this flawed viewpoint of so-called "practical materialists" is only an extension of the idea that Engels' basic viewpoint of materialism about the basic question of philosophy which he discussed in *Ludwig Feuerbach and the End of Classical German Philosophy* is just a generalization of the views of the old materialism and that Lenin's ideas in Materialism and Empirio-Criticism basically belong to mechanistic materialism.

Some western scholars criticized that Stalin's generalization of the basic features of materialism of Marxist philosophy had embarked a different path from Marx's views on practice, and therefore equated Marx's materialism with the old materialism, which blocked the way to people's understanding that Marx regarded the "practice view" as his primary revolution in modern philosophy. This kind of criticism has been common in recent years in the discussions of practical materialism among philosophical circles. The question here is actually how to evaluate the status and effect of practice in Marxist philosophy. Some scholars, when it comes to the effect and significance of the philosophical revolution achieved through Marxist philosophy, think that the reason why Marx was able to establish Marxist philosophy is that he replaced and denied the old materialism with practical materialism. Therefore, regarding Marxist philosophy as dialectic materialism, does not indicate the essential difference between Marxist philosophy and the old materialism. Based on that, they criticized Engels, Lenin and especially Stalin's viewpoints on the basic questions of dialectic materialism. We think that scientific practice did play an important role in the establishment of Marxist philosophy and held an important position on it, but this can never be interpreted as if practice is something that determines the very nature of Marxism and therefore denies that Marxist philosophy is dialectical materialism. The essence of the philosophical revolution achieved through Marxist philosophy is that Marx and Engels, on the basis of scientific practice dialectically and materialistically solved the basic question of philosophy- the relations between mind and existence, and achieved the unity of materialism and dialectics and the unity of materialistic dialectic view of nature and materialistic dialectic view of history. The very nature of Marxist philosophy is dialectic materialism. Some people who advocate for practical materialism "ontologized" practice, trying to replace materialistic ontology with practical ontology, which does not only confuse the original meaning of practice, but also eradicates material as the basis of materialism. Their attempt of replacing the relations between objectivity and subjectivity with the relations of material and consciousness confused the principles and boundaries between materialism and idealism. However, it does not make any sense to criticize Engels, Lenin and Stalin. The most important contribution of Engels' thought on the basic question of philosophy is that he provided a scientific standard of correctly distinguishing materialism and idealism. Lenin's new elaboration on it according to the new development of natural science has also been proved correct by numerous facts. Therefore, Stalin's generalization based on Engels' and Lenin's thought is also correct. Especially, we need to point out that Stalin did not deny the viewpoint of practice. He had clearly pointed out when he was commenting on the third basic feature of materialism of Marxist philosophy, that "our knowledge about the laws of the nature and our knowledge that has been tested by experience and practice are objective and reliable; in the world there is nothing that cannot be understood, only something that has not been understood but will be exposed and understood by the power of science and practice."[9] He further quoted Engels' famous argument against agnosticism from the view of practice in his work *Ludwig Feuerbach and the End of Classical German Philosophy*. Therefore, it is without any factual basis to say that Stalin completely denied the viewpoint of practice of Marxist philosophy.

Stalin's generalization of the basic features of materialism of Marxist philosophy has its contributions. He creatively combined Engels' basic thought on philosophical questions with Lenin's basic thought on materialism of Marxist philosophy and epistemology of his work *Materialism and Empirio-Criticism*. By doing that, Stalin made the theories of materialism of Marxist philosophy more integrated and systematic. However, there are some flaws in his viewpoints, but the flaws are not that he completely denied practice, but that he did not pay enough attention to it. Therefore, when he was elaborating on the basic viewpoints of materialism of Marxist philosophy, he failed to completely reflect on the basic viewpoints of Marxist philosophy, especially the view of scientific practice in Marxist philosophy. He also failed to completely reflect on the basic viewpoints of epistemology of Marxist philosophy. As a result, he did not demonstrate that consciousness has a motile reaction to material via practice emphasized by Marxist philosophy under the precondition that material is primary and consciousness is secondary.

---

9   Selected Works of Stalin, volume 2, p. 434.

5. The systematic demonstration of the basic principles of historical materialism

In *Dialectical and Historical Materialism*, Stalin had made a brief but comparatively systematic elaboration on the basic principles of historical materialism. He has also put forward some innovative ideas, which although enriched and developed historical materialism, still had some limitation and defects.

First, Stalin clearly explained the conditions of material life of society, the determinant forces of them and their effect in the development of society. This is one of Stalin's important theoretical contributions. He pointed out that the conditions of material life of society include geographical environment, population and the method of producing the means of life, among which, the geographical environment and population are the indispensable conditions that accelerate or retard the development of society. The method of producing the means of life is the chief determinant force of the development of society, which determines the nature of the social system and the physiognomy of the society. Although Marx and Engels, had pointed out as well the determinant effect of the conditions of material life of society on the development of society, but failed to clearly demonstrate the connotation of the concept. Their comments on the determinant forces of the conditions of material life of society mainly focused on the effect of the mode of production. Stalin's explanation on the conditions of material life of society is the enrichment and development of historical materialism. Some scholars think that Stalin's thought on the conditions of material life of society is undoubtedly right when he criticized the theory that geographical environment is the chief determinant force of social development and the bourgeois population theory. However, he had the major defect of underestimating the great influence and restriction of geographical environment and population growth in the social development. We think that this kind of criticism is over demanding of Stalin, because it was obviously from the perspective of the modern reality and contemporary people. At that time, environment and population issues were not as acute as they are now, so it is unblamable that Stalin's basic viewpoints focused on the determining effect of the materialist conception of history—the mode of production of society—on social development.

Second, Stalin systematically explained the theory of historical materialism that productive forces and relations of production are dialectically united. In this aspect, Stalin brought some theoretical innovation. According to it, he clearly defined productive forces and explained the determinant factors of productive forces and their status and effect. He pointed out, "the instruments of production wherewith material values are produced, the people who operate the instruments of production and carry on the production of material values thanks to a certain production experience and labor skill- all these elements jointly constitute the productive forces of society."[10] Among the determinant factors of productive forces, labors are the most important one. The development of productive forces starts from the revolution of the instruments of production. However, the revolution and development of instruments of production is achieved by people who conduct productive activities. The revolution of the instruments of production in turn increases labor skills. This important viewpoint of Stalin profoundly exposed the fundamental process and laws of the development of productive forces.

In the comments that the mode of production is the chief determinant force of social development, Stalin clearly pointed out that the mode of production is the unity of productive forces and the relations of production. At the same time, he also revealed in depth the three features of the method of producing the means of life of society. He pointed out that the first feature of production is that it never stays at one point for a long time but always in a state of change and development; that change in the mode of production will definitely lead to change in the whole social system, social ideas, political views and political institutions, which means a reconstruction of the whole social and political order. The second feature of production is that the change and development of production always start from change and development of productive forces with change and development of instruments of production in the first place. Next, in accordance to and in conformity with the changes, people's relations of production and their economic relations change. While the development of relations of production is dependent on the development of productive forces, it reacts in turn on the development of the productive forces, accelerating or retarding it. The third feature of production is that the emergence of new productive forces and of the relations of production in accordance with them does not take place isolated from the old system or after the elimination of the old system but within the old system. Similarly, it is not a result of deliberate and conscious human activities, but takes place spontaneously, unconsciously and independently of the will of men. The rise and development of new mode of production have their internal inevitability.

By observing the determining effect of mode of production on social development, Stalin elaborated on the basic principles of materialist conception of history about the mutual relations between productive forces and relations of production, profoundly exposed the fundamental laws of the development of mode of production in society, enriched and developed materialist conception of history.

10   Selected Works of Stalin, volume 2, p. 442, Retrieved from Marxist Internet Archive.

When he was elaborating on the basic principles of materialist conception of history about the mutual relations between productive forces and relations of production, by making case-by-case analysis on the paradoxical movement of productive forces and relations of production in capitalist society and on the root-causes of economic and social crisis in the capitalist society, Stalin explained the historical inevitability of replacing capitalist mode of production with socialist mode of production. At the same time, by making case-by-case analysis on the mutual relations between productive forces of society and relations of production in socialist society, he drew the conclusion that under socialist system, relations of production are completely compatible with productive forces. This conclusion is obviously incorrect and self-contradicted with his own basic viewpoint of historical materialism. Stalin's conclusion was to demonstrate the superiority of socialism compared to capitalism. However, in socialist society, there are still contradictions between relations of production and productive forces, which are independent and indispensable of any good wills. The denial of the contradictions between relation of production and productive forces did not only lead to serious metaphysics, but also made him unable to correctly understand the fundamental driving force of the development of socialist society and consciously reform the relations of production that are not suitable for the development of productive forces in time. This is the theoretical root-cause of the USSR's rigid economic and political system. Its serious results came later up more and more in Soviet Union's socialist system.

In addition, when Stalin was commenting on the third feature, although he talked about the relations between the economic base and the superstructure, he especially emphasized on the great effects of the new social ideas, new political institutions and new powers in the process of the new relations of production replacing the old ones. However, he did not further explain the basic principles of the relations between the economic base and the superstructure in the materialist conception of history, which is an inappropriate way of explaining materialist conception of history as it is a very important basic principle. It also made him having an incomplete comment on and generalization of the basic principles of materialist conception of history.

IV. Stalin's philosophical thought in his later years

After the World War II, under the leadership of Stalin, the people of Soviet Union quickly healed the wound of war and made great achievement in socialist economic construction. Faced with the new situations and problems in the process of the socialist construction, the USSR's theoretical world started detailed and long-lasting discussions around the main topic of the law of development in socialist society. Focused on some of the major theoretical problems, Stalin published two important works: *Marxism and Problems of Linguistics* in 1950 and *Economic Problems of Socialism in USSR* in 1953. By concluding the practical experience of economic construction of socialism, Stalin explained his views on the mutual relations between the economic base and the superstructure in socialist society and their features, demonstrated the laws of social development and the objectivity of economic law and finally further developed Marxist philosophy.

1. Stalin's philosophical thought in *Marxism and Problems of Linguistics*

In May 1950, organized by the *Pravda*, the Soviet Union started a discussion on linguistics in order to establish the right direction of the development of linguistics. At that time, the idealistic linguistic viewpoints advocated by the famous linguistic authority of Soviet Union's N.Y. Marr was in a dominant position in the linguistic world. It was praised highly as the real materialistic scientific viewpoint and the basis of linguistics of the USSR. Marr suggested that language is ideology that is in the sphere of superstructure and has a class character; that it is the tool of class struggle used by one class against the other. He also stated that the so-called masses' national language that has overstepped classes is just an unrealistic illusion; that mind can exist separately from language and that the communication between people can be achieved by mind only, etc. In January 1950, at the memorial meeting of the 15th anniversary of Marr's death, Marr's idealistic linguistic views were again highly praised. Focused on this situation, the Pravda published articles that criticized Marr linguistics, which started a large discussion on the problems of linguistics. From this discussion strong reactions aroused. Stalin also paid a lot of attention to it and joined the discussion in person. One after another, he published some articles to express his opinions. These articles were collected to publish in August 1950 named Marxism and Problems of Linguistics.

In *Marxism and Problems of Linguistics*, Stalin made a clear definition of economic base and superstructure and explained their relations, with the emphasis on the features and differences between superstructure and language.

Targeted at N. Y. Marr's wrong opinion that language has a class character and belongs to superstructure, Stalin clearly pointed out that language belongs to neither economic base nor superstructure. It is in essence just the tool of people's communication. Due to the complexity of the phenomena in social life, not every social phenomenon can be included in the sphere of economic base or superstructure, such as language, natural science, some methods of education and family, etc. To prove that language does not belong to the category of superstructure, Stalin made clear explanation of economic base and superstructure. He pointed out, "base is the economic system of a society at a certain stage of its development while superstructure is the society's ideas of politics, law, religion, art and philosophy and the political and legal institutions that go with these ideas."[11] We should say that Stalin's definition on economic base and superstructure is basically consistent with Marx's basic thought in *The Preface of a Contribution to the Critique of Political Economy*. Based on this understanding, Stalin explained why language is not included in the superstructure from four aspects and the mutual relations between superstructure and economic base. First, superstructure is determined by economic base; it changes with the change of the economic base. However, language does not change as the economic base changes. Second, superstructure that has developed on a certain economic base is at the service of economic base; the superstructure has great reactions on the economic base. However, language is different, as it is not a product of the economic base, but generated by the history of society and economic bases in hundreds of years. Language is also not created by any class to serve a particular class; it serves every class in the society as it does not only serve the old economic base and superstructure, but also the new economic base and superstructure. Third, superstructure is the particular product of a particular time during which particular economic base exists and functions; its life is not long-lasting. However, language is the product of different eras, which lasts much longer than any economic base or superstructure. Fourth, the essential difference between superstructure and language is that superstructure and productive activities do not have direct connection; that superstructure and productive activities are indirectly connected by the agents, which are economy and the economic base. However, language is not only directly connected with productive activities, but also directly connected with all human activities, with a more extensive effective range than economic base and superstructure.

Scholars both at home and abroad, especially some western scholars, expressed a lot of rejection and critique on Stalin's opinions on his definition of superstructure in *Marxism and Problems of Linguistics* and his elaboration on the mutual relations between economic base and superstructure.

63

---

11 Selected Works of Stalin, volume 2, p. 501.

For example, some scholars of our country think that Stalin's definition on superstructure is actually replacing superstructure with ideology by equating the two. Stalin exaggerated the effect of ideology and therefore decreased, even wiped out the great effect of political power, political organs and their institutions. Marx mentioned in *The Preface of a Contribution to the Critique of Political Economy* that ideology conforms to economic base, which was adapted by Stalin as that political and legal organs conform to ideology. This is one of Stalin's mistakes. We think that this critique needs some discussions, because Stalin's definition neither equated superstructure with ideology, nor decreased or wiped out the effect of the state political power and its institutions. From Marx, Engels to Lenin, they all thought that superstructure includes ideological superstructure and political superstructure; but not only the state political power and its institutions. They also thought that in a particular society, the state political power and its institutions are all built up under the instruction of the ideology of certain classes and used to serve their own economic base. Aren't the capitalist political power and its institutions built up under the instruction of the ideology of the bourgeoisie? Aren't the proletarian political power and its institutions built up under the instruction of the ideology of the proletarian class? Stalin's definition neither denied that the political superstructure must conform to the economic base nor denied the determinant effect of economic base on political superstructure. The superstructure he mentioned includes ideology and political and legal institutions that conform to the ideology. His original meaning was meant to demonstrate that particular political superstructure is built up under particular ideology. This opinion is correct and unblamable.

Some scholars think that Stalin's understanding of the relations between economic base and superstructure betrayed the materialist concept of history. That his way of determining the relations is completely mechanistic. In particular, that he thought that the superstructure disappears with the disappearance of the economic base on which the superstructure rises, which is not in line with Marx and Engels' thought that ideology is relatively independent and has its own comparatively independent history of development. This opinion of Stalin would cause cultural nihilism. As it is known to all, the October Revolution in Russia did not completely eliminate the cultural heritage from previous eras as the superstructure of the old economic base. Actually, this is a misunderstanding of Stalin's thought. What Stalin emphasized here is that superstructure definitely changes with the change of the economic base; that economic base has the determining effect on superstructure. He did not deny that superstructure is relatively independent. Because he was mainly talking about the difference between the comparable instability of superstructure and the comparable stability of language, it is natural that the emphasis was on the changeability of super-structure. This is determined by the aim of the argument and the perspective on which the issue was explained. Stalin pointed out that if economic base would be changed and finally wouldget eliminated, its superstructure would also get changed and eliminated. He also explained the two cases in which superstructure changes with the change of the economic base. First, as the economic base changes, so will the superstructure. The change here does not refer to elimination. Obviously he had realized that consciousness is comparable independent and culturally successive. Second, superstructure will disappear with the disappearance of the economic base. When he was demonstrating the elimination of superstructure, Stalin made it very clear that it is the political superstructure that would be eliminated. His original words were, "Russia eliminated the old basis of capitalism and established the new basis of socialism. To go with it, the superstructure on the basis of capitalism was eliminated and the new superstructure that subordinates to the basis of socialism was established. That is to say, the old political and legal institutions have been replaced by the new socialist institutions."[12] It is very clear that the old superstructure that has been elim-inated is, according to Stalin, the political superstructure such as political and legal institutions, but not social consciousness forms or culture. Based on this argument only, the conclusion that Stalin caused cultural nihilism is not solid. Similarly, the idea that Stalin's comment on the relations between economic base and superstructure is metaphysical and therefore constitutes betrayal of the materialist concept of history and lacks the due evidence.

Stalin made a relatively complete elaboration and new development on the basic principles of the relations between economic base and superstruc-ture from the perspective of the materialist concept of history, but he mainly focused on the basic principles. Once it comes to the detailed understanding of the basic contradiction of socialist society, his limitation was exposed. In *Marxism and Problems of Linguistics*, Stalin did not make a case-by-case analysis on neither the contradiction between productive forces and rela-tions of production in socialist society nor about that between economic base and superstructure. Generally, he still inclined to the theory of "entire-ly appropriate match." In addition, when he was discussing the problems of superstructure, he did not analyze case by case the relations between ideological or conceptive superstructure and political superstructure, which was one of the important reasons why his opinions have been criticized by scholars at home and abroad.

In *Marxism and Problems of Linguistics*, Stalin also had in-depth discus-sions on the forms of qualitative change, which enriched the principles of the law of quantitative and qualitative change of Marxist philosophy.

---

12   Selected Works of Stain, volume 2, p. 502.

From Stalin's major philosophical work *Dialectical and Historical Materialism* we can tell that he had always attached great importance to the study and discussion of the law of quantitative and qualitative change. In *Marxism and Problems of Linguistics*, he proposed the important idea of the two forms of qualitative change, which change the idea in his previous work that the only form of qualitative change is explosive leap. He thought that in addition to explosive leap, there is another form of the qualitative change of objects. This change of idea is Stalin's generalization of the USSR's 30-year experience of socialist construction and the generalization of features of development of things under the conditions of socialism.

At that time some linguists suggested that development of language relies on abrupt language revolution, which is also a reflection of the idea of the abrupt qualitative change. To argue against this viewpoint, Stalin pointed out that, "the law of transition from an old quality to a new by means of an explosion is inapplicable not only to the history of the development of languages; it is not always applicable to other social phenomena of a basis or superstructural character. It applies of necessity to a society divided into hostile classes. But it does not necessarily apply to a society which has no hostile classes."[13] The development of languages is a transition from one quality to another achieved by the long-term accumulation of the language's new quality and new structure and the gradual extinction of the old quality. From the perspective of the development of economic base and superstructure, for a socialist society that has hostile classes, explosion is a necessity. However, for a socialist society that has no hostile classes, the explosion is not a necessity. Under the conditions of socialism, the transition from individual peasants to collective farms is a qualitative change, but this qualitative change is achieved through the form of transition, not explosion. In the future, the transition from collective farms to the socialist ownership of whole people will also be achieved in the form of non-explosion. Furthermore, Stalin pointed out that under the conditions of socialism, when the economic system and superstructure are not suitable to the development of productive forces and relations of production, they will also need to be reformed by gradual changes. That is to say, with constant reform and adjustment, economic base and superstructure will be improved to a new level and finally transited to a new quality. All in all, the reform in socialist society does not need to be achieved by explosive qualitative change such as overthrowing the political power and establishing a new one. The gradual accumulation of new quality and the gradual extinction of the old are the new features of the development of objects in socialist society. This is determined by the particularity of the internal contradictions of objects and the particularity of their external conditions. The diversity of

---

13   ibid., p. 519, Retrieved from Marxist Internet Archive

the characteristics of objects determines the diversity of the forms of qualitative change. Stalin's enrichment and development of the law of quantitative and qualitative change is very significant for us to correctly understand the particular characteristics of various contradictions in socialist society and take appropriate measures to facilitate the development and reform of objects according to their fixed form of leap.

2. The philosophical evaluation of *Economic Problems of Socialism in USSR* written by Stalin

The issue of the law of social development in socialist society had always been one of the subjects which Stalin attached great importance to and studied in-depth on. Especially in his later years, he made comments on this issue many times. He pointed out that socialist society has its fixed objective laws, which can be used by people, but can never be eliminated. Therefore, we must respect the objective laws and act in accordance with them. These important ideas of Stalin were mainly reflected in his last work Economic Problems of Socialism in USSR in his later years.

First, he demonstrated the objectivity of the socialist economic law. The greatest contribution of Marxist philosophy is that it scientifically revealed the objective law of the historical development of society and explained that the development of human society is a natural historical process. Moreover, Marx and Engels demonstrated in detail the objectivity of economic law. However, from the 1920s, in the USSR's theoretical circles an idea of denying the objectivity of socialist economic law came up. It suggested that the economic law only exists in a society where production and economy are at an anarchic state such as capitalist society. But in a socialist society such as the USSR that practices planned economy, the economic law does not work and therefore disappears. Later, after seriously criticized, this idea faded out, but it did not completely disappear. Once there was a chance, it was once again put forward by some people in different forms. In 1930s, Stalin had criticized the idea of denying the objective laws for many times. He pointed out that Marxism is the science about the objective law of social development. However, after the Second World War, the Party and the government of the Soviet Union played a very important role in the recovery of national economy and the socialist construction. Therefore, in the early 1950s, some people of the theoretical circles suggested that the Republics of the USSR and their leaders are omnipotent and can do whatever they want. That they cannot only eliminate any existing economic law, but also create new economic law. Having targeted on this wrong idea of denying objective economic law, Stalin again emphasized on the objectivity of law. He pointed out that no matter, socialist society or capitalist society, they both have their fixed objective laws, which, as it is valid for the law of nature, are indispensable and independent from the will of men. People can understand them, study them and consider them in their activities, but can never arbitrarily deny them, not to mention change or transform them. That the political power of the USSR can complete the task of transforming the old society and establishing a new one "is not because it eliminated any existing economic law and 'created' anything new, but because it relied on the economic law that the relations of production must be suitable for the productive forces."[14] In the socialist society, no matter how authoritative the political power of the Party or the government is, they must act in accordance with objective law, making plans, principles and policies and considering their own activities and work on the basis of the objective law of social development. The superiority of socialism provides people with the possibility of consciously understanding and correctly making use of objective law. Therefore, "the law of planned development of national economy has made it possible for our planning organs to correctly plan social production. However, possibility and reality cannot be confused."[15] To change the possibility in to the reality, the objective law has to be respected and everything must be done in line with the objective law.

To explain the objectivity of economic law, Stalin further demonstrated the economic law's features that are different from the law of nature. He pointed out, "one of the features of political economy is that its law is different from that of natural science and not long lasting; that the laws of political economy, at least most of them, are working within a certain historical period, after which they will be replaced by new laws. However, the original laws are not eliminated, but out of power due to the rise of the new economic conditions. They left the stage, giving the position to the new laws, which are not being created by people's mind, but on the basis of the new economic conditions."[16] By understanding and grasping the feature of economic law, one can not only understand the difference between economic law and natural law, but also understand the root-cause for the emergence of new economic laws and the disappearance of the old and therefore profoundly demonstrate that as it is valid for the law of nature, economic law is also independent and indispensable of men's will. Furthermore, Stalin also pointed out that in natural science, it is more or less smooth to discover and apply the new laws. However, in the economic field, to discover and make use of the new laws that are conflicting with the interests of the degenerate power, one has to face its extremely strong struggle. Different from the law of nature, this is another feature of economic law.

---

14   Selected Works of Stalin, volume 2, p. 543.
15   ibid., p.544.
16   ibid., p.541.

Second, he commented on the mutual relations between productive forces and relations of production in socialist society. The USSR economist Yaroshenko thought that under socialist system, the independence of the relations of production has disappeared and become part of the productive forces. To argue against this wrong point of view, Stalin further elaborated on the mutual relations between the productive forces and the relations of production in socialist society. He pointed out that from the perspective of Marxism, social production is a whole with two inseparable parts, which are productive forces and relations of production. They are related with and working on each other. In any social formation, these are the two parts of social production. Otherwise, the social production cannot be carried out. Stalin also criticized Yaroshenko's one-sided viewpoint that with the existence of antagonistic class contradiction, the relations of production only work in a negative way by hindering the development of productive forces. Stalin pointed out, that the reaction of the relations of production on the development of productive forces is not only the hindered effect of the old relations of production on the development of productive forces, but also the promotion effect of the new relations of production on the development of productive forces. "The relations of production develop from the obstructer of productive forces to the major promoter of productive forces, and from the promoter of productive forces to the obstructer of productive forces - this character of development is one of the key elements of Marxist materialistic dialectics."[17] That the relations of production must conform to the productive forces is the subjective law that must be followed by any form of human society.

69

What is worth of notice is that Stalin made a new explanation on the idea that he was advocating for in the past. That is, that the relations of production are completely suitable for the productive forces in socialist society. He pointed out that in socialist society, the law of paradoxical movement of productive forces and relations of production is still in place. The productive forces are entirely appropriate for the relations of production in socialist society. However, the complete match of relations of production and productive forces cannot be regarded as particular in socialist society. In a certain period of time when the capitalist system was just established, the capitalist relations of production were also completely suitable for the productive forces. At the same time, the understanding of "full conformity" should not be absolutized. It should not be interpreted as if under socialism, the rule that the improvement of the relations of production is behind that of productive forces, disappears. Productive forces are the most active and revolutionary power in production. This kind of power, even under socialism, is unarguably ahead of the relations of production. Only after a period

---

17   Selected Works of Stalin, volume 2, p. 586.

of time can the relations of production be transformed to be suitable for the productive forces. "How, then, are the words 'full conformity' to be understood? They are to be understood as meaning that under socialism things do not usually go to the length of a conflict between the relations of production and the productive forces; that society is in a position to take timely steps to bring the lagging relations of production into conformity with the character of the productive forces. Socialist society is in a position to do so because it does not include the obsolescent classes that might organize resistance. Of course, even under socialism there will be backward, inert forces that do not realize the necessity for changing the relations of production; but they, of course, will not be difficult to be overcome without bringing matters to a conflict."[18] He also admitted that under the USSR's socialism, the full conformity of relations of production and productive forces promotes the rapid development of productive forces. However, if we rest easy and "think that there are no contradictions between our productive forces and the relations of production, while there certainly are, and will be, contradictions, we will see that the development of the relations of production lags, and will lag, behind the development of the productive forces."[19] Stalin's new explanation of the "full conformity" that he was advocating is undoubtedly a correction of his previous metaphysical thought. It is fair to say that it constitutes an important progress of his philosophical thought. However, because he had not completely given up the idea of "full conformity", this progress is very limited.

Some scholars at home and abroad criticized Stalin's philosophical thought in *Economic Problems of Socialism in the USSR*, thinking that the major defect of his philosophical thought expressed in this work is that he did not scientifically explain the basic difference between economic law and the law of nature. Stalin also regarded and observed the law existing in real life from the perspective of abstract sphere that is separated from human activities. This idea was mainly embodied in his viewpoint that under socialism, the relations of production must unconditionally conform to the productive forces as if history is not created by human activities but by laws. By doing so, Stalin completely denied the subjective initiative of men. This change of idea is Stalin's generalization of the USSR's 30-year experience of socialist construction and the generalization of features of development of things under the conditions of socialism the generalization of features of development of things under the conditions of socialism.We think that the first criticism does make some sense, because judging from Stalin's analysis on the nature of economic laws and their difference from the laws of nature, he did not grasp the essential difference between the two.

---

18   ibid., p. 577, Retrieved from Marxists Internet Archive.
19   ibid., p. 590.

About the differences between social laws and natural laws, Engels had made very clear comments in *Ludwig Feuerbach and the End of Classical German Philosophy*, elaborating that the most essential difference between social laws and natural laws is that social laws are embodied through purposive human activities while natural laws are the result of the spontaneous functions of various random natural powers of the nature. Stalin did not pay attention to it. He just explained the objective conditions of the formation of economic law, but did not mention that economic law is shown through the purposive human activities. One can not deny that this is one of Stalin's defects. As for Stalin's complete denial of the subjective initiative of men, we think this critique needs some further discussions. We do not think that Stalin denied the effect of men's subjective initiative on laws. In this book, he mainly criticized the wrong idea that denied the objectivity of economic law. That is why he emphasized that men cannot create or eliminate economic law and that it is completely necessary for laws to be independent and indispensable from men's subjective wills. At the same time, Stalin also pointed out in the book that one should not become himself the slave of laws by regarding them as fetish. He suggested that people are not absolutely powerless in front of subjective laws; that men can play a dynamic role in understanding and making use of objective law, to some extent keep the effect of laws within the limit and harness the laws to some extent. "Having come to know economic laws and relying upon them, society can restrict their sphere of action, utilize them in the interests of society and 'harness' them."[20] How does this mean the complete denial of the subjective initiative of men? It is fair to say that Stalin's understanding on the relations between objective laws and the subjective initiative of men is generally correct.

To sum up, Stalin's philosophical thought has the right aspect that has made contributions to Marxist philosophy, and the limited aspect that is metaphysical. To evaluate his philosophical thought, one must uphold a scientific attitude, practical and realistic, make analysis case by case and should never be metaphysical by completely denying everything.

20   ibid., p. 542, Retrieved from Marxists Internet Archive.

Chapter III

Stalin's Outlook of Socialism

What is socialism and how to construct socialism have always been the primary questions of the countries with backward economies and cultures after taking the proletarian political power and starting socialist construction. In the practice of Soviet Union's socialist construction, on the basis of absorbing Marx and Engels' theories of socialism, Stalin had gradually formed his own outlook of socialism. Stalin's outlook of socialism did not only have important influence on the USSR's socialist construction, but also provided some valuable theoretical heritage to other socialist countries for their practice of socialist construction. However, Stalin led the people of the USSR in the construction of socialism in such a big country with a large population but without any previous experiences to be used as reference. Therefore, he committed some obvious mistakes on the questions like what socialism is and how to build socialism. Some of these mistakes later evolved into the theoretical doctrines that restrained the vigor of socialism.

I. Stalin's discussions on the future of socialism

For a ruling party that has taken the proletarian political power, it is of great significance to clearly understand the country's future of socialism. After Lenin's death, Stalin took the great responsibility of leading the socialist revolution and construction of the USSR. In the arguments with Trotsky's opposition, Zinoviev and Kamenev's new opposition and Trotsky-Zinoviev united opposition, Stalin had formed a series of views on the future of socialism and developed the views of socialism's future of Marxism.

1. The view on the future of socialism formed in the arguments within the party

Around 1924, the situation in the world and in the USSR had greatly changed. In the world, the speed of revolution in capitalist countries had unexpectedly slowed down; the proletarian revolutions in some countries such as Germany, Italy and Poland failed one after the other and turned into low ebb; the capitalist world entered into a relatively stable period. At the same time, in the USSR, the NEP enhanced the economic and political power, but due to the permission of the existence of private capital, it also aroused wide concern that whether or not the NEP would weaken socialist construction. Under these circumstances, the questions were sharply raised, such as surrounded by the capitalist system, what the USSR's future would be, whether it would be possible or not to construct socialism economically and technically only with self reliance. On this issue, heated discussions with in the Russian Communist Party came up.

Based on the opportunistic theory of "permanent revolution", Trotsky held a negative attitude on the USSR's future of socialism. In 1922, in the preface of the book *The Year 1905* and in the postscript to the pamphlet "Program for Peace", Trotsky had made it clear that the Soviet Russia cannot build socialism by itself. He demonstrated from two aspects. First, that the Soviet Russia is a backward country with peasants making up most of the population. In such a country, the contradiction of the position of a workers' government can only be solved internationally- on the stage of the world proletariat. Second, that the Soviet Russia is surrounded by the capitalist world. In such a situation, it must manage to reach the agreement with the capitalist world to break the economic isolation. However, this kind of agreement can only make some progress on economy. The real development of the Russian economy would not possible until the proletariat would reach victory in some of the most important European countries.[1]

Stalin held heated discussions with Trotsky. Stalin's critiques on Trotsky's opinions were mainly from three aspects:

First, in May 1924 in the speech about *The Foundations of Leninism*, Stalin revealed the essence of the opportunistic theory of the "permanent revolution" based on Lenin's theory of socialist revolution. He pointed out, "formerly, the victory of the revolution in a single country was considered impossible, on the assumption that it would require the combined action of the proletarians of all or at least of a majority of the advanced countries to achieve victory over the bourgeoisie. Now this point of view no longer fits in with the facts. Now we must proceed from the possibility of

---

1   See The Political Views of Trotsky for further reference, volume 1, p. 177; volume 2, p. 302, Beijing, SDX Joint Publishing Company, 1979.

such a victory, for the uneven and spasmodic character of the development of the various capitalist countries under the conditions of imperialism, the development within imperialism of catastrophic contradictions leading to inevitable wars, the growth of the revolutionary movement in all countries of the world-all this leads, not only to the possibility, but also to the necessity of the victory of the proletariat in individual countries. The history of the revolution in Russia is direct proof of this."[2] Furthermore he pointed out, "but the overthrow of the power of the bourgeoisie and establishment of the power of the proletariat in a single country does not yet mean that the complete victory of socialism has been ensured. After consolidating its power and leading the peasantry in its wake, the proletariat of the victorious country can and must build a socialist society. But does this mean that it will thereby achieve the complete and final victory of socialism, i.e., does it mean that with the forces of only a single country it can finally consolidate socialism and fully guarantee that country against intervention and, consequently, also against restoration? No, it does not. For this the victory of the revolution in at least several countries is needed."[3] Obviously, when Stalin was criticizing Trotsky's points of view, he had realized that the victory of socialism in a single country is somehow different from the complete victory of socialism, but he failed to figure out what the real difference is.

Second, in December 1924, Stalin published The October Revolution and the Tactics of the Russian Communists, in which Stalin criticized Trotsky's idea that "a revolutionary Russia could hold out in the face of a conservative Europe" according to Lenin's thought of building socialism in a single country. Stalin thought that Trotsky's idea was tit-for-tat of Lenin's thought of building socialism in a single country. He pointed out, "it goes without saying that for the complete victory of socialism, for a complete guarantee against the restoration of the old order, the united efforts of the proletarians of several countries are necessary. It goes without saying that, without the support given to our revolution by the proletariat of Europe, the proletariat of Russia could not have held out against the general onslaught, just as without the support given by the revolution in Russia to the revolutionary movement in the West the latter could not have developed at the pace at which it has begun to develop since the establishment of the proletarian dictatorship in Russia. It goes without saying that we need support. But what does support of our revolution by the West-European proletariat imply? ... the sympathy of the European workers for our revolution, their readiness to thwart the imperialists' plans of intervention—is ... real assistance... Without such support, without such assistance, not only from the European

---

2　Collected Works of Stalin, first Chinese version, volume 6, p. 94, Retrieved from Marxists Internet Archive.

3　Collected Works of Stalin, first Chinese version, volume 6, p. 95, Retrieved from Marxists Internet Archive.

workers but also from the colonial and dependent countries, the proletarian dictatorship in Russia would have been stronglyunder pressure. Has this sympathy and this assistance, up to now, coupled with the might of our Red Army and the readiness of the workers and peasants of Russia to defend their socialist fatherland to the last—has all this been sufficient to beat off the attacks of the imperialists and to achieve us the necessary conditions for the serious work of construction? Yes, it has been sufficient."[4] On the basis of his comments, Stalin also pointed out three mistakes in Trotsky's theory: "firstly, …Trotsky does not appreciate the inherent strength of our revolution; secondly, …Trotsky does not understand the inestimable importance of the moral support which is given to our revolution by the workers of the West and the peasants of the East; thirdly, …Trotsky does not perceive the internal infirmity which is consuming imperialism today."[5]

By then, Stalin had differentiated building socialism in a single country and the complete victory of socialism by distinguishing the internal and external contradictions of the USSR. The differentiation he made reflected that his view on the future of socialism is scientific.

Third, in The Results of the Work of the Fourteenth Conference of the RCP (B) given on May 9, 1925 and the speech Questions and Answers delivered at the Sverdlov University on June 9, where Stalin commented on "what is socialism" and "how to build socialism". There, he pointed out, "socialism is the transition from a society with the dictatorship of the proletariat to a stateless society. To effect this transition, however, preparations must be made for altering the state apparatus in such a way as to ensure in fact that the society with the dictatorship is transformed into communist society. That purpose is served by the slogan of revitalizing the Soviets, the slogan of implanting Soviet democracy in town and country, the slogan of drawing the best elements of the working class and the peasantry into the direct work of governing the country."[6] From the perspective of the two contradictions in the USSR and the way to solve them, Stalin further pointed out, "socialist society is a producers' and consumers' association of those who work in industry and agriculture. If, in this association, industry is not linked up with agriculture, which provides raw materials and food and absorbs the products of industry, if industry and agriculture do not thus constitute a single, national-economic whole, there will be no socialism whatever."[7] Therefore, the relations between workers and peasants and between proletariats and peasants became the basic issue of building

4   ibid, p. 324, Retrieved from Marxists Internet Archive.
5   ibid, p. 325, Retrieved from Marxists Internet Archive)
6   Collected Works of Stalin, first Chinese version, volume 7, p. 133, Retrieved from Marxists Internet Archive.
7   ibid., p.167, Retrieved from Marxists Internet Archive.

socialism. The contradictions between the proletariat and peasants are the internal contradictions of Soviet Union. Although there are contradictions between the proletarians and peasants, they have the mutual benefits deriving from the basic issue of developing socialism. That is exactly the basis of the alliance of the workers and peasants, which is the essential method of building socialism. The USSR proletarians are completely able to use their own power to solve the contradictions with peasants and therefore build socialism by relying on the alliance of the workers and peasants. The contradictions between the socialist Russia and other capitalist countries are the external contradictions of the USSR. "They mean that, as long as capitalist encirclement exists, there is bound to be the danger of intervention by the capitalist countries, and as long as such a danger exists, there is bound to be the danger of restoration, the danger of the capitalist order being re-established in our country."[8] In the international scale, only with the joint efforts of several countries, or with the proletariats' victory of revolution in several major capitalist countries, it is possible to avoid the armed intervention of the capitalist countries or the restoration of capitalism and to achieve the final victory of socialism.

After the Fourteenth Congress of RCP (B), the debate within the party with Trotsky started to turn into the debate with the "new opposition" led by Zinoviev and Kamenev. On a meeting of the Political Bureau prior to the Fourteenth Congress of RCP (B), Zinoviev and Kamenev pulled Marxism to Dogmatism, suggesting that "the economically backward Russia cannot build socialism without the support of the western revolutions." Stalin explained his points of view when criticizing the opinions of the "new opposition". He thought that Zinoviev's and Kamenev's "new opposition" confused the USSR's contradictions at home and abroad. The contradictions in the country are the ones between the proletarians and peasants, which can be totally overcome by the efforts of the country. The contradictions out of the country are the ones between socialist countries and all capitalist countries, which can only be solved with the efforts of the proletariats from several countries. "Anyone who confuses the first group of contradictions with the second group of contradictions commits a gross error against Leninism. He is either a muddle-head or an incorrigible opportunist."[9] He also thought that Zinoviev's and Kamenev's "new opposition" confused the two formulations of the victory of socialism: the first is "the possibility of building socialism by the efforts of a single country, which must be answered in the affirmative"; the other is "the question whether a country in which the dictatorship of the proletariat has been established can consider itself fully guaranteed against intervention, and consequently against the restoration

---

8   ibid., p. 99, Retrieved from Marxists Internet Archive.
9   Collected Works of Stalin, first Chinese version, volume 8, p. 63, Retrieved from Marxists Internet Archive.

of the old order, without a victorious revolution in a number of other countries- which must be answered in the negative." "The organization of a socialist society by the efforts of a single country is impossible- which, of course, is correct."[10]

After 1926, Zinoviev and Kamenev integrated themselves as "the united opposition" and continued denying the future of socialism. In the report The Social-Democratic Deviation in Our Party delivered by Stalin at the Fifteenth All-Union Conference of the CPSU(B), he demonstrated the great significance of the future of socialism from four aspects. First, being clear of the future of socialism is the foundation of socialist construction. "We cannot build without prospects, without the certainty that having begun to build a socialist economy we can complete it. Without clear prospects, without clear aims, the Party cannot direct the work of construction…We must subordinate our forward movement, our practical work, to the basic class aim of the proletariat's constructive work. If not, we shall certainly and inevitably land in the quagmire of opportunism."[11] Second, being clear of the future of socialism is the foundation for the worker masses to consciously build socialism. "If the prospects of our constructive work are not clear, if there is no certainty that the building of socialism can be completed, the working masses cannot consciously participate in this constructive work, and cannot consciously lead the peasantry. If there is no certainty that the building of socialism can be completed, there can not be will to build socialism… the absence of socialist prospect for our constructive work certainly and inevitably leads to the weakening of the proletariat's will to build."[12] Third, being clear of the future of socialism is the foundation of fighting against the restoration of capitalism. Being clear of the future of socialism makes the willpower of socialism stronger and therefore prevents the capitalist elements from increasing. "For what does building socialism mean, if not overcoming the capitalist elements in our economy? Pessimistic and defeatist sentiments in the working class are bound to fire the capitalist elements' hopes of restoring the old order. Whoever fails to appreciate the decisive importance of the socialist prospects of our constructive work assists the capitalist elements in our economy fosters a spirit of capitulation."[13] Fourth, being clear of the future of socialism is the foundation of developing international revolution around the world. The significance of the USSR's socialist construction is never limited within the nation, it "is of tremendous international significance from the point of view of revolutionizing the proletarians of all countries. Whoever attempts

---

10   Collected Works of Stalin, first Chinese version, volume 8, p. 61, Retrieved from Marxists Internet Archive.

11   ibid., p. 248, Retrieved from Marxists Internet Archive.

12   Retrieved from Marxists Internet Archive.

13   ibid., p. 249, Retrieved from Marxists Internet Archive.

to do away with the socialist prospects of our constructive work is attempting to extinguish in the international proletariat the hope that we shall be victorious, and whoever extinguishes that hope is violating the elementary demands of proletarian internationalism."

2. The succession and development of the Marxist view on the future of socialism

Marxism's scientific exploration on the future of socialism is contained in the establishment and development of scientific socialism. From 1840s to 1860s, Marx and Engels made a series of scientific predictions on the historical necessity of socialism in their studies on the internal contradictions of developed capitalist economies and their historical trends with the example of Britain. After 1870s, Marx and Engels further extended the theoretical horizon of socialism studies based on the new changes of the economic and political situations in the world. Faced with the outstanding phenomenon of "cosmopolitism" emerged in the development of the capitalist economic relations, Marx and Engels from the perspective of the "world history", probed into the social development of the countries that were relatively lagging behind in economy and culture, and particularly, had the initial discussions on how these countries stride over the developing stage of capitalism. At that time, the capitalist economic relations had shown their dual characters, with one promoting the development of the productive forces in society and the progress of human civilization and the other bringing catastrophic results to human society. Therefore, when the countries that were relatively lagging behind in economy and culture were choosing their way of development, there unavoidably appeared the question: how to develop themselves by adopting and utilizing the achievements brought by the development of capitalist society and at the same time, how to avoid the disastrous vicissitudes brought to the human society by the development of capitalist society?

After the 1870s, although Marx and Engels' discussions on this issue were at the initial stage, these discussions were quite profound. People later concluded this study as the study on the development of the "oriental society", which means the study on the development of the countries lagging behind in economy and culture, or as the study on the issue of striding over the Crafting Gorge", which means the possibility of developing by only absorbing all the positive achievements of capitalist production but without going through any of its disastrous effects.

Their opinion on this issue is that even though there is the possibility that the countries that are relatively lagging behind in economy and culture will stride over the stage of capitalist development and directly go to socialism, it can only happen under the precondition that the proletariat of the developed capitalist countries have got the victory of revolution in advance or get it at the same time. Obviously, the issue of the future of socialism in the countries that are lagging behind in economy and culture had become a major subject of study and the theme of Marxism study at that time.

In the early 20th century, Lenin made creative exploration of the important topic put forward by Marx and Engels by combing the basic principles of Marxism and the new features of the changes in history and with times and by combing the Russian socialist revolution and the practice of construction. Based on the law of uneven economic and political development of capitalism, Lenin summed up the theory of victory of socialism in a single country. That is, "the victory of socialism is possible first in several or even in a single capitalist country." After expropriating the capitalists and organizing their own socialist production, the victorious proletariat of that country will arise against the rest of the world—the capitalist world— attracting to its cause the oppressed classes of other countries, stirring uprisings in those countries against the capitalists, and in case of need using even armed force against the exploiting classes and their states."[14] The victory of the October Revolution in Russia in 1917 was a great practice of the victory of socialism, making it true that the countries that are lagging behind in economy and culture directly transit to socialism and therefore changing Marx and Engels' early conclusion that the countries that are lagging behind in economy and culture will be able to transit to socialism only with the support of the victorious proletariat of the capitalist countries in advance or at the same time. Due to Lenin's early death, many of his theoretical visions could not be tested in practice and were not comprehensively and systematically studied and developed.

Leading the practice of the socialist economic construction in the USSR, Stalin succeeded Marxism's view on the future of socialism and further demonstrated Lenin's theory of victory of socialism in a single country. Stalin pointed out that although the law or uneven economic and political development of capitalism existed before the period of imperialism, it is still greatly different from the period of imperialism. The difference is: "the development of capitalism through free competition has been replaced by development through huge monopolist capitalist combines; that the old, 'cultured,' 'progressive' capital has been replaced by finance capital, by 'decaying' capital; that the 'peaceful' expansion of capital and its spread to 'vacant' territories has been replaced by spasmodic development, development through re-divisions of the already divided world by means of military conflicts between capitalist groups; that the old capitalism, the

14   Selected Works of Lenin, third edition, volume 2, p. 554, Beijing, People's Publishing House, 1995, Retrieved from Marxists Internet Archive.

development of which as a whole was on the upgrade, has thus been replaced by moribund capitalism, the development of which as a whole is on the downgrade."[15] Stalin thought that it was this difference where the uneven development in the period of imperialism came from. Uneven development and the level of the development are two different questions. In the period of imperialism, the difference between the levels of development of the capitalist countries is getting smaller and more even. This balance is nothing but the basis on which the effect of the law of uneven development gets stronger. The trend of balance in the level of economic development among capitalist countries makes it possible that some countries surpass other countries by leaping forward, have conflicts on places of origin of raw materials and market quota, and therefore create the conditions for the victory of socialism in one or two countries first. At the same time, Stalin made a thorough elaboration on Lenin's theory of victory of socialism in a single country, pointing out that the content of the theory is: none of the tasks, such as the proletariat taking the political power, depriving capitalists and organizing socialist production, are the final purpose; they are the means to fight against the rest of the capitalist world and to help the proletariats in the world to struggle with capitalism.

Having succeeded Marxism's view on the future of socialism, Stalin put forward some creative theories by combing the practice of the socialist revolution in Russia, developed Lenin's theory of the victory of socialism in a single country and made important contributions to scientific socialism. Following are his major contributions:

First, he referred to the two arrangements of the theory- victory of socialism in a single country: the question of socialism built by a single country and the question of the final victory of socialism. He also analyzed the two theoretical arrangements. Stalin thought that the theory of the victory of socialism includes two different theoretical arrangements, which are socialism built by a single country and the final victory of socialism. But the two arrangements ought to be distinguished. The reason of doing so is the social contradictions. In Stalin's opinion, there are two kinds of contradictions in the USSR: domestic contradictions and international contradictions. Domestic contradictions are the contradictions between the proletariat and peasants. The question of socialism built in a single country is actually the question whether or not the USSR can solve the internal contradictions, economically defeat the bourgeoisie and build the economic basis of socialism with its own power. "To create the economic basis of socialism means welding agriculture and socialist industry into one integral economy, subordinating agriculture to the leadership of socialist industry, regulating relations between town and country on the basis of an exchange of the products

15   Selected Works of Stalin, volume 1, p. 572, Retrieved from Marxists Internet Archive.

of agriculture and industry, closing and eliminating all the channels which facilitate the birth of classes and, above all, of capital, and, in the long run, establishing such conditions of production and distribution in order to lead directly and immediately to the abolition of classes."[16] Therefore, the USSR is completely able to build socialism. International contradictions are the contradictions between the socialist Russia and other capitalist countries. The question of the final victory of socialism is the question how to keep the socialist Russia that is being built away from extraneous risks and restoration of capitalism and how to solve the international contradictions and defeat the bourgeoisie in the world.

Second, Stalin talked about two important foundations of building socialism in a single country- domestic conditions and international conditions and demonstrated them. Stalin thought that the domestic condition of building socialism in a single country is organizing the whole national economy that includes industry and agriculture. With the dictatorship of the proletariat, the USSR actually has got the political basis of building socialism. And "the question of the relations between industry and agriculture, the question of the relations between the proletariat and the peasantry, is a fundamental question in the problem of building a socialist economy."[17] They constitute the economic basis of building socialism. If industry and agriculture could not consist the whole national economy, there would not be socialism. To consolidate the alliance of workers and peasants, the financial, tax and price policies have to be implemented in accordance with the interests of worker and peasant masses; industrial and agricultural production have to be rapidly developed; the country's socialist industrialization has to be achieved; the agricultural technical and socialist transformation have to be completed; agricultural economy has to be included in the system of socialist construction by general collectivization; and the contradictions and differences between urban and rural areas have to be eliminated. The international condition of building socialism in a single country is to have a period of "breathing" to get rid of the war. Stalin thought that after the World War I, capitalism was partially stabilized; the contradictions between the proletariat and the bourgeoisie within the imperialist countries, between imperialist countries and their colonies or dependent states, between the victorious and the vanquished countries had made the capitalist world week and feeble and therefore provided the USSR the possibility of establishing the international relations featured by the peaceful coexistence between the USSR and the capitalist countries and of starting a period of "breathing" without serious armed intervention.

---

16   Selected Works of Stalin, volume 1, p. 511, Retrieved from Marxists Internet Archive.
17   ibid., p. 386, Retrieved from Marxists Internet Archive.

Third, he talked about the two basic tasks of the proletarian revolution-"national" task and international task, and analyzed the relations between them. The "national" task of the proletariat is to achieve the victory of socialism in a single country while the international task is to help the proletariats around the world fight against capitalism. Stalin commented on the consistence and indivisibility of the two tasks. He thought that the revolution in the USSR is part of the revolution in the world. That they are closely related to each other. The national and international tasks of the proletariat in the USSR integrate into a common task of the liberation of the proletariat in the world; the interests of the socialism in the USSR and of the revolutions in other countries integrate into the common interests of the victory of the revolutions in the world. A single country has to rely on the support of other countries to take the political power and build socialism; a single country's final victory of the proletarian revolution also relies on the victory of the revolutions in several countries or all over the world. Therefore, a single country's victory of the revolution is the beginning and basis of the revolution in the world; a single country's victory of the revolution is not the final target, but the method and driving force of the development of revolutions in other countries.

II. Stalin's discussions on the issue of transition from capitalism to socialism

Stalin's view on the future of socialism is that socialism can be built in a single country. However, that a single country builds socialism needs to go through a transition period. Stalin's discussions on the transition period of capitalism transiting to socialism and how to build socialism reflected his basic outlook of socialism.

1. The views on the "transition period"

Ever since the victory of the October Revolution, the USSR had focused on the recovery of economy. According to the principles of socialism, the capitalist ownership was turned into socialist ownership and the capitalist large-scale industry was nationalized to make the Soviet political power start the construction of the socialist national economy and therefore the transition from capitalism to socialism.

During this period, the USSR was a country of dictatorship of the proletariat, with several economic forms existing at the same time. The form and way of transition were decided by the conditions. At that time, there were five different economic forms in the national economy. First is the patriarchal economy, which, to a great extent, is shown as the peasants' natural economy. The second is the small commodity production, most of which are the production of peasants for the sale of grain. The third is the private capitalism; the fourth is the state capitalism and the fifth is socialism. Among the five different economic forms, the peasants' small commodity production took the main position and became the basis of saving and restoring capitalism. The petty bourgeoisie in urban and rural areas are the Soviet political power's major risk of building socialism. On the contrary, the state capitalism is greatly significant for the transition to socialism. According to the situation in the USSR, Lenin made it clear that the major task of the Soviet political power is to overcome the spontaneous forces of the petty bourgeoisie and consolidate the economic form of socialism to make it the economic form that takes the majority with it and then to make it the only economic form that includes everything. The fundamental measure to complete these tasks was to make use of and to develop "the state capitalism under the dictatorship of the proletariat."

The reason is that the state capitalism is economically stronger than the peasants' economy; plus it is charged and supervised by the Soviet political organs, which, as a result, is beneficial to struggle with the spontaneous forces of the petty bourgeoisie and to promote the development of productive forces. According to Lenin's thought, the USSR turned into the NEP from the wartime communism. From 1926 to 1929, the development of the large-scale industry in the USSR had made full preparation for the socialist transformation. From 1929 to 1932, the early completion of the first five-year plan sped up the socialist construction; the socialist transformation of industry and agriculture had helped the USSR to build the basis of socialism. From 1932 to 1937, the socialist transformation of all forms of national economy was completed, meaning that the USSR had completed the transition from capitalism to socialism and basically established a socialist society.

Stalin elaborated on the meaning of the "transition period" during the recovery of the USSR's national economy and the socialist transformation, mainly from two aspects:

First, Stalin differentiated the "old meaning" of the "transition period" and its meaning "in the period of socialism". In the history of the USSR, the transition period was from the victory of the October Revolution to the year of 1936 when the socialist transformation was completed and the socialist society was established. In July 1930, in the political report of the Central Committee to the Sixteenth Congress of the CPSU(B), Stalin made it clear that the "transition period" that was lasting for a long time has different features at different historical stages. He pointed out, "our period is usually called the period of transition from capitalism to socialism. It was called a transition period in 1918, when Lenin, in his celebrated article, *'Left-Wing' Childishness and Petty-Bourgeois Mentality*, first described this period with its five forms of economy. It is called a transition period today, in 1930, when some of these forms, having become obsolete, are already on their way to disappear, while one of them, namely, the new form of economy in the sphere of industry and agriculture, is growing and developing with unprecedented speed. Can it be said that these two transition periods are identical, are not radically different from each other? Obviously not."[18]

So exactly what is the difference? Stalin differentiated the old meaning of the transition period and the transition period after entering socialism by comparing and analyzing the situations in 1918 and in 1930. He pointed out, "what did we have in the sphere of the national economy in 1918? A ruined industry and cigarette lighters; neither collective farms nor state farms on a mass scale; the growth of a 'new' bourgeoisie in the towns and of the kulaks in the countryside."[19] And what was it like in 1930? Stalin clearly elaborated, "what do we have today? Socialist industry, restored and undergoing reconstruction, an extensive system of state farms and collective farms, accounting for more than 40 per cent of the total sown area of the USSR in the spring-sown sector alone, a moribund 'new' bourgeoisie in the town and a moribund kulak class in the countryside."[20] Based on this analysis, Stalin emphasized, "the former was a transition period and so is the latter. Nevertheless, they are as far apart as heaven and earth. And nevertheless, no one can deny that we are on the verge of eliminating the last important capitalist class, the kulak class. Clearly, we have already emerged from the transition period in the old sense and have entered the period of direct and sweeping socialist construction along the whole front. Clearly, we have already entered the period of socialism, since the socialist sector now controls all the economic levers of the entire national economy, although we are still far from having completely built a socialist society and from having abolished class distinctions." The plan of the national economy of 1931 made at the end of 1930, also emphasized it, stating that the socialist form had taken the majority in the national economy; that the USSR had entered into the period of socialist offensive, which means the period of socialism. The coming 1931 would be the year in which the achievements and victory would be achieved by fighting against capitalism. The completion of the collectivization would make the socialist elements in rural areas become the majority over the private economic form; it would consolidate the alliance of working class and the peasant masses and establish the complete economic basis of socialism in the Soviet Union. All of these would be the most meaningful victory in the history of the world.

18 Collected Works of Stalin, first Chinese version, volume 13, p. 6, Beijing, People's Publishing House, 1956, Retrieved from Marxists Internet Archive.
19 ibid., p.7, Retrieved from Marxists Internet Archive.
20 Collected Works of Stalin, first Chinese version, volume 13, p. 7, Retrieved from Marxists Internet Archive.

Second, Stalin talked about speeding up to go through the transition period and building socialism. About this issue, Stalin mainly referred from the perspective of building socialism as soon as possible and surpassing the developed countries. Building socialism in the shortest period of time was the target of the USSR in the transition period. The year of 1929 was of great significance, because in this year, after the hardest struggle for peace, the USSR had achieved the preliminary results of socialist industrialization and collectivization and turned to the socialist transformation. In November this year, the Central Plenum of the CPSU(B) put forward the thesis of building socialism in the shortest period of time. The plenum pointed out: "the development of the socialist economic form, the increase of its proportion in the national economy, and its stronger influence on peasants (shown as the poor and middle size peasants consciously inclined to collectivization)–all of these tell that the policy of socialism attacking the capitalist elements have had the guarantee of the decisive victory; that in the country with the dictatorship of the proletariat, building socialism can be completed in the shortest period of time."[21] With the collectivization movement, the USSR's political power had laid solid foundation in agriculture and consolidated it, which had created decisive conditions for building socialist national economy. From the perspective of affirming the effect of collectivization movement, the Sixteenth Congress of the CPSU(B) stated that it is a meaningful step to transit to collectivization and an important stage for the USSR to build the basis of socialism.

The speed has to be guaranteed for catching up and surpassing the developed countries. Stalin had made some comments on the USSR's catching up the developed capitalist economies in a short period of time.

He said, "To slacken the tempo would mean falling behind. And those who fall behind get beaten."[22] According to the reality of the USSR, "we are fifty or a hundred years behind the advanced countries."[23] So, how to eliminate the distance? Stalin pointed out, "we must make good this distance in ten years. Either we do it, or we shall perish."[24] "But we do not want to be beaten."[25] "One feature of the history of old Russia was the repeated defeats it suffered because of its backwardness. Russia was beaten by the Mongol Khans. It was beaten by the Turkish beys. It was beaten by the Swedish feudal lords. It was beaten by the Polish and Lithuanian gentry. Russia was beaten by the British and French capitalists. It was beaten by the Japanese

---

21　For further reference, see the Collected Resolutions of the Congresses, Representatives Meetings and Central Plenums of the CPSU(B) volume 4, p. 72-73, Beijing, People's Publishing House, 1957.
22　Selected Works of Stalin, volume 2, p. 273, Retrieved from Marxists Internet Archive.
23　ibid., p. 274, Retrieved from Marxists Internet Archive.
24　Retrieved from Marxists Internet Archive
25　ibid., p. 273, Retrieved from Marxists Internet Archive.

barons. All beat Russia — because of its backwardness, because of its military backwardness, cultural backwardness, political backwardness, industrial backwardness, agricultural backwardness. They defeated Russia because it was weak and could be done with impunity…Therefore you are wrong; hence you can be beaten and enslaved. You are mighty—therefore you are right; hence we must be wary of you."[26] Can we avoid being beaten by avoiding the situation of falling behind? Stalin thought there are at least two possibilities. One is the victory of the October Revolution made the people of Soviet Union overthrow the rule of capitalism, take the political power, have their own motherland and protect its independence. "Do you want our socialist fatherland to be beaten and to lose its independence? If you do not want this, you must put an end to its backwardness in the shortest possible time and develop a genuine Bolshevik tempo in building up its socialist economy. There is no other way."[27] Stalin thought that the USSR workers' obligation on peasants required us to do so; our obligation on the working class in the world required us to do so.[28] The other possibility is that the development of the USSR's industrialization and the collectivization movement made the Bolsheviks grasp the skills and become experts themselves. "There are no fortresses that Bolsheviks cannot capture. We have solved a number of most difficult problems. We have overthrown capitalism. We have assumed power. We have built up a huge socialist industry. We have transferred the middle size peasants on to the path of socialism. We have already accomplished what is most important from the point of view of construction. What remains to be done is not so much: to study technique, to master science. And when we have done that we shall develop a tempo of which we not even dare to dream at present. And we shall do it if we really want to."[29]

87

2. The discussions on the basic foundation and building of socialism

In 1936, the features of the domestic life of the USSR were: the socialist transformation of all sectors in the national economy was completed; the socialist society was established; the question of "who will defeat whom" was basically solved; socialism had achieved victory in the USSR; the USSR had become a powerful industrial country that was able to satisfy the its needs of national defense. Evaluating the current situation, Stalin commented on the USSR's basic conditions of building and establishment of socialism, including three aspects:

---

26 Retrieved from Marxists Internet Archive.
27 Retrieved from Marxists Internet Archive
28 For further reference, see the above book, p. 274.
29 ibid., p. 275, Retrieved from Marxists Internet Archive.

First, Stalin thought the establishment of socialism in the USSR had basically achieved the first stage of the communist society mentioned by Marx and Engels. Stalin explained his view by analyzing the essential changes in USSR related to socialism that was established. He thought that the essential changes of the established socialism in the USSR were mainly the ownership forms, changes in the national economic system, the class structure in the society and so on.

In terms of the ownership forms, Stalin pointed out, "our Soviet society is a socialist society, because the private ownership of the factories, works, the land, the banks and the transport system has been abolished and public ownership has been put in its place. The social organization which we have created may be called a Soviet socialist organization, though not entirely completed, but fundamentally, a socialist organization of society. The foundation of this society is public property: state, i.e., national, and also co-operative, collective farm property."[30]

In terms of the national economic system, Stalin made it clear that the socialist system was established in every sector of the national economy in the USSR, including industry, agriculture and commerce. The USSR's industry "is now based on new, developed, modern technical equipment, with a powerful heavy industry sector, and an even including a developed machine-building industry. But the most important thing is that capitalism has been banished entirely from the sphere of our industry, while the Socialist form of production now holds undivided sway in the sphere of our industry."[31] The agriculture "now has mechanized production, conducted on a scale larger than anywhere else in the world, with up-to-date technical equipment, in the form of an all-embracing system of collective farms and state farms." "The kulak class in agriculture has been eliminated, while the sector of small individual peasant farms, with its backward, outdated technical equipment, now occupies an insignificant place."[32] As for the commerce sphere , "the merchants and profiteers have been banished entirely from this sphere. All trade is now in the hands of the state, the cooperative societies, and the collective farms. A new, Soviet trade–trade without profiteers, trade without capitalists–has arisen and developed."[33]

In terms of the class structure, due to the essential changes in the USSR's economy, the class structure had also changed. "The capitalist class in the sphere of industry has ceased to exist. The kulak class in the sphere of agriculture has ceased to exist. And the merchants and profiteers in the sphere of trade have ceased to exist. Thus all the exploiting classes have been

30 Stalin's Works (1934-1952), pp. 91-92, Retrieved from Marxists Internet Archive.
31 Ibid.
32 Ibid.
33 Selected Works of Stalin, volume 2, p. 393, Retrieved from Marxists Internet Archive.

eliminated."[34] In the established socialist society of the USSR, "the working class of the USSR is an entirely new working class, a working class emancipated from exploitation, the like of which the history of mankind has never known before."[35] Peasants are the entirely new peasants, who have got rid of exploitation. "It bases its work and wealth not on individual labor and on backward technical equipment, but on collective labor and up-to-date technical equipment."[36] The economic base of peasants is the collective ownership built on the basis of collective working. The intelligentsia "is an entirely new intelligentsia, bound up by its very roots with the working class and the peasantry", "the like of which you will not find in any other country on earth."[37] The change of the class structure means that the boundary between the working class and peasantry and between these two classes and the intelligentsia were disappearing ; thus the economic and political contradictions between them were shrinking or eliminating.

Because of these essential changes, Stalin thought that the USSR had basically achieved socialism and established the socialist system, which means the system of the first stage or lower stage of communism mentioned by Marx and Engels was set up. He said, "We have already achieved the first phase of communism. In other words Socialism... The fundamental principle of this phase of Communism as you know is the formula: 'From each according to his abilities, and to each according to his work.' Should our Constitution reflect this fact, the fact that Socialism has been achieved? Should it be based on this achievement? Unquestionably, it should. It should, because for the USSR socialism is something already achieved and won."[38]

Second, the establishment of socialism in the USSR meant that with the efforts of 10 to 15 years, the USSR could catch up and surpass the major capitalist countries. At the Eighteenth Congress of the CPSU(B), Stalin presented the final working report of the Central Committee of the CPSU(B). In the report, Stalin analyzed the development of the industrial technologies in the USSR, stating that the most important achievement of developing the national economy in the USSR is the completion of the transformation of industry and agriculture on the basis of new modern technologies. He mentioned, "there are no more or hardly any more those old plants in our country, with their old technique, and hardly any old agricultural farms, with their antediluvian equipment. Our industry and agriculture are now based on new, up-to-date technology. It may be said without exaggeration

---

34 Selected Works of Stalin, volume 2, p. 394.
35 ibid p. 395.
36 ibid.
37 ibid., p. 396.
38 ibid., p. 399.

that from the standpoint of the technique of production, compared from the standpoint of the degree of saturation of industry and agriculture with new machinery, our country is more advanced than any other country."[39] Just for this reason, by continuously developing the industry in the USSR, increasing the productive forces of labor and improving the techniques of production, the USSR will catch up and surpass the major capitalist countries in terms of the technical equipment in production and the speed of development, on the basis of which, the USSR in the future will economically catch up with and surpass the major capitalist countries in 10 to 15 years.

Third, Stalin thought that the establishment of socialism in the USSR means that the USSR has entered into the completely classless social formation and therefore can gradually transit to communist society. At the Eighteenth Congress of the Party, as Stalin was commenting on technical equipment in production and the speed of development in comparison with major capitalist countries, he had also emphasized that the USSR had to catch up with and surpass the major countries in terms of economic volume. He commented: "only if we outstrip the principal capitalist countries economically can we reckon upon our country being fully saturated with consumers' goods, having an abundance of products, and thus being able to make the transition from the first phase of communism to its second phase."[40] This idea of Stalin was later included in the third five-year plan (1938-1942) of the national economy of the USSR, which clearly pointed out: Due to the achievements made by the victory of the second five-year plan and socialism, the USSR has entered into a new phase of development with the third five-year plan. In this phase, it will be decisively significant to provide the working people with communist education and overcome the capitalist survivals in the mind of people the constructors of communism.[41] Accordingly the *Constitution of the Communist Party of the USSR* passed on October 31, 1952 had clearly defined the major task of the Party as: Gradual transition from socialism to communism and finally establish the communist society; continuously increasing the material and cultural level of the society; educating the members of the society with the spirit of internationalism and establishing brotherhood with the working people all over the world; making every effort to intensify the national defense of the USSR to prevent the invasion by the enemies.

---

39   Works of Stalin (1934-1952), p. 247, Retrieved from Marxists Internet Archive.
40   Works of Stalin (1934-1952), p. 251-252.
41   For further reference, see Collected Resolutions of the Congresses, Representatives Meetings and Central Plenums of the CPSU(B) volume 5, p. 10-11, Beijing, People's Publishing House, 1958.

3. The influence of Stalin's discussions on the transition period in China

There are both reasonable elements and mistakes in Stalin's discussions on the transition from capitalism to socialism, which have had great influence on the construction efforts in the transition period of China. The reasonable elements were mainly: first, Stalin's differentiation of the old meaning of the transition period and its meaning in the period of socialism had undoubtedly practical significance for the promotion of the socialist construction; second, Stalin's exploration on speeding up construction efforts to eliminate the backwardness and catch up with the developed countries in the process of building socialism in the USSR was undoubtedly very important, third, Stalin's analysis on the USSR's economy, politics and class structure which was generally in line with the social practice at that time, had also theoretical significance.

However, there were also some mistakes in Stalin's analysis. For example, he confused the transition period with the period of socialism; he one-sidedly emphasized on the speed. He advocated building socialism by running through the transition period in the shortest period of time, which reflected his impatience on establishing the socialist system and building socialism. His ideas that the establishment of socialism in the USSR meant the first phase of communism mentioned in Marx's and Engels' theories were basically achieved and that the USSR will transit from the first phase to the second only if it catches up with and surpasses the major capitalist countries reflected his impatience not only on the issue of the transition from capitalism to socialism, but also on the transition from socialism to communism. The reason why China went through a very short period of transition (1953-56) from new democracy to socialism can be related to the effect of Stalin's ideas.

After the foundation of the new China in 1949, Mao Zedong attached great importance to the issue of transition. He regarded the transition from the new-democracy society to socialist society as: "After the victory of the new-democratic Revolution, the construction of the new-democratic society will take a very long period of time until the material and spiritual conditions are completely mature; after then the question how to transit to socialism should be considered." Mao Zedong thought that one of the most important aspects of the transition from the new-democratic society to socialism was to quickly recover and develop production, transforming the agricultural country to an industrial country. Industrialization was the material precondition for China to enter into the socialist society. Accordingly on 18th February 1951, Mao Zedong drafted the inner-party circular titled *Main Points of the Resolution Adopted at the Enlarged Meeting of the Political Bureau of the Central Committee of the Communist Party of China*. In the first part, of this document he proposed the strategic idea of "three years for preparation and ten years for planned economic construction", in which he obviously meant the preparation for the transition that included the nationalization of industry and collectivization of agriculture. Only after the completion of the nationalization of industry and the collectivization of agriculture can the transition from new-democratic society to socialism could be considered. Because the tasks of nationalization of industry and the collectivization of agriculture could not be accomplished in a short period of time, thus the transition would also last long. Mao Zedong had made several comments on this topic. At the meeting of the Political Bureau in September 1948, Mao Zedong indicated that it may need 15 years to take the entire start an all-round offensive aiming socialism when he tried to make some predictions on the situation after the victory of the new democratic revolution. Later, Liu Shaoqi made further explanation on this issue, pointing out that the new-democratic economy is a transitional economy, which actually solved "the issue of 'who defeated whom' as stated by Lenin in the period of the NEP in the USSR."[42] Therefore, it the idea was it would need numerous steps for China, rather than a short period of time to complete socialist transformation. On the contrary in the early days of new China, Mao Zedong, after considering the time taken by the USSR to achieve the transition to socialism, believed that we would need 10 to 15 years of new-democratic construction and "after that we could start the transition to socialism."

92

However, after 1952, Mao Zedong's understanding on the issue of transition encountered great changes. After the foundation of the New China and after three years' efforts, the big bureaucratic capital was confiscated, the imperialistic forces in China were eliminated and the powerful socialist state owned economic sector was formed. At the same time, the counter-revolutionaries were relatively completely suppressed on the mainland; suppressed in the new liberated areas with the population of 300 million, the agrarian reform were completed; the proletariat had united the peasants and other small producers; the successful policy of uniting, educating and reforming were applied against the national bourgeoisie; thus the class relations in China had encountered historical changes. Under such historical conditions, Mao Zedong when annotating and commenting on a document of the Ministry of United Front Work as follows: "with the overthrow of the landlord class and the bureaucrat-capitalist class, the contradiction between the working class and the national bourgeoisie has become the principal contradiction in China; therefore the national bourgeoisie should no longer be defined as an intermediate class."[43] At the meeting of the Central

42　Selected Works of Liu Shaoqi, volume 1, p. 427, 428, Beijing, People's Publishing House, 1985.
43　Collected Works of Mao Zedong, volume 6, p. 231, Beijing, People's Publishing House, 1999, Retrieved from Marxists Internet Archive.

Committee Secretariat in September 1952, Mao Zedong changed his previous formulation of transiting to socialism in 10 to 15 years. He pointed out that it will need 10 to 15 years not to transit to socialism, but to basically establish socialism. He indicated that the limitation policy against national bourgeoisie which was put forward at the second plenum of the Central Committee in 1949 now has more content. Now in industry, 32.7% were privately owned and 67.3% were state-owned, which was thirty-seventy ratio; in commerce, there was a forty to sixty ratio. After five years' development, these ratios would even be smaller—the private will be much less than the state owned), though the private capital will be still still allowed to have some room for development. That is still not socialism. If that is what would be like in five year, what would it be like in 10 or 15 years? That we need to think about.[44] By then on, Mao Zedong had changed his original thought of transiting to socialism in 10 to 15 years into the idea of gradually transiting to socialism from then on. Mao Zedong's unrealistic new assumption and practice on time needed to transit from the new-democracy to socialism were undoubtedly influenced by Stalin's thought.

III. Stalin's discussions on the basic features of socialism

How can be socialism built by a single country? That was Stalin's discussion on the transition from capitalism to socialism. What kind of socialism can be built by a single country is another question that attracted a lot of Stalin's attention. In the practice of leading the USSR's socialist construction, Stalin's discussions on the basic features of socialism to some degree deepened his outlook of socialism.

1. The generalization of the basic feature of socialism

In the 1930s, the USSR started the national industrialization and the collectivization of agriculture, began the socialist transformation, implemented other measures and gradually established the first socialist system in human history. Just as Stalin pointed out at the Sixteenth Congress of the CPSU(B), "Clearly, we have already emerged from the transition period in the old sense and have entered the period of direct and sweeping socialist construction along the whole front. Clearly, we have already entered the period of socialism, since the socialist sector now controls all the economic levers of the entire national economy, although we are still far from having completely built a socialist society and from having abolished class distinctions."[45]

---

44 For further reference, see The Literature of the Chinese Communist Party, 1989 (6), p. 79.
45 Collected Works of Stalin, first Chinese version, volume 13, p. 7, Retrieved from Marxists Internet Archive.

Judging by a series of Stalin's speeches and works in the period of socialist transition and construction, his comments on the basic features of socialism can be generalized as the following aspects:

First, the public ownership of the means of production is the economic basis of the socialist relations of production. In the process of the nation's industrialization and the collectivization of agriculture, Stalin clearly thought that the political power of the USSR could not rely on two form of ownerships- public ownership and private ownership; believed that with the development of industrialization and the collectivization of agriculture, the policy of limiting, excluding and final elimination of the capitalist and the kulak economic elements should be achieved and that only single form single form of public ownership should be established Stalin commented on the issue of the public ownership of the means of production mainly from two aspects. One is to divide the ownership of the means of production into two basic forms- ownership by the whole people and the collective ownership and equated the state ownership with the ownership by the whole people. He thought that the Soviet socialist society's "foundation... is public property: state, i.e., national, and also cooperative or collective farm property."[46] In Stalin's period, the Constitution of the USSR also mentioned that state ownership is the main form of the socialist ownership; that the collective farm is another form of the public ownership and is the collective ownership of farm workers. In 1952, Stalin in Economic Problems of Socialism in the USSR thought that the ownership of the collective farms have become the obstacle of the development of productive forces. Therefore, measures must be taken to upgrade the ownership of the collective farms to the level of the ownership of the whole people and therefore simplify the forms of ownership. The other is that he commented on how to consolidate and protect the public ownership of materials of production. In 1932, Stalin drafted the resolution on Protection of the Property of State Enterprises, Collective Farms and Co-operatives and the Consolidation of Public (Socialist) Property, in which he pointed out: "The Central Executive Committee and Council of People's Commissars of the U.S.S.R. hold that public property (state, collective-farm and co-operative property),which is the basis of the Soviet system; it is sacred and inviolable, and persons committing offences against public property must be considered enemies of the people. In view of this it is a prime duty of the organs of Soviet power to wage a determined struggle against those who steal public property."[46] Stalin attached great importance to this issue in the process of the socialist construction. He made further comments on it in The Results of the First Five-Year Plan in 1933 and emphasized, "the sharp edge of revolutionary

94

46   Collected Works of Stalin, first Chinese version, volume 13, p. 344, annotation 51, Retrieved from Marxists Internet Archive.

law at the present time is directed, not against the excesses of war communism, which have ceased to exist for long, but against thieves and wreckers in public economy, against rowdies and pilferers of public property. The main concern of revolutionary law at the present time is, consequently, the protection of public property, and not something else. That is why it is one of the fundamental tasks of the Party to fight to protect public property, to fight with all the measures and all the means placed at our command by our Soviet laws."[47]

Second, the socialist economy is planned economy. Stalin thought that planned economy is what the public ownership of socialism needs and constitutes its fundamental feature which distinguishes it from the capitalist economy. The uneven development of capitalist economy is adjusted by the spontaneous forces of the market. The free competition under anarchy always leads to crisis. Planned economy cannot be carried out in capitalist countries, because it is necessary to have "a nationalized industry, a nationalized credit system, nationalized land, a socialist bond with the countryside, working-class rule in the country, etc."[48] However, the socialist economy is different. It is the most unified and collective planned economy with organization and leadership and therefore it is superior to capitalist economy. That is because "crises, unemployment, waste, destitution among the masses—such are the incurable diseases of capitalism. Our system does not suffer from these diseases because power is in our hands, in the hands of the working class; because we are conducting a planned economy, systematically accumulating resources and properly distributing them among the different branches of the national economy."[49] Stalin did not deny that capitalist countries also have plans, but he thought the plans of the capitalist countries are different from those of the socialist countries. The plans of the capitalist countries are "forecast plans, guess-work plans, does not bind anybody, and they cannot serve as a basis for directing the country's economy" while the plans of socialist countries are "not forecast plans, not guess-work plans, but directive plans, which are binding upon our leading bodies, and which determine the trend of our future economic development on a country-wide scale."[50]

Third, distribution according to work is the principle of socialist distribution of personal consuming products. On this basic feature of socialist system, Stalin commented from the perspective of criticizing equalitarianism that existed in the distribution system. He pointed out that one should

47   ibid., p.189, Retrieved from Marxists Internet Archive.
48   Collected Works of Stalin, first Chinese version, volume 10, p. 280, Beijing, People's Publishing House, 1954, Retrieved from Marxists Internet Archive.
49   Selected Works of Stalin, volume 2, p. 269, Retrieved from Marxists Internet Archive.
50   Collected Works of Stalin, first Chinese version, volume 10, p. 280, Retrieved from Marxists Internet Archive.

never require that the need of the members of the socialist society and their personal life are all average, equal or the same; that we must "abolish the wage equalization"; that in terms of the wage system, we must "discard the old wage scales" and "must draw up wage scales that will take into account the difference between skilled and unskilled labor, between heavy and light work." The reason is that this difference "would exist even under socialism, even after classes were abolished; that only under communism would this difference disappear and that, consequently, even under socialism 'wages' must be paid according to work performed and not according to needs."[51] For the first time, Stalin put forward that "'From each according to his ability, to each according to his work.' Such is the Marxist formula of socialism, i.e., the formula of the first stage of communism, the first stage of communist society." He also pointed out that "equalitarianism owes its origin to the individual peasant type of mentality, the psychology of share and share alike, the psychology of primitive peasant 'communism.'"[52] Stalin also elaborated that "from each according to his ability, to each according to his work" has shown the view of equalization of Marxism. The view on equalization of Marxism has something in common in the two social systems- communism and socialism. First is the equal political status of the laborers; second is that the laborers are equal in the materials of production. However, on the distribution of the personal consuming products, the view on equalization of Marxism is differently reflected in communist society and socialist society. That meansthat, in socialist society, it is the equal right for all laborers to get their wages according to their work while in communist society, labors have the equal right to get what they want according to their needs. Equalitarianism does not have anything in common with the socialist society of Marxism, because the "equality in Marxism means, not equalisation of personal requirements and everyday life, but the abolition of classes."[53]

Fourth, the Communist Party is the leading core of the socialist country. Stalin thought that in the socialist country, the Communist Party is the tool of the dictatorship of the proletariat, the leader and the instructor in the system of dictatorship of the proletariat, because "the highest expression of the leading role of the Party, here, in the USSR, in the land of the dictatorship of the proletariat, for example, is the fact that not a single important political or organizational question is decided by our Soviet and other mass organizations without guiding directives from the party."[54] In a socialist

51 Collected Works of Stalin, first Chinese version, volume 13, p. 54, Retrieved from Marxists Internet Archive.

52 Selected Works of Stalin, volume 2, p. 308, 309, Retrieved from Marxists Internet Archive.

53 Collected Works of Stalin, first Chinese version, volume 13, p. 314, Retrieved from Marxists Internet Archive.

54 Collected Works of Stalin, first Chinese version, volume8, p. 36, Retrieved from Marxists Internet Archive.

country like the USSR, the communist party can never share the leadership with other parties. "The position of our party as the only legal party in the country (the monopoly of the Communist Party) is not something artificial and deliberately invented. Such a position cannot be created artificially by administrative machinations, etc. The monopoly of our party grew up out of life, it developed historically as a result of the fact that the Socialist Revolutionary Party and the Menshevik Party became absolutely bankrupt and departed from the stage of our social life."[55]

Fifth, the dictatorship of the proletariat is the form which realizes the state's function in the socialist country. When discussing the changes in the forms of the state's functions, Stalin made it clear that "the forms of our state are changing and will continue to change in line with the development of our country and with the changes in the international situation. Lenin was absolutely right when he said: '…the transition from capitalism to communism will certainly create a great variety and abundance of political forms, but their essence will inevitably be the same: the dictatorship of the proletariat.'"[56] As the form of the country's function, the dictatorship of the proletariat has both the violent and non violent aspect. From these two aspects, Stalin elaborated on it as the form of the state's function. He pointed out that from the violent aspect, "the dictatorship of the proletariat is the rule-unrestricted by law and based on force-of the proletariat over the bourgeoisie, a rule enjoying the sympathy and support of the laboring and exploited masses."[57] From the nonviolent aspect, the dictatorship of the proletariat is "leadership of the toiling masses of the non-proletarian classes, it means also the building of a socialist economy, which is a higher type of economy than capitalist economy, with a higher productive forces of labor than the capitalist economy.[58] Therefore, in addition to "violence, unrestricted by law, in relation to the capitalists and landlords", it also includes "leadership by the proletariat in relation to the peasantry" and "the building of socialism in relation to the whole of society."[59] Later, at the Eighteenth Congress of the CPSU(B), Stalin very briefly generalized the three major functions of the dictatorship of the proletariat: first is to suppress the class that has been overthrown in the country; second is to protect the nation from invasion; third is to organize economic and cultural work.

---

55 Collected Works of Stalin, first Chinese version, volume 10, p. 102, Retrieved from Marxists Internet Archive.
56 Works of Stalin, volume1, p. 254, Retrieved from Marxists Internet Archive.
57 Collected Works of Stalin, first Chinese version, volume 6, p. 102, Retrieved from Marxists Internet Archive.
58 Collected Works of Stalin, first Chinese version, volume 7, p. 155, Retrieved from Marxists Internet Archive.
59 Retrieved from Marxists Internet Archive.

Sixth, Marxism-Leninism should enjoy the leading position in the field of ideology. Stalin argued that Marxism-Leninism serves as the scientific guidance for socialist construction, which has been proved by the victory of the socialist revolution under the leadership of the party. "Our Party alone knows in what direction to steer its course, and it is going forward successfully. To what does our Party owe its superiority? To the fact that it is a Marxist party, a Leninist party. It owes it to the fact that it is guided in its work by the teachings of Marx, Engels, and Lenin. There can be no doubt that as long as we remain loyal to these teachings, as long as we have this compass, we shall achieve successes in our work."[60] It should also be applied to our socialist construction. We must educate the staff in every department of the party and of the government with Marxism-Leninism. "The higher the political level and the Marxist-Leninist knowledge of the workers in any branch of State and Party work the better and more fruitful will be the work itself, and the more effective the results of the work."[61] Stalin repeatedly emphasized that Marxism-Leninism is a science that is developing; that when instructing the socialist construction, we cannot make it dogmatized. In *Marxism and Problems of Linguistics*, he pointed out, "Marxism is the science revealing the laws governing the development of nature and society, the science of revolution for the oppressed and exploited masses, the science leading to the victory of socialism in all countries, the science of building communist society. As a science, Marxism cannot stand still, it develops and it is being perfected. In its development, Marxism cannot but be enriched by new experience, new knowledge—consequently some of its formulas and conclusions cannot but change in the course of time, cannot but be replaced by new formulas and conclusions, corresponding to the new historical tasks. Marxism does not recognize invariable conclusions and formulas, obligatory for all epochs and periods. Marxism is the enemy of all dogmatism."[62]

2. Discussions on the theoretical basis and historical conditions of the basic features of socialism

Stalin's discussions on the basic features of socialism have inherited and enriched Marxism's outlook of socialism from the perspective of the practice of socialism in the USSR.

In the mid-19th century when Marx and Engels were demonstrating the law of the historical development of society that capitalism will definitely

---

60   Collected Works of Stalin, first Chinese version, volume 13, p. 332, Retrieved from Marxists Internet Archive.
61   Works of Stalin, volume1, p. 246, Retrieved from Marxists Internet Archive.
62   Works of Stalin, volume 2, p. 559, Beijing, People's Publishing House, 1962, Retrieved from Marxists Internet Archive.

be replaced by socialism, they also predicted the basic structure of the new society in the future, thinking that the basic features of the future new society will include the following six aspects:

First, the productive forces to be developed at a fast pace will further develop the material preconditions of socialism. Marx and Engels thought that in the future society, "the proletariat will use their own political power to take all the capital of the bourgeoisie step by step and having therefore all the means of production in the hand of the nation, which is the proletariat organized to be the ruling class, and to increase the total output as soon as possible."[63] Socialism is based on the great increase of productive forces and rapid development. The reason is: "with out this kind of development, there will be only the universalization of poverty and extreme poverty; under the circumstances of extreme poverty, the struggle for necessities will start again and therefore all the decaying stuff will again become alive; only with the universal development of productive forces can the universal communication between people be set up." As a result the system of general social metabolism, of universal relations, of all-round needs and individuals with universal capacities and individuals in a world-historical existence will be formed and the former restricted and one-sided development status of individuals will be surpassed."[64]

Second, the private ownership of means of production is eliminated; all the means of production are owned by the whole society and are used by all the members in the society; all production sectors will be administrated by the union of free and equal producers that are consisted of all members of the whole society. In the struggle for the establishment of the new social system, Marx and Engels have paid great attention to the necessity of eliminating private ownership and establishing public ownership. They also stated that "communists can generalize their theory with one phrase: eliminating private ownership."[65] Elimination of private ownership a constitute the basic path of replacing capitalism with socialism. It is no doubt that socialist society is "a society that is collective and based on public ownership of means of production."[66] The public ownership of means of production is the essential difference between socialism and capitalism.

Third, the anarchy of the general capitalist production is eliminated and the social production is put under the planning and regulation of the whole society. In any society, there are always an objective proportion and a corresponding relation between aggregate social production and aggregate

---

63   Selected Works of Marx and Engels, second edition, volume 1, p. 293, Beijing, People's Publishing House, 1995.
64   ibid., p. 86.
65   ibid., p. 286.
66   Selected Works of Marx and Engels, second edition, volume 3, p. 303.

demand. Marx pointed out, "the national collectivization of the means of production will be the national basis of the society that is consisted of the unions of the free and equal producers. These producers will conduct social labor according to the common and rational plans."[67] Clearly, Marx's and Engels' idea that in socialist society, commodity and currency are out of economic life was in line with the idea that the production in socialist society is planned. The planned social production that is on the basis of public ownership of means of production has overcome the contradiction between private labor and social labor, with social labor directly becoming part of labor and commodity and currency dropping out of the sphere of economic activities.

Fourth, the personal consuming products are being distributed according to work. The mode of production determines the way of distribution. Marx thought that "every producer gets his quota of means of subsistence according to his working hours." Therefore, the hours of labor will have two effects. The planned social distribution according to the hours of labor properly adjusts the proportion between various functions of labor and different demands. On the other hand, working hours is also the standard to measure every individual producer's quota in the labor in common, where people's relations with their labor and products of their labor are simple and clear no matter on production or on distribution."[68] Distribution according to one's work means that the laborer takes his consumption goods that are equal to the labor he provided. In Marx's mind, "the laborer gets a voucher from the society to prove how much work he has provided (excluding the work for public funds). With this voucher, he can get the consumption goods that take the same amount of labor from the social stock. Therefore, the labor he provided to the society is taken back in another form."[69] We can see that the idea of distribution according to one's work envisaged by Marx is achieved in the form of distribution in kind.

Fifth, with the elimination of classes and the class difference, nation starts to geteliminated too. Marx and Engels thought that the dictatorship of the proletariat is the nation in the transition period from capitalism to socialism. In the phase of socialism, the means of production are all taken by the society and the classes and class differences are being eliminated. Therefore, the nation as the dictatorship of the proletariat will lose the conditions of existence and start to gradually eliminate. It will be replaced by a unity of free individuals, which will exercise the function of administration to the society. In *Socialism: Utopian and Scientific*, Engels pointed out,

67   Selected Works of Marx and Engels, second edition, volume 3, p. 130.
68   Collected Works of Marx and Engels, first Chinese edition, volume 23, p. 96, Beijing, People's Publishing House, 1972.
69   Selected Works of Marx and Engels, second edition, volume 3, p. 304.

"at that time, the rule on people will be replaced by the administration of objects and the leadership of the process of production. The nation cannot 'be abolished' because it will eliminate itself."[70]

Sixth, every member in the society will have completely free development and give the rein to all of their talents and power. Marx and Engels believed that the distorted development of human beings- the continuous decrease of self-worth with the increasing growth of material wealth- is the biggest disadvantage in capitalist society. However, in socialist society, due to the elimination of exploitation, classes and class differences and the great development of productive forces in the society, people can completely and comprehensively develop themselves.

Marx's and Engels' prediction on the future society was made under the circumstances that they did not clearly distinguish socialist society and communist society or did not experience the practice of socialism. Therefore, their assumption of the basic features of the future society was under the precondition that the proletarian revolution achieved victory first in developed capitalist countries, which was also deduced according to the social and economic situations in developed capitalist countries. Later, the victory of socialism completely exceeded their expectations by firstly reaching victory in the country that was economically and culturally backward. According to the reality of the economically and culturally backward country, Lenin called the early phase of communist society the socialist society, of which he explored the basic features. On the basis of succeeding the basic features of the future society predicted by Marx and Engels, Lenin made new explorations on the basic features of the socialist society. First, there are two forms of public ownership in socialist society: state ownership and cooperative ownership. Second, the commodity-money relationship still exists in socialist society and commodity, price, market, profit and economic balance still play their part in the socialist society. Third, the distribution according to one's work is not based on the supply and direct exchange of products from the social stock, but resorts to the commodity-money relationship and trade. Fourth, there is still the social difference of labor in socialist society. Fifth, socialist society still needs the nation of dictatorship of the proletariat, army and various administrative institutions. Because Lenin was discussing the basic features of socialism mainly from the perspective of "going to" socialism, meaning the perspective of transition from capitalism to socialism, additional to his early death, many of his conceptions did not get any chance to be put in practice or systematically commented on with practice.

In the practice of socialism in the USSR, under the leadership of Stalin,

---

70   ibid., p. 755.

the people of the USSR completed the transition from capitalist society to socialist society, established socialist system and conducted socialist construction. Therefore, Stalin discussed the basic features of socialism in the process of the practice of socialism in the country that was economically and culturally backward. His explorations of the two forms of public ownership in socialist society-state ownership and cooperative ownership, on the principle of distribution according to one's work under the commodity-money relationship in socialist society and on the nonviolent effect of the dictatorship of the proletariat as one form of the administrative function in the socialist country were the innovation on the basis of succeeding Marx' and Engels' ideas of the basic features of socialism. Stalin's ideas were proved correct by the practice of socialism in the USSR.

3. The historical influence of the understanding on the basic features of socialism

Stalin's understanding on the basic features of socialism had great positive influence on the socialist construction in practice. That is his insistence on the socialist direction when it comes to the development of the country. The USSR rapidly achieved industrialization and collectivization of agriculture in a short period of time, made the public ownership of the means of production absolutely dominant in national economy, greatly improved people's materialistic and cultural life and fundamentally changed the backwardness of the country, making the USSR a great power which the capitalist world could not ignore and brought up completely the superiority and vitality of socialism.

However, due to Stalin's dogmatic and one-sided understanding of Marxism from many aspects, his understanding on the basic features of socialism also had some negative effect on the socialist construction in practice and therefore had a lot of bad influences on the socialist construction of the USSR.

In terms of the public ownership of the means of production, Stalin had realized that it has two forms in the socialist construction in a country that is economically and culturally backward, which is a development of the ideas of Marx and Engels. However, they absolutized then this understanding, thinking that the public ownership of the means of production can only have these two forms. What is more, he thought about the two forms, that the state ownership is superior to the cooperative ownership and the latter must transit to the former. Therefore, during the period of transition to socialism and the socialist construction, the USSR was in pursuit of pure socialist economy and of the complete elimination of non-socialist economy, advancing rashly again and again in changing the relations of production and ownership. In 1927, the socialist elements took 86% in industry, 95% in whole sale commerce, and 65% in retail commerce. From 1929, the attack against capitalist elements was started, a partial offensive turning into an all offensive. By 1934, the socialist elements had taken 99.1% in national income, 99.8% in gross industrial output value, 98.5% in gross agricultural output value and 100% in the commercial enterprises' volume of the flow of retail goods. By 1950, the percentage of the above four items had reached to 99.8%, 100%, 98.1% and 100% respectively. In the early 1950s, the USSR also acted vigorously in upgrading the cooperative ownership, getting collective farms merged, transiting to the ownership of the whole people and regarding the existence of collective farms as the obstacle of the development of productive forces and of the planned economy. As a result, the USSR's socialist economy suffered great losses.

In terms of the administrative system, Stalin dogmatically treated the thought of Marx and Engels, thinking that the socialist economy established in the USSR, a country that is economically and culturally backward, is also planned economy. This idea became the guiding ideology of the USSR's highly centralized planned economy and administrative system. Although we should see that the formation of the highly centralized planned economy and administrative system in the USSR was more caused by history, the theoretical limitation also had important influence on their establishment. The highly centralized planned economy and administrative system formed under Stalin's guiding ideology that "socialist economy is planned economy", had had positive influence on the socialist construction in the USSR. As one form of the socialist relations of production, it embodied the socialist quality of the economic and political system and guaranteed the direction of socialism in the development of economy and politics in the USSR from many aspects, such as insisting on the public ownership of means of production, planned economy, distribution according to one's work, the leadership of the Communist Party and the dictatorship of the proletariat as the function of the socialist country, etc. As one of the relations of production subordinating to the productive forces at that time, Stalin's idea guaranteed the establishment of socialism in the USSR in a short period of time from the aspects such as arranging the national layout of productive forces, mainly focusing on important projects of construction, etc. However, Stalin's thought that socialist economy is planned economy had caused serious defects and disadvantages of the economic and political system in the USSR, such as over centralization of decision-making authority, lack of activity in local areas and in enterprises, one-sided emphasis on mandatory plans and administrative measures, exclusion of marketing mechanism, prevalence of bureaucratic style, etc. Consequently, the promotion of this economic and political system seriously hindered the development of the national economy in the USSR, making socialism losing the vitality and vigor.

Stalin's explorations on the basic features of socialism also had great influences on the economically and culturally backward countries that went on the path of socialism. Many countries took the USSR as a good example, following its thought and practice to build socialism and thinking that "today's USSR will be our tomorrow". As a result, the vitality and creativity were suffocated, making the socialist construction suffer serious setbacks. The historical conditions and basic national conditions of the eastern European countries were greatly different from those of the USSR. However, during the process of them studying and copying the experience of socialist construction in the USSR, they ignored these differences and just copied the USSR mode. Therefore, they had great losses in the socialist construction. Our country had no exception. In the period of the first five-year plan in our country, the highly centralized planned economy was a copy of that of the USSR. Of course, under the international circumstances and historical conditions at that time, it was impossible for out party to exceed the traditional understanding on the basic features of socialism, or to break the basic frame of the USSR's highly centralized planned economy and administrative system. Our party had made the mistake of the "left" in the instructive ideology. Together with some incorrect understandings on the formation of socialism, the socialist construction was stagnated.

To sum up, Stalin was exploring the basic features of socialism on the basis of succeeding the ideas of Marx and Engels. In some aspects such as the basic form of the public ownership of the means of production, distribution according to one's work, the leadership of the party, etc, he developed Marx' and Engels' thought while in some other aspects such as the singularity of the public ownership of the means of production, planned economy, etc, he misunderstood their thought and therefore had non-scientific even distorted understandings on socialism.

IV. Stalin's discussions on the issue of socialist construction

How to build socialism and what socialism is, consist together the basic connotation of socialism. The understanding of what socialism is clearly is the precondition of how to build socialism. On the basis of his understanding of what socialism is, Stalin explored the theory and practice on how to build socialism, which again embodied his outlook of socialism.

1. Analysis on the starting point of socialist construction

That socialist construction must start from developing industry is one of Stalin's basic explorations on the future and basic features of socialism, and also one of his basic views on how to build socialism. As early as the period of the NEP when Lenin was establishing the policy of socialist industrialization, Stalin had put forward the tasks of socialist industrialization at the Fourteenth Congress of the CPSU(B), "a) in the direction of further increasing the output of the national economy; b) in the direction of transforming our country from an agrarian into an industrial country; c) in the direction of ensuring within the national economy a decisive preponderance of the socialist elements over the capitalist elements; d) in the direction of ensuring for the national economy of the USSR the necessary independence in the circumstances of capitalist encirclement; e) in the direction of increasing the proportion of non-tax revenue in the total state budget."[71] The basic tasks of socialist industrialization proposed by Stalin had shown three basic contents of industrialization: first, in the process of promoting a general increase in the national economy, transforming the USSR from an agrarian into an industrial country by increasing the gross industry output value while guaranteeing the leading position of industry in the national economy; second, at the same time of developing socialist industry, limiting and excluding private economy and guarantee the decisive superiority of socialist economy against private and capitalist economy; third, together with the development of socialist industry, gradually to get rid of the dependence on the capitalist world and guarantee the independence of the economy.

To achieve socialist industrialization, Stalin firstly established the central task of industrialization. That is to give priority to the development of heavy industry, especially machine-building industry. He said that "for industrialization, we should firstly develop the heavy industry in our country, especially the development of the machine-building industry", because it is

---

71 Collected Works of Stalin, first Chinese version, volume 7, p.280, Retrieved from Marxists Internet Archive.

"the center of industrialization and the foundation of industrialization."[72] In Stalin's opinion, the industrialization in capitalist countries usually started from developing light industry; after a long period of time, during which the light industry accumulated profits and gathered them in banks, the conditions for developing the heavy industry would be satisfied. However, this long time of waiting does not work for the Communist Party. Heavy industry is determinant in the large-scale industry. Without the development of the heavy industry, none of other industries would be built, not to mention industrialization. Particularly, for a country of dictatorship of the proletariat surrounded by capitalism, it will not be economically independent if it is not able to produce instruments and means of production or its economic development is enslaved to the developed countries that produce and export instruments and means of production. Only by developing the heavy industry can the USSR develop the whole industry, transportation and agriculture on the basis of new technology, get rid of the dependence on the capitalist economy in the world, increase its own economic independence and strengthen the power of national defense. In addition, Stalin took a further step, thinking that the socialist industrialization is actually the industrialization that sets up the support of industry to agriculture and the dependence of agriculture on industry in the first place. It is also the direct industrialization with the development of the national economy as a whole determined by the development of heavy industry. Stalin's proposition of giving priority to the development of heavy industry had far-reaching affect in the world. After the war, there appeared some disadvantages in the economic development in some socialist countries that had generally adopted Stalin's proposal in a certain period of time, which left the thought-provoking lesions to people.

Developing the socialist heavy industry at a fast pace became the path that had to be passed for the USSR to catch up with and surpass the developed capitalist countries in the early period of socialist construction. Stalin thought that the economy of the USSR is able to catch up with and surpass those of the capitalist countries, with the conditions of high speed and high accumulation. He emphasized that the industrialization can not be achieved with "a relatively slowly speed". The reason is that judging from the comparison of the situations in the USSR and in the developed capitalist countries, "suppose that our industry and technology were as developed as those of Germany, suppose that the proportion of our industry in the national economy as a whole was as big as that of Germany", "suppose that we are not the only country with dictatorship of the proletariat", then we would "be able to develop our industry with a relatively slowly speed."[73] The reality of the USSR's backward technology decided that the industry must be

---

72   Collected Works of Stalin, first Chinese version, volume 8, pp.113, 112.
73   Collected Works of Stalin, first Chinese version, volume 11, pp. 216,217, Beijing, People's Publishing House, 1955.

developed in a high speed. Judging from the economic reality in the USSR, the scattered small-peasant economy took the dominant position while the socialist large-scale economy was like a lonely island in the ocean. Without developing the socialist industry at a fast pace, withouttransforming economically and technologically the small-peasant economy into the socialist large-scale agriculture with modern technology, one can never say that the socialism was established. From the perspective of the superiority of socialist system, the feudal economy took about 200 years to prove its superiority over the slavery economy; the capitalist economy took about 100 years, which was amazingly fast, to prove its superiority to the feudal economy. To prove that socialist economy is superior over the capitalist economy in a short period of time, the high speed of development is required. Of course, although Stalin advocated for achieving industrialization at a fast pace, he also attached great importance to acting according to the national strength, thinking that concentrating on development without calculating the strength will definitely bring losses to the development and therefore to the socialist construction.

On the issue of the accumulation of funds needed by the high-speed development of industrialization, Stalin analyzed different methods of raising funds for industrialization in history. He thought that it cannot be adopted to get ill-gotten gains with dishonorable measures, such as Britain exploiting the colonies, Germany relying on the war indemnity, tsarist Russia selling sovereignty, etc. "We can only rely on ourselves to raise funds for socialist industrialization, not getting from any foreign loans but out of our own savings."[74] There are mainly two resources of accumulating funds on our own: "one is the working class that creates value and promotes industry; the other is the peasants."[75] From the perspective of industry, it is very important to increase the output, improve the quality and decrease the cost; the state-owned enterprises must make the technology and management rationalized in socialist society. From the perspective of agriculture, its potential should be fully used because in a certain period of time, agriculture will still develop on the basis of the previous technology. Stalin thought that there are two ways of raising funds from agriculture: one is the tax paid to the country by the peasants, including direct tax and indirect tax; the other is to rely on the scissors difference of the agricultural and industrial products. In addition, the funds needed for industrialization can also be raised by many other ways. For example, increasing the taxes of capitalist enterprises; nationalizing the enterprises that have been lent or leased at maturity and transforming them to socialist industrial enterprises; implementing the police of vodka monopoly and charging the special excise duty while

74 For further reference, see Collected Works of Stalin, first Chinese version, volume 8, pp. 114-115.
75 Collected Works of Stalin, first Chinese version, volume 11, p. 139.

combating excessive drinking; with the achievement of some performing loans, paying for some prewar debt as the additional interests in order to get loans for industrial development while persisting in the cancellation of the debt of the Tsar.

Stalin's thought on the starting point of socialist construction had promoted the development of the national economy in the USSR. With only two five-year plans, the USSR had basically established the socialist large-scale industrial system. However, the thought that the starting point of socialist construction was formed under certain historical circumstances. Therefore, it had some limitation in instructing the practice of the socialist economic construction. Later, it caused some mistakes in the socialist economic construction in the USSR and in other socialist countries.

2. The driving forces of socialist construction

When leading the socialist construction of the USSR, Stalin took the class struggle at this stage as the driving force of socialism and regarded the achievements of the socialist construction as the manifestation and results of the class struggle. He repeatedly emphasized that the more victorious socialism is, the sharper the class struggle will be. Only with class struggle as soon as possible can it promote the socialist construction.

Stalin's opinion on class struggle can be divided into two different periods: the period of transition and the period of socialism. His opinion on the class struggle in the period of transition is the starting point of his opinion on the class struggle in the period of socialism.

In the period of transition, although the implementation of the NEP only recovered and developed the national economy as well as consolidated and strengthened the socialist economic basis, it also increased the capitalist economic power. The basic power of socialist construction- the working class and the peasantry had both developed, but the absolute number of the middle class had also increased. The question "who beats down whom" had not been solved between working class and middle class and between socialism and capitalism. Under such circumstances, Stalin thought that with the development of socialist economy, the fight of capitalism has also strengthened. Class struggle was getting more and more intensified. "There have been no cases in history where dying classes have voluntarily departed from the scene."[76] Only with struggle and setbacks can the proletariat take progress to socialism. He further asserted that the class struggle is the decisive power for the progress of the socialist society. Any of the USSR's progress or any of the achievements of the USSR are the manifestation and results of the class struggle. On the question of how to eliminate class,

76   Selected Works of Stalin, volume 2, p. 140, Retrieved from Marxists Internet Archive.

Stalin came up with the formula of "eliminating class with the cruel class struggle of the proletariat", meaning elimination of class with stronger class struggle. Stalin thought at that time in the USSR, that the very last and most powerful exploiting class with the largest population was the kulak class. For these "blood-suckers", "vampires" and "spiders", "…the policy of eliminating the kulaks as a class must be pursued with all the persistence and consistency of which Bolsheviks are capable."[77] Based on that, Stalin thought further that "to speed up the development of industry and agriculture in the socialist construction, to increasingly exclude the capitalists in urban and rural areas and to arouse the mass to take part in the socialist construction and in the fight against capitalism, we must rely on the sharp class struggle".

By 1936, the USSR had basically finished the socialist transformation and entered into the period of socialism. After the class struggle in the transition period, the question of "who beats down whom" was basically solved. "Thus the complete victory of the Socialist system in all spheres of the national economy is now a fact."[78] "It means that the exploitation of man by man has been abolished, eliminated, while the Socialist ownership of the implements and means of production has been established as the unshakable foundation of our Soviet society."[79] In conformity with it, the class structure in the USSR had correspondingly changed. "The landlord class… had already been eliminated as a result of the victorious conclusion of the civil war. As for the other exploiting classes, they have shared the fate of the landlord class. The capitalist class in the sphere of industry has ceased to exist. The kulak class in the sphere of agriculture has ceased to exist. And the merchants and profiteers in the sphere of trade have ceased to exist. Thus all the exploiting classes have been eliminated."[80] What was left were the working class, peasant class and the intelligentsia. The working class is the one that is entirely new and has got rid of the exploitation; the peasants are the ones that have got rid of exploitation and the intelligentsia is the one that are closely related to the working class and the peasants and are entirely new. This means that "the economic contradictions between these social groups are declining, are becoming obliterated"; that "the political contradictions between them are also declining and becoming obliterated."[81] However, the class difference was still there. Stalin's opinions on the change of the class structure in the USSR and the idea that the exploiting class was eliminated were correct no matter in theory or in practice. However, he did not build socialism by following the right way. Instead,

---

77 Selected Works of Stalin, volume 2, p. 263, Retrieved from Marxists Internet Archive.
78 Works of Stalin, volume 1, p. 84, Retrieved from Marxists Internet Archive.
79 Retrieved from Marxists Internet Archive.
80 ibid., p. 85, Retrieved from Marxists Internet Archive.
81 ibid., p. 87, Retrieved from www. marx2mao.com.

with the announcement that the USSR had eliminated the exploiting class, Stalin also emphasized that "the further forward we advance, the greater the successes we achieve, the greater will be the fury of the remnants of the broken exploiting classes, the sooner will they resort to sharper forms of struggle, the more will they seek to harm the Soviet state and the more will they clutch at the most desperate means of struggle, as the last resort of doomed people."[82] Therefore, building socialism with class struggle became one of the basic contents of Stalin's outlook of socialism. Although he had seen the new features of the workers, peasants, intellectuals and their relations, he failed to make further analysis on the contradictions between them or to realize that the essential driving forces of the progress of socialist construction is to correctly handle and resolve the contradictions between them.

3. The discussions on the law of the socialist economic development

Stalin's discussions on the law of economic development under socialism can be read mostly in the book Economic Problems of Socialism in the USSR. In this book, he elaborated on the two important economic laws in the economic development under socialism: the basic law of socialist economy and the law that the national economy develops as planned and in proportion. First, on the basis of expounding the meaning of the basic economic law, he stated the content of the basic economic law under socialism. Stalin thought that out of the many economic laws that work in every form of society, the basic economic law is the one that plays the leading role. Its character is: there is only one basic economic law in every form of society; it shows the most basic causal relationship in the social economy; it also determines "all the principal aspects and all the principal processes" of the development of the social production."[83] Its main content is the unity of the purpose of social production and the methods to achieve the purpose. Stalin generally stated on the principle characters and requirements of the basic economic law under socialism: "the securing of the maximum satisfaction of the constantly rising material and cultural requirements of the whole of society through the continuous expansion and perfection of socialist production on the basis of higher techniques."[84] He emphasized that the basic economic law of socialism is the law that determines all the principle aspects and the entire principal processes in the development of social production. It is something essential that determines the social production; it also leads, controls and decides other economic laws.

---

82   ibid., p. 129, Retrieved from www. marx2mao.com
83   Selected Works of Stalin, volume 2, p. 567, Retrieved from Marxists Internet Archive.
84   Selected Works of Stalin, volume 2, p. 569, Retrieved from Marxists Internet Archive.

Second, Stalin put forward and demonstrated the law that the national economy develops as planned and in proportion. He thought that under socialism, by eliminating the basic contradictions of capitalism, the public ownership of socialism has united the sectors of the national economy with the enterprises as an organized whole with the same basic interests. Therefore it is definite that the national economy develops as planned and in proportion. The manifestation of the relations between the law that the national economy develops as planned and in proportion and the basic economic law of socialism is: the basic economic law of socialism determines the law that the national economy develops as planned and in proportion, whose functions will be given full scope to only when it is on the basis of the basic economic law of socialism. Focusing on the idea of equating the national economic plan with the economic laws in the academy of the USSR, Stalin further pointed out, "possibility must not be confused with actuality. They are two different things. In order to turn the possibility into actuality, it is necessary to study this economic law, to master it, to learn to apply it with full understanding and to compile such plans as fully reflect the requirements of this law."[85]

The commodity production and law of value under socialism was one of the many theoretical issues that was discussed most in the world of economics in the USSR from 1930s to 1950s. In the early 1930s, the idea that socialism is natural economy took a dominant position in the world of economics in the USSR. At that time, people regarded the NEP as retrogression. After that, although it was generally acknowledged in the circles of economists in the USSR that the commodity production will still exist for a quite long period of time, many people denied the effect of the law of value. Stalin's affirmation of the relations between commodity and money was just from the perspective of circulation. His official acknowledgement from the perspective of theory on the relations between commodity and money under socialism was in the early 1950s. In the book Economic Problems of Socialism in the USSR, he mainly elaborated on the reason why the commodity production relations exists, the quality of commodity production under socialism and the effect of the law of value on the socialist economy, etc.

As for the reason why commodity production exists under socialism, Stalin thought that the two forms of the public ownership under socialist system is the reason of the existence of commodity production. "Today there are two basic forms of socialist production in our country: state, or publicly-owned production, and collective-farm production, which cannot be said to be publicly owned...At present the collective farms will not recognize any other economic relation with the town except the commodity

---

85   Selected Works of Stalin, volume 2, p. 544, Retrieved from Marxists Internet Archive.

relation–exchange through purchase and sale. Because of this, commodity production and trade are as much a necessity with us today as they were, say, thirty years ago, when Lenin spoke of the necessity of developing trade to the utmost."[86]

In terms of the quality of the commodity production under socialism, Stalin clearly pointed out that the commodity production under socialism is the "special commodity production" that is different from the commodity production under capitalism. It is the reflection of the relations of mutual aid and benefit between the socialist working people, with the destiny of serving the socialist cause. The sphere of commodity production under socialism is just personal consuming products. Under socialism, the means of production are not commodity, nor is the working force. In Stalin's opinion, commodity production does not lead to capitalism at any time or under any conditions. Only under the capitalist system under which workers are exploited will commodity production lead to capitalism. Therefore, "commodity production must not be identified with capitalist production."[87]

As for the effect of the law of value in socialist economy, Stalin observed mainly from two aspects: area of production and area of circulation. He pointed out that in the area of production, the law of value has its influence. In the development of the national economy, the law of value is exercised in cost accounting and profitableness, because "consumer goods, which arc needed to compensate the labor power expended in the process of production, are produced and realized in our country as commodities coming under the operation of the law of value. It is precisely here that the law of value exercises its influence on production."[88] In the sphere of circulation, the law of value preserves the function as a regulator within certain limits. For the reason that the sphere of commodity production under socialism is personal consumption and that the means of production and working force are not commodity, "the sphere of operation of the law of value extends, first of all, to commodity circulation, to the ex-change of commodities through purchase and sale, the exchange, mainly, of articles of personal consumption."[89] Stalin also affirmed the operation of the law of value from the perspective of social practice, pointing out that the law of value "is a good practical school which accelerates the development of our executive personnel and their growth into genuine leaders of socialist production at the present stage of development."[90]

112

86   ibid, volume 2, p. 550, Retrieved from Marxists Internet Archive.
87   Ibid, Volume 2, p.548, Retrieved from Marxists Internet Archive.
88   Selected Works of Stalin, volume 2, p. 553, Retrieved from Marxists Internet Archive.
89   ibid., volume 2, p. 552, Retrieved from Marxists Internet Archive.
90   ibid., volume 2, p. 553, Retrieved from Marxists Internet Archive.

By studying on Stalin's explorations on the law of economic development under socialism, we can clearly see that there are many defects in his theories. For example, although he admitted the existence of the law of value under socialism, his elaboration still did not shake off the fetters of product economy, etc. However, it is undeniable that in the history of the development of Marxism, his theoretical discussions played an important role in promoting the development of Marxism.

Stalin's economic model and management system originated from the mistaken understanding related to the nature of the economic sphere and its laws. This is also related to Marxist understanding of economic laws and has also philosophical aspects. In this respect Stalin had a one sided approach.[91]

The thinking failure or skip that takes social development as the process of natural history is premised on the opinion that views the economic laws of society as natural laws. It is true that Marx mentions that the economic laws of society equal to natural laws in many places; for example, in *Capital*, he repeatedly refers to "the natural laws of capitalist production", "even when a society has got upon the right track for the discovery of the natural laws of its movement – and it is the ultimate aim of this work."[92] Lenin had stated, "Marx speaks of the economic law of motion of society, even referring to this law as a Naturgesetz – a law of nature."[93] However, the problem is that in what sense Marx considers the economic laws of society are natural laws. We think this is not understood in a comprehensive way. As the most important laws of society, they reflect the sociality, historicity and epochal character of human activity in a comprehensive manner.

The economic laws of society are different from natural laws: (1) the economic laws of society run through the relationship between man and man through the exchange between man and nature; (2) the economic laws of society are a process of the appropriation of "material exchange" in the form of man and by means of the inherent measure of man; (3) the economic laws of society are essentially practical, as the activity laws of man in economic practice, changing continuously along with the changes in the pattern of men's economic practice, and their realization also depends on the practice of man. Natural laws are the mechanical, physical, chemical and biological laws of nature, existing themselves blindly; when they are not cognized by men, natural laws appear to be opposite to men; once they are discovered, they can be utilized by men to conquer or lead natural forces with sciences. Obviously, natural laws and social laws are different in essence.

91   See Yang Geng: New Interpretation of Marxist Philosophy.
92   Marx, Capital (Translation of Vol. I of French Edition Revised by Yang Geng), p. 4.
93   Collected Works of Lenin. Beijing: People's Publishing House, 1984: 2nd Chinese Ed., Vol. 1, p. 105.

Chapter IV

Stalin Model and Its Socialist Economic System

The economic model and the economic system of socialism established by Stalin in the USSR constitute the most important economic reality in the economic and social development of the world in the 20th century.

Either any discussion related to the initial formation of the economic system during initial phase of the building of socialism or any discussion related to economic system reforms and economic system innovations under the conditions of established socialism, the issue of Stalin's economic model becomes an important part—directly or indirectly—of these discussions.

Today, at the moment we are entering into the 21st century, deeper studies on this unique economic model has great theoretical and practical significance to evaluate Stalin's achievements and mistakes in the socialist construction of the USSR. It is also important for those countries which are currently building socialism and passing through critical economic system reforms.

I. The historical conditions and theoretical background of the emergence of Stalin's economic model

Stalin's economic model did not come out of blue, nor was it an inborn set of ideas in Stalin's mind.

Generally speaking, it was the product of the economic and social development realities of Russia a certain period, a certain phase in the history of the economic development during building socialism. It is also a manifestation of Stalin's subjective understanding on the economic development laws under the conditions of socialism. This unique perspective is critical to correctly understand and evaluate Stalin's model.

1. The social and historical background of Stalin's economic model

The emergence and formation of the Stalin model is firstly directly related to the economic and political development realities in Russia. Judging from economic point of view, before the October Revolution, Russia's level of productive forces was relatively low. If we evaluate Russia as a whole, the level of economic development was also not high. In essence, it was still a "feudal imperialist" country and also a country where the small-peasant economy constituted the dominant position. The industry of Russia then was mainly based on backward and old technologies, industrial output far lower than West European countries.

The elements of modern capitalist economy only contributed about 20% of the GDP. The agricultural production basically relied on manual labor, and generally small production was quite scattered. In those days, Russia was a country characterized by underdeveloped agricultural production. At that time, Russia ranked fifth in military industries among major countries of the world. But compared with United States, Britain, Germany and France, its general industrial level was extremely low.

France's population was only 1/4 of Russia's, but its industrial output was 2.5 times of that of Russia. The absolute value of industrial products of United States was 13 times higher than that of Russia, which meant, if calculated on an average per capita, USA was 21 times stronger. In terms of production modes, Russia possessed various production modes coexisting such as the patriarchal production mode (primitive agriculture), small commodity production mode conducted by small producers, private capitalist economy, state-capitalist economy and socialist economy, among them the primitive agriculture mode and the small commodity production mode conducted by small producers constituted the dominant position.

In terms of economic structure, Russia having a vast territory and abundant resources, mining and raw material extraction industries took the larger part, while the processing industry and the high-grade sophisticated technologies remained at a lower level. In terms of technology and machinery there was also a huge gap between Russia and the developed capitalist countries at that time. In terms of finance and marketing systems, Russia was even more backward compared with the developed countries. Besides, in this backward conditions the Soviet Russia around the 1920s, Russia had left back two destructive wars and a civil war, which meant that to build socialism and catch up with the level of productive forces in the developed countries on such a basis, it was undoubtedly an extremely difficult task.

Judging from the political superstructure, before the October Revolution, Russia was a military feudal imperialist country under the despotic Tsar regime, mainly a feudal political system. 19th century Russia did not initiate all round capitalist economic reforms, the Tsar's regime had one-sidedly promoted the development of military industry and formed a huge military machine, thus Russia had evolved to a militaristic feudal imperialist country. Centralism was the very manifestation of the Tsar's feudal autocracy. This centralism also had great influence on the later political and economic system of Soviet Russia.

In terms of social classes, the Russian working class was a newly developing class and its peasant past was still fresh. Under the autocratic rule of the Tsar, on the one hand they lacked the experience and ability of administrating a country, on the other hand, they lacked basic education and culture, and especially the organization and training practice provided by the large-scale industry. In Russia then, peasants and small producers formed 70% of the population. The peasants were mainly subjects of natural or semi-natural mode of production mixed with serfdom conditions especially under the influence of the patriarchal system in Russia.

Commodity economy and commodity markets were underdeveloped, which meant self-sufficient regional isolated markets constituted the largest part of the economic life. Small type manorial manufacture (handicrafts) economy was the element in the "industry" life. I can certainly say that, in Soviet Russia with such immature and relatively small working class on one side and the small producers forming the great majority of the population and underdeveloped commodity economy and lacking the social practice of country-wide markets on the other side, constituted the breeding ground for the highly centralized systems, and caused the denial of commodity production and distrust for marketization (commodity exchange systems) of the economy.

Judging from cultural aspect, in Russia, either the workers or peasants, both classes had a very low level of literacy, including individual farm producers and the handicraftsmen. Before 1917, 75% of Russians were illiterate. By 1920, the illiteracy rate was still unbelievably high reaching 68.1% of the population. After the October Revolution, feudal culture, the small producers' social consciousness and psychology, capitalist and socialist cultures all coexisted, both in harmony and conflict. Due to the low level of literacy of the working people and their lack of self-management in social practice, the administration of the enterprises, administration of the society and the country could not be administrated properly; a democratic administration style lacked a sufficient social basis or strong support. On the contrary, practices of centralized management styles, even patriarchy and individualistic autocratic styles were rampant. Therefore, Stalin's socialist economic model and system was not something written on a blank new sheet of paper, but a product of Russian socio-historical reality under unique historical conditions. The inherited socio-historical and economic development mainly determined that Stalin's economic system had formed on the basis of low level of productive forces, underdeveloped commodity economy, low scientific and cultural level and strong feudal-patriarchal social consciousness in the superstructure.

2. The effects of the international environment on Stalin's system

The Soviet Russia was the first socialist country. After the victory of the October Revolution, it was encircled and militarily intervened by the western capitalist countries. Under certain historical conditions at that time, a world war had become inevitable. Russia encountered 1904 war with Japan and Tsar participated in the First World War, and after the 1917 October Revolution, due to military intervention by foreign powers Russia was still warring.

As soon as the Soviet political power was established, there came the three-year civil war which took the form of Patriotic War. The civil war had caused huge economic losses, great sufferings for people. Goods and materials were extremely scarce, especially the vital necessities of life such as food. With the NEP (New Economic Policy) of Lenin, Russia recuperated and re-gained its strength and its economy gradually reached to the prewar level. In 1929 an unprecedented huge economic crisis broke out in the capitalist world, which rapidly intensified various basic contradictions of the world capitalist system, in many regions of the world violent local wars were fermenting and occurring (China, Spain). Fascism and war conditions were rapidly developing. In the Second World War, the USSR fought another Patriotic War against German fascist aggressors, a life-and-death battle for people and the nation. For the victory in the war, the USSR paid a huge price. Above international environment of Soviet Russia, which was acutely insecure (since its birth) and which included foreign aggression threat was another cause behind the formation of Stalin's economic model and played an extremely important role in the implementation of closely commanded planned economy with highly centralized management system.

Faced by the above realistic and urgent threats, Stalin thought: "to guarantee the USSR's economic independence, to increase national defense capabilities, to establish and develop a strong material-economic basis to counter the armed subversion of imperialism, we should eliminate backwardness in the shortest period of time. Therefore, we should establish a highly centralized leadership and administration, form a highly unified thinking and action within the party and Soviet people and need to highly centralize our Soviet manpower, material resources and financial resources. All these need a unified and centralized source allocation system managed by the central authority. By doing so, the economic and material basis of socialism will be built faster by utilizing our scarce sources wholly. And politically the socialist political power will be guarded and the subversive attempts and armed aggression of the foreign capitalist countries will be countered, thus we will be able to smash down the destructive activities of our enemies at home and abroad."[1]

3. The level and characteristics of the subjective understanding on the classical theories of socialism in the Soviet Union

As the first socialist country in the world, Russia did not have any available concrete historical experience to use for reference in its economic and social construction which determined its construction to be an exploration including trials and errors. Marx and Engels, as the founders of scientific socialism theories, limited by the historical conditions of their age could not witness and study any socialist revolution and socialist construction. Their scientific predictions on the basic features of the future socialist/communist society were formed through their critiques of the "old world"-the capitalist world, in their struggle against capitalism.

119

For example, Marx argued that only after the full development of capitalism, during which the material basis for the socialist revolution gets matured, could the communist society be built smoothly. However, the social and political practice had exceeded the expectations of Marx and Engels. The socialist revolution firstly broke out in Russia, a country that was both economically and agriculturally backward, plus lacking capitalist civilization. Therefore, how to build socialism in a country with relatively low level of productive forces had become an entirely new question that needed new explorations by Russian Marxists after wrestling political power. It cannot be neglected that Stalin subjectively tried to follow Marx, Engels and Lenin's socialist thoughts as his theoretical guideline and aimed to realize some socialist principles and policies advocated by the founders of Marxism, fought to build socialism in the USSR as fast as possible. However, the problem was that in many aspects, Stalin and leaders around him followed a dogmatic approach instead of creatively studying the current realities of Soviet Union and ignored to creatively interpret the essence of scientific predictions on socialism, created by founders and other previous theoreticians of Marxism.

---

1   Stalin Collected Works Volume 6, p 127.

For example, when Marx and Engels criticized private ownership of production means, one essential nature of capitalism, they argued that in the future society, the public ownership of the means of production should be implemented and production should be organized on this basis; as one essential difference between communism and capitalism. However, the precondition of this assumption was that the revolution would happen in a country where capitalism had fully developed. Furthermore, after the victory of the revolution, there would be a relatively long historical period of transition to communism. Taking Marx' and Engels' scientific predictions as "the supreme rule", Stalin followed a hasty road aiming to complete the transition from capitalism to socialism, ignoring the reality that the level of material and intellectual/spiritual productive forces in Soviet Russia was quite low and that there in Russia, co-existed various production modes -which needed to be handled differently—developing simultaneously. Stalin aimed to exclude all the other production modes than socialism, evaluating them as direct and urgent obstacles of developing socialist economic mode, the consequence was striving to establish a single ownership system—type of socialist economic system, public ownership of means of production- type of socialist economic system, This single ownership system included two forms: ownership of means of production by the whole society managed by the state and ownership of means of production by a group in the society managed by its own leaders.

120

Another example was the understanding on the nature of socialist economy. The social production in the communist society foreseen by Marx and Engels should be regulated by a comprehensive unified plan according to predictions and surveys on social demand by people. Thus a product economy would be established which surpasses capitalist commodity production and market exchanges via currency, both losing their social and historical basis.

Lenin had also basically succeeded Marx' and Engels' thoughts, and advocated a planned economy for the Soviet Union. Although in the practice of NEP, Lenin had made an important progress, namely he had realized that commodity production, commodity exchange (market), money and markets will be needed in the transition period, his understanding also contained certain limitations.[2]

Lenin continued to believe that market and market mechanisms had emerged together with private ownership of means of production; that the commodity-money relationship has the nature of exploitation to some degree and these relations should only function with certain limits in the period of transition. Stalin mainly maintained these ideas of Marx, Engels

2 Product economy is believed to be the opposite of commodity production economy which neglects value.

and Lenin, arguing that socialist economy should be a "product economy", rather than a commodity economy, namely he closely related commodity economy with capitalist private ownership of capitalism. For him to build the "product economy" where social production would be conducted according to the social demand, a comprehensive and centralized planning system was required, and the whole economic activities in the society needed to be administrated with plans, mainly the mandatory ones.

In terms of distribution policies of socialist economic system, Stalin was also greatly influenced by Marx, Engels and Lenin. Marx and Engels had argued that in the highly developed communist society of the future, the distribution principle "from each according to one's ability and to each according to his needs" would dominate. However, according to Lenin, in the stage of socialism, which is the first stage of communism, since all the springs of wealth still cannot "flow abundantly" and because various differences in abilities possessed by the working people still continued to exist greatly, only the distribution principle "from each according to one's ability and according to his work" could be operated. The centrally designed salary grading system characterized by its quite egalitarian classification was the product of this principle of "distribution according to one's work" discovered by Lenin. Additionally, we can comfortably say that since Stalin's economic model included the single ownership form, and since other production factors which contributed to social wealth was not recognized, only labor's contribution as the single criterion was considered as the basis of distribution of created social wealth.

121

Marx famous argument said: In a higher phase of communist society, after the enslaving subordination of the individual to the division of labor, and therewith also the antithesis between mental and physical labor, has vanished; after labor has become not only a means of life but life's prime want; after the productive forces have also increased with the all-around development of the individual, and all the springs of co-operative wealth flow more abundantly—only then can the narrow horizon of bourgeois right be crossed in its entirety and society inscribe on its banners: From each according to his ability, to each according to his needs!

II. The impacts of the theory and practice of Soviet socialist economy

Below I will discuss the two causes or sources of Stalin's economic model, which cannot be related to the thoughts of Marx, Engels and Lenin. A very big part of Stalin's economic model was his own creation together with other the economic practioners and theorists of his era. Stalin formed his socialist economic theories by synthesizing all these ideas and developed them when leading economic practices of the country. Plus certain political struggles also effected his theoretical orientation. These theories were formed and practiced for a period of 30 years when he was in power. Following points are the concise description of major elements in his economic theory and practice.

1. Stalin's unique understanding and practice related to NEP

The theory of NEP discovered by Lenin can be regarded as the dividing line between Stalin's economic theory and Lenin's economic theory. NEP's unique interpretation by Stalin is also the starting point in the formation Stalin's socialist economic model. NEP, discovered and operated-for a certain time- by Lenin, due to his early death could not be completed and further developed by him. When succeeding and practicing this policy and theory, Stalin had made great changes and additions to it, which formed the starting point of his economic model.

The NEP was the system of economic policies put forward by Lenin after Russia had shattered the foreign armed intervention and conceived the problems of "war communism economic policy" and aimed to find a more proper way to achieve a stronger economic recovery. Its main contents were: replacing the policy of mandatory appropriation of grain surplus produced by farmers with a tax paid as certain amount of grain (tax in kind), and allowing farmers to trade the remaining part ; adopting the policy of developing several state capitalism tools or policies such as a building a comprehensive economic calculation and accounting system for the whole economy, leasing the state enterprises to private operators, checking and leading non-socialist actors (for example grain traders) and sectors of the economy by economic means, thirdly certain concessions for foreign trade and foreign capital investments or allowing Soviet-foreign joint-ventures. Thus SU aimed to repair the damages and problems by the war; secondly in order strengthen the already existing—but still relatively weak- socialist sector (SOE's) and socialist actors of the economy in the long term by immediately developing certain markets (commodity-money relationships) and developing state capitalism. For Lenin, to lead and manage small farmers' production and trade activities by macro economic tools, instead of administrative tools would mean an important type of state capitalism policy.

From 1921 on when the NEP was started, the economy of the USSR saw a relatively rapid recovery and development, making great achievements. However, there were divergent views within the party on the issue of how to correctly understand the essence, purpose and effect of the NEP. Especially after Lenin's death in 1924, whether or not to continue the NEP had became the focus of debate and competition—later conflict—among Soviet leaders. Therefore, Stalin needed to make new elaborations on the basic questions of the NEP.

First, about the essence of the NEP, Stalin had emphasized its socialist nature and transitional nature. At that time, within the party there was an opinion that the NEP in essence was capitalism that is permitted under certain undesired conditions and should be restricted and checked by the proletarian state. Stalin thought that this opinion was extremely mistaken. He pointed out that SU practicing NEP could never be equated with capitalism. The policies of NEP which permitted free trade (markets) and state capitalism in certain extent were "in essence tools to maintain and consolidate the solidarity and alliance between the working class and the peasantry, thus vigorously helped SU to develop socialist agriculture, prepared the solid material foundation for socialist industrialization. Namely NEP limited and checked capitalism and helped SU to finally beat down capitalism and develop socialism. He said, "NEP is a specific policy of the proletarian state aimed at permitting capitalism while the commanding height positions of the economy are held by the proletarian state, aimed at developing the struggle between the capitalist and socialist elements, aimed at increasing the role of the socialist elements to the detriment of the capitalist elements, aimed at the victory of the socialist elements over the capitalist elements, aimed at the abolition of classes and building of the foundations of a socialist economy. Whoever fails to understand this transitional, dual nature of NEP departs from Leninism."[3] These ideas and comments by Stalin were both succession and further interpretation of Lenin's NEP ideas.

Second, about the phases of the NEP, Stalin divided the NEP into two phases. The first phase was from 1921 to 1926. The major task of this first phase was: developing agriculture, in order to make a good start in building the socialist economic basis, thus create the advantageous conditions for the development of industry. For Stalin only based on advanced industry, could the economic basis of socialism be consolidated. Developing industry should start from agriculture. That is because the development of industry has three preconditions: "firstly, a domestic market—and our domestic

---

3   Collected Works of Stalin, first Chinese version, volume 7, pp. 302-303, Retrieved from Marxists Internet Archive.

market so far is predominantly a peasant market; secondly, it is necessary to have a certain degree of output of agricultural raw materials (sugar beet, flax, cotton, etc.); thirdly, it is necessary that the countryside should be able to provide a certain minimum amount of agricultural products to support the industry, food needs by the industrial workers."[4] Therefore, in the first phase of the NEP, the development of the national economy as a whole mainly depended on agriculture. The second phase was the period of entering into direct and comprehensive industrialization. The most outstanding feature of this second phase was: the main emphasis in economic work of Party was shifted to industry; the development of the national economy was mainly depended on the expansion of industry. The theory of the two phases of the NEP period was theorized by Stalin, but this idea was already analyzed in Lenin's works. From 1926 on Stalin started the second phase of the NEP. However, compared with Lenin's thought on the second phase of the NEP, there were many important changes in many aspects. Stalin did not exactly follow Lenin's ideas on the tasks of the first phase. Also Stalin followed different transition mechanisms when passing from the first phase to the second phase compared with Lenin's ideas. Actually, Stalin's practice in the second phase of the NEP to some degree had followed a separate path from Lenin's original thoughts. In 1928, Stalin publicly announced that the NEP had reached an end and SU had entered into the period of all-round socialist construction. The history has proved that Stalin's premature ending of the NEP had caused many negative effects on the development of economy and especially on agriculture in the USSR.

The ending of the NEP by Stalin manifested that Stalin had had his own explorations on the economic model and system of the USSR. With the ending of the NEP Stalin's economic model and system was rapidly and comprehensively established.

2. Stalin's theory and practice related to industrialization

Not long after the October Revolution, Lenin suggested the task of establishing highly developed large-scale industry to achieve Soviet Union's industrialization goal. He also stated the famous equation that "communism = the Soviet power + electrification." After Lenin's death, Stalin made a series of important explorations on the theory and practice of the socialist economic construction in the USSR, gradually formed the industrial sector based on the ownership of the whole people, collective sector of agriculture based on the collective ownership of peasants and a planning system mainly based on administrative measures (instead of using economic measures). That was the core content of Stalin's economic model. We can say that the theory of industrialization is the beginning of the formation of Stalin's economic model.

4   Selected Works of Stalin, first, volume 1, p. 460, Retrieved from Marxists Internet Archive.

At the Fourteenth Congress of the CPSU(B) in December 1925, Stalin explained and persuaded the congress for the general policy of industrialization. He thought that since the NEP had made very good effects, as a next step the main emphasis of economic construction should be shifted to industrialization. That is because the USSR's economic construction should be conducted under the conditions of international encirclement by capitalism. "To further consolidate the foundation of socialist system and finally defeat capitalism, our independent industrial system should be established. Therefore t industrialization should be the general line of our economic construction. Since the domestic economy had reached some development, the demand of the whole society for industrial products had greatly increased, but the supply of industrial products was seriously short. To eliminate the shortage of products, to satisfy the needs of the society for the industrial products, and speed up the economic development with currently available resources, the task of industrialization must be prioritized. The reasons he mentioned above emphasized the necessity and urgency of industrialization, the basic policy of which is: "to make all efforts to increase the total output value by the economy, especially the proportion of the industrial output in total output in order to transform S.U rapidly from an agricultural to an industrial country. "We should also limit, exclude and finally eliminate private sector of the economy; gradually eliminate our dependence on foreign capitalist economies by establishing our own independent and comprehensive economic system."

125

Stalin thought that industrialization should firstly be understood as the development of heavy industry, especially to develop the "nerve center" of the whole industry- the machine manufacturing industry. He pointed out that "the main emphasis should be given to the development of heavy industries such as oil and metal and mine extracting sectors. "All in all, we need to develop the production of the means of production and the machine manufacturing industry in our country. The path of socialist industrialization is special, that means socialist industrialization cannot take the path of the capitalist countries, which realized industrialization by firstly developing the light industry. On the contrary, our road should take the path of achieving industrialization firstly starting by heavy industry. Only by giving priority to the development of the heavy industry, can we provide our economy with more raw materials and machinery on the basis of new technology, thus we can increase our economic independence on the basis of large-scale socialized production and particularly improve our power of national defense and get prepared to shatter the attacks of imperialism. Therefore, heavy industry is the foundation of the foundation of the national economy, the core of the core; it must be put in the first place".

Stalin also emphasized: "the key of the industrialization in our country includes the concept of developing the industry wholly, especially the production of the means of production at a fast pace. Therefore, the investment volume for the basic construction of industry must be increased as much as possible. We should better have some hard time in the short run in order to increase the speed of development for future gains." He thought that developing industry at a fast pace is a necessity determined by the internal and external conditions of the USSR. "Judging from our external conditions, in order fully demonstrate the superiority of socialism and finally defeat capitalism, we must rapidly change the situation." "Leave back backward industrial technology of the USSR and catch up with and surpass the capitalist countries and their advanced technologies. Only by doing so can the victory of socialism all-across the world be guaranteed. On the other hand, since we are encircled by capitalist countries, the danger like invasion or the restoration of the old order is always there in the USSR." The backward industrial technology was a great disadvantage for USSR. "This backwardness would definitely make the USSR get beaten up." To keep the USSR remain invincible and guarantee the political and economic independence of our socialist country, it is an urgent issue to realize industrialization at a fast pace."

He also evaluated the internal conditions: the commodity production conducted by small producers, the backward and scattered production conditions still constituted the dominant position in the USSR. On the other side the large-scale socialist industry was just like a smaller island in the ocean. If the socialist large-scale industrial system could not be established rapidly, the foundation of socialist economy would not be solid and unable to guarantee the establishment of socialist large-scale agriculture using higher technologies. As a result, the alliance of working class and the peasantry and the collectivization of agriculture would lack a strong support. These conditions imposed that realizing industrialization at a fast pace, catching up with and surpassing the developed countries had become the life-and-death issue for the further development of socialism. With the high speed, the USSR should be able to go through the path that took the capitalist countries 50 to 100 years within 10 years.

In Stalin's opinion, in order to realize industrialization with the high speed, the biggest priority was the accumulation of the necessary funds. He listed different ways for raising funds practiced in the world history of industrialization. One was to accumulate funds by invading and exploiting colonies, like what Britain had done to develop itself. The second was to raise funds by frightening other imperialists to pay you compensation funds – or war indemnities- to avoid wars, like what Germany had done. Another was developing industry by using expensive massive foreign loans, like what Russia had done. The common feature of the above three methods was used by these capitalist countries was raising "additional funds" from overseas. Therefore, these ways cannot be adopted by a socialist country. Stalin argued that the USSR should take the fourth path. That is to rely on its domestic strong points and increase internal savings to accumulate funds. This kind of accumulation mainly has two sources: one is the working class which shoulders the industrial sector and the other is the peasantry. Specifically, one major source of socialist accumulation was to nationalize the property of landlords and capitalists and make them owned by the whole people, this could be a huge source for accumulation; the second is to cancel the foreign debts made by the Tsar and use these funds for industrial accumulation; third is to develop state-owned socialist industry, improve the production and operation of the state owned sector of the industry, enhance technologies, decrease costs, increase output values, improve quality, increase profits thus save more for accumulation; the fifth is to increase the food reserves by making use of the domestic trade market, by paying attention to use price leverages, eliminating the loopholes and avoid funds flowing into the pockets of the private capitalists (kulaks); the sixth policy would be to make use of the banking system as the leverage for accumulation, raise funds from Soviet people by issuing government bonds, improve the credit net and increase the rate of utilization of funds; the seventh way would be to take care of the fiscal budget, leave just enough funds as reserve, increase taxes and decrease expenditures; the eighth way would be to increase accumulation funds coming from agricultural sector. Peasants should pay taxes to the state and at the same time provide extra funds to industrial sector via prices scissors, namely the price of industrial products should be higher compared to prices of the agricultural products. Stalin argued that the price scissors policy should be gradually eliminated otherwise that would cause negative effects on development of industrial and agricultural production and expansion of their markets. An unlimited price scissors policy would also ruin the alliance between working class and the peasantry. However, price scissors should not be eliminated in one stroke instead needs to be gradually eliminated. Since the industry of the USSR was still "young", the improvements in the industrial technology and decreasing production costs cannot be achieved in a short period of time. So, industrial sector will need the support of agriculture. In the later period of industrialization, the funds coming from agriculture would largely go back to agriculture. With the mutual support between industry and agriculture, economy as a whole would develop harmoniously.

Stalin also considered several measures to avoid waste and unnecessary expenses by party and government organs. The planning departments should use the accumulated funds properly. First measure for them would be to make rational industrial plans by paying close attention to the economic situation, resources, reserves, markets and speed of development, and see that violent ups and downs in economy would not occur. Second was to avoid unnecessary government organizations and institutions. Otherwise, workers and peasants would bear those excessive expenditures caused by overstaffed government organizations and the huge government departments. Third was to persistently fight against extravagance and waste. Excessive celebration parties, gifts and opening ceremonies should be avoided. The activities of peculation such as corruption and stealing public sources should be severely cracked down. Last was to strengthen the labor discipline and increase the productive forces of labor in the enterprises. In the practice of industrialization, Stalin attached great importance to the application of science and technology, and promotion of people with knowledge and talents. He proposed the famous slogan "technology determines everything." The period of industrialization in SU was a period of serious shortages in technology. Stalin proposed that every party member should strive to become an expert in a particular industry and learn technologies. Stalin also paid great attention to the role of the intelligentsia, with special emphasis on cultivating a new intelligentsia emerging from working class families including peasants. In a workers union meeting he commented the following: "technology determines everything" "has helped us eliminate the shortage of technology, but it is not sufficient. To apply and make good use of the technology we need individuals with technological knowledge and cadres who are not only an expert in technology but also can use it with expertise. Therefore, to supplement our slogan "technology determines everything", we should add "cadres determine everything" these two will greatly promote our rapid industrialization."

Under the leadership of Stalin, the USSR achieved a rapid industrialization. It had started by 1926 and basically finished by the end of the 1930s. The proportion between industrial and agricultural output values, were 38 to 62 in 1926 and 61 to39 in 1940. Consequently the USSR had become one of the most powerful industrial countries in the world, which was an achievement worth of praise. However, there were also serious problems in Stalin's theory of industrialization. These problems later became serious defects in Stalin's model. These defects mainly were: over emphasizing higher output values; pursuit for high speed but neglecting economic benefits; a very highly centralized industrial and economic administration, administrative command instead of using economic incentives or preventions based on planned economy; one-sided development of heavy industry, etc. One important consequence of these defects was the ignorance of economics of scale in the industrial structure, these defects brought a heavy burden on country's finance, hindered consistent improvement in people's living standards, led to shortage of commodity supply in the markets and to a stagnant agricultural structure which could not be cured for a long time. The mistaken concepts formed in the practice of Stalin model had also brought many negative effects other socialist countries, which should be carefully analyzed to draw proper lessons.

3. Stalin's theory and practice related to agricultural collectivization

With the great progress in industrialization, the scattered and backward family based agricultural enterprises had become a major obstacle for the further development of the economy. In 1927, the USSR had faced a very serious grain crisis, consequently the issue of agricultural reforms was prioritized. The question was how could the small-peasant economy transformed into a large-scale farming thus provide a more solid foundation for industrialization and feed urban people? Stalin's answer was to achieve the collectivization of agriculture by organizing collectively owned farms. This idea was opposed by Bukharin and other people. Bukharin argued: "we should not start the construction of socialist agricultural sector firstly by organizing large-scale collective farms; instead we should start from the other end, the path of farmers' cooperative system." Bukharin also thought that Lenin's NEP policies should be continued and peasants should be led to the road of socialism via developing the commodity-money (market) relations. Stalin, on the other hand, argued that it would be hard to equip individual small-peasant enterprises with new technology and new machinery, thus individual small-peasant enterprises sector would not be able to meet the needs of urban population and industry. His other argument was that small-scale production sector actively nurtured a large amount of new bourgeoisie elements. He commented: "to build socialism, we should establish collective farming, and transform the small-scale production and eliminate the bourgeoisie (the kulak) elements in rural areas. To achieve that the only correct option is to promote the development of collective farms and the Sovkhozy (state farms). Stalin's and Bukharin's different views were mainly caused by the the different understandings on the NEP and the issue of how to combine rural and urban development. Actually, Stalin thought that the NEP was out of date and a new road to combine rural and urban development had become necessary. In 1928, Stalin officially announced the ending of the NEP and declared to start preparations for comprehensive collectivization movement. Judging historically, Stalin's theory and practice on the collectivization of agriculture has proven erroneous. Although this practice has brought some benefits, its general consequences were negative. Erroneous collectivization was also the major cause of the long-term backwardness and slow development of agriculture.

Stalin's one-sided pursuit of "the larger the better "and "the higher the better" in the degree of the public ownership" had caused severe problems. Also the way Stalin followed this policy, his mandatory style in leading collectivization movements brought profound effects to other socialist countries.[5]

To emphasize the necessity of the collectivization, Stalin made his explanation from the perspective of the relations between industrial and agricultural productions. He pointed out: "the Soviet power and socialism absolutely cannot be endlessly base itself on two different foundations, with one established on the basis of the largest united industry under socialism and the other established on the basis of the most scattered and backward small commodity and peasant economy. Therefore agriculture should be shifted to the basis of the new technology, step by step but constantly, making it able to catch up with the development of socialist industry. The backwardness in agriculture and the shortage of the output value of the agricultural products would posit a danger of breaking up the relations between urban and rural areas, between industry and agriculture and the alliance between working class and the peasantry. To avoid this risk, we must support agriculture on the basis of the development of industry and unite the scattered individual farmers to form larger farms, the collective farms. When the large scale socialist farms with advanced technology can be established and they can provide the necessary food and raw materials for the development of industry, this will lead us to a more developed market, which would in turn promote the development of industry, promote industry and agriculture harmoniously move forward". He also thought: "socialist system would not be compatible with the scattered and backward small-peasant economy. The foundation of socialist economy can only be consolidated on the basis of large-scale industry and large-scale agriculture; .. private economy and small-peasant economy are the hotbeds for capitalism."..."As long as the small-peasant economy still takes the dominant position, there exists the risk of capitalist restoration and make the socialist system unstable. To guarantee the victory of socialism in a single country, agriculture with public ownership should be developed with every effort and the collective farms must be established."

---

5   Sovkhozy, or Soviet state farms, began to be created in the early 1920s as an example of "socialist agriculture of the highest order". Kolkhozes, or collective farms, were regarded for a long time as an intermediate stage in the transition to the ideal of state owned farming. While kolkhozy were typically created by combining small individual farms together in a cooperative structure, a sovkhoz (state farms) would be organized by the state on land confiscated from former large estates (so-called "state reserve land" that was left over after distribution of land to individuals) and sovkhoz workers would be recruited from among landless rural residents. The sovkhoz employees would be paid regulated wages, whereas the remuneration system in a kolkhoz relied on cooperative-style distribution of farm earnings (in cash and in kind) among the members.

About the necessary conditions for complete agricultural collectivization, Stalin thought complete collectivization needs some necessary preconditions. The first is the support by Soviet political power, which will
help peasants in taking the path of collective farms. Second is to drive away
landlords and capitalists, nationalize their factories and land. The rich peasants also need to be cracked down and their machines and tractors should
be nationalized, machines and tractors should be utilized be by the poor
and middle peasants who will join the collective farms. Third is to build
an industrialized country and establish a new tractor and agricultural machinery manufacturing industry to support the collective farms. Fourth is
that the party must strive to form a unity of understanding and increase the
support of the peasant masses for its policies. Only by these conditions can
the comprehensive collectivization campaign start. By 1929, Stalin thought
that the above mentioned conditions were ready and USSR could start the
complete collectivization.

On the policies and principles of the collectivization, Stalin also had
some propositions. He suggested that in collectivization of agriculture, the
party's policy in rural areas would be: "the poor peasants are the main supporter of the working class, the middle size peasants should be won as the
ally and the kulaks should be treated as the enemy." This policy emphasized
on relying on the poor peasants and uniting with the middle size peasants,
to lead the great majority of peasants to the road of socialism. However, by
regarding the kulaks as the "class enemies", eliminating and suppressing
them, the size of political attack and class struggle was artificially enlarged,
which intensified the class contradictions to become acuter, thus caused
negative effects. As for the policies towards the middle size peasants, there
had also been extreme actions, and serious mistakes. For Stalin three principles should be followed in the collectivization of agriculture. First was
the principle of gaining voluntary support from the peasants in joining the
collective farms mainly by persuasion and education. The party should
avoid forcing the peasants with mandatory orders, never use violence. "We
should prove to them with their own experiences that the collective farms
can help them in getting rid of poverty and become prosperous and that
their collective farms will have an unparalleled superiority compared to
individual farming, thus make the peasants believe in the superiority of
socialism. There is no doubt that principle was right. However, in practice
this principle was often violated, by giving mandatory orders and use of
violence. Although the whole collectivization was completed within just a
few years through an intense campaign, there were endless troubles for a
longer time. The second principle was to achieve collectivization by stages and in groups according to various conditions in different regions of
the country. The USSR enjoyed a vast territory, with great differences in
natural conditions, cultures, economically, etc. in different regions, which

required different treatments in each particular region. The third principle was to transit to public ownership gradually and avoid overstepping. The main form of collective farms was the Kolkhozes, party should not directly jump to higher degree of collectivization by ignoring the masses' degree of mental preparedness. Stalin had criticized the hasty steps in collectivization, and criticized those who forced the peasants to transform their personal means of production, live stocks and houses to public ownership.

When discussing on the essence and features of collective farms, Stalin argued that the essence of the collective farms was socialism: "as an economic entity, collective farming is one of the economic forms under socialism."[6]

Only with collectivization, can the millions of individual peasants support the economy with machinery and tractors, which would be the leverage of the economic prosperity and which would develop agriculture along the road of socialism. This nature is determined by the relations within the process of collective production. In collective farms, the exploiting would be eliminated and that land and the basic means of production are owned by the public would determine the socialist nature of the collective farming.

The main types of collective farms in the USSR were the agricultural enterprises called Kolkhozes. Their basic characteristics were: first, the land and their agricultural machinery were state-owned; other means of production were community-owned (members of the collective farm); very few means of production were privately owned by the individual members of the farm; second, the government enjoyed a highly centralized leadership over the farms and also led them with plans. Major agricultural products were purchased by the state, purchasing policies and pricing took different forms; third, the collective farms enjoyed full responsibility for their profits and losses and carried independent economic operations. The members of the farm worked in groups and got payments on the basis of their working days according to the principle of distribution according to one's work. A small scope of private family business by the members was permitted.

6   Selected Works of Stalin, volume 2, p. 224.

III. The development stages of Stalin's economic model and economic system

Stalin's socialist economic model and system were produced under certain historical conditions and under certain domestic and international circumstances. Its formation, development and completion had taken a relatively long historical period, which can be generally divided into three stages: first was the stage of preparation (1924-1928); second was the stage of formation (1928-1936); third was the stage of consolidation (1937-1953).

1. The first stage (1924-1928)

At this stage, Stalin actively led a huge amount of preparation work for the formation of the new socialist economic model. From 1921 to 1924, Lenin had led the NEP policies in USSR by making use of the commodity-money (market) relations and developed state capitalism. NEP had recovered and developed the domestic economy to a great extent which laid a positive foundation for the modernization of industry and agriculture. After Lenin's death in 1924, as his successor, Stalin controlled the power and started to build socialism according to his own thinking orientation. In December 1925, Stalin presided over the Fourteenth Congress of the CPSU(B), at which the policy of the country-wide industrialization was decided. In April 1926, the CC of the CPSU(B) promulgated the detailed policies for industrialization, officially started the industrialization. In December 1927, the Fifteenth Congress of the CPSU(B) passed the resolution for the collectivization of agriculture, set the guidelines for the first five-year plan and started a reform in the economic management system. As the three pillars of Stalin's economic model and economic operation system, industrialization, collectivization of agriculture and planning system was basically formed. In 1928, Stalin officially announced that the period of the NEP was over and the USSR had entered into the new period of all round socialist construction.

2. The second stage (1928-1936)

At this stage, Stalin's economic model and system has started to get its form. From 1928 to 1932, the first five-year plan was implemented, which meant the planned administration of the whole national economy. As for the ownership forms only the state-owned ownership was in operation in industry. In enterprises the one-man leadership system was implemented. When we analyze macro operation the previous general management bureau and fourteen management syndicates were dismissed and replaced by three joint trusts directly attached to related ministry offices, which employed vertical management system. This meant the production and sales of the enterprises were under the unified management of theses three trust companies. At the same time, a strict system of economic accounting led centrally was set up. To support industrialization, the three major reforms were made known as "credit reform, tax reform and salary reform", to streamline the industrial operations. In 1930, the Party passed the resolution to quicken and deepen the construction of the collective farms. Given the goals of the first Five Year Plan, the state sought increased political control of agriculture in order to feed the rapidly growing urban population and to obtain foreign currency through increased cereal exports. Given its late start, the USSR needed to import a substantial number of the expensive—and largely Western—technologies necessary for heavy industrialization. Naturally, a substantial foreign currency reserve was necessary. In 1932, the first Kolkhozes' Operation Regulations document was issued, emphasiszing a highly centralized leadership in agricultural production. In 1935, The Soviet Presidium released the Kolkhozes' Consolidation Regulation, stating that the collectivization of agriculture had basically formed. In 1936, Stalin proudly announced: "since the USSR had basically realized industrialization and collectivization of agriculture, we had entered into socialist society."

3. The third stage (1937-1953)

134

This was the stage of consolidation and further improvement of Stalin's economic model and system. The Constitution of the USSR promulgated in December 1936 marked the establishment of Stalin's economic model and system. From 1937 till Stalin's death in 1953 this economic model and system saw some partial changes and revisions although the basic frame and main content was maintained. For example, the upper management departments were divided; the decision-making right for some enterprise managements was enlarged. Soviet Union began to use economic ways (a type of macro economic management) such as price and tax policies to stimulate and manage the economic life. But in general, these measures were all designed to consolidate and improve Stalin's economic model and system in its own logic and structure. After Stalin's death in 1953, the USSR also started a series of reforms on its economic system, but these reforms did not aim change the essential nature of the Stalin model. Only in 1989, with the disintegration of the USSR, the Stalin model was abolished.

The division and brief description introduction of the three stages aims to explain the formation and development of Stalin's economic model and system. To have a deeper understanding on this economic model and system, we will analyze its basic features in detail.

IV. The basic features of Stalin's economic model and economic system

The basic features of Stalin's economic model and system was the planned economic system utilizing administrative and mandatory management mode. This economic system can be further explained from the perspective of ownership forms, systems used in planning, system of distribution, strategies applied in economic development and foreign economic relations.

1. The practice of single ownership form: public ownership

Under Stalin's socialist economic system, the ownership structure of the means of production was wholly single: public ownership including collective ownership, non-public property forms and economic elements were almost non-existent. In 1937, the public sector of the economy produced the 99.1% of the national income, 99.8% of the total industrial output value, 98.5% of the agricultural output value, and 100% of the retail commodity turnover of the commercial enterprises. As for the forms of the public ownership under the Stalin model, there were only two: state-owned ownership and collective ownership enterprises.

The state-owned ownership was the major form of the public ownership. Its main features were as follows:

First, in socialist literature the ownership managed by the state as representing the whole working people is generally called the ownership by the whole people, and generally whole people includes the whole population since all citizens need to work to earn their living. Nominally the means of production are owned by all working people. Actually, there are two aspects in this system on the one side the working people are the owners—they have the possession of the means of production (whole of them), on the other side they are not the owners—for the reason that the public ownership owned by each individual is only effective when this ownership is integrated with other people's share, and only this integrated whole can constitute the public ownership. In the current development stage of socialist society the system of ownership by the whole people need to be under unified management by one social center. When there is a state, this social center can only be the state, who will own the public ownership of the means of production as the representative of the whole people. The natural resources, like land and mines, and the means of production of the state-owned enterprises are owned by the state. The state can use, move and transfer the state assets; it can also successfully raise or by mistaken acts depreciate the value of the state assets. The state enterprises in S.U which only conducted production did not have any say or control on the ownership management of the state assets, they were only responsible to complete the production plan.

Second, the ownership, possession, control and use of the means of production were realized by unified center, plus the ownership and management was also unified. The state and its management organs were the owners of the state-owned means of production, as well as the possessor, controller and user of them, which led the operation and management of the state assets and the state-owned enterprises. In conformity with the state's ownership the state naturally held the rights on the gains (profits) of these assets. The profits of the state-owned enterprises via production and other operational activities (trade, financial operations) were submitted to the state, in turn the state organs considering the needs their operations allocated and gave funds to them from the state budget. If any loss occurred in the operation of an enterprise, the state supported its debts and financial problems with grants.

Third, on the management of the state assets, the state's administrative power undertook a mixed function including both the management of the society and management of the state assets as the possessor of them (state assets). In this way the state administered the whole economy from a macroscopic perspective. The state's administrative powers was interwoven

with and overlapped with its usage of property right of possession of the assets. Thus the tasks of enterprise administration overlapped with the relations of property on the enterprise. This kind of administrative function actually existed on the economic basis: namely the possessor's ownership (property) on the state assets.

The collective ownership system under the Stalin model included various different forms in it, such as the collective farms in rural areas the farmer cooperatives for agricultural production, handicraft kolkhozes in towns and cities, cooperatives for handicrafts, etc. The collective ownership mainly existed in rural areas. It was the collective economic enterprise formed by peasants. The main means of production were collectively owned by the working people (as members) within the enterprise, thus means of production were possessed, controlled and used by this member collective. Each enterprise on the basis of unified kolkhoz enterprise management system, classified and defined farm works and applied unified accounting system, distributed the common gains according to the working hours (work points) among the workers. The governing body and leaders elected by the collective conducted the management. Although enjoying autonomous operation rights and full responsibility for their own profits and losses, this collectively-owned economic sector was still strictly controlled by the state. The agricultural and sideline products, what to be planted and what part to be sold to the state was decided according to the plans made by the state. The selection of the breeds (animals and plants), the portion of land to be used, even the methods of cultivation were usually specified by the government to a certain level.

The leaders of the collective (farm) economic organizations were always appointed by the relevant government level. Under Stalin's model, the state ownership was regarded as the highest level of the public ownership, the collective ownership as the one lower level of public ownership. Out of the two forms of public ownership, the state ownership took the dominant position in the economy. According to the statistics of the USSR in 1936, in the total production, the state ownership sector took up 91% while the collective ownership had a share of 8.7 % in the industrial output value. Assets owned by state ownership enterprises 97% of the total assets while the collective enterprises owned 2.6% of the total assets. In the total agricultural output value, the state ownership enterprises had a share of 76%, while the collective enterprises had a share of 20.3%. In the later years, the proportion of the share of state ownership enterprises had further increased.

The Stalin model also regarded the transition from collective ownership to state ownership as the criterion of socialist development. The backwardness of agriculture was a long-term problem existing in the economic structure of the USSR, and evaluated as the obstacle hindering continuous and rapid economic development, collective ownership was seen as the one reason leading to the insufficient supply of agricultural products, thus could not meet the increasing demand in the society. Therefore, the main solution was seen as elevating collective ownership to the ownership of the whole people, and the modernization of rural areas and the modernization of agriculture could help for this step. In his letter to Yaroshenko, Stalin wrote: "the task of the governing body is to act in a timely manner to solve the intensifying contradictions and take timely measures, so that the relations of production can conform with the growth of the productive forces, thus resolve this type of contradiction. What involves here is firstly some economic phenomena related to collective ownership, namely collective farms, secondly, the sphere of commodity circulation, etc. Of course, today we are still using these phenomena to develop the socialist sector of the economy, but at the same time we should see that they have started to hinder the vigorous development of productive forces in our country. They have started to form an obstacle, preventing the whole economic of the country, especially agricultural sector to accord with our nation-wide plans. Our task is to eliminate these contradictions by gradually elevating the ownership form collective farms to the ownership of the whole people, and also by gradually replacing the circulation of commodities by establishing the system exchange of products."[7] With this aspect, Stalin promoted

---

7   Selected Works of Stalin, volume 2, p. 228.

some pilot state-owned farms in the rural areas as successful models, to persuade member of collective farms for higher level of public ownership. As one important detail, we can see that the management forms applied in state-owned farms was very similar to those in the industrial state-owned enterprises.

2. Highly centralized departmental (ministerial) management system

Under Stalin's model, economy was mainly managed by the state. The government established various ministerial departments according to different sectors or sub-sectors, such as the Department of Coal-Mining Industry, the Department of Petroleum Industry, the Department of Chemical Industry, etc., either to directly manage the related state-owned enterprises or manage them via the middle-level institutions. All the important enterprises, such as the ones that were critical for the national economy and those enterprises that provide raw materials and equipment, and the enterprises that provide fuel and energy, main logistics enterprises and enterprises related to important consumer products, were under the management of the central authority. And the industries that operated in the local areas were under the management of the relevant departments in local governments. These departments were responsible for appointing the directors of these enterprises, including central and local ones, to manage the enterprise on behalf of the government.

Under this ministerial (departmental) management system, the economic decision-making right was highly centralized. The decision-making rights related to macro-economy, the decision of goals, speed of increase in production and decisions to arrange important proportions related different sectors of the economy, was completely assumed by the central authority. The decision-making rights related to micro-economic actors, meaning the decisions on production and commercial operation activities like investment, output and sales of the enterprises were also assumed by the government or by the department in charge of economic administration.

The funds needed or produced by the enterprises were centrally and strictly managed or allocated by the any violation of this rule by enterprises were administratively controlled.

The profits produced by the enterprises were all submitted to the central state funds. The commodities and the raw materials or half manufactured inputs needed by enterprises needed were also centrally allocated by the departments.

Without the ratification of higher management, the enterprise did not have the right to do anything about them. What or how much the enterprises produce should be in line with the central planning. The products were under the state monopoly of purchase and marketing and the price was also set by the state. The enterprise organization structure, the number of the staff, the level of salaries, etc were all ruled by the state. All in all, the state and its economic departments directly controlled the personnel issues, enterprise assets varlık, goods and materials, supply and marketing of the enterprises and decided the size, enterprise strategy, closing down, suspension of operation, mergers among them and change the line of production of the enterprises. The center also decided whether or not to establish a new enterprise. The enterprise was nothing but the executor of the orders of the central plan or the administrative department in charge. It was just the simple extension of central administrative organs, which only had the right to execute the orders from a higher level and and enjoyed very little decision-making right. When the enterprises had any problems that were out of their limit of functions and yetki power, they must ask the department in charge for instructions to handle the problems. The states managed economy with administrative measures. Every economic process or activitiy were all instructed, planned or intervened by the state, managing enterprises by economic leverages or by economic benefits which would favour the enterprise or its management was rarely used. The enterprises set up the departments within the enterprises with the reference of the administrative organs as a symbolic rank. The executives of the enterprises were also state's cadres with the rank that is corresponding to the rank in the enterprise. The higher administrative department in charge controlled the enterprise, appointed or dismissed the executives of the enterprise, namely the enterprise management didn't have any autonomy.

139

3. The centralized and unified system of planned economy

The Stalin model operated a planned economy. The national economy functioned under the instruction of the unified plan of the state. Every sector of the national economy, every economic region, the production, circulation, distribution and consumption, budget, finance and prices were brought into the plan of the state. The allocation of the means of production and labor force were decided by the plans. The development of every sector had to be in line with the unified plan. Just as what Kuybyshev said about the planning system of the USSR, "in our planning system…none of the economic, cultural or scientific sectors are out of the plan or our working range."[8]

---

8   Selected Speech of Kuybyshev, Russian version, p.226.

The plan in the Stalin model was the mandatory plan, which meant the plan with a mandatory nature that was legally binding, forcing the related institutions and enterprises to execute the orders. Stalin thought that with strict rules of awards and punishment, the execution of the plan should be one important criterion for assessing and choosing cadres. For those who harmed the plan, the government would investigate and affix the administrative responsibility, even the person concerned should bear legal responsibility.

At the state level, there was a huge planning organizationsystem (Gosplan) that was in charge of making the plan. The state appointed the Planning Committee, responsible for making the national plan. Every central department and every local department at every level had their own planning institution, which was led by the central department in Moscow and the national planning committee. To design the plan, first, the Communist Party in power proposed the major general goals of the economic development by taking into consideration the domestic and international situations and the need for the political and economic development. The political leadership –during their designing—started ing from the output value of the most important products, and then calculations were needed to achive that output amount, thus the draft of the plan was made. At the same time, each sector and each local area submitted their draft plans to the national planning committee, who, after evaluating and revising them would make the national plan. With the ratification by party and state the plan would be officially declared, explained, executed from top to bottom. The national planning committee and the planning organs in every sector or every region were responsible for supervising the execution of the plan.

Stalin's unified plan was a huge indicator system consisted of many indicators. From a larger perspective, there were categories like production, development of production technology, basic investment in construction sector, material and technology to be used , labor wages, consumption of raw materials, expenses of production, cost and finance. Under each category, there were many detailed sub-indicators. The important feature of this kind of plan was that it was centered around the products , not the value; that the planned indicators were made according to the variety and output value of the products such as steel, coal, machinery, etc. Currency and prices were only used as the tool of economic accounting, which functioned as the assistant criterion.

The plan was divided into three different kinds: long-term plan, mid-term plan and short-term plan. The long-term plan was the plan for the future, usually covering over 10 years; the mid-term plan was usually for 5 years, known as the five-year plan; the short-term plan was mainly the yearly plans, also including the quarterly and monthly plans. The three kinds of plans constituted the plan system, out of which the yearly plan took the central position.

Under the planned economy, the resources were allocated not by market, but by the state according to the plan. The resources of labor forces were distributed in a centralized way. The labor department of the state, according to the principle of full employment, allocated the social labor forces to each economic unit. The enterprises had not only to consider their own tasks of production, but also have their eyes on the protection of the social stability of the country and accept the labor forces allocated by the labor department of the state.

Although the enterprises had to a degree to decide the number, quality and variety of the labor forces, the decision-making right of the allocation of the labor forces were not in the hand of the enterprise but the department in charge and the national labor department. The administrative cadres of the enterprises were also allocated in a centralized way by the department in charge, and the personnel department. They also assumed the functions of assessing, choosing and transferring the cadres.

The financial resources—funds were collected and invested in a centralized way. The profits of the state-owned enterprises were all submitted to the state in the form of profit and tax. These two collected became the main source of the national finance. The state allocated these funds according to the centralized plan. The Department of Finance of the central government was the "major steward" of the funds, taking charge of the funds of the state and allocating them to each department, region and enterprise. The department of finance in each sector or each region was the administrator of the funds of their own department or region. The funds needed by the enterprises, including fixed funds and turning funds (working capital) , were all allocated from the state budget for them to use without compensation. The state set strict and detailed regulations and limits on the direction and usage of these funds. Under planned economy, central financial allocation played a more important role than credit and banks did. Banks were affiliations (extension) of the Department of Finance of the central government, functioning as a clerk, not as an agent to manage economic leverages.

Material balance planning was the major function of Gosplan (plan department) in the Soviet Union. This method of planning involved the accounting of material supplies in natural units (as opposed to monetary terms), which are used to balance the supply of available inputs with targeted outputs. Material balancing involves taking a survey of available inputs and raw materials in the economy and then using a balance-sheet to balance them with output targets specified by industry to achieve a balance between supply and demand. This balance was used to formulate a plan for the national economy. When the enterprises were making the production plan, they submitted their input demands to the higher authority level and get allocation after their demand is ratified by the higher authority. Under the planned economy, the economic activities were conducted vertically, with very little horizontal relations. There were very little direct relations among the enterprises and the relations were realized via the vertical relations. For example, the relations of ordering and buying goods among the enterprises that were subordinate to different departments could not be established unless the higher department ratified and coordinated the relations.

The planners had to include many types of goods and inputs into a single production planning sheet since it was impossible to create an individual balance for each of the approximately 24 million items consumed in the USSR.

Encouragement of black-market activity due to centrally planned resource allocation.

Low quality of goods due to isolation from the competitive world markets. The neglect of consumer needs and choices due to flaws in measuring the quality of goods.

The tendency of enterprise-level managers to understate productive capacity in fear of the "ratchet effect". This effect resulted from an enterprise overproducing in a given plan cycle. They would have to match their new level of higher production in the next cycle as the plan was 'adjusted' to fit the new data.

An anti-innovation bias (also from fear of the ratchet effect) "Storming" was the hurry to complete the plan at the end of a planning cycle resulting in poor production quality "Scattering" of resources (excessive spread) where too many projects (esp. construction) would have been started simultaneously and it took much longer to complete because of a lack of available inputs on time

4. The single mode of distribution—distribution according to one's work

To conform with the single public ownership, the single mode of distribution was conducted under this economic model: the distribution according to one's work, which means that the means of consumption is distributed according to the quantity and quality of labor and that one who does not labour does not deserve social support. There were two forms of the distribution according to one's work: the wage grade system of the administrative personnel ('staff') and the work points system.

The wage grade system of the administrative personnel ('staff') was conducted in all the production units that were under the ownership of the whole people including service sector. The wage grade of the administrative staff of the state, engineers and technicians and other staff was determined mainly by their job description. The wage grade of the workers was mainly determined by the degree of complexity and proficiency of the work. Monetary wages were given according to the different levels. Workers who assumed the work that was strenuous and harmful to health, the workers who worked in the heavy industries such as metal, coal, petroleum and machine manufacturing and the workers who worked in the areas with tough conditions should be given higher pay. The wage system was made and implemented in a centralized way, so was the increases in wages. The state regulated the total amount of the funds for wages nationwide and allocated the funds to each sector of the national economy in a planned way; each sector then allocated the funds to the affiliated enterprises within the limit of the funds for basic wages. The total amount of the funds for wages was mainly determined by the number of the enterprises and their technological structure, regardless of the efficiency in their operation. The enterprises with profits would not get more while the ones with losses would not get less. All enterprises were eating from the same "big pot." The staff's basic wages were under the centralized regulation of the country. When the policy of hourly wages was in use, people with the same skill scale in the same wage scale and with the same wage standard got the same wages as long as they went to work, no matter which enterprise they worked for, regardless of the enterprise's economic performance. This was a manifestation of equalitarianism. When the policy of piece rate pay was in use, the payment was paid according to the quantity of the products, regardless of the final economic getiri benefits. Stalin's policy of 'lower wages but more employment' had led to extensive employment of the male and female labor force. This policy had lowered the unemployment rate, but also the wage level in the society.

143

In addition to the monetary wages which was decided according to one's work, the staff of the state-owned enterprises also enjoyed other remunerations such as the social insurance, public medical care, free education, various subsidies, preferential treatment, apartments with very low rent, exemption from public service fees, etc. These kind of remunerations had become part of the staff's income. They were not distributed according to one's work, but according one's need. As a matter of fact, it was some kind of equalitarianism. Some of the remunerations were distributed according to posts and levels under the pretext called as: the needs for this job. The higher the post and the level, the more and better the benefits the cadre enjoyed.

5. The priority of heavy industry and the strategy of extensive economic development

After the victory of the socialist revolution Russia faced the backwardness of its economy, especially its level of industrial development, was far away from the level of the major capitalist countries. Therefore, the establishment of the Stalin's economic model under socialism inevitably needed to follow the economic development strategy of achieving industrialization as soon as possible and catching up and surpassing the advanced capitalist countries in terms of technology and economy. At the same time, the major way to achieve the strategic goal was definitely to give priority of the development to heavy industry. Stalin pointed out, "The center of industrialization, the basis for it, is the development of heavy industry (fuel, metal, etc.), the development, in the last analysis, of the production of the means of production, the development of our own machine-building industry."[9]

He thought only by doing so, it would be possible to realize the nation's industrialization in a very short historical period; it would be guaranteed that the national economy as a whole can be transformed on the basis of the prior development of technology; the socialist country would be economically independent with powerful national defense; the socialism would be victorious. Therefore, the Stalin model put the strategic emphasis of the economic development on the priority of developing heavy industry. With the highly centralized planning system and large amount of funds, goods and materials, human resources invested in the construction of the heavy industry, the heavy industry had developed with a very high speed while the development of the light industry and that of the agriculture was very slow. During the period of the first five-year plan (1929-1932), the investment in the basic construction of industry was 27.7 billion rubles (calculated according to the price in 1955), out of which 23.3 billion rubles was spent on the investment of heavy industry, taking up over 84%. During the second five-year plan (from 1933 to 1937), the investment in the basic construction of industry was 61.6 billion rubles, out of which 50.9 billion rubles was spent on the heavy industry, taking up 82.6%. Compared to 1913, in 1953, the heavy industry increased 45.46 times while the light industry only increased 7.82 times and agriculture only increased 46%. The proportion of the means of production in the total output value of industry was 33.3% in 1913 and increased to 60% in 1940.

Under Stalin's economic model, catching up with and surpassing the advanced capitalist countries in economy mainly referred to the quantity of products and speed of production development. Therefore, in the economic

---

9   Collected Works of Stalin, first Chinese version, volume 8, pp. 112-113, Retrieved from Marxist Internet Archive

development, the policy of extensive operation was exercised, emphasizing the growth of the output value and speed, but neglecting the economic benefits. The extensive operation mainly referred to expanding the production capacity and achieves rapid growth by constantly adding the quantity of production factors and establishing large amount of enterprises, instead of developing the economy by improving the productive forces of labor and the resource utilization rate. This was a path of high consumption, high increase, but low efficiency. In the USSR from 1928 to 1937, the staff increased to 6.3 million, which was 1.7 times of the original number. From 1929 to 1937, thousands of factories were built up. From 1930 to 1937, the annual increase of the industrial output value was at the average of about 20%. The products of the enterprises that were established or completely transformed in the first two five-year plans took over 60% of the quantum of output. The newly added output and output value were mainly from the investment of new manpower, material and financial resources. The economic growth was higher when there was more investment, lower when the investment was less.

Under Stalin's socialist economic model, the large amount of funds needed for the establishment of heavy industry and realizing industrialization were provided by the internal accumulation, mainly the profits and taxes from the state-owned industrial and commercial enterprises, agricultural tax and the scissors difference between the exchange of industrial and agricultural products, the policy of savings and the control of the increase of consumption.

The economic development strategy under Stalin's economic model had close relations with the highly centralized economic management system. The development priority of heavy industry and the strategy of extensive economic development required and established the highly centralized system of planned economy. The highly centralized administrative system of the central authority guaranteed the operation of the development priority of heavy industry and the strategy of extensive economic development.

6. The closure of foreign economic relations and the rigidity of self-development

Stalin's socialist model was an enclosed or semi-enclosed society, with its independent economic system and very little interaction with the outside world. This situation was formed for the following reasons. First, the capitalist world was extremely hostile to socialist countries from the beginning, making every attempt to blockade, sanction, even invade and subvert the socialist countries. Therefore, the relations between the socialist and capitalist countries were very intense, making it hard to handle normal economic, scientific and cultural exchange and cooperation between countries with different social systems.

Second, under the Stalin model, the understanding of building a socialism was inclined to keep the country distanced from the outside world. For example, in the 1920s, the USSR had overly emphasized that it was prepared in every aspect to establish socialism by itself, but failed to attach importance to Lenin's thought of making every effort to absorb external economic and technical facilities. Instead, it absolutized the relations between capitalism and socialism, thinking that the increase of the economic relations between the USSR and the capitalist world would also increase the reliance on it and therefore cause many new risks. Some people even thought that the USSR would become the affiliation of the world capitalist system by joining the world economic system. So the socialist economy of the USSR should not "be engaged in the general system of the capitalist development and become its affiliated enterprise."[10] Therefore, a series of measures should be taken to avoid the USSR being dependent on the capitalist countries, thus strive to establish an independent economic system that mainly relying on the domestic market.

After the Second World War, Stalin put forward that "The economic consequence of the existence of two opposite camps was that the single all-embracing world market disintegrated, so that now we have two parallel world markets…"[11] Thus there were the capitalist market and the socialist market. With the high speed industrial development, very soon these socialist countries would "be in no need of any imports from capitalist countries."[12] The theory of the two parallel markets and also two confronting markets had to a certain degree limited the economic relations between socialist countries and capitalist countries.

Third, on the basis of state ownership and collective ownership, the system of planned economy was inclined to autarky system. At that time, people generally thought that the purpose of socialist production was to meet the demand of people in the country; that the socialist production should pursue for use values rather (not) than value; that developing foreign trade was only an expedient way of ensuring the country's shortage of goods and materials. Plus, the foreign trade system under the state monopoly did not give the decision-making right on foreign trade to the Soviet enterprises, making the foreign trade separated from the production. For this reason the domestic and international prices of SU were far apart.

---

10   Collected Works of Stalin, first Chinese version, volume 7, p. 246.
11   Selected Works of Stalin, volume 2, p. 561, Retrieved form Marxist Internet Archive.
12   p. 562, Retrieved form Marxist Internet Archive.

As a result, the flexible development of the foreign trade was hindered. The departmental management system in the eceonomic administration set barriers between different departments, which made each industry have a separate regime and thus led to independent departmental kingdoms. Therefore, every department, every region, relatively larger enterprises and institutions established their own system and were only related with each other vertically from top to bottom. As a result, there formed the autarkic enterprise groups that lacked the horizontal relations in the whole industry.

For the reasons mentioned above, the socialist country under the Stalin model was basically autarkic, playing an inactive role in the international division of labor and in terms of collaboration with the world economy. The foreign trade neither took up a large proportion nor played an important role in the economy thus leading to an uneven foreign trade structure. For example, from the October Revolution to 1948, the USSR's volume of foreign trade had not reached the level of 1917. From 1939 to 1945, the annual volume of foreign trade was less than 1 billion rubles. As for the proportion of the USSR's volume of foreign trade in the GNP, it was only 1% to 2% from 1930s to 40s, 3% from 50s to 60s and less than 10% from 70s to 80s. However, in 1985, the proportion of the turnover of foreign trade in the GNP was up to 14.6% in the United States, 24% in Japan, 46% in Britain, 50% in Canada, 54.6% in Federal Germany and 13% in India. The small proportion that the USSR took up in the world trade was irrelevant to its national strength, with only 2.6% in 1950 and 3.8% in 1981. The GNP of the USSR was the second in the world, but its volume of foreign trade was over a long period of time lower than that of the United States, Federal Germany, Japan, Britain, France, Canada and even Italy. The development of trade relations with other socialist countries was regarded as the main part of foreign economic and trade activities, which led to the serious imbalance in the foreign trade areas. Among the exported products, raw materials took up over 60%, but machinery equipment only took up 15% to 20%, out of which only 3% was exported to the western countries. All these demonstrate that Stalin's economic system was closed or semi-closed.

V. The evaluation of Stalin's economic model

Stalin's economic model and management system demonstrated a particular rigidity in the aspect of self-development. That is to say, this economic model and management system were constantly dogmatized, standardized and rendered unchangeable, failing to initiate necessary reforms according to the practical situation and the development of the times. This rigidity was firstly presented in the understanding of the economic management system. For a long time, Stalin had thought that socialist productive forces and relations of production, secondly the economic base and the superstructure in S.U were completely harmonious with each other; that there were no contradictions between them, instead he saw only some insignificant contradictions that had little influences. Therefore, once the socialist economic model is established, there would be no need to have substantial reform related to it, but only needed consolidating and strengthening.

1. The rigidity of the economic model

Contrarily with the change of the international situation and domestic conditions, the traditional socialist model needed important reforms in order to adapt to the new historical conditions. However, the USSR had consolidated and strengthened the traditional model with a series of measures. For example, the promotion of the collective farms in rural areas, the attempt to gradually transit from collective ownership to the ownership of the whole people, the continuous strengthening of the system of central departmental management system, ignoring that the means of production are commodities and the regulating of the law of value in production sphere and lastly S.U had insisted on the economic management system which mainly employed administrative measures.

These measures had frozen the traditional model, making it a fixed model: Socialism became conservative towards any reform. It was deified and compulsorily promoted as the "universally applicable" example of socialism for all other countries. Every socialist country was required to completely follow the model. Once there was any violation, this country would be ferociously attacked. One typical example was the conflict between the USSR and Yugoslavia at the end of the 1940s. After the war, at the same time when Yugoslavia was learning from the experiences of the USSR related to socialist transformation and socialist construction, it decided some domestic and foreign policies that were different from those of the USSR which it thought would better fit to the features of this country.

In 1948, headed by the Communist Party of the USSR, the European Information Bureau of the Communist and Workers' Parties (Cominform) passed the resolution, condemning that the Communist Party of Yugoslavia had "broken with the Marxist theory of classes and class struggle" in terms of the internal affairs, and had become the "Kulak Party". In terms of the foreign affairs, it had betrayed the internationalism and "assumed a nationalist position." Therefore, Yugoslavian practice were labeled as "departing from Marxism-Leninism" and expelled from the Cominform.

The Communist Party of the USSR applied pressures on Yugoslavia, with the USSR being the first one to sever all relations with Yugoslavia. It also conducted blockade and military besiege on Yugoslavia. The people's democratic states of the East Europe also cut off the trade realtions with Yugoslavia one after the other, forcing Yugoslavia into a very difficult situation. Later, as required by the USSR, the people's democratic states of the East Europe started an all-round propaganda attack against "nationalism" and the "Titoists", which caused millions of members' quiting from the Yugoslavian party. Actually, it was a warning against East European countries to avoid them violating the policies and development model set and followed by the USSR. As a result, the conflict between the USSR and Yugoslavia and the struggles against "anti-Titoists" had directly hindered most socialist countries from seeking a path of socialist development that could fit to their own conditions. Consequently, except Yugoslavia, other East European countries, regardless of how different their national conditions were fromthe USSR, all strictly and exactly copied the model of the USSR in their socialist transformation and construction work.

Second, this rigidity was also manifested as bureaucratic style and inflexibility in the operation of the system. One of the outstanding features of Stalin's economic model was that the government was in charge of and very inflexible in many spheres. No region, no enterprise and no institution had any right to decide flexible measures to solve any problem; that everything, no matter if it's important or not, had to be reported to get ratification level by level, which was a waste of time and effort. Therefore, the system operated in very slow and stiff motion.

Without any authority over finance or personnel, the local governments could not lead the economic construction flexibly according to the local conditions and actual needs. If there was any important affair, it had to be reported to the department in-charge at a higher level, which would also need to consider the report and finally ratify it. Such a complicated "document trip" with many even tens of stamps of different departments in charge would take from months to years before the local government was authorized to do anything. The enterprises did also not have any decision-making rights. The personnel, finance and materials of the enterprise were also controlled by the plan department of the state and therefore did not adapt to the need of the market or to changes in the supply and demand relationship. Therefore they were not able to adjust the production factors of the enterprise in due time to improve the production and operation management. The staff employment of the enterprise was under the centralized allocation of the state, laborers without having the freedom of choosing or changing the job. If the enterprise wanted to improve technology and operation management, it still had to report to the higher-level department in charge for ratification. The regions, enterprises and individuals had all their hands and feet tied so that the operation of the national economy as a whole was rigid and stiff, without any vigor or vitality that they were supposed to have.

Stalin's economic model and management system were in a rigid and stagnant state for a long time which reproduced itself, and lacked any inner, inherent mechanism enabling self-transformation or self-reform. Thus it would finally collapse and be replaced by a new system that had more vitality.

2. The scientific evaluation of Stalin's economic model

It is not easy to impartially, and correctly evaluate Stalin's economic model and system, but we must make a fair and objective evaluation according to historical circumstances and historical facts. Objectively speaking, Stalin's socialist economic model made great achievements in a certain historical period and under certain conditions. The main achievement was the promotion of industrialization of the USSR and the fast-paced development of science, culture and education.

One of the outstanding features of Stalin's economic model and system was the operation of the highly centralized planned economy with the administrative orders. One strength of it was to transfer, collect and allocate various social resources to the greatest extent within the shortest period of time to deal with the urgent needs of the state and society. When there was a war or famine, or when the society was undergoing important changes, this way was very efficient. At the early stage of industrialization and economic modernization when the economic development was still at a low level, it was effective in laying the foundation for the modern industrial system, rapidly completing the primitive accumulation of social capital and satisfying the basic needs of the masses in a sufficient but at a low level. The rapid development of industrialization in the USSR at the early stage had proved this point. In the mid-1920s, although the USSR was the fifth powerful country in the world, its level of productive forces, production technology and people's life were still far less comparable with those of the developed countries. In terms of culture and education, it was even worse. However, in only 12 years from 1925 when the USSR set industrialization as the goal to strive for until 1937 as the second five-year plan was accomplished, the USSR had basically achieved industrialization. By 1937, the proportion of the total industrial output value in the total output value of industry and agriculture had increased to 77.4% from 42.1% in 1913. This number continued to increase to 85.7% in 1940. The production of the means of production had increased 9 times from 1913 to 1937, out of which, the machine-building industry and the metal-processing industry had increased 19 times while the chemical industry had increased 14.2 times. Although when we know today that it was not accurate to use the industrial output value as the standard to determine the level of industrialization, the USSR had in a short period of time established an industrial system that was relatively complete in range, it had enormously enhanced the level of technological transformation and equipment update and greatly improved the production capacity. For example, in the period of the first five-year plan, the USSR was only able to produce about 100,000 tractors, but by the time of the second five-year plan, it was able to produce over 600,000 tractors. The output of steel, pig iron, coal, petroleum and cotton cloth were 4.2 million tons, 4.2 million tons, 21.9 million tons, 9.2 million tons and 2.58 billion meters respectively. By 1937, the numbers were up to 13 million tons, 14.5 million tons, 128 million tons, 30.48 million tons and 3.47 billion meters respectively. In terms of the main products and their output, the USSR had caught up with or surpassed the advanced capitalist countries. In the period of the first five-year plan, the heavy industry increased at the average of 28.5%; the light industry had increased 11.4%. By 1937, the level of industrial production of the USSR had become the second in the world and the first in Europe from the fifth in the world and fourth in the Europe in 1913. The USSR had become the second powerful industrial country only after the United States, which was nothing but an industrial miracle. At the same time, the USSR also made a lot of efforts to develop science and education, bridging many gaps in science and technology. In 1920, the illiteracy ratio in the USSR was up to over 68%, but by 1939, the illiterates among the young and middle-aged people had basically been eliminated; the literacy rate of the residents was up to 87%. The USSR had also made great achievements in employment and medical care.

Under Stalin's economic model and management system, based on the advantages of highly centralized power which could rapidly arrange and allocate the limited resources available, the industrialization was basically realized before the Second World War. And this had strengthened the power of national defense, which provided strong material basis for the victory of the anti-fascist war. When the war broke out, this system was smoothly connected with the war-time system, urgently mobilizing and transferring personnel, material and financial resources. This system had enabled that the need of the war was the center of all work. The sectors related toward: production facilities for tanks, aviation and weapons were thus established. Compared with the numbers in 1940, in 1942, the proportion of defense spending in the the national income of the USSR had increased to 55% from 15%. In industry, the products for the need of war had increased from 26% to 68%. In 1942, the war products increased nearly %100 compared to the prewar period. In the last three years of the war, the USSR annually made 30.000 tanks, nearly 40.000 airplanes, 120.000 cannons and over 5 million various guns. All of these measures had played an important role in the final victory of the anti-fascist war. They also enabled USSR recover as soon as possible after the war and develop with fast pace.

Stalin's economic model and system had played a positive role in healing the trauma of the war, recovering the economic construction as soon as possible and enabling a fast economic recovery increase fast. During the World War, the USSR had suffered great losses. Over 20 million people died in the war; the economic losses were up to 2.500 billion rubles; over 1.700 towns, more than 70.000 villages, 32.000 enterprises, more than 10 farms and 65.000 kilometers railway were damaged in different degrees. Relying on the strength of the highly centralized economic management system, the USSR shifted its resources to most important spheres, thus rapidly got rid of the difficulties after the war. With only less than 5 years, the major economic indicators had bounced back to the level of 1940. By 1950, total industrial output value had increased 73% compared with the prewar levels of 1940. The output of pig iron, steel, coal and crude oil was up to 19.2 million tons, 27.3 million tons, 261 million tons and 38 million tons respectively. The electrical generating capacity had increased to 91 billion kilo-watt hours, which had surpassed the level before the war. In the early 1930s, the pace of economic development of the USSR had surpassed the western developed countries, with a great increase of people's living standard and the great improvement of the military power. The USSR's whole economic strength, science, culture and education were all in the leading position in the world.

152 The facts above show that Stalin's economic model and management system, under certain historical conditions and in the certain historical period, was not completely irrelevant, it rather had some, even substantial positive influences on the development of the backward countries. The achievements it has made in some aspects are also the facts known to everybody. Therefore, in our further studies on this model we should have fair and objective stand affirm and not evade the facts. Stalin led "patriarchal style political system, practice of 'one person alone has the last say', personality cult", high-handed oppressions even ruthless murder of people with different political views were the super-structural support for such highly centralized economic system. There are different ideas on this subject.[13] Once this political system started disintegration it became hard to maintain the former highly centralized economic system. The price and future troubles left by the highly centralized economic system were hard to accept. Its irrational aspects and disadvantages were mainly as follows:

The personalistic authoritarian system, life-long tenure of leading posts and designated successor system that Stalin created and practiced deviated from the democratic republic system The system of appointing posts according to grade[14], system of bureaucratic privileges, system of eliminating dissidents, system of manipulating cadres and the masses were also legacies of the feudal autocratic society.

---

13   Gao Fang thinks this is the most important aspect of Soviet system, which had hindered reforms.
14   Top-down appointment of leading cadres at all levels through layer by layer

The leader of the upper layer appoints the leader of the lower layer and the latter chooses his team to work with and appoints the leader of the furher lower layer.

3. Irrational aspects and disadvantages of Stalin's economic model

First, in terms of the main nature of the economy, Stalin model exercised planned economy, excluded market economy and emphasized non-marketization of goods and services plus production equipment and others. All the disadvantages of Stalin's economic model and management system originated from the mistaken understanding related to the nature of the economic sphere. This is also related to Marxist understanding of economic laws and has also philosophical aspects. In this respect Stalin had a one sided approach.[15]

The thinking failure or skip that takes social development as the process of natural history is premised on the opinion that views the economic laws of society as natural laws. It is true that Marx mentions that the economic laws of society equal to natural laws in many places; for example, in *Capital*, he repeatedly refers to "the natural laws of capitalist production", "even when a society has got upon the right track for the discovery of the natural laws of its movement—and it is the ultimate aim of this work."[16] Lenin had stated, "Marx speaks of the economic law of motion of society, even referring to this law as a Naturgesetz—a law of nature."[17] However, the problem is that in what sense Marx considers the economic laws of society are natural laws.This is not understood fully.

The economic laws of society are the laws of men's economic activity. As the most important laws of society, they reflect the sociality, historicity and epochal character of human activity I a most deeply manner. The economic laws of society are different from natural laws: (1) the economic laws of society run through the relationship between man and man through the exchange between man and nature; (2) the economic laws of society are a process of the appropriation of "material exchange" in the form of man and by means of the inherent measure of man; (3) the economic laws of society are essentially practical, as the activity laws of man in economic practice, changing continuously along with the changes in the model of men's economic practice, and their realization also depends on the practice of man. Natural laws are the mechanical, physical, chemical and biological laws of nature, existing themselves blindly; when they are not cognized by

153

---

15   See Yang Geng: New Interpretation of Marxist Philosophy.
16   Marx, Capital (Translation of Vol. I of French Edition Revised by Yang Geng), p. 4.
17   Collected Works of Lenin. 2nd Chinese Ed., Vol. 1, p. 105, Beijing: People's Publishing House, 1984.

men, natural laws appear to be opposite to men; once they are discovered, they can be utilized by men to conquer or lead natural forces with sciences. Obviously, natural laws and social laws are different in essence.

After the stage of the primitive societal development, the human society entered into the stage of the autarkic natural economy with agricultural production playing the leading role. The characteristics of this economy were that the supply-demand relationship was balanced internally and it was closed to extern. The trade (exchange) consisted mainly of the products and real objects; the trade did not include commodity, money and market. With the progress of human civilization, scientific revolutions, system innovation, mass production the as a result socialized trade and socialized consumption took the dominant position. The human society and man's economic practice then entered into the phase of market economy. The outstanding feature of market economy is to use the relations between commodity, money and markets when producing and exchanging commodities, this includes using markets as the basis and main instrument to allocate the economic resources of society.

Market economy is a stage that cannot be overstepped in the economic development of any society after capitalism is irreversibly established in the 18th century as a world system. And this world system continuously and forcefully urged precapitalist societies of the world in this modern direction. Since soscialism is a more modern system than capitalism, it is obvious that it should inherit and make use of past human practical achievments in economic sphere. Thus latest socialism researches after 1980's—though it is a new cognition in socialist theory and practice—suggest that commodity, money, socialized trade, socialized consumption and markets do not have any nature of political ideology. Stalin's fatal mistake was to equate market economy with capitalism and he wanted to eliminate it hastily. It is obvious that planning is an intelligent and rational tool to guide both social production and production of enterprises, since long capitalist states also make guiding plans and capitalist enterprises also make internal plans.

But Stalin made a general mistake on the nature of economy by elevating a rational tool (planned production) to the level of a holy concept which should be a single and only guiding model for the whole economic practice of a modern society. The concept of planned economy contained both the elements of late critical utopian socialism—which was only partially scientific but mainly futuristic—of the first half of 19th century and the remnant ideas from the human practice of natural economy. Especially when it was later cognized as the indispensable and essential part of development laws of socialism this planned economy theory became the foundation of Stalin's economic model. This cognition also included to evaluate it as the dividing line between capitalist and socialist development, consequently as the two confronting mega economic concepts. The planned system concept mainly meant to allocate economic resources with plans rather than the market, but became to over-determine every aspect of economic life. This fundamental cognition mistake and economic waste caused by his blindness was the root cause behind the later cul de sac faced by the planned economy of SU. This cul de sac or failure of the planned economic system was a historical necessity, which was caused both by the misunderstanding of the nature of economic laws (in general and in the socialist society) and opposing the practice of correct handling of economic laws when regulating commodities, commodity production, money and markets in the benefit of (three) socialist individual, people and socialist state.

Second, the economic management system was highly centralized led with administrative orders, which made the mechanism rigid and become outdated after a while. The plan was highly centralized with all power kept in hand of the central authority. Too many things were centralized in an overly rigid way, which caused huge waste of the economic resources and constrained the economic activities in every aspect of economic and financial life. That the all-inclusive plan was forced to be carried out by administrative orders, which could easily neglect the actual and new needs of the enterprises and the majority of the consumers. Therefore, on the one hand, the undesired products were largely overstocked; on the other hand, the consumer products and production input goods were in serious shortage, causing serious imbalances in the product structure, which put the social production and social life into the state of semi-stagnation and semi-paralysis. The basis of highly centralized economy with led by administrative orders was the single ownership structure. The uniform public ownership was one of the outstanding features of Stalin's economic model and the pillar of the planned economy. In industry, it was the single national ownership or the ownership of the whole people administered by the state; in agriculture, it was the single collective ownership, still mainly administered by the state. Due to economic administration methods and measures used, and high centralization, led by administrative orders and high status given to planning practice had turned the collective group ownership into the ownership of the whole people, which had also seriously effected the healthy development of the economy.

Third, the foreign trade was strongly inclined to closure, self-circulation. SU lacked external competition, undermined import of advanced technology and management technologies, rejected the use of foreign funds in a word its foreign trade and economic relations was at minimum. Though the self-development by closing oneself to the outside to some degree can be favorable for the economic independence of a country, on the other side this will to one-sided development, thus it will in the long run fall behind the development of the world economy due to the lack of interaction with the rest of the world and competition. In the globalization age (globally allocation of most resources) an economically closed country will also encounter disadvantages due to irrational resource allocation, higher resource costs, higher consumption of its own resources and decreasing profitability and efficiency. It will unnecessarily over-invest in certain sectors of economy or industry, though it could be wiser to cooperate with foreign partners.

Fourth, the economic structure was irrational and the development was uneven causing serious imbalances in the national economy. The strategy of prioritizing heavy industry was established to deal with war threat, thus large amount of resources were allocated to machine or tool manufacturing and raw materials extraction and processing industries. But light industry, food and consumer products industries were ignored for a long period of time. Such a super power, able to send satellites, establishes a space station could not even produce a qualified tea or coffee kettle, which reflected the true model of its economic development. Particularly, the rural population was sacrificed for the accumulation of industrial funds through price scissors policy (substantial difference between industrial and agricultural products prices). This had caused a long term stagnancy in agriculture. The agriculture had remained stagnant for decades, even gone backward. The output of grain decreased from 86 million tons to 82.5 million tons, with the grain output per capita decreasing from 540 kilograms to 435 kilograms, meaning a serious structural imbalance in the economy.

From 1913 to 1953, the industry of the USSR had increased 45.5 times while the light industry only 7.8 times.

Fifth, the extensive development mode which included fast development pace, high investment rates, high resource waste and low profit meant to unsustainable economic development. Such an economy could not produce material benefits for the people in the long run. The product quality lagged behind citizens' needs, while production costs were relatively high and economic system lacked cost efficiency. Though the enterprises, suffered manifold problems including lack of profitability, but still they couldn't use any initiative for reform, they didn't have any decision-making rights, meaning they lacked inner vitality. Evaluating from the microscopic perspective, the enterprises' production relied on plans, financial support from central finance, administrative management from above, which meant there was no self-functioning economic mechanisms, thus profit and loss figures were all unrealistic, making enterprises passive subjects. Such a model meant to an inefficient enterprise system leading to an instable economic basis. Evaluated from the macroscopic perspective, the investments did not turn into an effective production capacity or produce the demanded modern products, leading to over-stock. As a result, there formed the vicious circle:

investment → overstock → shortage → reinvestment → re-overstock → re-shortage, which finally caused a dead lock in the economic development in 80'ies.

I think the five disadvantages mentioned above can comfortably demonstrate the defects of Stalin's economic model. The necessity for economic development and social progress is an irresistible trend, therefore—when all other conditions were mature, and prior reform efforts had failed- this economic system was completely changed and replaced by the new economic system, which was an historical necessity.

Chapter V

Stalin's Theory and Practice on Socialist Planning and Market

The relations between plan and market are the key issue not only of Stalin's socialist economic model, but also of the characteristics of the operation of the model and system. In the later process of reforming Stalin's socialist economic model, the most important and fundamental problem is how to understand and deal with the relations between the plan and the market.

I. Stalin's theory on socialist planning

Stalin's theory of the socialist economic model, with industrial nationalization and agricultural collectivization as the basic system requirement, was directly target to achieve the economic growth and development under socialism with super fast pace, to catch up with western developed capitalist countries and to establish a strong socialist camp.

With what mean (tool) could we connect the basic system requirement and the economic development goal?

Stalin's answer was the socialist planned economy. Stalin thought that after the establishment of the socialist public ownership, also known as the socialist state ownership and socialist collective farms, only with the management system of planned economy and the mandatory plans could the expected goal of economic development be met within the shortest period of time. Thus the USSR, a country that was economically backward, could catch up with and surpass the developed capitalist countries. And only by doing that, the socialist state ownership and the socialist agricultural collective ownership be really consolidated and developed. There was no any other way except this. Based on such an understanding, Stalin succeeded

Marx, Engels and Lenin's thought on planned economy, made further development from many aspects and formed a relatively complete theory of planned economy.

First, Stalin regarded planned economy as one of the essential features of the socialist economic system. He pointed out: since we are constructing socialism, so we should take the needs of the whole society into consideration and consciously organize the economy nationwide according to the plan.

Stalin thought that the capitalist economic system was a private ownership system and the system under which capital employs labor; and pursues maximum profits, the capitalists must pursue life-and-death struggles, which formed the anarchy with free competition in the capitalist society and that this state of anarchy was one of the basic reasons that the capitalist society will be doomed to perish.

The socialist economic system is public ownership with people handling and making decisions on their own affairs. The basic economic law of the public-owned economy is "the securing of the maximum satisfaction of the constantly rising material and cultural requirements of the whole of society through the continuous expansion and perfection of socialist production on the basis of high technology."[1] As long as the aim of economic development in socialist society will not be to pursue maximum profits, there will not occur any life-and-death struggle in the society. There will not be any acute and irreconcilable contradiction between workers, between workers' organizations or between workers and the state; their fundamental interest will be harmonious with each other.

Therefore, the state can be the main body to propose, make and release plans and operate vertically from top to bottom with administrative orders to coordinate the whole process of economic operation. Just because the planning of socialism replaces economic anarchy, the socialist economy is superior to the capitalist economy. He said, "Crises, unemployment, waste, destitution among the masses—such are the incurable diseases of capitalism. Our system does not suffer from these diseases because power is in our hands… because we are conducting a planned economy, systematically accumulating resources and properly allocating them among the different branches of the national economy… That is what distinguishes us from capitalism; is that what constitutes our decisive superiority over capitalism."[2]

Second, for the first time Stalin made it clear that in socialist society there existed the law of planned proportional development. He thought that socialist economy does not aim maximum profit, but aims to guarantee the

---

1   Works of Stalin, volume 2, page 602.
2   CollectedWorks of Stalin, volume 13, page 32-33.

society's material and cultural needs will be satisfied to the greatest extent; in this way in the development of production there will not occur the intermission from upsurge to crisis and from crisis to upsurge, but the constant and orderly increase of production.

Socialist economy does not see periodic destructions in the developmentof technology which occurs simultaneously with the destruction of the productive forces, but there occurs constant improvement on the basis of advanced production technology. The law of planned and proportional development, which is the opposite of anarchy caused by competition and the anarchy of production under capitalism, can be achieved on the basis of public ownership of the means of production.

That is to say, only by following the law of planned and proportional development could the development of socialist economy be realized and the planning department could effectively organize production. Of course, when Stalin was emphasizing the law of planned proportional development, he did not confuse the objectivity of this law with the particular subjective planning activities. Instead, he strictly distinguished between the role of subjective planning with the law of planned and proportional development. The plan should offer the strategic goals, focal point and steps of the development for the economy but these goals can only be achieved by the subjective initiative of the planning department.

In Stalin's opinion, the economic law of planned and proportional development, and is the objective law which does not change with men's will, and its existence has certain internal reasons, and they are as follows:

First is the socialized large-scale production. The operation of socialized largescale production objectively requires the law of planned proportional development.

All the relations in the economy production, circulation, distribution must be conducted in a planned and proportional way.

Plus, the central government also possesses the ability to manage the economic life of the whole society in a planned and proportional way by acquiring correct information about the needs of the whole society.

Second is the socialist public ownership. The public ownership of the means of production enables the working people possess the means of production which eliminates the antagonistic contradictions between them and the exploiters. Therefore the fundamental interests of the state, the collectives and the individuals become consistent. This consistency of the fundamental interests (among three) makes the majority of the people accept and support the fundamental aim of economic activities: The aim of satisfying people's constantly growing material and cultural needs.

This consistency of the fundamental interests (among three parties) also make them consciously subordinate their partial and individual interests to the interest of the whole. This fact enables the sublation of the confrontation in the capitalist society, and people can enjoy harmony and order in the social andeconomic life. As a result, plan and proportionaldevelopment the two states that definitely exist in the operation of public-owned economy.

Just because the law of planned proportional development existed as the objective condition of the socialist economic life, Stalin repeatedly emphasized that this law, together with the basic economic law of socialism, the law of distribution according to one's labor contribution,-the two- formed the system of the socialist economic laws.

He pointed out that Marx had evaluated scientific laws, no matter the laws of natural sciences or laws of economics, as the reflection of the objective process that cannot be changed with men's will. People can discover them, study on them, consider them in their own activities and make use them for the good of the society, but men cannot change or abolish these laws.

Especially, men cannot make or create any new scientific law. Just based on this understanding, Stalin strictly criticized some researchers' view that the law of planned and proportional development made it possible that the Soviet people could eliminate the existing economic laws and create the new ones. He clearly pointed out that the yearly plans, the five-year plans and the objective law of planned and proportional development of the national economy must not be confused.

The former must correctly reflect the basic socialist economic law and the objective requirement of the law of planned and proportional development in order to get a good effect. Stalin thought that the law of planned proportional development demonstrates its effect around the basic socialist economic law. Stalin formulated the basic economic law of socialism that objectively exists as "the securing of the maximum satisfaction of the constantly rising material and cultural requirements of the whole of society through the continuous expansion and perfection of socialist production on the basis of higher techniques."[3] How to make the basic economic law of socialism function? One important point was to make use of the law of planned proportional development. Only by this law of planned and proportionaldevelopment and of distribution according to one's work can the basic economic law of socialism function.

The combined action of the basic socialist economic law, the law of planned and proportional development and the law of distribution according to one's labor contribution was the practical application of Marx's

3 Works of Stalin, volume 2, p. 602.

historical materialism. Namely one basic law of historical materialism: The relations of production must necessarily conform with the character of the productive forces.

Furthermore, Stalin designed the whole frame of the economic system through planning.

If I analyze its contents, in Stalin's era, the sphere of planned economy was extremely extensive and detailed, including every region, every sector, every enterprise and even every factory; from the whole process of social production and reproduction to every factor and link of the social reproduction; from economic life to culture, education and social development, almost everythingshould be designed by planned management.

The planned management had become a net that included everything. The plans included yearly plan, five-year plan, mid-term and long-term plans. The short term, mid-term and long-term plans were connected and formed a chain of plans. Judging from the methods, the forms of plans included mandatory plans and orientation plans, but the mandatory plans took the leading position. Once the plan was ratified by the legislature, it was legally effective and should be strictly executed. Judging from the procedure, the central administrative institution proposed the plan, which should be executed from top to bottom, and thecentralstate institutions evaluated and checked the execution of the plan at last. When the planned goals could not be completed, the leaders of the state-owned enterprises and the collective farms would have to bear administrative responsibility. They did not bear economic responsibility, since the punishment they faced was mainly related to their administrative posts. Judging from the goals, no matter it was short-term, mid-term or long-term plans, the main goal was to achieve the maximum total output with the fastest pace. The economic efficiency was not among the key criteria. Among the criteria the emphasis was on the development of heavy industry. The development of the light industry and agriculture needed to serve for the goal of maximum output in the heavy industry.

163

Stalin's planned economy theory was the important part of his whole theoretical system of socialism. He had formed his views of the highly centralized planned economy with his own thought and logic. To have a deep understanding of Stalin's planned economy theory, we should first have a deep understanding on the origins of the formation of this theory.

Stalin thought that it was an urgent necessity and was also certainly possibleto have a planned economy in the Soviet Russia. In terms of necessity, the origin of his planned economy theory was formed based on his theory of the threats posed by imperialism and his the theory of ever sharpening class struggle in the society. The threats posed by imperialism meant that the

USSR, as the first socialist country in the world, was not only economically backward, but also encircled by imperialism.

At that time, indeed the new-born Soviet power was faced with the economic and political pressures and isolation by the imperialist countries. There was also athreat of military intervention. This situation of encirclement made it very difficult for the Soviets to economically cooperate with the international trade and financial markets. Plus influence of imperialism might cause economic dependeny and hinder its healthy and secure economic development.

Politically, the new born Soviet power was also threatened by imperialism, which wanted to strangle it in the cradle at any time.

Furthermore, the world financial crisis in the capitalist world in 1929 had intensified the contradictions between the imperialist countries, which might cause a new imperialist war among them. To rapidly enhance its power to defend against the challenge posed by the imperialist countries, be prepared against the increasing world war threat, this new system certainly needed the highly centralized planned economic system.

The theory of ever sharpening class struggle in the society meant that Stalin regarded the relations between workers and peasants as an important issue of class struggle. In 1927, there occurred a grain procurement crisis in the USSR. Stalin had thought that it was because the kulak class did not want to sell their grain to the state; that they greedily waited the increase of prices to take advantage of it. They also tried their best to drive up the grain prices and sabotage the grain market led by the state. This was Stalin's analysis.

He said: "The procurement crisis is the expression of the first serious resistance under the conditions of NEP, undertaken by the capitalist elements of the countryside against the Soviet Government." For Stalin the grain procurement was an important question of socialist construction work related to grain procurement.[4]

For Stalin, the individual small peasant economy was the huge social foundation on which the inclination of capitalism was formed. Just for this reason, to transform the small peasant economy the collective farms should be established thus peasants should be led into the path of socialism,then the scattered and backward small individual peasants would choose to become the members of collective farms.

---

4 Collected Works of Stalin, first Chinese version, volume 11, p. 39.

Based on this approach the grain price should be determined by the government. and the peasants should not have an alternative market. This was assumed as a victory the proletariat against rural the capitalist class elements. The industrial nationalization could become the solid foundation of socialism only under the support of the planned economic system, without which it would be impossible to achieve successes in the rural collectivization movement. To insure the victory of the proletariat over the capitalist class in the rural areas, the system of the highly centralized planned economy should be built, this was regarded as the only guarantee for the stability of the socialist economic foundation.

In terms of possibility of planned economy: Stalin's theory of the unlimited rationality of the Soviet state or power and the theory of the consistency (harmony) of the fundamental interests (of three subjects) in a public ownership system were the origins of his planned economy theory.

For Stalin, the unlimited rationality of the state meant that although the USSR could not eliminate the existing objective economic laws, but it could create new socialist economic system on the so called "open book". After grasping the knowledge of the economic laws, the Soviet state could make use of them, could limit the sphere in which economic laws functioned and command them, could control and rule them.[5]

As long as the Soviet party or state was able to completely understand and make use of these laws, it could learn and understand all and gather all information resources about the complicated social and economic life to lead it. And Soviet party or state could use the information to make scientific predictions and decisions. But the rationality of the economy is restricted or hindered by blindness and spontaneity, which could be solved only by resisting the blindness and spontaneity. Try to control them with the unlimited rational planning capacity of the state. Only by doing that could the whole society have a healthy development. Just because of the existence of the state institutions which have unlimited rationality in their hands, it was certainly logical to operate this system of highly centralized planned economy from top to bottom.

165

The theory of the consistency (harmony) of the fundamental interest in a public ownership system: This theory is related with the method of economic management, it means that when the capitalist private ownership is replaced by the public ownership of the means of production, the fundamental interest of the state, the collectives and the individuals—all three—are consistent (harmonious) so that the mandatory plan and the administrative measures could be directly and operated without the need of the regulation of commodity economy (i.e. market) and the law of value.

---

5   See Works of Stalin (1934-1952), p. 600, 603.

II. Stalin's theory on market

The formation of Stalin's thought on planned economy is directly related with his understanding on the issue of market. One can say that it was just his opinion on market economy that urged him to form his idea on planned economy. So, Stalin's theory of the market is actually another aspect of his theory of planned economy. Otherwise, we cannot deepen our studies on his theory of planned economy. From the perspective of contents, Stalin's theory of market can be divided into two parts: the theory of commodity economy, the theory of currency and secondly the theory of the law of value.

1. Stalin's theory on commodity economy

Stalin clearly pointed out that the commodity economy had existed also after the October Revolution. But some people had still quoted Engels' words written in Anti-Duhring that once the majority of the society takes the means of production the commodity economy should be eliminated. Thus they wanted to prove that after the October Revolution, the commodity economy should be eliminated. Targeting this view of point, Stalin pointed out that in the USSR the existence of commodity economy at that time was very necessary. He also pointed out that Engels's conclusion was made under the circumstances of Britain where the industrial and agricultural production was highly socialized. This conclusion was not suitable for Russia, a country where the small-peasant economy was in the dominant position. Stalin's conclusion was: the victorious proletariat, "in order to ensure an economic bond between city and country, between industry and agriculture, commodity production (exchange through purchase and sale) should be preserved for a certain period. Thus commodity production would be the form of economic tie with the city which is alone acceptable to the peasants, and Soviet trade—among the three state, cooperative, and collective-farm—should be developed to the full and the capitalists of all types and descriptions ousted from trading activity."[6]

Therefore Stalin had his own explanation for the basis of the socialist commodity economy. That is, under the socialist system, the commodity production and circulation still was an objective necessity. The reason why they still had the objective necessity was that: Both two different forms of ownership—namely the public ownership of the means of production (or the ownership of the means of production of the whole people as stated in the constitution) and the rural collective ownership represented by the collective farms still existed. Related to the enterprises which were under the public ownership of the whole people, the means of production and their

6   Selected Works of Stalin, volume 2, p. 548.

produced commodities were the property of the whole people and managed by the state as the representative of people. In the collective farm enterprises, although land, agricultural machinery and other facilities belonged to the state, the products were the property of the farms, representing a group of farmers. Some small-sized means of production that was freely added by the farmer was also the property of the collective farm. The property of the collective farm enterprise was owned by the members of the farm. When they had economic relations with the state-owned enterprises and they would prefer to exchange their products as commodity to purchase the industrial products and means of subsistence they needed. That is to say, they were conducting the economic activities as independent commodity producers and commodity operators. If their identity as the owner of the commodities were ignored, if their rights and requirement of interest were denied, the state-owned enterprises could not get the agricultural products they needed. Therefore, the normal economic relations in the society would not work.

Of course, even though Stalin admitted that the products of the collective farms were commodity, he also came up with many conditions, which limited its very commodity character. First, for Stalin in the socialist society, the sphere of commodity production activities should only be limited to the personal consuming products. Second, the means of production should not be exchanged in the market as commodities. Third, the machinery and tractors cannot be sold to the collective farms or possessed by them. Otherwise the sphere of the commodity circulation would be enlarged, and this would hinder the collective farms from improving their level of the ownership to that of the whole people. Fourth, the surplus products of the collective farms should be excluded from the commodity circulation system and brought into the system of product exchange between the state-owned industry and the collective farms. For Stalin, this could be the method that was practical and effective for improving the level of ownership of the collective farms to the ownership of the whole people.

Stalin did not allow the existence of other forms of ownership (such as individual economy and private economy) which would exist side by side with public ownership, so he explained the reason why commodity economy existed in the SU was the existence of the two different forms public ownership, which were the collective ownership and the public ownership (ownership of the whole people) existed. He thought that the commodity circulation and its monetary economy should be gradually eliminated which was an unnecessary factor in the national economy. But this would only be possible in the future when the two basic components of production would be replaced by an economic system which controls all types of production and control the production of all consumption goods.

Specific type of commodity production

Stalin emphasized that the socialist commodity production was the "specific type of commodity production" that was different from the capitalist commodity production. For Stalin, thisspecialtyis expressed in the following aspects.

First, it was under a different economic system, so the system basis of commodity production was different. The capitalist commodity production was established on the basis of the capitalist private ownership of the means of production while the socialist commodity production was established on the basis of the socialist ownership of the means of production.

Second, it reflected different economic relations. The capitalist commodity production was the economic relations formed in the fight for maximum of profits among capitalists and in the exploitation of the surplus value produced by workers. The socialist commodity production did not have any capitalists taking part in it. All it involved was the relations of exchange of goods produced by the united socialist producers. The socialist commodity production basically reflected the economic relations between the socialist producers.

Third, it had a different sphere of production. Since the socialist commodity production was based on a different system and different conditions, the sphere of the socialist commodity production was strictly limited, which was mainly reflected as follows: labor-power is not a commodity; means of production were not commodities; the sphere of activities of the commodity production was limited to personal consuming goods; in the field of foreign trade circulation, the means of production produced by the socialist enterprises kept the nature of commodity both in essence or in form, but in the sphere of the domestic economic circulation, the means of production did not have the nature of commodity, but they only dressed by the outer skin of the commodity.

Stalin further pointed out the differences between the commodity production category and the capitalist production category. Stalin thought that they are two kinds of different things. He thought that it was not right to think that commodity production would lead to capitalism no matter under what conditions. It was not like something absolute, namely at any time or under any conditions. Commodity production should not be confused with capitalist production because they are two different things. In the human history commodity production was earlier than capitalist production. It exited under the slavery system and feudal system to serve them. Therefore, the existence of commodity production is bound to rely on the existence of the economic system around it; it cannot exist independently. On the other hand, commodity production can exist by relying on different economic system or on different conditions; it is not necessarily attached with one particular economic system. As for the emergence of the capitalist commodity production, it was because under the capitalist private ownership of the means of production, labor-power appeared in market as a commodity. Therefore, capitalists could purchase and exploit their surplus value, thus the commodity production was pushed towards capitalism and capitalist commodity production.

Although Stalin admitted that there were objective economic reasons for the commodity production to exist in the USSR, he emphasized that only the production of personal consuming products was the commodity production and denied that the production of the means of production was also a commodity production. He was also against to sell tractors to the collective farms and thought that with the development of the productive forces and the increase of productive forces of labor in the USSR, reform measures should be taken to gradually upgrade the collective ownership to the ownership of the whole people and finally eliminate the commodity production which he saw as an ideal situation.

Stalin also clearly discussed the future of the commodity production: For him the commodity production was incompatible with the next step in the future, it was incompatible with requirements of transition from socialism to communism. In his opinion, limiting the commodity production, shrinking the sphere of activities of the commodity circulation and expanding the sphere of activities of product exchange would make it easier for socialism to transit to communism. As a matter of fact, Stalin has regarded the elimination of commodity production and circulation as an important part of the historical task of transition from socialism to communism. With the continuous increase of the socialist factors in the society, the factors of capitalism and small-scale production would continuously disappear along with the constant expansion of the sphere of product economy and in turn the constant shrinking of the sphere of the commodity economy. Finally, the product economy would definitely replace the commodity economy and socialism would be able to transform to communism.

2. Stalin's theory on currency

Between the end of the 1920s and the early 1930s, since the USSR was just in the beginning of conducting the socialist construction, plus Lenin's early death, leaders and party members had a great theoretical divergence whether or not the commodity-money relationship should exist, although Lenin had pointed out the importance of the commodity-money relationship in the practice of the NEP. He even pointed out that the essence of socialist economy and the basis of socialism was using the products (not commodities) of the socialist "large-scale industry" ("socialized" industry) to exchange for the products of the peasants.[7] However, in terms of the whole academic institutions related to economics, the view of denying the need of commodity-money relationship under socialism was very popular. Although Stalin thought that the commodity-money relationship is not the mechanism of socialist economy and that only the centralized administrative planned economy was the law of socialist economy, he also disagreed with the opinion that the conditions of directly transiting to product exchange was realized or satisfied and the money would be called off very soon. He pointed out that "money is the instrument of bourgeoisie economy which the Soviet Government has taken over and adapted to the interests of socialism…the direct exchange of products can replace, and be the result of, only a perfectly organized system of Soviet trade."[8] Thus he regarded this as a solution of the future.

The view that denied the commodity-money relationship and thought money should be eliminated was denied by Stalin, but he still argued that money was essentially an instrument of the bourgeoisie. Therefore, on the one hand, Stalin emphasized that money would exist for a long time in the economic life of the USSR until the first phase of communism, namely until the phase of socialist development, was completed.[9] On the other hand, Stalin regarded money only as the instrument of economic accounting and calculation, completely ignoring its real social character. He pointed out that in the socialist economic activities, the essence of money's function is the instrument of economic accounting, because it serves the whole system of planned economy, it serves to enable the planned prices. But the planned price was calculated and decided by the state; but the enterprises, as the producers, did not have any right to decide on the prices. Therefore we can conclude that Stalin's view on money is fundamentally different from the role and definition of money in the market economy. On the one hand acknowledging the effect of money on the other hand negating the market economy has inevitably led him to regard money as the instrument of planned economy. As a result, ignoring the nature and function of money was the inevitable outcome.

3. Stalin's thoughts on the law of value in socialism

The idea that denied the existence of the law of value under socialism was quite strong among Soviet economists. Stalin criticized it, arguing that it was necessary for the commodity economy to exist between the industry under the public ownership and the agriculture under the collective ownership, therefore the existence of the law of value was inevitable. However,

---

7 Collected Works of Lenin, second volume 41, p. 376, Beijing, People's Publishing House, 1986.
8 Collected Works of Stalin, volume 13, p. 304.
9 Works of Stalin (1934-1952), p. 611

he also thought that in the USSR's economy, the law of value functioned in a specific transformed form.

First, he pointed out the necessary link between the law of value and the commodity economy. That is, the law of value is primarily the law of commodity production. Wherever the commodity production and commodity exchange exist, there must be the law of value. Once the commodity production disappeared, value and the law of value would disappear as well. Therefore when he was answering if the law of value existed under the socialist system in the USSR and if it functioned or not, he affirmatively said, "yes, it exits, and functions. At the places where commodity and commodity production exist, there the law of value must exist."[10]

Second, he pointed out the sphere within which the law of value was effective under the condition of socialist public ownership. That is to say, in the field of commodity circulation, mainly related with the personal consuming goods, the law of value played the role of regulator. He said: "In our country, the sphere of operation of the law of value extends, first of all, to commodity circulation, to the exchange of commodities through purchase and sale, the exchange, chiefly, of articles of personal consumption. Here, in this sphere, the law of value preserves, within certain limits, of course, preserves the function of a regulator."[11]

Third, he argued out that the law of value in the socialist economy was limited, which means that the law of value did not function as a regulator. This regulator role was played by the law of planned proportional development of national economy and the yearly plan, five-year plan and the overall economic policy of the country decided according to this law. Stalin said, "the law of value can be a regulator of production only under capitalism, with private ownership of the means of production, and competition, anarchy of production, and crises of overproduction." "there can be no doubt that under our present socialist conditions of production, the law of value cannot be a 'regulator of the proportions' of labor when it is distributed among the various branches of production."[12]

For Stalin, if the law of value was the regulator of the proportion of the labor's allocation between different production sectors of the USSR, it cannot be explained why the USSR developed the heavy industry which made less profits, sometimes even no profits instead of making every effort to develop the light industry that brings more profits. If the law of value would be free to act as a regulator in every production sector, the leading position of the production of means of production would be beaten by the production

171

---

10 Collected Works of Stalin, volume 2, p. 552.
11 Works of Stalin (1934-1952), p. 611.
12 Selected Works of Stalin, volume 2, p. 556, 557.

of means of consumption. However, giving up the leading position of the production of means of production meant eliminating the possibility of the continuous increase of the economy, because Stalin thought economy cannot increase constantly without putting the production of means of production in the first place. At the same time, Stalin while on one side denied the law of value as the regulator of production, on the other side he also accepted the influence of the law of value in the field of production: he said : "in our country consumer goods, which serve to compensate/pay the labor power expended in the process of production, are produced and realized as commodities which are under the operation of the law of value."[13]

Stalin's theory of the relations between plan and market.

To sum up, there are several characteristics of Stalin's theory of the relations between plan and market.

First aspect which looks from the perspective of system. Basically, Stalin regarded planned economy as the feature of the socialist system, the market economy as the feature of the capitalist system. Socialism equals to planned economy; capitalism equals to market economy. The law of planned proportional development is the internal law of socialism while anarchic competition is the internal law of capitalist economy. The process of socialism beating down capitalism is also that of planned economy replacing market economy.

Second aspect looks from the perspective of the operational mechanism. The high degree centralized planned operational mechanism becomes the leading operational mechanism under socialism. On this leading basis of the former, the market mechanism could be introduced to the exchange of consuming products as a supplement or temporary solution. The latter is limited to function between the public ownership and the collective ownership, due to the immaturity of the development of the socialist economic system in the USSR at that time. It was just a temporary arrangement at the certain level of the socialist economic development.

Third aspect looks from the mutual relations. The planned economy under socialism should only allow an extremely limited sphere for the operation mechanism of the market economy. Take money for an example, in the operation of planned economy, it only exists as an instrument of economic accounting or calculation tool. The law of value should not play the role of regulator of production, but only had its influence in the field of the exchange process and production of consumption products. Plus this—sphere limited—influence should also regulated or oriented by the law of planned proportional development.

---

13   Works of Stalin (1934-1952), p. 611.

Fourth aspect looks at the issue from the trend of the development of history. Market economy, commodity economy and their related extensions such as money and the law of value will all gradually get pale until getting totally perished as the socialist system gradually gets mature. The moment when the commodity and market economy perish will also be the moment when the communist system is established. Stalin clearly argued that both the market economy, commodity economy are not compatible with the requirements of transition from socialism to communism.

III. Stalin's treatment of the relationship between planning and market

In the practice of socialist economic construction of the USSR, with his theoretical points of view on the relations between plan and market, Stalin established the first highly centralized administrative planned system in the history of the development of socialism. Stalin completed the first and the second five-year plans and achieved socialist industrialization and collectivization of agriculture. He also resisted the invasive aggression of the fascist Germany to the USSR and got the victory of the Patriotic War. Of course, his mistakes on the theoretical understanding and policy had also caused many problems to the practice of socialist construction.

1. The practice of leading the USSR to complete the two five-year plans

Stalin made the first five-year plan of national economy of the USSR in 1927. At that time, he pointed outthat "the fundamental task of the five-year plan was to convert the USSR from an agrarian and weak country, which was dependent upon the caprices of the capitalist countries, into an industrial and powerful country, fully self-reliant and independent of the caprices of world capitalism."[14]

As the first socialist country in the world, although the USSR won the victory of the proletarian revolution, its economy was extremely backward at that time. Before the war, industry only took 42.1% of the total output value while agriculture took up 57.9%. The population in rural areas took up 80% of the total population. As Stalin had expected, the preparation and implementation of the first five-year plan (1928-1932) had turned the USSR from an agrarian country into an industrial country and laid the economic basis of socialism, which had a decisive significance.

---

14 Collected Works of Stalin, first Chinese version, volume 13, p. 157.

According to the first five-year plan, the total investments were nearly 66.5 billion rubles, with over 19.4 billion rubles on industry (including electrification investments), an increase over 3 times than the 5.2 billion rubles investment in the previous five years before the first five-year plan. Out of the investment, 78% was used to develop heavy industry. In the five years, the total industrial output increased 1.8 times; output of means of production increased 2.3 times; means of subsistence increased 1.4 times. Within this five years, it was planned to establish 1500 large enterprises and 42 large regional electrical power stations. With all the efforts of the people of the USSR, the plan that was supposed to be finished in five years was completed within four years and three months. The unprecedented industrial sectors were established, such as machine tool manufacturing, car manufacturing, tractor manufacturing, chemical industry, engine manufacturing and airplane manufacturing, etc. Industrial Sectorial distribution of industry gradually became reasonable. The total industrial output value in 1932 increased 1.02 times than the figure in 1928, with the average annual growth rate of 19.2%. Heavy industry increased 1.73 times, with the average annual growth rate of 28.5%; light industry increased 50%, with the average annual growth rate of 11.7%. Industry now took up 70.7% in the total output value the country. The proportion of heavy industry in industry increased from 47.5% to 53.4%. However, the first five-year plan was overly prematurely advanced, so the advantages of targeting the best option had turned into the disadvantages with the change of the objective conditions. For example, the reform to organize the rural collective ownership was too fast so that the activity of peasants conducting agricultural production showed a sharp decline, (the agricultural output decreased), which led to the serious disproportion/imbalance in the development of national economy. By 1932, the agricultural output had decreased to the lowest level in the recent history. Actually, the best expectations awaited from the first five-year plan were not entirely achieved.

At the Seventeenth Congress of the CPSU(B) in January 1934 passed the second five-year plan. The political target of the second five-year plan was to eliminate all the capitalist elements and completely eradicate the exploiting class and the class differences. The economic target of the second five-year plan was to complete the entire transformation of national economy and establish the foundation of the most updated technology for all the sectors of national economy. According to the plan, over 4500 large enterprises would be established, with the total investment of 137.5 billion rubles, an increase more than %100 than the number in the first five-year plan. The most outstanding feature of the second five-year plan was the attempt to elevate the development of the light industry to a more important status. After a working very hard work for four years and three months, the second five-year plan was completed in advance again. The total industrial output value in 1937 increased 1.2 times than the number in 1932, with heavy industry increasing 1.39 times and light industry increasing 9.9 times. The annual growth rate of the whole industry was 17.1% (plan target was 16.5%), among which the heavy industry increased 19% (plan target was 14.5%) and the light industry had increased 14.8% (plan target was 18.5%). With the initial adjustment of the structure of heavy and light industry, the supply-demand imbalances related to consumption products were relieved to some degree. Therefore, in 1935 and 1936, the USSR abolished the ration system related to foods and also the ration system for industrial consumption goods, which improved people's level of consumption.[15]

The early completion of the first and second five-year plan of the USSR basically established a relatively solid national economy, thus the country was transformed from the imperialist Russia, a backward military feudal country, into a socialist country with a relatively advanced level of socialist industrialization. Therefore, the USSR leaders have announced that socialism had achieved a complete victory. Its status in international arena was also greatly improved because of this. Without the success of the first and the second five-year plans, it would be impossible for the USSR to achieve the victory in the Second World War later. This has been proved by the victory of the Great Patriotic War of the USSR.

However, the second five-year plan did not meet the economic expectations as planned. Generally, the second five-year plan of the USSR could not completely achieve the target of improving the healthy proportion between the heavy and light industry of light industry.. Heavy industry still greatly surpassed the proportion of light industry; agriculture was still the weakest. Instead of promoting the light industry with a fast pace, the heavy industry was further promoted. Light industry could complete the 85% of its plan; agriculture could complete 76.9% of its plan; the heavy industry could complete the 121.3% of its plan. The so-called politically eliminating all capitalist elements in the society and all roots of exploitation and conducting complete collectivization in rural areas to a great extent were the infringement of the private interest of the peasant masses in the rural areas. And the nationalization of all sectors of economic life in the cities actually reflected the exaggerated emphasis on the public sector/public ownership in the USSR, almost all types of non-public business was eliminated.[16]

15 Collected Statistics of the National Economy Plan of the USSR, page 44, Beijing, Statistical Publishing House, 1957.
16 The Modern History of the USSR (1917-1945) edited by Zhang Yide, Changchun, Jilin Literature and History Press, 1988.

Stalin's theory of the relations between plan and market had played a decisive role in conducting the strategy of industrialization of the USSR with a fast pace. However, because Stalin has formed a one-sided view on the relations between plan and market and followed a dogmatic attitude in his practice of economic construction of national economy, the USSR has encountered many slips and mistakes.

2. Lessons of the Soviet practice

Below, I will evaluate on the lessons of Stalin's theory and practice of planned economy and his negative attitude to market in socialism.

First aspect, negative effect of the personal cult of Stalin on planned economy practice

Making plans to lead the economic life of the country aimed at reflecting the great initiative of the millions of working people who had stood for complete liberation by building socialism which would guarantee them to be the masters of their state of socialism and thus undertake the carrying out of the state affairs.

However, in reality in the practical process of designing the economic plan the leaders' standards and choices replaced the people's standard and determined the main policies and targets of the plan document. The right and status of the masses as the masters of the socialist state- one basic policy socialism- was not practiced, their real needs were not reflected in the plan preparation process, but the words uttered by Stalin became the decree.

"All of the policies", even "details" "were all determined according to the ideas and passion of the great Comrade Stalin."[17] When the Communist Party of the USSR and the government were discussing the policies and principles of the third five-year plan, Rykov, the member of the Political Bureau of the CPSU(B), strongly advocated catching up to major capitalist countries in productive forces of labor while Stalin strongly advocated that the per capita output was more important than the productive forces of labor as a target.

Although Rykov's proposition of improving the productive forces of labor was in line with Lenin's last words, although Stalin's proposition would lead to low economic benefit and shortage of working force in rural areas, the Eighteenth Congress of the CPSU(B) still accepted Stalin's proposition.

The leadership of the CPSU(B) was basically reduced to Stalin's individual leadership. When the first five-year plan was being made, the National

17 Selected Works of Voznesensky's Economic Theory, p. 347, Beijing, People's Publishing House, 1983.

Planning Committee (state organ) prepared two kind of drafts, first one with the minimum indicators (the basic plan) and the second with the maximum indicators (the best scenario plan). During implementation if favorable circumstances occur, and in every aspect the objective conditions are just as perfect good expected, then the best plan should be operated; if adverse circumstances occur such as poor harvest of crops, setbacks in the foreign economic relations and a sharp increase in the expenditures of national defense,etc, the basic plan should be operated. Of course if basic plan is to be implemented some targets needed to be lowered or some policies needed to be cancelled.

When the National Planning Committee submitted these two plans to the party Central Committee for examination and discussion, Bukharin, Rykov, Tomsky and other people, considering the slow development of agricultural production and the grain procurement crisis, advocated to implement the basic plan and also put forward a two-year special plan for agricultural development. However, Stalin categorically denied Bukharin and other people's proposition; and labeled Bukharin and others who support the basic plan as "the group representing the Right deviation in the party" and some others who did not agree with him as "conciliating with the Right deviation". Following Stalin's will, the Sixteenth Congress of the CPSU(B) passed the best version of the first five-year plan, which was ratified by the Fifth Congress of the Soviet parliament. The indicators and targets in the best version of the plan were 20% higher than those in the basic plan, proposing a progressive increase in the targets. Even so, Stalin was still unsatisfied with the pace of economic work, and again and again pushed to increase the speed. In 1929, he suggested to increase the annual growth rate of industry from 21.5% to 32.1%. In 1930, in the working report to the Sixteenth Congress of the CPSU(B), again he emphasized "speeding up and urged for earlier accomplishment of the five-year plan", increasing the control indicators in the plan for several times. Such extremely high indicators and targets, would be hard to achieve even the circumstances were the most favorable circumstances, not to mention the "natural and man-made calamities "which occurred in the USSR at that time. Here I will just mention two negative circumstances: the international wave of anti-USSR actions especially in Europe and the man-made resistance by farmers which reduced domestic agricultural production. The actual results by the end of 1930 had already manifested that it was impossible to reach the annual growth rate as planned. The growth rate was %33 lower than expected. It was necessary to calmly look into realistic facts and decrease the targets and find certain solutions. However, at the beginning of 1931, at the First All-Union Conference of Leading Personnel of Socialist Industrial Enterprises, Stalin again required to "complete the five-year plan earlier than planned (within 3 years) related to basic and decisive industrial sectors and increase the annual growth rate. As a result, the annual industrial growth was only 20% of the figure stated in the plan. Finally, faced with the hard facts, there was nothing to do but readjust the yearly plan of 1932.[18]

Second problem was caused by the guiding thought of the party and Stalin: Rigid understanding on the issue of class struggles

First, if we evaluate the guiding thought of the party, class struggle was almost one-sidedly absolutized. For Stalin, whether or not the USSR can complete the plans in the shortest period was directly related with the fierce competition between the socialist Soviet Russia and the western capitalist countries: the struggle between socialism and capitalism. Therefore, he directly and closely attached the pace of completing economic plan as a highly political issue and an issue of one of cardinal principles.

When there occurred some different opinions on the planning policies or target indicators oron the pace of executing the plan, etc, all these opinion differences were treated as the direct reflection of class struggles within the party and were resolutely opposed. In these debates, even the behaviors of "employing cruel struggles and hitting ruthless blows" was applied against those who advocated different opinions. For example, in the period of preparations of the first five-year plan, the focus of argument was the problem of speed. Georgy Pyatakov, Zinoviev and Rykov advocated the theory of curvilinear pace decrease related to industrial development. When a county enters the period of industrialization—as time passes—its speed of development will show a decreasing trend.

They thought that industry could develop at a fast pace only in the period of economic recovery.

On the other side Bukharin argued that industry should develop at a moderate rate in the short run, instead of aiming fastest short run growth rates. He said: "we must take as our point of departure not the minimum tempo of accumulation for next year or the next few years, but aim such a proportion that will guarantee the greatest speed of development permanently and over the long run."

If this approach is ignored and too much funds are invested in the large-scale industry, these would cause imbalances in the economy, especially imbalance between natural human sources and goods, thus due to this imbalance finally the speed of industrial development would slow down.

However, Stalin regarded the problem of speed as a supreme political issue (the struggle between socialism and capitalism), it was a life-and-death

18 The Modern History of the USSR (1917-1945), edited by Zhang Yide, Changchun Press, p. 194, 219.

question for Bolsheviks. He argued: "We are fifty or a hundred years behind the advanced countries. We must make up this gap in ten years. Either we do it or they will crush us."[19] For that reason, Stalin employed critical attacks against other key leaders who argued for slowing down the pace. He labeled them as"bourgouise economists", "leaders of the Right deviationist surrenderists" and even "the saboteurs". Bukharin, Rykov and Tomsky, after observing the slow development of agricultural production due to resistance and the grain procurement crisis, advocated a balanced and coordinated development between industry and agriculture.

As we have mentioned above Stalin absolutely denied their propositions. Stalin believed what he did was to uphold the most vital principle of socialism, to struggle with the enemy forces that sabotaged the socialist cause. Without this stern class position, the new born Soviet Russia would certainly be defeated by domestic and external class enemies.

Third problem was the usage of highly centralized management system of the administrative plan.

The Soviet planned economy was administered by a highly centralized management system. To ensure the achievement of the plans at a fast pace, Stalin opted for establishing a highly centralized management system. In other words the power was centralized in the hands of the central authorities while- lower bodies- the regional administrators and enterprise leading organs were deprived of decision-making rights. Following Stalin's instruction to further divide the central functional decision making organs, the number of these organs increased from 4 in the early 1930s to 25 in the 1940s. Thus in the Soviet Union there were about 25 central management organs—named as Commissariat—about 13 of them were responsible for leading industrial sectors. Each of them led one industrial sector, vertically managing the attached enterprises in almost every aspect. The chief industrial departments were those of (1) metals, (2) mines, (3) chemicals, (4) foodstuffs, (5) textiles, (6) leather, (7) clothing, (8) electric works, (9) polygraph (printing works etc.), (10) automobiles, (11) peat, (12) state constructions, (13) lumber and timber. At the head of all industrial sectors was the Highest Council of National Economy, a body of thirteen persons with the rights of a people's commissariat (minister).

Each of the 13 Commissariats above was responsible for planning and managing the production and reproduction of the enterprises and also managed the issues related to production factors like personnel, financial and material resources. The means of production that any enterprises needed were supplied by a unified allocation system controlled by a central special body. The products of the enterprises were transferred to Commissariat of

19   Selected Works of Stalin, volume 2, p. 274.

Trade. Enterprises received the non-manufactured and semi-manufactured products they needed from the Commissariat of Logistic and Supply. Profits of enterprises were submitted to the state and the losses were covered by the state's financial commissariat.

Enterprises were no more than implementing production tasks set by the state, implementing a one-sided simple economic activity. Zhang Yide wrote: "For example the important affairs of Ministry of automobiles or Ministry of Textile were decided by the Highest Council of National Economy, but of course the final decision was asked and ratified by Stalin."[20]

Fourth, implementation of plans and the management method was based on administrative leadership and mandatory plans.

a) Before the five-year plan was made, the Central Committee of the CPSU(B) and the Highest Council of National Economy released a specific instruction assessing the general tasks and direction of the economic planning. According to the spirit of this instruction, the National Planning Committee of the USSR would immediately start making the draft of the five-year plan containing targets and annual control figures and submit it to the Central Committee of the CPSU(B) and the Highest Council of National Economy for ratification. Simultaneously the planning units at every lower level also started making their draft plans at the same time and submitted them to upper levels. After the Central Committee of the CPSU(B) and the Highest Council of National Economy ratified the last draft it was discussed in the Soviet Parliament and legally promulgated Once the end plan document was promulgated every ministry, every region and even every enterprise all had to adjust their own plans according to this plan document. Even individuals felt to act according to plans. The central organs even directly led the yearly and quarterly plans of the enterprises and central organs even made monthly controls to guarantee the completion of the national plans. The enterprises were only restricted to make only action plans for their actual daily activities.

b) That the economic operation system of the USSR's planned economy contained a highly centralized administrative management style had another important aspect:

The method used in the execution of economic plans was administrative in such a sense that they ignored both the economic objectivity and majority of people's subjectivity, in other words their consciousness about their interests. One result of this was putting administrative measures and economic measures in an oppositional position. Here when I say economic measures I mean an attitude/management considering economic cause and effect when managing the economy and economic agents. Within this

---

20   The Modern History of the USSR (1917-1945), edited by Zhang Yide, Changchun, p. 288.

oppositional approach economic measures were ignored and the administrative measures were highly emphasized. The expressions of this approach or attitude were as follows: first, the raw materials, semi-products and technological supplied to the enterprises was realized in two ways, one way was planned central allocation, and the second way was non-centralized planned supply, but over 90% was realized by the way of planned central allocation. Thus enterprises were castrated as an economic agent, could not react to economic reality (namely to economic cause and effect) or market impulses.

Most of the goods (nearly all) were planned goods namely their production quantity and their prices were set central government organ. Only certain products were non-planned goods. Their production quantity were set by the People's Commissariat (Ministry) of Supply, or the regional Executive Committee of the USSR according to the autonomous management principle. That means autonomous management was very limited compared to centralized management mode/style.

Only less than 10% of the prices of the personal consumption goods were set by the People's Commissariat (Ministry) of Foods or local government.

Due to the detached type of relation between price and value in the Soviet economic system (this was one result of ignorance of economic cause and effect reality) enterprises had very little sense of cost value for their products. The prices of the means of production, the prices of the agricultural products of state-owned farms such as corns which were compulsorily sold to the state economic institutions were all lower than their cost values. But the prices of many other consumption products were higher than their cost values. Since the price setting was greatly detached separated from cost value, the enterprises which mainly produced (there is generally a basket of a product mix) first category products[21] mentioned above tried to cheat the planning authority by showing their total output value and net income less than the reality. Others which mainly produced second category products followed the reverse way in cheating. So economic reality and figures on the paper were largely divergent.

Due to this divergence between reality and figures on the paper the proportion of the industrial sectors in national economy was not truly reflected.

c) Third, the key or core criterion when setting the plan indicators (target figures) was not the enterprises' profit value, but the total output value. Even though the indicator system consisted a number of other indicators such as, quantity of goods produced, usage of new technology, productive forces of labor, number of staff, gross value of salaries, cost of products

---

21   First category products refers to those products which had prices lower than their prices.

(cost efficiency) and profitability, the criterion of the total output value enjoyed the most superior status. Either they produced finished products or the semi-finished products, the activity value of the industrial product or certain enterprise's product being processed, they were all accounted as the total output value by subtracting the part of the goods they have produced for their self-uses of the enterprises. This way of accounting system used by the Soviet enterprises law caused many overlapping or repeated calculations, which hindered to grasp the realistic situation, especially enterprise efficiency. "In addition, the enterprise managements generally aimed to use the loopholes of the planned system to earn easy rewards for their performance, one way they used in this respect was using expensive raw materials to increase the output value of their enterprises. Another way was producing more products that were easy to produce, or produce low quality and expensive goods. And some cheated the planning department by increasing the ratio of products which are produced for self-use in their product mix. In such a overtly administrative system it was very hard to lead the enterprises efficiently, please remember there were about 10 million different kinds of products to be produced by the Soviet planned economic system."[22]

Under the leadership of Stalin, the USSR employed the planned economic system, which played an important role in promoting the development of the socialist economy. Under the historical conditions at that time, planned economy has enabled the USSR become one of the most powerful economies of the world. On the other hand because Stalin's ideas on the relations between the plan and the market was the theoretical basis of the traditional planned economic system of the USSR and other socialist countries, his above ideas on the relations between the plan and the market has played a key role in the rigid economic system of the USSR and other socialist countries including China.

---

22   The Modern History of the USSR (1917-1945), edited by Zhang Yide, Changchun, p. 290.

Chapter VI

Stalin's Theory and Practice on Socialist Economic Development

Socialist revolution was first victorious in Russia, an economically and culturally backward country. However, the establishment, consolidation and development of socialist relations of production must have the corresponding material and technologicalbasis. To establish the material and technological basis of socialism, Stalin launched debates with Trotsky, Zinoviev, Kamenev and Bukharin one after the other, coming up with the theory of socialist industrialization and collectivization of agriculture. At the same time, to shatter the attack of the fascist imperialism, and to establish the material and technological basis that conformed with the requirement of the socialist relations of production, Stalin proposed the strategy of making use of science and technology to develop economy at a fast pace. Stalin's theory of the development of socialist economy was carried out in the USSR, making great achievements, but it also had some defects.

I. Stalin's thought and practice on socialist industrialization

In Stalin's opinion, to develop productive forces and establish the material basis of socialism, the socialist industrialization must be realized first. In Stalin's debates with Trotsky, Bukharin and other people, he did not only elaborate on the direction and speed of socialist industrialization, but also deeply analyze the source of funds for the industrialization in the USSR.

1. The development process of Stalin's thought on socialist industrialization

After Lenin's death, Stalin became the major leader of the party and the nation. As for the strategic goal of developing large-scale industry and realizing the national industrialization proposed by Lenin long time ago, there was not too much divergence within the Bolshevik Party. The divergence was how to achieve this goal, which was the problem of the path and policy of industrialization, on which there came serious confrontation and struggle. Stalin's thought on socialist industrialization was getting more and more mature in these debates and struggles.

The first debate was between Trotsky, Preobrajensky and Stalin and Bukharin. Trotsky first started from the situations in the country, thinking that large-scale industry is the "dominating factor" and the "basis of socialism"; that only by making efforts to develop state-owned industry, can the alliance of working class and peasantry and the proletarian dictatorship be consolidated so that the healthy development of national economy can be guaranteed. He pointed out, "the risk we are facing in practice is that the state-owned industry is falling behind the development of national economy."[1] The result of the struggle between the tendency of socialism and of capitalism was determined by the rate of development. "If the development of the state industry is lower than that of the agriculture, and the agriculture is increasingly dividing into two completely confronting groups... it is natural that this process will lead to the restoration of capitalism."[2] At the same time, from the perspective of the world, Trotsky emphasized the extreme importance of accelerating industrialization. "Comparing our total rate of development and the development rate of the world economy", "under the condition that the world economy and politics are confronting with each other, our development rate, also known as the increasing rate of the quality and quantity of our products, is determinant."[3] As for the source of the funds for industrialization, Trotsky thought the accumulation within the industry is an important source, but under the conditions that the workers have had very bad living conditions, this method should not be emphasized too much. "To increase the accumulation of the funds for industrialization, we must be determined... to carry out the policy of the redistribution of the national income."[4]

184

---

1   Speech of Trotsky, volume 2, p. 660, Beijing, SDX Joint Publishing Company, 1979.
2   ibid., p. 637-638
3   ibid., p. 643.
4   ibid., p. 832.

At the same time, Trotsky suggested investing in industry by stabilizing the currency, improving the circulation of the currency, limiting speculation and usury, extensivelyabsorbing private savings, carrying out long-term credit, etc; he also suggested that overcoming bureaucracy and reducing the losses caused by low working efficiency and inconsiderate plans. In addition, he recommended increasing the accumulation of funds by reducing the circulation expenses, accelerating the circulation of money and decreasing the nonproductive expenses. At the same time, he also thought that the funds accumulated from the foreign investment monopoly, foreign loans, concessions system and contracts of technical assistance should be correctly utilized as the supplementary sources of the funds for industrialization.

Preobrajensky thought the commercial crisis emerged in the USSR's economy in the early and mid 1920s was because of the shortage of industrial fixed funds; that the only way to overcome the crisis was to expand production by increasing the industrial fixed funds. So, where did the funds come from? Preobrajensky came up with the theory of "the law of the primitive accumulation of socialism". He thought that Russia was a country with very low level of productive force and the dominance of small peasants, so the accumulation of the funds for socialist industrialization cannot rely on exploiting colonies. The only way was to regard the small production as the "colonies" and even to make peasants break in order to provide funds to industrialization. "the task of the socialist country here was not to take less from the petty-bourgeoisie producers than that was taken by capitalism from them, but to take more from the extra income of the small producers who got the money because of the rationalization of the whole national economy, including the small-scale economy on the basis of national industrialization and the integration of agriculture."[5]

185

Stalin and Bukharin were strongly against the above opinion. They thought that in the national economy as a whole, the state owned economy that was playing the leading role and the peasant economy were contradicted with yet still closely related to each other. Without the accumulation from the peasant economy, the accumulation from the socialist industry would not be able to last long. The opposition lead by Trotsky only emphasized that the large-scale industry and the high speed were wrong. Only by developing circulation between rural and urban areas and between workers and peasants with a lot of efforts, activating agricultural economy, promoting the demand of peasants for consuming products and means of production and constantly increasing the capacity of the market, can the large-scale industry be provided with increasing accumulation, can the socialist industrialization and the rapid development of the whole national economy be promoted. They were against the policy of imposing heavy taxes on

5   Preobrajensky: The New Economics, p. 46, Beijing, SDX Joint Publishing Company, 1984.

peasants with mandatory administrative measures and increasing the price of industrial products, but they advocated for collecting progressive income tax from the rich bourgeoisie in the rural area. They also advocated for the policy of decreasing the price of industrial products, thinking that it can better satisfy the needs of the peasants, promote agricultural production and speed up commodity circulation and the combination of economy in rural and urban areas. Stalin's thought on industrialization had new development in this debate, but it was still not mature.

The second debate was between Stalin and Bukharin. It was during this debate that Stalin's thought on socialistindustrialization was relatively completely and clearly expressed. Bukharin thought the view that "transferring funds to the maximum from agriculture to industry can guarantee the maximum development speed of industry" was wrong; that "only with the combination of industry and the agriculture that has rapidly increased to the climax, can we keep the speed at the maximum in the long term" and that the development of industry must be "under the precondition that agriculture can have the real rapid accumulation."[6] He suggested that the pursuit of the high speed of industrialization did not mean that everything should be used for the basic construction. There was a problem of "the maximum" of accumulation and investment. When making the plan for the basic construction, we "must consider the reserve (foreign exchange reserve, money reserve, food reserve and commodity reserve)". We cannot just "stay on the theoretical level", or "play bureaucracy and games of number", or "build the factory of 'reality' with the 'bricks' of the 'future.'"[7]

Stalin was strongly against Bukharin's opinion above. He thought that to equip agriculture and transform peasants, we must greatly speed up the development of industry, impose heavy "tribute taxes" and limit private trade. Stalin did not only clearly put forward his opinion, but also made the critique on Bukharin's proposition on industrialization. Just as a foreign scholar had once said, at the end of the 1920s, "Stalin's mandatory and uncompromising decisions on development gradually took the dominant position within the party while the separation from Stalin's theory was regarded as the inclination to surrenderism and petty-bourgeoisie. In a certain period, the struggle against the Right deviation that was concealed from the party members and the masses was all over every field of the social life."[8] At the Joint Meeting of the Political Bureau of the Central Committee and the Presidium of the Central Control Committee, CPSU(B) at the end of January and the beginning of February, Stalin put forward to put the

6   Selected Works of Bukharin, volume 2, p. 279, Beijing, People's Publishing House, 1981.
7   ibid., p. 291-293.
8   Political Economy and Socialism of the USSR, p. 56, Shanghai, Translation Publishing House, 1983.

tolerance of the "Bukharin activists" to an end. At the same time, he called Bukharin's Notes of an Economist was "an anti-party article of eclecticism", which was aimed at delaying the development of industrialization. Stalin did not only criticize Bukharin's theory of industrialization from the perspective of ideology, but also launched the movement of "against the Right opportunism" in the USSR targeted at Bukharin's idea of industrialization. He also completely put his own ideas of socialist industrialization into the economic practice.

2. The development of heavy industry is the basis of industrialization

Stalin though it was the petty-bourgeoisie's view of socialism that the socialist system can be established and consolidated on the basis of backward small production. "The main task of the bourgeois revolution consists in seizing power and making it conforms to the already existing bourgeois economy, whereas the main task of the proletarian revolution consists, after seizing power, in building a new, socialist economy."[9] Where should we start to build the economic basis of socialism? Stalin thought it should first start from the socialist industrialization in the country. At the Fourteenth Congress of the CPSU(B) in December 1925, Stalin put forward the general line of socialist industrialization. He said at this conference that in the first phase of the NEP, the development of the whole national economy relied on agriculture. "Now we have entered into the second phase. The most important and outstanding feature of our economy is that the economic center now has shifted to industry", so we have to "put our focus on industry."[10] From the last half of the 1920s, there came the "commodity shortage" in the USSR's economy, which Stalin thought was also caused by the backwardness of industry.

Recovery and development of agriculture and provision of enough food, raw materials and market are the necessary preconditions of industrialization. Stalin quoted Lenin's words that"developing industry must start from agriculture."[11]

Since 1921 when the Soviet power was established, the recovery and development of agriculture were started. By 1925, agriculture had recovered 87% of the prewar level. In Stalin's opinion, the necessary conditions for socialized economy were satisfied.

---

9   Selected Works of Stalin, volume 1, p. 402. (Retrieved from Marxists Internet Archive)
10 Collected Works of Stalin, volume 8, p. 111.
11 Selected Works of Stalin, volume 1, p. 460.

In the process of industrialization, Stalin attached great importance to the effect of the means of production on the expansion of socialist reproduction. He pointed out, "a fast rate of development of industry in general, and of the production of the means of production in particular, is the underlying principle of, and the key to, the industrialization of the country, the underlying principle of, and the key to, the transformation of our entire national economy along the lines of socialist development."[12] And "The relatively higher rate of expansion of production of means of production is necessary not only because it has to provide the equipment both for its own plants and for all the other branches of the national economy, but also because reproduction on an extended scale becomes altogether impossible without it."[13]

Stalin thought that in capitalist countries, industrialization usually started from light industry. That was determined by the law of development of productive forces under capitalist system and the capitalist class' nature of pursuing profits. The reason was compared with heavy industry, light industry required less investment and had a faster capital turnover. Therefore it was easy to get profits. That was why the capitalists would like to first develop industry as the beginning of industrialization. Due to the regularity of the capitalist economic development, after a period of time, the profits accumulated by light industry would gradually flow into heavy industry, creating conditions for the development of heavy industry. This was a very long process of industrialization that could take decades even hundreds of years. However, for the USSR, to ensure the economy of the USSR was independent from the world capital while it was encircled by capitalism, not the development of any industry would count as industrialization. In the USSR, there were some people who thought the socialist industrialization is the development of any industry. There were even such "weirdoes" in the USSR who thought that Ivan the Terrible who had created some sort of industrial embryo was already an industrialist. By that logic, Peter the Great should have been called the first industrialist. Stalin was strongly against these formulations. He pointed out that not any one of the industries could be counted as industrialization. The center and basis of industrialization was to develop the heavy industry (fuels, metal, etc.). All in all, industrialization was the development of the production of the means of production and the development of the domestic machine manufacturing industry. He thought that only by giving development priority to heavy industry can the whole industry, transportation and agriculture be developed on the basis of new technology so that the whole national economy can develop at a faster pace; can we get rid of the dependence on the foreign capitalist economy and become economically independent; can the power of national defense

188

---

12   Selected Works of Stalin, volume 2, p. 76. (Retrieved from Marxists Internet Archive)
13   Selected Works of Stalin, volume 2, p. 589. (Retrieved from Marxists Internet Archive)

be strengthened. The USSR's "industrialization has the task not only of increasing the share of manufacturing industry in our national economy as a whole; it has also the task, within this development, of ensuring economic independence for our country, surrounded as it is by capitalist states, of safeguarding it from being converted into an appendage of world capitalism."[14]

Judging from practice, when the industrialization started, the USSR greatly increased investment in heavy industry. Before industrialization, from 1918 to 1928, the investment in heavy industry only took up 11.9% of the total investment. In the period of the first five-year plan, the investment increased to 32.0%. In the whole period of the industrialization, the proportion was about 30%, sometimes even reached 40% while the investment in light industry had never been higher than 7%, sometimes only 4%. The investment on agriculture has started to decrease since the first five-year plan. For example, in the period of the first five-year plan, the proportion of the agricultural investment was 15.5%; it was 11.8% in the period of the second five-year plan, 10.7% in the period of the third five-year plan and only 9.3% from 1941 to 1945. On the perspective of the outcome of development, there was a huge gap between heavy industry, light industry and agriculture. For example, from 1926 when industrialization started to 1940 before the war, heavy industry had increased 18.4 times with the average annual growth rate of 21.9%, but light industry had only increased 6.2 times with the average annual growth rate of 14.1%. In the same period, agriculture had only increased 26%, with the average annual growth rate of only 1.5%.

In the process of industrialization, Stalin tried to coordinate the relations between the development of heavy industry and that of light industry. As mentioned above, as early as the industrialization started, headed by Stalin, the central authority of the USSR's Communist Party had strictly criticized the so-called "super industrialization" policy, which is to achieve industrialization at a super fast pace by sacrificing agriculture and people's life. In 1927, the Fifteenth Congress of the CPSU(B) clearly pointed out that the development of heavy industry and light industry must be combined in the best way considering the proportions they took up. It was right to put the focus of heavy industry on the production of the means of production. At the same time, it must be estimated the risk that the state had too much funds laid idle on the large construction projects that would take years to be able to sell their products in the market. When the first five-year plan was completed, considering that heavy industry had already had the basis to some extent, but agriculture and light industry were comparatively backward and that the market supply was in short, Stalin had come up with some ideas of adjusting the policy of economic construction. In the report to the

---

14   Collected Works of Stalin, volume 8, p. 113. (Retrieved from Marxists Internet Archive)

Sixteenth Congress of the CPSU(B), Stalin pointed out, "we have already restored heavy industry. Now it only needs to be developed further. Now we can turn to light industry and push it forward at an accelerated pace. One of the new features in the development of our industry is that we are now in a position to develop both heavy and light industry at an accelerated pace."[15] This congress established the adjusted policy of developing agriculture and light industry at an accelerated pace, improving people's live and properly slowing down the pace of the development of heavy industry. However, the policy made at this congress had not been completed put into practice.

3. The pace of industrialization and the source of funds

In terms of the pace of industrialization, Stalin advocated for the fast-pace development. First, from the external and internal conditions of the USSR, Stalin analyzed the objective requirement of realizing industrialization with an accelerated rate. In terms of the external conditions, the USSR was a country with very backward technology while there were a lot of capitalist countries with advanced technology and under development. Stalin emphasized that the only way to insure the economic independence of the USSR and keep it from becoming an appendage of the capitalist countries was to transform the USSR from a country that imported equipment into a country that can make the equipment itself. "We are fifty or a hundred years behind the advanced countries. We must make good this distance in ten years. Either we do it, or we shall go under."[16] At the same time, Stalin also emphasized from the perspective of strengthening national defense that only by following the general line of industrialization can the USSR have great power of national defense to resist the invasion of imperialism. He said, "we could not know just when the imperialists would attack the U.S.S.R. and interrupt our work of construction; but that they might attack us at any moment, taking advantage of the technical and economic weakness of our country—of that there could be no doubt. That is why the Party was obliged to spur the country on, so as not to lose time, so as to make the utmost use of the respite and to create in the U.S.S.R. the basis of industrialization which is the foundation of its might."[17]

Judging from the internal conditions, although the period of the national economy recovery had finished in the USSR, it was still a backward agricultural country. There were a lot of defects in industry; heavy industry was particularly weak, not to mention a complete industrial system. At the same time, in Stalin's opinion, the scattered and backward small agricultural

---

15 Collected Works of Stalin, first Chinese version, volume 12, p. 289. (Retrieved from Marxists Internet Archive)

16 Collected Works of Stalin, first, volume 13, p. 38. (Retrieved from Marxists Internet Archive)

17 ibid., p. 168. (Retrieved from Marxists Internet Archive)

production still took the absolutely dominant position. Under such circumstances, if the USSR did not develop the socialist large-scale industry rapidly, economically and technologically transform the small-peasant economy into the socialist large-scale agriculture with advanced technology, there would be the possibility of restoration of capitalism within the USSR, which means that the USSR had not established socialism. For the USSR, "on the one hand, we in our country have the most advanced system, the Soviet system, and the most advanced type of state power in the world, Soviet power, while, on the other hand, our industry, which should be the basis of socialism and of Soviet power, is extremely backward technically."[18] Therefore, it was right to catch up with and exceed the advanced technology owned by the developed capitalist countries, not only from the perspective of establishing socialism, but also from the perspective of the independence of the USSR in the encirclement of the capitalism.

Although Stalin advocated for achieving industrialization at a fast pace, he especially emphasized that industrialization should be on the basis of national strength and carried out according to the ability of the country; that the economic construction cannot be separated from the basis of the national strength. He said, "Among us there is sometimes a fondness for drawing up fantastic industrial plans, without taking our actual resources into account. People sometimes forget that you can build neither industrial plans nor any "broad" and "all-embracing" enterprises without a certain minimum of funds, a certain minimum of reserves. They forget this and run too far ahead. And what does running too far ahead in the matter of industrial planning mean? It means building beyond your resources."[19]

191

To achieve the socialist industrialization, large amount of funds were needed. Therefore, Stalin listed the different ways of accumulating funds in the history of industrialization. First is to accumulate funds by invading and exploiting the colonies, such as what Britain did. Second is to accumulating by asking for the war indemnity, such as Germany. Third is to develop industry with slavery loans, such as the Tsarist Russia. The common feature of the three ways is they all relied on the "added capital" from abroad to establish the capitalist industrialized countries, but none of them is acceptable to socialist countries. The USSR is going to take the fourth path. That is to rely on the internal forces of the country, "to find funds for industry out of our own savings, the way of socialist accumulation, to which Comrade Lenin repeatedly drew attention as the only way of industrializing our country."[20]

18   Collected Works of Stalin, volume 11, p. 214. (Retrieved from Marxists Internet Archive).
19   Collected Works of Stalin, volume 8, p. 120-121. (Retrieved from Marxists Internet Archive)
20   ibid., p. 115. (Retrieved from Marxists Internet Archive)

There were mainly two sources for the accumulation of this kind. "First is the working class that created value and pushed industry forward; second is the peasantry."[21] Specifically, the main sources of socialist accumulation were: (1) robbing the property of landlords and capitalists, which was a huge source of accumulation; (2) abolishing the foreign debt of the Tsar and using the funds for industrial accumulation; (3) development of the nationalized industry; (4) developing foreign trade, expanding export and increasing foreign exchange reserve; (5) developing the domestic trade market, increasing food reserve, paying attention to the leverage of price, tightening the loopholes and preventing funds from flowing into the pocket of capitalists; (6) making use of the banking system, which is the leverage of accumulation to accumulate funds by issuing domestic government bonds, improving the credit network and improving the profit rate of the funds; (7) accumulation from agriculture. Among these sources of funds for industrialization, Stalin pointed out that "Nationalized land, nationalized industry, nationalized transport and credit, monopoly of foreign trade and state-regulated domestic trade—these are all new sources of "extra capital," which can be used for developing our country's industry, and which hitherto no bourgeois state has possessed."[22]

When the industrialization started, the USSR acutely increased the proportion of the accumulated funds used for the expansion of reproduction in the national income while correspondingly greatly decreasing the proportion of the funds for consumption. In 1925, the proportion of the accumulate funds was only 16%, but by 1932 at the end of the first five-year plan, this number had increased to 27% and kept at about 30% during the period of industrialization. This number before the war in 1913 was only 9%. The USSR also absorbed the funds from residents by taxes, government bonds and one-time donations. In the period of the first five-year plan, the total amount of paid tax by the residents increased 2.3 times and the issued amount of the government bonds increased 4.4 times. At the same time, the USSR also accumulated the funds by issuing notes. Under the circumstances that the industrial output valued increase one time but the agricultural output value almost did not increase at that time, the amount of currency circulation increased 4 times. It was originally planned to issue the notes of 1.25 billion rubles, but actually additional notes of 4 billion rubles were issued.

Stalin thought it was a good way of accumulating funds for industry from agriculture by making use of the scissors difference that existed in the prices of industrial and agricultural products. That was because, on the one hand, industry was still very young and needed to take the funds from agriculture; on the other hand, it would take some time for the rationalization

---

21   Collected Works of Stalin, first Chinese version, volume 11, p. 115.
22   Collected Works of Stalin, volume 7, p. 166. (Retrieved from Marxists Internet Archive)

of the technology of production in industry and the operationand management, so it was not possible for the price of the industrial products to decrease to a very low level. Stalin suggested the basic line that which the industry must follow. That is to gradually reduce the scissors difference, systematically reduce the cost of the industrial products and systematically reduce the price of the industrial products.[23]

However, at the same time, Stalin thought in order to "keep the rapid development of industry", it was necessary for the peasants to "pay more when purchasing industrial products, but to take less whey selling the agricultural products."[24] When the industrialization had started, the USSR immediately carried out the "compulsory sale of agricultural products to the state". Since the purchase price was very low, the so-called compulsory sale to the state was actually the tax in a different form, "something in the nature of a tribute". Generally, the price that the USSR paid to the peasants for the agricultural products was only 10% of the cost of the products, some even lower. From 1927 to 1940, the price for peasants to buy the industrial products increased 5.5 times, but in the same period, the price of the agricultural products had only increased 2.3 times.

When Stalin was talking about the sources of funds for socialized industrialization, he particularly mentioned vodka monopoly, which was a transitional method. As early as in the Lenin period, to raise funds to maintain the currency system and recover industry, the Soviet power had no choice but to conduct the vodka monopoly since it had no way to get foreign loans. Vodka is a disaster, bad for both people's health and the development of production. It would be more harmful if it was controlled by foreign capital. At the beginning of industrialization, the vodka monopoly was lasted, providing 0.5 billion rubles as the funds for industrialization. Stalin criticized that it was a huge mistake that some people assumed to build socialism wearing white gloves; that to insure the victory of the proletariat and the peasantry, there was no choice but to be infected with some dirty stuff; that as soon as there was the new source of funds for the development of industrialization, the vodka monopoly would definitely be called off.

Stalin said that the funds for industrialization were hard-earned so they must be reasonably used with particular attention. He said, living on the funds that we ourselves accumulate, we must be exceptionally frugal and restrained in spending accumulated funds; we must try to invest every kopek wisely, i.e., in such undertakings as it is absolutely essential to develop at the given moment.[25]

---

23   Collected Works of Stalin, volume 9, p. 175, Beijing, People's Publishing House, 1954. (Retrieved from Marxists Internet Archive)
24   Collected Works of Stalin, first Chinese version, volume 12, p. 45.
25   Collected Works of Stalin, volume 7, p. 249. (Retrieved from Marxists Internet Archive)

He thought it was extremely important to reasonably and economically spend the funds and the method was hard to grasp instantly. We must make every effort to keep the accumulation from getting scattered or embezzled. The funds should be spent for the best use and in conformity with the basic police of industrial construction. Therefore, Stalin suggested streamlining the administrative structure, to eliminate the phenomenon of extravagance and waste and to stop the "happy" stealing of the state property. He also pointed that the problem of absence had made industry lose thousands of working days millions of rubles in vain. It would harm industry and the working class if the phenomenon of absence was not eliminated or the productive forces of labor was not improved. To achieve industrialization and reduce the waste of the state funds, it was required to strictly conduct the regime of economy and avoid any unnecessary or non-productive expenditure. In June 1926, the Central Executive Committee and the People's Commissariat of the USSR particularly passed the resolution on the conduct of the regime of economy, which was required to be conducted in the strictest way in state-owned factories and cooperative economic institutions. It also required that the activities such as abuse, waste or not saving the funds of the state and the cooperatives must be firmly stopped; that the rationalization of every economic and administrative sector must be continuously strengthened.

4. A brief evaluation

When Marx explained the precondition of expanded reproduction in social production in the volume 2 of the Capital, he emphasized on the role that the means of production played in the expanded reproduction.Under the new historical conditions, Lenin made further development of Marx's thought. He thought that under the circumstances that the constant progress of technology had led to the increase of the organic composition of capital, the means of production that was used to produce the means of production increased the fastest. Second was the means of production that was used to produce means of subsistence. The slowest was the production of the means of subsistence. The prior increase of the means of production was mainly manifested in the prior increase of heavy industry. In November 1922, Lenin pointed out, "the salvation of Russia lies not only in a good harvest on the peasant farms—that is not enough; and not only in the good condition of light industry, which provides the peasantry with consumer goods—this, too, is not enough; we also need heavy industry." "Unless we save heavy industry, unless we restore it, we shall not be able to build up an industry at all; and without an industry we shall go under as an independent, country."[26] Therefore, Stalin's industrial thought was the succession of Marx and Lenin's thought.

---

26 Collected Works of Lenin, volume 43, p. 282. (Retrieved from Marxists Internet Archive)

Before the October Revolution, although the capitalist economy had had some development in Russia, it basically was just a backward feudalagrarian country, with very little modern industry and very weak material and technological foundation of national economy. By 1913, the output value of industrial products took up a little bit more than 40% of the total industrial and agricultural output value, only 1/3 being the means of production and mostly being the means of subsistence. The proportion of the modern large-scale industry was very low. The machine manufacturing industry only took up 6.8% of the total industrial output value. The whole industry, especially the large-scale industry was very much dependent on foreign capital. The major large modernized enterprises were all controlled by foreign capital with most of the industrial equipment relying on import.

The basis of industry, even though as weak as mentioned above, was still seriously damaged in the first World War and the period of the armed intervention of the foreign countries. By 1920 when the civil war was over, the industrial output value in Russia was only 13.8% of that in 1913 before the war, with pig iron taking up 2.4%, cotton yarn 5%, sugar 6.6% and vegetable oil 3.4%.[27] Faced by such a difficult situation, one of the important tasks of the Russian people led by Lenin was to recover the production and develop the large-scale industry. Lenin had attached great importance to establishing and developing large-scale industry, regarding it as the material foundation of establishing, consolidating and developing socialism. At the Third Congress of the Communist International, Lenin had clearly pointed out in the Outline of the Report on the Tactics of the Communist Party that "the material foundation of socialism can only be the large-scale mechanized industry that can transform agriculture at the same time."[28] That is because the large-scale mechanized industry is the manifestation of a more advanced way of social production. Only that socialist industry replaces capitalist production and petty-bourgeoisie production can be the biggest source of the power needed by beating down the bourgeoisie and the single insurance to guarantee the victory.[29]

From 1920 when the civil war was over, the Soviet government shifted the focus of work to the recovery of economy, making a series of policies to develop industry, such as giving permission to some daily-necessities-making enterprises of small-scale industry or handicraft industry to temporarily resume capitalist production, non-nationalization of some small enterprises, giving permission to concession of the state-owned enterprises, etc. However, by 1924, the industrial production had not reached to the level before the war.

27   The History of the National Economy of the USSR, volume 3, p. 77, Beijing, People's Publishing House, 1960.
28   Selected Works of Lenin, volume 42, p. 7, Beijing, People's Publishing House, 1987.
29   Selected Works of Lenin, volume 4, p. 13, Beijing, People's Publishing House, 1995.

Stalin's thought on industrialization had very obvious positive influence in practice. He led the USSR to successfully achieve the socialist industrialization. By 1925, the total industrial output value was up to 75% of the level in 1913 and surpasses the prewar level by 1926. In 1937, the socialist industry of the USSR took up 77.4% in the total output industrial and agricultural industry. In the industrial structure, the proportion of the means of production was 57.8%. By then, the USSR had completed the mission of industrialization within only 13 years. The same job took the capitalist countries decades even hundreds of years to finish. The industrialization of the USSR had made great achievements, no matter from the perspective of the annual growth rate or from the comparison with the capitalist countries at that time. From the first five-year plan to 1940, the whole in industry of the USSR increased 5.5 times, with the average annual growth rate of 16.9%, out of which, heavy industry increased 9 times, with the average annual growth rate of 21.2%. This was something that had never happened in the history of industrialization. The fast increase of industry of in the USSR and the financial crisis in the capitalist countries at that time had made a clear comparison. For example, in the period of the first five-year plan from 1929 to 1932, the industry of the USSR increased over one time while that of the United States decreased 42%, Britain 18%, Germany 39%, France 26% and 33% in the whole capitalist world. In 1938, compared with 1913,

the industry of the USSR increased more than 8 times while the United States only increased 20%, Britain 13.3%, Germany 31.6% and France -6.8%. Some scholars abroad also affirmed that the industry of the USSR had made great achievements in the Stalin period. The American author Strong said in her book The Stalin Era that "never in history was so great an advance so swift."[30]

However, Stalin's thought on industrialization one-sidedly emphasized on the development of heavy industry, seriously affecting the improvement of people's living standard. Mao Zedong in On the Ten Major Relationships had criticized the above mentioned practice of the USSR. He pointed out that the USSR's "lop-sided stress on heavy industry to the neglect of agriculture and light industry results in a shortage of goods on the market and an unstable currency."[31]

---

30 Strong: The Stalin Era, p. 38, Beijing, China Financial and Economic Publishing House, 1985. (Retrieved from Marxists Internet Archive)
31 Selected Works of Mao Zedong, volume 7, p. 24, Beijing, People's Publishing House, 1999. (Retrieved from Marxists Internet Archive)

II. Stalin's thought on agricultural collectivization and agricultural development

To avoid hindering industrialization, promote the development of the whole national economy, the socialist agriculture must be developed at a fast pace. However, one of the outstanding features of Stalin's thought on the development of socialist agriculture was to combine the agricultural development and the change of the relations of production and to regard the collectivization as the precondition and basis of the development of agriculture. Stalin's exploration and practice on the collectivization of agriculture strongly supported the development of industrialization and guaranteed the establishment of the socialist relations of production in the rural areas, but it had obvious defects in improving the productive forces in the rural areas.

1. The idea of developing agriculture by collectivization of agriculture

Lenin once pointed out, "in a country of small peasants…unless we achieve a practical and massive improvement in small-scale peasant farming, there is no salvation for us. Unless this basis is created, no economic development will be possible and the most ambitious plans will be valueless."[32] Therefore, the recovery and development of agriculture were a big problem that was directly related to the destiny of the Soviet power. The primary issue of the home and foreign policy was to develop economy of every sector with agricultural development as the first one. As the civil war was over and the NEP started to be conducted, Lenin determined that the primary task of the party was to adjust the relations between workers and peasants. Therefore, he made and conducted the measures from the two aspects, which satisfied the interest of the peasants as the producers of small commodity. By doing so, it also combined the interest of the workers and the peasants with the task of socialist construction and transformation. The first measure was to substitute the surplus grain appropriation system with the tax in kind and allow the peasants to pay the tax by freely selling their surplus products. The second measure was to solve the problem through the cooperatives and by further developing and improving the cooperative system. The initial practice of the agricultural cooperation strongly proved that Lenin's plan of cooperatives was right. At the beginning of the NEP, the agricultural production did not immediately start to expand. Plus there came the serious drought in 1921, making the agricultural production further in decline with the continuous decrease of the output. It was from 1922 when the agriculture of the USSR really started to recover. Due to the right

197

---

32   Collected Works of Lenin, volume 4, p. 354. (Retrieved from Marxists Internet Archive)

policy at that time, the grain output was 72.47 million tons in 1925, which was 95% of the output in 1913 and a 60% increase compared with the number in 1920. In the one-year period from 1925 to 1926, the total agricultural output value reached 9.746 billion rubles, which was 95.3% of the total agricultural output value in the 1913-1914 year period.

After Lenin's death, the agricultural socialist transformation of the USSR was led by Stalin. At that time, the industrialization of the USSR was rapidly developing, but the agriculture, which was based on individual economy, developed very slowly. As the major sector of agriculture, the output of grain had not been 91% of the prewar level until 1927. The amounts of grain as commodity was even less with only 37% of the pre-War level and the tendency of decreasing continuously. To change this situation, at the Fifteenth Congress of the CPSU(B) at the end of 1927, Stalin put forward the issue of transforming agriculture with the collectivization of agriculture and new technology. He pointed out that the solution of agriculture was "to turn the small and scattered peasant farms into large united farms based on cultivation of the land in common, to go over to collective cultivation of the land on the basis of a new and higher technique."[33]

As for how to achieve the economic development of agriculture of the USSR via the collectivization of agriculture, Stalin had different methods in different periods. In the mid 1920s, he had clearly said that under the new conditions that the proletariat had got the political power and had the economic lifelines in hand, they must develop along the other road, on which different forms of cooperatives were united by the small business owners in the rural areas. Here Stalin was trying to complete the reform of the social system in rural areas in the USSR by organizing cooperative as it was a gradual approach.

In the mid and late 1920s, Stalin still thought that at the current stage, the focus was on further improving the individual economy of the middle and small peasants, but as a supplement, the collective farms must be established and the state-owned farms must be developed. The individual economy still had the potential of development, which should be helped to improve the productive forces of labor, increase the output per unit area, replace the wood plough with the iron one and provide the small and medium size machinery. In addition, the individual economy can also be helped by the provision of large-size machinery via the agricultural instrument rental station, the supply of seeds and fertilizer, the assistance of agricultural science and technology, the peasants' participation in the cooperatives and signing the forward purchasing contract with them. It was also pointed out it was wrong to think that the individual economy should be struggled

33 Collected Works of Stalin, volume 10, p. 261. (Retrieved from Marxists Internet Archive).

against and eliminated rather than supported; it was also wrong to think that individual economy was nothing but the ignorance of the collective and state-owned farms.

However, in April 1929, in *The Right Deviation in the CPSU(B)*, Stalin systematically criticized the economic proposition of Bukharin and other people, especially the plan of comprehensively developing individual economy and reducing the pace of development of the collective and state-owned farms. He thought that the conditions for the USSR to develop collective and state-owned farms with large quantity was satisfied and required to launch the masses' movement of establishing collective and state-owned farms. In November 1929, Stalin wrote *A Year of Great Change*, in which he emphasized on the fundamental change from the small-peasant economy to the socialist agriculture when talking about the productive forces of labor and the achievement of industrial construction. He thought that the new and decisive feature of the present collective-farm movement is that the peasants are joining the collective farms not in separate groups, as was formerly the case, but by whole villages, volosts, districts, and even okrugs, which means that the middle peasant is joining the collective farm. And that is the basis of that radical change in the development of agriculture.[34]

Some foreign scholars divided Stalin's thought of the collectivization of agriculture in the 1920s into two totally different phases. For example, the former Soviet Union scholar Medvedev thought that the large-scale collectivization of agriculture in the USSR at the end of 1920s had "declared the war to the peasant economy, just a year ago, it was against by nobody else but Stalin himself."[35] Actually, Stalin's thought on the transformation of the rural areas in the USSR was greatly different from the practice, but in terms of building the socialist economic foundation in rural areas, the theory and the practice were still related with each other and in the same direction. Just as what he said, "The Party's task: to extend and consolidate our socialist key positions in all branches of the national economy, both in town and country, pursuing a course towards the elimination of the capitalist elements from the national economy."[36]

How should the collectivization of agriculture be carried out? Stalin thought that the small-peasant economy was the economy that at crossroads. To transform from the small-peasant economy to the large-scale agriculture, there were two roads. One was the capitalist road that made the bourgeoisie in urban areas became rich by breaking most of the peasants, which was firmly denied by Stalin. The other was to bring the peasants to

34 Collected Works of Stalin, volume 12, p. 118,Retrieved from Marxists Internet Archive.
35 The Road of the Collectivization of Agriculture and Its Lessons, Rural Life, March 11, 1989.
36 Collected Works of Stalin, volume 19, p. 256. (Retrieved from the Marxist Internet Archive)

the road of common development of socialism by attracting the peasants to participate in the socialist construction via the collectivization, which was fully agreed by Stalin. At the beginning of the collectivization of agriculture, Stalin used to assume to unite the thousands of hundreds of peasants around the socialist industry and gradually lead them to the road of collectivization by various forms of cooperative system, ranging from sales cooperative, trading cooperative and productive cooperative (collective farms). He used to clearly point out: under the new conditions, when the proletariat is in power and holds in its hands all the basic threads of our economy, development must proceed along a different path, along the path of uniting the small proprietors of the villages in all kinds of co-operative societies, which will be backed by the state in their struggle against private capital; along the path of gradually drawing the millions of small peasant proprietors into socialist construction through the co-operatives; along the path of gradually improving the economic conditions of the small peasant proprietors (and not of impoverishing them).[37] Just because of this, the cooperative had a great development. The commodity supply to the rural areas held by the consumers' cooperative had increased from 25.6% in the year period of 1924-1925 to 50.8% in the year period of 1926-1927.

Stalin thought that the small-peasant economy was fragile and backward with very little strength. It was unable to take new agricultural machinery and techniques, cultivate the new land, expand the cultivated area or largely improve the output. It also had very low productive forces of labor and the commodity rate of agricultural products. To the natural disaster, the small-peasant economy had no way to resist. Some peasants, out of different reasons, lived a very poor life so that they had no choice but to borrow the usury and get exploited by the kulak, making the life more difficult. Between 1927 and 1928, the USSR had a very serious grain procurement crisis. The most important reason of the crisis was the backwardness of the small-peasant economy. Stalin thought, "the basis of our grain difficulties lies in the increasingly scattered and divided character of agriculture. It is a fact that agriculture, especially grain farming, is growing smaller in scale, becoming increasingly less remunerative and less productive of marketable surpluses. Whereas before the revolution we had about 15,000,000 or 16,000,000 peasant farms, now we have some 24,000,000 or 25,000,000; moreover, the process of division tends to become more marked."[38] The scattered small-peasant economy was not conformed with the needs of socialist industrialization or not good for the development of the productive forces. Therefore the collectivization of agriculture must be achieved.

---

37 Collected Works of Stalin, volume 5, p. 263. (Retrieved from Marxists Internet Archive).
38 Collected Works of Stalin, volume 11, p. 156. (Retrieved from Marxists Internet Archive)

Stalin also elaborated on the reasons to promote the all-embracing collectivization. First, the USSR cannot be established on two different economic bases for a long time. He asked if, in a very long time, the soviet Power and the socialist course can be built on two different basis, or specifically, on the basis of the largest and the most unified socialist industry and of the most scattered and backward peasants' small commodity economy? No, they cannot. If things went on like this, one day that whole national economy would break up. Second, the small-peasant economy had had not extra space to develop. Stalin thought that most of the small-peasant economy cannot make any reproduction that can be expanded every year. Not only that, it cannot even conduct the simple reproduction. Therefore, only by transforming this kind of agriculture into the large-scale agriculture, making it able to accumulate and expand the reproduction, can it be the agricultural basis need for the development of the large-scale industry. To do that, there were two ways, the capitalist way and the socialist way. The Soviet power can choose nothing but the socialist way, which means the all-round collectivization of agriculture.[39] Third, the problem of the grain procurement and the industrial accumulation should be solved by conducting the all-round collectivization of agriculture.

Correspondingly, Stalin thought that the cooperatives, collective and state-owned farms are the only solution of the agricultural problems of the USSR. As the industrialization had taken great progress, the number of staff and the urban population sharply increased, with the increase of demand for grains. The increase rate of agricultural production and the supply of grain had become less and less conformed with the needs of the national economy in the period of the construction of industrialization. The productive forces of labor and the commodity rate of the small-peasant economy were very low, so in order to solve the grain problem, "the way out lies…in passing from small, backward and scattered peasant farms to united, large socially-conducted farms… capable of producing the maximum amount of marketable grain" and making "the transition from individual peasant farming to collective, socially-conducted economy in agriculture", because the "large-scale farming, irrespective of whether it is landlord, kulak or collective farming… produce the maximum quantity of marketable grain."[40]

In Stalin's opinion, Soviet Union could push the peasant economy into the socialist economic construction system, establish the Sovhoz and co-operative production system and practice the scientific method of intensive agriculture by using the advanced machinery and tractors. Therefore, Stalin optimistically thought that if the development of the collective farms

39 Collected Works of Stalin, volume 12, p. 129-130.
40 Collected Works of Stalin, volume 11, p. 77, 73. (Retrieved from Marxists Internet Archive)

and state farms was accelerated, "there was no reason to doubt that in about three years' time" Soviet Union "would be one of the world's largest grain producers, if not the largest."[41]

2. The ways and means of the collectivization of agriculture

In the process of the collectivization, Stalin emphasized that it must be conducted on a voluntary basis with the demonstration of typical examples; that it must be conducted in accordance with the different conditions in different regions without mandatory orders, over-simplification, impatience or premature advance. He used to point out that the way out is to unite the small and dwarf peasant farms gradually but surely, not by pressure, but by example and persuasion, into large farms based on common, co-operative, collective cultivation of the land with the use of agricultural machines and tractors and scientific methods of intensive agriculture.[42]

At the beginning of the collectivization of agriculture, Stalin emphasized the policy of "relying on poor peasants, consolidating the alliance with middle peasants and the strong objection to the kulaks". In March 1919, at the Eighth Congress of the Party, Lenin pointed out in the opening remarks that in a country of small peasants, the most difficult and arduous task was how to treat the middle peasants. He also pointed out, "we have entered such a stage of socialist construction. At the moment we must make the detailed basic rules that have been tested out by the working experience in rural areas to instruct and guide out action in order to make sure our position of consolidating the alliance with the middle peasants."[43] Stalin pointed out that Lenin's slogan was the most accurate and appropriate expression of the party's guideline; that reaching an agreement with the middle peasant, which meant forming an alliance with the middle peasant, was not a short-term of occasional policy but a long-term one. By combining the practice in rural areas, he also emphasized Lenin's slogan. And with a short formula, he also expressed his thought: (1) relying on the poor peasant; (2) reaching agreement with the middle peasants; (3) non-stop fighting against kulaks. These ideas accurately grasped the three-in-one task in the work in rural areas. The three aspects cannot be separated or taken out one with the other two left. Otherwise it would be very easy to make mistakes. With the operation of the NEP, how would the class structure be changed in the USSR? In the mid 1920s, Stalin pointed out the unique form of differentiation in rural areas. As for the differentiation under capitalist system, the number

---

41 Collected Works of Stalin, volume 12, p. 118. (Retrieved from Marxists Internet Archive)
42 Collected Works of Stalin, volume 10, p. 261. (Retrieved from Marxists Internet Archive)
43 Collected Works of Lenin, , volume 36, p. 117, Beijing, People's Publishing House, 1985.

of poor and rich peasants increased while the middle peasants were melted away, but under the Soviet power, the poor peasants gradually decreased, the rich peasants increased a little bit and the middle peasants also increased with some poor peasants upgrading to the middle peasants. However, the land nationalization, the elimination of the private ownership of the land, the state's policy of tax, credit and cooperation and the raid development of the socialist industry all had certain influence and limitation on the spontaneous process of differentiation and therefore led the rural economy to the road of socialist transformation.

Between 1927 and 1928, the USSR had the grain procurement crisis. The grain procured at the end of 1927 struggled to reach 4.91 million tons, which was 210 tons less than that of 1926, but the commodity grain the state need was 8.2 million tons. Different from the background of the grain crisis at the beginning of the civil war, this crisis broke out under a good economic situation. In August 1926, the National Planning Committee made and submitted the control figure of the 1926-1927 year period to the Labor and Defense Council, estimating that the procurement of grain could increase 9% than the last year period, and the commodity rate of all agricultural products would increase 18% with 16% increase of the commodity rate of grain. The emergence of the grain procurement crisis was completely out of Stalin's expectation. For example, on October 23, 1927 when Stalin was talking about agriculture, he did not see the difficulty of the procurement that was coming.[44] Until March to April of 1928, Stalin admitted that the grain procurement crisis at the end of 1927 was out of his expectation.[45]

203

When the grain procurement started, Stalin proposed three ways out to solve the grain problem. First was to establish the collective farms; second was to develop the state farms; third was to improve individual peasant economy. He thought the focus at the current stage was still to further improve the small and middle peasant economy. There was still some possibility for the development of the individual peasant economy and the possibilityshould be well achieved by some assistance.[46] Therefore, the Soviet government should help it improve productive forces of labor and the output per unit area. Stalin pointed out: all the data show that the yield of peasant farms can be increased by some 15 to 20 per cent in the course of a few years. At present no less than 5 million wooden ploughs are in use in our country. Their replacement by modern ploughs alone would result in a very considerable increase in grain production in the country. This is apart from supplying the peasant farms with a certain minimum of fertilizers, selected seed, small machines, etc. He even optimistically thought that on this

44   Collected Works of Stalin, first Chinese version, volume 10, p. 169-172.
45   Collected Works of Stalin, first Chinese version, volume 11, p. 31.
46   ibid., p. 157.

basis, within three or four years, the grain would increase no less than 100 million puds. The grain procurement crisis had made the forward purchase contract attached with great importance. Stalin thought the contract system is "is the best method of raising the yield of peasant farms and of drawing the peasants into the co-operatives."[47]

Stalin was against the view that the individual should be fought against and eliminated rather than supported. He pointed out that the individual economy still had potential; that the Soviet governmentshould let it take advantage of the potential to the maximum and gradually lead it to the road of collectivism. Of course, peasants were small producers, who, for thousands of hundreds of years, were used to individual possession and individual production. This mentality and habits cannot be changed in a short period of time. Lenin once pointed out, "it will take generations to remold the small farmer, and recast his mentality and habits. The only way to solve this problem of the small farmer—to improve, so to speak, his mentality—is through the material basis, technical equipment, the extensive use of tractors and other farm machinery and electrification on a mass scale.[48] Stalin persisted on Lenin's thought. On November 5 1927, he pointed out in the interview with the foreign workers' delegations, "all-embracing collectivization will come when the peasant farms are reorganized on a new technical basis, through mechanization and electrification, when the majority of the working peasants are organized in co-operative organizations, and when the majority of villages are covered by a network of agricultural co-operatives of a collectivist type."[49]

What is in relation with the ideas mentioned above was Stalin's estimation on the class structure of the USSR back then. In 1926 when Stalin was working with Bukharin to have the debate with the opposition led by Trotsky, he used to have the following demonstration: "differentiation in the countryside cannot assume its former dimensions, the middle peasants still constitute the main mass of the peasantry, and the kulak cannot regain his former strength, if only for the reason that the land has been nationalized, that it has been withdrawn from circulation, while our trade, credit, tax and cooperative policy is directed towards restricting the kulaks' exploiting proclivities, towards promoting the welfare of the broad mass of the peasantry and leveling out the extremes in the countryside."[50] The NEP to some degree allowed the existence and development of the capitalist relations of

47   Collected Works of Stalin, volume 11, p. 79. (Retrieved from Marxists Internet Archive)
48   Collected Works of Lenin, second Chinese version, volume 41, p. 53. (Retrieved from Marxists Internet Archive)
49   Collected Works of Stalin, volume 10, p. 193. (Retrieved from Marxists Internet Archive)
50   Selected Works of Stalin, volume 2, p. 453-454. (Retrieved from Marxists Internet Archive)

production, permitted the existence of private and rented enterprises so that the NEP men can continue the production and the private market economy can be recovered, but these were all under the supervision and control of the Soviet political power. Their development was not directed to capitalism but to the transition to socialism by making use of the development of capitalism within certain limits. At the Plenum of the Central Committee, CPSU(B) in 1928, Stalin asserted categorically that the proportion of the kulaks was 5%. What is worth noticing is that when the slogan of speeding up the attack on the kulaks in 1927, the formulation of the kulak problem in principle was still restricting the exploitation and fighting against exploiting kulaks with administrative measures. In the Plenum of the Central Committee in July 1928, the idea of canceling the NEP was firmly denied and the"counter-revolutionary stereotype" was called off. The plenum required to continue the attack on the kulak, but also made it clear that it can never be done by exploitation. Stalin personally also advocated for the policy of restricting the kulak in that period. He said at the Fifteenth Congress of the CPSU(B), "those comrades are wrong who think that it is possible and necessary to put an end to the kulaks by means of administrative measures, through the GPU: give an order, affix a seal, and that settles it. That is an easy way, but it is far from being effective. The kulak must be defeated by means of economic measures and in conformity with Soviet law."[51] Until June 1928, in the grain procurement crisis, Stalin emphasized criticized the attempt to turn the struggle against the kulaks into the exploitation on them, thinking that under the conditions at that time, exploiting kulaks was stupid and separated from the line of the party.

With the development of industry, the number of staff and the population sharply increased. Plus the grain was needed to exchange for the import of machine and equipment, the demand for commodity grain also increased. However, the agriculture developed comparatively slowly, presenting less and less conformity with the development of agriculture. Under such circumstances, Stalin's ways and means of the collectivization of agriculture also had great changes.

Stalin thought there was another practical reason for the emergence of the grain procurement crisis at the later half of the 1920s. In January 1928 when he was making an inspection tour in Siberia, his first question was that the kulaks hoarded up grains. He suggested to solve the problem of grain procurement with the 107 Clause of the Criminal Law of the Russian Federation and other emergency measures, and created the "Siberia-Ural" method. In April 1928 when Stalin was analyzing the reasons of the grain procurement crisis, he pointed out more clearly that the shortage of supply

---

51　Collected Works of Stalin, volume 10, p. 266. (Retrieved from Marxists Internet Archive)

of industrial products, the backwardness of the small-peasant economy and the disorganization of state procurement were all the general conditions and basis that caused the grain procurement crisis; that the major cause was that the kulaks had hoarded up large amount of grains due to the harvest in the last three years and waited to sell them at a high price. Therefore, he asserted, "the procurement crisis is the expression of the first serious action, under the conditions of NEP, undertaken by the capitalist elements of the countryside against the Soviet Government in connection with one of the most important questions of our constructive work, that of grain procurements."[52] In April 1929, Stalin again clearly blamed the difficulty of procurement to poor harvest and the kulaks' disturbance.

Just based on the above understanding, Stalin did not only advocate for speeding up the collectivization of agriculture, but also actively proposed the all-embracing collectivization. Stalin firstly criticized Bukharin's proposition of the economic policy in rural areas of the USSR. When the grain procurement crisis happened, Bukharin, Ryikov, Tomsky and some other people thought that we should slow down the pace of the industrialdevelopment and the construction of the collective and state farms; that we should help individual peasants develop production via the cooperatives and that we should increase the price of the grain procurement, rapidly eliminate the scissor difference, make the market "normalized" and make compromise to peasants to keep the alliance of the working class and the peasantry. However, Stalin was against this opinion. He pointed out: that some people even "counterpose collective farms to co-operatives is to make a mockery of Leninism and to acknowledge one's own ignorance."[53]

Engels and Lenin had repeatedly emphasized the voluntary basis of the collectivization of agriculture, stressing on persuasion and education instead of using administrative measures or coercion. Stalin also used to put forward that it was wrong to force the peasants to join in the collective farms with mandatory orders even violence. However, in the practical process of the collectivization of the USSR, especially from the end of 1920s to the beginning of 1930s, the principle was just violated with a lot of "excesses". At the Plenum of the Central Committee in July 1928, Bukharin said in his speech, "the problem now is to eliminate threat on our alliance with the middle peasants-that is what we have been looking for." "We will never again plan to use the emergency measure."[54] However, Stalin had a completely different attitude at this Plenum of the Central Committee. Although he still admitted that the "emergency measure" should be abandoned, the

---

52 Collected Works of Stalin, volume 11, p. 39. (Retrieved from Marxists Internet Archive)
53 Retrieved from Marxists Internet Archive) Collected Works of Stalin, first Chinese version, volume 12, p. 117.
54 Selected Works of Bukharin, volume 2, p. 268, 269.

next he emphasized and pointed out that the "emergency measure" is the only measure that must be taken to save the country. He also made it clear that it cannot be guaranteed that the "emergency measure" would not be used again forever.[55] In the debate with Bukharin later, Stalin even suggested, "that is the usual trick of the opportunists: on the pretext that excesses are committed in carrying out a correct line, abolish that line and replace it by an opportunist line."[56] Just because of the "excesses", the all-embracing collectivization of agriculture was accelerated. Within the two year from June 1927 to June 1929, the total number of collective farms increased from 14800 to 57000, increasing over 3 times. The proportion of the collectivized peasant's household increased from 0.8% to 3.9%, which was more than four times improvement of the level of collectivization. From the second half year of 1929, the collective-farm movement entered into the phase of all-embracing collectivization. Within three months from July 1929 to September, the collective farms increased 10400, increasing from 57000 to 67400; the collectivized peasant's households increased almost one time and reached to two million, with the collectivization level improving from 3.9% to 7.6%.[57]

About the forms of the collective farms, Stalin concluded the experience from practice, thinking that the basic form of the collective farm was neither the joint farming nor the agricultural commune. It was the artel. The reason was that the joint farming was the lower form of the collective-farm movement without making the means of production transferred to public ownership. As for the agricultural commune, the public ownership was applied not only in production, but also distribution, which, according to the conditions at that time, was not ready to be carried out. The artel were just between the two. That is to say, the basic means of production was owned by the public, such as the land-use right, machine, other instruments, farm animals and economic constructions were under the public ownership while the garden beside the house (small vegetable or fruit garden), house, part of milking livestock, etc were owned by the individual peasants. Therefore this is the form that was most conformed with the productive forces at that time. In the construction of the collective farms led by Stalin, family was no longer the independent economic unit, but not everything was owned by the public in the rural areas of the USSR.

After Stalin won the debate with Bukharin, thecollectivization of agriculture of the USSR reached the climax. However, some people, intoxicated with the victory of their action on the kulaks, turned to the middle

55 Collected Works of Stalin, first Chinese version, volume 11, p. 151-152.
56 Collected Works of Stalin, volume 12, p. 82.(Retrieved from Marxists Internet Archive)
57 The Socialist Economic History of the USSR, volume 3, p. 470, Beijing, SDX Joint Publishing Company, 1982.

peasants, depriving them of the election right and properties with violence. In some regions, in the one-sided pursuit of the percentage of the number of the collective farms, some collective farms were established with forces. As a result, these collective farms that were rapidly established disappeared quickly; some peasants who had rashly embraced the collective farming, now tried to avoid the evil consequences of it. Some backward villages just mechanically copied the methods used in the advanced regions, blindly willing to "catch up and surpass"the advanced regions. Some other regions, instead of consolidating the form of artel farms stipulated in the Standard Regulations of the Collective Farms, attempted to jump to the form of agricultural commune, though the technology was underdeveloped andcertain machines were in short, without considering that the form and level of the collective farming should must with the level of the productive forces. For example, in some regions, the houses, all of the small livestock and poultry were all "communized". In 1930, Stalin wrote the article Dizzy with Success, initially analyzed the mistakes mentioned above.

Later at the Seventeenth Congress of the CPSU(B), he made further conclusion and pointed out, "the future commune will arise on the basis of a more developed technique and of a more developed artel, on the basis of an abundance of products... It would be criminal artificially to accelerate the process of transition from the artel to the future commune. That would confuse the whole issue, and would facilitate the work of our enemies."[58]

208

About the class structure in the rural areas of the USSR, Stalin made the speech Concerning Questions of the Agrarian Policy in the USSR at the plenary meeting of the agrarian experts held at the end of 1929 and declared to shift from the policy of restricting the kulaks to the policy of eliminating the kulak class. On February 9, 1930 when Stalin was answering the questions of the students of the Sverdlov University, he said, "from the moment we passed to the policy of eliminating the kulaks as a class, this slogan became the chief slogan; and in the areas of incomplete collectivization the slogan of restricting the kulaks changed from an independent slogan into a subsidiary slogan, an auxiliary of the chief slogan, into a slogan which facilitates the creation in these areas of the conditions for a transition to the chief slogan."[59]

Also in this year, the USSR passed the resolution: On the Consolidation of the Socialist Transformation in the All-Embracing Collectivization Regions and the Measures of Class Struggle with the Kulak Class. As regulated in the resolution, in the regions of all-embracing collectivization, the local political authority had the right to confiscate the kulaks' property and expel them to the outlying areas. According to the statistics of the scholars in the USSR,

58   (Retrieved from Marxists Internet Archive) Selected Works of Stalin, volume 2, p. 334.
59   (Retrieved from Marxists Internet Archive) Collected Works of Stalin, volume 12, p. 164.

from the early 1930 to the fall 1932, over 240000 kulak families were banished from the regions of all-embracing collectivization, taking up about 1% of the total farm households.

In 1933, Stalin pointed out at the First All-Union Congress of Collective Farm Shock Brigadiers that collective-farm is the only right path so all the members of the collective farms were demanded to "work conscientiously; to distribute collective-farm incomes according to the amount of work done; to take care of collective farm property, to take care of the tractors and machines; to see to it that the horses are well looked after; to fulfill the assignments of your workers' and peasants' state; to consolidate the collective farms and to expel from the collective farms the kulaks and kulak agents who have wormed their way into them."[60]

After only a few years of the campaign for collectivization of agriculture, at the Eighteenth Congress of the CPSU(B) held in 1939, Stalin announced that "the collective farmingsystem has been finally consolidated and established. Socialist economic system now is the only form of our agriculture."[61]

3. A brief evaluation

Stalin's thought and practice for the collectivization of agriculture insisted on the fundamental direction of transiting from small-scale agriculture to the large-scale agriculture, from individual economy to collective economy, which was in line with the law of the social economic development. The movement of collectivization of agriculture led by Stalin established the collective farms by organizing millions of thousands of scattered middle and small peasant households and changed the economic structure in rural areas. The establishment of the basis of socialist economy in rural areas was nothing but a huge social transformation. At the same time, the collectivization of agriculture in the USSR had made contributions to the victory of the Great Patriotic War in the USSR. Just as what Stalin said, "our collective farms and State farms have stood the trials of war with credit. Under difficult war-time conditions the Soviet peasants work in the fields without folding their hands, supplying our army and population with food and our industry with raw materials."[62]

There are also some defects in Stalin's thought and practice of the collectivization of agriculture, such as the separation from the actual level of productive forces of the USSR, one-sided pursuit of promoting the relations of

60   Collected Works of Stalin, Volume 13, p. 219.(Retrieved from Marxists Internet Archive)
61   Works of Stalin (1934-1952), p. 253.
62   (Retrieved from Marxists Internet Archive) ibid., p. 413-414.

production, ignorance of the principle of voluntary participation and mutual benefit and inappropriate measures on kulaks and middle peasants, etc. Due to these mistakes, the agriculture of the USSR was seriously affected. By the early 1950s, some products had not reached to the highest level in the history of the Tsarist Russia. Mao Zedong once pointed out, "The USSR's method made the peasants suffer a lot. Their method like the so-called compulsory sale to the state took too much from the peasants with a very low price. Their accumulation by this way seriously affected the peasants' enthusiasm for production."[63]

At the same time, in Stalin's opinion, the collective farm was under the collective ownership, which was between the private ownership and the public ownership with a nature of transition. Stalin was not satisfied with the collective farms that have been achieved, but actively proposed to transit them to a higher level of ownership. In the early 1930s, when he was analyzing the peasants of the collective farms, he wrote: "the position of the members of collective farms is that they are no longer individual farmers, but collectivists; but their consciousness is still the old one—that of private property owners."[64]

Later, in *Economic Problems of the USSR*, he made it more clearly, "take, for instance, the distinction between agriculture and industry. In our country it consists not only in the fact that the conditions of labour in agriculture differ from those in industry, but, mainly and chiefly, in the fact that whereas in industry we have public ownership of the means of production and of the product of industry, in agriculture we have not public, but group, collective-farm ownership... It therefore cannot be denied that the disappearance of this essential distinction between agriculture and industry must be a matter of paramount importance for us."[65]

III. Continuously raising and continuously improving socialist production on the basis of high technology

In the process of the socialist construction in the USSR led by Stalin, he attached great importance to science and technology. Later he clearly pointed out to continuously increase and improve socialist production on the basis of high technology. To develop science and technology, Stalin had a profound elaboration on how to transform and value the science and technology staff and how to import science and technology from abroad.

63   Collected Works of Mao Zedong, volume 7, p. 29-30.
64   (Retrieved from Marxists Internet Archive) Collected Works of Stalin, first Chinese version, volume 13, p. 188.
65   Collected Works of Stalin, volume 2, p. 591-592.

1. "Bolsheviks should grasp technology"

After the victory of the October Revolution, the Soviet power rapidly achieved the nationalization of bank, railway and large-scale industry and grasped the most advanced methods of production in Russia under the leadership of Lenin. In Lenin's opinion, the real and only foundation of socialism can only be the large-scale industry, which can be the solid foundation of socialism only by combining with the modern science and technology. Since at that time, electrification was the sign of advanced science and technology, Lenin regarded electrification as the major symbol of the technological basis of socialism. He did not only clearly put forwardthe famous equation that "communism is the Soviet power plus electrification", but also directly lead to make the first long-time development plan of the national economy in the USSR, establishing the target as developing the large-scale mechanized industry and innovating technology on the basis of electrification. Lenin pointed out, "we in Russia have a far more concrete knowledge of this than before; so that instead of speaking about restoring large-scale industry in some indefinite and abstract way, we now speak of the definite, precisely calculated and concrete plan of electrification... Without it, no real socialist foundation for our economic life is possible."[66] Led by Lenin, the science and technology of the USSR was rapidly recover and developed.

In the process of socialist construction led by Stalin, he was attaching great importance to science and technology. Earlier than the industrialization, Stalin had had a clear understanding of the important role that science and technology played in the economic construction. He said, "The simple development of state industry is not enough now...The task now is to push forward the re-equipmentof our state industry and to expand it further on a new technical basis."[67] In 1925 when Stalin was leading the USSR to start the socialist industrialization, he especially emphasized that the socialistindustrialization should be combined with the development and application of science and technology. He pointed out, "What does it mean by making our country industrialized? It means turning out our country from an agrarian country into an industrial country. It means establishing and developing our industry on the basis of new technology."[68] In Stalin's opinion, without the support of science and technology, the economic development and industrialization would be impossible.

---

66 Collected Works of Lenin, second Chinese version, volume 41, p. 302. (Retrieved from Marxists Internet Archive)
67 Collected Works of Stalin, first Chinese version, volume 7, p. 211. (Retrieved from Marxists Internet Archive)
68 Collected Works of Stalin, first Chinese version, volume 9, p. 157.

Not long after the industrialization, the USSR started the collectivization of agriculture. The basis of agriculture in the USSR was very weak, seriously affecting the development of other sectors of the national economy. Stalin tried to promote the progress of agricultural technology by industrialization. He thought that conducting the collectivization of agriculture at the same time of industrialization was important to encourage agriculture to use new agricultural equipment and technology and finally lay the material and technological foundation of socialism. At the same time, to make the agricultural development conform to the rapid development of industry, the small-peasant economy must be completely transformed by turning the scattered small peasant households into the united large farms based on joint farming and carrying out the collective farming system on the basis of new technology. Stalin emphasized that industry is a key; that the backward and scattered agriculture can only be transformed on the basis of collectivization with the help of that key.[69]

Stalin especially emphasized on the importance of grasping science and technology to the socialist construction. In 1928, at the Eighth Congress of the All-Union Leninist Young Communist League, Stalin focused on thequestion and demonstrated it. He thought that to building socialist large-scale agriculture needs to master agricultural science and building socialist industry needs to master the corresponding science; that without high level of science and technology, the development of the socialist agriculture and industry would be beyond the imagination. He pointed out that one should understand that the conditions of struggle now are different from that in the civil war, in which period it was possible to capture enemy positions by dash, courage, daring, by assaults. "Today, in the conditions of peaceful economic construction, cavalry assaults can only do harm."[70] To master science, one important way is study, study with persistence and patience and study from all other people. Stalin especially criticized those who are proud of uneducated, pointing out these people, instead of learning hard, were proud of their backwardness; that they think they are workers "at the bench" if they are illiterate or cannot write grammatically; that if they learn to read and master science, they become alien elements who have "broken away" from the masses and no longer the workers. Stalin seriously pointed out, "We shall not advance a single step until we root out this barbarism and boorishness, this barbaric attitude towards science and men of culture."[71]

69   Lenin and Stalin: on Socialist Economic Construction, volume 2, p. 551, Beijing, People's Publishing House, 1951.
70   Selected Works of Stalin, volume 2, p. 40-41.(Retrieved from Marxists Internet Archive)
71   ibid., p. 40. (Retrieved from Marxists Internet Archive)

Stalin thought the development of science and technology is related to the consolidation of socialist system. He pointed out, one of the important tasks that the party is faced with is transforming all the sectors of national economy on the basis of the new modern technology. Otherwise, the all-offensive of socialism cannot be conducted. That is because to beat down and completely eliminate the capitalist elements in urban areas, we have to not only rely on the new artel and ownership, but also rely on new technology and our own technological advantage. At the same time, Stalin thought that the development of science and technology is also related with the question if the USSR can catch up and surpass the advanced capitalist countries. He thought that the level of industrial development in the USSR is still falling behind the advanced capitalist countries. To eliminate the backwardness, the new technology must be used in the whole national economy of the USSR and all the sectors of national economy must be transformed on the basis of the new modern technology.

In the early 1930s, targeting on the lack of techniques of production and the low level of education and expertise, Stalin put forward the slogan that"in the period of transformation, technique decides everything". In February 1931, focusing on the various phenomena of backwardness caused by the lack of technological equipment so that the various need of the state cannot be satisfied, and focusing on some disappointing phenomena that some leaders of the enterprises were happy to be a laymen and satisfied with only signing documents and orders, Stalin pointed out, "Bolsheviks should master the technique. It is time for the Bolsheviks to become the experts ourselves."[72] The practice had proved that in the period of transformation, technology was of decisive significance. The slogan that "technique decides everything" reflected the objective fact, so it was correct. Encouraged by this slogan, the machine manufacturing industry of the USSR was established, so were the heavy machine manufacturing industry, tractor making industry, airplane making industry, etc. The production of the metal cutting machine increased from 1783 in the 1927-1928 year period to 17666 in 1932, increasing over 9 times.[73] As a result, thousands of modernized new factories were established; thousands of old enterprises were transformed on the basis of new technology; the railway transportation also started the technological transformation of electrification and mechanization; the building industry was equipped with new technology; new tractors and agricultural machine were constantly transported to rural areas. Within just a few years, the phenomenon of lacking technology and equipment had basically all gone.

72   Selected Works of Stalin, volume 2, p. 275
73   Liashenko: History of the National Economy of the USSR, p. 297, Beijing, People's Publishing House, 1960.

Stalin attached great importance to the role of science and technology in the economic development and growth. Until a few years before he died, he still thought that the continuousincrease and improvement on the basis of high technology is the way of achieving the goal of socialist production.[74]

Science and technology in socialist construction are of "decisive significance", but socialist society also created the best conditions for the development and application of science and technology. Socialist constructors should make as much use as possible of the good condition to fully bring the science and technology into the construction. Stalin said, "I think that our country, with its revolutionary habits and traditions, its struggle against conservatism and stagnation of thought, provides the most favorable environment for the flourishing of science. There can be scarcely any doubt that philistine narrow-mindedness and routine, which are characteristic of the old professors of the capitalist school, are fetters on science. There can be scarcely any doubt that only new people who are free from these defects are capable of full and free creative activity in science. In this respect, our country has a great future before it as the citadel and nursery of free and unfettered science."[75]

Stalin also made the appeal that "mass campaigns of revolutionary youth on science". He called for the rationalizationmovement of production and operation management, opening a right path for the development and application of science and technology. This rationalization movement actually was to greatly promote the operating method of using new technology and new forms of labor organizationin this movement, thousands of hundreds of people became the constructors and inventors of socialist rationalization. With the further development of the movement, it incorporated more and more extensive and detailed contents in order to rationally manage the economy on the scientific basis. The contents ranged from emphasizing on labor discipline to conducting strict responsibility system and one-man system in enterprises; from emphasizing on the regime of saving to the task of operating and consolidating the economic accounting system in enterprises; from emphasizing that leaders had to become experts to the question of the whole system of leadership, etc. All of these undoubtedly had important influence on the socialist construction of the USSR.

74 Selected Works of Stalin, volume 3, p. 569.
75 Collected Works of Stalin, first Chinese version, volume 7, p. 74. (Retrieved from Marxists Internet Archive)

2. Importing and making use of advanced foreign technology

To develop science and technology in the home country, the advanced technology must be imported from abroad. After Lenin's death, Trotsky and some people thought making use of the western capital and technology would make the USSR economically dependent on the capitalist countries and "be controlled" by them. Stalin criticized this opinion, "to depict a socialist economy as something absolutely self-contained and absolutely independent of the surrounding national economies is to talk nonsense."[76]

As a matter of fact, the policy of importing technology was started from Lenin period. In the period of the NEP, to accelerate the recovery of economy, Lenin suggested to conduct the concession system, which means, under the condition that the state sovereignty and interest were not violated, under some conditions, concession out some mines, forests and oil fields that were not able to operate to the foreign capitalists to operate. He thought that under the concession system, part of the valuable products were paid to the lessee, which was undoubtedly a kind of tribute that the country of working class paid to the bourgeoisie, but it can make up the shortage of the funds for construction and guarantee the introduction of foreign capital and advanced technology and equipment, which was good for recovering industry, increasing products and improving people's living standard. On November 23, 1920, Lenin signed the Concession Decree, which regulated the general economic and legal conditions for concession. In March 1921, the Tenth Congress of the CPSU(B) further regulated that any sector of the national economy, as long as it can improve the productive forces of Russia, can be the lessee. The concession period was usually 20 years with various beneficial conditions. However, due to the bad influence of many negative factors from home and abroad, the concession system did not have too much development in terms of introducing foreign technology.

By 1927, the world trade had had some new development and the technology of the capitalist countries had made great progress. Just as Stalin said, "capital has prospered not only as regards the growth of production and as regards trade as well, but also in the field of improving methods of production, in the field of technical progress and the rationalization of production; moreover all this has led to the further strengthening of the largest trusts and to the organization of new, powerful, monopolist cartels."[77] Stalin pointed out that the USSR would like to the technology from any country-France, the United States, Britain or Germany, and try to collect all the strengths of the machines of other countries on one machine and produce

---

76 Collected Works of Stalin, first Chinese version, volume 9, p. 118. (Retrieved from Marxists Internet Archive)
77 Collected Works of Stalin, first Chinese version, volume 10, p. 233. (Retrieved from Marxists Internet Archive)

a lot more better machines. However, the historical conditions at this time had changed a lot from the conditions at the time when Lenin came up with the concession system. At that time, the USSR was faced with serious economic difficulties, especially the shortage of money and technology; but by the 1930s, the USSR had overcome the economic difficulties and the national economy as a whole had started developing on the basis of a full recovery. The instructive ideology of the development of the whole national economy had become that on thebasis of material and technological transformation in every sector of the national economy, with planned and large-scale socialist economic construction, establishing independent and powerful material and technological basis, catching up and surpassing the most developed capitalist countries in the world in terms of economic strength. At the same time, in the enterprises of concession, because the capitalists pursued higher profits, the exploiting and corrupt behavior got more and more serious. Since these were usually small enterprises, it was not easy for them to use new technology. Therefore, from 1982, the USSR started to call off the enterprises of concession, replacing them with technological assistance.

Stalin made some correct policy of introducing large amount of advanced technology and equipment from abroad. In December 1927, the Fifteenth Congress of the CPSU(B) passed the Resolution on Drafting the First Five-Year Plan, which clearly pointed out that the USSR must expand the economic connection to the maximum with the capitalist countries, because this connection (expanding foreign trade and international credit, conducting the concession system, attracting the foreign technology, etc) will strengthen theeconomic power of the USSR, make it more independent in the capitalist world and expand the basis for the further development of socialism in the USSR. Stalin himself also thought, "We are looking attentively at the United States, because this country was in very high level of science and technology. We hope that the American scientists and technicians can be our teacher and we can be their students in terms of technology."[78] Actually, it was possible and necessary to replace the enterprises of concession with the acceptance of technology assistance and establish it as the major form of making use of the western financial crisis in this period. As for the possibility, it was mainly because the major western capitalist countries, driven by profit, forced by the serious financial crisis, would like or raced to provide technology assistance to the USSR; on the other hand, the economic development in the USSR did not only need these technologies urgently, but also accumulate certain financial and technological power to be able to accept the assistance. As for the necessity, it mainly refers to that the assistance had many advantages under the new economic situation

78   Collected Works of Stalin, first Chinese version, volume 13, p. 136.

compared with the concession system. The biggest advantage was it can introduce the western advanced technology, equipment and technicians with some favorable conditions at the same time; it also very easy for the USSR government to lead the whole national economy according to the plan. In Stalin period, the subjective conditions and ability were all met to accept the large amount of technology assistance, so this form developed very fast in practice. By 1929, the USSR had signed over 70 technology assistance agreements with foreign capitalists, with the fields ranging from metal, machinery, metal processing, fuel power, petroleum and chemicals, transportation, agricultural machines, agricultural irrigation, automobile and airplane manufacturing and many other important economic sectors. By 1931, the USSR had accepted 124 projects of technology assistance, with the total value of 83 million rubles.[79]

From 1937 when the Second World War broke out, the USSR, as an important anti-fascist member, made new development on introducing the foreign technologies. According to Stalin's design, the USSR should firmly seize the historic opportunity to make good the distance of 50 to 100 years with about ten years. "Either we do it, or we shall go under."[80] The American scholar Grossman thought, "What closely related to the large amount of accumulation of funds is the extensive and organized acceptance and absorb of the western technology. To certain degree, the process of the accumulation of capital is also the process of introducing technologies. Not only that, a lot of equipment, especially the sophisticated pieces were directly introduced from abroad, no matter in the past or right now."[81] Sarton also thought so, "from 1936 to 1941, the USSR and the United States had singed many very important agreements that were not open to public, including aviation, petroleum, chemical industry and some technological sectors of the USSR that were not modernized." "Similarly, after 1942, according to the Concession Decree, the United States exported large amount of modern technologies to the USSR, making the economy of the USSR smoothly enter into the 1950s." From 1929 to 1945, the USSR had signed altogether 216 technology assistance agreements with the western companies.[82] In the Stalin period, the introduction and utilization of the western advanced technology and machinery equipment did not only reach to an unprecedented size, but also had great economic effect.

217

79 The History of the Socialist Economy of the USSR, volume 3, p. 426.
80 Collected Works of Stalin, first Chinese version, volume 13, p. 38.(Retrieved from Marxists Internet Archive)
81 The European Economic History, volume 4, p. 116, Beijing, the Commercial Press, 1991.
82 Sarton: Western Technology and the Economic Development of the USSR (1930-1945), p. 528, Beijing, China Social Sciences Press, 1980.

3. People and cadres are the most valuable and decisive factor

The development of science and technology and the foster and training of cadres and experts for the socialist economic construction cannot do without the intelligentsia. As early as in 1921, as the central task of the party had turned from the war into the peaceful construction, Stalin had put forward, "now, the Party cannot dispense with experts; in addition to utilizing the old specialists it must train its own experts." "Without this we shall be unable to build."[83] In 1928, Stalin again said that the working class would not become the real master of the country if they failed to get rid of illiteracy, to train their own intelligentsia, to master science or to manage economy according to the scientific principles. In 1931, the rapid development of industry of the USSR greatly increased the demand for engineers and technicians and for industrial conducting personnel, which greatly brought out the problem of the intelligentsia. Under such circumstances, Stalin thought that in order to train the working class' own intellectuals, the gate of various schools should be opened.

As the problem of lacking technology and equipment was solved, another contradiction that was mentioned by Stalin as early as in 1928 started to stick out. That was the contradiction of lacking cadres for industrial construction. For example, it took only 11 months to build up the Stalingrad Tractor Factory, but it took over a year to master this factory because many of the engineers, technicians and workers did not know how to use the new technology or anything about the line production. The reason of this phenomenon is the increase of the cadres who can master the technology was far less that the improvement of technology. With the victorious completion of the first five-year plan, the contradiction of the shortage of cadres capable of mastering technologies became more outstanding. In May 1935, Stalin pointed out, "'technique decides everything,' which is a reflection of a period already passed, a period in which we suffered from a dearth of technique, must now be replaced by a new slogan, the slogan 'Cadres decide everything.' That is the main thing now."[84] Therefore, "the training of new cadres for socialist industry from the ranks of the working class and the laboring people generally, cadres capable of providing social and political, as well as production and technical, leadership for our enterprises is a cardinal task of the moment."[85]

218

83　Collected Works of Stalin, first Chinese version, volume 5, p. 86. (Retrieved from Marxists Internet Archive)
84　Selected Works of Stalin, volume 2, p. 371. (Retrieved from Marxists Internet Archive)
85　Collected Works of Stalin, first Chinese version, volume 12, p. 201. (Retrieved from Marxists Internet Archive)

In the 1930s, the USSR came up with the slogan "in the period of trans-formation, technique decides everything." Many people just mechanically-understoodthe slogan, thinking that the request of the slogan was met only with more machines. Stalin pointed out, "that is not true. Technique cannot be separated from the people who set the technique going. Without people, technique is dead. The slogan "In the period of reconstruction technique decides everything," refers not to naked technique but to technique in the charge of people who have mastered the technique."[86]

Stalin criticized the attitude of bureaucracy to cadres and people, point-ing out that the slogan "cadres decide everything" required our leaders to take a considerate and caring attitude toward the workers. No matter their work is "large" "medium" of "small, no matter which sector they are work-ing in", the leaders should take care of them, helping them when they need support and encouraging them and promote them to make progress when they have made some achievement. However, in reality, people took an indifferent and bureaucratic attitude toward the people and cadres, which was absurd. Stalin thought that the reason was people had not learnt how to valued people and cadres. He said, "it is time to realize that of all the valuable capital the world possesses, the most valuable and most decisive is people, cadres. It must be realized that under our present conditions 'cad-res decide everything.' If we have good and numerous cadres in industry, agriculture, transport, and the army—our country will be invincible. If we do not have such cadres—we shall be lame on both legs."[87] Promoted by the slogan that "cadres decide everything", the USSR took a series of mea-sures to foster and train engineers, technicians and skilled workers. In the period of the five-year plan, the higher industrial institutions increased 9 time and the secondary technical schools increased 3 times, training near-ly 100,000 engineers and technicians for the large-scale industry. To train skilled people from workers, the workers'preparatory classes were started in universities; the factories also organized the movement of mastering sci-ence. With the social technology tests, thousand of hundreds of workers became the experts in their industry. In the period of the second fie-year plan, this team, consisted of the USSR's own cadres capable of mastering technology, people and workers, grew a lot bigger and greatly promoted the socialist construction of the USSR.

In November 1936, Stalin in the report *On the Draft Constitution of the USSR* further analyzed the team of intelligentsia of the USSR. He thought that the structure of the team of intelligentsia had undergone great changes, with 80% to 90% of the intellectuals coming from the working class, peas-antry and other classes of labors. The nature of the intellectuals' activities

---

86 Works of Stalin, volume 1, p. 26. (Retrieved from Marxists Internet Archive)
87 Selected Works of Stalin, volume 2, p. 373. (Retrieved from Marxists Internet Archive)

had also changed. In the past, they had no choice but to serve the rich people; now, they serve the people since the exploiting class no longer existed. Therefore,Stalin drew the conclusion that "our Soviet intelligentsia is an entirely new intelligentsia, bound up by its very roots with the working class and the peasantry"; that "It is now an equal member of Soviet society, in which, side by side with the workers and peasants, pulling together with them, it is engaged in building the new, classless, socialist society."[88] Undoubtedly, Stalin's comments on the rank of the intelligentsia were the important part of his theory of socialist construction. At the same time, Stalin also thought that techniques and intellectuals, under certain conditions, can create "miracles" and bring "great benefit", but they also can cause great harm. "Having this experience we are far from underestimating the good and the bad sides of the technical intelligentsia and we know that on the one hand it can do harm, and on the other hand, it can perform 'miracles.'"[89]

To train people, in addition to sending large amount of excellent young people and advanced producers to the higher educational institutions and special technical schools to study, the party and the government of the USSR also decided to pick up large amount of outstanding people to study abroad. In April 1928, the Plenum of the Central Committee, CPSU(B) decided that in order to expand and improve the work of sending experts abroad to study the most updated technology, it especially needed to send the most outstanding young experts and the students from the higher technical schools to study abroad. The large amount of new experts had played a very important role in making use of the western technology to develop the industry of the USSR. In the socialist construction of the USSR, not only that many scientists and technicians went abroad, it also introduced large amount of scientists and technicians from western countries. In the crisis of capitalism in the 1930s, the number of foreign experts, engineers and technicians increased very fast. By 1928, there were 379 foreign experts working in the USSR and 505 scientists and technicians. By 1932, the former had increased to 1910, growing over 4 times compared with the number in 1928; the latter increased to 10665, increased over 21 times of the number in 1928.

Evaluating and promoting the talented intellectuals that were not the members of the party was one of Stalin's important ideas. He criticized those who had a sectarian tendency in executing the cadres' policy that "some comrades think that only Party members may be placed in leading positions in the mills and factories. That is the reason why they not infrequently push aside non-Party comrades who possess ability and initiative

---

88   ibid., p. 396. (Retrieved from Marxists Internet Archive)
89   ibid., p. 358. (Retrieved from the Marxist Internet Archive)

and put Party members at the top instead, although they may be less capable and show no initiative. Needless to say, there is nothing more stupid and reactionary than such a 'policy', if one may call it such."[90]

Stalin elaborated on the great significance of socialist emulation of improving the level of education and technology of all working people and of promoting the further development of science and technology in socialist construction. In April 1929, the Sixteenth Conference of the CPSU(B) passed the Appeal for Emulation to the Workers and All Laboring People, fully affirming the decision on the emulation at the Ninth Conference of the CPSU(B) in 1920 and appealed every construction sector to organize the emulation. In May the same year, the Central Authority of the CPSU(B) passed the resolution on organizing socialist emulation. Therefore, the masses' movement of the socialist emulation started with vigor and vitality. Stalin highly valued the socialist emulation, thinking that this movement is the way of building socialism on the basis of the maximum enthusiasm of the masses; that it is the working class' leverage of turning the economic and cultural life of the country on thebasis of socialism. On August 30, 1935, Stakhanov, a miner at the Central Irmino Mine in Donets Basin hewed a record-setting 102 tons of coal during his shift, exceeding 13 times of the quota. This brand new record had made the Stakhanov Movement, named after the initiator, rapidly spread to the whole country, pushing forward the socialist emulation to a higher level. It broke the old opinion on technology; it also broke the old technical standards, designing ability and production plan and set an example of high productive forces of labor that capitalism cannot reach. Stalin pointed out, "Stakhanovites are innovators in our industry, that the Stakhanov movement represents the future of our industry, that it contains the seed of the future rise in the culture and technical level of the working class, that it opens to us the path by which alone can be achieved those high indices of productive forces of labor which are essential for the transition from Socialism to Communism and for the elimination of the distinction between mental labor and manual labor."[91]

Stalin also put forward the view that science does not recognize fetishes. Some people talked about science, saying that the data of science contained in technical handbooks and instructions, contradict the demands of the Stakhanovites movement for new and higher technology standards. Stalin criticized their view, thinking that the data of science had always been tested by practice and experience. Science which has severed contact with practice, with experience — what sort of science is that? Stalin said, "Science is called science just because it does not recognize fetishes, just

90   Selected Works of Stalin, volume 2, p. 288. (Retrieved from Marxists Internet Archive)
91   Selected Works of Stalin, volume 2, p. 377-378. (Retrieved from Marxists Internet Archive)

because it does not fear to raise its hand against the obsolete and antiquated, and because it lends an attentive ear to the voice of experience, of practice."[92]This view of Stalin had great significance for understanding the role of science and technology in building socialism.

Some of Stalin's thought on promoting development of science and technology was very important, because people later fully understand the crucial role of science and technology in socialist economic construction and how to make use them. Thephenomenal achievements on science and technology made in the Stalin period have been fully affirmed even by some western scholars; they also laid the solid foundation for the science and technology of the USSR staying in the high rank in the world in the long term. However, there were also some major defects in Stain's thought and practice on science and technology. For example, he wantonly interfered with the scientific studies and took a rude attitude towards the scientific discussions. The later materials have shown that Stalin had interfered in the fields like geology, medical science and biological genetics, on which he made the most serious damage. He overly politicized the scientific studies and the natural science into different classes. For example, in the literature of natural science in the USSR, there were the formulations like the proletarian biology and capitalist biology. Stalin highly valued the science and technology related to military and heavy industry while comparatively ignored that for civil industries which caused them remain underdeveloped in the Soviet Union's economic history.

222

92   Selected Works of Stalin, volume 2, p. 384. (Retrieved from Marxists Internet Archive)

Chapter VII

Stalin's Theory and Practice on Political System of Socialism

According to the predictions of Marx and Engels, the proletarian revolution would firstly win victory in the countries where the industry was more developed like Britain and France. But the facts occurred so that the party of the of the working class was victorious in backward Russia. Before the victory of revolution, Russia was a country where the level of socialized production was low and the most of the population was peasants. The level of social and economic development of Russia was still very low, people had the social mentality and habit of relying on the "Savior". These conditions determined that instead of directly copying the design of Marx and Engels in establishing the new state system after the victory of the proletarian revolution, the special national conditions of Russia should be taken into consideration. Led by Lenin and Stalin, the Russian Bolsheviks creatively applied the theory of Marxism into the revolutionary practice of Russia, and started the difficult exploration and construction of the socialist political system.

I. The initial establishment of Soviet socialist political system and Lenin's reform in his later years

1. The characteristics of the socialist political system in the early period

With the victory of the October Revolution, Russia established the first proletarian revolutionary rule in the world- the Soviet power, and established the first new socialist system in human history. However, the new born Soviet power was faced with very complicated domestic and international situations. Internationally, there was the powerful armed intervention of the imperialism; domestically, there was the crazy attack of the class enemies. The domestic and international reactionary forces acted in collusion, trying to strangle the new born revolutionary power in the cradle. Just faced with these fierce struggles, the Bolsheviks started the great task of establishing the socialist political system.

First, the Soviet system was established. Soviet was one political organ of the revolution (Soviets of Workers' Deputies) created by the workers, soldiers and working masses in the February Revolution. It was consisted of the representatives that were generally elected by the factories, armies and working masses. It had the functions of discussing state affairs, making decisions, legislation and also executed the decisions and laws. It also led an armed force of people. After the February Revolution, the Soviet organ actually functioned as a political organ which counterbalanced and checked the Soviet government. Lenin thought it would be the form of the state of the future Russian proletarian dictatorship. In the famous *The Tasks of the Proletariat in Our Revolution (The April Theses)*, he pointed out, "the Soviets of workers, soldiers, peasants and other deputies are not understood, not only mis-understood in the sense of their class significance and their role in the Russianrevolution, is not clear for the majority." "The masses must be made to see that the Soviets of Workers' Deputies are the only possible form of revolutionary government."[1] At the same time, Lenin especially emphasized that the Soviet power should inherit the principles of the Paris Commune. That is, the Soviet's political form should not be "a parliamentary republic", but the political form that takes charge of both legislation and administration (executive). However, in actual practice, when the Second All-Russian Congress of Soviets of Workers' and Soldiers' Deputies elected the two supreme authority—the All-Russian Central Executive Committee and secondly People's Commissariat, it did not decide which one of the two organs would be the organ using the "combination of the legislative and executive powers" and which would take the supreme power of the state.

---

[1] Selected Works of Lenin, third edition, volume 3, p. 47, Marxists Internet Archive.

Therefore, there occurred the heated struggle when the Soviets realized the state power, especially the legislative right. At last, with Lenin's persistence and endeavor, in 1918, the Constitution of the Russian Federation clearly stipulated that the People's Commissariat has the right to issue laws, orders, instructions and take any necessary measures to insure the normal and fast operation of the state affairs, but the important laws that are of great political significance to the overall situation decided by the People's Commissariat should be ratified by the All-Russian Central Executive Committee. If these problems (including military and diplomatic affairs) were urgent, the People's Commissariat would be able to directly make the decision, but the All-Russian Central Executive Committee reserved the right of inspection and abolishment of those decisions. In 1924, the Constitution of the USSR has re-affirmed this principle.

After the victory of the October Revolution, the Russian masses rose up, smashed the old political apparatus and conquered the political power in the political form of Soviet assemblies. However, since the newly established Soviets were scattered all over the country and were still immature organizationally and without clear division of power, there appeared the phenomenon that these local/regional Soviets operated on their own, seriously independent from the central state. To strengthen the leadership of the central leadership and establish a complete system of Soviet assemblies all over the country. In the early 1918, the People's Commissariat issued the Rights and Obligations of the Soviets, emphasizing the leadership of the CC. It also stipulated that all the regional Soviets should execute the instructions of the CC, thus this decree has established the centralized Soviet system.

Second, the single-party leadership system was established. After the victory of the October Revolution, Bolshevik party invited the left wing of Socialist-Revolutionary Party to join the new government but was declined, so the new government only included the Bolshevik party. To unite the other progressive parties Lenin had often expressed that it would better to share the political power with other revolutionary parties and once more invited the left wing of the Socialist Revolutionary Party to join the government. After many negotiations, some members of this Party joined the All-Russian Central Executive Committee, the People's Commissariat, the All-Russian Extraordinary Commission for Combating against Counter-Revolution and Sabotage (Cheka for short) and some local Soviet administrations. However, this situation of unity was soon broken by the Treaty of Brest-Litovsk, which the Socialist Revolutionaries rejected. They thought it was a national betrayal and surrender. As a result, when the treaty was ratified at the Fourth Congress of All-Russian Soviets in March 1918, they all withdrew from the People's Commissariat. Later, the two parties had serious divergence on the peasant policy. In July 1918, the leader of the left wing Socialist Revolutionary Party proposed the non-confidence vote for the government and launched a military rebellion. After this rebellion was suppressed, the two-party coalition was replaced by the single party state. As early as April 1918, the Russian Communist Party (Bolshevik) had started establishing its party organizations in every province, county and town, firmly expanded its political power throughout the country, the single-party leadership system was extended to all regions.

Third, a highly centralized leadership was established. High degree of centralization in the leadership system was the most important feature of the new born Soviet state. Before the October Revolution, Lenin had the idea of establishing a top-to-bottom system of administration. He also wanted to employ the strengths and advantages of the parliamentary system and the direct democracy system, thus the new socialist democracy, would inherit some elements of of the "primitive democracy." He wrote: "the transition from capitalism to socialism is impossible without a certain "reversion" to "primitive" democracy (because how else can the majority, and then the whole population without exception, proceed to discharge state functions?)"

However, after the victory of the October Revolution, the principles of the socialist democracy saw some application, but this democratic development was very soon halted by the foreign armed intervention and the domestic armed rebellion. To deal with the urgent situation, on September[2], 1918, the All-Russian Central Executive Committee announced that the Republic of Soviets was a "unified military camp". On November 30, it also announced the establishment of the Council of Workers' and Peasants' Defense. Lenin was the first chairman of this Council. The members included the chairman of the All-Russian Central Executive Committee, the chairman of the Soviet Republic Revolutionary Military Committee, the People's Commissar for Transportation, the deputy People's Commissar for Grain, the chairman of the Extraordinary Commission of Production and Supply and a representative from the All-Russian Trade Union Association, etc. The Council of Workers' and Peasants' Defense had the full authority (including legislation) to manage personnel and material resources of the country for the war purposes. In fact, it was the wartime supreme organ of decision making and execution. In conformity with that realistic task, a highly centralized leadership was employed. All the important decisions of the country were directly decided by the Political Bureau of the Party Central Committee and the Revolutionary Military Committee. Strict organizational discipline and the vertical leadership from top to bottom were used. Plus, within the party the decisive position of the supreme leading organs was intensified; the highly centralized leadership system was also intensified. After the civil war had ended, even though there were some changes in the leadership system, the high degree centralization was still kept.

Fourth, the system of centralized appointment system of the cadres was established. Before the October Revolution, Lenin used to think a system, in which the state leaders would be directly elected anddisplaceable at any time. Lenin said, "the people need a real democratic republic of workers and peasants, meaning a republic where anyone in power must be elected according to the will of the people and be dismissed or replaced at any time."[2]

Lenin thought that in a proletarian country, a full election system should be implemented for the public/state officers. However, in the practice after the October Revolution, Lenin gradually realized that it was not practical to conduct this kind of election system. After analyzing the result of "Constituent Assembly elections" realized at the end of 1917 (yet under the bourgeoisie rule) Right wing SRs—with tricks—got the overwhelming votes and wree overrepresented, leaving out left wing SRs who were part of the coalition government with the Bolsheviks. (See election results) The Constituent Assembly convened on 18 January 1918. However, the other parties refused to give their support to the soviet republic. The All-Russian Central Executive Committee dissolved the Assembly the next day, declaring that the All-Russian Congress of Soviets as the governing body of Russia. Thus, Lenin had realized that the bourgeoisie and the petty-bourgeoisie democrats may take vantage of the election system to act against the Soviets. At the same time, due the situation of intense military and political fights, it was actually very hard to conduct the democratic election of government cadres. Therefore, after the second half of 1918, Lenin decided to replace the election system of cadres with the appointment system. After the new law was passed, the CC of the RCP (B) appointed a large number of leaders and cadres to various organizations of the party, the Soviets, the Red Army and the trade unions at all levels and the economic enterprises. It was required by the objective situation at that time to replace the election system with appointment, but it also brought some problems. Some cadres ignored the criticism of massesand refused the supervision of the masses; some cadres even discriminated those people with different opinions, even punished those who had criticized them, etc.

---

2 Collected Works of Lenin, second Chinese version, volume 29, p. 457.

Party of the Proletariat (Bolsheviks)	9.02 million=25%
Petty-Bourgeois democratic parties (Socialist-Revolutionaries, Mensheviks, etc.)	22.62 million=62%
Parties of landowners and bourgeoisie (Cadets, etc.)	4.62 million=13%

**Free election results 3 weeks after Bolsheviks
came to power in October 1917**

Fifth, absolute subordination f state organs to the party was established. Around the October Revolution, Lenin repeatedly emphasized that the masses should be promoted to participate the administration of the state power, Soviet Union should establish a special school in which the working masses could learn how to govern the country. However, analyzing the results of the practice Lenin had realized that in a country where most people are illiterate, it would be impossible for everyone to take part in the administration of the state power. He pointed out, "the result of this low cultural level is that the Soviets, which by virtue of their program are organs of government by the working people, theyare in fact organs of government for the working peopleled by the advanced section of the proletariat, but not by the working people as a whole."[3] Lenin thought people's advanced participation in the work of government should gain experience, developing from low level to the higher level. At the lower stage, people can only participate in the work of government through their vanguard, which is the Bolshevik Party.

In the whole democratic revolution period, the trade unions used to play a very important role in educating the masses, developing worker's consciousness and leading the workers' movement. Before the October Revolution, there were over 2000 trade unions, with up to 20 million members. And the trade union organizations enjoyed their own organizational system, including propaganda work, their own finance, liaisons and the workers' armed forces. Therefore, Lenin paid great attention to the issue of the trade union's position and their role effecting the state power. After the victory of the October Revolution, Lenin initially advocated the idea of "nationalization of trade unions." He pointed out, "today we can no longer confine ourselves with proclaiming the idea of dictatorship of the proletariat. The trade unions have to be governmentalized; they have to be fused with state bodies. The work of building up large-scale industry has to be entrusted entirely to trade unions."[4] However, after one-year practice of

228

---

3   Selected Works of Lenin, third edition, volume 3, p.770.
4   Collected Works of Lenin, volume 35, p. 438, Beijing, People's Publishing House, 1985.

the governmentalization of trade unions, there occurred many problems, mainly caused by some leaders of the trade unions who had a low level of culture, political, management and administrative qualities. Therefore Lenin quickly realized that it would not work to have the trade unions governmentalized too early, he realized that he had overestimated the qualities of the working class. He pointed out: "we cannot merge the trade unions with the state bodies at once, at one stroke. It would be a mistake;" ...."if the trade unions arbitrarily to attempt to take over government functions now, they would only make a mess of it."[5]

At the end of 1920, since the civil war had almost ceased, the RCP (B) turned the focus of work into economic construction. Therefore, the question how to organize production and manage the enterprises was prioritized again. In those days Trotsky and some other leaders had suggested to immediately conduct the "nationalization of the trade unions", turning trade unions into state organs which would be in charge of production management. They also emphasized on conducting the "military methods and militarization of labor life" in the production process, which would turn the trade unions into the mandatory organs empowered with full authority of socialist construction. This time, Lenin strongly rejected this proposition, since Lenin's opinion on "nationalization of trade unions" had completely changed. In December 1920 Lenin in his speech *The Trade Unions, the Present Situation and Trotsky's Mistake* put forward the theory of the proletarian dictatorship and elaborated on the relations between the trade unions and the state. He pointed out that the proletarian dictatorship is "a complex arrangement of cogwheels."[6] Under this arrangement, the trade union is a school of administration, a school of education and a "school of communism" "standing between the party and the state". It is not a state organization and therefore it is not proper to place unions above the party and the political power. Instead, dictatorship of the proletariat cannot be exercised by a mass proletarian organization, unions should be one of the "transmission belts" running from the vanguard of the class to the mass of class and vice versa. The theory of the proletarian dictatorship is the theoretical generalization of the socialist political system. This idea by Lenin, scientifically elaborated the position and role of the party, the Soviets, the trade unions and other organizations in the state power, which gave a solid cognition for the establishment of the party's leadership to the state.

---

5   Collected Works of Lenin, volume 35, pp. 438, 439.
6   Selected Works of Lenin, third edition, volume 4, p. 369.

2. Lenin's thoughts on the political reform in his later years

The Soviet Russian socialist political system, born in the revolution and formed in the war, had played an important role in suppressing the reactionary rebellion, shattering the foreign armed intervention and stabilizing the Soviet power. However, as the civil war was over and the period of peaceful economic construction started, the defects of the system were exposed. Just as the Tenth Congress of the RCP (B) had pointed out, since the extreme centralization was required, there formed the overstaffed bureaucratic organizations which bred bureaucracy and the negative tendency of separation from the masses. Under such circumstances, "the battle type command system usually took the form of suppressive character; the necessary authority turned into the excuse of various corrupt behaviors; the necessary austerity of the party organs weakened the party's spiritual life."[7]

At that time, there were a lot of manifestations of bureaucratism in the organs of the party and the Soviet government and the most important were as follows.

First, the power was overly centralized.

The high degree of centralization formed at the civil war period was not halted. On the contrary, it tended to get intensified. The major sign was that the local powers was passed and centralized at the CC of the party, finally al the powers were centralized in the hands of Political Bureau of the CC consisting of a few people. Plus it was also very outstanding that the powers in the center were centralized in one persons' hand. For example, Lenin was the member of the Political Bureau (actually person in charge of the party's affairs), the chairman of the People's Commissariat, the chairman of the Committee of the National Defense and the chairman of the Committee of the National Economy, with the power of the party, the government, the army and the economy centralized in his hands.

Stalin was the member of the Political Bureau, the member of Organization Bureau, the People's Commissar for National Affair, the People's Commissar for Workers' and Peasants' Inspection, and later he was elected the general secretary of the Secretariat of the RCP (B). A proper centralization of power might be good to improve the efficiency of work, but over centralization has weakened the basis of democratic system and brought extremely bad consequences to the party, to the nation and the people.

---

7   Collective Resolutions of the Congresses, Conferences and Central Plenums of the Communist Party of the USSR, Volume 2, p. 52, Beijing, People's Publishing House, 1964.

Second is the separation from reality and the masses. Many members of the Communist Party and the staff of the government, after taking some leadership role, became fond of issuing orders. They were sitting up high in the leading position, far away from reality, conducting no investigation or study, not solving anything that was urgently needed in the socialist construction. They were also indifferent to masses' difficulties and didn't care or hear what the masses were thinking, therefore were seriously separated from the masses and lost their trust.

The Povolzhye crisis in the spring of 1921 had fully proved that. At that time, even the Putilov Industrial Plant, the "workers' fortress" in Petrograd, with a bright revolutionary tradition, had went to strike. The sailors of the Baltic fleet that was once called "the pride and glory of the Russian revolution", also launched the Kronstadt Rebellion.

Third, the organizations were overstaffed. At the beginning of the establishment of the Soviet state power, the institutions and personnel were both streamlined. For example, when the People's Commissariat was firstly established, it had only ten committees under it, but the Soviet Russia managed the whole countryand social life, especially its economic affairs mostly with administrative measures. With the development of the national economy and the increase of the military, political, cultural and other tasks, the administrative institutions and their staff were also greatly increased. By 1922, there were 120 various committees under the central-level Soviet organs. The number of staff of the Central Committee, had increased from 15 in 1919 to 602 in 1921. With the increase of institutions and staff, the bureaucracy was also bred. Large amount of the national organs' staff "were sucked down intowriting and signing papers, jawing about decrees, drawing up decrees—and in this sea of paper live work is being drowned."[8] To solve the problems in the socialist political system, Lenin spent lots time and efforts in his later years. Lenin and the CC of the RCP (B) took a series of positive measures.

A series of positive measures by Lenin

First was to place large number of outstanding workers to top positions in the state organs in a planned, organized and purposeful way. In 1920, when the civil war was about to finish, Lenin pointed out, "we shall not drive out the old officials—just as we did not drive the experts out of the army, but we have attached worker commissars to them… Workers must enter all the government establishments so as to supervise the entire government apparatus."[9] According to Lenin's proposition, large number of outstanding workers was sent to the government offices. As the figures show, by

---

8 Collected Works of Lenin, volume 42, p. 387.
9 Collected Works of Lenin, volume 42, p. 140, Beijing, People's Publishing House, 1986.

the end of 1920, workers had taken up 61.6% in the central and provincial presidium of the Committee of the National Economy, in the administrative parent bureaus and committees, enterprises and administrative departments of the factories.

Second was to intensify the connections between the staff of the government offices and the masses. Lenin said, "one of the greatest and most serious dangers that confront the numerically small Communist Party which, as the vanguard of the working class, is guiding a vast country in the process of transition to socialism (for the time being without the direct support of the more advanced countries), is isolation from the masses."[10]

In order to strengthen the connections with the masses, the Eighth Congress of the RCP (B) held in March 1919 decided to instruct the members of the Communist Party and directors of the government organs that they should report the work to their electorates at least every two weeks. Those who do government in a row should go back to work in the factory for at least one month. All members of the Communist Party should be the members of the trade unions and help the trade unions. In 1921, the Tenth Congress of the RCP (B) strongly re-emphasized that in order to prevent the government getting separated from the masses, the staff that was doing the work of the Soviet or the Party should be sent to work in factories or rural areas. In addition, Lenin also attached great importance to the complaint letters and visits by the masses to officers.

Third measure was to enhance quality of the state organizations and improve the work of the government establishments, which was mainly manifested in the following aspects.

First was to streamline the organizations and cut down the staff. Lenin thought that the bureaucracy and the overstaffed organizations were inseparable facts. Therefore as early as 1918, Lenin had warned for the streamlining of the government organizations. After that, there was a wave of institutional reform nationwide, but it was not very successful. In 1922, Lenin conducted a research of the Soviet government establishments and found that a lot of government institutions did not cut their size but instead increased it. As a result, he proposed to "completely revoke" the semi-aristocratic institutions with "a nature of toys" and ruthlessly drive away the extra officers in order to streamline the government organizations to the minimum, thus increase their work efficiency.

Second was to establish the system of individual responsibility and accountability of the managers. After the October Revolution, the Soviet

10   Selected Works of Lenin, third edition, volume 4, p. 626.

government establishments used to conduct the system of collective management, which led to the phenomenon that everybody took the responsibility actually meant no body took the responsibility. Therefore, the Ninth Congress of the RCP (B) made the decision in April 1920, asking the government organizations from top to bottom to start a new system: "Certain individuals should take certain responsibility for a certain work. In the process of discussing or making decisions, the collective management should be applied, but in the process of execution, the collective management must unconditionally give way to the one-man system."[11]

Third was to clarify the functions of the state's oppressive (violence) organs. This aimed at preventing them from abusing their power and violates people's interests. After the civil war, the political situation got better, so Lenin thought the activity sphere of the state's oppressive organs should be properly narrowed down. On December 1st, 1921, Lenin drafted the resolution guidelines of the All-Russian Extraordinary Commission for Combating Counter-Revolution and Sabotage for the Central Political Bureau of the RCP (B), and proposed six principles, including narrowing down the functions of the All-Russian Extraordinary Commission for Combating Counter-Revolution and Sabotage and restricting the right of arresting, etc.

Fourth was to enlarge democracy within the party and improve the leadership qualities of the party. With the civil war coming to an end, in March 1921, the Tenth Congress of the RCP (B) put forward the policy of conducting the "workers' democracy" within the party. The workers' democracy mainly included activating the party life, canceling the system of cadres' appointment and putting the party's leading organs under the supervision of the whole party.

To further enlarge the democracy within the party and prevent the power being over centralized in the hands of few party leaders, Lenin also came up with the proposition of enlarging the Central Committee. He suggested turning the Central Committee into the "highest conference of the party", making the Central Committee the organization that has the supreme decision-making right bu also every member would have the right to ask anyone any questions. To make sure that the Central Committee really uses the supreme decision-making right and strengthen the democratic basis in the process of making decisions, Lenin suggested to add 50 to 75 workers and peasants that had undergone the tests of revolutionary work to join in the Central Committee. This would provide a solid mass foundation for the party decisions, thus prevent it becoming a privileged group. This measure would also prevent the Central Committee from making arbitrary decisions

233

11 Collected Information Resolutions of the Congresses, Conferences and Central Plenums of the RCP (B), volume 2, p. 10.

based on individual and occasional factors Participation of young workers into the CC would also function as a cushion effect which could diminish polarization among strong and dominant leaders (like between Stalin and Trotsky). In terms of improving the party's leadership, Lenin and the C.C of the CPSU(B) put forward the proposition of division of labor between the party and the government. The phenomenon of lack of distinctions between the party work and the government work had emerged since the new political power was born. With the establishment of the one-party system and due to the civil war, this phenomenon became more problematic and widespread. After the civil war, to solve this problem, Lenin made a lot of efforts. In his *Letter to Molotov for the Plenary Meeting of the Central Committee, RCP (B)—Plan of the Political Report for the Eleventh Party Congress* Lenin wrote in March 1922, targeted on the issue of the relation between the party and the government, he sharply pointed out: "currently the extremely important task is, we should distinguish much more precisely the functions of the Party (and of its Central Committee) from those of the Soviet government; increase the responsibility and independence of Soviet officials and of Soviet government institutions, leaving to the Party the general guidance of the activities of all state bodies, without too frequent, irregular and often petty interferences."[12]

The Eleventh Congress of the RCP (B), according to Lenin's suggestions made the resolution, which initially established that the leadership of the party to the Soviet government was mainly: first, choosing leaders and cadres and educating party members; second, explaining the significance of the NEP; third, struggling against the prejudices that hindered the regular economic development. In addition, since the leading bodies at every level were busy in the work of economic recovery after the civil war, especially that the leaders at all levels had too much work to do, the realization of this important was negatively affected. This phenomenon could not be corrected properly.

Fifth was to establish and improve the control ve system related to the party and the government.

As early as in the period of civil war, Lenin had realized that under the circumstances that the country was administered by the minority advanced elements representing the mass of people, there could be a risk that the advanced quality of the party members could degenerate, if due attention was not paid. Therefore, he suggested to intensify the control of the cadres of the party and the staff of the Soviet government, by improving the control system of the party and the government. In September 1920, according to Lenin's suggestion, the Ninth Conference of the Party decided

---

12 Collected Works of Lenin, volume 43, p. 64.

to establish the Control Committees of the Party from central to the regions at every level. Lenin thought the control committees should be consisted of the cadres with prestige in the party so that they could carry out the control functions more effectively. The control committee at every level should be parallel with the party committee at the same level; the central control committee should also enjoy all those rights as the Central Committee does. In addition, Lenin also especially emphasized the strong independence of the members of the control committee, thinking that the control committee could function as an organizational guarantee, only if the members of the control committee could use their rights independently.

II. The formation of the highly centralized Soviet political system in the Stalin period and its features

In reality the socialist political system of the USSR was established in the Stalin period. Therefore people also call it Stalin's political system. After Lenin's death, in the struggles against various oppositions within the party, Stalin gradually became the actual leader of the socialist construction of the USSR. In the development of the socialist construction of the USSR, Stalin has made important contributions to development of Lenin's theory of socialist political system, but he failed to apply these correct theories and ideas in the practice. In many aspects, he has deviated and followed a separate way from Lenin's basic thought, making the defects of the original political system become worse and even go to the extreme. This practice of him has finally led to the highly centralized political system.

1. The struggles within the party and the formation of the highly centralized political system

After Lenin's death in 1924, within the RCP (B) there was serious divergence on a series of important issues such as the party's line and policies. Just in these sharp struggles, Stalin gradually consolidated his absolute leading authority within the party and established the highly centralized political system.

The first struggle was around the issue of inner-party democracy. It was between the CC majority headed by Stalin, Zinoviev and Kamenev and the opposition led by Trotsky. This struggle, to be exact, had started before Lenin's death. In summer-autumn of 1923, the Trotsky opposition group wrote to the CC to criticize the work of the CC, pointing out that the system that was basically formed before the Twelfth Congress and consolidated after it, compared to the system at the most critical period of the wartime communism, was a lot farther than the workers' socialist democracy. Therefore, the letter asked to enlarge the inner-party democracy. At the beginning, the two sides discussed the issue of inner-party democracy, on which they did not have too much divergence. Both sides advocated for further developing and enlarging the inner-party democracy. In December 1923, Political Bureau of the CC and the presidium of the Central Control Committee passed the resolution of developing the inner-party democracy. However, Trotsky was quite unsatisfied about it. After the above meeting, he published the article New Policy in *Pravda*, criticizing that Bolsheviks have qualitatively changed; that the bureaucracy was getting more and more serious and that the phenomenon of separating from practice and the masses were more and more widespread. In January 1924, the Thirteenth Party Conference of the RCP (B) concluded this debate. The Trotsky opposition was denounced of having the petty-bourgeoisie tendency in the issue of party democracy.

The second struggle was related to different evaluations of the party history. After Lenin's death in January 1924, Trotsky wrote some articles to express his condolence for Lenin's death, which were published under the title *On Lenin* in April 1924. In September, he collected the articles and speeches from his early years into a book and wrote a preface to it preface was titled as *The Lessons of October*. This preface article and the book *On Lenin* aroused a fierce inner-party struggle, because Trotsky deliberately exaggerated his contributions to the October Revolution and undermined Lenin's position and role in those past days. He criticized Zinoviev and Kamenev's mistakes in history by mentioning their names. He also anonymously criticized some leaders within the party, which caused the anger of many old Bolsheviks. The party organizations at different places gathered together passed resolutions and released announcements to denounce the Trotskyism. In January 1925, at the Central Plenum of the CPSU(B), Trotsky was given a serious party warning and expelled from the posts as the chairman of the Revolutionary Military Committee and the People's Commissariat responsible from the Army.

236

The third struggle was around the issue of "socialism in a single country." After the Trotsky led opposition, this time the new opposition led by Zinoviev and Kamenev was soon formed within the CPSU(B). The new opposition thought that the technology and economic level of Russia were too backward so it was not possible for the SU to build socialism independently. In December 1925, at the Fourteenth Congress of the CPSU(B), Stalin criticized the views of the new opposition. He emphasized that the USSR had possessed the basic initial conditions of building socialism. The congress denied the line and proposition of the new opposition and expelled some of their key members from the Central Committee. For example, Kamenev was demoted to the non-voting membership of the Political Bureau. After the congress, Zinoviev and Kamenev were dismissed from their posts as the chairman of the Leningrad Soviet and the deputy chairman of the Council of Labor and Defense and the People's Commissariat respectively. As the new opposition was cracked down, they felt too weak so they approached to the Trotsky opposition and formed an alliance with them.

In April 1926, Trotsky and Zinoviev met on the issue Between May and June in the same year, the Trotsky-Zinoviev allied opposition started to form. The main view of the allied opposition was still "socialism cannot be built in a single country". Trotsky's original theory of "permanent revolution" actually served as the theoretical basis for this view. At the same time, he also came up with the proposition of "super-industrialization", arguing that the industrialization in the USSR was too slow. The funds for the "super-industrialization" must be accumulated by further increasing the prices of industrial products and imposing taxes on peasants. The allied opposition also had some critical opinions on the issue of inner-party democracy, denouncing that the CC majority damaged the inner-party democratic system, harmed the inner-party democracy, controlled the inner-party debates and therefore seriously bred bureaucracy. When the Trotsky-Zinoviev allied opposition was formed, they distributed their leaflets everywhere, made speeches, propagated their own program and held semi-overt secret meetings on a regular basis. Targeted at these activities of the opposition, in July 1926 the CC of the CPSU(B) decided to expel Zinoviev from the Political Bureau. In October the same year, it decided to dismiss Trotsky from the membership of the Political Bureau and Kamenev from the alternate membership of the Political Bureau. After that, the struggle had lasted some time. On November 7 1927, which was the tenth anniversary of the October Revolution, the allied opposition organized demonstrations in Moscow and Leningrad, turning the contradictions between the two sides from an inner-party debate to an open confrontation. On 14 November, the Joint Meeting of the Central Committee and the Central Control Committee, CPSU(B) decided to expel Zinoviev and Kamenev from the Party. In December, the Fifteenth Congress of the Party made a resolution to expel 75 key members of the Trotsky-Zinoviev allied opposition, including Kamenev from the party. At that point, the Trotsky-Zinoviev allied opposition was completely disordered in terms of organization.

The fourth struggle was between Stalin and Bukharin on the road to be followed and method of socialist construction. After Bukharin was defeated, Bukharin was also expelled from the Political Bureau and dismissed from the chief editorship of Prevda and from his posts in the Communist International. Therefore, after a series of inner-party struggles, the CC headed by Stalin defeated the Trotsky opposition, the new opposition of Zinoviev and Kamenev, the Trotsky-Zinoviev allied opposition and the Bukharin opposition one after the other and Stalin firmly consolidated his position within the party.

Among the four major inner-party struggles, Stalin basically held the right views and propositions in the first three, but had many mistakes in the struggle methods. It is fair to say that different opinions within the party and struggles were a very normal thing. In the history of the CPSU(B), the divergences and struggle within the party had never stopped, but the previous inner-party struggles were all solved in a satisfying way. The reason is that, throughout the inner-party ideological struggles of the past, the Bolshevik Party led by Lenin, at the times of inner-party struggles, was paying attention to developing the inner-party democracy and insisting on democratic centralism, and avoided those methods of struggle which would be employed against enemies. Plus, at that time, leading members did not see anything unusual to have inner-party struggles, but regarded as the sign of a healthy democratic life within the party.

However, after Lenin's death, there occurred a lot of anomalies related to inner-party struggles of the CPSU(B). Two sides in the debate often overly exaggerated the mistakes and inaccuracy, only focusing on one point and ignoring the rest. The two sides also often took many vulgar and violent methods, exaggerating the mistake to the maximum and attacking each other. As a result, the struggles became increasingly fierce and finally developed to an antagonistic situation.

After the oppositions were defeated one by one, to prevent the new oppositions occurring, the inner-party democracy of the CPSU(B) was further damaged. Maybe because the past struggles were not evaluated cooly. Since then, in a very long period of time, there had never occurred any confrontations of ideas or debates of different opinions. The inner-party democracy existed in name only. The members of the party did not have the right to discuss the party policy; they had no right of say related to the appointment of the leaders or cadres; they also did not have the right to inquire and check the words and behavior of the party leaders. All these above led to an abnormal situation, such that the central or local leading behaved arbitrarily and power was centralized in their hands.

With the victory of Stalin over the oppositions, the personal cult on Stalin started to emerge and develop. Since the exaggerated celebrations of Stalin's 50th birthday in December 1929, the articles of flattering Stalin were nothing new in newspapers. In 1934, the Seventeenth Congress of the CPSU(B), which was called "the Congress of the Victors", made a series of revisions in the Party Constitution, subordinated the Central Control Committee to the Central Committee and gave more powers to the general secretary of the party. All these, combined with the negative effects of the highly centralized centrally administrated controlled economic system, directly led to the establishment of the highly centralized political system of the USSR.

In 1936, the USSR passed the new Constitution, known as the Stalin Constitution later, declaring that socialism was basically built, which meant that the highly centralized political power of the USSR has gained the lagal form of Constitution.

2. The strengthening of the leadership of the party related to the state organs and various social organizations

In 1922, the situation of one party system and only one party possessing the power was formed in the USSR which manifested itself in the practice/employment of the state power. The one-party system of the USSR has lasted till the disintegration of the USSR. It is certain that the realistic issue of one-party system in the SU is related with the issue of relations between the party and the government. Although Stalin made some theoretical discussions theoretically and had many correct explanations, this problem was never properly solved in practice.

First, in dealing with the relations between the party and the government, the party became the actual supreme authority while the Soviet government organs were just a "rubber stamp" which obeys the instruction of the Central Committee of the Party. In terms of improving and developing the Soviet system, Stalin had made some contributions. Before 1936, the administrative divisions in the Soviet Russia was not clear and the institutional structure was not complete, so the organizational structure of the state authorities at all levels were not unified; the relationships between higher and lower administrative levels were not clear too. With Stalin's efforts, the 1936 Constitution to a great extent solved this problem. First, it stipulated and defined the Soviet government system at every level, including the Supreme Soviet of the USSR, the Union Republics and the Autonomous Soviet Republics, the territorial, regions, autonomous regions' Soviets, districts' and cities' Soviets, etc.

Secondly, the organizational structure was clearly defined. For example, the Supreme Soviet used to have three chambers: the Congress of the Soviets, the Central Executive Committee and the Presidium of Central Committee. Now it would have two chambers, the Supreme Soviet and its Presidium.

Thirdly, the functions of the Soviet assemblies and their relations were clearly defined. As said in the 1936 Constitution, the legislative power in the USSR was exercised exclusively by the Supreme Soviet of the USSR, this new step had ended the unclear situation. Before that the Central Executive Committee and its Presidium and the People's Commissariat had also issued laws. It was also stipulated in the Constitution that the Soviet assemblies of different levels should conduct democratic centralism system. On the one hand, the lower Soviets should follow and execute the instructions of the higher Soviets; on the other hand, the lower Soviets joined in the work of higher Soviets by electing representatives. The 1936 Constitution fixed the new election system as universal, equal, direct and anonymous. If we evaluate these new regulations from the perspective legal development they showed the expansion of democracy in the USSR and reflected the progress of the society. However, these reforms did not cause substantial changes, did not improve the status of the government/state in the Soviet political system did not improve the status of the government/state authority as expected. On the contrary, it remained to be the subordinate organ of the party, in reality party strictly guided legislation and state operation.

Many of the laws and decrees were actually drafted, discussed and decided by the CC instead of the legislative organ. For example, the first five-year plan was made by the Political Bureau according to the guidelines of the Fifteenth Party Congress. The first five-year plan was later voted and decided at the Sixteenth Conference of the Party, and submitted to the Fifth Congress of the Soviet assembly for ratification.

The second five-year plan was made according to the instruction of the Seventeenth Conference of the Party and voted and ratified by the Seventeenth Congress of the Party, plus the Central Executive Committee and the People's Commissariat.

240

The third five-year plan was also first ratified by the Eighteenth Congress of the Party. In addition, there was another outstanding example, related to the making of the 1936 Constitution. Originally, making the new Constitution was supposed to be the primary task and the first responsibility of the Soviet assembly, but the whole process of formulating the Constitution was conducted within the party and revised and edited by Stalin in person. The Eighth Congress of the Soviet assembly was just a formality. More seriously, in the later period of Stalin's rule, many major acts of party organs and party leaders and many policies made by the party had greatly exceeded and infringed the sphere stipulated in the Constitution and other state laws. The CC and some leaders could infringe or by-pass any decisions made by the state organs at any time, which caused serious political chaos. For example, in January 1939, Stalin, undermined the related laws of the Soviet assembly, secretly telegraphed to the regions, affirming and supporting the corporal punishments done given to "people's enemies."[13]

The situation of the party replacing the government was not only restricted with the CC. but was more serious in local (lower) levels. In Stalin period, the chairmanship of the Soviet Assembly Executive Committees at all levels was usually held by the second secretary of the Party Committee

13 Issues about Stalin, volume 1, p. 271, Hangzhou, International Communist Movement Institute, Hangzhou University, 1979.

at the same level. Therefore, it was unavoidable that these standing organs of the Soviet Assemblies at all levels have become subordinated to the corresponding party committees. Plus, the deputies of the Soviet assemblies were almost decided by the system of appointment, so the Soviet deputies at all levels were controllable by the party. All in all, in Stalin period, especially the later period, the Soviet assemblies as state organs only existed in name, not performing any major functions. It is fair to say that it totally contrasted the requirements of the construction of political system of socialist democracy.

Second, looking to another aspect of the relations between the party and the government we can say all the government departments were over-topped by the party. Thus Party directly commanded and led the work of the government organs at all levels. Normally, the CC of the party should neither be an organ enjoying special power privileges within the party, nor is the organ of supreme state power. But in Stalin period, the CC enjoyed the right to directly issue orders to the government. Many major issues that were supposed to be solved by the government organs were decided by the CC of the party and issued for execution in the name of the CC. For example, the grain crisis issue in 1927 was completely dealt by the CC of the party while the People's Commissariat that was supposed to take charge of the work was laid aside. Examples like this can be found everywhere. If we look at economic construction sphere, there were tremendous amount of decisions that were made either directly by the CPSU(B) or by the CPSU(B) and the government in joint meetings. For example, the important resolutions released only by the CPSU(B) were: The establishment of Urals Mining Industry Syndicate (May 1930), On Completing the Industrial Five-Year Plan (June-July 1936), Plan of Complex Reconstruction of the Rivers: Volga, Don and Dnieper to Prepare Measures to Maintain the Caspian Sea Level and to Begin Constructing Volga-Don Connection (March 1939) etc. The important resolutions and orders jointly issued were: Plan of Construction of the Volga Power Plant (March 1932), The Struggle Against the Drought and Irritation of the Left Bank of the Lower and Middle Volga River (May 1932), Construction of Kuibyshev Reservoir on Volga River and the Reservoirs on Kama River (August 1937), Measures on the Stable Yields in Drought Area of the Southeastern USSR (October 1938), etc. In addition, things like method of improving the grain seeds, abolishing the allotment system on bread and some other kinds of food, even the breeding of horses were decided by the CC. The state organs were only informed later.

To ensure the "specific and actual leadership" of the party, Stalin established a system which included parallel leadership organs attached to the central and local committees of the party. In 1934, a leadership organ in charge of leading and managing the economy and production was established which were attached to the central and provincial committees of the CPSU(B), they controlled and led a parallel state organ in charge of the same work.

Attached tothe Central Committee of the CPSU(B), the Department of Agriculture, the Department of Industry, the Department of Transportation, the Department of Finance and Trade Planning, the Department of Political Administration and the Department of Newspapers and Periodicals were established which were parallel to state organs in charge of the same work. Attached to party committees in the Union Republics, in the provinces, regions and cities, these parallel leading departments were also set up. Although some minor changes now and then were made, this parallel system has never changed. During the Great Patriotic War, in 1941, to meet the needs of the war, an extraordinary organ of state power the State Defense Committee was established tocommand of everything. Therefore the system of complete integration of the party and the government was finally established. After the war, although there were some changes in the structure of the party organizations, this system started in 1934 has remained.

Third, the relations between the party and civil society. Here we see that the special interests of the masses including many social organizations and iniative of social associations were ignored. Social organizations were turned into appendages of the party, running errands for the party and government. Trade union for example, when Lenin was alive, the trade unions enjoyed substantial powers and directly participated the administration of economic construction affairs. However, under Stalin's era their powers were transferred to party organizations and to state economic administrative organs. Plus the party organizations intervened in the works of the trade unions, undertook most of the problems that were supposed to be solved by the trade union. On the surface it seemed that the party's leadership to the trade union was strengthened and the relations between the party and the masses became closer, but in fact, it was just another important expression that the party was more and more separated from the masses.

In Stalin period, the Congresses of the Trade Union Federation that was held every year was now held at an average of every six years, with the longest interval of 17 years. In fact, the trade union's original mission of protecting the interest of the working class and defending their reasonable requirements were lost, more and more they became an organization "run by the party" as an administrative organ of executing the party's resolutions. As long as the interests and requirements of the working class cannot be protected or reflected by the trade union, it is not possible for the workers to regard the trade union as the organization "of their own". That is why during the drastic changes in the East Europe in 80ies, many opposition groups flaunted the banner of "independence or autonomy".

All in all, in Stalin period, under the general thought line of the CPSU(B), the legislative and administrative power were actually taken by the leading organs of the party and outsatnading party leaders. The party led all the state organizations and social organizations under its the organization. This finally formed the situation that the power of the party exceeded any other power and the party organization was superior to any other organization.

3. Stalin strengthened the power of central state organs over federally led entities

According to Marxism, the state's organisational structure is the reflection of national realities on the state system. Therefore, if any proletarian dictatorship country adopts a unitary system or a federal system is determined by the national situation and particular conditions of that country. In principle Marx and Engels were against federal system, but under special circumstances, if proletariat could not overcome the national question by another solution federal system would be an exceptional way to solve the problem. Applying Marxist views, and combining Marx's views with the actual situation of the national questions in Russia, Lenin put forward the proposition of adopting a federal system. It was started with the *Declaration of Rights of the Working and the Exploited People* written in January 1918 This was an unprecedented event in the world history. This proposition, together with the declaration, was written into the 1918 Constitution of Russia. And in 1922, at the First Congress of the Soviet assembly, the Union of Soviet Socialist Republics was founded and the federal system was established as the state system.[14]

The USSR began to practice the federal organizational system as the state system, but the party's principle of organization was the system of democratic centralism. Because of this reality there occurred differences and contradictions between the federal system and the principle of democratic centralism. When Lenin was alive, in dealing with two type of contradictions first between the central state and the local components belonging to the federal structure and second contradictions between the principle of federal organization system and the principle of democratic centralism, the following principles were followed as solution: the principle of national self-determination, the principle of national equality, the principle of voluntary cooperation and the principle of democratic centralism.

243

14   USSR included 16 Union Republics united under a federal state system, including the federal Russian state. The other Republics were not federal states but included some autonomous regions based on national identity.

In practice, Lenin paid a lot of attention to promote the national republics to exercise their self-determination right, and strongly supported them against the Russian chauvinism. He suggested the party Central Committee not to interfere to the affairs of Union Republics or appoint too many Russian people who will be leaders in Union Republics' party and state organs. He also advocated a double-subordination system in state affairs: first, local state organs of Union Republics, should be subordinate to central state in Moscow and secondly subordinated to the local Soviet assemblies. In terms of the inner-party organizational relations, Lenin suggested that the local/national party organizations of the Union Republics should have the decision-making power on the local/national affairs. In terms of the management of the national economy, Lenin on the one side advocated a system of unified leadership and on the other side allowed autonomy both to admistrative levels and local/national state organs of the Union Republics.[15]

We should say that these principles and methods were proper to solve the 2 contradictions between the central state and the local state organs of the Union Republics, and between the federal system and the democratic centralism policies. However, at that time, due to several ambiguities related to administrative divisions and ambiguities related to task and power division between the higher and the lower organs there often occurred the situation of insufficient cooperation and management conflicts.

244

When Stalin was in power, he did not follow Lenin's above principles. On the one hand he strengthened centralization in the party, on the other hand made every effort to weaken the powers of the Union Republics, provinces, cities and regions, finally the federal organizational system only existed in name. Actually, the total Soviet syatem was turned into a unitary system centered around Russian nation and Moscow.

Following are Stalin's measures when he strengthened the central organ of the federal state

First, the state administrative regions were re-divided. After Stalin assumed the power, to rationalize the relationships among administrative regions and strengthen the leadership of the central authority to the local areas, he re-divided the administrative regions. First (during 1923-1929), town level was abolished and attached to districts; the country and province levels were abolished and they were attached to regions.

Second (in 1930), the region level was abolished and subordinated to oblast. All in all, the policy in arranging divisions aimed to strengthen the leadership of the central authority and reduce the number of levels. . The 1936 Constitution stipulated that the decisions for the establishment of

15 There were 27 provisions in which 16 Union Republics have transferred their state soverignty to central state.

new territories, oblasts, autonomous republics and autonomous regions in a Union Republic must be ratified by the central state, but the right of adminstative sovereignty (to practice independent local state authority) and the right to secede would belong to the Union Republics.

Second, the central state's powers of managing the local economies of Union Republics were strengthened. The 1924 Constitution of the USSR had stipulated that the central state organ of the USSR only has the right to formulate economic management principles and general plans. But by the 1930s, the central state did not only have the right to formulate the economic plans for Union Republics, but also directly controlled the personnel, finance, material, production, supply and sales affairs of the large local enterprises in Union Republics through central departments in Moscow. This system left very little decision-making rights to Union Republics. According to the statistics, in 1936, industrial production value of 15 Union Republics only amounted to about 10% of the total value of the USSR industrial production, which had seriously affected the economic development of the other 15 Union Republics.

Third, the legislative power of the central state was strengthened.

It was stipulated in the *1936 Constitution* that: "Legislation on the judicial system and judicial procedure; criminal and civil codes" belongs to central state. Constitution also said: Control over the observance of the Constitution of the USSR and ensuring conformity of the Constitutions of the Union Republics with the Constitution of the USSR" belongs to central state.

In addition, the right to issue important laws and decrees also belonged to the central state of the USSR. However in the past, the central state only decided the guiding principles of these laws and the Union Republics formulated their own laws accordingly.

Fourth, the central state's powers related to local personnel appointments were enlarged.

After Stalin took power, in order to strengthen the powers of the central state, on the one hand, he established a general system of appointment of cadres; on the other hand, he greatly strengthened the personnel management rights of the central state such as appointing or dismissing the senior cadres in local areas. Even the directors and managers of some important enterprises were all appointed by the central state department in charge. The *1936 Constitution* also stipulated that: "Procurators of Union Republics, Territorial administrations and Regions, as well as Procurators of Autonomous Republics and Autonomous Regions are appointed by the Procurator of the USSR for a term of five years." The powers used by these Procurators cannot be interfered by local state organs, they are independent and subordinate solely subordinate to the Procurator of the USSR (Central state organ). However in the past, the Procurator's office of any Union Republic was not subordinated to the central procurator office of the USSR.

In addition, in Stalin period, due to lack of clear distinction between the party and the government and because party held the key position in power structure, the leadership over the local state organs was usually applied by the central organs of the party. The central organs of the party in Moscow usually appointed sent the major party leaders to the other Union Republics to lead the local party organization. Thus a high degrre of the integration between the party and the government was achieved and the leaders of the central organs of the party also became the leaders of the central organs of the 16 states. That is to say, the so-called federal system could not survive.

4. The aspect of dictatorship was extremely employed in the state system and the democratic supervision system was weakened

At beginning of the establishment of the Soviet state system, great efforts were paid to construct a socialist democratic and legal state system. Around 1922, the Soviet Russia issued the Civil Law and the Criminal Law, Agrarian Law, Labor Law, etc, which initially formed the relatively complete legal system. At the same time, Soviet Russia also issued the Regulation for Court Organization Regulation, the Regulation for General Procurator and the Regulation for Lawyers Institutions, ond others. In 1925, the Third Congress of the All Union Soviet assembly passed the resolution on Adopting the Revolutionary Legal System, which established the legal system of the peaceful period. All these new laws and regulations had played an important role in beating down crimes, stabilizing public order kamu and protecting people's democratic rights.

As the main leader of the socialist construction, Stalin had made great contributions in designing socialist democracy and building the socialist legal system, but unfortunately, just as his socialism theories, Stalin's practice of socialism also included sharp contradictions hard to reconcile. On the one hand, he tried to build the socialist legal system, but on the other hand, he crudely damaged the past achievements he has madein this respect. Thus he caused a series of terrible results, such as the distorted development of the organs of the state dictatorship, deprived people from their democratic rights and almost eliminated the system of democratic supervision by people. If we trace its sources, on the one hand, it was the result of his one-sidedly exaggeration of the functions of the country of the proletarian dictatorship; on the other hand, it was the result of the complicated domestic and international inputs of the era.

Since 1928, there occurred the grain procurement crisis, the Shakhty incident and frequent conforntations which caused Stalin to mistakenly evaluate the situation of the class struggle at that time. He thought that the further the Soviet Union advanced towards socialism, the fiercer would be the fury of the remnants of the defeated exploiting classes, the more would they attempt the most desperate means of struggle."[16]

Under the influence of this mistaken estimation, Stalin escalated the emphasis of dictatorship, namely activated the repressive apparatuses of the state. The national security organ was the main component of the repressive apparatuses in the Stalin period. The predecessor of the USSR national security organ is the All-Russian Extraordinary Commission for Combating Counter-Revolution and Sabotage. Under the leadership of Felix Dzerzhinski, Cheka effectively attacked on the counter-revolutionaries and played an important role in maintaining the stability of the Soviet power. Later the name of this organization was often changed. After the Second World War, it was called the Ministry of the State Security. Especially in the 1930s, under the guidance of Stalin's thought of intensifying class struggle and the state's function of suppression with violence, the state security organ was given certain privileges and has developed in a distorted way. In the 1930s, the state's security organ had developed into a huge and self-contained institution controlled by Stalin. It overtopped the party and the state, without the supervision of the state and party organs, and was called "the state of the state". It could arrest any cadres of the party and the government, including the members of the Central Committee and the party leaders at any level. It could also undertake the whole legal judicial procedures from arrest, investigation, trial, custody to sentencing. In addition, it also was given the right to conduct "special procedures", which means handling the case not according to the normal legal procedures. For example, the indictment could be sent to the defendant overnight; the defendant did not have to attend the trial; no appeal after the judgment; immediate execution of the defendant who was sentenced to death by shooting, etc.

The state security organ had an unlimited power, thus it could employ unlimited criminal evils. The highly centralized state power and the distorted status of the repressive apparatuses severely damaged people's right of mastering their own affairs and weakened the system of democratic supervision. Stalin thought that the control of the state should be everywhere and on everything. In the whole Stalin period, there occurred only very limited actual progress in the aspects of making people the master of their own affairs and expanding the right of people's supervision. On the contrary, there occurred some retrogression in many aspects.

---

16 Works of Stalin, volume 1, p. 129.

The most important expression of people's mastering their own affairs is that the working people have equal rights to elect and be elected, and can exercise their rights to administer the country via the Soviet Assemblies. However, in Stalin period, the state organ—the Soviet asswemblies played less and less important role and became the stamping machine of the resolutions of the party. The vast masses could not exercise their rights to administer the country via the Soviet asswemblies at all. More seriously, related to state officers as the system of appointment was prevalent the election system gradually existed only in name. Since the list of the candidates of Soviet deputies were designated by the higher authority and the election was the single-candidate election, the working people's equal right to elect and be elected was actually infringed. Another important expression of people mastering their own affairs is that the masses can exercise the right to affect the state via social mass organizations that represent the particular interest of social group or a profession. However, Stalin overtly stressed the functions of the state, completely ignored of the various positive functions of the social group activities, suspecting that these activities and associations could confront the party. In practice, Stalin paid efforts to weaken the functions of these organizations, and turned them into appendages of the party and the government. In the 1930s, many excellent leaders of trade unions were put into prison with the charge of "syndicalism deviation", "anti-partyism", etc. and killed. Therefore, it was impossible for the masses exercise the right to administer the country via their own mass organizations.

248

That people's rights to be the masters of their own affairs were infringed meant the loss of the system of democratic supervision. If people cannot choose their deputies, they also do not have the right to dismiss or change them at any time legally. As a matter of fact, in the Stalin period, no law related to dismissing deputies was issued. Not only that, after Stalin came to power, the method of election also changed. In the past, the elections were conducted according to industries and occupations. In Stalin period, the elections were conducted according to communities.

In a country where the party was organized mainly due to working sites this election system in essence restricted the relations between electorates and deputies, thus electorates were hardly able to supervise the deputies. The biggest move of Stalin for weakening the system of democratic supervision was the "reform" of the inspection and control organs. When Lenin was alive, to prevent the party from degenerating and state organs becoming bureaucratic and to avoid corruption, the Workers' and Peasants' Inspectorate (for the state affairs) Inspection and the Central Control Committee (for the party affairs) were established to realise the supervision on the party and the government establishments. And to establish an effective mechanism of power restriction, Lenin suggested upgrading them to the parallel status with the Central Committee of the Party. However, after Stalin came to power, he weakened this control system. The Workers' and Peasants' Inspectorate was turned into the Soviet Control Committee led by the People's Commissariat (the government). The Central Control Committee of the party was downgraded to the organization whose members were appointed and an organ led by the Central Committee of the Party. The aim of the control was changed from the supervision on the party, party leaders and the government organs and their staff to the inspection of the realization of the resolutions of the central leading organs. In addition, Stalin also avowedly changed Lenin's style of including worker and peasant masses in the Workers' and Peasants' Inspection to conduct the democratic supervision. He ordered that the Soviet Control Committee of the People's Commissariat of the USSR should only employ experts and those people with expertise to conduct the supervision; that all the work of supervising and inspecting should only be done by the control staff appointed by the state control organ. Thus obviously the vast masses were kept outside of the work of supervision. What Stalin had done did not only violate Lenin's creative thoughts in his later years, but also caused potential harm to the construction of a socialist state system and legal system in socialist countries.

5. The formation stages of the cadres management system in the Stalin period

Stalin attached great importance to the role of cadres in the socialist construction. He pointed out, "After a correct political line has been worked out and tested in practice, the Party cadres become the decisive force in the work of guiding the Party and the state."[17] He had e proposed the famous slogan "cadres decided everything." Under his active promotion and direct leadership, the CPSU(B) started training cadres at an accelerated pace as the primary and the most important task, initiated the new era of training cadres at a large scale. At the same time he also elaborated on the standards and policies of choosing cadres, and pointed out that the cadres' political quality and performance should both be taken into consideration when choosing and appointing them. He especially emphasized that the cadres should have the knowledge of science and technology and become experts of industry. Therefore, he suggested a positive approach towards intellectuals and fully affirmed their role in socialist construction. In addition, Stalin also paid attention to the average age of the cadres, argued that young cares are more sensitive to new things and eager to excel. So, "that is why we must boldly and in timely manner promote young cadres to leading posts."[18] Guided by these

17   Selected Works of Stalin, volume 2, p. 458.
18   Works of Stalin, volume 1, p. 245.

ideas, even with him taking charge in person, the CPSU(B) designed a lot of policies to improve the cadres' political quality, cultural level and expertise and set mechanisms to choose bright cadres who would be appointed as the leaders of different departments. Stalin's propositions did not only encourage the vast cadres' enthusiasm, but also trained thousands of outstanding cadres for the USSR. According to the statistics, in 1928, there were only 90000 experts that had received higher education. By 1937, there were 9.6 million educated cadres in the country and 4.2 million of them were technical cadres. These high-quality cadres have laid solid foundation for the development of the socialist construction and the great victory of the Patriotic War.

In Stalin period, the USSR formed a system of cadres management system and established a huge reservoir of cadres of scientists and experts. This was one of the important contribution by Stalin to the political construction task. However, he also made many serious mistakes in this respect.

Mistakes in cadres system

First, Stalin over stressed on the appointment system (in contrast to election) and centralized the right to appoint and dismissing of cadres in the hands of the central party organs. The system of appointment had started as early as in the period of Lenin, which was mainly one result of the civil war and the backwardness of the culture of Russia. After the civil war, according to the change of the situation, Lenin suggested appointing cadres mainly according to election system with the appointment system as the complementary method. But Stalin did not follow Lenin's proposition. Under his leadership, the election system only existed in name. In Stalin period, the appointment system was not only conducted for the government organs, even in the election of the Soviet, there existed "the appointment and mandatory appointment of Soviet candidates."[19] This was even for the party cadres. The individuals appointed party organizations at all levels undoubtedly were without exception appointed by the higher organization. Targeting this, Bukharin sharply criticized that there was not any party committee secretary that was elected, instead they were all appointed by Stalin's circle. Plus, because the party was raised to sole power owner, the party organizations actually took every right to appoint or dismiss government cadres. In Stalin period, the party organizations did not only take the right to appoint or dismiss the Soviet assembly candidates but also selected the people who would lead the enterprises.

It is fair to say that under special circumstances, especially in the period of the civil war and the Patriotic War (1941-45), it was necessary that the

---

19   The Collected Resolutions of the Congresses, Conferences and Central Plenums of the CPSU(B), volume 3, p. 266, Beijing, People's Publishing House, 1956.

party appointed the leaders and cadres for certain important departments of the government and army so that the party could command the war in an organized way to defeat the enemies. But to continue the same appointment system and generalize it for all times was not a proper way in the practice of party leadership over state affairs, in fact this was a mechanical understanding of party leadership. Centralizing the power to appoint in the hands of the party organizations has led to negative consequences. This was neither good for the development of the socialist democracy.

In fact, the 1936 Constitution of the USSR had established the new election system for Soviet citizens.

Stalin could have taken this opportunity to establish a democratic system of elections for selecting government cadres, but he did not do that. Instead, he kept the old appointment system and further centralized the right to appoint and dismiss. This was a serious mistake of Stalin related to building the contingent rank of cadres.

Second, another serious mistake of Stalin in the construction of the rank of cadres is the concurrent system of the party and the government cadres.

Stalin thought the concurrent system of the party and the government cadres is one of the important conditions to ensure the flexibility and orderliness of the party's leadership over the government organs.

In Stalin's era, the leaders of the party organizations at all levels were either "elected" to Soviet assemblies or to high level government/state organs. Stalin himself were holding several positions at the same time, the leadership of the party, the government and the army was centralized in his hands.

Another important failure was the—de facto—life-long tenure system. Since there were no limit to the job terms of the leaders, they held their posts life long tenure. Not only Stalin was the party and state leader until he passed away, all other important leaders held their posts till to the end.

Stalin also promoted a privileged cadres system. The most outstanding expression of this problem was the abolishment of the upper limits related to the salaries for the leaders and senior cadres. They were also provided with other side payments and other advantages such as special shopping malls and summer houses etc. After 1933, Stalin started a special payment system for concurrent jobs. This system included the leaders and cadres of the city level and above. That is to say, a cadre could hold concurrent posts and get paid for all of them, which was one form of cadres' privilege. These mistaken systems above has undoubtedly caused some cadres regard the posts as an instrument to reach both power and money, which reinvigorated the decayed sense of hierarchy and bureaucracy of the old society.

6. The leadership functions of the secretaries in the party commitees was strengthened

Collective leadership is one important manifestation of the principle of democratic centralism of the proletarian party, and the most important principle of the leadership of the proletarian party. Lenin attached great importance to this principle. When he was in power, all the major issues were decided after the collective organ discussion. According to statistics, from 1918 to 1924, the party held seven congresses and six conferences; from 1917 to 1922, the All-Russian Congress of Soviet was held for ten times. As for the party central committee plenums, meetings of the People's Commissariat and meetings of the Council of the National Defense, they were more frequent. Just between 1919 to 1922, Lenin had led up to 296 meetings of the party Political Bureau. In the first few years after Lenin's death, Stalin, who held highest authority in the central committee of the party, still followed the principle of collective leadership. However, with Stalin's position getting stabilized within the party, he gradually started to abandon the principle of collective leadership, weakened the democratic supervision system of the party.

The primary expression of the party's collective leadership is that the party holds the General Congresses on a regular basis and makes it the institution where the will of the whole party can be expressed and the major policies can be made. However, since after the Seventeenth Congress of the Party, Stalin gradually damaged the system of holding the party congresses on a regular basis. According to the Party constitution, the congresses of the party should be held at least every three to five years, but the previous regulation was once a year. Even so, the last regulation was still not followed. The intermission of the plenums of the party central committee and other party organs became longer and longer. The Eighteenth Congress of the Party was held after five years. The intermission between the Eighteenth and the Nineteenth Congress of the Party was as long as 13 years. The meetings of the Central Committee and the Political Bureau were always replaced by the "five people group" or "seven people group" appointed and invited by Stalin, which meant that the collective organ meetings of the party had turned into Stalin's endorsement meetings, where he made long talks and demanded approval.

Stalin's infringement of the principle of the collective leadership was at the same time meant he was strengthening the functions and power of the secretariat of the party organs, including that of the central committee.

Normally the main responsibility of the secretariat is to lead the every-day organizational and executive work. Secretariat and its organ should be subordinate to the Political Bureau and the Organizational Bureau of the Central Committee. However, since April 1922 when Stalin was elected as the general secretary of the party Central Committee, he started to gradually expand the actual power of the secretariat. After Stalin became the general secretary, the critical powers held in the secretariat organization's hands was the right to appoint cadres for the central government organs, provinces, factories and villages. He merged the Party's personnel section, the Registration and Distribution Department with the

Department of Organization and Inspection, the two departments were under the general secretariat at that time, working as one organ: Orgbureau with the powers of "recommending", appointing and promoting the leaders and cadres of the party, government, trade unions, factories and cooperatives.

At the same time, the secretariat also dispatched large amount of inspectors to inspect the work of party and government organs and attached republics. At that time, the number of staff of the secretariat organ was 767. In 1930, Stalin again "reformed" the secretariat, and divided Orgbureau as the Registration and Distribution Department and the Department of Organization and Inspection.

253

The Department of Organization and Inspection was in charge of keeping contact with the party organizations in the local areas, control and inspect their work. The Department of Distribution was in charge of appointing and dismissing the leaders of all enterprises related to industrial production sectors (at that time, there were heavy industry section, light industry section, transportation section, agriculture section, foreign affairs cadres section, finance and planned trade section, the Soviet administrative section, finance section). Stalin's "reform" of the secretariat created the embryo of designing the departments of the party Central Committee according to production sectors.

In 1934, the new party Central Committee officially established about seven departments that should lead the production sectors, but the decisions to be made by them was actually still in hands of the secretariat. In addition, since the conferences and meetings of the central committee of the party and other leadership organs could not be held in their normal intervals, the secretariat and its organs actually became the supreme authority of the party. The secretariat did not only have the right to decide the time of holding the congress of the party and the plenum of the central committee, the number of Soviet assembly deputies and how they will be elected; it also had the right to decide on the major issues, issue specific regulations and execute them. Even the candidates of the Central Committee were decided by the secretariat. It should also be pointed out that the work of the secretariat was actually led by the Stalin and a few persons near to him. Therefore, the decision-making and execution rights were actually used by a few people, especially by Stalin, who was the member of the Political Bureau and the Organization Bureau and the general secretary of the Central Committee. From 1941, on Stalin held the posts of the chairman of the People's Commissariat, the chairman of the Council of National Defense, the People's Commissar for Defense (Defense Minister), the supreme commander of the Army of the USSR. Thus holding the power of the party, the government and the army, Stalin completely abandoned the principle of collective leadership.

III. The reasons for the formation of the highly centralized political system in the Stalin period

The formation of the highly centralized political system of the USSR in the 1930s was not only because of Stalin's personal will and unlimited power. It also had its profound social and economic basis.

1. Influence of the backward productive forces and culture

According to the design of Marx and Engels, socialism should be established on the basis of generally developed socialized production, but due to many special historical and realistic reasons, socialism was first victorious in Russia, a country with backward economy and culture. We should say that Lenin has developed Marxism with the idea that the proletariat of the backward country takes the power first and creates the conditions needed for socialism with its power. However, the problems brought by the drastic changes in a society are very complicated. I think especially the backward productive forces and culture have determined that the socialist system born in a backward country was bound to have the property of incompleteness, thus highly centralized political system was just the external reflection of it. The influences of the backward productive forces and culture on the socialist political system of the Soviet Union were manifested in the following aspects.

First, the backward productive forces and culture made individuals and groups lack of self-consciousness, which caused the social mentality of the worship of authority.

This is one of the fundamental reasons that formed the highly centralized political system in the USSR. the worship of authority is the universal social mentality caused by "the personal dependence" in the pre-capitalist societies. Marx had discussed this issue long time ago. In *Economic Manuscripts of 1857-1858*, Marx mentioned three major social forms:

"Relations of personal dependence (entirely spontaneous at the outset) are the first social forms, in which human productive capacity develops only to a slight extent and at isolated points. Personal independence founded on objective[sachlicher]dependence is the second great form, in which a system of general social metabolism, of universal relations, of all-round needs and universal capacities is formed for the first time. Free individuality, based on the universal development of individuals and on their subordination of their communal, social productive forces as their social wealth, is the third stage. The second stage creates the conditions for the third.

Patriarchal as well as ancient conditions (feudal, also) thus disintegrate with the development of commerce, of luxury, of money, of exchange value, while modern society arises and grows in the same measure."[20]

The "personal dependence" refers to the reliance of people on other people. In different historical periods, different nations and regions, individual's dependence on others take different forms. The "personal dependence" discussed by Marx above mainly refers to the individual's dependence, subordination to others after the emergence of the private ownership. Marx included it as "patriarchal, ancient (and feudal)."

255

The fundamental cause of these type of social relations was the backwardness of the productive forces and the culture, demonstrating themselves as underdeveloped commodity economy (markets), low level of the socialization of production, and the dominant position of natural and semi-natural agricultural economy, generally low cultural level of the society, popularity of the despotic culture, obedience to the supreme power of the Tsars, etc. According to Marx socialism was born in Russia when this society was mainly in the first great form and when it just entered the second great form.

The result of "personal dependence" of an individual generally speaking, is his loss of independence due to dependence to other people. Thus, the person will lack self-consciousness. People who lack self-consciousness never realize the personal interest. Even though they have, they will not dare to consciously and boldly pursue for it. They are always used to depreciate and depress themselves, and regard making contribution and sacrifice for authority as their task, and regardobedience as a virtue. In their life, they will always seek authority of others on himself. No matter in a family and village, or as big as the country, they will always seek an authority or a

---

20 Collected Works of Marx and Engels, volume 46 (A), p. 104, Beijing, People's Publishing House, 1979.

supreme ruler. Even though there isn't one, people need to create one. For them authority and social hierarchy are unquestionable, so they never dare to stand up against various type of authorities, not to mention freely express their own requests. Unless they are highly disturbed, they will not take the risk to stand up. However, once they succeed, the first thing they are going to do is to make themselves the authority, making other people worship and obey them. The worship of authority went to top in the dark rule of the Christianity in the middle ages in western world. The main aim of the Christianity and some other religions was to strangle the tiny little self-consciousness remained in people's mind, making them self-deny and self-depreciated. They gave all the virtues and power to the God, making the God the dominator of human beings and object on which people depend.

Before the victory of the October Revolution, Russia, generally speaking, like Europe in the middle ages, was at the stage of "personal dependence" in its historical development. The belief of Orthodox Eastern Church was Russian people's main guide and basis of their life. Therefore, in a country like this, it is no wonder that the highly centralized political system was formed. Before the October Revolution, Russia had never experienced a full capitalist development; the people's cultural quality, values, spirits and religious traditions were never elevated to the level of developed countries in Western Europe; the vast masses generally had the mentality of appreciation to the Tsar-the wise emperor. People were used to being instructed and led by a certain heroic figure. It was just this backward productive forces and cultural awareness that became the social foundation of the highly centralized political system formed in the Stalin period. Therefore, that the history "chose" Stalin had both the fortuity and the necessity. Second, the backwardness of the productive forces and the culture will definitely widen the political gap between the group of leaders and other members among the revolutionary ranks.

And the widening of this political level gap is a very important factor that formed the highly centralized political system. As the science for the liberation of the proletarian class and all humanity, Marxism does not only have the broad and profound contents and thoughts, but also an accurate logic and a complete system. Therefore, this broad system of knowledge can only be mastered by the those intellectuals with a high cultural level who can grasp the general law of the development of history and lead the proletarian cause to victory. However, before the October Revolution, there was a huge gap between Russia and the western developed countries in economy and culture. Russia's industrial output value only took up 12.5% of that of the United States; the industrial productivity of labor was only 11% of that of the United States; 75% of the residents in the country were illiterate; only 1% of the residents were working in science, culture and education. Even by 1926, with the great efforts of the party and the government, the national economy of the USSR had only reached to the prewar level. Among the residents aged between 19 and 46, half were still illiterate. People working in science, culture and education were less than 2% of the employed citizens. Under such backward circumstances, only very few revolutionary intellectuals could understand and master Marxism comprehensively. Parallel to this, within the party there has formed a thought trend that was completely different from the democratic system.

According to the principle of democracy, it should be allowed so that the thoughts can come from grass root members and go upwards for evaluation and discussion. But due to the special conditions of Russia, this was upside down. Therefore, within the party, the members were divided into different levels according to their cultural level, level of political awareness and ability. According to Lenin's division, the revolutionary ranks was divided into four levels, namely the small group of prestigious, talented and experienced leaders, party, class and masses. In such a backward country as Russia, the difference between complex features of Marxism and the low cultural level of individuals in the revolutionary ranks have determined that Marxism could be disseminated by a group of leaders consisting only a very few people. This has definitely widened the political gap between the group of leaders and other members and this wide gap was bound to lead to the high centralized system.

The highly centralized political system as a historical phenomenon did not only exist in the USSR, but also in some other socialist countries after the Second World War The root causes were the objective factors such as the backward productive forces, underdeveloped commodity economy and backward culture. Of course, the USSR as the first socialist country in the world, having this highly centralized political system which contrasted the socialist principles has also other historical reasons, which will be discussed below.

2. The extensive existence of small peasantry and issues related to maturity of the proletariat

The extensive existence of the small peasants is the class basis for the formation of the highly centralized political system. Lenin thought, "Russia is an agrarian country and one of the most backward countries in Europe". In 1913, the individual peasants (not including the kulaks/rich peasants) and the individual handicraftsmen took up 66.7% of the whole population. The isolated and scattered way of production of the small peasants, with family as the unit, determined that they consciously regarded the patriarchal system and autocratic monarchy as unalterable concepts and that they were used to worship unfounded ideas and idols. They could neither form a political organization nor propose a new program to replace the feudal system. Generations of the Russian peasants lived in the illusions about the Tsar, hoped that there was a sagacious monarch relieve people from suffering, which was the breeding ground for the centralization. After the victory of the October Revolution, the Soviet power allocated to peasants the land confiscated from landlords and kulaks. Therefore, the poor working peasants mostly had become independent small producers, and part of the poor peasants had become middle peasants. During the period of the victory of the October Revolution to the collectivization of agriculture, the Russian peasants were still small producers under the effect of patriarchal thoughts and who were still afraid of the destructive power of the market. In the early period of collectivization, the peasants resisted it, but with the establishment of the collectivization of agriculture and after the state's control of all the activities of production and operation of the collective farms, this time peasants connected their destiny with the state, therefore regarding the state the leaders of the country as their God.

The proletariat of Russian had started to grow very late. The Russian industrialization started in the 1830s when the industrialization of Britain and France was nearly over. The serious survivals of the slavery system were still preserved in Russian factories, where workers did not have any freedom. Between 1830s and 40s when the proletariat in some European countries started to stage in the political arena, the Russian proletariat was just at the early stage. The Russian proletariat still had very strong small-peasant consciousness, with illusions on the Tsar in their struggle against the bourgeoisie. From the end of the 1920s to the early 1930s, the rapid industrialization of the USSR made millions of peasants pour into cities from rural area and join the rank of workers. They still kept the small-peasant consciousness. In terms of mentality and cultural level, although they were enthusiastic and hard-working, they lacked the spirit of innovation and the consciousness of democracy. They were also more used to mandatory orders and submission. Therefore, it was very natural that the working class in such a mood could easily become the social foundation of personal cult and administrative orders from above.

3. The influence of the special tendency: The party building thought of Bolsheviks

In the history of Russia, the Tsars were famous for their tyranny, their dark and terrifying autocratic monarchy had lasted hundreds of years in Russia. The highly centralized autocratic monarchy was also the main trend in the Russian history. The several major transformations in the Russian history were all achieved when the autocratic monarchy was on the top and in a top to down way. The highest leaders and the officers at every level of Russia were used to this way of ruling. Under the autocratic monarchy, there was not any bit of democracy in Russia. The Tsar government violently suppressed on the democratic progressive personages and blocked and strangled progressive thought, forcing the revolutionary parties and organizations have to follow secret activities. Faced by this cruel rule , Lenin suggested building a strictly disciplined and militant revolutionary party. He emphasized that the proletariat can effectively play its role of organization (its major function) only by strict discipline within the party and by conducting the principle that the minority subordinates the majority and that the lower level subordinates to the higher level and apply the principle of democratic centralism.He regarded the proletariat's unconditional organizational centralism and extremely district discipline as one of the basic conditions of defeating capitalism. Lenin even analyzed the tendency which resisted against centralism as "the fixed and fundamental character of opportunism on the organizational question."[21] With the development of the proletarian struggle, Lenin also realized the disadvantages of the overly centralized power structure within the party. Therefore, he started to emphasize the centralism should re-written as "democratic centralism", which was written into the party's program passed at the Fourth Conference of the Party in 1906 as the basic principle of the party life. However, under the conditions of harsh political struggle, the party organizations were not established on the basis of democratic election system. The centralism was still the dominant tendency in the Bolsheviks' party building thought. The supreme power of leading the party was still actually in the hands of only a few professional revolutionaries. Following centralism strictly and having centralized power and decision system, was positive and effective for conquering and consolidating the political power led by the party. However, once this system was established, it has remained with a huge inertia and resistance. Thus it has caused an outstanding influence on the leadership system of the party after the victory of the revolution, even on the leadership system of the state.

---

21   Selected Works of Lenin, third edition, volume 1, p. 507.

4. The dual influence of the militarist historical tradition and the perilous international environment

The whole history of the Tsarist Russia is the history of invasion and expansion. The influence of militarism had penetrated into every field of the Russian society and became one important aspect of the Russian historical traditions. Marxism has always been against the theory of the determinism of the geographical environments, but it has never denied the great effect of geographic environment on the development of the society. In the 15th century when Russia got rid of the control of the Mongolians and developed into a centralized feudal principality, the country and its territories were in danger of invasion by foreign enemies. In the north, Sweden, this powerful Northern European country, was guarding the sea gate of the Baltic; in the east and south, there were the threats of the Tatars and Turks now and then; in the west, it was the East European steppes without any military barrier. The Russia Principality at that time, as a land-locked country, did not have any sea gate at all, which seriously affected the economic development of Russia. Faced by such difficult conditions, the Tsars of every generation all took "national security" and seeking for a sea gate as the primary task, which was the motive for invasions and expansion. According to the statistics, during over 370 years from 1547 when Ivan IV became the first Tsar to the 1917 the last Tsar Nicholas II, the Russian governments frequently had wars of various sizes with over 20 countries. Among them, there were 36 wars that were of large size with over tens of thousands of troops. As the wars went on, the territory of the Tsarist Russia had also expanded. By the time of Nicholas II in 1917, the territory of Russia had expanded from 2.7 million square meters at the time of Ivan IV to 22.8 million square meters, becoming a military superpower that spanned Asia and Europe with 1/6 of the world's land area. The long-term wars and invasions had caused militarism to penetrate into every corner of the society. From economy to politics, the formulation of the policies and the operation of the system were all designed around the need for military goals. Even people's social life, values and the education of art were imbued with the spirit of militarism. By the end of 19th century and the beginning of 20th century, the Tsarist Russia had developed into a real (military feudal) imperialist country, meaning that its greediness could not be satisfied by external expansion only and aimed to fight for the world hegemony.

Analyzing the 370 years' history of the Tsarist Russia, it is not hard to tell that the secret of Tsar's victories in various wars and its constant expansion was the highly centralized system that was effective in running of economy at wartimes and in unifying the ideology and activities of the society at a high level. Therefore, from the first Tsar Ivan IV, the centralized political system had started to form. With the efforts of the Tsarsand especially with the reforms by the Peter the Great, (1872-1725) the autocratic system was finally completed and established. Thus it can be seen that the autocratic monarchy is the essential product of the Tsarist Russia to meet the needs of military expansion. Lenin had sharply pointed out: the whole history of Tsarist Russia's "autocracy is one of wholesale grabbing of local, regional, and national lands."[22]

As the sound of the gun of the October Revolution went to the air, the history of the dark rule of the Tsar was over and the Russia saw the dawn of the new era. The Soviet assemblies, as the unity of the new democracy and new power, fully manifested the natures of socialism—that is people to be masters their own affairs. However, the historical tradition of militarism, with its relatively stable ideology, was not possibly to disappear from people's mind easily with socialist reforms. Plus the dangerous international environment of Soviet Union was the catalyzer of the restoration of the militarism. From the first day the Soviet power was established, revolution and war had become the two major issues that it had to face. First was the three-year civil war and then came the encirclement of the imperialist countries and the constant partial attacks. Especially when the world financial crisis broke out in 1929 and the German fascists came to power in 1933, the USSR was shrouded in the shadow of war. This dangerous international environment made Stalin and the CPSU(B) realize that "the new imperialist war was coming day by day." In January 1934, Stalin pointed out during the Seventeenth Congress of the CPSU(B): "we have to take every measure to protect our country from any unexpected event." The coming war made the young Soviet think that it had no choice but to resort to the old way of the Tsar government. Although the nature of the coming war was different, the requirement of war related to the political system its militarization or high degree of centralization. Only with the highly centralized political system could the personnel, human, material and financial resources be gathered in order to ensure that the party, the whole country could be kept highly unified in the sphere politics, ideology and activities. Only in this way could the powerful material foundation for the war could be built and developed.

However, we must point out that the historical tradition of militarism is the internal cause of the formation of the highly centralized political system of the USSR, the dangerous international environment was the external cause of the formation of this system. Such a high level of centralization in Stalin's period, even his personal dictatorship, could not be formed without the deep rooted historical tradition of militarism. Also this highly centralized political system would not last after the war without this tradition. In fact, from Stalin to Brezhnev, the influence of this militaristic ideology could be observed everywhere. Before the breakout of the Second World

---

22 Collected Works of Lenin, volume 16, p. 299, Beijing, People's Publishing House, 1988.

War, the USSR launched the Soviet-Finnish War and formed its eastern front; after the war, it had secret negotiation in Yalta about China and many other countries of the world. The USSR's self-centered mentalisty, great-power chauvinism, and hegemonism demonstrated itself in its treatment and relations with the third-world countries including socialist countries. Her acts and mentality were all the expressions of the historical tradition of the Tsarist Russia's external expansionism and militarism. Therefore, as long as this spirit of militarism could not be overcome, the highly central-ized political system of the USSR could not be fundamentally changed. Of course, the dangerous international environment also added fuel to the fire of the formation of the highly centralized political system. This dan-gerous international environment made the leaders of the USSR continue the concept of considering the crisis threating the survival of USSR from a geopolitical perspective and activated the thought of militarism that had deep roots in the mind of some USSR leaders. For example, Stalin in his speech of the Patriotic War, he used the name of famous high-ranking mili-tary officer of Tsar's who had led external expansion in order to inspire and encourage the Red Army soldiers. He also named the orders of the Red Army (i.e. Order of Suvorov) and the highest military institution, which undoubtedly promoted sympathy for the militaristic tradition of Russian people. Therefore, the dangerous international environment and the histori-cal tradition of militarism has interacted and complemented each other, and finally promoted the formation of the highly centralized political system.

5. The influence of Stalin's personality

Historical materialism emphasizes that the masses are the creators of history. On the other side it also admits the important role of the outstanding people in history. The highly centralized political system was formed as the result of interaction of many factors such as the backward productive forc-es, complicated domestic and international environment, special cultural traditions, etc. But we cannot deny that the formation of the highly cen-tralized political system bears the particular personal formation of Stalin, especially his personality. If we can say that the historical traditions of the Tsarist Russia and practical conditions above has provided the possibility of the formation of the centralized political system, then we can say that Stalin's effect personally has made it become the reality. Stalin's personali-ty was extremely contradictory. On the one hand, he was loyal to the prole-tarian cause and Marxism-Leninist thoughts and had the courage to firmly fight against various counterrevolutionary forces, but on the other hand, he was suspicious, ruthless, capricious, proud and too arbitrary. These defects of his personality, when combined with power, had great impact on the party's and the government's system of leadership. Lenin has expected this situation. He said, "Comrade Stalin, having become Secretary-General, has unlimited authority concentrated in his hands, and I am not sure whether he will always be capable of using that authority with sufficient caution." "Stalin is too rude and this defect, although quite tolerable in our midst and in dealing among us Communists, becomes intolerable for a Secretary-General post."[23] Therefore he suggested that the Central Committee should remove Stalin from the post of general secretary and he added: This circumstance (Ed. of Stalin) may appear to be a negligible detail. But I think that from the standpoint of safeguards against a split (of the party) and from the standpoint of what I wrote above about the relationship between Stalin and Trotsky it is not a [minor] detail, but it is a detail which can assume decisive importance."

The future development has proved Lenin's prediction.

In 1922 when Stalin was elected the general secretary of the party, he started to reorganize the institutions of the Central Committee and continuously expanded his power. Especially after his victories in the inner-party struggles and after some achievements were made in socialist construction, the defects of Stalin's personality were also exposed. Claiming all the credit to himself, Stalin became more and more arrogant and arbitrary. He also re-established the organizations of the party and the government to free his personal will, thus elevated himself and these new organs above the party and the government. In 1941, he took the position as the chairman of the People's Commissariat and the Chairman of the Council of National Defense, holding the power of the party, the government and the army in his hands. He carried out a patriarchal leadership style and finally formed his intention of highly centralized political system.

263

IV. Stalin's contributions and defects in the theory of socialist political system

During the 30 years under Stalin's power, he made a lot of theoretical discussions related to the theory of the socialist political system. These discussions have not only enriched the socialist political system theory, but also became guiding thoughts in the theory and practice of the socialist political system in Soviet Union after the mid-1920s and deeply effected other socialist countries. However, Stalin's thoughts contained certain distortions on the theory of the socialist political system, which not only departed from both the scientific principles of Marxism and scientific spirit but also caused great harm to the world socialist movement in practice.

---

23 Collected Works of Lenin, volume 43, p. 339, 340.

1. Stalin's contributions to the theory of socialist political system

Stalin's contributions to the theory of socialist political system can be roughly summarized as the following:

Firstly, Stalin further deepened the thought on the structure of dictatorship of the proletariat. The theoretical system of the dictatorship of proletariat was cleared in Lenin's struggle against certain mistaken ideas of Trotsky. After the death of Lenin, Stalin inherited and further developed the main contents of Lenin's thoughts on this issue.

Stalin argued that the structure of the dictatorship of the proletariat consisted of two elements: the vanguard of the proletariat (party), secondly the Soviet assemblies and other mass organizations especiallythe Soviet assemblies were the most all-embracing mass organisations of the working classes.. The vanguard of the proletariat is the "directing force" category in the system of the dictatorship of the proletariat.And the broad mass organizations including Soviet assemblieswere the two way "transmission gears" or "levers" in of the structure of the dictatorship of the proletariat. He stressed that these two the "gears", and the "directing force" were essential for the proletariat, because without them, the proletariat could neither win nor gain the long-term consolidation of dictatorship of the proletariat in the struggle to overthrow the bourgeoisie, in the struggle to consolidate proletarian political power, and succeed in the practice of building socialism.

In *On the Foundations of Leninism, On the Several Issues of Leninism* and other works, Stalin systematically explained the component parts of the system of the dictatorship of the proletariat. The party is the vanguard of the proletariat and the directing force in the structure of the dictatorship of the proletariat. Stalin argued that the party is the advanced detachment , the political leader and its headquarter in the battles of the working class. It is due to the party's leadership that the proletariat can become strong team with leadership and organization and gains the courage to attack all the reactionary forces to ultimately overthrow the rule of the bourgeoisie and establish the dictatorship of the proletariat. It is due to the party's leadership that the proletariat can consolidate the dictatorship of the proletariat to build socialism. Stalin further deepened Lenin's idea that the party is "the highest form of class unity of proletarians."[24] He pointed out: "the party is not the only organization of the working class. The proletariat has many other organizations absolutely necessary to the smoothly carry its struggles against the capital"[25], such as the trade unions, the cooperatives, the plant organizations, the parliamentary groups, the Communist Youth League, and so on. Most of these organizations are non-party organizations, but under certain conditions were

24 Selected Works of Lenin, vol. 4, version 3, p.160.
25 Selected Works of Stalin, vol. 1, 265.

absolutely necessary to the working class. Because without them, the proletariat could neither consolidate its positions in a variety of class struggles, nor complete their historic mission. But who could organize, coordinate and design a line of action for so many loose organizations?

Stalin argued that this task could only be done by the party of the proletariat, because the party not only fully absorbed all the outstanding individuals of the working class and their experience, revolutionary spirit and the boundless loyalty to the cause of proletariat, but also Party employed Marxism as its ideological weapon which distinguished this party from all other non-proletarian parties and mass organizations. Therefore, "the party is the highest form of the organizations of proletarian class, which is higher compared to other forms of organization of the proletariat (the trade unions, the consumer and agri-production cooperative associations, and state organizations)."[26] However, as he emphasized, the party's leadership over other organizations was not imperative. But party should employ all means of persuasion to the members of these organizations to make these non-party organizations be close with the proletarian party in their work, thus they could voluntarily accept the party's political leadership.

Soviet assembly organ is the form of state within the dictatorship of the proletariat. It is one of the most appropriate forms to link the working people to participate in state administration and to implement the dictatorship against the enemies. Stalin pointed out: "The Soviet assemblies are a mass organisation of all the working people of town and country. They are a non-Party organisation. The Soviets are the direct expression of the dictatorship of the proletariat. It is through the Soviet assemblies that all measures for strengthening the dictatorship and for building socialism are carried out."[27] Soviet assemblies are the bond connecting millions of working people and the proletarian vanguard, which embody the unity of the new democracy and the new dictatorship. Stalin has made many expositions on the Soviet assemblies along with Lenin's thoughts, some of which still have important guiding significance for us. For example, he pointed out that the aim of Lenin's emphasis on Soviet assemblies' role was to "establish the Soviet democracy", and further develop the enthusiasm, initiative and organization of the proletariat. And when the task of building socialism was gradually completed in the Soviet Union, the slogan of active Soviets should be replaced by strengthening Soviet assemblies so that they can improve the work of the Soviet state organs and to try prevent them from retrogressing "back to the corrupt bureaucratic system of the ordinary bourgeois state."[28]

---

26   Collected Works of Stalin, vol. 10,pp. 90-91.
27   Selected Works of Stalin, vol. 1, 412.
28   Collected Works of Stalin, vol. 11, p. 217.

What are the roles of the mass organizations in the system of the dictatorship of the proletariat? Stalin argued that these organizations included the trade unions, the cooperatives and the Youth League and so on. The trade unions are the organizations for all members of the working class, linking together workers from all walks of life and becoming the party's bond to contact the masses of workers and on the other side the advanced elements' bond to contact those elements who lag behind. Stalin pointed out that the trade unions were the communist schools whose basic task was to select the outstanding elements from their own ranks to lead the all the tasks of state administration. Trade unions can help the party to educate the working masses with the socialist and communist faiths. The cooperatives were mainly the organizations for the farmers, but also "primarily link combining the workers (consumers) and farmers."[29] Stalin also especially pointed out that the cooperatives had special significance for the consolidation of the dictatorship of the proletariat. Cooperatives facilitate the contacts between the proletarian pioneers and the peasant masses, creating the conditions of leading the peasant masses onto the track of construction of socialism. The Youth League is a mass organization for young workers and peasants and its basic task is to help the party educate the younger generation with the socialist spirit and provide the reserved army of young people for all other proletarian mass organizations. Stalin also emphasized that during the period where the dictatorship of the proletariat was launching a wide range of cultural and educational work, the Youth League would play an irreplaceably positive promoting role.

In Stalin's view, the dictatorship of the proletariat should be realized under the leadership of the party and through the Soviet assemblies and various other masses organizations. All these masses organizations closely linked the party with the masses of workers and other working people from all aspects and offered ultimate support for realization of the dictatorship of the proletariat directed by the party. Stalin clearly stated: "The party's mission is to unify the work of the proletarian mass organizations without exception and lead their actions to one goal—the liberation of the proletariat."[30]

Only in this way, the majority of the proletariat and other working people could be brought together to form a strong cohesive force. Only thus we can ensure the ultimate goal of liberation of the proletariat. However, when discussing the party's directing the dictatorship of the proletariat, Stalin also stressed that the party should not directly implement this dictatorship, here Soviet assemblies', trade unions' role was critical. Secondly, Stalin theoretically distinguished between the two different concepts of "the leading role of the party" and "the dictatorship of the proletariat."

29 Selected Works of Stalin (I), vol. 1, p.412.
30 Ibid, 413.

Stalin pointed out: "In this sense it could be said that the dictatorship of the proletariat is, in essence, the "dictatorship" of its vanguard, the "dictatorship" of its Party, as the main guiding force of the proletariat." But he added: "But this, however, must not be understood in the sense that a sign of equality can be put between the dictatorship of the proletariat and the leading role of the Party (the "dictatorship" of the Party), that the former can be identified with the latter, that the latter can be substituted for the former."[31] Stalin explained this distinction mainly from the following four aspects:

Firstly, the dictatorship of the proletariat, in its content, is broader and richer than the "dictatorship" of the party. Although the Party carries out the dictatorship of the proletariat, and in this sense the dictatorship of the proletariat is, in essence, is the "dictatorship" of its Party, this does not mean that the "dictatorship of the Party" (its leading role) is identical with the dictatorship of the proletariat, that the former is equal in scope to the latter. The Party carries out the dictatorship of the proletariat, but it carries out the dictatorship of the proletariat, and not any other kind of dictatorship. Whoever identifies the leading role of the Party with the dictatorship of the proletariat is substituting "dictatorship" of the Party for the dictatorship of the proletariat."

He pointed to another aspect of the distinction the leading role of the party and "the dictatorship of the proletariat."Not a single important decision is arrived at by the mass organisations of the proletariat without guiding directives from the Party.The dictatorship of the proletariat consists of the guiding directives of the Party plus the carrying out of these directives by the mass organisations of the proletariat, plus fulfilment of these directives by the population. Here, as you see, we have to deal with a whole series of intermediary steps which are by no means unimportant elements of the dictatorship of the proletariat. Therefore, between the guiding directives of the Party and their fulfilment lie the will and actions of those who are led (i.e. the class) the willingness (or unwillingness) of the class to support such directives, its ability (or inability) to carry out these directives, its ability (or inability) to carry them out in strict accordance with the requirements of the situation. It scarcely needs proof that the Party, having taken the leadership into its hands, must carefully consider the will, the condition, and the level of political consciousness of those who are led. Therefore, whoever identifies the leading role of the Party with the dictatorship of the proletariat is substituting the directives given by the Party for the will and actions of the class."[32]

---

31   Selected Works of Stalin, vol. 1, p. 415.
32   Ibid, p. 417.

Thirdly, Stalin discussed another aspect: "The Party is the direct governing vanguard of the proletariat; party is the leader" (Lenin) In this sense the Party takes power, the Party governs the country. But this must not be understood in the sense that the Party exercises the dictatorship of the proletariat separately from the state power, without the state power; it does not mean that the Party governs the country separately from the Soviet assemblies, not through the Soviet assemblies.".. "It is not true to say that our Soviet institutions …for instance our army, our transport, our economic institutions, etc., are Party institutions, that the Party can replace the Soviets and their ramifications, It is not true to say that the Party can be identified with the state power." ... "This does not mean that the Party can be identified with the Soviets, with the state power. The Party is the core of this power, but it is not and cannot be identified with the state power."[33]

Fourthly, for Stalin the concept of dictatorship of the proletariat is a state concept. Stalin understood it as the regime by virtue of direct violence. He said, "The dictatorship of the proletariat itself must contain the concept of violence." "No violence, no dictatorship."[34] The proletarian party is different. The party's leadership can not rely on force and violence, but only on the party's correct theory and policy, on its persuasion and people's trust. That is to say, the party, the working class and the relationship between its masses organizations can neither be built on the basis of the unlimited power nor through violence to the working class and its masses organizations to coerce them into obeying the leadership of the party, but should rely on the long-term work of the party and through the party members to persuade people into obtaining the trust and support of the masses of the class to voluntarily accept the party's leadership.

In addition, Stalin also explained Lenin's using the concept of "the dictatorship of the party", pointing out that the dictatorship of the party "is not "in the strict sense of the word ("power based on the use of force"), but Lenin used this term in the figurative sense, in the sense of party's undivided leadership."

Whoever identifies the leadership of the Party with the dictatorship of the proletariat, is in fact giving to the Party the function of employing force against the working class as a whole. This mistaken understanding violates the elementary requirements of correct mutual relations between the vanguard and the class, between the Party and the non-Party members of the working class.

33   Selected Works of Stalin, vol.1, p. 418.
34   Ibid, p. 419.

Stalin's correct ideas when distinguishing between the concepts of the leading role of the party and the dictatorship of the proletariat, in his practice did not help him to solve the issue of the dividing the party affairs and state (dictatorship) affairs. The same applies for his practice related to party's leading role in the realization of the dictatorship of the proletariat through Soviet assemblies as argued by Lenin. But we can say that he made an important step forward on the issue of "why we indeed need the division of the party and the (state) dictatorship" in socialism.

Thirdly, Stalin further clarified the functions, development and changes related to the socialist state.

Stalin advocated that the theory of Marx and Engels related to the demise of the proletarian state after the establishment of the public ownership had started from the assumption that the victory of socialism would occur in all or most countries of the world at the same time. But this was not suitable for the specific circumstances that socialism only won victory in the Soviet Union and which was surrounded by aggressive imperialism. Therefore, after the establishment of public ownership in the proletarian country, the state could not die. He noted that after Soviet society entered into the period communism: "state will be preserved unless capitalist encirclement shall have been liquidated and the danger of military attacks from without eliminated; of course the forms of our state will change once again with a change of the internal and external setting. No, it will not be preserved and will wither away if capitalist encirclement shall have been liquidated and replaced by Socialist encirclement"[35], the state would lead to extinction.

While elucidating that socialism would keep the state, Stalin further clarified the functions, development and changes of the socialist state according to the historical mission of the dictatorship of the proletariat and combined his analysis with the history of the development of the Soviet state. In Stalin's view, in order to the overthrow capitalism and achieve the goal of emancipation of the proletariat, we should not only overthrow the regime of bourgeois, but also thoroughly smash the old state apparatus of bourgeois and replace them with the new proletarian state. However, it was not enough. In the process of the existence and development of the proletarian state, some old state functions according to the needs of the proletariat should be reserved but their form should change.. Stalin stated that the functions of the dictatorship of the proletariat were mainly three aspects: the first was to repress against the overthrowed of class; the second was to defend the country against foreign aggression; and the third was to organize work in the spheres of economy, culture and education. The functions of the Soviet socialist state should change with the development and the external

35   Selected Works of Stalin, vol. 1, p.471.

environmental changes. Thus, he proposed that the development of the socialist state in the SU has experience two main stages:

Two main stages of the Soviet state

The first stage was from the October Revolution until the elimination of various exploiting classes. The basic task of this period was to suppress the resistance of the exploiting classes, to organize the national defense to against the violations of the armed intervention, to restore industry and agriculture, and to prepare conditions to eliminate all elements of capitalism. Therefore, the socialist state in this period mainly implemented two basic functions, namely, the repression of the domestic opposition of the overthrown classes and to defend the country to against external aggression. These two basic functions were similar to the states in the past human history on the surface, but there were differences in principles: "the former states supported the exploitation of the majority for the interests of a minority while we were working for the interests of the majority and suppress a small number of exploiters; the states of the past was against the foreign aggression to protect the wealth and privileges of a small number of exploiters while we oppose foreign aggression in order to protect the labor products of most workers. The second stage included the elimination of urban and rural capitalist elements until the complete establishment of the socialist economic system and the new constitution of 1936. In the end of this period, the system of exploitation was eliminated. And exploiters were no longer there thus the state's basic task was to organize socialist economy, to eliminate the last remnants of the capitalist elements, to organize the culture revolution and to prepare a fully modernized military to defend the country. Correspondingly, the functions of the socialist state have changed. In the country, the function of the implementation of violence to suppress had died, what replaced this suppression was the new function: the state should protect socialist property from thieves and pillagers. The function of the military defense of the country against attacks from without has been preserved in its entirety remain, so were the army, the punishing agencies and the investigating apparatuses of the state should not be directed against the internal but external enemies. In this period, the function of economic coordination and cultural education by state organs also has remained and received full development.[36]

Fourthly, Stalin made a series of theoretical views on ensuring the leadership of the party.

When elaborating the system of the dictatorship of the proletariat, Stalin gavea series of theoretical views on ensuring the leadership of the party. Stalin believed that to ensure the correct leadership of the party, these

36   Selected Works of Stalin, vol. 2, p. 468-471.

should be ensured: the lines and policies developed by the party should be correct and in harmony with the interests of the working class; the lines and policies of the party should be mastered by the masses and gain their active support; the party should not only develop the lines and policies but also specifically lead the implementation of these lines and policies. Among these three conditions, the most critical was that the party should develop the correct lines and policies. Thus, Stalin specially studied on how the party could design correct line and policies. He wrote: to ensure the political parties of proletariat making no politic mistakes, firstly should base themselves on the laws of the development of production and the laws of the social economic development when developing their general guding-lines and practical activities; secondly, the proletarian parties when developing their lines and policies should correctly consider the consciousness of, which was the essential condition to ensure the correctness of lines and policies. Stalin, starting from Lenin's point of view of the "mutual trust" between the party and the masses, pointed out that when developing the lines and policies, the party "should listen to the opinions of the masses, pay careful attention to the revolutionary instincts of the masses, study the struggle practices of the masses and and on this basis test the correctness of its own policy; that, consequently, it must not only teach the masses, but also learn from them."[37] Therefore, when developing and implementing their lines and policies, the party should not only persuade the masses, but also learn from them.

271

"After developing the correct political line tested in practice, the cadres of the party become the decisive forces of the leadership of the party and the state." [38] In Stalin's view, the correct political line must be implemented by a number of cadres with high political quality, strong sense of responsibility and strong operational capability. Otherwise, even the best political line will become a dead letter. So he asked the party cadres not only to strengthen their Marxist theoretical and political level, but also to improve the level of operational capacity and scientific skills. He pointed out that if the party cadres could not become the experts in all walks of life or were not familiar with the economic management, then the "so-called leadership of the party would probably degenerate into a bunch of ridiculous command, an that will weaken and reduce the party's leadership. While making important explanations of the above four aspects, Stalin also discussed the issues of promotion of democracy in the party, and on the role of criticism and self-criticism. Stalin pointed out that the aim of democracy was to raise awareness and enthusiasm of the masses. In this way they could not only participate in the discussion of the party's major issues, but also participate in the work of the party's

---

37   Selected Works of Stalin, vol. 1, p. 420.
38   Selected Works of Stalin, vol. 2, p. 458.

decision-making and work of leadership. All this will enhance the sense of ownership of the party members. Starting from the needs of the actual struggle, Stalin emphasized the highest principle of the inner-party democracy as to safeguard the interests of the party. The party's interests are above the formal democracy. It was necessary to unify 2 aims: the promotion of democracy and safeguard of the interests of party. On the issue of criticism and self-criticism, Stalin argued: "criticism and self-criticism are the foundation of both the party and the proletarian dictatorship, and a very important force to keep us moving forward. Therefore, "self-criticism to us is like air and water" Stalin emphasized: "it isnecessary to emphasize criticism from above criticism by the Workers' and Peasants' Inspection, by the Central Committee of our Party and so on as well as the criticism to the party by the ordinary workers and peasants."…"even if the criticism is only five percent to 10 percent true, it should be welcome and be carefully listened to."[39] In addition, Stalin also emphasized the importance of the criticism to the leadership from the masses. He pointed out: "continuous victories in socialist construction would gradually increase the prestige of the party and prestige of its leadership, which may lead to the separation of the party's leader from the masses. This risk is very risky and could even destroy the party. Therefore, "in order to move forward and to improve the relationship between the masses and the leaders, party should always open the door of self-criticism.It should make it necessary for the Soviet people to 'blame' their leaders and criticize their faults, thus avoid leaders become conformists."[40]

272

2. The defects of Stalin's thoughts on the socialist political system

Most of Stalin's thoughts on the socialist political system given above-have upheld and developed Marxism-Leninism to a large extent. However, although his discussion on the theory of socialist political system was deep-and complex, we can say that his many correct expressions were out of touch with real practice. And these expressions also lack sufficient consistency, often showing certain colors of pragmatism. What is more important is that Stalin's ideas lack dialectics. There is a serious tendency to idealism and metaphysics. We can notice defects specifically in the following areas:

Firstly, his ideas exaggerated the dictatorship functions of the proletarian state. In the classic works of Marx, there are broad and narrow senses of the concept of "dictatorship of the proletariat." The broad concept refers to the state power established after the victory of the proletarian revolution. Proletariat should "shatter the former state power and replace it by a new and truly democratic one," the proletarian democracy. According to Lenin, dictatorship and democracy are complementary and inseparable.

---

39   Ibid, p. 30.
40   Selected Works of Stalin, vol. 2, p. 9-10.

The narrow concept of the proletarian dictatorship specifically refers to the function of violent suppression of the anti-regime and anti-socialist elements by the proletarian state power. Lenin pointed out: "according to vulgar bourgeois standpoint the terms dictatorship and democracy are mutually exclusive. Failing to understand the theory of class struggle, and accustomed to seeing in the political arena the petty squabbling of the various bourgeois circles ....the bourgeois conceives dictatorship to mean the annulment of all the liberties and all guarantees of democracy, tyranny of every kind, and every sort of abuse of power in the personal interests of a dictator."

In Stalin's writings, both the two concepts of dictatorship of the proletariat were used. However, he often equated and confused the two. For example, in his conversation with the delegation of American workers in September 1927, he said: "The fundamental idea of the dictatorship of the proletariat as the political domination (rule) of the proletariat and as a method of overthrowing the reign of capital (economics -ed.) by violence was created by Marx and Engels."Here, the words "political domination" by Stalin obviously refers to the state power while the "by violence" obviously refers to repression of capitalism by violence. But Stalin took them as the same thing. Meanwhile, Stalin also one-sidedly attributed the functions of proletarian state to the functions of dictatorship.And he limited the functions of dictatorship only by violent repression, and was often in favor of "maximizing" violent repression apparatus to suppress the bourgeoisie and the eradicate capitalism.[41] He regarded it as a main way and method to advance in socialism. In this way, he emasculated Lenin's thought that the dictatorship of the proletariat is the new type of democracy and a new type of dictatorship, which only targeted a few, but did not target a domestic class, under normal conditions. This was not only a departure from the basic principles of Marxism bus also constituted a risk for the future and destiny of socialism in the USSR.The practice of the Soviet Union and other socialist countries has proven this defect and risk.

Stalin's exaggeration of the dictatorship functions of the proletarian state was simplistic and included absolute distortion of the explanations of the Marxist-Leninist theory on socialism. Theoretical errors were often disguised under the cloak of Marxism-Leninism, which made difficult to identify his theory as it is. For example, in *Concerning Questions of Leninism*, Stalin wrote: Leninism is the theory and tactics of the proletarian revolution, and the basic content of the proletarian revolution is the dictatorship of the proletariat, then it is clear that the main thing in Leninism is the question of the dictatorship of the proletariat, Leninism is the elaboration of this question, the substantiation and concretisation of this question.

---

41   Selected Works of Stalin, vol. 2, p. 134.

I think we should discuss this issue carefully and ask: is the dictatorship of the proletariat, basic problem, the starting point and the essence of Leninism ? In this statement, Stalin simply attributed the wealth of ideas of Leninism and Lenin to the issue of dictatorship of the proletariat. In this statement Stalin simply attributed the wealth of ideas of Leninism and Lenin to the issue of dictatorship of the proletariat. When Stalin specifically discussed the nature and functions of the dictatorship of the proletariat, he repeatedly referred to Lenin's following idea: "revolutionary dictatorship of the proletariat is rule won and maintained by the use of violence by the proletariat against the bourgeoisie, rule that is unrestricted by any laws." When Lenin wrote the article "The Proletarian Revolution and the Renegade Kautsky in 1918, he used this sentence with a different intention:

Here, the words "unrestricted by any laws"means that the dictatorship is not subject to the legal constrains of the bourgeois Provisional Government of Kerenski. In fact, Lenin did not mention that the dictatorship of the proletariat will not be "unrestricted by any laws" at any time or period. But, Stalin took this sentence as a basis for applying it any time without any concrete analysis of the period or conditions and extended it to the entire historical period of the dictatorship of the proletariat. This is essentially exposed Stalin's one side: His denial of democracy and contempt for the laws.

274   Stalin occasionally referred to Lenin's view as: This new state "must inevitably,"..."be a state that is democratic in a new way (for the proletariat and the propertyless in general) and dictatorial in a new way (against the bourgeoisie)."..."dictatorship of the proletariat is the highest type of democracy in a class society"[42], and the Soviet system should be "the most fully democratic system". But Stalin failed to dialectically unite the proletarian democracy and the dictatorship of the proletariat. He thought democracy was just democracy—independent—and dictatorship was just the dictatorship. There was no necessary linking the two. In practice, he regarded the proletarian democracy and dictatorship of the proletariat as mutually antagonistic and exclusive. This not only distorted Lenin's ideas onthe dictatorship of the proletariat, but also brought great harm to the building of socialist democracy and the socialist legal system (rule of law).

Secondly, Stalin incorrectly raised the idea that the party and other forms of organization are mutually exclusive.

Although Stalin further elaborated on the structure of the proletarian dictatorship and clarified the status and roles of the proletarian party and other forms of proletarian organizations, he did not theoretically solve the issue of relationship between the strengthening of party's leadership and promoting the positive roles of Soviet assemblies and other organizations.

---

42   The Collected Works of Stalin vol. 10, p. 87.

Instead, he mistakenly believed that "the apparatuses of the state and public organisations have considerably grown and gained in strength. The trusts and syndicates, the trading and credit institutions, the administrative—political and cultural—educational organisations, and, finally, the co-operatives of all kinds, have grown and expanded considerably, having absorbed hundreds of thousands of new people, mainly non-Party people. But these apparatuses are not only growing in personnel; their power and influence are growing too. And the more their importance grows the more palpable becomes their pressure on the Party, the more persistently do they try to weaken the Party's leadership, and the stronger becomes their resistance to the Party. The forces in those apparatuses must beregrouped and the leading people in them must bedistributed in such a way as to ensure the Party's leadership in the new situation."[43]

Therefore, he stressed the need to strengthen the party's leadership. He said that the party cadres's leadership on the above mentioned state apparatuses should no more be "in general" but it should be "specific and concrete." These ideas of Stalin in fact, contradicted his ideas in another speech: "However, party exercises it (proletarian dictatorship) not directly, but with the help of the trade unions, and through the Soviet assemblies and their ramifications."

Undoubtedly, this has caused important ills and led to overlapping of party and state.This mistake made the party a hurricane which swept all other organizations. 275

The above idea to put the party in opposition with other proletarian organizations advocated by Stalin was not accidental. First, when he explained the structure of dictatorship of the proletariat, this idea can also be seen.

As he talked about the relationship between the Soviet assemblies and other proletarian organizations, Stalin only mentioned that the party led and coordinated other proletarian organizations, but did not mention the "palpable pressure" and "resistance" imposed by such organizations on the party.

He avoided discussing how to get the people participate in the administration of national economic life, political life, cultural life and social life. In his view, these organizations (other proletarian organizations) were "Gears" and "Levers". They are the means of which the Party is closely linked with the class and with the masses.

He pointed out: "The highest expression of the leading role of the Party, here, in the Soviet Union, in the land of the dictatorship of the proletariat, for example, is the fact that not a single important political or organisational

---

43   The Collected Works of Stalin, vol. 7, p. 142.

question is decided by our Soviet and other mass organisations without guiding directives from the Party. In this sense it could be said that the dictatorship of the proletariat is, in essence, the "dictatorship" of its vanguard, the "dictatorship" of its Party, as the main guiding force of the proletariat."[44]

This conception actually regarded the Soviet assemblies and other proletarian mass organizations like administrative organs which should simply carry outparty's resolutions and implement its decisions as the vassals of the party.

This has deprived them from their vital functions of protecting interests of the people and reflecting their reasonable requirements.

Second, the emergence of thismistaken idea is intrinsically linked with his one-sided exaggeration of dictatorship against enemies and his ignoraning of true democracyamong the people.

Classic writers of Marxism-Leninism claimed that the dictatorship of the proletariat is always the dialectical unity of conducting dictatorship to enemies and democracy for the masses. However, Stalin split the necessary link between the two, and regarded proletarian dictatorship and democracy as something opposite and mutually exclusive. He only talked about dictatorship and neglected emphasis on democracy, even when he talked about main aspects of the dictatorship of the proletariat. Its alliances and leadership to other laboring and exploited masses, Stalin wrote: "The utilisation of the rule of the proletariat in order to ... consolidate the alliance of the proletariat with these masses and to draw these masses into the work of socialist construction, and to ensure the state leadership of these masses by the proletariat."[45]

276

In fact what he said above was related to alliance and democracy but he chose to use the term "the dictatorship of the proletariat" In fact, he saw democracy more as something formal and a method, a tool and style of work, and rarely as the essential requirement of socialism. He even thought that the expansion of democracy was only a "concession" by the party when it was compelled to. It was under the influence of the above ideas that Stalin came to the conclusion that expanding democracy for the people, and strengthening the roles of Soviet assemblies and roles of other proletarian organizations would weaken the leadership of the party.

Thirdly, the theory of the proletarian party was distorted in many ways.

Stalin was the first leader who made a clear affirmation on the one-party issue. In 1922, the Soviet Union had already formed the communist party's one-party political system. However, Lenin did not regard the one-party

44   Collected Works of Stalin, vol. 8, p. 36.
45   Stalin, Concerning Questions of Leninism, p. 31.

system which was formed in the special conditions- as the inevitable law of socialism. It was Stalin who reached this conclusion and elevated this phenomenon to the level of theory. In 1927, he explicitly declared that the Soviet Union would implement the system of one-party leadership. To this end, he emphasized that the exploiters in the SU was deprived of the right of establishing their own political organizations, and that though there were debates about different views between workers and peasants, "Such conflict of opinion can only serve to strengthen the monopoly of the Communist Party. Such a conflict of opinion cannot provide nourishment for other parties within the working class and among the toiling peasantry."[46] In 1936, he announced that after socialism was established in the Soviet Union, exploiting classes were eliminated, so "there is no basis for the existence of several political parties" … "In the USSR there is ground only for one party, the Communist Party. In the USSR only one party can exist, the Communist Party, which courageously defends the interests of the workers and peasants to the very end."[47] This has led the political system of the Soviet Union which has been a one party—rule of the Communist Party, as a long-term reality.

In terms of the principle of the party's leadership, Stalin made the mistake that the party replaced the government. Although he correctly distinguished the two categories: "the party's leadership" and the "the dictatorship of the proletariat", and advocated the concept that the party cannot and should not replace the state power (dictatorship of the proletariat). But he mistakenly equated or reduced the concept of party leadership to its instructions, and improperly evaluated the practice of solving major problems of socialist construction according to party instructions as "the greatest performance of the party's leadership."[48] In practice the party issued instructions related to all trivial details, thus the general leadership of the party became "day-to-day"and "direct, specific and trivial leadership."

In an article published in 18th issue of Communist in 1925, Stalin commented on a Trotsky's statement which said: "the party should apply the general leadership, but should not directly participate in administration." Stalin sharply criticized this idea and wrote: "But, this means that the party does not exist." Thus, Stalin maintained that the party should lead, intervene in and arrange everything, and many of his other speeches also prove it.

For example, in June 1925, when Stalin talked on "most serious risks that are weakening the party's leadership", he said: "in the new conditions if we continue to have the concept of leadership in general" as before "it

---

46   Collected Works of Stalin, 1st Chinese edition, vol. 10, p. 105.
47   Selected Works of Stalin, volume 2, p. 408.
48   Collected Works of Stalin, vol. 8, p. 36.

will only be an empty talk." Because, Stalin thought the construction work had become "a complex and diversified" work. Thus, in the new conditions, party workers should implement "concrete and specific leadership."[49]

Obviously, his such remarks contradict Lenin's principle that the party's leadership should be a general leadership to state organs. But Stalin insisted: "Yes, in our country the Party guides the government. And the Party is able to do so because it enjoys the confidence of the majority of the workers and working people generally and has a right to guide the organs of government in the name of that majority."[50]

In addition, Stalin also declared: as the core of state power, the party should administer : "It must not be forgotten that we are a party in power.... the slogans of the Bolshevik Party has ...the force of practical decision, the force of law, and must be carried out immediately."[51] He argued: "cadres of the party are commanding officers of the party, and because our party is the party in power, they are commanding officers of leading organs of the state."[52] These ideas actually laid the theoretical foundation for the party acting on behalf of the government.

Stalin distorted Lenin's basic principle of democratic centralism. Democratic centralism is the basic norm of life within a Marxist party, which Lenin had consistently adhered to, and here, democracy and centralism are an organic whole. However, Stalin separated and even opposed democracy and centralism, placed a one-sided emphasis on centralism, discipline and unity of the party, ignoring or damaging inner-party democracy.

After the death of Lenin, faced by the opposition groups accusing him for undermining democracy within the party, he critized Lutovinov: "He wants the 'real' democracy, and he required that at least all the major questions, should be discussed from the the bottom to up by each branch of the party...but, comrades, we are now in power and we have 400,000 members and no fewer than 20,000 Party units, and I don't know what consequences the implementation of this system will bring about. If we implement this system, our party will become a debating society which would be eternally talking and decide nothing. But, our party should at first be a party in action, for we are in power."[53]

In this way, with this pretext Stalin deprived the large number of party members and the party's branches of the right to discussing major issues, and denied basic norms of democratic life within the party. What was

---

49   Collected Works of Stalin, vol. 7, p. 143.
50   Collected Works of Stalin,vol. 10, p. 92-93.
51   Collected Works of Stalin,vol. 12, p. 58-59.
52   Selected Works of Stalin (II), p. 458.
53   Collected Works of Stalin, vol. 5, p. 181-182.

inner-party democracy for Stalin? "Inner-Party democracy means raising the activity of the masses of Party members and strengthening the unity of the Party, strengthening conscious proletarian discipline in the Party.[54]

This concept not only separates the dialectical relationship between democracy and centralism, but distorts Lenin's basic spirit of democracy. This is a mistake in which discipline replaces freedom and in which centralism replaces democracy. In addition, he justified his ideas and practice by making one-sided emphasis on internal and external conditions for implementing democracy. He pointed out that democracy was not a static thing in any condition at any time, "it was sometimes impossible and meaningless to carry out democracy."

For him, to allow inner-party democracy, two conditions were required: "first, the intensification of our constructive work in general, and of industrial construction in particularand the the strengthening of a militant, solid, united and indivisible party that can firmly and confidently direct our construction work."

These ideas and views of Stalin actually indefinitely postponed the implementation of democracy. They were an excuse for his restricting inner-party democracy and practice personal authoritarianism.

V. Rational rethinking on Stalin's political system

There has been a serious dispute in the theoretical circles about how to evaluate the highly centralized political system formed in Stalin's era and how to treat its historical impacts. What lessons can be learned? We believe that Stalin's political system should be understood and evaluated from the perspective of Soviet Union's historical conditions at that time, and everything exists in time, place and conditions, and we cannot simply affirm or deny everything. That is one basic approach of dialectical materialism.

1. Historical achievements of Stalin's political system

Although the highly centralized political system formed in Stalin's era—as the first model of socialist political system—was quite criticized in history, we have to admit that its basis and nature are socialist. The fact that this system has emerged and was smoothly operated in a certain historical period indicates that it after all has its own objective rationality. If we evaluate this system in a fair, objective and realistic way, we cannot deny the huge

---

54   Collected Works of Stalin, vol. 8, p. 131.

achievements it made in history. These achievements can be summarized as follows.

Firstly, this system basically guaranteed the political stability of the proletariat and the Soviet regime under the extremely complex and grim circumstances home and abroad.

During the Stalin period, the Soviet Union was sieged by imperialism, which together with all other reactionary forces was ready to strangle the nascent Soviet regime in the cradle. Especially after Hitler, the German fascist leader, came to power in 1933, it was enveloped in the haze of wars. Meanwhile, a large-scale movement of collectivization was conducted. In dealing with the issue of peasants, especially in the treatment of rich and middle peasants, there emerged the ultra-hasty and ultra-left tendencies, igniting a fierce class struggle within the society. The sharp struggle within the party became more intense because of this problem. In addition, the Soviet Union had a vast territory and included many nationalities, with highly unbalanced political, economic and cultural development in different regions. The majority of the republics had their own special historical and cultural traditions and also specific political and economic interests, and also a long history of ethnic conflicts. In this extremely complex and challenging domestic and international situation, it was overriding and also fundamental to consolidate political power, protect unity and maintain stability, and the highly centralized political system did play its proper role in this regard. The fact shows that during the period ruled by Stalin, Soviet Union's political situation was basically stable, and the whole country and the whole party also maintained a high degree of unity. Although some localized social unrest and ethnic frictions occasionally took place, the overall atmosphere at that time left the impression that the entire society was mentally sound and people lived a peaceful life. The superiority of the socialist system was highlighted, and society maintained stability, compared with the capitalist world at that time, especially with the social unrest and instability caused by the worldwide capitalist economic crisis in 1930s and the chaos of rampant fascism.

Secondly, such a system corresponds or adapts to the large-scale socialized production in many ways.

The practice of the Soviet Union proves that the appropriate concentration of power is conducive to the large-scale socialized production. The increasing socialization of production process, socialization and concentration in the means of production objectively requires that the government should appropriately intervene in the operation of various economic sectors and conduct macroeconomic forecasting and management related to national economy. In addition, the appropriate concentration of power becomes advantageous mainly in that it can quickly and effectively collect human, financial and material resources of the country for the large-scale construction of material aspect of modernization. This advantage is particularly obvious in countries with backward economy and culture. The Soviet Union developed within a very short time from an agricultural country before the founding of the union to a large industrial power second only to the United States then, and created the "Industrial Miracle" of the Soviet Union, which shocked the whole world. During World War II, suffering severe wounds of wars and without any external assistance, it was first in recovery and rapidly developed its productive forces, creating another miracle in the industrial development. Compared with 1913, its national income increased by 12.67 times in 1953, while US grew by 2.03 times, Britain 0.71, and France only 0.54. These remarkable achievements have to be said to be related to the effect of such a political system in a certain historical period. What is particularly worth mentioning is that in terms of fields such as nuclear and aerospace technologies, the Soviet Union used administrative means to organize research and collaboration and allocate manpower and resources, causing it to keep pace with and in some respects even surpass the United States, which had the modern scientific and technological power. This more fully demonstrates that the highly centralized political system has advantages in some aspects.

Thirdly, this system guaranteed the victory of the Great Patriotic War of the Soviet Union.

The experience of human history indicates that the highly centralized political system is a very effective means to cope with wars. It can unify spirits of all the people around the country at a critical time and can maximize the concentration of the country's human, material and financial resources to meet the needs of wars in a very short period of time. It can be said that the highly centralized political system has created conditions for the victory of the Great Patriotic War. According to incomplete statistics, during the first eight days after the war began, 5.3 million people enlisted in the army, and by the end of 1941, the newly-formed army divisions amounted to as much as 400; within the several months after the war began, over 1500 important enterprises and 10 million people was moved from the western theaters to the rear. Throughout the war, there were no less than dozens of large-scale battles like the Battle of Moscow and the battle of Stalingrad, in which as many as 100 to 150 divisions or even more were involved and nearly ten thousand aircrafts and tanks as well as tens of thousands of artillery were used each time. Moreover, in these battles, the offensive zone often reached 500 to 700 kilometers wide and 300 to 500 kilometers deep, and they lasted for several months. Such large-scale military mobilization, strategic transfer and military buildup are rare in all histories of wars. These would have been simply unimaginable if there was no strict organization and discipline or high concentration of power as the lever. After the German-Soviet War broke out, it only took the Soviet Union four years to drive the invasive German armies out of its national borders, and it defeated the fascist Germany and Japan with its allies and became an important force in the world anti-fascist war. Practically speaking, these remarkable achievements are inextricably linked with the highly centralized political system.

Although the highly centralized political system enabled interest gains and prestige for the Soviet Union in a specific historical period, it, as one manifestation of the nature of the socialist political system, was far from being a mature, complete and perfect system and its demerits are as eye-catching as its merits. As Anne Louise Strong commented, "This is a vibrant history of the great era, perhaps the greatest of time... It produced millions of heroes, also some demons. Insignificant people today can recall the time and cite its evil. However, those alive after the struggle and even many people who died because of the struggle endured the scourge and thought that this was part of the costs of the construction."[55] However, as a true Marxist, one should not list mistakes of the history or even pay the price unnecessarily and silently. The correct approach is to be good at finding problems and identifying root causes, and then to define the right medicine—find a specific way to solve the problem. The Soviet Union has been disintegrated for over two decades. From the perspective of summarizing historical experience and lessons, for Marxists in real socialist countries it is necessary to re-examine drawbacks and harms brought by the Stalinist political system itself from a new point of view, which is of great value for the healthy development of the socialist system.

2. The main disadvantages of Stalin's political system

Although Stalin's political system played a positive role in the history of the Soviet Union, its disadvantages were increasingly evident with the development of history. These disadvantages are manifested in the following aspects.

Firstly, power was excessively concentrated and unrestricted, which impeded the development of socialist democracy and the proper establishment of the socialist legal system.

And this is the most typical feature of Stalin's political system it is its most important drawback. During Stalin period, all the power both inside and outside the party, especially the right of appointment and removal, were concentrated in the hands of the central committee. For ordinary cadres

282

---

55 Anne Louise Strong, The Stalin Era (Beijing: World Knowledge Publishing House, 1979), 2.

and people, the right to vote and democratic supervision written in the Constitution was a castle in the air. The people could not exercise supervisory power. Among the state, organs there lacked mechanisms of checks and balances of power. Stalin's political system looked like a pyramidaltower in appearance. In the top of the tower was Stalin, as well as the secretariat organs of the CC and national security agencies under his direct leadership. In the upper part of the tower were high-ranking officials of the central ministries and secretaries of party branches and directors of government organs appointed and "recommended" by the secretariat of the CC. In the middle and lower part of the tower were ordinary cadres and people. Whether within the top or the middle and lower level of this pyramidal power structure, there was a lack of separation and checks and balances of powers.

The mechanism of supervising and restricting power was in no way there. Inside the structure were only various major institutions established in accordance with state functions. Even though the institutions were organized as committees, they were often controlled by one person or a few people (one person leadership system). For example, Stalin concentrated the party, state (governmental), military, economic, and other powers in himself, almost undertook all the powers of the country. Party leaders at all levels also served as persons people in charge of Soviet assembly, the government and other mass organizations of working people besides they were both the user and the self-supervisor of power. It is clear that the system that concentrates supervision and implementation of power in one person only existedc in the era of absolute monarchy, though the class nature and the social system reflected by the Soviet was totally different from the absolute monarchy.

Montesquieu wrote in *The Spirit of the Laws*, according to long term experience, ones that are often in power like to abuse their power till they are restricted. To make them not abuse their power, another power should be used to stop their power." In Stalin's political system, since concentration of power was emphasized and rational division and supervision of power was ignored, inevitable result was concentration of power in the hands of a few people and even one person.

However, once one person holds the limitless and unchecked power, he or she will overtop the party, the state and the law, resulting in personal authoritarianism, cult of personality and even she/he inevitably tramples socialist democracy and legal system. From the political practice of the Soviet Union for 70-odd years, owing to the intense concentration of power and no separation between the party work and the government work, the authority and power of the party has been superior to that of laws and the party's leader has overtopped the highest authority of the party (congress) and the state. During the Stalin period, Stalin not only outmatched the party and the country, but also could be free to overturn laws, regulations and statutes formulated by any institution. In the seventh congress of the party, Kirov even declared that Stalin's words were "the party's laws". In this environment of personal authoritarianism and personal interventions challenging laws, people's democratic rights were infringed and even the legal system itself lost its meaning. Vishynsky, Prosecutor General of Soviet, said, "We should remember the words of Stalin: in social life and in our own lifetime, there is always such a moment when laws become obsolete and should be shunted aside."[56] With absence of democracy and rule of law, it was inevitable that violence and terror penetrated the whole society. It was obvious that Stalin had conducted five large-scale activities of purges-related to party, and in each party purge, a large number of cadres and members were arrested, killed, imprisoned and exiled. Soviet historian R. A. Medvedev wrote: "The scale of Stalin's terror was unmatched. According to the most cautious estimates, from 1936 to 1939, political prisoners persecuted were no less than four to five million people, among whom at least half a million people were executed immediately (the first to be executed were responsible cadres), and the rest were sentenced to long imprisonment. Repression and killing from 1937 to 1938 were so rampant that sometimes one thousand people were shot dead according to the sentence of the court only in Moscow in one day. The daily registered number of executed people in Lubyanka, the internal prison in the Central Headquarters of People's Commissariat for Internal Affairs (NKVD), was as many as two hundred."[57] Among these suppressed people were also Central Committee members, opposition leaders, war heroes and distinguished scientists, tens of thousands or even hundreds of thousands of ordinary farmers, workers, employees, junior officers, engineers and technicians.

Secondly, huge size of state and party organs and officers, their isolation from masses led to division of privileged and common people.

The highly centralized political system in which the party replaced the government inevitably led to countless departments and over-expanded organizations and a huge army of officers. In terms of the size of state organizations, in the early 1950s, the Ministry of Agriculture in the Soviet Union had as many as 422 bureaus, divisions and departments. Number of such ministries in the Soviet Union was 43. Please note that these numbers do not include paralel organs of the party's leading organizations at all levels. The overexpansion of organizations and huge army of officers not only reduced the efficiency of state organs, but also increased the burden on the society. Khrushchev pointed out in the conference of the Supreme Soviet of the USSR in April 1954: Although tax authorities in some areas were repeatedly downsized, there were still so many tax units that staff salaries

56 Boris Levitchi (ed.), Stalinist Terror in 1930s, Beijing: People's Publishing House, 1981, p. 35.
57 R. A. Medvedev, Let History Judge (II), p. 381.

completely exceeded the total amount of tax paid in these regions. Such a large number of staff who received salaries, bonuses, or other supports from the government not only tightened the budget finance, but also was bound to increase the burden on the masses. The overexpansion of organizations and cadres also cause cadres being isolated from masses. Thus those who ought to be servants of the peoplebecame masters of the people, accordingly breeding the bureaucratic tendency.

No separation between the party work and the government work, organizational/functional overlapping, and unclear responsibilities and rights, all these directly brought about chaos: different policies ordered by different departments on the same subject, passing the buck, and doing drag, abuse of power and all types of bureaucracy. The appointment system of cadres and the high concentration of power have inevitably caused cadres to only submit to their superiors and become seriously isolated from the people. In addition, the vertical subordination and unlimited power of superiors often ledto a strange grouping: upper and lower cadres often formed a feudal relationships with personal dependence, thus inside institutions occurred "Small Families" and "Small Groups" whose basic feature was nepotism/interest and which aimed to expand group privileges by use of positions and power. These were the specific performance of bureaucracy and also a chronic disease which had long plagued the Soviet's political and economic development.

285

Thirdly, intertwining of the party work and the government work, the party substituting the functions of the government, organizational overlapping, and unclear responsibilities and rights has greatly decreased the administrative efficiency of the government.

Above were an obvious feature of Stalin's political system and even more were its major drawbacks, which already existed as early as the establishment of the Soviet regime. Both Lenin and Stalin at times correctly described the relationship between the leadership of partyand the proletarian dictatorship; however, in practice, Stalin in his practice departed from Lenin's and his own ideas. Moreover he stereotyped and polarized the practice of intertwining of the party work and the government work , the party substituting the functions of the government. The party directly—on a great scale—led the Soviet assemblies, the government and various mass organisations of working people, and furthermore theparty implemented day-to-day and specific leadership to the state via by-passing them. In order to realize this type of direct leadership, Stalin created leading party departments which directly led related/parallel government organizations. This led to a peculiar phenomenon of two sets of paralel authoritative organizations as a characteristic the structural form of the political system: the party and the government organisations. Intertwining of the party work and the government work, the party substituting the functions of the government, organizational overlapping, and unclear responsibilities and rights has greatly decreased the administrative efficiency of the government.

In the Stalin's political system, because the party directly controlled the state power and exercised the executive leadership of the state placing itself above the state and the government, the inevitable result was the underdeveloped-ness of the state and the government, thus they could not establish and develop their due authority. Moreover, both the government and the party tried to manage the administrative affairs and there was no clear division of responsibilities and rights between the two, which led to a strange fact: neither of them alone managed what they should normally manage and both of them managed what should not be managed by the two. This fact caused the disordered, chaotic and low efficient operation of the state apparatus. At the same time, administrative organizations of the state were faced with difficulties to effectively perform their normal functions, therefore when they were assigned an additional work they refused to accept and superiors decided to add new departments to do this additional work. This naturally formed a vicious cycle that the lower the efficiency of administrative departments were the more departments needed to be increased, and the more the departments increased, the lower the efficiency was.

In addition, imposing administrative tasks to party organizations was definitely hazardous. Originally the missions of the party, as the vanguard detachment of the proletariat, is to formulate the general route of the state, guidelines and policies, and undertake overall leadership of the state. At the same time, the party is also the cradle of fostering politicians of proletariat and leadersof socialist construction. If any socialist party in power indulges itself with specific administrative affairs and reduces itself to an administrative agency of the state, its own development and improvement would be negatively affected, and its ability to control and lead the overall situation will be weakened. Moreover in the long term the image and authority of the party will be risked, any big failure related to an admistrative issue will lead to direct accusation of the party which is detrimental to building socialism which is a long term task. Fourthly, the top-down appointment system of cadres was implemented, leading to the bad tendency of cadres only feeling responsibility to their superiors rather than to inferiors and people. For a proper socialist country the election system and the tenure system should be one of the basic principles of democracy and they are one of the greatest achievements of human civilization inherited and created by the bourgeoisie when it fought against the feudal monarchy. Unfortunately, though the socialist system is superior than the capitalist system, Stalin's political system did not inherit this fruit of civilization, and on the contrary, it was largely backwards in this respect. In Stalin's political system, party and state leaders at all levels were finger pointed by the appointment system. According to investigative report submitted to the Plenum meeting of the Central Committee of CPSU(B) held in February-March, 1937, it was mentioned that standing members of provincial committees and the Central Committees of attached republics were all appointed. The Party Constitution said that the elected secretaries of the party committees should be approved by a higher organ of the party, but it practice many of them were directly appointed they were approved by higher authorities before being elected. The same applies for the standing members of the Soviet assemblies. Moreover, in Stalin's system, due to the mistaken cadres (officers) retirement system, officers could be promoted but not demoted, leading to lifelong tenure system of cadres in practice. Within the organs of the Soviet party and government, not only Stalin himself, but also some high-ranking officials including the central to the local governments did not want to "retire" from their official position until their death.

Because of the top-down appointment system of cadres, promotion and demotion of cadres totally depended on the will of superiors, which inevitably led to a series of problems. First, it allowed the team of cadres to form the atmosphere of being responsible only for superiors rather than the people, thus cadres were seriously isolated from the masses. It stimulated cadres to first care about their own promotion and statuses, instead of interests of the masses. Because of this, when implementing state policies, they often performed their duties superficially without regarding the actual effects of their work, and some even used their power for personal gains. Second, it allowed cadres to generally lack initiative, resulting in a large number of blind, submissive, unenergetic cadres. Thirdly, it allowed the emergence of dependent relationship of cronyism in among the cadres. It also stimulated some people good at seeking personal gains to flatter and win the favor of superiors by all means for the purpose of being promoted and become rich. In addition, top-down appointment system easily caused a series of feudalistic elements such as the privilege system, patriarchy, and hierarchy revive in the socialism.

Defects in Stalin's political system indeed brought a grave disaster to the construction of socialism in the Soviet Union and the world socialism as a whole. After 70 years of practice, Soviet's socialism finally came to an end. Although reasons behind are complex, it is undeniable that weaknesses in Stalin's political system is one of the most direct causes for the disintegration of the Soviet Union. The practice of Soviet's socialism for 70 years proves that undemocratic politics, unequal social status and low administrative efficiency were bound to affect the people's enthusiasm, impede scientific and technological invention and innovation and negatively influence the transformation of science technology to actual productive forces , ultimately leading to economic stagnation and decline in the development of productive forces. Today, we re-examine the history of the Stalin period from the perspective of the reality, and it is not difficult to find out that many chronic and stubborn problems in the Soviet Union after Stalin's death were intrinsically linked with his system.

Chapter VIII

Stalin's Theory on Class and Class Struggle in the Socialism Period

In the Stalin's theoretical system of socialist thoughts, the most distinctive one is his theory of the class struggle. All through his 30-year rule in the Soviet Union, this theory was his guiding thought. He had constantly stressed that the class and the class struggle were "something that cannot be forgotten for even a second". He also proposed the formula "to eliminate the classes by means of fierce (violent) proletarian class struggles." He led the party, the country, the army and everything with this thought. In developing the cause of the socialism of the Soviet Union, this also caused serious damages, and greatly tarnished the reputation of socialism. The theory also influenced other socialist countries to different degrees, leaving us a profound lesson.

I. The formation and development of Stalin's theory of class struggle

1. Stalin's arguments on the class struggle in the transition period

Lenin held several discussions on the issues of the class and class struggle in the transition period, in which he analyzed the social status of the classes in different periods. Since after the implementation of the new economic policy, Lenin when analyzing the relations among classes at that time, clearly pointed out that the social system was based on the main alliance between the working class and the peasant class. In this certain social context since "Nepman" class elements were allowed, namely these "Nepman" bourgeoisie elements should be considered as joining this alliance.

This special situation of the classes determined that the class struggle still existed in the society, but on the other side the task of suppressing the resistance of the exploiters was "apparently completed in general and this task had decreased to secondary status."[1] Lenin believed that "after the victory over the bourgeoisie politically and the consolidation of this victory through military means, the victories against bourgeoisie should be demonstrated as the successes in the organization of the national economy, and in the organization of the production and organizing proletarian control and accounting."[2] In Lenin's view, the class struggle would still exist during the transition period after the proletariat has seized the power, but due to changes in the class combination and relations in the society, the form of class struggles should naturally change. The violent oppression form of the past should be replaced by economic successes which will lead us to achievement of the final victory in the class struggle. During several years after the death of Lenin, Stalin not only followed Lenin's New Economic Policy in the economic sphere, but also followed Lenin's advices on the theory and tactics of the class struggle. I should say that Stalin's understandings on the situation of social classes in the Soviet Union were more realistic and his responses were also quite cautious.

In the mid-1920s, the Soviet party and government had made a major change in the rural policies, namely began to clear the remnants of the war communism (economic policy) in rural areas (this includes political approach towards peasants). The party adopted a series of measures to promote the further development of the individual peasant economy. For instance, reduction of agricultural tax and reduction of restrictions of renting fields and hiring laborers, etc. These policies enabled a positive development in agricultural economy, strengthened the economic strength of the middle peasants and middle peasants became the central class in rural areas. Meanwhile, the kulaks—rich peasants—class were also among benefiters. At that time, the "new opposition" group with Zinoviev and Kamenev as their leaders exaggerated the danger of kulaks in rural areas, accuses that most figures in the CPSU (Bolshevik) Central Committee possessed "kulak tendencies" and started strong attacks against Bukharin who had played an important role in designing the new rural policies. The "new opposition" demanded more pressure or restrictions against kulaks, proposing some ideas which were in fact the policy of resuming to the old war communism economic policy in the rural areas.

---

1 The Collected Works of Lenin, vol. 34, Chinese Version 2 (Beijing: Renmin Press, 1985), p.121.
2 Ibid., pp.123-124.

At this point of time, the issues or debates on how to assess the situation of social classes in the Soviet Union after the implementation of the new economic policy and debates on how to properly carry out (handle) the class struggle were in essence a debate on how to approach and evaluate the NEP. Related to this debate, Stalin's attitude was clear. He insisted on Lenin's New Economic Policy and argued clearly that those concessions in rural policies were necessary, correct and undoubtedly consistent "within the new economic policy decision of the party."[3] So he tried to demonstrate his stand which insisted to follow the NEP.

Stalin argued that under the conditions that the proletariat has mastered the power, the issues of the classes in the society and the class struggle should be mainly considered as the following:

Firstly, he analyzed the changes in the balance of class forces in Russia during the period when national economy was recovering.

Stalin pointed out that the implementation of the new economic policy, had not only enabled the Soviet national economy to recover, but also promoted the growth of the urban and rural capitalist class elements and enabled the growth of capitalist economy. In this situation, balance of power between classes had undergone significant changes: Firstly, the forces which were aiming to build socialism were increasing, which mainly reflected in the gradual growth of the ranks of the working class. As an independent class, the class consciousness of the working class was strengthening; especially their consciousness of being the ruling class had greatly improved. At the same time, the poor peasants living in the rural areas had begun to organize themselves. The middle peasants had become the majority in rural areas. Secondly, with the growth of economic power of capitalism, the absolute number of capitalist elements was as also increasing. The socialist components of the national economy were growing, so the dissatisfaction towards the Soviet power was also ascending. Thirdly, the members of intellectual group had fractured. Their many members had started to consider it a glorious and creative career to participate in large construction projects, so with positive feelings they were getting closer to the proletariat. On the other side the intellectuals with rural roots and who were part of toiling classes welcomed the Soviet state who supports the rural education, so they could possibly ally with the Soviet power for a long time in the future.

3   The Collected Works of Stalin, vol. 7, 1st Chinese version, p.295.

Secondly, he emphasized that the class contradictions and class struggle issues should be evaluated only specifically

When it started comprehensive rural changes, the CPSU (Bolshevik) Central Committee repeatedly emphasized the general policy of relying on the poor peasants, uniting with the middle peasants and fighting against the kulaks. Stalin pointed out that the tendency of booming of the middle peasants in the rural areas was very obvious, and since the middle peasants was becoming the basic rural class and the main force in of the rural economy, socialism could not be built if the proletariat could not form a solid coalition with this class.

The poor peasants in rural areas were still the main target to ally, staunch supporter of the Soviet power, so the state should aid them, improve their material conditions, and help them to become an independent political force in rural areas. The strength of kulaks (rich peasants) had also increased driven by the new economic policy. They were the major representative of the rural bourgeoisie class. Therefore, the party policy should try to distance kulaks from the middle peasants and guide poor peasants against the kulaks. Stalin believed there were three main class struggle fronts in the Soviet Union:

The first was the struggle between the entire working class (as represented by the state) and the whole peasants.

Stalin argued that the two basic classes of society as the workers and peasants shared common interests related to fundamental issues and they could easily form alliance, but their interests contradicted in some specific issues, such as in the prices of industrial and agricultural products, the conflict related to the burden of agricultural tax. These issues inevitably led to certain degree of contradictions between workers and peasants in the Soviet state under the leadership of the proletariat.

The second was the struggle between the entire working class (as represented by the state) and the kulaks.

It was mainly reflected in fact that the Soviet state would like the kulaks to take the main agricultural tax burden while kulaks were trying hard to transfer this tax burden upon the shoulders of the poor and middle peasants. The Soviet state made fair and reasonable prices when buying agricultural products, butthe kulaks were doing everything possible to store the products, raise the prices artificially and tried to reap huge profits.

The third was the contradiction between the poor peasants and kulaks.

Stalin believed that the open struggle between exploiting on fight against exploiting, namely open struggle between poor peasants and kulaks should still exist during the recovery period. Therefore, the state should organize and lead the poor peasants' fight against kulaks, but he stressed that the state should not deliberately incite or artificially intensify this contradiction, i.e., the class struggle.

Thirdly, Stalin advocated using different methods of struggle when dealing with different class conflicts. Stalin made detailed analysis of class contradictions of the epoch. He argued that although there were some certain contradictions between the peasants and the working class, since they share the same interests on fundamental issues, among them "negotiations and mutual concessions" should be adopted to adjust their relations. "In no case contradictions among them should be driven to get intensified or led to a conflict-oriented course." In dealing with the contradictions between the working class and the kulaks, Stalin had warned against two mistaken tendencies: the first was underestimating the danger of the kulaks; the second was its exaggeration. For him both tendencies were harmful. Underestimating the danger of kulaks would inevitably lead to the denial of class struggle in the rural areas, which meant the loss of revolutionary vigilance. On the other hand the exaggeration of the danger would instigate class struggle in the countryside. Both mistaken attitudes would damage the current favorable NEP policy. Therefore, party should be alert against these two mistaken tendencies.

Stalin believed that the "new opposition" exaggerated the effect of capitalist development to the relations between poor peasants and kulaks. This tendency actually instigated class struggle in the countryside, which was very harmful. This attitude was in fact meant "to restore the poor peasants' committees to deprive the kulaks, which equals to announce civil war in the countryside, which can destroy all our construction work."4 When evaluating the increasing power of the bourgeois (capitalism) Stalin pointed out that the party should allow the existence of (capitalism) bourgeoisie under certain conditions and within some certain limitations. The party on the one side should use their knowledge and experience in favour of building socialism and on the other side employ economic means to restrict them. It could be possible to win part of them to a so that Soviet-oriented attitude, final victory over them could be won step by step. When evaluating the differentiation of attitudes among intellectuals, Stalin had warned that not all intellectuals were dissatisfied with the Soviet system. In the current situation the party should apply the policy of uniting with those intellectuals who have working class and urban-rural laborer roots who were willing to approach closer to proletariat and the Soviet power.

---

4 Ibid., p.278.

Fourthly, he proposed that it was inappropriate to simply employ administrative measures when struggling against kulaks.

Stalin pointed out that in the fight against kulaks, the Soviet party and state should employ economic means and act lawfully in the frame of the Soviet legal system, the Party should reject solely relying on simple administrative means. In this epoch some people in the CPSU (Bolshevik) believed that only by mobilizing the National Political Security Bureau could the kulaks be eliminated. Stalin radically rejected this erroneous view and emphasizing that the correct way was to "take appropriate measures to limit and isolate kulaks economically". Of course, some administrative means could also be necessary, "but the administrative means should by no means substitute economic measures."[5]

Stalin's above views were certainly correct. With a serious Marxist scientific approach, Stalin could still correctly analyze the situation of social classes in the Soviet Union, he could wisely distinguish among different characteristics of class struggles. Every class difference or struggle inevitably possesses different nature. He argued that class struggles should assume "unique forms" due to specific historical conditions, namely things should be different under the dictatorship of the proletariat. But if I make a general evaluation Stalin's above ideas, though they were only in their new formation, though still immature and incomplete, they were of great value and should be fully affirmed.

294

2. Stalin's theory of "ever intensifying class struggle"

From autumn 1927 to spring 1928, a serious crisis related to grain purchasing of the state had occurred in the Soviet Union's, which seriously affected the domestic grain supply and damaged its grain exports. According to statistics, the grain purchased by the state was more than 4.2 billion puds at the end of 1926, but roughly 300 million pood at the end of 1927 with 100 million pood less. Significant reduction of grain supply not only affected social stability in the cities, but also greatly threatened the industrial development. Therefore, the issue of grain had become an acute problem. In order to prevent the crisis of grain supply and increase grain purchases, the CPSU (Bolshevik) Central Committee Political Bureau decided to launch a nationwide campaign to enhance grain purchases with "extraordinary measures". The state applied the Section 107 of the Soviet Penal Code which was passed in 1926 to the purchase of grain, i.e., with this law government could send speculators to court and the state could confiscated the grain products. These extraordinary measures played a certain role in the increase of grain purchases. On the other hand violent and excessive acts of searching, arresting and confiscation of grain had occurred especially in major grain-producing regions.

5　Ibid., p.266.

The thoughts among the main leaders of the CPSU (Bolshevik) Central Committee on whether extraordinary measures should be taken or not were different. Some ideas were radically different. Most people of the Central Committee at that time thought that the main reason was the inefficiency in the level of organization, namely leadership mistakes.

This understanding was reflected in the wording of the resolution, which evaluated the crisis: the resolution passed in the Joint Plenary Session of the CPSU (Bolshevik) Central Committee plus the Control Commission in April 1928. The resolution said: "the errors in the practical implementation of the plan of industrial distribution (delay in the distribution of industrial products), the errors of the general policy (too light rural tax for the rural upper class, the large price gaps between grains and other agricultural products, and so on), the current facts such as lag of growth in the industrial products production. Besides problems of organization and lack of enthusiasm in the leading administrative organs—this problem includes the party organs—which still play an extremely important role... are the causes of serious economic difficulties If we can timely and properly use major economic means to maintain a balance and eliminate the administrative shortcomings of both state and party organs we can well overcome these difficulties."[6]

The resolution also criticized the mistaken and excessive practices which had occurred during the execution of "extraordinary measures" and urged firm correction of them.

The resolution had defined aims and limits of "extraordinary measures" in a detailed form. The resolution had emphasized: these mistaken and excessive acts practiced by some organization of the party and the Soviet state organs in some regions should absolutely be avoided. The party should struggle against them firmly, because these mistaken and excessive practices actions will cause long-term and adverse consequences both in economy and politics.

The resolution had also clearly stated "all above criticized practices which have aimed both the kulaks and the middle peasants" were part of those excessive acts. The resolution also aimed to balance the above critique saying : in fact these acts have occurred in our work related to surplus collection.".. at the moment "current extraordinary measures in force cannot be reversed into normal means." And finally, the resolution affirmed "the correct line to fight against the kulaks, and NEP economic policy, and said: "only on the basis of the 'NEP'—which is the only correct form of combining large-scale socialist industry with the small-scale rural economic sector) and only by the strict implementation of revolutionary laws of the proletarian state can we realize the slogan of 'continue to attack the kulaks' of the 15th Party Congress."[7]

Stalin had led this plenary session and supported the above resolution, but in fact he was holding the different views with the basic spirit of this resolution. With the occurance of the crisis Stalin was alarmed and had closely followed the developments. He had urged other leaders for the initiation of the "extraordinary measures" and had sent many of the Central Committee members to the countryside. In 1928, he had made an inspection tour to Siberia, and invented the so-called "Ural–Siberia" method of grain purchase, he had urged harsh practices and mobilized the local officials to implement the "extraordinary measures" strictly, namely with no habituation.

This uncontrolled attitude of him was disappointing and had never occurred after since he became the top leader of SU. The reason behind this extraordinary attitude and understanding of the crisis was that Stalin had linked some domestic economic events with the class struggle since the beginning. He believed that the real cause of the crisis was the destructive attack initiated by kulaks. In January 1928, Stalin said during his visit to the Siberian grain-producing area: "the kulaks are reluctant to distribute the grain in their hands. They are just waiting for price hikes. They seem to act like crazy speculators. This is true, but they do not only want price increase, but aim to make it two times higher than the price set by the state." "We can be sure that the slowing down of the gain purchases will exist as long as there are the kulaks."[8] On April 13, 1928, Stalin stressed in his report titled as "The Work of the April Joint Plenum of the Central Committee and Central Control Commission": "the crisis of grain purchase reflects a serious attack to the Soviet by the rural capitalist elements related to one of the most important construction issues—the issue of the grain purchase under the new economic policy. Comrades, this is the class background of this crisis..."[9] A month later, Stalin made a more clear evaluation on the crisis in his speech to the 8th Conference of the Soviet Union Communist Youth League. He said: this crisis of grain purchase "wakes up all of our organizations, breaks the so-called theory of 'equilibrium" and once again forcefully points to the existence of the class enemy. These enemies do not fall asleep, so it is necessary to strengthen the power, vigilance, revolutionary nature of the working class to fight against these enemies."[10] In July, he made a report titled "On the Issue of Industrialization and Grain" for

---

7   Ibid., p.428.
8   Collected Works of Stalin, vol. 11, Chinese Version p.1, 4, 6.
9   Ibid., pp.39-40.
10   Ibid., p.59.

the CPSU (Bolshevik) Central Committee meeting. He pointed out in the report that: "all improvements we have achieved and our slightly significant achievements are the performances and results of our domestic class struggle". "The advances towards socialism will definitely lead to the resistance and revolt of the exploiters, in turn the revolt by the exploiters, will certainly result in the necessary intensifying of the class struggle."[11]

The crisis of grain purchase and his evaluation on the causes of the crisis as two motive forces had caused a dramatic change in his cognition, evaluation and attitude of Stalin related to certain issues related to class struggle: His estimations on the situation of current and future mid-term domestic class relations, his ideas on the status and role of class struggle in the domestic social life under the dictatorship of the proletariat and his ideas related to the forms and methods of class struggle, etc, had encountered a shift.[12]

In October of that year, Stalin analyzed the root of the class struggle in the Soviet Union, and proposed the task of "digging out the roots of the capitalism." In his view, the roots of capitalism was hidden in commodity production and small-scale production in the rural areas. In the Soviet Union, the small-scale production was prevalent and even dominant, especially in the period of NEP. Stalin quoting from Lenin said: "The small-scale production massively and rapidly generates capitalism and the bourgeoisie, forming the basis for capitalist restoration." .... "Anyone who did not understand this point was "Rightist". The so-called "Rightists" "underestimate the strength of our enemies and the strength of capitalism, does not notice the danger of the capitalist restoration, and cannot understand the mechanism of class struggle under the the the dictatorship of the proletariat."[13]

297

At the beginning of 1929, Stalin once again explained his theory of intensifying class struggle when he criticized Bukharin's so-called idea that "Russia could grow into socialism"[14][15]

---

11   Ibid., pp.149-150.
12   Here, we can make a simple anology with Mao's reaction to the crisis in 1957, when rightist elements of China had stirred certain counter-revolutionary events.
13   Ibid., p.199.
14   Bukharin, since 1922 had developed an idea that Russia could develop towards socialism with gradual economic struggles against the bourgeoisie elements.
15   Since the beginning of 1920s, Bukharin had analyzed discussed the theoretical and practical issue of the"growing into socialism" and made a clear definition of his understanding on this issue. He said we havetalked too much about revisionist ideas on the issue of growing into socialism. We Marxists have a different understanding of it"it is impossible to accomplish our task by shear laws and violent measures. It is a long-term organic process, strictly speaking, it is a long process to grow into socialism"..."Ours is clearly distinctive from the "growing into socialism" proposed by revisionism and the difference lay in when to grow into it..." Refer to The Selected Works of Bukharin, vol. 1, p.63, Beijing: Renmin Press, 1981.

Stalin believed that there were two real causes for the intensification of domestic class struggles: firstly, we were advancing in our offense strategy and the status of socialist elements and practices are ascending in industry and agriculture. What accompanies this growth is that part of the rural and urban capitalists are getting marginalized. Secondly, the capitalist elements will not automatically exit the stage of history. They resist and revolt because their share is declining but their absolute population still sees a growth. Our march forward and insistitance on our offense policy will reduce the capitalist elements and marginalize them. In history, the perishing classes did never exit the stage of history automatically, instead they have attempted to exhaust all their residual power to maintain their survival. They have always resisted desperately, and this is the root root of the intensifying class struggle. Taking the crisis of the grain purchase and the Shakhty affair[16] as evidences Stalin had argued that these two issues were the attacks of rural and urban capitalism against socialism.

These attacks had demonstrated that the proletarian class enemies were re-deploying their forces in an attempt to maintain the old system and fight against the new system, which had inevitably led to the intensification of the class struggle.

When criticizing Bukharin, Stalin not only elaborated the reasons for the intensifying class struggle, but also discussed the ways to eliminate the classes. He compared the arguments of of Bukharin and the theory of Lenin, criticized: "Bukharin thinks that under the dictatorship of the proletariat the class struggle must *die down* and *come to an end* so that the abolition of classes may be brought about. Lenin, on the contrary, teaches us that classes can be abolished only by means of a stubborn class struggle, which under the dictatorship of the proletariat becomes even fiercer than it was before the dictatorship of the proletariat."

"The abolition of classes, says Lenin, requires a long, difficult and stubborn *class struggle*, which, *after* the overthrow of the power of capital, *after* the destruction of the bourgeois state, *after* the establishment of the dictatorship of the proletariat, *does not disappear* (as the vulgar representatives of the old socialism and the old Social-Democracy imagine), but merely changes its forms and in many respects becomes even fiercer."[17]

"The abolition of classes *by means of the fierce class struggle of the proletariat*—such is Lenin's formula. The abolition of classes *by means of the extinction of the class struggle and by the capitalists growing into socialism*—such is Bukharin's formula."[18]

16   Fifty-three mining engineers and technicians, including some top officials and three German engineers, were accused of acts of sabotage and treason dating back to the 1920s and taking part in a conspiracy directed from abroad (involving French finance and Polish counter espionage.
17   Collected Works of Stalin, vol. 24, p. 315.
18   Collected Works of Stalin, vol. 12, 1st Chinese version, pp.30-31.

Accordingly, Stalin emphasized that only "through a brutal proletarian class struggle" and the reinforcement of the class struggle and organs of the proletarian dictatorship could we achieve the proletariat society. In order to prove his claim, he quoted Lenin's words in 1919 as the "theoretical evidence", saying that "the elimination of classes should need a long, difficult and stubborn class struggle. After the overthrow of the capitalists, after the smashing of the bourgeois state and the establishment of the dictatorship of the proletariat, the class struggle does not just disappear but changes its form and become more violent in many ways."[19]

In April 1929, Stalin further pointed out that under the dictatorship of the proletariat, the class struggle becomes more fiercer than the past. Only through the brutal class struggle could the bedrock of capitalism be eradicated. He stressed that the Soviet Union was undergoing a new changes in social classes mevzilenmesi configuration. He commented: "now the "Shakhty elements" exist in all of our industrial sectors. In the countryside, the capitalist elements, i.e. the kulaks had accumulated the necessary capital and have the power to resist the Soviet regime. This situation could not but lead to the intensifying of the class struggle. If the Soviet economy should be transformed on the basis of the socialism, the socialism should "start an overall attack aiming capitalist elements."[20] In Stalin's view, every step forward in the development of socialism was bound closely with the class struggle, because in history, the dying classes had never exited the stage of history automatically. When they faced their doom, they had to "exhaust all their residual power to maintain their survival."[21] Thus he believed in the proletarian class struggle to eliminate classes, which was his socialism and socialist construction theory.

Stalin took the theory of class struggle as the main theoretical weapon to criticize Bukharin's "Rightist" thought. He repeatedly ridiculed Bukharin did not understand "the mechanism of the class struggle under the dictatorship of the proletariat." He opened all the old books against him giving texts from Lenin in which Lenin criticized Bukharin. Bukharin was severely accused as declaring the slogan of "domestic peace" under the dictatorship of the proletariat. For him Bukharin, did not see the change of the form in the class struggles in those days, thus advocated to follow the main form of economic struggles and using economic competition method against the private sector merchants and kulaks in order to gradually marginalize, and eventually eliminate them. Bukharin was advocating the so-called "the theory of the extinguishment of the class struggle". He said Rykov and Bukharin's objection of the "emergency measures" against

---

19   Collected Works of Lenin, vol. 36, Chinese Version 2, p.376.
20   Collected Works of Stalin, vol. 12, 1st Chinese version, p.14.
21   Ibid., p.35.

kulaks (rich peasants) was the "policy of the bourgeoisie liberalism", and firmly negated Rykov's advocacy that "the main idea of the Five-Year Plan is the growth of the labor productivity" and saying it was "not the Five-Year Plan but the Five-Year Nonsense if the party agrees with this proposal"[22]

Since then, Stalin argued and gave reasons for the issue of the sharpening domestic class struggles for many times. In November 1929, in his speech for the 12th anniversary of the victory of the October Revolution, he mentioned: "the last hope of the world capitalists' dreaming of the restoration of capitalism in the Soviet Union—'the sacred principle of private property' is shattered and becoming naught. The peasants, being seen as the nourished materials by them, are leaving the praised banner of 'private ownership' massively…the last hope of the restoration of capitalism is shattered. For this reason, the capitalist elements in our country desperately attempt to mobilize all the forces of the old world to oppose socialism, thereby sharpen the class struggle."[23] In 1930, at the 16th Congress CPSU (Bolshevik), he stated again the reason for the intensified class struggle: "we have launched a massive attack to the capitalist elements and significantly moved our socialist industry forward and started the establishment of the state-run farms and collective farms. These phenomena will affect the exploiting class. Often, what accompanied these phenomena are the bankruptcy of the dying class, the class of the rural kulaks and the shrinking of the sites of the small-scale urban bourgeoisie at all levels."[24] Obviously, all of these cannot but make the class struggle more acute and a more intensive resistance to the Soviet regime's policy, by the dying class.

300

Faced by the fierce attacks of Stalin, Bukharin also fought back. Bukharin has strongly refuted the viewpoint that the more forward the socialism moved, the more intensified the class struggle becomes. He said that this strange theory took the fact of currently intensifying class struggle and generalized it as an inevitable law of the social development. "A conclusion could be obtained from this strange theory that the more forward we moved to the socialism, the more difficulties we might have and the more intensified the class struggle becomes. It seems we should start a nation-wide civil war, or starve or being killed in the war at the front door of socialism." However, due to various reasons, finally Bukharin and his supporters have failed to persuade party and people and Stalin won the victory against the "Rightists", which allowed Stalin's theory of class struggle becoming the dominant thought of the Soviet party.

22   Collected Works of Stalin, vol. 12, 1st Chinese version, p.73.
23   Ibid., pp.118-119.
24   Ibid., pp.306-307.

Under the guidance of the theory of ever intensifying class struggles, since the second half of 1929, the Soviets had changed the policy of limiting the trend of the exploitation by the kulaks and began to implement a policy to eliminate the kulaks. The Soviets Union only deprived the of their means of production, but also exiled them and tried to reform them ideologically through forced labor and excluded the private sector merchants from functioning in the domestic circulation of goods through state's administrative measures. Through various coercive means, till 1931 when the First Five Year Plan was completed ahead of schedule, the capitalist elements (men) within the Soviet Union were basically wiped out, but Stalin did not give up his theory of ever intensifying class struggle, on the contrary, he said: "just because they are dying and facing the doom, they will go on from one form attack to another, sharper form, appealing to the backward sections of the population and mobilizing them against the Soviet regime."[25] Thus, in those days Stalin, intentionally or unintentionally expanded the "front" of the class enemies. He pointed out in the conclusion speech of the First Five Year Plan talks that the remnants of the dying classes —the private industrialists and their servants, the private merchants and their pawns, the former nobles and priests, the kulaks and their lackeys, the former White Guard and police officers, policeman and gendarmes, all kinds of bourgeois intellectuals of a chauvinist type and all other anti-Soviet elements have been tossed out. But these "have beens" have wormed into our various government offices and trading organizations, factories, mainly into collective and state farms and even into the party." "They carried with them hatred for the Soviet regime, of course sharp enmity towards new forms of economy, new life and new culture." Under these conditions "all this may provide for a revival of the activities of the defeated groups of the old counter-revolutionary parties—the Social Revolutionaries, the Mensheviks, and the bourgeois nationalists of the central and border regions... the Trotskyites, and the Right deviationists..." This analysis essentially classified all the people against Stalin and those with different views with Stalin into the ranks of the class enemies, which laid a foundation for the later "Great Purge".

With the completion of the second Five-Year Plan ahead of schedule and the completion of socialist transformation of the economy, Stalin announced that socialism was established and the exploiting classes were eliminated in November 1936. This conclusion was realistic and was also of great significance, but unfortunately, he did not give up his erroneous theory of ever intensifying class struggle, even after he announced the elimination of all classes. Instead, he made a speech that the class struggle would be more acute as the socialism advanced on this new basis. In 1937, he said in the report of "On the Party's Shortcomings at Work and the Ways

25   Collected Works of Stalin, vol. 13, 1st Chinese version, p.190.

to Eliminate Trotsky and Other Double-dealers": "We must remember that the more hopeless the position of the enemies becomes, the more readily they will clutch at extreme measures as the only measures of the doomed in their struggle against Soviet power. One must remember this and be vigilant" This argument was clearly self-contradictory when he claimed that the class struggle was more acute after the elimination of exploiting classes. In order to justify himself, Stalin presented two reasons: First, the direct support of foreign imperialists. He stressed that the remnants of the defeated classes are directly supported by foreign enemies: "Capitalist encirclement-it means that there is one country, the Soviet Union, which has established at home a Socialist order, and that there are, besides, many countries, bourgeois countries, which continue to carry on the capitalist form of life and which encircle the Soviet Union, waiting for the opportunity to attack it, to crush it, or, in any case-to undermine its might and to weaken it."[26] Thus, "as long as we are surrounded by capitalist countries, there would be assassinators, spies, saboteurs and murders sent to our rear areas by the foreign agents."[27] Second, Contemporary Trotskyism is not a political trend within the working class, but an unprincipled and intellectually devoid band of wreckers, diversionists, intelligence agents, spies, and killers; a band of sworn enemies of the working class in the hire of the intelligence service organs of foreign states. Such is the indisputable result of the evolution of Trotskyism in the past seven or eight years. Such is the difference between Trotskyism in the past and Trotskyism in the present.

302

They have been a group of assassinators, spies, saboteurs and murders, totally an unscrupulous, unprincipled, and thoughtless gang. Stalin also emphasized that the Trotskyites were involved in sabotage, assassination and espionage, acting under the directions of foreign intelligence agencies.

Under the guidance of the theory of ever intensifying class struggle, the phenomenon Stalin repeatedly stressed became a reality throughout the Soviet Union, that is, "the class struggle was stirred up" on all fronts and "the class struggle was artificially provoked and incited." While the capitalism was declared to be eradicated in cities and countryside, "the Great Purge" started in the Soviet Union, blasting through both the party and the army. To make a summary of this practice, especially to defend the terror policy which put all people into scare, Stalin further deepened and developed his arguments on the class struggle under the proletarian dictatorship. His argument of ever intensifying class struggle eventually became a systematic theory.

---

26 Selected Works of Stalin (1934-1952), p.153.
27 Selected Works of Stalin (1934-1952), pp.141-142.

In summary, we can see that Stalin's theory of class struggle under the proletarian dictatorship encountered two important turning points. The first step (from the late 1920s to early 1930s): In the late 1920s, in order to meet the changes in economic policies (NEP) and anti-rightist movements in the party, Stalin presented a series of views distinct from the previous ones on the issue of class struggle by using the economic crisis of grain supply. Thus he tried to establish a theoretical support for a line which I can term as "revolution" from above. Second step: On December 1, 1934, Kirov, a member of the Central Committee Political Bureau (Bolshevik) of the Communist Party of the Soviet Union (CPSU), the general secretary of Central Committee, the first secretary of Leningrad State, was assassinated. Stalin immediately waged a nation-wide "purge" after this incident. To provide a theoretical support for the "the Great Purge", Stalin further enriched and developed his theory of class struggle, and pushed it to a more ridiculous position. After these two drastic events Stalin's theory of class struggle under the proletarian dictatorship has become systematic. During the world anti-fascist war, the Soviet army and people began to have more contacts with the outside world, the Soviet Army had operated throughout Europe. After the war, frequent exchanges occurred between the Soviet Union and other countries. In this new context, to guard against foreign ideological and cultural influence, Stalin launched a massive "anti-cosmopolitanism" and campaign against "fawning" on the West (1946) campaign after the war. Thus a new content was added to the theory of class struggle which was basically formed in the 1930s. In the following decades, Stalin's theory of class struggle not only worked as the Soviet Communist Party's basic guiding ideology, but also a guidance followed by almost all socialist countries. Class struggle was seen in everything, behind everything and everything was judged and examined by the theory of class struggle. All the problems-academic-cultural-social life would easily come to be directly linked with the class struggle. This theory's deep effect was an important theoretical source of "left" lines of communist parties and has formed long-term thinking and study (inceleme) mode which gained deep roots. It became very hard to rectify its above effects in the Soviet Union and other socialist countries.

II. Stalin's major contributions to the theory of class struggle and its errors

1. Stalin's contributions to the theory of class and theory of class struggle in the socialist period

The theorists have always attached critical and negative attitude against Stalin's theory of class and his theory of class struggle in the socialist period. Then, did Stalin ever make contributions to the theory of class struggle in the socialist period? Was there anything right? Our answer is positive.

First, Stalin generally analyzed the class division in the socialist society with a proper approach.

Marxist classical writers- Marx and Engels has argued that "the existence of classes is only bound up with particular historical phases in the development of production (Letter to Weydemeyer in 1852)..."[28] In the process of development of productive forces, the different positions in relation to means of production is the fundamental standard to classify the classes. Stalin basically followed these standards for the class analysis when analyzing the class composition of socialist society. He pointed out that, as the capitalist economic elements in all the sectors of the national economy had completely vanished and socialism had achieved a complete victory in all sectors of the economy, and as the socialist public ownership has become the unshakable foundation of the society and therefore, the class structure of the societ in the socialist period would inevitably change accordingly as the economic system has changed.

In November 1936, Stalin declared in his report of "On the Draft of the Soviet Union's Constitution": Due to the realization of socialismand establishment of a socialist system, all the exploiting classes has been eliminated, and a man's exploitation of others was eradicated in the Soviet Union; there are only the working class, peasantry and intellectuals in the society who has undergone a fundamental change. Stalin pointed out that, in the socialist Soviet Union, the working class, who had liberated themselves and has been free from oppression and exploitation, was leading a large-scale socialist construction. It has become the leading class instead of being oppressed and exploited by the capitalists. Farmers were no longer the small producers class either. They have shaken off exploitation and most of them have become members of collective producers. Their work and private property were not on the basis of private economy, individual labor process and backward technology, but on collective ownership, collective work

---

28   Selected Works of Marx and Engels, vol. 4, 2nd edition, p.547, Beijing: People's Publishing House, 1995.

and modern technology. After the socialist transformation, the intellectuals has an entirely new, working intelligentsia, the like of which you will not find in any other country on earth, who maintains a close relation with the working class and farmers, who serve the people and socialist construction. Thus, they enjoyed the equal rights with other citizens of the Soviet Union. In addition, Stalin also emphasized that, in spite of the difference between these three groups that constituted the socialist society, a) the dividing lines between the working class and the peasantry, and between these classes and the intelligentsia, are being obliterated, and that the old class exclusiveness is disappearing. This means that the distance between these social groups is steadily diminishing. Secondly, they signify that the economic contradictions between these social groups are declining are becoming obliterated.

And lastly, they signify that the political contradictions between them are also declining and becoming obliterated.[29]

Second, Stalin indeed presented a proper analysis of the class relations in the Soviet Union. Were there class struggles in the Soviet Union after the exploiting classes were eliminated and fraternal cooperation occurred between workers, peasants, and intellectuals? Stalin gave a positive answer. Combining with the analysis of international and domestic environment of the Soviet Union, Stalin pointed out that the Soviet Union, the only socialist country which was sieged by the imperialist countries, was faced with the class struggle against the imperialist countries, and this international struggle, to some degree, was reflected in the domestic class relations. This effect was mainly reflected among the people who were ideologically weak-shaped, greedy for money, bribed by the imperialist countries and among some which act as their agents, and among the dissidents in the party holding different opinions who acted as their spies, as well as some remnants of the bourgeoisie elements who wished to destroy the socialist cause in collision by the international enemies. In response to this risk, Stalin demanded that the people should be vigilant and should not ignore the remaining existence of class struggle. We also believe that, due to the influence of foreign imperialist powers, the class struggle remained in the Soviet Union after the elimination of the exploiting classes. The analysis of Stalin associating the domestic class struggle with the international class struggle was in line with the actual situation of the Soviet Union and Lenin's theory of class struggle under the proletarian dictatorship. We should say that Stalin has made contributions in this regard, but unfortunately this view was imbued with unlimited expansion and absolution of class struggles.

---

29 Selected Works of Stalin (I), p.237.

Thirdly, Stalin has developed the theory of new driving force of the socialist development. Marxist classical writers have argued that the class struggle was the direct driving force of social development in a class society. Marx and Engels argued clearly in the "Communist Manifesto" that the history since the disintegration of the original communal society was all the history of class struggle, which was the driving force of development of a class society. In the late 1870s, in the famous "A Circular Letter to August Bebel, Wilhelm Liebknecht, Wilhelm Bracke, and others", Marx and Engels solemnly declared, "In nearly 40 years, we have always stressed the class struggle, which is the direct driving force of history, and in particular the class struggle between the bourgeoisie and the proletariat as the great lever of the modern social revolution; it is therefore impossible for us to co-operate with people who wish to expunge this class struggle from the socialist movement."[30]

What is the direct driving force promoting the social development in the socialist society? Stalin examined this issue and the classical writers thus advanced some correct theoretical views. When commenting on the issue of new driving force of socialist development (socialist society), Stalin wrote: "the new driving forces of socialist society that were unknown before and were absent in previous social-economic formations, namely: the moral-patriotic unity of the peoples of the USSR, Soviet patriotism."[31] Stalin also discovered the special role played by self-criticism in the development of the socialist society: "the party requires self-criticism as a means of proper leadership of the country, its significance as an objective law in the development of the socialist society."

The driving force of socialist development was later summarized into four points based on Stalin's speeches in the Soviet Union: moral and political consensus, the friendship between nationalities, Soviet patriotism, fourth criticism and self-criticism. It should be said that these four points on the driving forces of socialist development served as a groundbreaking contribution to Marxist theory of class struggle, which has greatly promoted Marxism.

2. Stalin's major errors in the theory of class struggle

Based on his major arguments on class struggle and his practice, under Stalin's rule the major errors in his theory of class struggle were manifested in his theory of "ever intensifying class struggle" in the socialist period, specifically in the following areas:

Firstly, Marx and Engels' proposition that class struggle as "the direct driving force of history" was changed into an "eternal power", which excessively emphasized the status and role of class struggle in the socialist period.

---

30   Selected Works of Marx and Engels, vol. 3, 2nd edition, p.685.
31   Selected Works of Stalin (I), p.237.

Classes and class struggle idea is undoubtedly an important issue in the Marxist theory. Marx and Engels, the founders of Marxism, attached great importance to the research of class and class struggles and the historical role of class struggle since the birth of their theory. Marx has argued that the class is in a historical category. The classes came into being after the man was separated from the animal kingdom and stepped into the human society. There was no class division in primitive human times, let alone the class struggle. When the future communist society comes, both the exploiting class and all other classes would be eliminated, and there will naturally no longer be class struggles. Clearly, when it comes to the whole historical development of human society, the class struggle can't be a universal driving force of historical development.

Strictly speaking, Marx and Engels never or seldom discussed the class and class struggle issue in socialism/communism. Marx and Engels had expected that the socialist revolution would succeed first in Britain, France, the United States, Germany, and other developed capitalist countries, which would be followed by a transition period. The first phase of communist society (socialism) would eventually come into being after the gradual elimination of classes and class differences under the proletarian dictatorship. Thus, it is difficult to find any argument on class and class struggle in the socialist period in their writings. The class and class struggle they mentioned were mainly related to the transition period, that is, the class struggle after the proletariat's seizure of power and the period before the completion of socialist construction. When talking about the class struggle in this transition period, Marx and Engels stressed that the proletariat should provide a reasonable social environment after the seizure of power and should ensure that the class struggle was conducted in the most reasonable and most humane way.[32]

After the October Revolution in Russia, based on the specific conditions of Russia, Lenin had stressed that the political prerequisites of socialism were there and the struggle for socialism was not necessarily to be linked with the class struggle, since the proletariat had achieved state power as the ruling class. For Lenin, the main task had shifted from the class struggle to the economic construction under the rule of proletarian state power and the creation of socialist economic base, and the promotion of productive forces to a highly-developed modernized level and socialized level. Upholding the Marxist historical materialism, this argument defended and developed the Marx's principle that the productive forces are the ultimate decisive power of any social development.

---

32   Selected Works of Marx and Engels, vol. 3, 2nd edition, p.98.

Stalin did not consider Lenin's ideas deeply, this was a great mistake of him. He thought that the possible intense class struggle needed in the transition—before the completion of socialist transformation—should also be throughout the whole socialism period. He argued that throughout the whole socialism period and under the proletarian dictatorship, the class struggle would become more and more important, as a most primary issue and should determine all other spheres of life including the party, the state, and the army. Stalin wrote: "I think that, under the proletarian dictatorship, there is no single political or economic, which does not reflect the existence of a class struggle in urban or rural social life"; "the progresses and moderately significant achievements of our socialist construction are all the performance and results of our domestic class struggle";[33] the class struggle is the decisive power in promoting our socialist development: Is it not obvious that our whole forward movement, our every success of any importance in the sphere of socialist construction, is an expression and result of the class struggle in our country?

Although Stalin had also developed certain new ideas on the "new driving forces" of socialist development, he simply prioritized class struggles as the driving force of socialist development, which was reflected in his handling of contradictions. He argued that the significant achievements in the socialist construction were all the results of domestic class struggles. This understanding was clearly inconsistent with the real situation in the SU.

Second, Stalin misjudged the situation of class struggle in the socialist period and regarded the class struggle as the basic task of developing socialist construction. Thus, Stalin believed that, with the development of socialism, the class struggle would more and more intensify and the class enemies would be in deeper disguise, therefore its magnitude would expand wider and wider, it would be increasingly more important to smash the class enemies. The class enemies had not only permeated with the society, but infiltrated into the state power, even into the leadership organs of the party, into the top leading group. The enemies carried "party identity cards", which was their power. Since Stalin believed that the class struggle was the main issue in all aspects of social life, all kinds of "class struggles" could be observed in the Soviet Union during his rule.

Stalin's analysis related to the Soviet domestic class situation in his report of "On the Draft Constitution of the USSR" in November 1936 was generally in line with the reality. However, he failed to understand the contradictions among the 3 groups: the working class, peasantry and intellectuals. Nor could he clearly define the position of remnant exploiting classes

---

33   Collected Works of Stalin, vol. 11, 148-149.

which were abolished. Soon later he argued that in March 1937, that there were still remnants of the defeated classes, who wanted to continue their deadly struggles in the future. Stalin emphasized that the faster the growth of the Soviet national power, the more intense would be the resistance of the class enemies. I suggest this was a self-contradictory argument. Where were the class enemies? In fact, Stalin confused the contradictions among people and the contradictions in the party ranks with the contradictions between ourselves and the enemy. Stalin launched "the Great Purge" based on this confusion, leading to a large number of infringements of law and socialist freedoms.

Third, Stalin revised the Marxist theory on the state and the theory of proletarian According to Marx's theory, the state would inevitably disappear with the disappearance of classes. The proletarian dictatorship as a state would only exist in the transition period between capitalism and socialism/communism after the proletariat wins the political power. For the proletarian dictatorship, both Engels and Lenin emphasized the principle of majority ruling the minority. After the proletariat wins the power, "a special apparatus, special machinery for suppression, the "state" is still necessary, but this is now a transitional one, no longer a state in the usaual sense."[34] Lenin wrote the term state in apostrophes.

Before and after the October Revolution, Lenin presented many arguments on the proletarian dictatorship. Lenin defended the necessity of repressive functions of proletarian dictatorship, during the period when the proletarian regime was not yet consolidated, especially during the civil war and foreign military intervention periods. If the resistance of bourgeoisie was not defeated, the bourgeoisie would return and the proletarian regime would collapse.Thus, Lenin defined the policy of the civil war as follows: "The dictatorship of the proletariat is not bound even by its own laws; this dictatorship rested on force not laws."[35] When the proletarian dictatorship gains stability or the economic construction has gained significant basis, the proletarian dictatorship should turn to peaceful and lawful and use soft power. Because of this, Lenin added, "The proletarian dictatorship... is not only violence against the exploiters, and not even mainly violence."[36] According to the Marxist point of view, the ultimate goal of proletarian dictatorship is to destroy all classes and class differences, but to achieve this, the fundamental task is to concentrate all the power on the development of economic forces and the improvement of labor productivity. The issues of

---

34   Collected Works of Lenin, vol. 31, Chinese version 2, p.86, Beijing: People's Publishing House, 1985.
35   Collected Works of Lenin, vol. 35, Chinese version 2, p.237.
36   Collected Works of Lenin, vol. 37, Chinese version 2, p.11, Beijing: People's Publishing House, 1986.

social development in socialism can't all be solved only by class struggle. On this point, Lenin proposed specific ideas. He said: "In any socialist revolution, after both the task of the proletariat's seizure of power is finished and the repression of exploiters' resistance are basically finished, the fundamental task is to build an economic system that surpasses those that exist in capitalist societies. This fundamental task equates with raising the rate of labor productivity."[37]

Stalin has amended Marxism and Leninism on the issue. First, Stalin put forward a proposition claiming "demise of the state will not happen by the weakening of the state power, but by its maximum strengthening."[38] This was not an "automatic demise" of proletarian state as advocated by Engels and Lenin, but the theory of artificial "annihilation" of the state which Engels and Lenin have criticized. Certainly, determined by objective conditions, the disappearance of classes and states is a "natural" historical process. Obviously, Stalin fell into historical idealism on this issue.

Additionally, Stalin quoted Lenin's sentence "The dictatorship of the proletariat is not bound even by its own laws" and interpreted it as the universal concept related to proletarian dictatorship. This was not in line with Lenin's ideas and estimations. Lenin also argued that strengthening of the proletarian socialist legal system should be a "firm slogan" of Bolsheviks and criticized the "vulgar bourgeois argument" which argued that "the dictatorship is to abolish all the freedom and democracy, to trample any freedoms at will and achieve the dictators' narrow personal by the abuse of power."[39]

Fourth, Stalin mistakenly proposed the formulation of "eliminating the classes by the fierce proletarian class struggles."

In regard with the trend and forms of class struggle, Stalin believed that the faster the socialist development, the more intense gets the class struggle. As the class enemies become crazier, they should be more severely cracked down. In order to eliminate the class enemies, any means or methods could be used, which was not in consistent with Marxist-Leninist principles on the elimination of classes.

Lenin's statement that the class struggles "became more brutal in many ways" after the establishment of proletarian dictatorship was proposed limited for a certain period. His statement was not a general formula. First, Lenin's theory of class and class struggle referred mainly to the transition period. For instance, when he wrote his article "Greetings to the Hungarian Workers", he suggested: "The abolition of classes requires a long, difficult

---

37   Collected Works of Lenin, vol. 3, 3rd edition, p.490.
38   Collected Works of Stalin, vol. 13, 1st Chinese version, p.190.
39   Collected Works of Lenin, vol. 39, Chinese version 2, p.371.

and stubborn class struggle, which, after the overthrow of capitalist rule, after the destruction of the bourgeois state, after the establishment of the dictatorship of the proletariat, does not disappear (as the vulgar representatives of the old socialism and the old Social-Democracy imagine), but merely changes its forms and in many respects becomes fiercer."[40] Another example is his argument in "The Documents Prepared for the Second Congress of the Communist International": "When the proletariat comes to power, the class struggle between the proletariat and the bourgeoisie doesn't end; on the contrary, the battle will become particularly widespread, intense and cruel."[41]

From Lenin's statements, we can easily see that here he analyzed the class and class struggles of the transition period. He wrote: "That is why Marx spoke of an entire period of the dictatorship of the proletariat as the period of transition from capitalism to socialism." In December 1921, he wrote clearly in "The Draft Outline of the Role and Tasks of Trade Unions under the New Economic Policy": "there must be classes in the transitional period from capitalism to socialism", and "the class struggle is inevitable as long as there exist classes."[42]

Second, the class struggle Lenin mentioned refers to that in the transitional period, when he wrote about the class and class struggles in the socialism period.

311

In the case of "socialism means the abolition of classes" that we often mention, when we look into Lenin's "The Economy and Politics in the Era of Proletarian Dictatorship", we will find that in this article the socialism Lenin referred was not the first phase of communist society, but the transitional period to socialism. And Lenin said that the society where difference exists between workers and peasants could not be called a socialist society. In other words, Lenin believed that a socialist society will have no classes, let alone class struggles, which was in line with Marx and Engels' views. Third, when it comes to the elimination of classes, Lenin had pointed out long ago, "In order to completely eliminate the classes, the exploiters must be overthrown, including the landowners and capitalists. Both their ownership and any private ownership of production must be abolished. And the difference between cities and countries, physical workers and mental workers must be removed. There will be a very long way to run. To accomplish this cause, we must greatly develop the productive forces, must overcome the resistance of numerous small-scale remnants... must overcome the strong old forces and conservative forces associated with these

---

40   Collected Works of Lenin, vol. 36, Chinese version 2, p.376.
41   Selected Works of Lenin, vol. 4, 3rd edition, p.239.
42   Collected Works of Lenin, vol. 42, Chinese version 2, p.367.

remnants."[43] Lenin's argument was exactly the same as that of Marx and Engels. Engels also pointed out long ago that the division of classes was based on the less developed productive forces, and that the highly developed productive forces were the prerequisite of the elimination of social classes. Therefore, the elimination of classes can not only rely on harsh class struggle. It can be seen from this that Lenin did not advocate that the process of elimination of classes going through a fierce class struggle. Instead, the classes can be eliminated by the development of productive forces. After the civil war, Lenin rarely talked about the cruel class struggle. Instead, he used to talk about how to restore the economy, how to develop the productive forces, and how to create labor productivity which is higher than capitalism. Therefore, we can't see any similarity with the conclusion that Stalin made when we compare the writings of Lenin , especially in his writings in his later years.

Stalin only emphasized on the elimination of classes through class struggles, but failed to mention the highly developed productive forces as the base of elimination of classes. His clasping of historical idealism was bound to cause "left" errors in practice.

3. The analysis of the birth of "ever intensifying class struggle"

Why did Stalin put forward the theory of "ever intensifying class struggle?" Why did Stalin's unique theory of class struggle undergo a series of mistakes in practice? These questions have always remained hot and difficult for many theorists. Nowadays there is a very popular point of view which argues that Stalin's theory of class struggle had aimed to destroy his rivals and the opposition. This was an important reason for Stalin to repeatedly stress this theory, but is not the only reason. In fact, there were complicated reasons for Stalin to put forward the theory of intensifying class struggle. It is absolutely biased if the reasons are attributed only to one point.

Firstly, a certain range of class contradictions and class struggle were the external factors that Stalin put forward this erroneous theory.

It has been 70 years since Stalin put forward the theory of "intensified class struggle", so Stalin is definitely thought to be out of ill personal intentions when he put forward this theory, if we judge and analyze his theory by using the current vision and standards of today. But if the historical facts are reconsidered, it is not difficult to find that Stalin put forward this theory against a special historical background. At that time, a certain degree of class struggle remained in the Soviet Union, and was very intensive in some spheres. After the October Revolution, the Tsar remnants, reactionary

43   Selected Works of Lenin, vol. 4, 3rd edition, p.11.

landlords, capitalists and international imperialists gathered together and never stopped their destructive activites. regime. In the three-year civil war, the Soviet regime basically put down the Kolchak, Denikin and other insurgents, and defeated the foreign armed intervention. Since then, in the recovery period of national economy, the domestic class contradictions were eased because of the Soviet New Economic Policy. But Stalin gradually abandoned the New Economic Policy after 1927 and turned to the massive collectivization campaigns in the rural areas. Due to mistakes in and the impetuous implementation of these new policies, the domestic class contradictions became sharp once again. For instance, there were more than 700 arsons and other violent incidents in 1927, and the number reached 1,027 in 1928; in 1929, there were over 620 terrorist incidents in Central Asia, and the terrorist incidents in Ukraine were 3 times that of 1927; and the terrorist incidents in October 1929 were equivalent to the sum of that in 1928. In these terrorist and violent events, a large number of party cadres and activists were killed, including 544 Soviet grass-roots cadres, 412 social activists, and 46 rural correspondents.[44] In addition, a world-wide anti-Soviet wave was started. In 1927, British-Soviet diplomatic relations were severely broken the assassination of Soviet ambassador to Poland, and other similar cases came one by one. In 1929, the largest economic crisis broke out in the capitalist world, in which the fascist forces began to rise in many countries. Some fascist parties seized the regime, while the United States and other imperialist countries implemented the policy of appeasement to shift troubles to others. The existing contradictions and struggles at home and abroad fully reflected the severe class struggles that the Soviet Union was faced with. These contradictions and struggles possibly aroused the vigilance of Stalin, who unfortunately did not conduct in-depth detailed analysis for these events. The class struggles were regarded as a common phenomenon in society and the principal contradiction dominating and influencing all the other contradictions. The mode of thinking that treated problems in a superficial way eventually came up to a conclusion that expanded and intensified class struggles was needed. This was only Stalin's mode of thinking, but the serious class struggle was reflected when considered from another point of view. Therefore, a range of class struggles, to a certain extent, were surely the external factors for Stalin's erroneous theory.

313

Secondly, the mistakes in Stalin's philosophical views were the epistemological roots of his erroneous theory.

Mao Zedong criticized Stalin's philosophy in "The Conference of Secretaries of Provincial, Municipal and Regional Party Committees in January, 1959. According to one fundamental law of dialectics, namely the unity of opposites, opposites are both in struggle and unity, opposites

---

44   Keming Liu and Hui Jin, The Soviet Politics and Economy over Seventy Years, p.329.

are mutually exclusive and interrelated. Under certain conditions, they can transform to one another. Mao Zedong said, "Stalin had many metaphysics and had taught metaphysics to many people. In *The Concise Guide to the History of CPSU (Bolshevik)*, he wrote about dialectics, but he put [the theory of] contradictions only at the very end (fourth row). We should say that the most fundamental problem of dialectics is the unity of contradictory opposites. The first law that he talked about was the relationship between things, as if all things were related for no reason. In fact, how are things related? The relationship is actually between the two aspects of a contradiction. In everything there are two aspects in opposition to each other. And when he talked about the fourth law was the internal contradiction in things. Again, he only talked about the struggle between opposites, but not about the unity of opposites."

"Stalin could not understand the struggle and unity of opposites... He recognized either struggle or unity and did not recognize the unity of opposites, so he made mistakes in politics."[45] It can be said that Mao Zedong's comments on Stalin's philosophy deeply reveal the epistemological roots of Stalin's mistakes. In Stalin's many writings typically represented in his *On the Dialectical Materialism and Historical Materialism*, something metaphysical can be found everywhere. He often simplified things which are universally linked into two mechanical and opposite extremes, and the struggle of opposites was simply summarized into one "eating" or "destroying" the other. As Mao Zedong criticized, "In their view, a war is a war, and peace is peace. These two things are mutually exclusive and not linked. They thought awar cannot be transformed into peace; peace cannot be transformed into a war."... "In reality, they also have an internal connection between them. That is why at times these oppositions are also united. When we [seek to] understand problems we cannot see only one side. We should analyze it from all sides, look through its essence."[46]

These flaws in Stalin's philosophy caused him inevitably to make either-or conclusions in understanding and analyzing problems. Thus, Stalin disobeyed the general laws of social development and the essence of socialism, and it is not surprising for him to make mistakes in the theory of class struggle in the socialist society.

Thirdly, Stalin's misunderstanding of means of realization of socialism is the intrinsic cause for this mistaken theory he proposed.

Although Stalin styled himself as the student of Lenin, he did not grasp the essence of Lenin's ideas. As the practitioner of socialism, Lenin's ideas has changed and enriched with the development of practice. Shortly after the victory of the October Revolution, he himself once said, for Russia,

45 Selected Works of Mao Zedong, vol. 7, p.194-195.
46 Ibid., p.194.

the era in which socialist programs were discussed according to books had passed, and today socialist programs should be talked about only according to experience. The so-called "according to experience" is to constantly re-cognize socialism in practice. Therefore, we often see that Lenin had different writings or discourses about some theories of Marxism under different circumstances in different periods of time, which reflects his spirit of seeking truth from facts. However, Stalin did not completely understand the essence of Lenin's ideas, and tended to stay in a certain stage of development of Lenin's thinking.

For example, in the beginning of the implementation of the New Economic Policy (NEP), Lenin and many other leaders had the same ideas with Lenin's original ones, which held that NEP was a strategic (tactical) retreat after the Soviet Union had suffered serious problems from War Communism economic policy. However, with the development of practice, Lenin's these ideas of NEP had changed fundamentally. He no longer considered the wartime communism as the "revolutionary way" of socialist construction, and now he regarded NEP as a prudent, slow, gradual and roundabout way. In November, 1922, he clearly suggested that Russia through implementing the NEP would transform to socialist Russia. As another example, in terms of class struggle, he talked a lot about fierce, acute and long-term problems in class struggle during periods of revolution and three-year civil war, but with the arrival of peace, he seldom talked about, or strictly speaking, gradually abandoned the argument of intensified class struggle after the proletariat seized political power. Nevertheless, Stalin did not understand the profound changes in Lenin's thought development, and many of his thinking only stayed in the earlier stages of Lenin's thought. He maintained that NEP was a temporary retreat in the process towards socialism, and when this retreat could not continue, it was time that socialism launched a general attack on capitalism. Thus, as early as the Fourteenth Party Congress in 1925, he started to adjust NEP and started an attack on non-socialist elements. In 1928 when the crisis of grain supply and Shakhty affair occurred one after the other, he thought that this temporary retreat of NEP came to an end. In 1929, he officially announced to abandon NEP and launch a general attack on capitalism. As for the issue of class struggle, his ideas only stayed at a stage where the class struggle was still sharp after the proletariat seized power. Although he repeatedly stressed that class struggle should not be triggered during the period of economic recovery, this was not his real intention and he only set the practice of not stirring up class struggle as a tactic to restore the economy. Once the conditions and the time were ripe, he launched the fierce class struggle. Therefore, I believe that Stalin's misunderstanding of means of realization of socialism is the intrinsic cause for his theory of intensified class struggle in socialism, and as long as time and conditions permitted, this theory would come into being sooner or later.

Fourthly, personal political purposes are the important causes for Stalin's repeated emphases on this theory and the final formation of the theory of intensified class struggle under socialism.

It has remained a hot debate whether the theory of intensified class struggle guided Stalin's Great Purge in the 1930s or this theory was created because of the need to conduct the Great Purge. We are convinced that we should approach this issue from a dialectical perspective, rather than make an either-or answer. First, this theory was not put forward in the Great Purge in the 1930s. In addition, around 1928, Stalin's prestige and status in the party were unmatched, and it was unnecessary for him to eliminate oppositions through class struggle. Moreover, at that time, the opposition led by Trotsky and Zinoviev was overthrown, and Bukharin's status and political abilities were far from enough to confront Stalin. Therefore, it was far-fetched to believe that the theory of intensified class struggle proposed by Stalin aimed to overthrow oppositions. Secondly, many historical doubts before and after the Great Purge indicate the following: Stalin's repeated emphases on this theory and the final formation of the theory of intensified class struggle under socialism were indeed out of the need of his own political purposes. There are at least three reasons worth considering: First, the assassination of Kirov. It was reported that in the election of members of the Central Committee in the 17th Soviet Communist Party Congress in 1934, Kirov got the most votes with only three negative votes, whereas Stalin got the least votes with 292 negative ones. What was more, some cadres met Kirov before the conference and demanded him to replace Stalin. If Kaganovich- who was the leader of the counting committee had not tampered with the election result, Stalin might have lost power.The counting committee had destroyed the ballot papers. Soon after, Kirov was assassinated, and the real reason behind has remained a mystery. Second, the 17th Congress of the Communist Party of the Soviet Union has always been world-famous for being "the Congress of Victors," but 83 out of 139 members and alternate members of the Central Committee elected in this congress were arrested and executed with the charge of "People's Enemies." The 1108 out of 1966 delegates were executed shot in a variety of charges. Whether evaluated from their origin or their loyalty to the Soviet, they were absolutely reliable. However, it is difficult to understand why they did not betray the revolution and the party during the special time such as the October Revolution and the Civil War. And on the contrary, strangely they had become counter-revolutionists when socialism was thriving. As representatives of the party members, they were elected into the 17th Congress of the Communist Party of the Soviet Union which was regarded as "the Congress of Victors", but they were labeled enemies of the people, which is apparently contradictory in itself.

Third, in November 1936, Stalin made a clear statement in his *On the Draft Constitution of the Soviet Union*: All the exploiting classes were eliminated within the Soviet Union and the phenomenon of exploitation of people by other people was eradicated and eliminated. A few months later, however, he made a conclusion that with the development of socialism, class struggle would be more acute. It is not convincing that these two diametrically opposed conclusions can be put together, no matter what explanation lay behind. *The History of CPSU* republished in 1938 said, "There remain now few remnants of the exploiting classes which have almost been eliminated and it is only a matter of today's recent time to totally eradicate them." In 1939, Stalin in the 18th Congress of the Communist Party of the Soviet Union said, "The most significant achievement in the social and political development of our country is the complete elimination of remnants of the exploiting classes"[47], and the period from 1937 to 1938 was the peak period of suppressing and eliminating oppositions including Trotsky, Zinoviev, Bukharin, and 1939 was the final stage. If we link Stalin's speeches in 1938 and 1939 and compare them with the situation in the Soviet Union, we will find out that remnants of the exploiting classes to suppress referred by Stalin were the opposition groups. If we string together the above three doubts, it is not difficult for us to judge that repeated emphases on and the final formation of the wrong theory of intensified class struggle under socialism are indeed partly formed for the suppression of opposition groups.

In addition to the above four reasons, Stalin's personality also had played some part in the formation of this theory. His special experience caused him to advocate violence and lack trust in others. Khrushchev recalled that Stalin sometimes said to others, "Why are you always sneaking?" or "Why do you always have asquint eyes and do not dare to frankly look me in the eyes today?"[48] This skepticism always caused Stalin to speculate and fear murder by others. Historian Roy Medvedev wrote: "There were usually several bedrooms in the villa where Stalin lived, and there was a set of bedding in each bed. He himself made the bed. Before sleeping, he often checked the space under the bed. In order to facilitate this check, lights in his bedrooms had no shades and wires were long enough to lie on floors. His villa had two exits which were closely guarded throughout the year."[49] In addition, his character was very hard, which in a large degree influenced how he dealt with others. In order to rationalize his behaviors, it is understandable for him to propose the mistaken theory of intensified class struggle.

---

47   Selected Works of Stalin (1934-1952), p.247.
48   Zhichao Lu, ed., Re-understanding of Stalin's Issues, p. 42, Beijing: Social Sciences Academic Press, 1994.
49   R. A. Medvedev, Let History Judge (II), p.531.

III. The practice of Stalin's theory of class struggle and its serious consequences

After the death of Lenin, under the guidance of the theory of class struggle Stalin led and launched a series of domestic class struggles, which mainly included the following major events.

At first, in 1925-26, Stalin struggled against "the New Opposition" in the party led by Zinoviev and Kamenev. From the late 1920s to early 1930s, the struggle became as the movements of the rural collectivization and the elimination of kulaks. In 1927 and early 1928—after setting the crisis of grain supply rooted in rural areas and the Shakhty Affair in the Donbass region—Stalin announced that he abandoned the NEP and launched an all-out attack against capitalism. The main task of this class struggle was to eliminate kulaks and latent "Partners of Shakhty group". On March 10, 1928, the state security bureau of the Soviet Union announced that it cracked a "Case of Counter-revolutionary Sabotage by Experts of Bourgeois" in a mining area of Shakhty in Donbass, and Stalin believed that this sabotage clearly reflected the seriousness of the domestic class struggle.

In the mid-1930s, beginning with the assassination of Kirov in 1934, the Soviet Union launched "the Great Purge", which lasted for as long as four years, culminating in 1937 and 1938. "The Great Purge", with four major trial cases of "Trotsky-Zinoviev Joint Headquarter"[50], "the Parallel Headquarter"[51], "Rightists-Trotsky Headquarter"[52] and "Tukhachevsky affair"[53] as the axis, radiated all classes in all the sectors of the whole society of the Soviet Union.

50 In August 1935, the Special Court composed of the Procuratorate and the Supreme Court of the Soviet Union, after the hearing, declared: "Trotsky-Zinoviev Joint Headquarter" was a counter-revolutionary terrorist center, which planned the murder of Kirov and was ready to murder Stalin and other leaders. Then 16 defendants were sentenced to death at court and immediately executed.
51 In the preliminary hearing of the case of "Trotsky-Zinoviev Joint Headquarter", defendants suddenly began to supplement that they had "Guilty Connections" with Pyatakov, Radek, and others. In January 1937, 17 people including Pyatakov and Radek were brought to trial by the Military Commission for participating in the so-called "Parallel Headquarter", which planned terrorist actions (one was the assassination of Kirov), spying, attempting to split the motherland and restore capitalism, and other charges. The result of the trial was that Pyatakov, Radek and other 11 people were sentenced to death and immediately executed.
52 In January, 1937, in the trial of Pyatakov, Radek and others, counter-revolutionary crimes of Bukharin, Rykov and others were also uncovered. In March, 1938, the Soviet Supreme Court tried Bukharin, Rykov and other 19 people for murder, espionage, splitting the motherland and other charges. In addition to original leaders of the so-called "Rightists", defendants included the original "Trotskyites", so this trial was called "Rightists-Trotsky Headquarter". After a hasty trial by the court, 17 people including Bukharin were sentenced to death and others to imprisonment.
53 During the trial of "the Parallel Headquarter", in the absence of any strong testimony from Radek and others, the Military Court confirmed that Tukhachevsky (the most outstanding military strategist in the Soviet Union, ranking first among five Grand Marshals of the Soviet Union) and others formed a military group related to "the Parallel Headquarter", and participated in murder, splitting the motherland, collaboration and other crimes. In June 1937, through a brief secret trial of the Military Court, Tukhachevsky and other seven senior military leaders were secretly executed.

After the war, especially the campaign of repression occurred in the late 1940s. In the fall of 1949, the Soviet authorities announced that they identified the so-called "Leningrad Event"; in January 1953, the Interior Ministry also announced that it uncovered "the Case of Doctor Murder", and then a large number of doctors in the Kremlin were accused of murder and were arrested.

Stalin claimed that these movements were struggles against the bourgeoisie and "enemies of the people". Then, what consequences on earth did this so-called "Revolutions" and "Purges" result in?

1. Repression and exploitation of peasants and devastation of the agricultural economy

It is difficult to have accurate statistics about the number of people who were hurt in the "Agricultural Revolution" in the Soviet countryside from the late 1920s to the early 1930s. There were actually two types of people who were harmed by this "Revolution": one type was kulaks who were eliminated in the process of collectivization, and middle peasants, poor peasants and farm laborers who were labelled as "Small Rich Peasants" or "Kulak supporters" and were persecuted for being reluctant to join collective farms with various reasons; the other was people who starved to death in the terrible famine (1932-33) in the Soviet countryside during the later period of the collectivization movement.

319

In the process of the all out collectivization, hundred thousands of rich peasants and their children were suppressed or eliminated. Tens of millions of middle peasants and poor peasants were suddenly forced to hand over their farm tools and animals as well as land allocated to them. They lost their basic means of subsistence and independent status of producers at once, and were no longer peasants in the original sense. Unprepared, they had to change their lifestyle. People who showed dissatisfaction or resistance to this behavior were harmed in varying degrees. Many were persecuted as kulaks or quasi-kulaks. The problem was more serious in the regions of ethnic minorities, where the collectivization movement was combined with forcing pastoralists to settle down and force them to hand in and sell their livestock. This led to the reduction in livestock and caused many deaths of hunger.

After the establishment of collective farms, interests of farm members were jeopardized, and their enthusiasm for production fell. From 1932 to 1933, severe famine took place in North Caucasus region and in Ukraine and other regions, and many farm members were caught in hunger after exhausting their grain reserves. Some people went to other places to make a living, and some secretly cut ears of wheat from the farms at night and took them home to eat. To stop this behavior, in August 1932, Stalin personally formulated the decree On the Protection of Socialist Property, which regulated that people stealing farm property would be charged by maximum penalties—execution and their all property would be confiscated. If people committed a less serious crime, they would be deprived of liberty for more than 10 years and all their property would be confiscated. The decree said these punishments could not be reversed or pardoned. Konchalovsky and Lipkov wrote that: Within less than five months, 54645 people were sentenced by this decree and 2,110 were sentenced to death.[54] Since then, the persecution was intensified. In the North Caucasus, 43% of the rural party members were "cleaned out of" the party. On May 8, 1933, Stalin signed the directive and said that the Central Committee received reports from various areas, which demanded that approximately 100,000 farmer families should be immediately expelled from their regions. The Central Committee believes that class struggle will inevitably be acute, but this practice of expelling is already out of date. It only allowed 12,000 farmer families to move out.[55] Stalin's instructions had some excesses but he did not reduce the pressure on farmers. Some farm members even turned over their seed grain and their reserve grain in order to fulfill the tasks decided by the state. As a result, a large number of farm members suffered from hunger and many of them starved to death. We lack the exact how many peasant deaths were caused by Stalin's movement of transforming peasants. A US expert on SU Mark Harrison held that in this campaign of collectivization, some people were persecuted and some had moved to cities and towns, so all together 3 million rural households which amounted to circa 15 million people were reduced in the rural areas of the Soviet Union.[56]

2. Suppression of intellectuals and its burden on science, technology, literature and art

Stalin had started an all out attack on capitalism, and this target of course included those intellectuals of the past society, the so-called "bourgeois experts".

In March 1928, the Bureau of Political Security announced that it cracked down a "Counter-revolutionary Destructive Case by Bourgeois Experts" in the mining area of Shakhty in Donbas. Stalin claimed that this case has clearly indicated the seriousness of the domestic class struggle. In July 1928, under the directions of the General Prosecutor A. Vyshinsky, the Shakhty event was brought to a public trial.[53] defendants were basically the mining engineers, and most of them were old experts. They were accused of

54   Pravda, 26 May 1964.
55   Pravda, 16 September 1988.
56   Historical Issues 2 (1988): p. 5.

causing mine accidents, engaging in sabotage activities, maintaining secret contact with the original owner of the mine, buying unnecessary foreign equipment, and so on. The outcome of the trial was 11 people being sentenced to death, 4 people were acquitted, 4 people were placed on probation and others were sentenced to 1 to 10 years' of imprisonment.

In April 1929, Stalin in the Plenary Session of the Central Committee pointed out, "We must not think that the so-called Shakhty Affair is accidental. There are partners of Shakhty in all the industrial sectors now," and the bourgeoisie's secret sabotage undoubtedly proved "the bourgeoisie members are far from laying down their weapons, and they are gathering their strength for a new attack against the Soviet regime."[57] According to Stalin's instructions, the class struggle of revealing "partners of Shakhty " was set off around the country. The main object of the struggle was the Soviet intelligentsia, especially those technical intellectuals from Tsarist Russia together with a group of cadres of the Central Committee of CPSU (Bolshevik). Under Stalin's instructions, one after the other "Shakhty" gangs were uncovered. The most important events were the "Ukrainian Liberation League", "Labor Peasant Party" and "Industrial Party". In the trial of these cases, many senior intellectuals and technical experts within and outside the party were sentenced and even executed by shooting without sufficient evidence.

Under the guidance of Stalin's theory of class struggle, the prevalent atmosphere of class struggle in science and blindly employing the label of bourgeois pseudo-science to different and new academic views has devastated the world-leading scientific disciplines in the Soviet Union. This attitude has greatly prevented the healthy development of new science branches in the Soviet Union. Meanwhile, some pseudo-scholars and some grass-root people who won the favor of Stalin behaved arrogantly and monopolized the field of science by labelling others politically or "bludgeoning", and became real scholar-tyrants. For example, the group of Lysenko, placing themselves behind their vulgar scientific concepts attacked wildly against Nikolai Vavilov, and caused the persecution of this world-famous geneticist thus destroying the emerging genetics branch in the Soviet Union. Nikolai Vavilov, was sent to exile. He was sentenced to death in July 1941. In 1942 his sentence was commuted to twenty years' imprisonment; he died in prison in 1943, of starvation. Some other scientists, especially some social scientists and writers, though they were not directly persecuted, were so cautious that they could not freely express their true academic views, and they were forced to cultivate a slavish psychology obedient to Stalin. The same atmosphere prevailed for a while after Stalin's death, too. For example, the prominent writer A. Fadeyev wrote in the letter to the CPSU

57   Collected Works of Stalin, 1st Chinese edition, vol. 12, p.15.

Central Committee before ending his life in 1956, "It is impossible for me to live any further since the art to which I have given my life has been destroyed by the self-confident, ignorant leadership of the Party and can no longer be corrected"...."After Lenin's death they brought us down to the level of children; they destroyed us. They threatened us ideologically and called this "the Party spirit". And now, when everything might be corrected, primitivism and ignorance—along with a disgraceful share of self-assurance—manifest themselves in those very ones who are supposed to correct everything."[58]

3. Repression of military leaders and its burden on the national defense

"The Great Purge" also greatly damaged the army, thus the Soviet Red Army suffered a devastating blow. In his book Hitler's War on Russia, German historian Paul Karell Schmidt provided the following figures. From 1937 to 1938, Stalin killed nearly 35,000 Red Army commanders, almost 80 % senior officers: three out of five Marshals; 13 out of 15 group army commanders; 57 out of 85 front army commanders; 110 out of 195 army teachers; 220 out of 406 brigade commanders; all the commanders of military regions.[59]

The majority of executed senior generals of the Red Army had outstanding talents. For example, Tukhachevsky was the youngest among the five marshals in the Soviet at that time, and died only at the age of 44. He had joined the Russian Communist Party in 1918. Lenin's sharp eyes could catch such talents, he identified the extraordinary military talent of this young man who was only 25 years old and promoted him. Fully up to the expectation, Tukhachevsky won remarkable military battles crushing the White Army of Krasnov, Kolchak, Denikin and Antonov, and was promoted to be the deputy commissar of NKO and the commander-in-chief of the armed forces. In the early 1930s, he successfully led the modernization of the Soviet Red Army. However, in Stalin's "Great Purge", this military general who had a remarkable military talent and made great achievements in domestic wars could not survive.

4. Repression of leaders and cadres in the party and the state

In 1929, after Bukharin, the last opposition group within the party, was defeated, Stalin in fact became a dictator who almost had unlimited powers, and centralized the power of the party, the state and the army in his own hands. However, when he established this absolute authority, he was

---

58   Foreign Social Science Information 18 (1991).
59   Socialism Abroad Journal, issue 2 (1988).

not unanimously supported by comrades inside and outside the party. But he had popularity among the majority of party members and the masses. Many of the old Bolsheviks were worried about his autocracy and brutality, and even his loyal assistants and the staff who had worked with him felt dissatisfied and were critical of him, though could not express their ideas or feelings. In the early 1930s, with the upsurge of campaigns against the "partners of Shakhty," and after that the so-called "anti-party groups" within the party which did not applaud Stalin's authority and policies were attacked. However, these groups did not constitute a threat to Stalin. The key to the problem was that there were some figures resisting Stalin's policies and authority. Their representative was Sergei Kirov, and his supporters were Ordzhonikidze, Kuibyshev, Kalinin and some alternate members of Politburo.

A lot of Kirov's ideas and views showed certain independence at that time, and he had differences with Stalin in dealing several important issues. For instance, in handling the issues of "Ryutin Group" and the recovery of Zinoviev's party membership, Stalin's opinion was resolutely rejected by Kirov. In 1933 in the Politburo meeting, Kirov advocated some more flexible policies and he also believed that Stalin's ruthless suppression of all the dissidents was wrong. Moreover, in Leningrad, where he led the party, Kirov resolutely resisted taking any repressive measures to the supporters of opposition groups, and he readmitted some of them to the party.

Kirov was assassinated in Smolny Institute, in the state office where he worked, on December 1, 1934, in the end of the year when the 17th Congress was held, and the murderer Leonid Nikolayev was arrested on the spot. Kirov's death shocked people around the country, and in mourning, the people strongly demanded that the murderer should be toughly sanctioned and the truth should be uncapped. Stalin and the Central Government also attached great importance to this case. On that day, Stalin led others to go to Leningrad and personally interrogated the killer, and required immediate investigation on the case. All the facts about the assassination of Kirov had not been identified even after Stalin's death, but it became the fuse for the most tragic and the darkest history of the Soviet Union—"the Great Purge".

In this shocking political disaster, what suffered most was the team of cadres, especially senior cadres. For example, 14 figures from among over 20 members of the Central Committee elected in the 6th Congress of the Communist Party of the Soviet Union in 1917 who had led the great October Revolution, were treated unfairly or lawlessly executed in "the Great Purge". From among 27 members of the central committee elected in the in 1922, when Lenin was still alive (Lenin's last Congress) 17 were subjected to Stalin's repression. The 17th Congress of CPSU (Bolshevik) held in 1934 was regarded as "the Congress of Victors". However, the vast majority (accounting for 70%) of members of the central committee elected in this congress were labeled "enemies of the party and the people". 51 out of 71 members of the central committee were executed in "the Great Purge"; 47 out of 68 alternate members were executed. 1.108 out of 1.966 party member representatives attending the congress, that is, more than half the total number of people, were arrested for "counter-revolutionary" activities. From the 154 Leningrad member representatives led by Kirov in the 17th Congress only 3 people were left by 1939 and one of them was Stalin. Among 21 members of the People's Committee chaired by Molotov in 1937, 16 were executed. Local cadres at all levels also suffered from this massive "purge", and some state leaders were almost completely eliminated. During World War II, due to factors such as the war, the repression and "purges" were relatively relieved, and the control over thoughts and intellectuals was also relaxed, in this atmosphere humanist critical thoughts had risen to a certain degree. Stalin still could not tolerate this new phenomenon of the era. After the war, he decided to start a purge among the intellectuals. In August 1946, the Central Committee of CPSU (Bolshevik) agreed on the Central Committee resolution titled of On Two Magazines of Star and Leningrad. This esolution criticized that the two magazines were publishing too much about the Western ideas and were insufficient to reflect the Soviet (socialist) spirit, and decided to close down Leningrad and restructured the editorial department of Star. Then the party launched a movement of eliminating bourgeois ideology. Consequently many prominent intellectuals were labeled and suffered a wide variety of penalties. This campaign soon spread to other areas. In the fall of 1949, Soviet authorities announced that they have revealed the so-called "Leningrad Event". In this event, Voznesensky, the first vice chairman of the USSR Council of Ministers (prime minister), and Kuznetsov, secretary of the Leningrad State leading party committee and secretary of the CPC Central Committee, were executed for treason, and soon after people closely related to them were also arrested. In January 1953, the Interior Ministry announced that it uncovered "the Case of Doctor Murder", and then a large number of doctors in the Kremlin were accused of murder and were arrested. At the same time, the press repeatedly made broad propaganda in order to dig out hidden "class enemies" and the theory of intensified class struggle once again became popular and alarm bells were ringing everywhere. If Stalin did not die in that year, it was hard to predict that how long this new campaign would continue.

"The Great Purge" not only swept all the areas of the society in the Soviet Union, but harmed foreign communists working and living there in those days. A large number of well-known leaders of the Comintern and main leaders of foreign communists were harmed and executed, especially the

German communists. What particularly worth mentioning is the damage given to the Polish Communist Party. The Polish Communist Party was one of the most efficient combating and influential parties in the international communist movement, but it suffered from Stalin's repression due to different views with him in certain issues. Between 1937 and 1938, also leading members of other countries were ordered to come to Moscow for accusations and were arrested or executed., thus it was not only the activists, party members, and leaders of the Polish Communist Party working in Moscow were arrested and executed. Stalin dissolved the Polish Communist Party for "enemy spies infiltrating the party's leadership", bringing huge losses to the Polish people's struggle against fascism.[60]

Stalin won through many challenges, struggles on after the other. He eliminated all real and potential opponents, ultimately established and consolidated the system of his personal dictatorship. Under the guidance of his theory of ever intensifying class struggle, serious consequences have occurred in the Soviet Union which have ruined the reputation of socialism in front of the people across the world, thus greatly damaged the popularity of socialism. For decades, Stalin's theory of class struggle not only was the basic guiding ideology of the Soviet Communist Party, but also became the common guideline implemented by almost all socialist countries. Everything became an issue of class struggle, and everything was approached from the perspective of class struggle. The unlimited spread of this theory was the important cause that hindered the Soviet Union and other socialist countries overcome the "Left" guiding thought for a long time.

325

60   Changbin Jiang, The Political Critical Biography on Stalin, p.560, Chengdu: Sichuan People's Publishing House, 2001.

Chapter IX

Stalin's Theory of Party Building

The victory of the Russian October Revolution has enabled the Russian proletarian party to conquest power and became the ruling party for the first time in history. The character and the leadership style of the party—how it leads the masses—is quite important, and it has even direct effects on the nature of the socialist regime. These characteristics of the Marxist party will also affect its development prospect and its revolutionary career. Lenin had paid great attention to strengthening the party's self-construction after the victory of the October Revolution and formed the theory of self-building of the ruling party. After Lenin's death, Stalin defended Lenin's theory on party building, cumulated fresh experience in this sphere during socialist revolution and socialist construction. We can comfortably say that he has enriched the Marxist theory on party building in many aspects. On the other side in practice Stalin deviated in applying the correct theory on building the proletarian party and even infringed his own correct ideas.

I. Stalin's struggle to defend Lenin's theory of building the ruling proletarian party

1. The systematic discussion on the characteristics of the new proletarian Party

In the process of leading the Russian Revolution, Lenin adhered to the thought that the proletariat should build its own independent political party, which was first proposed by Marx and Engels. Lenin also developed new ideas on the function of the party, ideas on the necessity of building the party in an orderly manner. Lenin also proposed the theory of building a new type of proletarian political party, thus he had further enriched and developed the theory of Marxist political party. On January 21, 1924, Lenin died. The Central Committee of the CPSU (Bolshevik) was then faced with the serious issue of how tomaintain and hold high the great banner of Leninism. In these days Trotsky and others wrote some important articles—*Lessons of the October Revolution*, *On Lenin* and others, which had caused confusions on the truth of Leninism. In order to eliminate their negative impacts and defend the banner of Leninism, the Central Committee of the CPSU (Bolshevik) led by Stalin carried out a resolute theoretical struggle. In this respect Stalin published his famous works Mourning Lenin, On Lenin and On the Foundations of Leninism and other articles which strongly criticized Trotsky's errors, demonstrated Lenin's contributions to Marxism. Especially in the article *On the Foundations of Leninism*, Stalin systematically discussed the basic content of Lenin's doctrine on the new type of proletarian party.

Stalin pointed out that in the revolutionary era when the proletariat was preparing to overthrow imperialism and preparing to seize the political power, it should build a new, militant and revolutionary party different from the old type of political party advocated by the revisionist wing of the Second International before the era of revolution. This should be the Leninist party, with the following characteristics:

2. New type of Leninist Proletarian Party

Firstly, the party should be the vanguard of the working class.

Stalin argued that the party should not only absorb all advanced characteristics of the working class, at the same time the party should study their experience. The party should have the revolutionary spirit and the spirit of boundless loyalty to the proletarian cause, should arm the proletariat with revolutionary theories and laws of revolution and social development. Only in this way can the new political party stand at a higher level and be farsighted, guide the proletariat, become political leader and thus be the headquarter of their battle. However, the party being the vanguard is not enough and it should also contain the forces of this class. Party should maintain close contacts with the class, educate them so that they see it as their own party, aa a part of them, educate them in such a manner that they will deeply care about the healthy development and consolidation of the party, relate their own destiny with that of the party and voluntarily accept the party's leadership. Stalin had always stressed the class character andopposed any denial of this basic quality of the party by any pretext. On the other hand, he had insisted that proletarian parties were only a part of the proletarian class, a force composed of advanced elements of this vanguard class, and that the vanguard nature of the proletariat should never be substituted or confused with the vanguard nature of the proletarian parties.

Secondly, the party—as a tool—is the organized force of the working class.

Stalin argued that if the party will truly lead the class struggle, it must be both the vanguard of the working class as well as the organized force of the class. He pointed out that under the conditions of capitalism, the party's tasks were comprehensive and complicated, and only when it can become the organized force of the class could it fulfill these tasks. When expounding on this character Stalin wrote: "the party is not only the sum of all the organizations of the party, is also a unified system of these organizations, it is a unified whole formed by these organizations. There should be the organs of superiors and subordinates are leading, the principle that minority should obey majority, and actual resolution that all party members must perform."[1]

He noted that only when these conditions are met the party will be able to lead the struggles of the working class in a planned and organized manner.

Thirdly, the party is the highest and most advanced organizational form of the proletarian class.

Stalin argued that in addition to the party organization, there are a lot of other necessary proletarian organizations for the smooth realization (as "transmission gears") of the struggle against capitalism. They are trade unions, many type of cooperatives, the plant cell basic organization its groups in the parliament, the non-party women's groups, publishing companies, the cultural and educational organizations, the Youth League, fighting organizations organized during revolutionary fights and state organizations when the proletariat seizes power—the Soviets (as its parliamentary organ), and so on. These organizations are certainly necessary to the working class under various conditions. Stalin asked: "But who decides the lines of the

---

1   Selected Works of Stalin, vol. 1, p.264.

work when carrying our tasks, i.e., who implements the general leadership for so many organizations of the proletariat? Where should we build a central organization which can generalize the all the experiences of the class, form a general direction for them and lead these organizations towards this direction with a unified leadership, with such a leadership which enjoys the needed will and authority?"..."This organization is the proletarian party." This is because the party has all the required conditions for this: "Firstly, because the party posseses the advanced elements of the working class, and these advanced elements having direct contacts with the non-party organizations of the proletarian class in most cases can lead them; secondly, because the party is the gathering point of the advanced elements of the working class.

It it is the best school to cultivate the leaders of the working class who can lead these various "transmission gears" organizations of this class; thirdly, because the party is the best school which cultivates the leaders of the working class, where they become the experienced and prestiged members of this class, it is the only organization which can mobilize call for the leaders of the struggle of the proletariat, thus the party can be able to transform these various non-party organizations of proletariat to its agencies which serve the party to closely relate with the class."[2]

Fourthly, the party is the tool of the dictatorship of the proletariat.

In Stalin's view, the reason why the proletariat needs the Party is because the party is the combat command center which essential for the successful master of power, and also for consolidating and perfecting this dictatorship. Only this kind of party which can organize the proletarian masses in full, only this kind of party which can mobilize all the leaders of the whole proletarian movement in its of struggle can realize the revolutionary dictatorship of the proletariat.

For Stalin "the Party carries out the dictatorship of the proletariat" and therefore "whoever identifies and equals the leading role of the Party with the dictatorship of the proletariat will aim to substitute the directives (leadership) given by the Party with the will and actions of the class."

And Stalin concluded: "With the elimination of classes and the demise of the dictatorship of the proletariat, the party will certainly disappear."

Fifthly, the Marxist party should demonstrate a unified will which is incompatible with the existence of organizational factions.

Stalin argued that the party should have a unified will and iron discipline which are indispensable for winning and maintaining the dictatorship of the proletariat, but this unified will and iron discipline does not exclude

2   Selected Works of Stalin, vol. 1, pp.266-267.

criticism and debates in the party. On the contrary, the unity and iron discipline of the party are the premises for inner-party democracy. He stated: "after the debate has ended, criticism has been completed and the party resolution is formulated, the unity of will and unity of action by all party members is a necessary condition. Without this condition, we cannot expect unified party or a party with iron discipline."[3]

All this means that the existence of organized factions in the party will hinder the unified will, thus weaken and undermine the party discipline. Therefore, all such factional activities should be avoided.

Sixthly, the party can be consolidated by "cleaning" the opportunist elements from among their ranks.

Stalin had argued that the proletariat did not have an isolated existence. Various elements belonging to petty bourgeois social strata would use various opportunities to enter into the party, thus bring with themselves the sentiments of opportunism, such as corruption, unsteadily corruption and hesitation to the party.

These elements are the main source of factionalism and disintegration of solidarity in the party and the main source of various phenomenon of slackness and internal maladies of the party. If we fight against imperialism with such "allies" among our ranks means we are faced with two kinds of enemies. Therefore, these opportunists should be eliminated from the party. In the fight against opportunist elements, Stalin favored ruthless attacks against them including expelling them. He argued that it would be a corrupt and dangerous theory to employ inner-party thought struggles (political and theoretical debates) to "overcome" these opportunist elements or to "eliminate" opportunist elements in a Marxist party. "We should conduct relentless struggle against these opportunists and to expel them from the party."..."the party can be consolidated by cleaning opportunists from among its ranks."[4]

331

The above six points advocated by Stalin give us the general characteristics of the new type of proletariat party of during the era of proletarian revolution. We cannot ignore that this conception of him was necessary and beneficial for maintaining the unity and solidarity of the Communist Party of the Soviet Union after Lenin's death. It is also clear that he had defended Lenin's theory of Marxist party building. Meanwhile, these thoughts of him offer many useful thoughts for perfecting the self-construction of the proletarian party during the era of dictatorship of the proletariat.

---

3   Ibid.,p.269.
4   Selected Works of Stalin, vol.1, p.272.

3. Stalin's ideas on the basic conditions for the Communist parties to achieve Bolshevisation

When leading the Central Committee of the CPSU (Bolshevik) Committee in its fight against the Trotskyites, Stalin was also very concerned about the education and health of the international communist movement. If we remember the international situation in those days, the revolutionary development in Western Europe was at low ebb and world capitalism had entered into a relatively stable period, therefore, opportunist thoughts were spreading within the Communist Parties in many countries. Considering this situation, Stalin leading the 5th Congress of the Communist International which was held from June to July 1924, proposed the idea of "Bolshevisation" of world communist parties, which was a timely act. In the conversation with the German Communist Party Haier Zucker in February 1925, Stalin specifically explained his ideas on the basic conditions of achieving Bolshevisation. The two leaders had mentioned twelve points on this subject:

Firstly, the communist parties should be transformed to the highest form of the joint action of the proletarian class. It should undertake the mission to lead the proletariat and its all other forms of organizations. It should not be regarded as the accessory of parliamentary elections and the trade unions.

Secondly, the party and its leaders should be armed with Marxist revolutionary theory which is indivisible and this theory should be closely linked to revolutionary practice.

Thirdly, when deciding on the slogans and tactics of the struggle i, the party should carefully analyze the specific internal and external conditions of the revolutionary movement and take the revolutionary experiences of various countries into consideration, they should reject memorized formulas and never use historical analogies when making decisions.

Fourthly, the party should observe and judge the correctness of its slogans and tactics in the test of practice of revolutionary struggle of the masses.

Fifthly, all the tasks party should be re-considered according to new revolutionary methods, this could be the main way to eliminate the traditional effects of the Social Democratic Party. Communist parties should lead the working class masses gain their class education, namely the rising revolution would train and educate the broad masses. Party should trust the capacity of working class masses.

Sixthly, communist parties should be good at relating the highest principle and the most extensive masses in their work.

Otherwise, it is impossible for the party to educate the masses, nor learn from them, nor guide the people or elevate them to the level of party's understanding and to the level of party's practice, otherwise communist parties will not be able hear or consider their voices and or understand their urgent demands.

Seventhly, communist parties should be good at combining both the irreconcilable revolutionary attitude and the maximum flexibility and cooperative attitude in their work.

Eighthly, the parties should never cover up their mistakes nor be afraid of criticism and should be good at learning from their mistakes, in this way they should improve and educate their cadres.

Ninthly, the parties should be good at selecting and recruiting advanced elements from among soldiers for their grass-root party committees.

Tenthly, the parties should always aim to improve their social class composition in their own organizations in order to eliminate the yoz corrupt opportunist elements, this policy will provide them maximum unity in understanding and activity.

The eleventh the parties should develop the iron proletariat discipline in all aspects of party work. The foundation of this discipline could only be the following: the consistency in its ideas, the clarity of goals in its practical activity, the unity of action and the conscious attitude of the majority of party members and the masses. The twelfth, the parties should always check the results of the implementation of their own decisions and specific directives. 333

Finally, Stalin had stressed "talking on the success of Bolshevization would be empty talk without these conditions.[5]

The twelve points discussed and proposed by Stalin has expounded Lenin's theory on the new type of proletarian party. These points were also the generalization of the experiences of Marxist party building for the international communist movement. The two leaders had strongly emphasized elimination of the opportunist trend within the Communist International. This was the content Bolshevization effort of the communist parties in this specific historical context. This effort can easily be evaluated as the contribution made by Stalin to the defense and spread of the theory of Leninist party.

5   Collected Works of Lenin, vol. 7, 1st Chinese version, p.37.

II. Stalin's new contributions to the theory of building the ruling party

During the 30 years when he led the Soviet power, Stalin had advocated and enriched the Marxist ideas of party building. He mainly developed the ideas on party's leadership in socialist construction, ideas on upholding the Party's solidarity and unity, ideas on inner-Party democracy and ideas on critique and self-critique in the party. Of course there are other aspects which he had developed.

1. His ideas on the party's leadership of the state power during the period of socialist construction

It is one of Lenin's basic principles of party building that the socialist cause should stick to party's leadership in its course of development. Stalin largely inherited and developed this theory after he assumed the party leadership.

When elaborating his ideas related to the system of proletarian dictatorship, Stalin discussed the contents and the components—mutual relations among these components—of the system of proletarian dictatorship. In relation with this issue he also demonstrated the status and roles of the party related to the state power, in the period of socialist construction.

He wrote: "the only thing which can unify and guide the work of proletarian masses can be the proletarian vanguard and the proletarian party.

Only the proletarian party—the Communist Party can play the major leading role in the whole system of the dictatorship of the proletariat."[6]

The comparatively long-term consolidation work of this dictatorship could not proceed exist if without the main leading ship—the party.

To further develop and guarantee party leadership over the state power, the Soviet Constitution included special articles which in legal form stipulated the leading role of the party for the first time in the 1936 Constitution of SU under Stalin's direct suggestions. Article 126 in Chapter 10 under "The Basic Rights and Obligations of the Citizens" in the Constitution stipulated: "in order to fit the interests of workers and develop the autonomous nature and political initiative of the mass' organizations, all Soviet citizens have the right to participate in various social organisations, namely trade unions, cooperatives, youth organizations, sports associations, also in defense, culture, technology and science organizations. Besides the most active and most conscious citizens belonging to working class, peasants

---

6   Selected Works of Stalin, vol. 1, p.413.

and working class intellectuals have the right to voluntarily participate the Communist Party of the Soviet Union, i.e., namely the vanguard of the working class which fights for the building communist society and which is the core of leadership of all the social groups and the state organs of the working people."

Stalin pointed out: "I should admit that the new draft of constitution retains the system of the dictatorship of the working class as well as the leadership of the Soviet Communist Party now with unchangeably."[7]

Party leadership over the state power

Stalin argued that the party leadership over the state power includes the following contents:

The first is the implementation of political leadership.

Stalin argued that the party leadership over state power should mainly demonstrate itself in that the party determines the line and policies of the whole state its organs.

The party should ensure the correctness of this (state) line and the effectiveness of its implementation. He explained: "the party should provide the main principles and general policies when any (state) government agency is designing the working plans in the spheres of industrial, agricultural, commercial and cultural construction works, and the party should guide the nature and direction of these works during the implementation."[8]

Moreover, when making decision designs the party should be good in choosing the right policy priorities and aim to ensure its good implementation. Stalin wrote: "To ensure the Party's correct leadership, besides all other conditions, the party should have the correct line; besides masses should understand the correctness of the party's line and actively support this line; the party should not only develop the general line, but also lead the accomplishment of this line at every moment."[9]

The second is the implementation of organizational leadership. For, Stalin after the correct political line is established and it is proven, the cadres of the party become the decisive force in the party's and state's leadership. Therefore, the party's leadership over the state power should be "primarily reflected in the issue that the Communist Party is trying to employ those true leaders who are faithful to the cause of the proletariat and are willing to wholeheartedly serve for the proletarian class, it should as well employ its excellent cadres to important positions of the state through the Soviet

7   Selected Works of Stalin, vol. 2, p.408.
8   Collected Works of Stalin, vol. 10, 1st Chinese version, p.93.
9   Collected Works of Stalin, vol. 12, 1st Chinese version, p.297.

and the Congresses of Soviets"[10] This means that after the party establishes the correct line, there must be numerous cadres in all levels who grasp the political line of the party, are good at practical work and who are engaged in implementing this line. Thus the leadership of the party is guaranteed through leadership in organizational matters—through providing the right cadres. Otherwise, the correct political line will become meaningless.

The third is to implement the leadership in the sphere of ideology.

Stalin spefically emphasized the importance of party leadership in the thought sphere. He said: "In the work of any department of the state and the Party, the higher the political level and the consciousness of Marxism-Leninism by the cadres the more efficient will the work and more achievements will the work have. Conversely, the lower the political level and the consciousness of Marxism-Leninism by the cadres, the more likely we will suffer setbacks and failures. Thus the staff will degrade to vulgar and short-sighted elements advocates in handling of the affairs and the more likely they will degenerate—which is a theorem."[11] In addition, Stalin also specifically emphasized the role of the theoretical (thought aspect) and political work during implementing the economic works of the party and state, he argued that in practice, politics and economy were inseparable. These two should co-exist and work together. Who ignored and separates economy and politics in practical work, emphasizes economic work, but weakens the political work or vice versa, would definitely fail and do harm.

The fourth aspect is to implement supervision and inspection. Stalin believed that "the task of the party should not be limited to developing the general line but it should also check the actual implementation of this general line at every moment. It should lead the implementation of the general line, namely make amendments on the current economic development plan in the process of its practice in order to perfect it and correct and prevent errors."[12] He criticized the mistaken working style of some leaders in the Polish Communist Party who only paid their attention to the establishment of the line but neglected the necessary care for the implementation of this line, Stalin commented: "He read out these resolutions with a muzaffer lider havasında triumphant air, regarding that the leadership of the party lies in the fixing of an excellent resolution. He does not know that, determining the resolution is only the first step and the beginning in the party leadership issue. He does not know the essence of party leadership is not this perfect resolution but rather the implementation and achievement of the resolution."[13] He advocated that the party should supervise and inspect the

---

10   Collected Works of Stalin, vol. 10, 1st Chinese version, p.93.
11   Selected Works of Stalin, vol. 2, pp.461-462.
12   Collected Works of Stalin, vol. 12, 1st Chinese version, p.300.
13   Collected Works of Stalin, vol. 6, 1st Chinese version, p.234.

responsible authorities and departments, correcting their mistakes in the implementation, thus avoid the shortcomings in their work. Party should both support and guarantee the success of their work.

When explaining the viewpoint above, Stalin was the first socialist leader who theoretically distinguished the relationship between the leadership of the party and the dictatorship of the proletariat, namely he emphasized that the leadership of the party could not and should not substitute replace the state power.

In short, Stalin's idea that in the course of building socialism, Marxists should uphold the party leadership (in theory and practice) not only greatly enriched and developed the theory of Marxist party building, but also played a positive role in consolidating and expanding the dictatorship of the proletariat, in this way he successfully led the completion of socialist construction.

2. Stalin's practice of democratic centralism and his efforts to improve inner party life

The principle of democratic centralism is the most essential part of Lenin's party building theory. Stalin, in the early stage of his ruling, had advocated this principle both in theory and practice. On this issue Stalin had given many meaningful elaborations.

Stalin believed that inner party democracy aims to raise the enthusiasm and self-consciousness of party members, which constantly enables and promotes the participation of the mass of party members. Thus they will contribute to the party's discussion of major affairs of the party, contribute to decision-making process actively. Namely democracy aims to promote the leadership qualities of all members and guarantees that they undertake their duties more consciously and with enthusiasm. To consolidate and perfect the dictatorship of the proletariat and to carry out the socialist construction, the enthusiasm of the whole working class needs to be raised. Thus, the party itself must start the first step and should resolutely practice democracy within the party. The party organizations at all levels must attract the largest majority of party members to the discussion of country construction issues, otherwise, country construction will not be based on the initiative of the working class".

In order to promote inner party democracy, Stalin advocated several measures. Firstly, the remnants and habits of the war time existing in the minds of some of the state staff should be eliminated, they should no longer regard the party as an organ of the state, but as an independent organism focusing on its own tasks. Secondly, on the one side the burden of bureaucracy in the state organs with nearly one million employees and on the other side the burden of bureaucracy inthe party organs with two or three million workers should be eliminated.

Thirdly, the cultural and thinking level of many of party branches which lag behind should be improved, and the active staff should be rationally allocated among various regions of the Soviet land.[14] In addition, Stalin also learned the lesson that in the past the long debate within the party delayed the party's central work. He pointed out that the party should oppose formal democracy and to oppose regarding democracy as endless debates among few people and oppose regarding democracy as freedom of various inner party grouping structures. He stressed that the party's interests are above any formal democracy, the formal democracy is meaningless, but the true interests of the party should be advocated above all. Therefore, the promotion of inner party democracy and safeguarding of the interests of the party should be unified.

338

3. Collective leadership system which practices criticism and self-criticism in itself

Stalin argued that it was an important aspect of socialist construction to adhere to collective leadership principle and carry out criticism and self-criticism in the party committees. In his conversation with the German writer Emil Ludwig, he said: "According to the experience of our three past revolutions, we know that within one hundred personal decisions, those decisions without collective review and modification in the party committees, about 90 were one-sided". Therefore, the party must adhere to the principle of collective leadership in its work. "If the individual is allowed to make decisions, then we will commit very serious errors."[15] Being against with the complacency mood and bureaucratic habits in the practical work with the party, Stalin argued that the party cadres to carry out criticism and self-criticism and strive for self-correction. He pointed out: "If we do not frankly and sincerely expose and grasp the shortcomings and mistakes in our work with the proper Bolshevik attitudes, we will block our way forward. We have to move forward. It is just because of this, we should take the sincere revolutionary self-criticism as one of our most important tasks,

14   Collected Works of Stalin, vol. 5, 1st Chinese version, pp.312-313.
15   Selected Works of Stalin, vol. 2, pp.300-301.

and otherwise, we can neither move forward nor develop."[16] In the process of criticism and self-criticism, the errors related to party work, whether they are errors of ordinary party members or the party leaders should be promptly identified and corrected. If we say "struggles can only be carried out under the condition that the prestige of the leaders should not be harmed, this view actually denies that any struggle can be carried out within the party"[17], because the struggles and the correction of the errors within the party could not be carried out without damaging the prestige of some leaders to some extent.

In Stalin's eyes, criticism and self-criticism were the basis of both the Bolshevism and health of the proletarian dictatorship system -especially of its political system-. He said: "The party, the classes, and the masses should be correctly educated with self-criticism. Bolshevism can't come into being when the party, the classes, and the masses are not correctly educated."[18] He evaluated self-criticism as demonstrating the power of our party not its weakness. Criticism and self-criticism will only strengthen the party "we need self-criticism as we need air and water."[19] If the party is not afraid of criticism and self-criticism, if it does not cover up its mistakes and shortcomings in its work, if it teaches and educates the cadres with their mistakes in the work, if it corrects the mistakes in a timely manner," the party will be invincible. On the contrary, the party will be doomed to failures and disintegration if it "conceals it own mistakes, covers up the long-existing problems, ignores its shortcomings with false and seemingly-dissatisfying pretexts , fails to tolerate criticism and self-criticism, indulges itself with complacency and blind arrogance, and if it lies only on the laurels."[20]

339

4. Stalin's ideas on guarding party's unity and solidarity

Lenin attached great importance on guarding solidarity and unity of the party all through his party life. And Lenin had severely criticized Stalin's inappropriate and brutal practices on this issue. After the death of Lenin, Stalin acted according to Lenin's criticism in the early stage of his leadership. We can say he applied relatively democratic principles and practices when dealing with inner party contradictions and struggles, thus cared to safeguard solidarity and unity of the party. Stalin argued that the basic requirement of democratic centralism was to strengthen the party discipline over its members while secondly the inner-Party democracy should be promoted, namely he stressed more on party discipline when interpreting

16   Collected Works of Stalin, vol. 10, 1st Chinese version, p.284.
17   Collected Works of Stalin, vol. 8, 1st Chinese version, p.6.
18   Selected Works of Stalin (II), p.56.
19   Selected Works of Stalin (II), p.7.
20   Ibid., p.622.

and applying democratic centralism. He said: "If there is no iron discipline within the party, the proletarian dictatorship can't achieve its missions of supressing the exploiting class and transforming the sınıflı toplumu class society into a socialist one."[21] And the grupçu factional activities would inevitably "break up the party's committees, split the party into minor separate departments, and weaken both the party and the proletarian dictatorship."[22] Therefore, the factional activities should be avoided to maintain the solidarity and unity of the party.

In dealing with the issues of inner-party struggle, Stalin advocated persuasion and education, and opposed to employ exclusion against those who had different ideas. He said: "I am against this policy, not because I pity those who have different ideas, but because such a policy would result in intimidation, menace, and other systems that contradict the spirits of self-criticism and initiative principle."[23] He stressed that the different views within the party should primarily be treated with thought struggle. And disciplinary measures shouldn't be taken until the thought differences developed into infringement of the party resolutions, or until they developed into factional separate activities. But the disciplinary punishment should not aim to kill a member with one strike. Those who are expelled from the party for disciplinary reasons could still be allowed to return to the party and serve as a leader if they admit their mistakes. In the fierce inner-party struggles, some party members suggested that "removal" be taken against those "Left". This idea was vetoed by Stalin, who said: "The 'removal' policy is very dangerous to the party... it is infectious: if a man is removed today, another one will be removed tomorrow, the third man.. the day after tomorrow... then who will be left within the party?"[24] As Stalin had adopted the right policy in dealing with the contradictions within the party in the early stage of his leadership, the party's solidarity and unity were in good shape.

I think, Stalin's arguments on the principle of democratic centralism, which have proven their correctness would definitely be helpful to the construction and development of the proletarian ruling party. But unfortunately, when we evaluate whole of Stalin period and the whole ruling periods of the Soviet Communist Party, the principle of democratic centralism was not fully followed, it was sometimes simply or extremely undermined.

340

---

21   Collected Works of Stalin, vol. 10, 1st Chinese version, p.91.
22   Collected Works of Stalin, vol. 8, 1st Chinese version, pp.131-132.
23   Collected Works of Stalin, vol. 7, 1st Chinese version, p.40.
24   Ibid., p.317.

III. The party should be good at selecting and training its cadres

As a major strategic issue in party building of the ruling party, the issue of cadres remains an important guarantee of correct the party leadership. Marxism-Leninism not only acknowledges the decisive role of the people in creating history , but also recognizes the great significant role of the leading organs, cadres and leaders in socialist construction and the practical activities of the party. As Lenin emphasized, for the ruling Communist Party, the keys to the work all lied in the correct selection of personnel and in the supervision of leading administrative organs.[25] Stalin had also advocated many correct and important ideas in this regard.

1. Stalin's formula of "cadres decide everything"

Stalin believed that the party's correct leadership over the state power includes both the formulation of correct policies, and also in the correct selection and training of party cadres.

As "our party is in power, the party cadres who are the party's leading officers are also the leading officers of the state leadership organs. They are also the decisive forces of the party leadership and state leadership after the political lines are established and tested in practice."[26] Stalin said, "After the correct lines are established, after the right decisions are made, the success depends on the organizational work, depends on the struggles to implement the lines set by Party, depends on the proper selection of good talents... otherwise the party's correct lines and correct resolutions would be seriously damaged. Besides, after the correct lines are proposed, the organizational work decides everything, including the future fate of political lines. In other words, the organizational work will belirleyecektir decide the successful realization or failure of political lines."[27] Accordingly, Stalin put forward the famous formula of "cadres decide everything." He pointed out that perfect talents and cadres were the most valuable and decisive capital, they are the most precious capital above all others. So everyone should be aware that "cadres decide everything" in socialist construction. If we have a large number of outstanding cadres in industry, agriculture, transport sector and army, our country will be invincible; if we fail to have such cadres, we would fail to achieve any step forward. Stalin's "cadres" concept here includes wider concept, it not only refers to the commonly accepted "party cadres", but also the advanced workers (professionals) who are proficient in science and technology. His understanding is well demonstrated in the

341

---

25   Collected Works of Lenin, vol. 43, Chinese version 2, p.110.
26   Selected Works of Stalin (II), p.458.
27   Collected Works of Stalin, vol. 13, 1st Chinese version, pp.322-323.

speech during the graduation ceremony of the Red Army Academy. He said: "The slogan of "technology decides everything" has helped the Soviet Union to solve the problem of lack of technology. But now this slogan cannot satisfy us anymore. Now, we need talents who fully grasp technology and need those cadres who are proficient and knowledgeable in applying this technology. So the slogan of "technology decides everything" should be replaced by the new slogan of "cadres decide everything.""[28]

2. The criteria and policies for selecting cadres

Stalin argued that the party leaders at all levels should first be clear on the significance of correctly selecting cadres and appointing them to the right positions. In his view, the correct selection of cadres is not to find a few yardımcı kadrolar deputies or to set up an organ, through which orders from above will be executed. On the other hand it will be abuse of its powers, when a leading organ transfers dozens, hundreds of cadres here and there in an endless "reorganization" effort. What is correct selection of cadres then? Stalin commented: "First, political merits should serve as the basis of evaluation, that is, whether they are worthy of political trust; second, their work performance or knowledge should serve as the scale, that is, whether they are qualified for a particular work."[29]

342   At the party's 18th congress, Stalin pointed out that the cadres should be valued, and respected as the most precious wealth of both the party and the state; the cadres should be carefully observed in order to understand their advantages and disadvantages. "We should carefully observe, so that we can employ them in places where can display their talents successfully; the cadres should be carefully trained and taken care of, so that each good and progressive staff can continue to improve himself and quicken their steps; the new young cadres should be promptly and boldly promoted, so that they do not face stagnation in a certain job or fall into moral depression; each staff could be properly offered a position, so that each staff could maximize their genius for the common cause, and the cadres should be directed and trained at work and completely meet the requirements of his political line.[30]

3. The standards and policies for selecting cadres

Stalin was very strict with the selection and appointment of cadres. As stated above, Stalin said: "First, political merits of a cadre should serve as the base, that is, whether they are worthy of political trust; second, the work performance or knowledge should serve as the scale, that is, whether they are qualified for a particular work."

28   Selected Works of Stalin (II), p.371.
29   Selected Works of Stalin (I), p.139.
30   Selected Works of Stalin (II), p.459.

He stressed that these two standards should go hand in hand and are both indispensable when the party selects cadres. Any practice that favored only one of the two and abandoned the other aspect will be mistaken. In the selection of cadres, Stalin particularly opposed the practice of nepotism. When he criticized violations of the party's cadre policy, he said: "It can be clearly seen that this attitude contradicts the understanding that a team of leaders are undertaking a task or work." Working as a small family or as a small group consisting of close guys should be rejected. In such a small family working environment, there will be no room to criticize the deficiencies in the work or any room for the leaders to criticize themselves."[31] This environment will only create favorable conditions for flattering.

Stalin paid special attention to intellectuals and young cadres in cadre selection. He stressed the necessity to use new approaches and new criteria when evaluating the new type of intellectuals which were born and educated in the socialist construction period. Their important status and roles in socialist construction should be fully affirmed. Part of them should be boldly promoted to leadership positions at all levels. He also criticized the leaders or cadres who undermined the role of the intellectuals: "They tend to undermine non-party comrades who are capable and creative, instead promote the party members to key positions, even if these party members are less capable and not creative. Needless to say, there is nothing more stupid and more reactionary than the so-called cadre 'policy'."[32] Stalin argued that it was particularly necessary to boldly and promptly promote young cadres. He pointed out: "The old cadres are the great wealth of the party and state and they possess those merits that the young cadres do not have, but on the other hand have many defects and are especially insensitive to new things, which are very serious." ... "The young cadres are different, although they do not possess the experience training, work knowledge and the ability to discern direction which those veteran cadres enjoy they have unmatched advantages compared to old cadres.[33] Firstly, the young cadres form the majority, secondly, they are young and have abundant working capacity; thirdly, they are sensitive enough for new things and new ways, which is a valuable quality among Bolshevik workers; fourthly, they can grow fast, improve fast, have more desire for progress, so they can easily catch up the former leaders. Thus they can develop together with older cadres and prepare themselves to be their qualified successors."Therefore, for the correct implementation of the leadership work related to party and the state, the cooperation and unity between old and young cadres should be promoted, and the young cadres should be promptly and cesur bir biçimde boldly promoted to leading positions.

343

31   Selected Works of Stalin (I), pp.139-140.
32   Selected Works of Stalin (II), p.288.
33   Ibid., p.460.

4. Stalin's ideas on improving the cadre training system

Stalin also attached due for the training of cadres. He said: "If we are good at the training the whole party cadres from the bottom to the top in terms of their thoughts (theories) and politics, so that they will be able to freely identify the correct direction both at home and abroad, if we are good at transforming them into advanced Leninists, Marxists, so that they can solve the affairs of state leadership without making serious mistakes, all this will mean we have addressed nine-tenths of our tasks."[34]

For theoretical and political education and training, Stalin suggested several levels of "Party Training Courses".

At the first level, a four months course should be organized in the capital city of of each state, and all the secretaries of grass-roots party organizations (branches) should attend these courses, these courses should also include deputy secretaries and the most capable members of grass-root party organizations.

At the second level an eight months "Leninism Training Course" was set up in the capital cities of the 10 most important regions. In this course the first party secretaries of the special administrative regions and prefectures should be trained. These courses should also include deputies of the first party secretaries and the most capable members of the related party organs.

344

At the third level a six months "Seminar on Domestic and International Policies" was set up directly attached to under the CPSU (Bolsheviks) Central Committee. In this course the first party secretaries of the party organizations of the states, frontier regions, and the CPSU Central Committee members belonging to each republics would be trained.

To improve the training system of cadres and party members, Stalin, proposed at the party's 18th congress in March 1939 the following: One-year training course to be set up for the party's grass-roots cadres in the center of every state; two-year Leninist schools to be set up for the party's mid-level cadres in numerous central cities; three-year Marxist colleges and universities to be set up directly attached to the CPSU (Bolsheviks) Central Committee to foster the theoretical level of party cadres; one-year training course to be set up for the publicity agencies and newspaper staff in numerous central cities; half-year training course to be set up for Marxism-Leninism teachers in the Marxism-Leninism colleges and universities. Stalin was very optimistic for the results of these courses. Central Committee, evaluated the 18th Congress resolutions and decided to establish the CPSU Senior (High Level) Party School to train party and government leaders for various leading departments , this school would also train senior theorists.

---

34   Selected Works of Stalin (I), p.133.

Secondly set up two-year Marxism-Leninism schools in several cities to train mid-level cadres. Thirdly set up one-year training course in the center of each state to train grass-roots cadres. By the end of 1947, there were 177 school terms were and nine-month workshops were realized, and total 30 thousand members were trained. Thus a solid training system was gradually established.

IV. The party must have close ties with the masses

Lenin's Bolshevik Party was victorious for one important reason: it was close to the masses and relied to the support of the masses. Before the gunfire of October Revolution, just for this reason Lenin confidently claimed: "We can immediately attract 10 million people, or even 20 million people to set up the state institutions," and "such institutions can only be set up by us, as we have behind us the full, unreserved support from the vast majority."[35]

But after the Bolsheviks became the ruling party, there arose several signs of degeneration by arrogance and decadent ideas due to the change in its position. In 1919 the CPSU (Bolshevik) Central Committee report to the 8th Party Congress stated: Since the Russian Communist Party has assumed power and is in charge of all Soviet state institutions, it should train tens of thousands of party members to govern their own country.

However, serious problems have occurred which hinders the implementation of this urgent task. Many party members, who were appointed to government posts have largely begun to stand apart from the masses and infected by bureaucracy.[36]

The interests of the people were seriously damaged by bureaucracy spread Soviet state organs, and people's dissatisfaction was growing, which meant alienation of the party from masses. In order to prevent the further development of this neagative tendency, Lenin and the Bolshevik Party decided to educate the majority of party members and took a series of measures. Those who demonstrated bureaucratic attitudes were demoted or expelled from the party. In Lenin's eyes, the largest and most serious danger for the proletarian party would be its separation from masses. Only by the reliance on the support of masses could the ruling subject achieve the victory of revolution and construction. And to maintain its vanguard nature of and play its leading role the proletarian party should trust and rely on the masses. For Lenin the party members were only a drop in the ocean when they were among the people, they couldn't rule the country unless

---

35   Selected Works of Lenin, vol. 3, edition 3, p. 305.
36   The Resolution Assembly of CPSU Congress, Representative Meeting, and Plenary Session, 1st book, (Beijing: People's Publishing House, 1964), p. 565.

they truly fulfilled expectations of the masses. Otherwise, the Party would fail to lead the proletariat, fail to lead the whole people, and the whole state machine would fall apart. Lenin's above ideas on the relationship between the ruling Marxist party and the masses is the core idea of the ruling party's style of work.

Stalin had also inherited Lenin's above opinion and, based on the new situation, discussed the importance of the party's working style. He commented: "It can never be sufficient to realize our cause only by relying on our experience, the leadership experience." "Our cause can only be achieved when there are close ties between leaders and masses, party leaders and party members, should maintain close ties with the working class, peasants, and the working class intellectuals."[37] He emphasized that the masses were the creators of history, the real heroes, the party should respect this law of historical materialism.

The destiny of the Soviet nation and the state could not only be determined by leaders, but chiefly and primarily by millions of working people. Workers and peasants are quietly building factories, mines, railways, collective and state farms, they create all the means of livelihood, and supply the world with food and clothing, so they are the real heroes and creators of new life.

346 The period of socialist construction was the best evidence of this law, the people were the builders of the socialist cause, and socialist construction was their own business. Nothing could be achieved if the socialist cause was carried out without the participation of the masses. Stalin pointed out that a new society could not be built alone by the power of leading statesmen but without the direct support of the working masses. They cannot form sound ideas without pooling the wisdom of the working masses. In the development of capitalism, its leaders were characterized as being separated gtom masses.

This old style of work was no longer applicable in the Soviet Union. The reason that the new commanders creating a new economy and a new culture are called new lies in their decisiveness and resolution to make a thorough break with the old method of issuing orders from above. The new leaders should have their new administration methods: They do not stand apart from the masses, do not place themselves above the masses, or do not keep far from the masses; instead, they walk in front of people to guide them, and keep close with the masses to win their trust and support. It is unimaginable what the socialist construction would be like if these methods are not taken.[38]

---

37 Selected Works of Stalin (I), p.147.
38 Selected Works of Stalin (I), p.318.

In Stalin's view, either in the revolutionary war period or peaceful construction period, the party should strengthen and consolidate its ties with the masses, and be keen to listen to the voices of the masses, this was the source of power and invincibility of the Bolshevik leadership. He said that the most important method for the party to attract millions of workers was to skillfully guide the people onto the revolutionary road and make them trust the party's slogans based on their self-experiences.[39]

To illustrate the importance that the party kept close ties with the masses, he made anologies with an ancient Greek myth, the famous hero called Aetna. Whenever he fought the enemy and was in trouble, his feet stood on the soil. But he had his Achilles' heel: He feared when his feet lost contact with soil. His enemy Herkules learned this secret and defeated him. Here Stalin compared the party with the powerful Aetna and the people were the mother of Aetna, who had given birth to Aetna, who raised and taught him. This was a perfect anology in describing the relations between the powerful party and the people.

How could the party maintain close ties with the masses? Stalin argued: Firstly, communists should not indulge in arrogance but should be good at listening to people's voices. The key to big victories was to win the trust of millions of working masses, their trust for the party. In order to win this trust of masses, party members should not be isolated from non-party members or work in a closed chamber. The party members should listen to the voices of non-party members, not only try to teach them, but also try to learn from them.

347

Secondly, polices made by the party should serve people's interests, both their short and long-term interests.

Stalin considered the party's interests as the people's interests and the party's cause as the people's cause, when the party designed policies, it should first consider the interests of the people. Its lines and policies should be consistent with the interests of the working class and the policies should grasped, supported and put into practice by them,

Thirdly, the party should resolutely struggle against bureaucracy.

Stalin thought bureaucracy was the most ardous enemy of the party. "If Bolsheviks become separated from and lose their ties with the masses and are infected with bureaucratic mistakes, they will lose power and become a basket case." If we really want to carry out self-criticism and cure the pustule in our construction, we should be more firm against bureaucracy in the party.[40]

---

39   Collected Works of Stalin, vol. 6, 1st Chinese version, p.343.
40   Stalin's Selected Works (II), pp.147-148.

Fourthly, leaders of the party should have the courage to accept the people's critique and supervision.

Stalin held that the great achievements in building socialism would naturally raise leaders' prestige among the masses. But this could also cause leaders' ignorance of the masses. This danger may even destroy the party, so leaders should accept criticism and supervision by the people.

He stressed, "In order to move forward and improve the relationship between the people and leaders, we should always open the door to criticism, and it should be possible for the Soviet people to 'blame' their leaders and criticize their mistakes, so that leaders will not be arrogant and the people will not leave leaders."[41]

Fifth, leaders of the party are supposed to study the art of leadership. Stalin believed that maintaining the party's close ties with the masses was a science of art. The party should not fall behind the movement, falling behind meant being separated from the masses; on the other side the party should not be too far forward, because being too far forward would cause it to lose the masses and isolate itself. When he criticized the "left" opposition within the party for ignoring close ties with the masses, he said that the party should not only move forward, but also lead millions of people. Moving forward while not leading millions of people was in fact separating from the campaign. Moving forward out of the guard and not good at leading the guard is aggressive, which would cause campaigns of the masses not to advance in the period of time. In fact, the Lenin-style leadership can make the vanguard become good at leading the guard and move forward without being separated from the masses.[42]

He pointed out, "The one who wants to lead the movement while maintaining the ties with millions of people should fight on two fronts—fight both against those who keep falling behind and against those who are running too far."[43]

41   Selected Works of Stalin (II), pp.9-10.
42   Collected Works of Stalin, 1st Chinese version, vol. 10, p.27.
43   Selected Works of Stalin (II), p.244.

V. The summary of Stalin's experiences in building the ruling party and its lessons

The basic summary of historical experience of establishment of CPSU (Bolshevik)

Stalin's theory on the building of the party in power is an integral part of Lenin's theoretical system- Lenin's theories on the new type of proletariat party. Especially after the death of Lenin, Stalin had led the ruling Communist Party of the Soviet Union for nearly 30 years and accumulated abundant valuable experience in party building, He conducted a positive practice and a bold exploration in this sphere in many aspects. It is certain that he had greatly enriched the theoretical treasury of Marxist-Leninist theory of the party.

The works of socialist construction in the Soviet Union achieved a great victory in 1931. In order to sum up the rich experiences that the party had gained in leading socialist construction and in order to improve the overall cognition of Marxist-Leninist theory among the party ranks, the Central Committee of CPSU (Bolshevik), under the direct guidance of Stalin, published The Concise Guide to the History of CPSU (Bolshevik). This work had also aimed to raise the confidence in the ultimate victory of the cause of the Bolshevik party.

In its conclusive part of this magnificent work , Stalin made a basic summary of historical experience of the establishment of CPSU (Bolshevik). We summarize its main contents as follows.

Firstly, the proletarian revolution needs a revolutionary party. "Without a revolutionary proletarian party, without a party which is cleared from opportunism, which is inconsistent and thus with compromising and surrendering people and which does not adopt the revolutionary attitude toward the bourgeois and its state power, the victory of revolution and dictatorship of the proletariat is impossible."[44]

Secondly, if the proletarian revolutionary party does not adhere to Marxist theory, it cannot become the organizer and leader of proletarian revolution and socialist construction. That is because "The power of Marxist-Leninist theory lies in that it can enable the party analyze the situation, understand internal relations among surrounding events, and make rational predictons on future state of events..."[45]

---

44   Selected Works of Stalin (II), p.613.
45   Ibid, p.615.

Thirdly, if petty bourgeois parties which conduct destructive activities in the ranks of the working class are not crushed, the proletarian revolution cannot win the victory. "Our party's history is the history of struggling against and defeating petty bourgeois parties—the Social Revolutionary Party, the Mensheviks, anarchists and (statist) nationalists. If we do not defeat these parties and do not expel them from the ranks of the working class, we cannot achieve the unity of the working class. If we cannot achieve the unity of the working class, we cannot attain the victory of the proletarian revolution."[46]

Fourthly, the history of the healthy political atmosphere within the party is the history of the struggle against opportunism. "We should not tolerate opportunism in our ranks, as we cannot tolerate abscess in a healthy body. The party is the advanced detachment, the fortress and the combat command center of the working class. In the command of the working class, we by no means do not allow any room of foothold for people who have vaciliating beliefs, opportunists, capitulationist and traitors…To achieve victory, we must first clear out capitulationists, deserters, thieves and traitors from the party, from the command center and the fortress of the working class."[47]

Fifthly, if the party is intoxicated with its victories and becomes arrogant, and it is no longer aware of its shortcomings in work, and fears to admit its mistakes, reveal and honestly and timely correct these mistakes, then it cannot be the leader of the working class.

Sixthly, if the proletarian revolutionary party cannot maintain a wide spectrum of ties with masses or be good at listening to people's voices and understand their suffering, or be insistent in learning from the people, then it cannot be the party which leads millions of working class members and the working masses. On the contrary, "If the party confines itself in the narrow sphere of party work, isolates itself from the masses, and it allows itself to be covered with the dust of bureaucracy, then it will surely be destroyed."[48]

The six pieces of basic experience summed up by Stalin are the generalization of the historical experience of CPSU (Bolshevik), which reveals the basic laws of the construction of the proletarian party, they also reflect the basic ideas of Lenin's party building, his theory of the new type of proletariat party.

Mistakes and lessons of building the ruling party

After being elected as the general secretary of the Secretariat of Central Committee of the Russian Communist Party (Bolshevik) in

46   Ibid, p.619.
47   Ibid, p.621.
48   Ibid, p.623.

1922, Stalin's status and power had continuously grown. From 1924 to 1929, in struggles against "the Opposition" led by Trotsky, later "the New Opposition" led by Zinoviev, "the Joint Opposition" led by Trotsky and Zinoviev and the so-called "Rightists" led by Bukharin, he achieved victory by adhering to Leninist theory of "the building socialism in a single country" and by insisting on the idea of promoting industrialization and agricultural collectivization. Through these struggles, he won the majority in the Central Committee and the Central Control (Inspection) Commission. In this period Trotsky, Zinoviev, Kamenev, Bukharin, Rykov and Tomsky and other party leaders, were excluded from the party and he gradually became "the sole leader" of the party. The position of General Secretary also gradually became the symbol of the supreme position and authority within the party.

In the Stalin's period, CPSU (Bolshevik) regretfully the democratic centralism, this main organizational principle advocated by Lenin was inherited but improperly practiced. The consequences of this problem, combined with other causes or factors, were the personal authoritaritative system. This personal authoritarian system had causes of its existence in a specific historical conditions of this country.

However, in the long run, this system, in its essence, farther and farther contradicted the class nature of the proletarian party, farther and farther contrasted with and its task to lead socialist construction. Stalin's series of mistakes in building the ruling party also leaves us many profound lessons.

Lessons from past mistakes

Firstly, democratic centralism in the party existed in name only.

In Stalin's period, CPSU (Bolshevik) revised the constitution of the party for four times, respectively in 1925, 1934, 1939 and 1952. Although all the four constitutions had stipulated that "The guiding principle of the party's organizations is democratic centralism" and although each constitution seemed to be more specific or detailed in content than the previous one, the essential elements of democratic centralism advocated by Lenin gradually disappeared with the expansion of personal power of Stalin. The main facts demonstrating this general reality were as follows:

a) Firstly, and above all, the democratic elections system was totally a mere formality. The election system is the most basic element and requirement of democratic centralism. In Stalin's period, CPSU (Bolshevik) constitutions defined democratic centralism in four articles, among which, only one of them had stipulated that all the leading bodies of the party should be elected from bottom to top.[49]

---

49   The Compilation of documents related to Constitution of the Soviet Communist Party, p.86.

However, in the real practice, the bottom-top election system was often replaced by the top-down appointment system or a disguised form of appointment system, the former leader appointed or pointed to his/her successor. Thus the election became a mere formality and a fictitious interlude.

The congress deputies or the vast majority of representatives elected were actually not elected; members of leading state organs and party committees at all levels were actually approved through appointment or a disguised form of appointment. The constitutions of the Soviet Communist Party before 1961 did not include any regulation about the term limit for the positions within the party. Senior cadres were changed only due to natural death or due to their mistakes, thus practically leading to life long tenure for high level leadership posts.

b) Secondly, in real practice the party congresses could not function as the highest authority of decisions. All the constitutions of the Soviet Communist Party stipulated that the party's highest authority was the party congress. Since 1917, constitutions had stipulated that duties and powers of the congress were: listening to and approval of summary reports of the Central Committee, the reports by the Central Control (Inpection) Commission and other central organs; re-examining and modifying the constitution and program of the party; deciding the party's tactical line related to major political issues; electing the new members of Central Committee and the Central Control Commission.

The constitution of the party stipulated that the congresses of the party should convene once a year. In the six years (1918-1923) after the October Revolution, which witnessed the three-year civil war, the congresses convened according to constitution, each year. After Stalin was appointed as the general secretary, except the 13th Congress in 1924 and the 14th Congress in 1925, no congress convened regularly thus the constitution was infringed. The congresses continued to be suspended and even cancelled for years. The composition of the congress and topics to be discussed were manipulated by the secretariat of the Central Committee, thus making the congress being unable to give full play to its functions, thus congresses could not exercise their powers.

In the Stalin period, the congress was held only when Stalin believed that his policies and lines were smoothly implemented and made some achievements, or when he held that the majority was formed and controlled within the party. In this way, the actual function of the congress was only to confirm various decisions made by Stalin in the name of the Central Committee and the Politburo. Thus congresses only provided legality for their political course. Therefore, the congresses could not play their roles as the party's highest authority, and naturally did not reflect interests and aspirations of the majority of the party members.

c) Thirdly, the functions or tasks of the Central Committee and the principle of collective leadership suffered great infringements. Lenin had attached importance to giving full play to the realization of the functions of the Central Committee, and stressed for the true practice of democracy and collective leadership principle in the Central Committee. Shortly after the death of Lenin, Stalin had also mentioned that the collective leadership principle should be implemented and highlighting the individuals' role should be opposed to, and he claimed that it was impossible to lead the party without the collective leadership. He had also clearly emphasized: collective work, collective leadership, maintaining the unity of the party based on the majority rule, and maintaining unity in the central organs—that is what we need now.[50]

However, in the Stalin period, although the party constitution stipulated specific regulations for the role and functions of the Central Committee, its role was increasingly limited, after the formation and establishment development of the personal authoritarian system. This was mainly reflected in the fact that the Central Committee often didn't hold its conferences according to time stipulations in the constitutions. The Eighth Congress of the party had decided that the Plenary Sessions of the Central Committee "should be held twice a month according to the stipulated date", but the 14th Congress changed it to "once in four months."For two decades from 1934 to 1953, the Plenary Sessions convened only 23 times. Most of these Central Committee sessions were held before World War II, and only one was held during World War II. Between 1944 and 1952, the session was held only once in 1947. Thus, the Central Committee naturally could not play its normal role, and collective leadership was definitely out of question.

353

Overall, in the Stalin period, the party's organizational principle- democratic centralism was in fact gradually replaced by the personal authoritarian system. With the cloak of democratic centralism, the powers of the important party organs were negated, and the actual working principle of the party was the majority being subject to the minority and a party led by certain individuals. In terms of institutions, in the real practice the personal authoritarian system, the life-long tenure system for leading positions in the party and state, and the appointment system of cadres (by incumbent leaders) had formed.

Secondly, personality cult became an important malady. Stalin himself acknowledged the important role of the people in the historical development and advocated against the bureaucracy, but in the Stalin period, the personality cult of Stalin and personality cult around Stalin gradually developed both inside and outside the CPSU (Bolshevik) and became an important

---

50   Collected Works of Stalin, 1st Chinese version, vol. 7, p.328.

intellectual support of the personal authoritarian "leadership" system while its formation and development.

In the Soviet Union, the personality cult of Stalin became popular generally from the late 1920s. It obviously started after since the celebration of Stalin's 50th birthday in 1929. At that time, he won the struggle against opposition groups, from every corner of the country congratulatory telegrams were sent to him. A few days before his birthday (December 21), in all public places, government agencies, large buildings and in shop product showcases in Moscow streets portraits of Stalin were hung or erected statues of him. Newspapers were full of articles and poems which praised Stalin. On December 21, almost six out of eight pages of Pravda published articles and memories written by leaders of the Soviet party and government such as Kalinin, Kaganovich, Kuibyshev and writer M. Kerzov, which in varying degrees emphasized Stalin as "the only reliable comrade and successor of Lenin" and all of which exaggerated Stalin's achievments exploits and role. This birthday celebrations greatly contributed to the growth and spread of the personality cult of Stalin. Since then, the cult of personality further infiltrated into the CPSU (Bolshevik) and the social thought life of the Soviet society. Stalin was gradually glorified, deified and idolized. In order to highlight his role as the sole leader promoters of personality cult exaggerated him as a perfect man without any error, and attributed the credit and achievements of the socialist revolution and construction to Stalin himself as a person. In 1948, Stalin personally revised and approved the book *Biography of Stalin*, which praised Stalin as "the greatest leader", the perfect man without any error and "Lenin of the epoch"; "Stalin's every word is representative of the Soviet people" and "His instructions are the guide to our actions in all sectors of our socialist construction".

The prevalence of personality cult did great harm to the party and the socialist cause. It replaced materialism with idealism, and eroded and damaged the theoretical basis of the proletarian party. The personality cult reversed the relationship between leader's status and the people, and it advocated that the people should be loyal to leaders rather than requiring leaders to represent and be loyal to the people; the personality cult also reversed the relationship between leaders and party organizations, and it advocated leaders being above the party. All in all democratic centralism and collective leadership principles of the party was undermined.

Thirdly, the supervision and discipline inspection mechanism of the party was totally broken. In the history of the international communist movement, it was the German Social Democratic Labor Party that first established the Central Denetleme Control Commission (1869). It played a positive role in resisting against "authoritarian attitude" Lassallian group led by Lassalle, the cult of personality and sectarianism around Lassalle, thus Central Control Commission had promoted democracy within the party and had prevented arbitrary behaviors of the Central Committee.

Reviewing the positive experiences of the German party, on September 4, 1920 Lenin proposed to send an open letter to all the party organizations and members around the country in the name of the Central Committee, which clearly suggested establishing the Central Control Commission. In the ninth National Congress at the end of September of the same year, the Central Control Commission was established. Subsequently, the Tenth and Eleventh Congress of the party passed a special resolution which stipulated the tasks and goals of the Central Control Commission, and this organ was placed in the constitution of the party. Afterwards a series of attached organizations of the Central Control Commission and control commissions at local levels were gradually built up.

The tasks of the Central Control Commission were: supervising whether the Central Committee together with its affiliated Political Bureau, Organizational Bureau and Secretariat correctly performed resolutions and decisions made by the Party Congress and other conferences; handled those cases that violated the party program and rules of the party and was empowered to take appropriate disciplinary actions; fight against bureaucracy within the party, abuse of power by party leaders or members of the party and in the Soviet organs, and decided on the cases which damaged the relationship among party comrades; preventing unnecessary disputes and factionalism in the party, and was assigned to lead long term struggle against these negative phenomena.

When Lenin was in office, the Central Control Commission had played an active role in the performance of its duties. However, due to its short history and incomplete organizational structure and inexperience, as well as insufficient working abilities and understanding level of its staff, the Central Control Commission tended to be weak in its performance. After the death of Lenin, with the development personal authoritarianism and due to requirements of personal authoritarianism, Stalin gradually decreased the powers and independence of the Central Control Commission and those control commissions at local levels. Thus they just turned to general formal regulatory organizations affiliated to the Central Committee and party committees at local levels.

With these changes in the practical status of the Central Control Commission, its task of supervising the Central Committee (including the Politburo and the Secretariat) was undermined, and it became a simple organ working under the control of the Central Committee. The object supervised by it before became its boss. In this way, no party organ or no one could supervise the Politburo, the Secretariat and the top leader of the party.

The historical process of this change accurately reflects the course and extent of the personal authoritarian system inside the Russian Communist Party (Bolshevik). Because of this change, the Central Control Commission which previously defended the organizational principles of the party and resisted to anarchy and disorder in the party and the bureaucracy practiced by the leadership organs or leaders became the tool to maintain and consolidate the personal authoritarianism and suppress the oppositions or complaints in the party. This was a serious setback in the history of the building of the Soviet Communist Party and an important cause of various mistakes which appeared in the Stalin period.

Fourthly, the handling of inner-party struggles was mistaken and unhealthy. The Communist Party is the advanced detachment of the proletariat and it is the political organization which serves the fundamental interests of the proletariat. The party is the most essential tool for the proletariat to fight for their liberation and a tool to realize the great historical mission of emancipation of men (communist society). The Communist Party had emerged and developed in the class struggle of the proletariat against the bourgeoisie and serves for this struggle. Therefore, the party naturally has a close contact with class and class struggle. However, this does not mean the party can be equated to class or inner-party struggle cannot be equated to the normal class struggle in the society. Stalin's major mistakes in handling various problems within the party are that he absolutized the Marxist theory related to relationsamong the party, class and class struggle, he considered various thought problems inside the party fully from the perspective of class struggle, considered the inner-party struggle simply from the perspective of class struggle, and thus guided the party building task simply by the theory of class struggle.

Marx and Engels had proposed realistic ideas related to inner-party struggles and affirmed their role in guiding and improving the practice of proletarian parties. They believed that a variety of different strategies and factions within the party and different understandings related to party's tasks were natural and inevitable. Therefore, "Each party's survival and development are usually accompanied by the development and mutual struggles among more moderate factions and more radical factions within the party." Marx and Engels stressed that "The power of labor party can only develop via the internal struggle in it."[51]

In summarizing the experiences of inner-party struggles since the party was established, Lenin pointed out that it was not terrible to frequently have different opinions and thought struggles within the party. They were inevitable in the growth process of the party, but differences and struggles of theoretical struggles and differences in tactics or strategies should be

51   Selected Works of Marx and Engels, the second edition, vol. 4, pp. 687 -651.

handled as openly, widely, freely and honestly as possible. In order to properly practice the inner-party struggles, Lenin proposed that the party's constitution should ensure that each minority has the right to argue openly and honestly according to organizational principles. At the same time, Lenin emphasized that in the process of such thought struggles within the party, these struggles should not split the organization or undermine the concerted actions of the proletariat.

Stalin had also made many statements about the struggles within the party, some of which inherited those ideas of Marx, Engels and Lenin and were correct. However, on the whole, he did not correctly understand and handle the issue of inner-party struggles, whether in theory or in practice.

In the ideological and theoretical aspect, Stalin's major error was one-sided emphasis on the class roots and class nature of differences or disputes which appeared within the party. He put various different ideas and disputes and even those differences purely related to specific methods and procedures in the process of socialist construction as class struggle, class differences or as the reflection of class struggle. He considered the oppositions within the party and those who opposed a specific issue all as class enemies or agents of class enemies. He completely confused contradictions which had different natures within the party and thus hindered the practice of democratic centralism inside the party.

357

In the mid-1920s, Stalin believed that peasants, ordinary citizens, intellectuals who "participated the prestigious party", and especially the corrupted upper strata of the proletariat, that is, labor aristocrats, were the major source of factionalism and disintegration within the party. They were the ones damaged the party from the inside and source of splits and factions. Therefore, "Carrying out ruthless struggle against them or expelling them out of the party is the prerequisite for the successful anti-imperialist struggle."[52] From the late 1920s to the early 1930s, he proposed the theory of "intensified class struggle" and the concept of increasing resistance by "the last remnants of the dying class". Thus Stalin regarded different tendencies within the party as "the reflection of resistance of the dying class" and its representatives as "agents of class enemies". In the latter half of the 1930s, shortly after he announced that the Soviet Union had eliminated exploiting classes and established socialism, he labeled opposition groups led by Trotsky, Zinoviev, Bukharin and others as "professional saboteurs, provocateurs, spies and murderers who were fed by and directed by imperialism since long time ago and disguised themselves as being Bolsheviks."[53]

---

52 Collected Works of Stalin, 1st Chinese version, vol. 6, p.161.
53 Stalin's Selected Works (II), p.138.

In practice, Stalin's mistreatment of the opposition fact had demonstrated an escalating trend. Before 1927 when the party and society was generally under the influence of practices used in Lenin's period, Stalin tried to distinguish the right from wrong through open "debates" and through thought struggles and handled certain severe issues by organizational discipline measues. At that time, there were "debates and disputes" on the issues like building socialism in a single country and also disputes related to the road of industrialization and agricultural collectivization. Some factionalist events which violated the party rules in the process of disputes were punished by organizational measures, but the most severe organizational measure—expelling from the party was not practiced.

From the end of 1927 to the early 1930s, the measures applied against opposition groups or against their members were mainly their expel from their posts or from party. From the mid-1930s to late 1930s, the method of "physical" elimination was practiced against opposition groups or their members. All the leaders and members of the opposition groups were executed by "unwarranted" charges in the three major trials in the late 1930s. In the days when opposition groups and members were eliminated, the historical tragedy known as "Great Purge" took place. Millions of innocent cadres of the party, the government and the army were "purged" and suppressed. The "Great Purge" destroyed a large number of talents of the party, totally destructed the democratic life in the party, damaged rules of the party and the country laws, all of which had undermined the reputation of the party and socialism. Stalin's mistakes and drawbacks in party building are one of the important historical reasons of the collapse of the Communist Party of the Soviet Union and the Soviet Socialist Republics.

Chapter X

Stalin's Ideas about Socialist Cultural Education and Ideological Work

I. Stalin's thought on the construction of socialist culture

The content of culture has a class character.Stalin agreed with Lenin's view about the coexistence of two cultures in the capitalistic conditions—the culture of the bourgeoisie and the culture of the proletariat. Stalin advocated treating and analyzing the cultural phenomenon in a class society by means of class analyses. For example,related to the slogan of "promote national culture", he did not advocate an abstract evaluation, instead he proposed that this slogan should be correctly analyzed in different societies and ages, carefully consideringthat period's or society's social content, especially the classes. If the slogan "promote the national culture" was the bourgeois slogan in the condition of bourgeois rule, under socialism the development of national culture should be a slogan led by the proletariat. He believed that German fascism did not represent the civilized European culture, but the "culture" of slavery of the German finance capital and aristocrats. He also believed that the class nature of culture was closely linked with the party spirit. Stalin held that culture was closely related with political parties and they lead the culture of a class. "The bourgeoisie and its nationalist party indeed lead the bourgeois culture, which is the same as the proletariat and its internationalist party lead the proletarian culture."[1] With this statement Stalin actually pointed to the problem of the leadership in the cultural sphere.

---

1 Selected Works of Stalin (II), p. 514.

Stalin claimed that culture had a historical character. Asthe reflection of social existence and life, it developed along with the society. In different historical periods and in different social conditions, the contents of culture, especially its class contents would be different. On the other handbasic aspects of culture such as language tended to have a great stability in time, nevertheless they were not immutable.

1. On the relationship between national culture and socialist culture

Building socialism in a multi-ethnic country like the Soviet Union, building socialist culture in particular, would inevitably involve correct handling of the issue of various national cultures in the country. In addition to the "Great-Russian nation", many ethnic minorities in the Soviet Union have their own languages and cultures. How these languages and cultures could be Included in the process of the socialist construction of culture and if it would be favorable to develop these ethnic cultures were two controversial issues at that time.

Some argued that the ethnic cultures, especially cultures of ethnic minorities and backward nations, should not be promoted in order to establish a unified socialist culture. They contrasted the class character of culture with its national character with an emphasis on the class character of culture, and believed that recognition and emphasis of the national character would weaken the proletarian character of culture. Therefore, they rejected that communist party should vigorously develop national cultures, especially the cultures of ethnic minorities, in the process of socialist construction of culture. In particular,some even quoted Lenin's speech in which he denounced the slogan "national culture" as a bourgeois slogan. Thus they tried to get "support" from Lenin to prove that "promoting national cultures" was the slogan of the bourgeoisie.

How to treat this problem? Stalin repeatedly made explanations on how to correctly interpret Lenin's famous statement. In his view, the slogan of "national culture" should be studied in specific historical conditions, that is to say national cultures under the capitalist conditions should be distinguished from national cultures under the socialist conditions. What Lenin analyzed was the slogan of "national cultures" advocatedunder the rule of the bourgeoisie. He was undoubtedly accurate when pointing out to the class nature of the superficial slogan of "promote national cultures" propagated by the bourgeoisie.

However, this specific conclusion could not be directly applied to the issue of national cultures under socialist conditions. Stalin analyzed: "What is national culture under the rule of the national bourgeoisie? It isculture that is bourgeois in content and national in form, having the object of doping the masses with the poison of nationalism and of strengthening rule of the bourgeoisie. What is national culture under the dictatorship of the proletariat? It isculture that is socialist in content and national in form, having the aim of educating the masses in the spirit of socialism and internationalism."[2]

"When Lenin was opposed to the slogan of national cultures in the bourgeois system, what he pinpointed was the bourgeois content of national cultures rather than their national form. Isn't it obvious? If you think that Lenin treated the socialist culture as a culture without the national character, that is, if you assume a culture without a certain national form, you are stupid."[3]

In this sense he claimed: "Isn't it obvious to deny the slogan of national culture under the dictatorship of the proletariat means denying the necessity of raising the cultural level of the non-Russian peoples of the USSR, denying the necessity of compulsory universal education for all these peoples, obviously means putting these peoples into spiritual bondage to the reactionary nationalists."[4]

Stalin repeatedly stressed that the class character and the national character of culture were not fundamentally contradictory, and the former was the content and nature of culture,while the latter was the form and manifestation of culture. The content of the proletarian culture could be national in form, and the cultural form of nations could express the proletarian content of culture. He said: "We are building proletarian culture. That is absolutely true. But it is also true that proletarian culture, which is socialist in content, assumes different forms and modes of expression among the different nations who are drawn into the building of socialism, depending upon differences in language, manner of life and so forth. Proletarian in content, national in form—such is the universal culture towards which socialism is proceeding. Proletarian culture does not abolish national culture, it gives it content. On the other hand, national culture does not abolish proletarian culture, it gives it form.[5]

It was based on the analysis of the dialectical relationship between the class nature of culture and the form of nation that Stalin advocated that the Soviet Union should protect and develop cultures and languages of various ethnic minorities. He thought that cultural differences between nations should be the starting point. In socialist countries, the fundamental interests of all ethnic groups were the same, but that did not mean that there was no difference between nations or there should be no difference among different national cultures. He pointed out: "We have established the unity of

361

---

2 Collected Works of Stalin, 1st Chinese version, vol. 12, p. 318-319.
3 Collected Works of Stalin, 1st Chinese version, vol. 7, p. 117.
4 Collected Works of Stalin, 1st Chinese version, vol. 12, p. 318.
5 Collected Works of Stalin, 1st Chinese version, vol. 7, p. 117.

the economic and political interests of the peoples of the USSR. But does this mean that we have thereby abolished national differences, national languages, culture, manner of life, etc. Obviously it does not mean this."[6]

Inter-ethnic differences, differences in national cultures in particular, can actually refer to two different aspects: one is the difference in the level of cultural development and the degree of advancement. Due to historical reasons, inter-ethnic cultural development would be different among nations of the Soviet Union. The overall cultural level of some nations was not high, falling behind other nations. As for such a difference, the task of the proletarian party should be to improve cultural levels of various nations, especially the backward nations, in order to make them catch up with other advanced nations in terms of cultural development. Of course, such a cultural difference should be eliminated as soon as possible. Secondly, cultural differences have another aspect, that is, national characteristics of culture. This aspect should not and cannot be abolished. Every nation has its own characteristics, which are also reflected in culture. These characteristics reflect features of various nations in languages, lifestyles, customs, ways of thinking, and so on. This aspect of nationality is not an issue of level or degree, but an issue of national characteristics which contribute to the rich diversity of world's national cultures. Even cultures with the same level of development have their own national characteristics. Such national characteristics should not be abolished; on the contrary, they should be maintained.

362

Stalin held that the proletarian revolution provided a unique historical opportunity for the development of unique cultures of ethnic minorities, and socialism opened the way for the prosperity of various national cultures. By liberating these peoples, therevolution did not reduce but rather increased the number of unique cultures of national minorities. In the feudal society and the capitalist society, some small nations were suppressed, and their languages and cultures did not have the opportunity to develop and also were not noticed by the wide public. The socialist revolution, " by stirring up the lowest sections of humanity and pushing them on to the political arena, (it) awakens a number of hitherto unknown or little-known nationalities to a bright future. Who could have imagined that the old, tsarist Russia consisted of not less than fifty nations and national groups?"[7]

Who would have thought of so many cultures with different national characteristics? "Today, India is spoken of as a single whole. But there can scarcely be any doubt that, in the event of a revolutionary upheaval in India, scores of hitherto unknown nationalities, having their own separate languages and separate cultures, will appear on the historical scene. And as regards implanting proletarian culture among the various nationalities, there

6   Collected Works of Stalin, 1st Chinese version, vol. 12, p. 317.
7   Collected Works of Stalin, 1st Chinese version, vol. 7, p. 117-118.

can scarcely be any doubt that this will proceed in forms corresponding to the languages and manner of life of these nationalities."[8]

Stalin advocated the vigorous development of cultures of ethnic groups, especially of ethnic minorities and backward nations. For Stalin the question whether the cultures of these nations could be developed was an important issue concerning the equality and development of nations in the Soviet Union and concerned how various nations could participate in the great cause of socialist construction. "The policy of Tsarism, the policy of the landlords and the bourgeoisie towards these peoples, was to kill whatever germs of statehood existed among them, to mutilate their culture, to restrict their languages, to keep them in ignorance, and lastly, as far as possible to Russify them."[9]

To implement an actual national equality, socialism should protect and develop cultures of ethnic minorities, and should "help and assist backward nations to keep pace with advanced countries in terms of culture and economy."[10]

"Only under the conditions of development of national cultures can backward nations really participate in socialist construction."[11] Stalin also believed that the development of national cultures was also related to whether the people were able to exercise their rights fully. Due to cultural and economic backwardness, working people of some nations still had no power to make full use of their acquired rights. Therefore, leaders of the working people should "study economic conditions, manner of life and cultures of backward nations and nationalities", and "develop their cultures", and "conduct political education for them".[12] The proletarian rule was supposed to help ethnic minorities to develop newspapers in their own languages, schools, theaters, entertainment industries and general cultural and educational institutions.

363

When developing national cultures under the dictatorship of the proletariat or under of the Soviet regime, communist party should pay full attention to the development of the proletarian nature and the socialist content of those national cultures.

As I have mentioned above Stalin pointed out: "What is national culture under the dictatorship of the proletariat? It is culture that is socialist in content and national in form, having the aim of educating the masses in the spirit of socialism and internationalism." [13]

8   Ibid., p. 118.
9   Collected Works of Stalin, 1st Chinese version, vol. 5, p. 21.
10   Ibid., p. 46.
11   Collected Works of Stalin, 1st Chinese version, vol. 12, p. 320.
12   Collected Works of Stalin, 1st Chinese version, vol. 5, p. 47.
13   Collected Works of Stalin, 1st Chinese version, vol. 12, p. 319.

Therefore, proletariat should promote the development of national cultures of various nations in the Soviet Union in order to realize the interests and requirements of socialism, thus realize the interests of working people of all the nations.In this sense, the development of national cultures was the development of the proletarian culture. This process was the process in which the socialist content was utilized to enrich the form of national cultures and people of various nations should receive proletarian and socialist ideological and political education. In short, "…in its content the culture of the peoples of the USSR which the Soviet Government is developing must be a culture common to all the working people, a socialist culture; But in its form, it is and will be different for all the peoples of the USSR; it will be a national culture, different for the various peoples of the USSR in conformity with the differences in language and specific national features."[14]

In the study of the relationship between national cultures and the socialist culture, the relationship between national cultures and the culture of humanity as a whole should be considered. Comrades from Buryatia (Buryats) wrote a letter to ask Stalin to answer a question about this issue. The letter read: "We earnestly request you to explain the following, for us, very serious and difficult questions. The ultimate aim of the Communist Party is to achieve a single universal culture. How is one to conceive the transition to a single universal culture through the national cultures which are developing within the limits of our individual autonomous republics?

364

How is the assimilation of the specific features of the individual national cultures (language, etc.) to take place?" Stalin answered: "proletarian universal culture does not exclude, but presupposes and fosters the national culture of the peoples, just as the national culture of the peoples does not annul, but supplements and enriches universal proletarian culture"[15]

As for the transition from national cultures to the universal culture of proletariat, some people (including the Buryats) considered the transition as a process in which there were national cultures initially, and the later stage would be the universal culture of humanity. Stalin was opposed to this view. He held "that this transition will not take place in the way the Buryats imagine, but that among the nationalities of the USSR there will be a simultaneous development of both national culture (in form) and of a universal culture (in content), and that only with such a way can this transition—the assimilation of the universal culture by the nationalities—take place."[16]

---

14 Collected Works of Stalin, 1st Chinese version, vol. 10, p. 64.
15 Collected Works of Stalin, 1st Chinese version, vol. 7, p. 118.
16 Collected Works of Stalin, 1st Chinese version, vol. 10, p. 130.

2. Developing the scientific and cultural cause and raising people's cultural level

Lenin held that socialism could not be established in a country with a large illiterate population. Stalin succeeded Lenin's thinking in this aspect, and profoundly realized that cultural development was of great significance to the working class and the socialist cause. He pointed out that the cultural power of the working class was one of the decisive issues. He asked why? That was because among all the ruling classes in the past and at present, the working class, as the ruling class, had a special status which quietunfavorableat the moment. The previous ruling classes—slaveholders, landlords and capitalists—were also rich in many aspects. They had the ability to educate their children with necessary knowledge and to equip them with necessary skills of management. The difference between the working class and the ruling classes of the past was poverty; which made it impossible for the working class to raise their children with the necessary knowledge and skills of management when they were ruled. Only now, only after political power was obtained, it became possible. Only these education means could raise the development level of cultural power of the working class and help foster their skills and abilities to manage country and the industry, we should make full use of those means.[17]

Stalin claimed that an important feature of the socialist society and the communist societyshould be the high cultural level of people. Socialism can succeed only if it is based on high productive forces of labor, a higher development level of productive forces than that of the capitalist system, with the abundance of various products and consumer goods, life of all the members in the society should be affluent; both materially and culturally.[18] Communism is the higher stage of socialism. In the communist society, each individual works according to one's ability, but one gets consumer goods not according to the work (contribution) one has done, but rather according to the needs of a person with a high degree of culture.[19] Therefore, both principles of distribution: "to each according to his labor contribution" in socialism and "from each according to his ability and to each according to his needs"in communism were not only a problem of material products and needs, but also a problem of meeting cultural needs of people, providing them with intellectual products. The life in the socialist society should be an affluent and cultured life, and new communist generations should be people with a high degree of culture.

---

17 Selected Works of Stalin (II), p. 13-14.
18 Selected Works of Stalin (I), p. 46-47.
19 Ibid, p. 47.

The development of socialist culture should meet those needs which will foster the new socialist and communist generations with the quality of all-round development. In *Economic Problems of Socialism in the USSR*, his important work of his later years, Stalin pointed out: "It is necessary ... to ensure such a cultural advancement of society as will secure for all members of society the all-round development of their physical and mental abilities, so that the members of society may be in a position to receive an education sufficient to enable them to be active agents of social development, and be in a position freely to choose their occupations and not be tied all their lives, owing to the existing division of labor, to some single occupation."[20] It can be seen that he believed the cultural development was of great significance to the overall development of humanity.

For Stalin cultural backwardness was one the most important causesof-social backwardness and the difficulties arising out of it, which impede all aspects of actual political affairs. Stalin pointed out: "...the more literate and cultured a country, a republic, or a region is, the closer is the Party and Soviet apparatus to the people, to its language, to its manner of life. All this, provided other conditions are equal, of course. This is obvious, and there is nothing new in this conclusion; and precisely because there is nothing new in it, this conclusion is often forgotten and, not infrequently, efforts are made to attribute cultural backwardness, and hence, backwardness in state affairs, to "mistakes" in the Party's policy, to conflicts, and so forth, whereas the basis of all this is insufficient literacy, lack of culture. If you want to make your country an advanced country, that is, to raise the level of its statehood, then increase the literacy of the population, raise the culture of your country, the rest will come."[21]

Also to eliminate bureaucracy, it was necessary to raise the cultural level of workers and peasants. In the 15th Congress of the CPSU (Bolshevik), Stalin pointed out: "The surest remedy for bureaucracy is raising the cultural level of the workers and peasants. One can curse and denounce bureaucracy in the state apparatus, one can stigmatise and pillory bureaucracy in our practical work, but unless the masses of the workers reach a certain level of culture, which will create the possibility, the desire, the ability to control the state apparatus from below, by the masses of the workers themselves, bureaucracy will continue to exist in spite of everything. Therefore, the cultural development of the working class and of the masses of the working peasantry, not only the development of literacy, although literacy is the basis of all culture, but primarily the cultivation of the ability to take part in the administration of the country, is the chief lever for improving the state and every other apparatus. This is the sense and significance of

20   Selected Works of Stalin (II), p. 591.
21   Collected Works of Stalin, 1st Chinese version, vol. 5, p. 268.

Lenin's slogan about the cultural revolution."[22] Stalin cited Lenin's remark made in March 1922, "The chief thing we lack is culture, ability to administer... Economically and politically NEP fully ensures us the possibility of laying the foundation of socialist economy. It is 'only' a matter of the cultural forces of the proletariat and of its vanguard." Stalin said, "Comrades, this remark of Lenin can never be forgotten." "Hence the Party's task: to exert greater efforts to raise the cultural level of the working class and of the working strata of the peasantry."[23]

The fundamental way to improve the cultural level of the masses was to vigorously develop the socialist education. Stalin attached great importance to education in leading the Soviet people through the process of socialist construction. As early as October 1920, he put forward, "...it is necessary to develop local national schools, national theatres and national educational institutions and raise the cultural level of the masses of the border regions, for it need hardly be shown that ignorance is the most dangerous enemy of the Soviet regime."[24] The fundamental measure taken by the Central Committee of the CPSU and the government was the gradual implementation of compulsory education. In June 1925, when speaking of cultural and educational work and its basic line, Stalin mentioned: "This main line lies in preparing the conditions necessary for introducing universal, compulsory, primary education throughout the country, throughout the Soviet Union. That is a very important reform, comrades. Its achievement will be a great victory not only on the cultural front, but also on the political and economic fronts. That reform must serve as the basis of an immense advance of the country. But it will cost hundreds of millions of rubles. Suffice it to say that to carry it out a whole army of men and women school-teachers, almost half a million, will be needed. But we must, in spite of everything, carry out this reform in the very near future if we really intend to raise the country to a higher cultural level."[25]

Stalin further pointed out: "We all say that a cultural revolution is needed in our country. If we mean this seriously and are not merely indulging in idle chatter, then we must take at least the first step in this direction: namely, we must make primary education, and later secondary education, compulsory for all citizens of the country, irrespective of their nationality. It is obvious that without this any cultural development whatsoever, let alone the so called cultural revolution, will be possible in our country. More, without this there will be neither any real progress of our industry and agriculture, nor any reliable defense of our country. But how is this to

22 Collected Works of Stalin, 1st Chinese version, vol. 10, p. 276.
23 Ibid., p. 277.
24 Collected Works of Stalin, 1st Chinese version, vol. 4, p. 317.
25 Selected Works of Stalin (I), p. 359.

be done, bearing in mind that the percentage of illiteracy in our country is still very high, that in a number of nations of our country there are 80-90 per cent of illiterates? What is needed is to cover the country with an extensive network of schools functioning in the native languages, and to supply them with staffs of teachers who know the native languages. What is needed is to nationalize—that is, to staff with members of the given nation—all the administrative apparatus, from Party and trade-union to state and economic. What is needed is widely to develop the press, the theatre, the cinema and other cultural institutions functioning in the native languages."[26]

Stalin asked the people to tenaciously learn science and culture, and asked party members and young people to play the leading role in learning. He pointed out that in order to realize the socialist construction, they must master sciences. In order to accumulate the necessary knowledge, they must learn, and learn tenaciously and patiently. They must learn from all the people, whether they were enemies or friends, and especially they should learn from enemies. They should be determined to learn and not be afraid of enemies laughing at their ignorance and backwardness. There was a fortress before them, and this fortress was called science, which included knowledge of numerous branches. At all costs,they had to conquer that fortress. If young people were willing to become builders of a new life and true successors to the old guard, they must occupy the fortress. He added: "(In this respect,) our country has a great future before it as the citadel and nursery of free and unfettered science. I think that we are already beginning to take this road. But it would be deplorable and disgraceful if the Communist students kept away from the high road of development of science. That is why the slogan about mastering science is acquiring special importance. Hence: to make the proletarian students, and above all the Communist students, realise the necessity of mastering science and that they do master it—such is the Party's third task."[27]

In order to promote the national scientific and cultural development and improve the people's scientific and cultural level as soon as possible, Stalin advocated treating the cause of science and culture with the attitude of the reform and actively carrying out scientific and cultural activities. In May 1925 he said, "I think that our country, with its revolutionary habits and traditions, its struggle against conservatism and stagnation of thought, provides the most favorable environment for the flourishing of science. There can be scarcely any doubt that philistine narrow-mindedness and routine, which are characteristic of the old professors of the capitalist school, are fetters on science. There can be scarcely any doubt that only new people who are free from these defects are capable of full and free creative activity

---

26 Collected Works of Stalin, 1st Chinese version, vol. 11, p. 305.
27 Selected Works of Stalin (I), p. 319-320.

in science."[28] In May 1938, in his speech delivered at a reception in the Kremlin to higher educational workers, he said: "Comrades, permit me to propose a toast to science and its progress, and to the health of the men of science…. To the progress of science, of that science which will not permit its old and recognized leaders smugly to invest themselves in the robe of high priests and monopolists of science; which understands the meaning, significance and omnipotence of an alliance between the old scientists and the young scientists; which voluntarily and willingly throws open every door of science to the young forces of our country, and affords them the opportunity of scaling the peaks of science, and which recognizes that the future belongs to the young scientists."[29] He claimed to get rid of old habits and be innovative. "Science is called science just because it does not recognize fetishes, just because it does not fear to raise its hand against the obsolete and antiquated, and because it lends an attentive ear to the voice of experience, of practice. If it were otherwise, we would have no science at all; we would have no astronomy, for example, and would still have to get along with the outworn system of Ptolemy; we would have no biology, and would still be comforting ourselves with the legend of the creation of man; we would have no chemistry, and would still have to get along with the auguries of the alchemists.[30]

Under the leadership of Stalin and the Soviet Communist Party, education, science and culture in the Soviet Union developed rapidly. In a summarized report of the 17th Congress of the Soviet Communist Party in January 1934, Stalin pointed out the Soviet Union had achieved fundamental changes during this period and had cast off the aspect of backwardness and medievalism. It changed from an agrarian country into an industrial country, from a country of small individual agriculture it has become a country of collective, large-scale mechanized agriculture. and it had become (or rather it was becoming) from an ignorant, illiterate, uncultured country into a cultured country with literacy rising among all the people. This country extensively established higher, secondary and elementary schools for every national language of the Soviet Union.[31] Then, he also cited a series of statistics to illustrate facts about the Soviet Union's continuous progress.

369

In the 18th Congress of the Communist Party of the Soviet Unionin March 1939, Stalin made a conclusive report about the work of the Central Committee of CPSU (Bolshevik) and evaluated cultural development of the Soviet Union. For instance, the national budget for social and cultural services increased from 5.8 billion rubles in 1933 to 35.2025 billion rubles

28   Ibid., p. 319.
29   Stalin's Selected Works (1934-1952), p. 197.
30   Stalin's Selected Works (I), p. 55.
31   Collected Works of Stalin, 1st Chinese version, vol. 13, p. 271.

in 1938. The People's cultural level had improved significantly. In order to illustrate it, he listed some tables and respectively presented figures in the report. In the table with the title "Rise In the Cultural Level of People", he listed the changes in the total number of students at all levels of schools, the increase in the number of public libraries and the number of books in these libraries' inventories, the rise in the number ofclubs, and the growth in theaters, cinemas, and rural cinemas. The second table was "Schools Established in the Soviet Union between 1933 and 1938". The third table was "Young Specialists Graduating from Higher Educational Institutions". In short, "As regards the cultural standard of the people, the period under review has been marked by a veritable cultural revolution. The introduction of universal compulsory elementary education in the languages of the various nations of the USSR, an increasing number of schools and scholars of all grades, an increasing number of college-trained experts, and the creation and growth of a new intelligentsia, a Soviet intelligentsia—such is the general picture of the cultural advancement of our people."[32]

3. Cultivating a new generation of socialist intellectuals and transforming the main contents of socialist culture

In human history, since the emergence of the division of mental and physical labor, intellectuals, as main bearers of mental work, have played a very important role in human cultural development. Without the participation of intellectuals, the socialist cause cannot achieve victory. Thus, the socialist construction, especially the cultural construction, cannot not be achieved without a new generation of socialist intellectuals.

Stalin discussed the position and the role of intellectuals in the society and analyzed their class nature. He pointed out: "I do not underestimate the role of the intelligentsia; on the contrary, I emphasize it. The question is, however, which intelligentsia are we discussing? Because there are different kinds of intelligentsia."[33] He believed that intellectuals in a class society should be distinguished from intellectuals of a classless society, because in a class society intellectuals served for the ruling class. He made a specific analysis about differentcontexts before and after the revolution. "The intelligentsia has never been a class, and can never be a class—it was and remains a stratum, which recruits its members from all classes of the society. In the old days the intelligentsia recruited its members from the ranks of the nobility, of the bourgeoisie, partly from the ranks of the peasantry, and only to a very inconsiderable extent from the ranks of the workers. In our day, under the Soviets, the intelligentsia recruits its members mainly from the ranks of the workers and peasants. But no matter where it may recruit

32 Stalin's Selected Works (I), p. 234.
33 Ibid., p. 14.

its members, and what character it may bear, the intelligentsia is nevertheless a stratum and not a class."[34] Improving the scientific and cultural level of workers and peasants was consistent with the policy of cultivating a great number of working class intellectuals. Thus communism was gradually resolving the contradiction between mental and physical labor,, greatly improving the cultural and technical level of manual workers. "In reality the elimination of the distinction between mental labour and manual labour can be brought about only by raising the cultural and technical level of the working class to the level of engineers and technical workers. It would be absurd to think that this is unfeasible. It is entirely feasible under the Soviet system…. The young generation of the working class has all the opportunitiesfor comprehensive technical education."[35]

Stalin severely criticized the mistaken view of despising intellectuals and treating them as dissidents. He pointed out that "whether in agriculture or industry, there are countless people willing to get involved in the construction and desire to lead the construction in our country, whereas there are incredibly very few people able to conduct and lead the construction. On the contrary, we are very ignorant in this area. In addition, some people are even determined to praise our illiteracy. If you cannot read or often have wrong spelling and boast of your own backwardness, you are an 'industrial' worker and win honor and respect. If you get rid of uncultured situation and know words and science, you are not one of us and not a worker any more, and you are 'out of' the masses." "I think if we do not eliminate this barbaric and uncivilized thinking phenomenon and the barbaric attitude toward science and cultured people, we cannot step forward. Ifthe working class cannot get rid of the uncultured conditions, if it cannot create its own intellectuals, if it does not master science and is not good at administer the economy based on scientific principles, it will not truly become the master of the country."[36]

With the further development of the Soviet socialist construction, the Soviet Union formed a huge team of socialist intellectuals and a socialist intelligentsia. In his report about the Soviet Constitution in November 1936, Stalin said, "Now, we will start to talk about the problem of intellectuals and the problem of technical workers, cultural workers and all the staff, etc. In the past period, intellectuals of our country also have undergone a tremendous change. They have no longer been stubborn old intellectuals that regard themselves as a supra class but actually serve for landlords and capitalists. Our Soviet intellectuals are entirely new intellectuals that are

---

34 Stalin's Selected Works (I), p. 102.
35 Ibid., p. 48.
36 Selected Works of Stalin (II), p. 40.

closely linked with the working class and peasants."[37] On the one hand, the composition of intellectuals has changed. 80% to 90% Soviet intellectualsare workers, peasants and other laborers. On the other hand, the nature of intellectual activities has changed. "They are now members with equal rights in the Soviet society, where they march forward side by side with workers and peasants to build a new socialist classless society."..."Thus, they are completely new working class intellectuals, who cannot be found in any country in the world."[38] In the summarized report about the work of the Central Committee of the CPSU (Bolshevik) in the 18th Congress of the party, Stalin said that "As a result of all the great cultural work in our country, has emerged and formed a new Soviet intelligentsia involving a large number of people, who come from the working class, peasants and from the ranks of staff in the Soviet Union, and who don't know what shackles of exploitation are. They hate exploiters and are determined to faithfully serve the people of all Soviet nations."[39] "In my opinion, the generation of this new socialist intelligentsia of the people is one of the most important achievements of the Cultural Revolution in our country."

II. Stalin's thought on the cause of developing socialist education

372

1. The importance of socialist educational undertakings

The central task when Stalin came to power was to consolidate the dictatorship of the proletariat and build socialism. In order to consolidate the Soviet socialist state system under the conditions of backward economy and culture, he attached great importance to the issue of education. When talking about the general nature of socialism, he regarded the educational undertakings as one of the necessary conditions to realize socialism, pointing out: the necessary conditions for the realization of the socialist society were sufficiently advanced productive forces, besides the socialist consciousness of the people and people's socialist education.[40] He put the nation-wide literacy level and cultural level as the standards to measure whether the Soviet Republics were well-developed. He emphasized that improving the national cultural level of the all the ethnics was significantly important for the establishment of the party and Soviet organs. He stated: if we aim to transform our republics into advanced ones, i.e. to republics with developed systems, it is necessary to improve people's literacy skills and the cultural

37   Stalin's Selected Works (I), p. 87.
38   Ibid., p. 87.
39   Ibid., p. 236.
40   Collected Works of Stalin, vol. 1, 1st Chinese version, p. 308.

level of the country, then everything else would be easier.[41] In those days the primary task was to train the new socialist industrial leaders with the backgrounds of working class and the general workers and who could also be able to be the political and social leaders.[42] "It is necessary to know that education is a weapon whose effects depend on who hold it in hands and whom it fights for."[43]

2. Launching the plan to eliminate illiteracy and the nation-wide campaign to popularize compulsory education

The Soviet Union at that time was an illiterate and semi-literate country. In order to build socialism and consolidate Soviet governance organs in such a country, to improve the cultural level was the primary task at that time. Stalin initiated a new plan to eliminate illiteracy and a nation-wide education campaign, establish Russian and local literacy committees and mobilize thousands of people to participate in fighting illiteracy. Meanwhile, from the aspect of the consolidating the relations between party, between the Soviet governance organs and the broad masses, Stalin emphasized the need for compulsory education, pointing out that eliminating illiteracy, gradually implementing compulsory education and secondary education for the citizenof republics was the major issue relating to the Soviet regime. He believed that education must be vigorously popularized, because only the popularization of education could block the channels to generate new illiterates, eliminate the source of illiteracy. Stalin said: "Firstly, we should make primary education compulsory for all citizens regardless of ethnics, then comes to secondary education. Obviously, otherwise, any cultural development… is impossible, not to mention the so-called Cultural Revolution. Moreover, if we don't do so, there will be neither real growth in industry and agriculture, nor a reliable national defense."[44]

373

Emphasizing the implementation of primary education and compulsory education was not only a "very significant reform" in the cultural front, but was also a "great victory" in the political and economic front. In Stalin's leadership, both the task of eliminating illiteracy and the literacy education campaign had made great achievements. The nation-wide quality and the level of education had generally improved.

41 The Collected Works of Stalin, vol. 5, 1st Chinese version, p. 268.
42 The Collected Works of Stalin, vol. 12, 1st Chinese version, p. 201.
43 Stalin's Selected Works 1934-1952, p. 22.
44 Collected Works of Stalin, vol. 11, 1st Chinese version, p. 304.

3. Building schools and strengthening the construction of educational bodies

In order to popularize education, Stalin personally instructed the Soviet governmentto issue a decreefor establishing local-regional educational bodies, new schools and which would expand the network of rural schools. During the Stalin era a relatively complete education system was basically formed.

It was also important to identify the status and role of teachers and strengthen the construction of educational bodies. During the period when the Soviet economy was recovered, the CPSU (Bolshevik) attached great importance to the issue of cultivating teachers. The 13th CPSU (Bolshevik) Congress proposed in the resolution of the Final Report on the Central Committee: "All the organizations in the party should pay great attention to the preparatory works of the First Soviet Teachers' Congress, promote the participation of the local rural teachers—to the highest extend—to this Congress" … "We should do our utmost to enable the Congress to practically complete the significant task, it undertakes."[45] Stalin in the his letter to teachers of the 1st Soviet Teachers' Congress explicitly pointed out: "the team of people's teachers is an essential part of the labor force who is building a new life according to the socialist principles."[46] He affirmed that the people's teachers are the laborers of building socialism and affirmed the status and role of the people's teachers in a courteous manner. With his presence, the First Soviet Teachers' Congress was held from January 12 to 17, 1925 in Moscow.

4. Implementing educational reforms

From the 1920s to the 1930s, under Stalin's instructions, the Soviet People's Committee and the CPSU (Bolshevik) had released a series of resolutions to reform the contents of the primary and secondary education. These reforms covered the teaching system, teaching content, teaching methods, the compilation of the textbooks and so on. In his Report Delivered at a Meeting of the Active of the Moscow Organisation of the CPSU(B.), April 13, 1928 in Moscow, Stalin pointed out "our leads and our red experts are not trained well in our higher technical schools", "because they only learn things from books. They are the experts of books but with no practical experience and are divorced form production". The exports we need should be "outstanding not only in theory, but also in actual experience, and in close contacts with production process."[47] In July, CPSU

---

45   Collections of Resolutions of the Soviet Communist Party Congresses, Meetings and the Central Conferances, vol, 3, p. 412.
46   Collected Works of Stalin, vol. 7, 1st Chinese version, p. 5.
47   Selected Works of Stalin, vol. 2, p. 29.

(Bolshevik) adopted the resolution "On the New Task of Improving the Training of New Experts", drew up plans for training experts, expanded the network of schools, institutions of higher education and specialized secondary schools. The resolution included reform plans for the educational system, curriculum and teaching methods of institutions of higher education and plans to improve the social political education among college students. In 1930 and 1932, the CPSU (Bolshevik) adopted "Resolution on Primary and Secondary Schools" and "Resolution on the Teaching Curricula and Systems of Primary and Secondary Schools". Thus started the comprehensive reform in the Soviet educational system, curriculum and teaching systemsaccording to these two resolutions.

5. Efforts to develop education in ethnic minority areas

Before and after the October Socialist Revolution, Stalin was very concerned about the ethnic issues and the education for the ethnic minorities. He systematically discussed the issues of education among ethnicpeoples in several articles such as: *Marxism and National Question, On the Abolition of Ethnic Restrictions, Political Tasks of the University of Orient* and some other articles. He argued: the issue of the education among ethnic people is an important part of the implementation of national equality. He pointed out: "it is a necessary condition to solve the racial issues to implement the ethnic equality in all aspects (language, schools, etc.)"[48]

He believed that the implementation of education for ethnic peoples was the main content of ethnic equality and the implementation of the ethnic equality was a necessary condition to solve the issue of peaceful coexistence and fraternal collaboration of peoples. Rapid training of ethnic minority cadres was one of the tasks of the education for ethnic peoples and one important condition of the establishment of the Soviet Autonomous Republics. He pointed out that "we should rapidly cultivate the cadres with local origin" and "use local people who are familiar with the lifestyle, customs, habits and language of the local inhabitants as much as possible in all Soviet institutions of the border area nations.[49] "All the administrative organs in the border areasnations should be consisted of their own people who understand their language and living habits."[50]

He believed that compulsory education should be implemented in ethnic minority areas and if the communists of the border areas want to eliminate people's ignorance and want to spiritually link the central and border areas of Russia, compulsory education should be implemented there.[51]

48   Selected Works of Stalin, vol. 1, p. 114.
49   Collected Works of Stalin, vol.4, 1st Chinese version, p. 317.
50   Ibid., p. 358.
51   Ibid., p. 317.

He also planned the steps for the popularization of compulsory education in the ethnic minority areas: firstly, "we should make primary education as compulsory education for all citizens regardless of ethnic, and then proceed to secondary education."[52] Schools and ethnic educational institutions should be developed in the ethnic minority areas. "Only complete education can help the highlanders[53] to sustain and reach higher level of culture. This is why they should firstly start from the establishment of schools and cultural and educational institutions in their own autonomous republics."[54] When talking about building schools in the ethnic minority areas, he stressed: "promoting native languages" in lectures given in the University of the Peoples' of the East, and cultivating talentsfrom ethnic minority areas to be employed in the ethnic minority areas, thus strengthen the construction of the ethnic language teaching bodies.

III. Stalin's thought on socialist ideological education work of the whole people

1. Studies on theoretical building of Marxism-Leninism and theoretical education

Marxism is proletariat's scientific world view, the guiding thought of the Marxist proletarian party, and also the theoretical basis and ideological guidance of the socialism thought. The primary task of the socialism thought is to establish a solid foundation for Marxist theory and determine the guiding position of Marxism in the ideological field of superstructure. Thus, we must build the Marxist theory, and also carry out the education of Marxist theoryamong the majority of party cadres and the masses.

Stalin discussed the natural characteristics of Marxism. He scientifically defined Marxism in his book *Marxism and Problems of Linguistics*: "Marxism is a science about the developing laws of nature and society, it is a revolutionary science about the oppressed and exploited masses, is a science about the victory of socialism in all countries and is the science about the construction of communist society."[55] This definition emphasized the scientific nature of Marxism, highlighted the characteristics of Marxism as the proletarian world view and emphasized the status and role of Marxism in the socialist revolution and construction. He then pointed out: "Marxism, the science, cannot be stagnant—it is in continuous

---

52 Collected Works of Stalin, vol. 11, 1st Chinese version, p. 304.
53 Such as Ingush, Ossetian, Chechen Kirgizh, Kabardin, Beslan and Kazakh people.
54 Collected Works of Stalin, vol. 4, 1st Chinese version, p. 358.
55 Stalin's Selected Works (II), p. 559.

development and completion. Marxism in its development can not but is enriched with new practice and new knowledge. Thus, any of its individual formulas and conclusions can not but change over time and replaced by new formulas and new conclusions, thus adapt to new historical tasks. Marxism does not recognize the unchangeable conclusions and formulas which absolutely adapt to all times and periods. Marxism is the enemy of all dogmatism."[56]

Stalin, exposed the characteristics of Leninism (Lenin's thoughts) and expounded the important position of Leninism in the history of the development of Marxism. He was opposed both to parallel Marxism and Leninism or treat them as two things far apart. He said: Such a formulation of the question might lead one to think that Marxism is one thing and Leninism another, that one can be a Leninist without being a Marxist. Such an idea cannot be regarded as correct. Leninism is not Lenin's teaching minus Marxism. Leninism is Marxism of the epoch of imperialism and proletarian revolutions. In other words, Leninism includes all that was taught by Marx plus Lenin's new contribution to the treasury of Marxism, and what necessarily follows from all that was taught by Marx (teaching on the dictatorship of the proletariat, the peasant question, the national question, the Party, the question of the social roots of reformism, the question of the principal deviations in communism, and so forth). It would be better, therefore, to formulate the question in such a way as to speak of Marxism or of Leninism (which fundamentally are the same) and not of Marxism and Leninism.[57]

377

Stalin attached great importance the function of the theory of Marxism, and commented that this scientific theory had great significance in guiding the undertakings of building socialism. He pointed out: "You know that theory, if it is genuine theory, gives practical workers the power of orientation, clarity of perspective, confidence in their work, faith in the victory of our cause. All this is, and necessarily must be, immensely important in our work of socialist construction"[58]. "In the work of any department of the state and the party, the higher the level of political telents and awareness of Marxism-Leninism among the staff, the more efficiency of the work itself and more achievements their work will bring; Conversely, the lower the level of political telent and the awareness of Marxism-Leninism among the staff, the more likely to suffer setbacks and failures, the more likely the staff will corrupt into a vulgar and short-sighted handlers of affairs and the more likely they will degenerate—which is a theorem."[59]

---

56   Ibid.
57   Collected Works of Stalin, vol. 7, 1st Chinese version, p. 204-205.
58   Selected Works of Stalin, vol. 2, p. 210-211.
59   Stalin's Selected Works(I), p. 246-247.

Stalin attached great importance to the building of the Marxism-Leninist research institutions, personally reviewed the compilation and publishing works related to Marxism-Leninism. With the suggestion of Stalin, On May 31, 1924, the Soviet Union established Lenin Institute. In 1930, in order to strengthen the comprehensive study of Marxism-Leninism, the CPSU (Bolshevik) Central Committee decided to unit Marx and Engels Institute and Lenin Institute into Marx Engels and Lenin Institute which was placed under the CPSU (Bolshevik) Publicity Bureau and responsible for compiling and publishing Works of Marx and Engels and Works of Lenin. Works of Marx and Engels and Works of Lenin were reprinted and republished for many times under Stalin's direct supervision, which provided theoretical guarantee for ideological and theoretical building.

In the 5th Congress of the Third International (Comintern) five months after Lenin's death, "Marxism" and "Leninism" were changed to "Marxism-Leninism" for the first time[60]. In the document titled as Outline of the Publicity Work of the Comintern and its Branches adopted before the closing of the Congress on July 8, 1924, it was pointed out that: "One of the principal tasks of the Comintern and its Branches is to turn this advanced theory-Marxism-Leninism to common property of their parties' members." "Making every communist understand significance of mastering Marxist-Leninist theory is the precondition of publicity work."

378

Stalin attached great importance on the theoretical training and education of the party members party and government cadres: "the task of propaganda of the Party and education to cadres with Marxist-Leninist is to help cadres from all sectors master Marxism-Leninism and its scientific theories on the laws of social development."[61] He discussed the issue of the relationship between cadres' professional knowledge learning and learning of the Marxist theory: "the training and formation of our young cadres are usually implemented related to individual professions or related to individual scientific and technological branches, which is necessary and appropriate. A medical expert is not necessary to be a physics expert or an expert in botany at the same time. Or vice versa. However, there is one scientific knowledge which should be learned by Bolsheviks in all the scientific departments. That is they should learn Marxist-Leninist theories on society, laws of social development, laws of development of the proletarian revolution, laws of development of socialist construction and the laws leading to the victory of communism… Instead of being experts in his major science branch, a true Leninist should be a statesman and social activist who is closely

---

60   Here, the term of "Marxism Leninism" should be translated as Marxism-Leninism by literal translation according to Russian or English and other Western language (its Russian is Марксизм ленинизм, English is Marxism Leninism).
61   Stalin's Selected Works (I), p. 247.

concerned with the fate of the country, grasps and is good at applying the laws of social development and actively strives to become an participant in the political leadership. Of course, this is an additional but promising burdenfor a Bolshevik expert."[62]

In order to make a better study of Marxism-Leninism, the 13th CPSU (Bolshevik) Congress passed a resolution, entrusting a task to the Central Committee to take all measures to rapidly publish Works of Marx and Engels, Works of Lenin, Selected Works of Marx and Engels, Selected Works of Lenin andother classicMarxist works. Since then, the CPSU (Bolshevik) Central Committee had paid more attention to the problemsin the publication of the classic works and issued several decrees in this direction.

Stalin attached due importance to the improvement of party's propaganda work and education of party and government, which we can evaluate as a contribution to Marxist Party education theory. The CPSU (Bolshevik) Central Committee had discussed Marxist Party education issues for several times with the participation of the party propagandists from different republics. After the publication of the *Concise Guide to the History of the CPSU (Bolshevik)* in September 1938, the CPSU (Bolshevik) Central Committee developed a well-known resolution, i.e., the "Resolution on the Task of Party's Propaganda Work After The Publication of the Concise Guide to the   379
History of the CPSU (Bolshevik)."

According to this famous resolution and with reference to the famous resolution of on the Shortcomings of the Party's Work of the CPSU (Bolshevik) Central Committee plenum in March 1939, the CPSU (Bolshevik) Central Committee instructed a series of measures to eliminate the shortcomings ofthe task party's propaganda and to improve education to party members and cadres with Marxist-Leninism.The March plenum resolution included the following concrete measures: Centralizing party's propaganda task, thus unifying the previous separate propaganda departments and press work in a unified organ: CPSU (Bolshevik) Central Bureau of Propaganda, secondly, establishing respective centralized propaganda departments in the party structures in each republic and regions. The March resolution argued that the propaganda work in small publicity groups was not correct, but it was appropriate for the individual party members to independently study the basic Marxism-Leninism. Therefore, the party's attention should be on the propaganda of publication and the organization of lectures. It also proposed to start a one-year training course for grass-roots cadres in the center of every republic, a two-year Leninism education for middle-level cadres in some central cities and a three-year Marxism-Leninism education

---

62   Stalin's Selected Works (I), p. 247.

in Moscow for improving those party cadres with higher theoretical level. For propagandists and newspaper staff, the resolution instructed to establish a one-year training course plus a six months review workshop in the Marxism-Leninism College. And the successful trainees would guide the Marxism-Leninism courses to college and university students throughout the country. [63]

2. How to strengthen the socialist ideological and political education?

The ideological and political work, especially the ideological and political education is an important part of the socialist ideological work. In the history of Communist movement, Stalin, for the first time, put forward the concept of "political and ideological work" and made a scientific description of it. He pointed out at the 17th Party Congress in 1934: our tasks in the political and ideological aspect are: firstly, improve the party's theoretical level to a higher level; secondly, strengthen the ideological work in all departments of the party; thirdly, constantly publicize Leninism in the party ranks; fourthly, educate the non-party activists in the party organizations and its surroundings with Lenin's internationalist spirit; fifthly, criticize boldly instead of concealing the tendencies among some comrades who have lost faith in Marxist-Leninism; sixthly, continuously expose the idea and remnant attitude of faction mentality which is hostile to Leninism.[64]

380

Stalin has further developed Lenin's theory of education which includes political, ideological, social and historical spheres. He emphasized the importance of educating broad masses in ideological and political spheres. Lenin, was the first Marxist who clearly expounded the theory of "education", arguing that the socialist political consciousness would not emerge spontaneously in the movements of the working-class, instead it should be educated "from without"..."only from outside their economic struggle, from outside the sphere of relations between workers and employers."

Stalin inherited this theory saying: "it must be spoken out to explain a thought that: the spontaneous workers' movement without socialism is like groping in darkness—even thought they can reach the destination one day, who knows when and how much to suffer. Therefore, socialist consciousness means a lot to the workers' movement."[65]

Stalin wrote: "Lenin's education theory means educating the party with Marxist theories and win broad masses' sympathy to Marxist and socialist theories and ideals."

63 Stalin's Selected Works (I), p. 248-249.
64 Collected Works of Stalin, vol. 13, 1st Chinese version, p. 321.
65 Selected Works of Stalin, vol. 1, p. 28.

When expounding on education Lenin mainly emphasized the role of intellectuals in the creation of socialist theories, whereas Stalin mainly emphasized the role of proletariatin education. He pointed out: "It also must say that the embodiment of the sense—the Social Democratic Party should educate socialism into the workers' movement and lead the movement rather than sitting on the sidelines and lag behind of the spontaneous workers' movement."…"It is the minor group of the Social Democratic intellectuals who support the creation of socialist consciousness, but it is the whole Social Democratic Party who educates socialist consciousness into the workers' movement, thus enables the spontaneous struggle of the proletariat to gain the nature of self-consciousness."[66]

The most important thing in the education of socialist consciousness is the education of socialist ideals. Lenin attached great importance to the education of socialist ideals and made several famous comments on the issue. Stalin also emphasized the education of socialist ideals. He said: "it could be concluded (actually) that the proletariats should improve their thoughts and understandingon their true class interests and the ideal of socialism, on the other side avoid trivializing this ideal or avoid it being affiliated to spontaneous movement. This practical conclusion was built on the theoretical foundation laid by Lenin. As long as we accept the premise of this theory, any contamination by opportunism will be eliminated. The significance of Leninist thought lay here."[67]

The cultivation of socialist consciousness is closely related with the education of collectivism and patriotism. In his interview with British writer-Herbert George Wells, Stalin explained the meaning of collectivism and its relationship with socialism. He pointed out: "there should not be irreconcilable oppositions between the individual and the collective and between individual and collective interests. This is because collectivism and socialism do not deny individual interests, instead it combines individual personal and collective interests. Individual interests can not be excluded from Socialism. Only socialism can fully satisfy individual interests."[68] Evaluating the Great Patriotic War of the Soviet Union, Stalin explained the Soviet patriotism during the War and its relationship with socialism. He believed that patriotism was a huge spiritual force—"the labor contributions in the rear of Soviet fronts, as well as the immortal contributions of our soldiers at the front, has originated from the vibrant Soviet patriotism."He explained that this patriotism was on a new basis which closely combined the interests of working masses and socialism. "The strength of Soviet patriotism lies in that the basis of patriotism is not racial prejudice

66   Selected Works of Stalin, vol.1, p. 28.
67   Collected Works of Stalin, vol.1, 1st Chinese version, p. 48-49.
68   Stalin's Selected Works (I), p. 5.

or ethnic prejudice, but the Soviet people's faith and loyalty to their Soviet motherland and fraternal amity among workers of all nationalities. In this Soviet patriotism, the ethnic traditions of all nations are harmoniously combined with the common vital interests of all the Soviet workers."[69] Aiming at the aggression of the German fascists, he pointed out "the reason why the Russians hate the German invaders, is not because they are from different race, but because they make our people and all freedom-loving people suffer countless disasters and sufferings. There has been a folk saying in our country: 'wolf was not hunted because it's ugly but because it ate sheep.'"[70]

For him, during the whole period of the dictatorship of the proletariat, the cultivation of people's socialist consciousness was to promote a new socialist spirit contrasting and surpassing the old traditional culture. Stalin said: one of party's major tasks during the period of the dictatorship of the proletariat is to carry out the task of transforming the older generations and educating a new generation with the idea of dictatorship of the proletariat and socialist spirit. The legacy of old social habits, customs, traditions and prejudices passed from the old society are the most dangerous enemies of socialism. These traditions and habits control millions of working people, which sometimes overshadow the proletariat and sometimes cause great threat to the existence of the proletariat. Therefore, in order to fight against these old traditions and habits, we must overcome them in all aspects, and educate the new generation with the spirit of proletarian socialism—these are our party's current tasks. The victory of socialism cannot be achieved without implementing these tasks.[71]

Stalin also specially dealt the education of the young people with the spirit of socialism: the mission of the Communist Youth Leagueis to help the party in educating the younger generation with the socialist spirit. As our reserve army formed by the young people, the Communist Youth League supplies and trains young people for other proletarian mass organizations plus for government departments. After the consolidation of the dictatorship of the proletariat, when the proletariat undertakes the task of all round cultural education, the Communist Youth League has a special importance. Stalin attached great importance to cultivating young activists saying; "let the intellectuals in the Communist Youth League play an important role in educating the masses of youth and make young people "cement"close contacts with people." In his speech to the rural activists of Communist Youth League in April 1925, he stated: please ensure that the Communist Youth Leaguewins a large number of young activists from rural areas and educates these activists politically, in order to make them the executives of

69 Stalin's Selected Works (II), p. 395.
70 Ibid., p. 396.
71 Collected Works of Stalin, vol.6, 1st Chinese version, p. 217.

proletarian policies in rural areas and to make them the cement combining the proletariat and the working peasants."[72]

In socialist education, the education for firm faith in the construction of socialism and confidence in the idea that socialism can be definitely established in a single country, was specifically important. After the October Revolution in Russia, the expectations for a victorious workers' revolution in Western Europe did not occur. Then, could socialism be established in a single country which already won victory of the socialist revolution? In those days this question was the general concern inside and outside of the party. Russia could not build socialism without a clear solution to this question. In handling this question, Stalin emphasized the solution: peoples' belief in the victory of socialist construction and elevated this idea to a level of conception. He argued, "capitalists do not only struggle in the economic aspects, but also struggle in the sphere of the proletarian thought, attempt to transmit the thoughts of disbelief in socialist construction and spread doubts related to the future of our socialist construction and aim the most unstable elements in the ranks of our party. It should be pointed out that it is a desperate effort."[73] Thus Stalin criticized Trotsky's theory of "permanent revolution", stating this theory essentially reflected the lack of confidence in Soviet people to build socialism on their own. He wrote: "the source of the theory of "permanent revolution"is the disbelief in the strength and skills of the revolution and of proletariat in our country. Later, in his closing (summary) report to the 18th Congress of the Party, Stalin emphasized: "the essence of this summary report lay in that it proves our socialist construction could achieve success."..."The main conclusion is that the working class in our country has eliminated the phenomenon, the exploitation of man by man, established the socialist system, thus to prove to the whole world the correctness of our cause. This is the main conclusion, because it strengthens the confidence in the strength of the working class and the final victory of the working class."[74]

383

3. Vigilance for textbooks related to the spheres of ideology and social sciences

The social science textbooks in various disciplines play an important role in education, especially political and ideological education. The educational role of the textbooks is universal and systemic. Therefore, the compilation of the textbooks is not only an important part of education but also an important aspect of the work of spreading socialist thoughts. The Central Committee of the CPSU and its main leaders paid attention to the issue of

---

72   Collected Works of Stalin, vol.7, 1st Chinese version, p. 66.
73   Selected Works of Stalin, vol.1, p. 360.
74   Stalin's Selected Works (I), p. 260.

textbook, and even directly involved into and intervened in the compilation of textbooks. Lenin said in 1922: "I do not deny the benefits of the textbook. I said not long ago, it is better for our writers to pay less attention to newspapers and make fewer political noises, but compile textbooks."[75] In the resolutions of the 10th and 11th Congresses, the CPSU (Bolshevik) stressed: "it is necessary to spend all efforts to compile and publish the Marxist textbooks and mobilize and organize our forces to carry out and finalize this task." After the death of Lenin, in Stalin's leadership the compilation of the social science textbook had made great achievements.

In the 1930s, the Supreme Soviet and the CPSU (Bolshevik) CC released a series of resolutions, making special provisions on the teaching curricula and systems in primary and secondary schools as well as in institutions for high education, and on the compilation of textbooks including the teaching of history and geography in primary and secondary schools. From February to March 1937, the CPSU (Bolshevik) Central Committee made the decision to compile the specialized textbooks for each discipline in the social science sphere. In August 1934, Stalin, Zhdanov and Kirov jointly wrote Suggestions on the Textbook of Soviet History. Stalin discussed the meaning of compiling textbooks in this document: "what mentioned here is the compilation of textbooks in which every word and definition should be wrestled, not like the irresponsible articles in the journals or newspapers".[76] He criticized that "the compilers of the Soviet History have blindly copied the ruhsuz trite way and completely unscientific definitions of the bourgeois historians, forgetting that they should teach our youth with Marxism and science-based definitions."[77] Finally, he proposed two principles when compiling the Soviet history textbooks: "the Soviet history textbooks we need are, firstly, the history of the large Russians should not be separated from the history of people from other ethnics of Soviet; secondly, the history of people from all the nationalities of Soviet Union should not be separated from the entire European history and the history of world generally."[78] The next day after writing this opinion, they jointly wrote the Suggestions on the Outline of the Textbook 'Modern History'. The Suggestions was very detailed and it proposed the division of the stages in modern history. It suggested "some appropriate definitions and terminology should be adapted."[79]

Stalin attached great importance to the compilation of the textbook of history of the Soviet Communist Party. In 1931, Stalin once wrote a long letter to the editorial of the journal of Proletarian Revolution on a number

384

75   Collected Works of Lenin, vol.43, Chinese version 2, p. 115-116.
76   Stalin's Selected Works (I), p. 21.
77   Ibid., p. 20.
78   Stalin's Selected Works (I), p. 21.
79   Ibid., p. 23.

of issues of the history of Bolshevism, proposing that the future task of the editorial board was to improve the level pubblications related to the history of the Bolshevik Party to a proper height and take the research on the history of the Bolshevik Party into a scientific track. With impetus of this letter, there were some deeper works on the history of the CPSU (Bolshevik) Party, among which, the *History of the All-Union Communist Party (Bolsheviks), Short Course* which was published in 1938 was the most representative one.

The *History of the All-Union Communist Party (Bolsheviks), Short Course* described the history of the Soviet Communist Party with the Marxist point of view and is known as the encyclopedia of the basic knowledge of Marxism-Leninism. This book was proposed by Stalin and compiled by the CPSU (Bolshevik) Central Committee Ad Hoc Committee. Stalin led the compilation of this book. In his notes to the editors of the textbook of the history of the CPSU (Bolshevik) Party, he analyzed the main reasons why the textbook of the CPSU (Bolshevik) was dissatisfactory. He wrote: the "description of the CPSU (Bolshevik) is not combined with the country's history, only include simple description of historical facts but does not include the Marxist principles". Furthermore, there was a problem of the structure and also problems of division of the stages in history. In response, Stalin made several important suggestions: Firstly, before each chapter, there should be a brief historical introduction of the country's economic and political conditions; secondly, the Marxist principles should be explained when describing the historic facts and struggles. He also prepared an outline according to his understandings related to the division of the stages in history. In particular, he personally wrote a very important chapter, for this book known as *On Dialectical and Historical Materialism*, and reviewed the final version of the entire book.

After the publication of the *History of the All-Union Communist Party (Bolsheviks), Short Course*, the CPSU (Bolshevik) Central Committee made the resolution on how to publicize the *History of the All-Union Communist Party (Bolsheviks), Short Course* after its Publication, regarding the publication of this book was "the biggest event in the life of the Bolshevik party. The book scientifically discussed the history of the Communist Party's, summed up the experiences of the party, was the most important tool to arm the party members with Marxism-Leninist theory and a tool to improve the level of the publicity of the Marxist-Leninism to a high degree. The book offered the party a united understanding on the party's history. It was the crystallization of the CPSU (Bolshevik) Central Committee's explanation on the basic problems of the history of the CPSU (Bolshevik) and history of Marxism-Leninism. It eliminated the harmful phenomenon of publicizing Marxism and Leninism separately and clarified the inseparable unity of the

Marxist and Leninist theories. It narrated the party's history based on the basic thought of Marxist-Leninism and taught Marxism-Leninism on the basis of the historic facts, overcoming the shortcomings of "telling the history of the CPSU (Bolshevik) party based on certain historical figures" in the old textbooks. It had surpassed the simplicity and vulgarity in the interpretations of historic issues. The publication of the *History of the All-Union Communist Party (Bolsheviks), Short Course* had a tremendous impact not only inside of the Soviet party and the country, but also in the world communist movement. It was translated into many languages and studied by Communist Parties in different countries. Communist Parties in many countries had also made decisions on studying the *History of the All-Union Communist Party (Bolsheviks), Short Course*. Communist Party of China used this book as the education material for its cadres. In May 1941, Mao Zedong pointed out in his famous speech "Transforming Our Learning": "the *History of the All-Union Communist Party (Bolsheviks), Short Course* should be taken as the central material in the study of Marxism-Leninism. The *History of the All-Union Communist Party (Bolsheviks), Short Course* has been the highest integration and summary of the world communist movement since a hundred years and it is the only typical combination of theory and practice"[80]

386

The reason Stalin was so strict on the history textbooks was not because he had addiction to history or science, but out of the ideological considerations. History was not just a professional study of this discipline, but also an issue of historical viewpoint. The basic viewpoint of the history and the world history of a single party and a single country plays a decisive role. Therefore, it was not the issue of writing any historical text, but rather the education of the historical viewpoint, for the party and people.

Philosophy textbooks

Philosophy is the core content of Marxist socialism thought. The compilation of the philosophy textbooks is directly related to the elaboration, understanding and education of the Marxist philosophy. The text *On Dialectical and Historical Materialism* in Chapter Four of the *History of the All-Union Communist Party (Bolsheviks), Short Course* written by Stalin systematically and in popular language had elaborated Marx's philosophy for the first time. Later, the book was published as a booklet, becoming a hand book of Marxist philosophy.

Stalin also dealt with the compilation of textbooks in the history of philosophy. There occurred a discussion in the Soviet Union around 1940s on the Vol. 3 of the *History of Philosophy*, Stalin personally participated in this discussion. The *History of Philosophy* was collectively compiled

80   Selected Works of Mao Zedong, vol.3, version 2, (Beijing: People's Publishing House, 1991), 802-803.

by the Institute of Philosophy of the Soviet Academyof Social Sciences. This book systematically exposed the history of philosophy including the Marxist philosophy from aspects of the stand, viewpoint and methodolgy of Marxism. In Vol. 3 of the book on the German classical philosophy, there were some erroneous tendencies, such as ignoring the contradiction between Hegelian progressive dialectic and his whole conservative arbitrary understanding; the limitations of the Hegelian dialectic was also not discussed, and the contradiction between Hegelian idealism and his materialist dialecticswas not emphasized. Also the reactionary nature of the social and political points of view of the German idealist philosophers were not properly discussed, and so on.

The CPSU Central Committee in the resolution on the Shortcomings of the Scientific Work Related to Philosophical Studies criticized the author of the third volume as giving a one-sided, non-Marxist evaluation of German classical philosophy, especially Hegelian philosophy, exaggerating its significance in the history of philosophy. The resolution also decided to revoke the original grant of the Stalin prize for writing of this volume. In addition, in the 1940s, a great discussion on philosophy occurred related to the book, the History of Western Philosophy by Alexanderovski. In June 1947, the CPSU CC authorized the secretary of the Central Committee Andrei Alexandrowitsch Zhdanov to organize the discussion on "History of Western Philosophy". Zhdanov had criticized that the book had deviated-from party's principles, gave much emphasis to the inheritance aspect compared to the the development and sublation aspect in history of philosophical thoughts , and not that the book did not highlighted the significance of great changes occuring in the history of philosophy by the works of Marx and Engels, and so on. Zhdanov also sharply criticized that the scholars of philosophy in the Soviet Union lacked fighting spirit and separated from the realities of the world and Soviet Union. Although there were some serious flaws in this discussion on philosophy, it had a significant positive impact on the development of Soviet philosophy, enabling the scholars of philosophy recognize the problems and overcome dogmatism, escapism and the mistaken attitude of liberalism against negative tendencies. A creative study atmosphere was promoted.

In his later years, Stalin dealt with the compilation of the textbooks on political economy. *The Textbook of Political Economy* compiled by the Institute of Political Economy of the Soviet Academy of Sciences was written by experts under the direct leadership of the Stalin-led CPSU (Bolshevik) CC. In November 1951, the CPSU (Bolshevik) specially organized a discussion participated by hundreds of economists and social scientists in order to assess the draft of this textbook. The participants extensively discussed on the draft and raised suggestions for improvement. Stalin attached great importance to this discussion. After receiving the files of the discussion, he wrote his own opinions on the issues discussed. This was his famous book *Economic Problems of Socialism in the USSR*.

Stalin also made a principled instruction on how to improve the errors of the textbook, omissions and other issues, which greatly improved the content and structure of the textbook.

4. On the role of press in the ideological work

Press is an important medium of mass communication and also an important carrier of thoughts in modern society. Stalin paid great attention to the important role of press in the ideological work. He had personally engaged in the editiorial work of journals and newspapers in his early revolutionary career. Whether in the period of revolutionary struggle against the Tsar or during the period of leading the socialist construction, he had attached great importance to the irreplaceable role of press in publicizing socialist views among the masses and its organizitional role and had offered many valuable suggestions on how to run press well and give full play to the role of press in publicizing and organizing works.

Stalin believed that press had more advantages compared to pamphlets in the aspect of revolutionary propaganda and should be fully utilized.

As early as in September 1901, Stalin in the first issue of the "Struggle" wrote to the editorial department of the newspaper: "the effect of propaganda by theses kind of pamphlets which can only answer some specific questions is very small in most cases. Therefore, it is necessary to establish a publication organ which can answer all the daily questions. This is a well-known truth which does not need us to prove. In Georgia's labor movement, the time of using periodicals as one of the leading means of the revolutionary work has come." [81]

He added: "as the newspaper of the Social Democratic Party organ, it should lead the workers' movement, indicate the road to help them not to make mistakes. In short, the primary responsibility of the newspaper is to get to the masses of the workers as close as possible, try to influence them and consciously make itself the center and leader of the masses of workers."[82]

Stalin analyzed the nature and function of the press. He said, "The press is not a mass institution or organization; however, it establishes a subtle relationship between the Party and the working class. In terms of power, this relationship is no less important than any other mass communication organization. Someone said that the press was the sixth powerful nation. I don't know what exactly this nation is, but it is powerful, without doubt.

---

81   Collected Works of Stalin, vol.1, 1st Chinese version, p. 4-5.
82   Ibid., p. 7.

The press is the most powerful weapon for the Party to deliver its word to the working class every day. No other way can establish the spiritual connection between the Party and classes. No other way can be as flexible as the press."[83] Referring to the press as the "spiritual connection" between the Party and classes was quite vivid and accurate.

Stalin further underlined the significant role of the press as a "collective organizer". He wrote: although its significance in agitation is profound, its role in organization is the most urgent factor in our current party construction work. The point is that we shall not only use the press for agitation and supporting rebellions, but first of all we shall use the press all over the country, and throughout all industrial and agricultural areas, among all the general staff, agency staff, and its correspondents. Therefore, in this way the Party and all industrial and agricultural areas are connected, thereby giving full play to the interactions among the Party and the people in all industrial and agricultural areas.[84]

After the revolution he wrote: "Right now, the urgent task of the press is to make it the collective organizer of the Party and the Soviet regime, and an agent connecting the laboring masses and uniting them around the Party and the Soviet regime."[85] He believed, the press, of course, could carry out some supplementary tasks, "but by no means can we tolerate that the supplementary tasks undermine its main task—its organizational role in the great undertaking: the Party construction and organize the whole people"[86] In March, 1929, Stalin wrote a congratulatory speech for the first issue of Agriculture: "Wish it accomplishments in the development of agriculture and in theoretical research based on Marxism-Leninism."…"Hope that it will become the organizational center for active workers and socialism constructors and lead the arduous undertaking of agricultural socialist transformation in our country."[87]

How to run the press and how to understand its role in the ideological work? This was a question often considered by Stalin. He has many bright expositions in this regard.

Stalin believed the press should aim at realities, rather than abstract theories. In May 1929 he talked about the press coverage about labor competition campaign, saying: "More and more articles and reports about competition appear in our newspapers. People always talk about the philosophy of competition, the roots of competition, and the possible outcomes of competition, etc. However, we rarely see reports that coherently describe how

---

83   Collected Works of Stalin, vol. 5, 1st Chinese version, p. 166.
84   Ibid., p. 230.
85   Ibid., p. 231.
86   Ibid., p. 232.
87   Collected Works of Stalin, vol. 11, 1st Chinese version, p. 285.

the masses compete, what millions of workers experience when they are competing, and how the working masses regard competition as a cause of their immediate concern. However, for us, these very aspects are crucial parts of competition."[88] He also talked about how to run magazines for college students, proposing that magazines should be "close to college students." He said, "Magazines should take attracting proletarian students to participate in the work of the Soviet power and the Communist Party as its basic task. Only when the magazines actually become magazines supported and read by college students can they achieve this goal… College students should realize that it is a magazine of their own."[89] He also mentioned that the political columns in youth journals or newspapers need to explain the fundamental questions about the Party and the Soviet system , instead of repeating words that other magazines have said. Columns such as "College Life", "Literature", "Science and Technology" should be greatly expanded, because these columns are the very places where college students can actively contribute and practice their talents. "Only by getting acceptance among college students can magazines accomplish their tasks and become the real magazine for Soviet college students."[90]

Stalin discussed the style of publicity (propaganda). He believed that newspaper articles should have a militant style. In September 1904 Stalin wrote: "I have read Galyorka's pamphlet Down With Bonapartism. It's not bad. It would have been better had he struck harder and deeper with his hammer. His jocular tone and please for mercy" rob his blows of strength and weight, and spoil the reader's impression. These defects are all the more glaring for the reason that the author evidently understands our position well, and explains and elaborates certain questions excellently. A man who takes up our position must speak with a firm and determined voice. In this respect Lenin is a real mountain eagle."[91]

Stalin also believed that the newspaper articles should be popular. In June 1925, Stalin, Molotov and Andreyev wrote a joint letter to the members of the editorial department of Komsomol Truth, talking about the style of writing. They pointed out that: "To make Komsomol Truth newspaper more popular, contributors are required to write in a simple and precise way and use as few foreign words as possible, as Lenin does. In the last resort, if some foreign words must be used, contributors can attach a mini dictionary of foreign words as a supplement to Komsomol Truth, or at least they can give some proper explanations in the articles."[92]

---

88 Collected Works of Stalin, vol. 12, 1st Chinese version, p. 99-100.
89 Collected Works of Stalin, vol. 7, 1st Chinese version, p. 6.
90 Ibid., p. 7.
91 Collected Works of Stalin, vol. 1, 1st Chinese version, p. 47.
92 Collected Works of Stalin, vol. 7, 1st Chinese version, p. 130.

To make workers and farmers get involved inrunning newspapers is an important idea of Stalin's. He thought, the foremost significance of involving in running newspapers is that it can make newspapers, a sharp weapon of class struggle a weapon that emancipate people. Only by promoting workers' letters, correspondents and farmer correspondents can realize this transformation. Only as an organized power can they play the role of conveying and transmitting the voice of the proletariat as a newspaper, the role of revealing the defects of the Soviet society, and the role of an inexhaustible soldier when improving socialist construction. The fundamental principle is that correspondents should be independent.

Newspapers should be good at criticizing properly and master several different ways of critical activities. In June 1928, Stalin were satisfied that newspapers have made some achievements in criticism. Newspapers had become more active and vigorous in their work. The staff in the press, such as worker correspondents and farmer correspondents had started to become an important political force. "True, our press still continues at times to skate on the surface; it has not yet learned to pass from individual critical remarks to deeper criticism, and from deep criticism to drawing general conclusions from the results of criticism and making plain what achievements have been attained in our constructive work as a resultof criticism. However, it can scarcely be doubted that advances will be made in this field as the campaign goes on."

391

Then he criticized the tendency of criticizing for criticism's sake. He said: "It must be observed, further, that even those organs of the press which, generally speaking, are not devoid of the ability to criticize correctly, that even they are sometimes inclined to criticize for criticism'ssake, turning criticism into a sport, into sensation mongering. Take Komsomolskaya Pravda, for example. Everyone knows the services rendered by KomsomolskayaPravda in stimulating self-criticism. But take the last issues of this paper and look at its "criticism" of the leaders of the All-Union Central Council of Trade Unions—a whole series of impermissible caricatures on the subject. Who, one asks, needs "criticism" of this kind, and what effect can it have except to discredit the slogan of self-criticism?"[93]

Besides newspapers, Stalin also fully evaluated the role of cinema films. He said: "Films are the most important tool for publicity. Our task is to control this undertaking."[94] In his letter to the State Administration of Film Studios, Stalin wrote: "The films that the Soviet power can control are an enormous power." "It is very likely that films can influence the masses spiritually. It helps the working class, the Party, the workers of socialist education to organize the masses to fight for socialism, and improve their

93 Ibid., p. 119.
94 Collected Works of Stalin, vol. 6, 1st Chinese version, p. 191.

level of education and ability for political struggle." "The Soviet regime expect from you to achieve new accomplishments, shoot new films, like Chapaev[95] that extols the great historical events in which Soviet workers and farmers fought for political power. Motivate them to accomplish new tasks, and remember both the past achievements and difficulties during the process of the construction of socialism." In the end, "the Soviet regime hopes your experts probe deeply into the most 'important' aspect (as said by Lenin) and most massive new field of all arts—movies."[96]

5. The work in the literary and artistic field and socialist ideological education

Stalin paid attention to the development dynamics in literary and art circles, considering this work in the literary and artistic fields as an important battle line of socialist ideological education. According to him, literature and art has undoubtful ideological importance and has connections with political life and political sphere. About the ideological and political importance of work in literature and art sphere, he explained them specifically. He believed: For those ideological spheres like literature and art, when one judge their political nature, one should not simply apply some inner-party concepts, such as "left-leaning" or "right-leaning", because literature is not an inner-party phenomenon. Instead, it is a much broader social phenomenon. The political nature of literature and art should not be expressed by class and state concepts."

In 1929 Stalin wrote in a letter: "I think the proposal arguing there are leftists and rightists in literary and artistic circles (including theatrical circles) is incorrect. Now in our country, concepts like 'right-leaning' or 'left-leaning' are only party related. To be exact, they are inner-party concepts. 'Rightists' or 'leftists' are people who deviate from the line of the Party and lean to one side or another. Therefore, too apply these concepts in non-party and wide fields like literature, art and drama will be very weird. It would be plausible if we restrain to use these concepts within some literary and artistic groups we have organized in our party. It is possible that in these groups there are 'rightists' and 'leftists.' But in the current stage of literature and art, if we apply these concepts for various schools even against anti-Soviet and anti-revolutionary literature and art circles, that would reverse everything. If we adopt class concepts like 'Soviet', 'anti-Soviet', 'revolutionary', 'anti-revolutionary' in literature and art circles, that would not be more correct."[97]

---

95   It is a story about Vasily Ivanovich Chapaev (1887-1919), a Red Army commander who became a hero of the Russian Civil War. The plot is based on the novel of the same name by Dmitri Furmanov, a Russian writer and Bolshevik commissar who fought together with Chapaev.
96   Stalin's Selected Works (I), p. 30.
97   Collected Works of Stalin, vol. 11, 1st Chinese version, p. 280

Stalin paid attention to the social and political importance of literature and art sphere. He believed that literary description should reflect the real image of the Soviet society and the Society people. Literature and art should play the role of spreading and protecting the image of the Soviet. Once Stalin wrote a critique to criticize the famous writer Demyan Bedny (Yefim Alekseevich Pridvorov), because he had passed the line when he described the problems of the Soviet society and turned his critic to a slander against the Soviet people. Stalin wrote: "Now the whole world admits that the center of the revolutionary movement has moved from Western Europe to Russia. Filled with hope, revolutionists all over the world look at the Soviet. They take it as the base of liberation of workers all over the world, and admit that it is their only motherland. Revolutionary workers throughout the world unanimously acclaim the Soviet working class. They all hail it as their leader because it implements the most revolutionary and positive policies that proletariats in other countries have always dreamed about. Leaders of revolutionary workers throughout the world are assiduously studying the instructive history of the Russian working class... and you? You didn't try to understand this great process, didn't improve yourself to shoulder the responsibility of extolling the advanced proletariat. Instead, you announced to the whole world: Russia used to be a bottle filled with ugliness and dejectedness; now Russia is a complete backward village. Laziness and desire to stay in the comfort zone are the characteristics of almost all nations of Russia. Therefore, they are also the characteristics of the Russian workers who accomplished the October Revolution. That is your so-called Bolshevik critic! Not at all, respectable comrade Demyan. That is not Bolshevik critic; that is a slander to our people, and an insult to Soviet, to the Soviet proletariat, and to the Russian proletariat."[98]

393

Stalin believed that literature and art should arouse fighting spirit among the people. This will help to reduce the discouraged, the complainants and the suspicious people. As for novels depicting wars, he opposed the exaggeration of 'horror' in the wars. He said: "As for novels depicting wars, they must be seriously chosen before being published. In the book market appear many novels depicting the 'horror' of wars and arousing antipathy against any war (not only imperialist wars, but also any other wars). Those capitalist and pacifist novels are of little value. What we need is not novels that make readers learn about the horror of imperialist wars, but those that can make readers realize we shall bring down the capitalist governments that organize such wars."[99]

---

98   Collected Works of Stalin, vol. 13, 1st Chinese version, p. 24-25.
99   Collected Works of Stalin, vol. 12, 1st Chinese version, p. 154.

As for non-proletarian artistic works, Stalin did not simply prohibit them. Instead, he advocated creating better works which compete against them. He said: "Of course, 'openly criticizing' and prohibiting non-proletariat works is very easy. But the easiest way is not the best. The point does not lie in prohibition, but in that through competition we can create genuine Soviet works, interesting, and full of artistic content, so that those inferior non-proletariat works, including old ones and new ones, will be replaced and squeezed out of the stage. Competition is a major matter, because only through competition can our proletarian literature come into being and get its shape."[100]

The Stalin-led CPSU Central Committee believed that to promote socialist construction, it was necessary to greatly develop the creation of literature and art. In 1930s, the Party Central Committee believed that 'RAPP'[101] was impeding the abundant creation of literature and art. Thus the party had decided to cancel it, establish a unified Soviet Writers' Union, and set up a Communist organizational branch in the Union. This would help the development of Soviet literature and art, plus help that the party leads literature and art.

394

Stalin vigorously supported young writers. He rejected various excuses to suppress their creative enthusiasm. He believed, one shall not be too fastidious towards the young writers' works. Instead, one should judge their value by from their inclination. At that time a youngster called E. Mikulina wrote a pamphlet *Emulation and Labor Enthusiasm of the Masses*. Stalin wrote the preface for the pamphlet . Someone wrote a short critic targeted at the pamphlet, saying that it made some serious mistakes, and 'deceived comrade Stalin,' and should be prohibited from publishing. This matter came to Stalin and he wrote a reply letter. In this letter, Stalin stated: "to evaluate the value of a work, one should focus on its overall inclination rather than some details. He questioned: Can some details determine the value of this pamphlet and neglect its overall inclination? The famous contemporary writer Sholokhov made some serious mistakes in his work *And Quiet Flows the Don* gave some untruthful information about Stepan Astakhov, Aksinia Astakhova and Grigori Panteleevich Melekhov. However, can we conclude that *And Quiet Flows the Don* is a useless book and ban it from publishing? He said, Micoud Lena's *The Competition of the Masses* lied in it transmitted the spirit of competition and touched readers with this spirit. That spirit, though some mistakes, which was the crucial point.

As for the tendency of suppressing young writers, Stalin criticized that severely. He said: "I didn't regret at all for writing the preface for a nameless person's pamphlet... I firmly oppose the tendency of only writing prefaces

100 Collected Works of Stalin, vol. 11, 1st Chinese version, p. 281.
101 RAPP: Russian Association of Proletarian Writers.

for 'eminent' figures in literature."[102] "In our country there are hundreds of thousands of talented youngsters. They spare no efforts to climb up from the bottom in order to contribute to our construction. However, their efforts usually turn out in vain because they are often suppressed by the arrogance of some 'eminent' figures in literature, also by the mercilessness and bureaucracy of some organizations, and the jealousy from their peers which cannot be evaluated as competition). Our task is to tear down this wall, so that countless young writers can have their way out. The reason why I wrote the preface for a nameless writer is to attempt to make some contribution in solving this task."[103] Finally, Stalin said that he did not oppose the critics about the mistakes in Micoud Lena's book, but firmly objected to push this definitely talented writer into an abyss and discourage a talent.

Stalin also wrote a letter to express his opinions about two novels in response to requests. He expressed similar ideas. "I've read both novels: Shooting and A Day of Our Lives. Neither of these two novels contains any 'petty bourgeoisie' or any 'anti-Party' stuff... Admittedly, there are some remains of radicalism of some youth league. Readers without much experience may even believe that it is not the Party that corrects the mistakes of the youth, but the truth is other way around. But it is not this mistake that composes the major features and fundamental essence of these two books. Their fundamental thoughts lie in that they sharply point out the defects in our government offices and they believe that these defects can be corrected. These are their major points and value. This value remarkably overshadows and deeply covers those tiny and, according to me, minor shortcomings."[104]

IV. Lessons of the ideological work to be drawn from the Stalin era

Stalin not only gave us abundant successful experiences in the sphere of ideological work, but also left us some painful lessons. Negative aspects are mainly his personal intervention in academic debates and his tolerance for personality cult. Summarizing these lessons can give us warnings and enable us do a better job in ideological work.

1. Stalin's intervention in the academic field

One feature of the ideological work during Stalin administration was that the Central Committee of CPSU (Bolshevik) or Stalin himself directly got involved or intervened in ideological theoretical studies, literature, art and scientific research activities. The direct involvement of the Central Committee of CPSU (Bolshevik) in academic debates provide any Marxist

395

---

102   Collected Works of Stalin, vol. 12, 1st Chinese version, p. 120.
103   Collected Works of Stalin, vol. 12, 1st Chinese version, p. 103.
104   Ibid., p. 175-176.

ruling party with experience and lessons related to ideological work, namely how to properly deal with the relationship between academic issues and political issues and how to manage the ideological work in socialist countries.

During the late 1920s and early 1930s, among the Soviet philosophy circles underwent a debate between the young philosophers represented by Mitin and on the other side the Deborin school. This debate was caused directly by the speech Stalin delivered in the conference of Marxist experts on agricultural issues. In the speech he criticized that the theoretical study fell behind the practice of socialist construction, and required that theoretical experts should conduct new research on economic and political issues, class issues, speed of construction, and on the policies of the Party based on new demands put forward by practice.

They should form new ideas which can help to get rid of the backward situation that theories could not be successfully applied to practice. The speech evoked strong repercussions in the Soviet theoretical circles. Based on this speech, some scholars Mitin and others put forward critics against the leaders in philosophy circles, saying that they were only indulged in explaining the history of philosophy, and did not delve into the practice of socialist construction, ignored the Leninist party principles, and looked down on the philosophical heritage of Lenin. During the debate, Stalin took the side of the young philosophers. On December 29th, 1930, he conducted a talk with the branch committee of the Party organized in the Red Professor's Institution, commented that the mistake committed by the Deborin School was "Menshevik Idealism." Deborin School was propagating Idealism from the stance of Menshevism and was an idealist revision of Marxism. Stalin instructed to check thoroughly what mechanists, Deborinists and other revisionists were doing, covering all their works, and criticize everything they wrote, and said. This had turned a normal academic debate into a vigorous mass type critical campaign.

In 1940s, Soviet philosophers had some differences and debates on the relationship between Marxism and previous philosophies, and the relationship between Marxism and other specific sciences. The Central Committee of CPSU directly or indirectly intervened in these two discussions. The central administrators responsible from ideological work of the party expressed their opinions about these specific academic questions during the debates and also put forward clear views about some general questions such as the situation and tasks of philosophical battle line, principles of Marxist party, the selection of philosophical topics. Of course, though they had intervened too much their views had generated positive practical impact.

As for the relationship between Marxism and previous philosophical thoughts, it was true that some Soviet philosophers during 1920s to 1940s, especially some veteran philosophers could not evaluate this issue well. The dominant tendency was to exaggerate the significance of some old philosophies, especially the role of Hegel's philosophy in the formation of Marxism, and undermine the revolutionary meaning of Marx's breakthrough in the history of philosophy. The third volume of the text book *History of Philosophy* and later Alexanderlovski's *History of Western Philosophy* published in 1940s were criticized for this approach.

As for the relationship between Marxism and specific sciences, the CPSU (Bolshevik) attached importance to the instructive role of Marxism in specific science spheres. Theoretically speaking, this was doubtfully correct. However, due to some incorrect understandings, it gave rise to a series politically motivated interventions in scientific researches. The Party criticized the so-called "cosmopolitanism" trend in physics research, then criticized the Morgan school in biological genetics, and then criticized cybernetics, which opened all fields of modern natural sciences to vulgar critique. Consequently the once enthusiastic situation in Soviet philosophy circle had disappeared; philosophers' and natural scientists' enthusiasm to think about philosophical questions diminished. The latest scientific researches on latest natural sciences, such as the theory of relativity, quantum mechanics, cosmology and biogenetics was negatively influenced.

Among them biogenetics branch suffered the most: it had received a crushing blow when the party criticized the Mendel-Morgan school. That not only resulted in its stasis for quite a long time, but also made it retrogress to the level back in 19th century. In the debate between the Mendel and Morgan school and Michurin School, Stalin supported Lysenko from the Michurin School who had criticized the Morgan school from the political perspective. Lysenko strongly accused the theories of genetics, and Malthusian population theory, and labeled them as "anti-science and anti-people," "idealist," "agnostic," "reactionary," and "pseudo-science." CPSU Central Committee once published an editorial in its organ, calling all the scientists and theoreticians in the Soviet Union be like Lysenko— "strive for the development of science, for the Soviet Union's prosperity and leading position in science, overcome the hostile influence of the theories of bourgeois reactionary nature and surpass the bourgeois culture." It led to the shutdown of the labs related to Morgan school. The scientific research for theories of genetics and related schooling were prohibited. A group of famous scientist got dismissed or removed from office.

The attitude of CPSU Central Committee and Stalin himself towards these academic debates indicated that, during socialist construction how to properly deal with the relationship between academia and politics is an important issue that needs further exploration. Academia and politics are complicated spheres, no matter themselves or their relationship. On the one

hand, academia and politics are related. Sometimes academia has some political influence, especially when some academic theories of certain social
sciences usually contain some political value, while on the other side the
political situation in the society will definitely influence the development
of the academia. No matter in what kind of society, this risky relation un-
deniably exists, especially in socialist society where the proletarian party
politics has broader implications. A mistaken approach will certainly affect
various fields of the society in different degrees, including literature and art
circles and the whole academic sphere.

We can say it was necessary and inevitable for Stalin led CPSU Central
Committee to pay attention to and lead the debates in literature and art and
academic sphere. On the other hand, academia, is basically different from
politics. They are two different social phenomena with their own rules that
should not be mixed. Academic activities may be influenced by politics, but
it has its own laws. If we follow these rules, it will develop healthily; if we
violate these laws and make it subject to careless political intervention, its
development will be damaged. Therefore, the complexity of the problem
lies in how to properly treat and handle their on the one side related but on
the other side differentiated status. To completely isolate academia from
politics, especially to isolate social subjects and social theoretical research
from social politics, will be incorrect and unrealistic. But if we simply
equate them and handle academic questions in the way we handle political
questions, it will be a serious mistake.

What forms should the leading and guidance of literature and art and
academia take, and how to lead literature and art and academia according
to their own laws is the key point. In this aspect, Stalin and CPSU Central
Committee took the simplest from—to intervene directly into debates of literature and art and academia. The common practice was that when the debate rose to a certain degree or took certain "longer" period, CPSU Central
Committee would make a finalizing judgment, or Stalin himself would propose his "authoritative" views, made a clear-cut verdict on the debate and
criticized the "wrong side" severely along with starting administrative measures. action. Of course this approach would influence literature and art and
academia strongly and directly. We can say this intervention did exert some
positive influence. It indeed gave a clear direction to academic research of
social sciences and creation of literature and art, and could quickly correct
the error of orientation. Moreover, the general policy direction that Stalin
and the CPSU (Bolshevik) had given in many cases were basically correct.
They were all intended to make academic research and literature and art
creation adhere to the leading position of Marxism-Leninism, and to make
them combine with the socialist construction and serve it. However, it is
also obvious that using such simple and rough ways to influence and guide

theoretical circles and literature and art circles had apparent negative side effects and severe sequel.

The major consequence of political intervention of academic debates was that the enthusiasm of the intellectuals was pushed down, especially their enthusiasm for creation. Due to improper critique of academic spheres and using political criteria to judge a certain academic school or trend of thought, the atmosphere of free debate had gradually disappeared while dogmatism, subjectivism prevailed, resulting in adverse consequences such as rigid thinking, and academic stagnation. The characteristic of intellectual activities is that creators should have relatively high autonomy and freedom of creation. If they are worried about making political mistakes all the time, and dare not explore boldly in theoretical research, it will lead to the stagnation of theoretical research. This phenomenon itself was a disaster in ideological sphere. Ideology, as a system of values, has its stability, but the vitality of ideology is that it itself encounters changes with the development of social life. Adherence to basic stuff does not mean a simple repetition of the well-known past conclusions. If we use an excessive, exaggerated and even far-fetched approach to check the political problems in the academia and literature and art, noacademic work or literature or art would be tolareted. The life of academia and literature and art will perish.

Meanwhile, the government's direct involvement and intervention into literary and artistic creation and academic debates will easily lead to an atmosphere that is not conducive to academic research and literary creation in the society. That is to say, it will also negatively effect the whole society, making people treat academic questions and literary creation questions with narrow political point of views. As a result, a surveillance and a negative vigilance will be shaped among the people and in the society, which will suppress intellectuals. Moreover, taking the people as the referee for judgment is usually harsher and less tolerant for academic innovation. Once such an atmosphere is formed in the society, academic research and literary creation will be even more difficult. Even if any concrete intervention by the CPSU Central Committee and Stalin might be minor, the stress and negative vigilance spontaneously formed in the whole society, its pressure will inevitably be much more higher.

If we carefully review some critique cases in the ideological sphere in the Soviet Union, they were not directly put forward by Stalin or CPSU Central Committee. Instead, some critiques were initiated by lower level researchers or observers in the society who spontaneously complained aiming certain scholars and even doing that exaggeratedly. Essentially such criticism had emerged from the society and spread everywhere. Sometimes these complaints went so far that Stalin had to speak out for the writer or creator to ensure that they were politically correct. Stalin had also criticized people who made groundless accusation about theories or literary works with political motives and protected some young writers. However, we can also ask isn't this problem of exaggerating academic questions originated from Stalin's political intervention in the academia?

2. Tolerance for personality cult in the ideological work

The most prominent characteristic of Stalin administration was the prevalence of personality cult. All the publications and all propaganda materials were filled with extolments to Stalin. The ideological system then existed in the Soviet Union was deeply marked by the personality cult of Stalin. Personality cult without doubt was an important thing related to certain ideas.prevalent among the people. Although fundamentally speaking it was a problem related to the party's leadership system, a problem of organizational principles (policies) implemented by the party, it primarily was caused by that some powers of the Party was too concentrated in the hands of an individual. Meanwhile, it was also a problem related to certain ideas believed by people, a major force that widely and deeply influenced great majority of people's mind in a certain period of time. On the other side if we study Stalin's ideological theories and practice without dealing with the issue of personality cult, one cannot comprehensively and profoundly understand the ideology of the society in that period.

It is obvious that the personality cult around Stalin exerted negative influences on the ideological spheres of the Soviet society. In this period flooded with personal cult, not only zeal and motivation but also ignorance and illiteracy prevailed. Ignorance in such a big country like the Soviet Union, caused that a person's wisdom replace the wisdom of millions of people. Stalin had become the highest authority of ideology then. If any society forms an environment or mechanism making all minds, especially those able minds stop thinking and blindly follow a person's thinking, then the society would become more and more ignorant. No one will say the words that the leader didn't say nor write those sentences that the leader didn't write, while the words the leader said have to be said thousands of times and his sentences in a document will be written thousands of times. This would definitely turn a society into one where all minds will stagnate.

Personality cult phenomenon in the socialist society's ideological sphere or in the forms of consciousness in a socialist society is not just a peripheral or secondary element, but an inherent factor related to people's conviction. Faith is the core of ideology; communist faith is the core of socialist ideology. Therefore we can say, actually, the personality cult around Stalin by people was a form of people's communist faith. As the leader of the proletariat, the leader of socialism, Stalin had become a symbol of that faith. Such form of worship was interwoven with the people's faith in Communism, of course, had inevitably caused harm to communist faith itself, lowered the grade of this high faith, and turned it into idolatry. But the dangers threating the communist faith usually manifest themselves in an indirect even in opposite forms rather than in a direct and obvious way. People may not feel or realize such negative impacts, but will recognize them afterwards. During the formation and development of personality cult, it may happen that: people's personality cult towards the leader of the revolution largely strengthened their faith in Communism. Unprecedented enthusiasm and energy can be mobilized, thereby people feeling the happiness of success. But it was at that very period that people were so intoxicated and indulged that they overlooked the potential dangerous factors in that zealous faith.

Personality cult was a common phenomenon not only in the Soviet Union but also in a group of other socialist countries then. The prevalence of this common phenomenon of course does not equal to its rationality, but at least it indicates that such phenomenon was not accidental, and personal factor cannot explain it completely. In fact, the respect and worship for the leader of the revolution arises inevitably from a massive real foundation, which to some extent inevitably manifests itself in ideological life of socialist parties and socialist societies. The socialist revolution and socialist construction requires a strong socialist ideology, which not only is based on the theoretical findings of Marxism, but also based on the faith in socialism and communist values, the pursuit for socialist goals, based on rational belief in the leaders leading the process, and the trust and worship for these leaders. Of course, the trust and worship for these leaders do not equal to personality cult. But personality cult also contains the trust and worship for the socialist leaders. There is no impassable chasm between the latter and the former. In fact, under historic circumstance then, generally this transition or confusion has happened. Leaders consciously or unconsciously became a symbol of the socialist ideology. Thus the image of leaders and the language of leaders became indispensable factors of the socialist ideology. Once, Stalin was quarrelling with his son, he shouted: "Who do you think you are? You think you are Stalin?" "Do you think I am Stalin?" "No!" And he pointed to the picture of Stalin on the wall, "He is Stalin." The reasons why leaders have tolerated that worship cannot merely attributed to self-intoxication or self-need. It is also related to that they subjectively wanted to protect people's faith in socialism, and to protect socialist ideology.

We must analyze the impact of personality cult to communist faith historically, concretely and specifically. We cannot cancel or ignore the positive influence of personality cult at that historic period and people's enthusiasm for all things. Personality cult is indeed incorrect, especially when judged from today's perspective. However it did exist in history. If through it people strengthened their faith in Communism and became communist sacrifiers in their behaviors, we should study this issue starting from facts rather than basing ourselves on abstract theories. When the Bolshevik veterans resisted against the aggressive enemies utilizing slogans "For Stalin!" could we say they were victims of personality cult ignoring that they were real communist militants? Could we criticize Stalin for his personality cult mistake and close our eyes to that truth, the Soviet people's faith in Communism in Stalin's era? If we evaluate the issue historically, I think we cannot draw such a conclusion.

Today, we should adopt a historical and fully analytical attitude when evaluating and observing the phenomenon of personality cult in the Soviet Union and in some other socialist countries and its impacts. On the one hand, we should start from the basic Marxist point of view thus firmly deny the personality cult phenomenon, recognize the harm that personality cult brings about, and summarize the lessons. On the other hand, we have to get rid of emotional evaluations towards personality cult, thus historically and specifically reveal the roots of the formation and development of personality cult, analyze the role that personality cult played in ideological sphere and its specific working mechanism. Only with such an approach can we truly understand and avoid the negative impact of personality cult to the ideological construction.

Chapter XI

Stalin's Thoughts on
World Economic and Political Relations

The economic and political configuration of the world is a complex and a vast sphere of study which covers extremely rich contents, extremely broad field and a variety of subjects. Lenin, in the study of monopoly capitalism, had made a scientific study on the relationship between imperialism and the colonies in the early 20th century and wrote his well known work in which he also analyzed the relationship between the world economy and politics—Imperialism, the Highest Stage of Capitalism. Stalin developed Lenin's ideas, in the new conditions and made various new analyses on the major basic contradictions in in the the world economy and world politics, i.e. the contradiction between imperialism and the colonies, on the internal contradictions possessed by the capitalist countries and the contradiction between capitalism and socialism. The "Center" and the "Periphery" conflict in the World Economic and Political System.

It was Stalin who firstly explicitly catogorized the relationship between the developed capitalist countries and the colonies in the structure of the world economy and politics as the relationship between the "center" and the "periphery". The "center" refers to the "European capitalism" while the "periphery" refers to the "colonies that the European capitalism relied on."[1] The relationship between the "center" and the "periphery" means the relationship of plunder and being plundered in economic sphere and the relationship between crisis and revolution in the relation between the European capitalism and its colonies. Stalin analyzed the relationship between the "center" and the "periphery" on the basis of his analysis on the internal and external contradictions of imperialism and according to the facts of the development and changes in the relationship between the world economy and politics during 1920s to 1950s.

1   Collected Works of Stalin, vol. 10, 1st Chinese version, p.185.

I. "Center" and "periphery" in world economic and political relations

As early as in the mid-1800s, Marx had already studied capitalism as a world system when investigating the capitalist production relations. He argued that when destroying the colonies and their social economic pattern which was the combination of small farming and the cottage industry the capitalist countries were mandatorily making them the countries of raw materials and their product markets, forming a "global capitalist system with as the result of large machined factory system which became dominant" in order to "make part of the earth to become a major agricultural area to serve the other part which mainly engaged in industrial production."[2] Obviously, the "part mainly engaged in industrial production" became the "center" in the capitalist world system at that time while the other "part which mainly engaged in agricultural production" became the "periphery", and the relationship between them was mainly demonstrated as "serving" and "being served", i.e. the relationship of "exploiter" and other "being exploited".

In the period from the late 19th to the early 20th century, the "free" competitive capitalism rapidly developed into monopoly capitalism and capitalism became the global system where a few "advanced" countries practiced colonial oppression and the financial yoke on most of the backward countries and nations. At this time, Lenin explicitly divided the various nations in era of imperialism into oppressing nations and oppressed nations and divided the whole world into two categories: one was a small number of countries exploiting and oppressing other people; the other one was the large number of weak colonial countries and nations. Obviously, the former was the "center" in the capitalist world system while the latter was the "periphery". Lenin did not use the terms of "center" and the "periphery", but he made in-depth analysis of the antagonistic basic pattern consisting of the "center" consisting of small number of developed capitalist countries and the "periphery" with large number of developing nations as the basic relationship in the world economy and politics and also revealed the law that the development of capitalism was uneven in different capitalist countries.[3]

Stalin inherited and developed Marx's and Lenin's ideas, specifically termed the relation between European capitalism and the colonies in the the world economic and political system in the early 20th century as the relations between the "center" and the "periphery." On November 5, 1927, he commented on the political relationship between Europe and the colonies in his talk with the workers' representatives from Germany, France, Austria and other countries. He said: "What are Europe and the colonies? They are

---

2 Collected Works of Marx and Engels, vol. 23, 1st Chinese version, pp.494-495.
3 Collected Works of Lenin, vol. 28, 2nd Chinese version, p.88.

the center and the periphery of the capitalist system. The center of Europe is 'restless' and its periphery is more 'restless.'[4] Stalin, in his other writings and talks, made several arguments on this basic pattern the contradictions inherent in imperialism—the world system.

Stalin's analysis on the contradiction between the "center" and the "periphery" was based on the analysis of the internal contradictions of imperialism. In Stalin's view, there were two main internal contradictions in imperialism: One was the internal contradictions of the capitalist countries, i.e. "the contradiction between labor and capital"; the other was the contradictions between different capitalist groups and between the various capitalist states (countries). "The contradiction between labor and capital" demonstrated itself as working class using various means and forces to fight against the "monopolistic trusts, syndicates, banks and financial oligarchs in the industrialized countries". Stalin argued that in this struggle, the common means adopted by the working class, such as the trade unions, the cooperatives, supporting political parties in the parliaments and parliamentary struggle, and so forth, had become completely inadequate, and the working class should pick up the new weapon: the revolution. The sharpening of the contradiction between the domestic laboring class in the capitalist countries and the capitalist class leads the working class to a revolution. The contradiction between the capitalist groups and between the various capitalist countries referred to the contradictions when the various financial groups and imperialist powers were competing for raw materials and fighting for other countries' territories. Stalin pointed out: "Imperialism is the export of capital to the sources of raw materials, the frenzied struggle for monopolist possession of these sources, the struggle for a re-division of the already divided world, a struggle waged with particular fury by new financial groups and powers seeking a "place in the sun" against the old groups and powers, which cling tenaciously to what they have seized. This frenzied struggle among the various groups of capitalists is notable in that it includes as an inevitable element imperialist wars, wars for the annexation of foreign territory. This circumstance, in its turn, is notable in that it leads to the mutual weakening of the imperialists, to the weakening of the position of capitalism in general, to the acceleration of the advent of the proletarian revolution and to the practical necessity of this revolution."[5]

Stalin further analyzed the contradiction between the "center" and the "periphery" based on the analysis of the internal contradictions of imperialism, i.e., the contradiction between the developed capitalist countries and the colonies. He summed up this contradiction as between "a very small number of dominant 'civilized' nations and more than a billion people in

4   Collected Works of Stalin, vol. 10, 1st Chinese version, p.185.
5   Collected Works of Stalin, vol. 6, 1st Chinese version, p.65.

the colonies as well as the dependencies", regarding the nature of the contradiction was that "imperialism is implementing the most shameless exploitation and the most cruel oppression to more than a billion people in the very large number of colonies and the dependencies. The purpose of such exploitation and oppression is extracting excess profits." The result of the development of this contradiction must be "the emergence of proletarian class, the generation of local intellectuals, the awakening of national consciousness and the strengthening of the liberation movement." "The growth of the revolutionary movement in all colonies and dependent countries without exception clearly testifies to this fact. This circumstance is of importance for the proletariat inasmuch as it saps radically the position of capitalism by converting the colonies and dependent countries from reserves of imperialism into reserves of the proletarian revolution."[6]

Stalin's analysis on the "center" and the "periphery" shows very clearly that imperialism not only made the proletarian revolution an inevitable practical problem but also established the advanced conditions to direct attack capitalism. This analysis explicitly pointed out to the main contradiction of that era in the relationship between the world economy and politics, which offered a strong ideological weapon for the proletariats in the colonies and the dependencies to understand the situation and fight for their liberation.

406   The existence and development of the "center" and the "periphery" phenomenon in the world's economic and and political configuration in the era of imperialism clearly demonstrated itself as a turbulent era. "Turbulence" was the general characteristics of the era of imperialism, but there was also relatively stable periods during its generally turbulent development. This relatively stable periods of capitalism did not mean imperialism got stronger but instead it proceeded to a more serious disorder. This meants Stalin analyzed the changes in the world's economic and and political configuration and changes in the pattern of the "center" and the "periphery" from the perspective of relative stability of the capitalist system in the 1920s.

In December 1925, Stalin made analysis on the development of capitalism in his political report to the 14th CPSU (Bolshevik) Congress, arguing that capitalism had already got rid of the post-war chaos and crisis in trade, production and finance. But the Bolshevik Party termed this new situation as "the local stability or the temporary stability". Stalin interpreted this formulation. He pointed out: "Production in all the advanced countries of Europe is either making progress compared with 1919, It is growing, reached in some places 80-90 per cent of the pre-war level, or is keeping on one level. Only in Britain are there some branches of production which have not yet straightened themselves out. In the main, if we take Europe as

---

6 Ibid., p.66.

a whole, production and trade are making progress, although they have not yet reached the prewar level. If we take the production of grain, we find that Britain has reached 80-85 per cent of the pre-war level, France 83 per cent, and Germany 68 per cent. In Germany, the production of grain is rising very slowly. In France it is not rising, and in Britain it is sinking. All this is compensated for by imports of grain from America. Coal output in Britain in 1925 amounts to 90 per cent of the pre-war level, in France to 107 per cent of the pre-war level, in Germany to 93 per cent. Steel production in Britain amounts to 98 per cent of the pre-war level, in France to 102 per cent, in Germany to 78 per cent. Consumption of raw cotton in Britain is equal to 82 per cent of the pre-war level, in France to 83 per cent, in Germany to 81 per cent. Britain's foreign trade shows an unfavourable balance and amounts to 94 per cent of pre-war; that of Germany is slightly higher than in 1919 and also shows an unfavourable balance; that of France is now higher than the pre-war level—102 per cent. The level of European trade as a whole, taking 1921, was 63 per cent of the pre-war level, but now, in 1925, it has reached 82 per cent of that level. The budgets of these countries balance in one way or another, but the balance is obtained by imposing a frightful burden of taxation upon the population. There is a fluctuation in the currency in some countries, but, in general, the former chaos we saw cannot be observed."[7]

We can understand that the relative stability of capitalism referred by Stalin was the recovery and development of the capitalist production and trade as well as the consolidation of the bourgeois regimes to some extent.

The rise and establishment of USA as a world economic power center Stalin studies the change in the pattern of the "center" and the "periphery" in his analysis on the pattern of the capitalist world economy and politics. Firstly, he explained the shift of the "center", when arguing the reasons for the relatively stable situation of capitalism. He believed that: The centre of financial power in the capitalist world, the centre of the financial exploitation of the whole world, has shifted from Europe to America. Formerly, France, Germany and Britain usually formed the centre of the financial exploitation of the world.That cannot be said now without special reservations. Now, the centre of the financial exploitation of the world is mainly the United States of America. That country is growing in every respect: as regards production, as regards trade, and as regards accumulation."[8]

Stalin used some data to prove his view. "The output of food has exceeded the pre-war level and has reached 104% of the pre-war level in the U.S. Although the output of coal is only 90% of the pre-war level, there is a large amount of oil production and reserves. He has to been pointed out that the output of oil had seen 70% increase. The output of steel has increased

7   Ibid., p.220.
8   Collected Works of Stalin, vol. 7, 1st Chinese version, p.221.

to 147% which is 47% higher than the pre-war level". "Depending on the output to the European countries, there is a huge trade surplus in the foreign trade which has reached 143% of the pre-war level. About 5 billion portion of the total 9 billion gold reserves are in the US. The North America's currency is the world's most stable one. The US is the only country whose ratio of the capital export is growing. The exports by Germany and France is very small and Britain has greatly reduced its capital exports."[9] Europe has purchased her temporary stability at the price of financial subordination to America, which is leading to a colossal increase in the burden of taxation, to the inevitable deterioration of the conditions of the workers, and to the revolutionisation of the European countries; secondly, because of a number of other reasons—about which I will speak later—that make the present stabilisation undurable, unstable"

The cost of temporary and relative stability of the capitalist world was "their subordination to the US capital and the Western European countries' financial subjection to the US The debts by Western European countries to US reached 26 billion rubles, indicating that relying on the capital inflows from the US (partially from the UK), the European countries have gained ground to a certain extent."[10]

Secondly, Stalin also explained the growth of revolutionary elements in the "periphery" of the world to illustrate "instability" factors.

That meant the "instability" elements had nurtured in the internal landscape of the capitalist countries. Stalin also believed that the attacks to the relative stability of capitalism was not only the Western European countries' financial subjection to the US" not only based on the domestic factors, but also by the world-wide factors, i.e. "their stepping up the oppression and exploitation aiming colonies and dependencies" would inevitably increase the crisis and revolutionary movements in those countries[11] and this would negatively affecting the relative stability of capitalism.

In addition, through his analysis on the shift "center" in the relationship between the capitalist world economy and politics, Stalin further explained potential risks capitalism faced and the "unstable" factors threating relative stability. He said: the number of the main countries in the exploitative world had narrowed to the extreme. Previously, the main exploiters were Britain, France, Germany and some others including the U.S., and now, it was narrower. The world's major financial and political exploiters and world's major creditors were the US, other areas where it controlled including its main supporter was the UK. Thus, although European countries still continued to exploit their colonies, on the other side they were

408

9   Ibid., pp.221-222.
10   Ibid., p.222.
11   Ibid., p.224.

financially dominated and exploited by the US. In this sense, the world's major exploiters reduced but the countries exploited had increased, which was bound to intensify the contradictions of the capitalist world system and create a strong blow on the stability of capitalism. Looking from the perspective of the development of the contradiction between the "center" and the "periphery", the capitalist world demonstrated some major facts: the development and growth of the industry and proletariat in the colonies, the overall improvement of the level of national culture and the increase in the number of intellectuals in colonies, the growth of the national revolutionary movements in the colonies, the general crisis of imperialism, the liberation struggle against the British imperialism in India and Egypt, the liberation struggle against the French imperialism in Syria and Morocco and so on. Based on these facts, Stalin concluded: "The current powers are facing the risk of losing their main backyard—the colonies. This was another factor threating thee consolidation of stability. Some undeveloped regions ...have begun to enter direct combat with imperialism. And imperialism cannot comfortably overwhelm and suppress its own colonies."[12]

Stalin's analysis on the dual pattern of "center" and "periphery" in the relationship between the capitalist world economy and politics, as well as the analysis of the "instability" factors in the capitalist system plus the change in the appearance of the contradiction between the "center" and the "periphery" still bears important theoretical significance for our discussion on today's capitalist world pattern.

II. Capitalism and socialism in world economic and political relations

For Stalin, in the world's economic and political configuration existed the "central" and "peripheral" divide and secondly another worldwide pattern as contradiction between two different social systems—capitalism and socialism. The contest between capitalism and socialism reflected itself in economic, political and cultural fields. Stalin made detailed analysis on this issue. Although some of his ideas had defects, generally speaking, his analysis still provides some valuable references for our understanding of the relationship between capitalism and socialism.

---

12 Collected Works of Stalin, vol.7, 1st Chinese version, p.224.

1. Stalin on the contradiction and opposition between capitalism and socialism

After the October Revolution in Russia, the socialist construction in the Soviet Union had made bright achievements when the capitalist world was plagued with crises and almost stuck in a desperate situation. With the overall economy continuing to grow, people's living standards were rapidly rising and the former agricultural country was transforming to an industrial country within a short period, Soviet Union became the world's first socialist country which was able to compete with capitalist countries. Repeated crises of capitalism and successive victories of socialism fully revelaed the contradiction and opposition between the two different social systems. It was in such a historical condition that Stalin began his study on the pattern of capitalism and socialism divide in the world's economic and political configuration.

An unprecedented severe crisis broke out in the capitalist world in 1929, which gave a heavy blow to the capitalist economy and intensified various contradictions in the capitalist world. Contrastingly the socialist construction was vigorously developing in the Soviet Union. In the political report of the 16th Congress of the CPSU (Bolshevik), Stalin analyzed the plight in the capitalist world and the prosperity in the socialist Soviet Union, and revealed the contradiction and opposition between capitalism and socialism. Stalin held that the capitalist economic crisis which broke out in 1929 was a crisis of overproduction. The crisis had two important features: First, it was worldwide. The reason why the economic crisis was "the world's general crisis is that it has influenced all or almost all industrial countries and even including France which kept stealing war compensation of several-billion-Marks from Germany into its own economy was not able to escape from economic depression... It is the world's general crisis, also because industrial and agricultural crises occur simultaneously, and the agricultural crisis has now spread to raw materials and food production in major agricultural countries."[13] Second, the development of the general crisis was uneven. "Although it is universal, the time and the depth in which it hits different countries vary."[14] The industrial crisis began in countries like Poland, and it took one year to spread to other countries; the agricultural crisis had the earliest obvious sign in countries such as Canada, the United States and Argentina, and the industrial crisis had occurred later; different countries went through different degrees of the crisis.

410

---

13 Collected Works of Stalin, 1st Chinese version, vol. 12, pp.209-210.
14 Ibid., 210.

The reason why the capitalist economic crisis presented features of universality and its uneven development occurred in special historical conditions. Below are the four areas analyzed by Stalin. First, the crisis severely hit major capitalist countries and the bastions of capitalism—the United States possessing no less than half of the world's production and consumption, had greatly expanded the scope and extent of the impact of the crisis. Second, in the process of the expansion of the economic crisis, the industrial crisis of major capitalist countries and the agricultural crisis of agricultural countries not only occurred simultaneously, but had intertwined with each other, effecting the entire economy. Third, the development of capitalism into the monopoly capitalism determined that the monopoly capitalism would inevitably impose economic losses for the majority of working people, so that the crisis spread deeper. Fourth, the economic crisis of capitalism would develop further on the basis of the general crisis of capitalism. The general crisis of capitalism had started as early as imperialist wars, and which had undermined the foundation of capitalism and promoted the emergence of the economic crisis. "The general crisis of capitalism" mentioned by Stalin here is what he explained in his Economic Problems of Socialism in the USSR.

It is the general crisis of the world's capitalist system and it includes both the overall economic crisis and the overall political crisis."[15]

Based on his analysis on the depth and formation of the capitalist economic crisis, Stalin uncovered the opposition between capitalism and socialism first from the perspective of the plight of capitalism and the advantages of the Soviet Union. In his view, the First World War and the capitalist economic crisis had promoted the decadence of capitalism and undermined its balance, and capitalism was not the only and all-inclusive world economy any longer. In addition to the capitalist economic system, there was a new socialist economic system which was growing in prosperity and which confronted the capitalist economic system, and its existence pointed to the decadence of capitalism and shook its foundation. Besides, it also undermined the bases of imperialism in colonial and dependent countries; imperialism was losing its prestige in these countries. Imperialism could not impose whatever it wanted against colonies. That was because in colonies and dependent countries was emerging a younger capitalism of their own, which could effectively compete with old capitalist countries. This fact has intensified and complicated the fight for sales markets. From the point of view of capitalist countries themselves, "War has left a heavy negative legacy in most of the capitalist countries—enterprises are often working under capacity and unemployed labor reserves has changed into millions of unemployed people forming a standing army of the unemployed. All

---

15   Stalin's Selected Works (II), p.616.

these caused deliver many difficulties for capitalism before the 1929 crisis, and were bound to complicate the situation."[16] Thus, in Stalin's view, the outbreak of the 1929 capitalist economic crisis had increased the economic power of socialism and deepened the antagonism between capitalism and socialism while destroying the basis of the world's capitalist system.

Next, analyzing the contradiction between capitalism and socialism, Stalin revealed the appearances of this opposition. He pointed out that the 1929 capitalist economic crisis not only intensified various conflicts in capitalist system, but also sharpened the contradiction between the capitalist world and the Soviet Union. This contradiction was between the entire capitalism and those countries under socialist construction. "Whenever conflicts in capitalism began to become more acute, the bourgeoisie turned their attention to the Soviet Union to see if a conflict or all conflicts could be resolved by toppling Soviet Union"[17], because the bourgeois feared that the existence of the Soviet would revolutionize the working class and colonies and the influence of capitalism would be reduced further. The result was bound to deepen the opposition between capitalism and socialism. This opposition was further deepened by the effect of "two contrary trends": one was "capitalist countries implement the policy of destroying economic links between them and the Soviet Union, and starting provocative attacks against the Soviet Union, and openly and covertly prepare for armed intervention against it"; the other was "workers in capitalist countries sympathize and lend support for the Soviet Union, and plus economic strength and political power of the Soviet Union was growing, and its military defense force getting strengthened, and the Soviet state was consistently implementing the policy of peace."[18]

Before World War II, Stalin's analysis on capitalism and socialism as two opposing social systems from the perspective of economic and political status of the current world capitalism was of great significance for guiding economically and culturally backward countries to fight for the victory of the socialist revolution and take the socialist road. However, Stalin had a one-sided view of this opposition, he misunderstood the relationship between capitalism and socialism, namely ignoring their long term coexistence and mutual need. Related to this error since the second half of the 1930s, he had developed a strong view that the Soviet Union was able to solely rely on itself in areas such as technology and human resources, and had begun to diminish links with capitalist countries, which caused a slower economic development in the Soviet.

412

16   Collected Works of Stalin, 1st Chinese version, vol. 12, p.217.
17   Collected Works of Stalin, 1st Chinese version, vol. 12, p.223.
18   Ibid., p.224.

2. Stalin's ideas on the formation of two parallel opposing world markets

After World War II, the world's economic and political configuration underwent dramatic changes. First, when fascist Germany, Italy and Japan suffered serious defeat and the old imperialist countries like Britain and France were greatly weakened, economic, political and military power of the United States were greatly enhanced. The United States became the dominator of the world. Second, after 20-odd years of fast development, the international status of the socialist Soviet Union was greatly improved, and its political influence and military strength were enormously enhanced. The success of China's revolution and the establishment of the people's democratic systems in a series of countries in Eastern Europe caused socialism to become a world system and form a powerful socialist camp by breaking through the range of a single country. Third, the birth of a range of socialist countries set an attractive example for the revolutionary struggle of oppressed people in colonial, semi-colonial and dependent countries. Both movements of national liberation and national independence have flourished, and the imperialist colonial system had collapsed. The world's economic and political development in the early post-war period has formed the US-led capitalist camp and the Soviet-led socialist camp. The opposition between these two camps was the major feature of the world's economic and political configuration after the war. Stalin was inspired by this new developments, and formed the theory of two parallel opposing world markets in Economic Problems of Socialism in the USSR. Stalin held that after World War II: "The economic result caused by the existence of two opposing camps is that the unified and all-encompassing world market has collapsed. Therefore, there are now two parallel and also opposing world markets"[19], which were respectively the capitalist world market and the socialist world market. The two main reasons for the formation of two parallel and opposing world markets are: First, the US-led imperialist countries impose economic blockade on socialist countries. The United States, Britain and France contribute to the formation and consolidation of the new parallel world markets, and of course, it was not out of their intentions. They imposed economic blockade on the Soviet Union, China and people's democracy countries in Europe that did not join the "Marshall Plan", in order to stifle them. In fact, instead of obeying them, this new (socialist) market was consolidated.[20] Second, socialist countries set up cooperative relations. After the war, socialist countries "join hands together in economy, and establish economic cooperation and mutual assistance. The cooperation has shown that no capitalist country can provide people's democracy countries

413

---

19   Stalin's Selected Works (II), p.594.
20   Ibid., p.594.

with real and qualified help like the Soviet Union. The problem is that not only this help is extremely inexpensive and technically first-class, but also this cooperation is based on the mutual help and a sincere desire to achieve common economic upsurge. As a result, these countries can have a high speed of industrial development. We can say with confidence that at such a speed of industrial development, these countries will have no need to import goods from capitalist countries and also will feel necessary to export their surplus goods to other countries."[21]

Based on the above analysis, Stalin further claimed that the existence of two parallel opposing world markets definitely brought about the following new phenomena: the range of the world's resources fought for by major capitalist countries had narrowed expanded rather than expanded; conditions of the world market for major capitalist countries were deteriorated rather than conducive; under capacity production status in the enterprises of these countries increased rather than reduced. Therefore, Stalin put forward two questions when discussing with economists: One was "Can we assert that the well-known argument which Stalin put forward before World War II, that is, the argument of a relatively stable markets in the general crisis of capitalism, is still valid?" The other was "Can we assert that the well-known argument which Lenin proposed in the spring of 1916, that is, the argument that 'capitalism, on the whole, develops more rapidly than before' though it decays, is this argument still valid?" His answer to both questions was "due to the new conditions produced by World War II, these two arguments are supposed to be invalid."[22] The negative answer to the two questions made by Stalin not only abandoned his right judgment of "relative stability" of capitalism before the war, but also denied Lenin's view that capitalism developed faster than before. Stalin's new view denied the historical materialistic view that the relations of production in monopoly capitalism on the one side gain some factors which can adapt to the development requirements of productive forces, while on the other side they still possess some elements which are incompatible with and hinder the development of productive forces. It deviated from the fact that monopoly capitalism was developing after the war.

Finally, Stalin concluded that "When the world market has been divided and the range of world's resources that major capitalist countries (US, Britain and France) fight for has begun to narrow, the economic development cycle of capitalism—the increases and decreases in production—will definitely exist. However, the production growth in these countries will be realized on the basis of continuing reduction, because their production will continue to fall."[23]

414

21   Ibid., pp.594-595.
22   Ibid., p.595.
23   Stalin's Selected Works (II), p.615.

Stalin's statement about the two parallel opposing markets objectively reflects the basic pattern of two major different social systems of capitalism and socialism in the world's economic and political configuration in the early post-war period, and fully affirms the necessity and importance of economic and technological exchanges and trade among socialist countries. In one sense, his theory was a new development of Lenin's principle of peaceful coexistence and policy of opening up. However, judging from the other conclusion by him Stalin one-sidedly opposed socialism and capitalism and lacked the understanding of the long-term coexistence of two major social systems of socialism and the capitalism worldwide, so he separated the unified world market possessing organic economic relations and simply combined his the two parallel economies/markets concept to the political pattern of two opposing camps. Stalin's understanding of this theory gave rise to the unilateral opening up practices in the socialist practice which artificially restricted the opening up of socialist countries only within the socialist camp and weakened their exchanges and cooperation with capitalist countries in economic, technological and trading spheres. It was bound to negatively affect the global socialist development and negatively affect the world peace and human progress. The socialist construction of the Soviet Union during 1927-45 was carried out exactly when it was isolated from the world market, the overall process of the world's economic development, and isolated from the general process of development occurring in the world's science and technology and human civilization. Thus, the Soviet Union in the later decades, due to its practice led by this theory—without being able to reform its closed model—has lagged behind the world levels in economic and technical aspects for a long time and lost the momentum of development.

415

3. Stalin's discussion on basic economic laws of the two different social systems

In the 1920s, many scholars in the Soviet academia believed that economic laws only existed in the capitalist society, and economic laws disappeared with the demise of the capitalist society, and there were no economic laws in the socialist society; in the 1940s, scholars had a new understanding of the nature of economic laws and began to admit the objective nature of the socialist economic laws, but they mixed state policies, plans and economic laws. In the conference about economic issues held by the CPSU Central Committee in the early 1950s, some people still denied the objective nature of economic laws, and held that history gave a special role to Soviet government and they and their leaders could abolish, formulate, create and transform economic laws, which was endorsed by the majority of debaters. About these views on the nature of economic laws in the Soviet academia, Stalin clearly pointed out that economic laws, as well as the laws of natural sciences, are objective. They are objective laws that reflect the process of economic development, they do not change according to people's will.[24] However, the economic laws had characteristics different from natural laws: "One of the distinguishing features of political economy is that its laws, unlike those of natural science, are impermanent, that they, or at least the majority of them, operate for a definite historical period, after which they give place to new laws. However, these laws are not abolished, but lose their validity owing to the new economic conditions and depart from the scene in order to give place to new laws, laws which are not created by the will of man, but which arise from the new economic conditions."[25]

As for the application of economic laws, Stalin thought there was a class interest background in a class society, because "in the natural sciences sphere discovery and application of new laws are more or less smooth. But different from that, in the field of economics, the discovery and application of the new laws that will violate the interests of the descending social force faces extremely strong resistance from this social force."[26]

Stalin emphasized that in addition to their objectivity, economic laws can be discovered and known. People can find economic laws, know them, rely on them, and use them to serve the society's interests, shift the destructive effects of certain economic laws to another direction, limit their influences in a certain range, and give full play or open room to other beneficial and effective laws. But economic laws cannot be created or eliminated, nor can they be changed. If we deny the objectivity of economic laws in socialism, and think the Soviet regime is omnipotent can manage everything, we will fall into chaos and contingency. That idea is not conducive to social development.

Based on the analysis above, Stalin further discussed the basic economic laws in different social systems, analyzed the most fundamental economic relations in the society, and explained the antagonism between capitalism and socialism in terms of fundamental economic laws.

Stalin argued that the characteristics of the basic economic laws of capitalism indicated: "The basic economic laws of capitalism are such laws that they do not determine a certain aspect or certain process of capitalist production, but determine every major aspect and process in the development of capitalist production. They determine the essence and nature of capitalist

416

---

24   Stalin's Selected Works (II), p.573.
25   Ibid.
26   Ibid., p.575.

production."[27] The law of value, law of competition and the anarchic state of production, the law of uneven and combined development, and the law of average rate of profit are not basic economic laws of capitalism, because they only reflect a certain aspect of capitalism "Most appropriate to the concept of a basic economic law of capitalism is the law of surplus value, the law of the origin and growth of capitalist profit. It really does determine the basic features of capitalist production. But the law of surplus value is too general a law; it does not cover the highest rate of profit, the securing of which is a condition for the development of monopoly capitalism. In order to fill this hiatus, the law of surplus value must be made more concrete and developed further in adaptation to the conditions of monopoly capitalism, at the same time bearing in mind that monopoly capitalism demands not any sort of profit, but precisely the maximum profit. That will be the basic economic law of modern capitalism."[28]

Therefore, the major characteristics and requirements of the basic economic laws of today's capitalism can be expressed as below: "to guarantee the maximum capitalist profits by exploiting the majority of the population, making them broke and poor, enslaving and plundering people of other nations, especially the ones of backward countries, using wars that ensure maximum of profits and militarizing their national economies."[29]

From Stalin's statements about the basic economic laws of capitalism, we can see that they are closely connected with the temel principal contradiction that exists and plays role in capitalist society. There are three major principal contradictions in the world of capitalism: the contradiction between the proletariat and the bourgeoisie, the one between imperialism and colonies and dependent countries. The main root why the big imperial powers have contradictions with each other is that they all want to maximize their own profits. Within the range of a single country, the bourgeoisies all want to exploit and oppress the proletariat; worldwide speaking, the monopoly bourgeoisies in imperialist countries all want to exploit and oppress the proletariat in backward countries. Stalin regarded this as "one of the meanings" of the basic economic laws of capitalism, and gave one example of "many startling examples" to explain the relationship between the basic economic laws of capitalism and contradictions of the capitalist world.[30] He pointed out that capitalists in capitalist society are not only standard-bearers of advanced technology, not only revolutionists related to production technologies, but they are also the opponents of advanced technology. How can we explain that? "That can only be explained by the

417

27   Ibid., pp.599-600.
28   Stalin's Selected Works (II), p.600.
29   Ibid., p.601.
30   Ibid., p.601.

basic economic laws of modern capitalism, i.e. with the necessity of acquiring maximum profits. When new technology signals maximum profits to capitalism, capitalism will advocate new technology; when new technology no longer signals maximum profits, capitalism opposes new technology and turns to conventional manual labor."[31] Thus Stalin distinguished the major characteristics and requirements of the basic economic laws of capitalism in different periods according to different stages of capitalism, and explained the emergence and development of the principal contradiction in capitalist society from the aspect of basic social economic relations.

Besides by thoroughly analyzing the basic economic laws of capitalism, Stalin expounded the basic economic laws of socialism. He believed that unlike those of the basic economic laws of capitalism, the major characteristics and requirements of the basic economic laws of socialism can be expressed as below: To meet the constantly rising material and social and cultural needs of the society as much as possible by constantly increasing and perfecting socialist production with advanced technology.[32] Therefore, the antagonism between the basic economic laws of socialism and those of capitalism manifest themselves as: socialism is to meet the constantly rising material and social and cultural needs of the society as much as possible rather than to seek maximum profits; socialism does not have an intermittent production pattern in which economy waxes and wines, but has an ever-increasing production pattern; in socialism, production does not suffer from periodic intermittent state of technology development brought by destruction of social production, but keeps perfecting itself based on highly advanced technology. Stalin also criticized the mistaken view which considered "the economy developing according to certain plans and certain proportions" can be included in the basic economic law of socialism. He pointed out that: "If we only highlight the development of economy developing in a planned manner, on the other side not clear about the aim or goal of the economy, then the proportional development of national economy and planned development of the national economy, such a law cannot produce any positive effects. The law that national economy should develop in a planned manner will produce due (positive) effects only when national economy is managed for a certain task. To argue for such a law: "national economy should develop in a planned manner" if we formulate this law in such a wording, then the task of the economy will be ignored This task of the economic development is contained only in the basic economic laws of socialism as I have mentioned above... Therefore, only when the law that national economy should develop in a planned manner, is in accordance with the basic economic laws of socialism, it can play its role properly."[33]

31   Ibid., p.602.
32   Ibid., p.602.
33   Ibid., pp.602-603.

418

Stalin's statements on the antagonism between capitalism and socialism related to basic economic laws can be evaluated as are a major contribution to Marxist economics.

4. About the economic relationship between socialism and capitalism

Ever since the beginning socialist construction in Soviet Union, it was faced with the issue whether to interact economically with capitalist countries or not. Based on his thought that "the entire political, economic and spiritual life of human race is becoming more and more international under capitalism" Stalin added: "socialism will make them completely international," Thus, Stalin argued for the inevitability of developing an economic relations with capitalist countries for the benefit of Soviet Union.

Back in 1921, when Stalin explained how CPSU (Bolshevik) could promote socialist economic construction he had emphasized the necessity and inevitability of developing economic relations with capitalist countries. He pointed out: "First, Russia is an economically backward country. If it does not exchange its raw materials for western countries' machines and equipment, it will be very difficult to organize transportation, develop industry and electrify both urban and rural areas on its own. Second, until now Russia is a socialist island surrounded by some hostile capitalist countries which have advanced industry. If next to Russia are an industry-developed Soviet (socialist) power or some Soviet powers, it would be easy to establish co-operative relationships with these countries, we can exchange our raw materials with machines and equipment with them. However, the case today is not like that, so before proletarian revolution gains victory in one or several industrialized capitalist countries, Soviet Russia and its leading party have to find a way to establish economic co-operation with western capitalist groups that are hostile against us, thus we can obtain necessary technology and equipment. Concession system and foreign trade are means to achieve this goal. If not, it will be difficult to achieve crucial accomplishments in economic construction and our electrification plan."[34] Stalin also clearly realized that this process was "difficult and painful".

In April 1923, in "National Factors in Party and State Affairs" a draft Stalin presented to CPSU (Bolshevik) Congress, discussed and approved by the 12th Congress of CPSU (Bolshevik) and the Central Committee, Stalin further argued that it was an inevitable trend to have economic interactions with different countries worldwide. He argued that more than a century ago in the development of capitalism appeared the trend of internationalizing of economic activities. The last one hundred years of capitalist development

---

34 Collected Works of Stalin, vol. 5, 1st Chinese version, p.87.

witnessed the intensification of this trend, "and with the link of international division of labor and interdependence growing in all aspects, various different nations are connected with each other."[35] This process reflected the vigorous development of capitalist productive forces, promoted the elimination of barriers among different nations and alleviate conflict interests among different nations, all these prepared the material basis necessary for the future socialist economy worldwide. Stalin clearly argued that all these were " progressive processes." Therefore, in this world wide trend in which all countries of the world are developing their economy, socialist countries by no means can stand alone "isolated" and reject mutual relations among different countries. Therefore Soviet Union needed to develop economic relations with capitalist countries, just like those capitalist countries which needed to strengthen their international economic exchanges, this is determined by the internationalization of economic life.

Later, in the practice of Soviet Union's socialist construction, aiming those people who were confused on this issue Stalin clearly pointed out: "It cannot be more stupid to think that socialist economy is a thing that is totally isolated and independent from other economies."[36] According to Stalin, that socialist Soviet should develop economic relations with capitalist countries is not determined by any subjective wish, he added "this is a necessity and there is no other alternative". It is an objective process determined by the laws of general human society and laws of economic development. To ignore this objective process and imagine a socialist construction, isolated and outside world economy would be to forsake socialism and ruin socialism. Stalin also explained the necessity of having mutual relationships from another aspect: "capitalist countries need to have economic exchanges with socialist countries". He added: "We receive credits from German capitalists. But we receive them not because of our bright eyes, but because the capitalist countries need our oil, our grain and our market for the disposal of their machinery. It must not be forgotten that our country constitutes one-sixth of the world, that it constitutes a huge market, and the capitalist countries cannot manage without some connection or other with our market. All this means that the capitalist countries depend upon our economy. The dependence is mutual."[37] Therefore, Soviet Union should work on this "need" of them and develop socialism through exchanges with capitalism.

Apparently, Stalin's statements about the necessity and inevitability developing economic relations with capitalism were made under the circumstances when Soviet Union was seriously surrounded by capitalist countries and when there was no other socialist country in the world, yet. But many

420

---

35   Ibid., p.149.
36   Collected Works of Stalin, vol. 9, 1st Chinese version, p.118.
37   Collected Works of Stalin, vol. 9, 1st Chinese version, pp.117-118.

recent researches suggest that he only considered this necessity as a temporary need and did not realize that the development of the economic relations with capitalist countries should be a long-term basic policy for socialist countries.

When discussing the economic relations between socialism and capitalism Stalin compared the relationship between the concept of "dependency" and "independence." He commented: ""dependency" refers to the mutual interdependence of economies of different countries"…"But this dependence is mutual. Not only does our economy depend upon the capitalist countries, but the capitalist countries, too, depend upon our economy, upon our oil, our grain, our timber and, lastly, our boundless market."

"Can we argue that there will be no export or import in a socialist economy? Is it possible that there will be no import of products that we don't have, or there is no export of our home products? No, we cannot reject all these. And how can we evaluate this export or import? They are manifestations that some countries rely on some other countries. They are manifestations of economic interdependence."[38] "Independency" means that a country enjoys autonomy when managing its own economy in the development of world economy. But every country, as an independent economic unit, needs economic exchanges with other countries. The dependency among countries and the independency of a country should be separately analyzed. In reality, that a country depends on other countries' economies does not mean it has no independency of its own, it does not mean that it has lost its independency, nor does it mean that it will become "a little screw" of international capitalism. Moreover, Stalin commented: "A distinction must be drawn between the dependence of some countries on others and the economic independence of these countries Denying the absolute independence of individual national economic units does not mean, …denying the economic independence of these units."[39] Stalin clearly stated that in the economic exchanges with capitalist world, Soviet Union should rely on the development of its domestic markets, rely on the optimal relation between its domestic industry and agriculture. Only by enhancing its independence could the Soviet Union avoid to become a screw in the system of capitalist development, or float in the orbit of capitalist development, and avoid to become an economic appendage for the development of world capitalism.

However, Stalin was not completely clear on the above concept of "independence." He tended to understand it as economic self-sufficiency or self-contained, and aimed to become independent of capitalist states. Accordingly, Soviet Union of those days had to import equipment, in order to cease to do that in the future, in the lon run it should be independent

421

---

38   Ibid., p.118.
39   Ibid., p.119.

economically and technologically. As a result, influenced by this thought, when Soviet Union's technological level and machinery & equipment were greatly improved, the Soviet academic community generally believed that the Soviet Union had become an economically independent country, that it already had all the necessary technical equipment for its own economy and national defense.

Stalin's ideas on the relation between world economy and politics had greatly promoted the development of the socialist Soviet Union, and left a valuable heritage. However, his theories on this issue had some limitations, which signals the need for further and deeper studies on the on the issue of relations between the world economy and development of socialism.

Chapter XII

Stalin's Theory and Practice on the International Communist Movement

After the death of Lenin, Stalin assumed the leadership of the CPSU (Bolshevik) and also practically became the leader of the international communist movement. Due to the huge reputation of the Soviet Union as the world's first socialist country and due to the special status of the CPSU (Bolsheviks) in the Communist International which began in 1919, Stalin's thought and theories have influenced and even dominated the entire route and policy of the international communist movement. Throughout this period of the international communist movement, we can see, on the one hand, the indelible historic achievements of Stalin and the Communist International led by him in the spreading of Marxism-Leninism, the struggles against all kinds of opportunism and against "left-wing infantilism" and the purification of the ranks of the proletarian revolution. Plus these achievements include helping or leading communists of many countries to establish and strengthen their proletarian revolutionary parties; includes supporting the revolutionary struggle of the workers of capitalist countries and supporting people's struggles for national independence and liberation movements in the colonial and semi-colonial countries and saving of human civilization in the world-wide anti-fascist struggle.

On the other hand, we should also see that there was a obvious "left" dogmatism which existed in the activities of the Communist International and activities of other communist Parties guided and effected by Stalin's leadership, especially in the mid-Communist International period. This "left" dogmatism trend highlighted in the following areas: Firstly, Stalin underestimated the potentials of the development capability of capitalism and its ability of self-regulation, was over optimistic when evaluating the situation of the world revolution and committed "left" adventurist or offensive errors when designing the revolutionary strategy; secondly, he advocated a high degree of centralization of decision power within the Communist International activities system, thereby stifling the national parties' independence and creativity; thirdly, he underestimated the impact of the Social Democratic Party among the working classes and adopted closed-doorism and sectarianism in the implementation of the revolutionary united front policies and in the relations between us and the social democratic parties of the world. History has proven that these "left" errors mainly led by him have caused heavy losses to the international communist movement.

We should treat the theory and practice of Stalin's international communist movement dialectically. Totally positive or negative evaluation would be unrealistic and worthless. Evaluating form the aspect of their consequences we should admit that besides positive impacts significant negative impacts are in no way can ve ignored. To sum up the historical experiences and to learn lessons, this chapter focuses on the analysis of Stalin's mistakes related to above issues

I. Erroneous judgment of the revolutionary situation and the implementation of the "left"-leaning political line of rushing ahead

According to Marxism, designing the strategies of the proletarian revolutionary struggle need to take mainly the objective analysis of the developing trend of the capitalism as the premise. In other words, only the scientific assessment of the objective situation of the capitalist countries and the whole world can we work out the correct strategy of the revolutionary struggle. However, in the process of the designing the changes of the national policies of the local communist parties and the Communist International, Stalin made obvious mistakes in the judgment of the international situation, especially his "third period theory"[1] which completely divorced from the realities and changes of the objective situation. And the "offensive strategy" drawn up accordingly caused serious damage to revolutions in other nations.

The proletarian revolution broke out in many European countries which were inspired by the victory of the October Revolution. At the same time, those oppressed nations of the Oriental countries saw a new upsurge in the national liberation struggles against imperialism. During that period, the leaders of the communist parties all over the world, including Lenin, held

---

1   The third period theory was promulgated at the 6th World Congress of the Communist International.

extremely optimistic attitude or ideas towards the victory of the world socialist revolution, regarding that the world capitalism was facing a general
deep crisis, thus the conditions of the world proletarian socialist revolution
was mature, estimating "the international world revolution is approaching
and will outbreak within days"[2], and believing the establishment of an international Soviet republic was not far off and Europe would become the
communist Europe. Therefore, the Communist International called all the
communists to start an offensive against the bourgeoisie, mobilizing workers, called all the communists to seize power and establish the dictatorship
of the proletariat.

However, from the fall of 1920 to the spring of 1921, the international
situation had undergone major changes. The proletarian revolution had
changed towards the low ebb, while the bourgeoisie was using the opportunity to the take the initiative of offense. In autumn 1920, the movement of
the Italian proletariat's occupation of the factories failed; In March 1921,
German parties suffered a setback in the offensive March Action Event,
thousands of workers were jailed, and tens of thousands fired and black-
listed, so did the struggle of the British miners. Meanwhile, the post-war
economies of the capitalist countries were reviving. In this situation, Lenin
assessed the situation and realized that the European proletariat could not
achieve quick victories, and the Soviet Russia surrounded by capitalism
better should follow peaceful coexistence strategy against the major capitalist countries. Based on this, Lenin advocated in the 3rd Party Congress of
the Comintern to abandon the "left" mistaken "offensive strategy." On the
4th Congress in October 1922, the idea of world revolution was no longer
regarded as realistic and the strategy was changed.

But Stalin, plus the leaders of the Communist International and the leaders of the local communist parties were neither completely freed from the
"left" dogmatism nor gave up the illusion that "the world revolution will
win quickly". They believed that the stability of capitalism was only temporary and the climax of the revolutionary wave would come very soon.
Therefore, the strategies to guide the revolutionary activity were still keen
to be offensive. Between September and October 1923, in the meeting
which discussed the situation on the German revolution of the Communist
International Executive Committee, Stalin had advocated that the turning
point in the development course of the German revolution had arrived,
the conditions for victory were becoming ripe, and called the German
Communist Party and the left wing Social Democrats to seize the power
immediately and establish a united coalition government. Stalin, at that
time, expected the establishment of Soviet power in Germany, thought that

2   Collected Works of Lenin, vol. 48, Chinese version 2, p.359, Beijing: People's Publishing
House, 1987.

the character of the German revolution was socialist and needs the dictatorship of the proletariat. He pointed out in the letter appointed by the "Red Banner Newspaper"—the German communists' central organic newspaper that the outbreak of revolution in Germany would be the most important world event. The victory of the German revolution would have more significant impacts on the European and American proletariats than the victory of the Russian revolution achieved six years ago. The victory of the Russian Revolution would definitely turn the center of the world revolution to Berlin from Moscow. However, these optimistic estimates did not match the situation in Germany and these optimistic estimates had exaggerated the degree of maturity of the revolutionary situation and underestimated the power of the enemy, which caused heavy losses for the revolution. After the failure of the German revolution, Stalin and other Communist International leaders did not seriously learn from its practice but attributed the failure to the betrayal of the social democrats and the "right" opportunism among the communist ranks, thus continued to follow or went further with their "left" dogmatic guiding line when applying Marxist theories.

In 1927, Stalin made an over-optimistic estimate related to the revolutionary situation. On August 1, 1927, Stalin declared in the speech of "International Situation and the Defense of the Soviet Union": "the crisis and the extinction of the capitalism are brewing up from the maturity and stability of capitalism."[3] He criticized Zinoviev saying: Zinoviev thinks that once there is stabilization, the cause of the revolution is lost. He does not understand that the crisis of capitalism and the preparation for its doom grow as a result of stabilization. In his view, the relative stability of capitalism which started by the mid-1920s had begun to collapse. On November 5, 1927, Stalin, when receiving a delegation of foreign workers said that the conditions for a new leap of revolution were ripe and there were a series of signs which prove an upsurge of a new revolution wave. At the 15th Congress of the CPSU (Bolshevik), Stalin mentioned a lot of events which he thought undoubtedly indicated that Europe was entering into a new period of revolutionary upsurge. These events included: "the general strike and the miners' strike in Britain, the revolutionary activity of Vienna workers; the revolutionary demonstrations in France and Germany due to the murder of Sacco and Vanzetti; the success of the election campaign of German and Polish Communist Party; the obvious differentiation that is taking place in the British working-class movement, whereby the workers are moving to the Left while the leaders are moving to the Right, into the camp of avowed social-imperialism, the degeneration of the Second International into a direct appendage of the imperialist League of Nations, the decline of the prestige of the Social-Democratic parties among the broad masses

---

3   Collected Works of Stalin, vol. 10, Chinese version 1, p.45.

of the working class, the universal growth of the influence and prestige of the Comintern and its sections among the proletarians in all countries, the growth of the prestige of the USSR among the oppressed classes all over the world, the "Congress of the Friends of the USSR."

In short, the "stability tends to collapse, the anti-colonial revolutionary movements increase and the sign of new revolutionary upsurge emerges in Europe"[4] Stalin thus asserted: "We are at the eve of a new revolutionary upsurge both in the colonies and the metropolises of the world (both in the center and periphery). Stabilisation is giving rise to a new revolutionary upsurge."[5]

Stalin also made a new estimation related to the situation in the capitalist countries that the growth of production and productive forces, the expansion of the world trade and the improvement of the industrial technologies did not indicate the stability of capitalism but rather indicated the increasing of the crisis of capitalism. Stalin said: "capitalism might reach the prewar level, might exceed that pre-war level, might rationalize its production, but that this did not mean—did not by a long way mean—that the stabilization of capitalism could as a result become firm, that capitalism could recover its former, pre-war stability. On the contrary, this very stabilization, the fact that production is growing, that trade is growing, that technical progress and production potentialities are increasing, whereas the world market, the limits of that market, and the spheres of influence of the individual imperialist groups, remain more or less stable—precisely this is giving rise to a most profound and acute crisis of world capitalism, a crisis which is fraught with new wars and which threatens the existence of any stabilization at all."

427

Thus, Stalin drew the conclusion that this period of partial instability would lead to the full instability of capitalism which was moribund and decadent.

Bukharin and Stalin differed in the assessment of the situation. As one main leader of the Communist International, Bukharin had made a different estimate in the draft outline of the "International Situation and the Task for the Communist International" submitted to the 6th Congress of the Communist International in 1928. He believed there was no new phenomenon indicating that the capitalism is shaking, and on the contrary, "capitalism was reconstructing itself and was maintaining itself more or less securely." He also stressed that it was not correct to evaluate the capitalism and the general crisis of the capitalist system superficially: "I think the following ideas are mistaken that the capitalism is collapsing in all the countries, or in most capitalist countries." Bukharin did not agree with Stalin's prediction that the capitalist world was giving birth to a new revolutionary

---

4   Collected Works of Stalin, vol. 10, Chinese version 1, p.247.
5   Ibid., p.243.

upsurge. He believed that the revolutionary situation had shifted directly to the periphery areas to the East and the colonies. The internal contradictions of the capitalist system were acute which demonstrated themselves by the strong shaking of capitalism in the periphery areas of the world. However, Bukharin's observation and views were regarded as Hilferding's view of "the recovery of the capitalism" or "possibility of organized capitalism" by Stalin.[6] Therefore, according to Stalin, "the delegation of the CPSU (Bolshevik) was obliged to introduce about twenty amendments to the theses" put forth by Bukharin."[7]

Later, the resolution agreed in the 6th Congress of the Communist International according to Stalin's thoughts which he had advocated since the 5th Congress. The resolution defined the period of capitalism as "the Third Period", i.e. the period when a new revolutionary upsurge was coming and the capitalist system was collapsing. According to the analysis of the resolution "due to the shrink of the capitalist markets, due to the existence of the Soviet Union, the anti-colonial movement, the growth of contradictions among imperialists, especially the contradiction between the rapid development of capitalist productive forces and the shrinking of the markets would inevitably lead to a new period of conflict which would cause the outbreak of an imperialist war among imperialist countries, the war of the imperialist countries headed against the Soviet Union, the wars of national liberation against imperialism, the wars of imperialist interventions and sharpening of class struggles.

During this period, due to the intensification of international conflicts, due to left attitudes strengthening among the working classes and the sharpening of class struggle within the capitalist countries, and the development of the anti-colonial movement in China, India, Egypt, Syria and other countries will increasingly shake the stability of the capitalism and inevitably extremely sharpen the general crisis of capitalism.

In short, the resolution adopted by the Communist International stressed: "the Third Period" intensifies the international conflicts and the internal contradictions of the capitalist countries and promotes the anti-colonial movement, which was bound to further aggravate the collapse of the stability of the capitalism, the development of the contradictions of this stability dramatically intensifies the general crisis of the capitalism.

After the 6th Congress of the Communist International, Stalin also took on various occasions to stress the theory of "the third period". In December 1928, Stalin pointed: Jules Humbert-Droz (a Swiss communist) forgets that

---

6   Collected Works of Stalin, vol. 12, Chinese version 1, p.20.
7   Ibid., p.19. Stalin said this draft was hastily distributed to Comintern delegates without being priorly discussed by the Soviet delegates.

the struggle of the working class is now taking place on the basis of a stabilization which is becoming shaken, forgets that the battles of the working class not infrequently bear the character of counter-battles, of a counter-offensive and a direct offensive against the capitalists. Humbert-Droz fails to see anything new in the battles of the working class in this period."[8]

In April 1929, Stalin again summarized "the third period" as "a growing period of the conditions of a new revolutionary upsurge, i.e., the working class is preparing to fight the upcoming class struggle."[9] In May the same year, Stalin pointed out more optimistically that "the class contradictions in all countries are intensified. The revolutionary crisis in Europe is growing. The conditions of a new revolutionary upsurge are ripe... New signs will occur in France, England, Czechoslovakia, the United States, India and China tomorrow. The earth of the world capitalism will soon burn up."[10]

Until July 1929, the 10th plenary meeting of the Communist International Executive Committee officially recognized that "the Third Period" would result in the development of the revolutionary upsurge in all the countries and clearly stated out "in this period, the general crisis of capitalism is growing and the internal and external contradictions of the imperialism are intensified, inevitably leading to the imperialist war, large-scale class struggles, the revolutionary upsurge of the capitalist countries and the great colonial anti-imperialist revolutions."[11]

The theory of "the Third Period" formed according to Stalin's assessment of the world strategic situation became the main basis guiding line of the proletarian revolutions in all the countries by the Communist International. Stalin stressed repeatedly at that time that "this issue is decisively significant for all the branches (parties) of the Communist International", and "all the strategies of the everyday political work of the communist parties should be decided according to this strategy."[12]

Later Ku Xining (a specialist in Comintern headquarters) evaluated the idea of "the Third Period" in his article titled: "the New Era and the change of the Policy of the Communist International" "the strategies of the Communist International saw a firm change which was effected by the leadership of Comrade Stalin, and these changes had a decisive effect on all the policies of the Communist International."[13]

---

8   Collected Works of Stalin, vol. 11, Chinese version 1, p.257.
9   Collected Works of Stalin, vol. 12, Chinese version 1, p.20.
10   Material of Edition and Translation of the Works of Marx-Lenin, vol.10, p.35, Beijing: People's Publishing House, 1980.
11   K. Bela, Edition of Files of the Communist International, Russian Version, 1933, p.876.
12   Collected Works of Stalin, vol. 12, Chinese version 1, p.20.
13   The Communist International, Russian version, 1930, p.2.

However, Stalin's assessment of the situation was in contrast with the objective reality. He saw the potential economic crisis and the crisis to be caused by the war which will come out of the rapid development of the capitalism, but ignored the analysis of the new phenomena and the new features shaping in the post-war capitalist countries. After World War I, capitalism began to transit from the private monopoly to the state monopoly, greatly enhanced the state's intervention policies related to economic policies. Although this new feature could not eliminate the inherent contradictions of capitalism and crisis, it had obviously improved the ability of capitalism to regulate and maintain itself to some extent. In addition, the rationalization of production process and the utilization of the new technologies had also contributed to the rapid development of capitalist production. Although in 1929, the severe capitalist world economic crisis took place, the revolutionary wave did not climb to the climax.

The strategies drawn up according to the theory of "the Third Period" brought serious harm to the communist parties and the workers' movements in all countries. Because of the far optimistic estimate of the revolutionary situation, the communist parties of all countries decided to achieve the dictatorship of the proletariat as their immediate goals, without calculating the real balance of forces between the capitalist-imperialist enemy forces and us, thus blindly followed the offensive strategy. In those countries where the communist parties held the legal status, their leaderships ignored to follow proper legal policies to win over the masses through their daily economic struggles, instead they chose the policies of urgently and directly (without intermediate steps) organizing general political strikes, started anti-government political demonstrations and marches, which caused defeats and unnecessary bloodshed. In those countries where the democratic revolution was not been fully completed and the communist parties were still illegal, the communist parties followed the tactic of insurrection and establishing a "worker-peasant dictatorship" as their central tasks, namely implemented the "left" adventurist policies without considering the urgent requirements of the democratic revolution and the national revolution, thus caused heavy losses for the revolutionary forces.

The two "left" lines which formed in the CPC history between 1928-1934 were directly related with the guidelines drawn up by the Communist International at that time, namely the impact of the theory of "the Third Period". After the great failure of the Chinese Revolution in 1927, the revolutionary situation had obviously ebbed.

But in 1929, Stalin and the Communist International had asserted that a new revolutionary upsurge had begun, suggesting the CPC to take a direct offensive line. In 1929, the Communist International successively sent three letters to the CPC Central Committee in Shanghai in February, June and

October, evaluating that "China has entered into a period of deep national crisis" and proposing to shift "the militarist war against the warlords into a countrywide class civil war (class war)" and "overthrow the joint bloc government of the bourgeois and the landlord classes." "The immediate task of the Chinese Communist Party is to prepare and concentrate all forces in the process of struggle to meet decisive battles in the nearest future."

According to the assessment of the situation by Stalin and the Communist International, the 2nd Plenary Session of the 6th CPC in Shanghai in February 1929 pointed out: "the world revolution has entered the Third Period" and the "volcanoes of the world revolution are going to explode". Soon, in June 1929, under the auspices of the Li Lisan leadership, the CPC Central Committee made a resolution, proposing: "we should firmly ensure the implementation of the correct international line" and advocated adventurist and slogan of "occupy Changsha city, win Wuchang city, join Forces in Wuhan, water our horses in the Yangtze River". Till the second half of 1930, the damages and falseness of the "left" line of the CPC leadership were evident in the actual work, but the Communist International still emphasized the "the 'right' mistakes as the main danger in the CPC" and repeatedly instructed the CPC leadership to "uncompromisingly struggle against the right opportunism". Such instructions by the Communist International not only hindered the CPC to correct the "left" line, but promoted the "left" line which caused heavy losses.

II. The implementation of a high level of centralization and the suppression the independent autonomy and creativity of various countries' parties

The complete liberation of the proletariat is a common cause of the international proletariat. With the development of local national workers movements, the organizations and political parties of the working class have been an important component of international proletariat movement and world socialism. Evaluating the social status and historical mission of the proletariat under the capitalist system, Marx and Engels held the opinion: "the working classes of all the countries should hold highly the banner of internationalism and strengthen the mutual ties and cooperation among themselves to achieve international solidarity of the working class and oppose the common enemies."

So, in the realization of this proletarian international cooperation, what principles should be followed? What ways of organization should be applied to deal with the relationships between the proletarian political parties, between the international joint/central organizations and the local/national parties in different countries? According to Marx and Engels, the international nature of the proletarian revolution should be reflected through parties' local/national revolutionary struggles. Since the local/national conditions of countries varies widely and their situations are complicated, (though their ultimate goal is the same) their specific revolutionary tasks and their strategy and tactics are different at different historical stages, thus the national interests represented by them will also be different.

Therefore, the international unity and solidarity the working class parties of all countries need to follow the principle of independence. Engels had argued that the independent action and development of the working class and its political parties was an important premise in the healthy growth of the international workers' movements. Thus, the real and correct internationalism should be based on the independency of local/national organizations and healthy and loyal international cooperation can be achieved only between equals. In his letter to Laura Lafargue, 20 June, 1893, Engels said explicitly that relations between the socialist parties can only be based on the principle of full equal rights. "International organization can only exist between nations whose existence, autonomy and independence in internal affairs are therefore already included in the concept of internationalism."

The organizational form of the First International was the principle of unity and national independence. The Second International that was established when Engels was alive, and it set up a permanent body of the Socialist International Bureau for coordination, but it still inherited the fine tradition of proletarian international solidarity on the premise of the independence of socialist parties in various countries. Thus Second International was not established as a global or international party of workers and socialists.

This organizational form of the Second International was affirmed by Engels and Lenin at that time. However, due to the collapse of the Second International in the historic moment of the outbreak of World War I, Lenin changed his view about Second International's loose organizational form, and held that this form could not fit the needs of fierce class struggles and the revolutionary epoch and should be abandoned. In order to establish a new type of revolutionary proletarian parties completely different from the social democratic parties of the Second International, namely to establish politically and ideologically unified, strictly disciplined and combat-efficent parties which could have unity of will and action Lenin proposed a new form of international unity and cooperation.

Thus Lenin led the socialist movement to replace the loose inter-party relations of the Second International with a highly centralized form of organization when the Comintern was established in 1919. Based on his theory of the world revolution, Lenin expected to realize the goal of establishing an "international Soviet" regime, through an international communist party with a strong centralized leadership and iron discipline. However, even he had stressed a centralized organizational policy for the Comintern, he did not ignore the independence of parties struggling in different countries.

The seventeenth article of the Terms of Admission into Comintern wrote: "All decisions of the Communist International's congresses and of its Executive Committee are binding on all affiliated parties." However, Lenin stressed that "In all work, the Comintern and its Executive Committee should certainly consider various conditions for struggle and activities of parties, so decisions that all parties must obey should be limited to feasible problems."[14]

Lenin was also vigilant against the tendency of hegemonic position of Russian Communist Party. Although he emphasized the special role that Russian Communist Party could play in the Comintern, he also warned that it "should never give orders from Moscow." In the first years of the Comintern, because of Lenin's correct leadership and his democratic style, different views were allowed to exist. Representatives of various countries could be free to express their views in the Comintern, deliver open criticism to some resolutions and actions of the Comintern and make independent decisions in leading revolutionary activities in their own countries. However, after the death of Lenin, Stalin, ignoring Lenin's warning, tried to shape and transform other parties according to the mode and style of the Russian Communist Party. He formed such a situation that the CPSU (Bolshevik) could "fully intervene" in other parties affairs, namely he strengthened the privileged and key status of the CPSU (Bolshevik) in the Comintern, thereby undermining the independence of other parties, preventing them from exploring their own revolutionary roads. This in essence ran counter to the principles of internationalism.

This was mainly demonstrated by the Bolshevization movement in the Comintern pushed by Stalin implemented. In Stalin's view, in order to build a new international communist party, it was necessary to build the communist parties of other countries by employing Lenin's party theories taking the Russian Bolshevism as a model. The slogan and the task of "Bolshevization" were formally put forward in the Fifth Congress of the Communist International in 1924. The outline of Tactics passed by this congress pointed out: "one of the most important tasks for the Comintern at this stage is to Bolshevize its branches." What was Bolshevization? In accordance with the outline of Tactics, Bolshevization was to apply all the things that had international significance and common sense (at present and in the past) to the various branches of Comintern. In the interview with a German communist Herzog in February 1924, Stalin, while affirming the significance of Bolshevization, claimed that a party must have 12 basic conditions in order to realize Bolshevization:

433

14   Selected Works of Lenin, vol. 4, version 3, p.254.

1) The Party must regard itself not as an appendage of the parliamentary electoral machinery....but as the highest form of class association of the proletariat, the function of which is to lead all the other forms of proletarian organisations, from the trade unions to the Party's group in parliament.

2) The Party, and especially its leading elements, must thoroughly master the revolutionary theory of Marxism, which is inseparably connected with revolutionary practice.

3) The Party must draw up slogans and directives not on the basis of stock formulas and historical analogies, but as the result of a careful analysis of the concrete internal and international conditions of the revolutionary movement, and it must, without fail, take into account the experience of revolutions in all countries.

4) The Party must test the correctness of these slogans and directives in the crucible of the revolutionary struggle of the masses.

5) The entire work of the Party, particularly if Social-Democratic traditions have not yet been eradicated in it, must be reorganised on new, revolutionary lines, so that every step, every action, taken by the Party should naturally serve to revolutionise the masses, to train and educate the broad masses of the working class in the revolutionary spirit.

6) In its work the Party must be able to combine the strictest adherence to principle (not to be confused with sectarianism!) with the maximum of ties and contacts with the masses (not to be confused with khvostism!); without this, the Party will be unable not only to teach the masses but also to learn from them, it will be unable not only to lead the masses and raise them to its own level but also to heed their voice and anticipate their urgent needs.

7) In its work the Party must be able to combine an uncompromising revolutionary spirit (not to be confused with revolutionary adventurism!) with the maximum of flexibility and manoeuvring ability (not to be confused with opportunism!); without this, the Party will be unable to master all the forms of struggle and organisation, will be unable to link the daily interests of the proletariat with the fundamental interests of the proletarian revolution, and to combine in its work the legal with the illegal struggle.

8) The Party must not cover up its mistakes, it must not fear criticism; it must improve and educate its cadres by learning from its own mistakes.

9) The Party must be able to recruit for its main leading group the best elements of the advanced fighters who are sufficiently devoted to the cause to be genuine spokesmen of the aspirations of the revolutionary proletariat, and who are sufficiently experienced to become real leaders of the proletarian revolution, capable of applying the tactics and strategy of Leninism.

10) The Party must systematically improve the social composition of its organisations and rid itself of corrupting opportunist elements with a view to achieving the utmost solidarity.

11) The Party must achieve iron proletarian discipline based on ideological solidarity, clarity concerning the aims of the movement, unity of practical action and an understanding of the Party's tasks by the mass of the Party membership.

12) The Party must systematically verify the execution of its decisions and directives; without this, these decisions and directives are in danger of becoming empty promises, which can only rob the Party of the confidence of the broad proletarian masses.

In the absence of these and similar conditions, Bolshevisation is just an empty sound.[15]

From the perspective of Stalin's basic conditions for Bolshevization and provisions of relevant documents adopted by the Comintern, the basic spirit was to make communist parties of other countries learn from the experiences of the Bolsheviks and build them into fighting organization. However, Stalin and other leaders of the Comintern, under this tactic, changed the Bolshevization movement into a mistaken practice of strengthening the hegemonic control of the Comintern and strengthened the special status of the CPSU (Bolshevik) in it, thus suppressed the necessity of independence of parties in other countries.

435

1. Natures of the Bolshevization movement

First, the sanctification and dogmatization of the Soviet experience.

Outlines adopted by Stalin and the Comintern have stressed that general principles of Leninism should be applied to specific situations in specific countries. The experience of the Russian Communist Party should be combined with the practice of specific countries during the implementation of Bolshevization movement. Especially, other sections were required to shape and transform their parties by modeling the Russian Communist Party. Outlines of the Comintern had specific uniform requirements not only in big issues from theory to strategy, but also in detailed work plans and checks for the implementation of the central decisions. The main aim was not the consideration of the specific situations in various countries, but "unification" which referred to shaping parties by a specific model. Coupled with the factor that communist parties were relatively young at that time, the inevitable result was copying the experience of the Soviet party. The result was that dogmatism had increased and the autonomy and creativity of other parties were suppressed.

15　Collected Works of Stalin, 1st Chinese version, vol. 7, pp.35-37.

In addition, Stalin on many occasions emphasized that it was a primary task of the Bolshevization to adjust and replace leaders of parties of other countries. In September 1924, he pointed out in his article On the International Situation: "the current task is to make the western communist parties become the true Bolshevik party and foster real practical and revolutionary cadres who can revolutionize the entire party with the spirit of educating the masses and preparing for revolutions."

Stalin also applied his understanding on the inner-party struggle practice of the CPSU (Bolshevik) to the Communist International, and saw the removal of the so-called opportunists, the right wing in particular, as the main content of the Bolshevization. For example, Stalin urged the Czechoslovak Communist Party as follows: "its new task should be when fighting against the 'ultra-leftists', we need to wage a resolute struggle against the danger from the right, so as to completely isolate the rightists and eliminate them. It is the task of this party and the way out of the crisis to unify true revolutionists within the party and completely eliminate the right-wing group. If we do not do that, we will never be able to Bolshevize the Czechoslovak Communist Party."[16]

Though Stalin said that it will be improper to adopt the attitude of rejecting other comrades with different ideas, the Bolshevization movement carried out by the Comintern in fact selected and removed party leaders in various countries according to the loyalty to the Comintern line and the Russian Communist Party and excluded all the dissidents.

436

What was more, in the implementation of the Bolshevization, the Comintern greatly strengthened the centralism and the special status of the CPSU (Bolshevik) in the Comintern. According to the program of the Comintern, the organizational requirements of the Bolshevization was to strengthen the "international center" of the Comintern to enable "the overall leadership", thus form a highly centralized system according to the mode of the Russian Communist Party. "In any case, practices of each party doing things in his own way, groups in parties and so on should be avoided."[17] and this policy was directed against the independence of parties. In this case, the Executive Committee of the Comintern (ECCI) constantly expanded its power and demanded to intervene in the internal affairs of parties of all the countries. For example, it had the right to dispatch plenipotentiaries and instructors with "the most extensive rights" to lead the member parties. These instructors they had the responsibility to supervise and direct all activities of member parties. Those parties were required to "unconditionally obey the stringent international disciplines" and "unconditionally submit to the Executive Committee of the Communist International".

16   Ibid., p.57.
17   Bela Kun, The Compilation of Documents of the Communist International, Russian version, p.495.

Stalin not only agreed with this approach, but also forbade others to hold different views. Togliatti, leader of the Italian Communist Party, once made a sharp criticism related to the internal democratic life of the Comintern in the 6th Congress of the Comintern and called for more democracy and "more transparency". Because his speech clearly violated the ideas of Stalin and the CPSU (Bolshevik), it was attacked. Some communist parties objected to the interventions by the Comintern, and Stalin made it clear: "As for the rights of the Comintern and its intervention in affairs of member parties, I strongly disagree with the view of narrowing those rights claimed by some comrades. Some people wish to make the Comintern an organization which indifferently observes what is happening within member parties and patiently record events. No, comrades, it could not be an organization on the planet. It is the fighting organization of the proletariat, and it has inextricable links with labor movements. It has to intervene in the affairs of parties and assist revolutionists in their struggles against their enemies. Anyone that denied the leading right of the Comintern and thus denied its right of intervention serves the enemies of communism.[18] Thus, any requirement and action of independence from parties in all countries were considered to be outrageous. For instance, after the failure of the German Communist Party in the presidential election, the left-wing group led by Maslov-Fischer, without the permission of the Executive Committee of the Comintern, "decided all by itself" to dispatch a delegation to seek contacts with communist parties in countries including Britain, France, Poland and Norway. Such behaviors were criticized by the Comintern; on the contrary, they were rebuked as attempts to "shift to the West" and establish "the Fourth International." Maslov, Fischer and others lost the trust of leaders of the Comintern and the CPSU (Bolshevik) because of their independent behaviors, and were soon ousted.

At the same time, the CPSU (Bolshevik) had the largest number of voting rights in the congress of the Comintern and had the most advantageous position in the Executive Committee and its departments. Another problem due to Soviet majority representatives of other parties needed to win the trust and the support of the Executive Committee, thus for a person to be elected into the Executive Committee needed personal good contacts to some the Executive Committee members. They could not be elected into the Executive Committee only by the support of congress delegates. Additionally, all the important decisions of the Executive Committee of the Comintern needed the approval of the Political Bureau of CPSU Central Committee in advance, therefore the relationship between the Comintern and members parties was in fact the relationship between the CPSU (Bolshevik) and other parties. Strengthening of the determinant position of the CPSU (Bolshevik) in the Comintern put other parties in a subordinate

18   Collected Works of Stalin, 1st Chinese version, vol. 7, pp.57-58.

position. Thus, it led to such an awkward situation: Member parties of the Comintern had no right to intervene in and comment on domestic policies and inter-party disputes of the Soviet Union; on the contrary, strategies and inter-party affairs of other parties were reported to the Political Bureau of the CPSU (Bolshevik) Central Committee by Soviet representatives of the Comintern, and the Political Bureau of the CPSU (Bolshevik) Central Committee Soviet's suggestions usually became the instructions of the Executive Committee of the Comintern, which were required to be implemented by other parties.

2. The theory of "socialism in a single country"

The theory of "socialism in a single country" further enhanced the special status of the Soviet Union in the Comintern. In the dispute with the Trotsky-Zinoviev opposition, Stalin's theory of "socialism in a single country" finally won in 1927. This theory has inherited and developed Lenin's theory of building socialism in backward countries, and also reflected the enthusiasm and self-confidence of building socialism by the masses and become a motive force for socialist construction. Thus, it bore a positive effect at that time. Unfortunately, when the theory of "socialism in a single country" was widely accepted at home and abroad, Stalin set interests of establishing socialism in the Soviet Union above the interests of the world wide revolutionary struggles. He especially forced other parties to regard the interests of the Soviet Union as the realization of the maximum interests of the world proletariat. Activities of the Communist International became the tool to realize this aim, thus other parties' tasks of striving for the victory of socialism in their own countries were reduced to a secondary and subordinate position. The attitude of member parties towards the Soviet Union, and the Soviet Party became a standard to measure the Bolshevik character of member parties. Aligning with "correct side" related to the inner-party struggles of the Soviet party was another criterion of Bolshevik character.

3. Defending the Soviet Union

From the premise that socialism could be built in a single country, Stalin made the following assertions: The international proletariat should promote the victory of socialist construction in the Soviet Union and defend the only country of proletarian dictatorship in the world, because the Soviet regime in Russia was the very base, fort and protector of the revolutions worldwide. This approach became the new guiding principle of the Comintern.

The program adopted by the Sixth Congress of the Comintern in 1928 declared that the Soviet Union had become "the leading force in the world revolutionary movements" and "the revolutionary base of international movements of all oppressed classes, the leading force in the world revolutionary movements". Stalin even equated "defending the Soviet Union" with "internationalism" and treated it as the "watershed" and "touchstone" of revolution and counter-revolution. In the joint conference of the Central Committee of CPSU (Bolshevik) and the Central Control Commission in 1927, Moscow, Stalin pointed out in the speech entitled "the international situation and defending the Soviet Union": "the proof of the revolutionary nature of a group, and a political party is not based on their statements or declarations, but based on their actions, practice and actual plans. There was a standard that could be set as the watershed to measure the revolutionary or counter-revolutionary nature of political parties. Currently this standard isdefending the Soviet Union, namely, the unconditional and absolute defense of the Soviet Union against imperialist attacks."..."who absolutely, unconditionally, openly and faithfully defend the Soviet Union is a revolutionist, because the Soviet Union is the world's first proletarian revolutionary country where socialism has been established. Who is absolutely, unwaveringly, unconditionally committed to defending the Soviet Union is an internationalist, because the Soviet Union is the base of the world revolutionary movements. If we do not defend the Soviet Union, we cannot defend and advance the world revolutionary movements."[19]

Since the interest of the Soviet Union was elevated to the top interest of the whole international proletariat, then the domestic and foreign policies of the Soviet Union in a large part should determine the tactics and activities of the member parties. For example, after Stalin suddenly decided to sign The Soviet-German Non-aggression Treaty on August 23, 1939, the Soviet Union's foreign policy underwent a major change. In order to avoid a negative effect on the Soviet-German relations, the Soviet Union no longer mentioned fascist Germany as the common enemy of the whole world and as the chief culprit launching the World War II. On the contrary, Soviet Union condemned Britain and France as war mongers and treated them as the target of attacks. After fascist Germany invaded Poland in September 1939, the Comintern, acting in the interests of the Soviet, drafted and adopted a resolution titled "Outline of the Situation" and wrote a "Document of Instructions" to other parties. In early November, Comintern issued The Manifest on the Celebration of the 22nd Anniversary of the October Socialist Revolution, demanding other parties to support The Soviet-German Non-aggression Treaty and fight against Britain and France which are responsible for the World War II. These sudden changes in the foreign policies of the Soviet Union and changes in the tactics of the Comintern made other communist parties belonging to the Comintern and especially European communist parties fall into confusion. For instance, Delin, western scholar studying the history of the Bulgarian Communist Party, once described:

19   Collected Works of Stalin, 1st Chinese version, vol. 10, p.47.

"this zigzag in Moscow's foreign policy was not beneficial to the Bulgarian Communist Party who followed it. Only within two years, the Bulgarian Communist Party first objected to and then supported and then again fought against Nazi Germany and its aggressive forces. Therefore, that seriously affected the prestige of European communist parties among the people and weakened their effect in the anti-fascist struggle.

What was worse, Stalin forcefully involved the parties of other countries in the inter-party struggle of the CPSU (Bolshevik). From the mid-1920s to the 1930s, the CPSU (Bolshevik) lived a severe inner-party struggles, first against Trotsky, then Zinoviev and finally Bukharin. All these figures had held important posts in the Comintern, so they had contacts with leaders of fraternal parties and their words and deeds inevitably affected them. When the leaders of fraternal parties supported their views in their speeches, they perhaps only aimed to express their support for the Comintern. However, when people like Trotsky, Zinoviev and Bukharin became targets of inner party struggles in the CPSU (Bolshevik), those leaders of fraternal parties who once supported their views were also implicated and baselessly became victims as "opportunists" or enemies. For example, Klement Gottwald, one of the main leaders of the Czechoslovak Communist Party once wrote articles to support Trotsky, and when Trotsky was criticized within the CPSU (Bolshevik), Klement Gottwald was labeled as "rightist" in the Czechoslovak Communist Party. Stalin not only accused Klement Gottwald, but also criticized Guttmann, another leader of the Czechoslovak Communist Party, for his protection for "rightists" and ordered the Czechoslovak Communist Party to ideologically and organizationally smash the "rightist" group.

440

Henryk Walecki, leader of the Polish Communist Party, "unequivocally" supported the opposition in the CPSU (Bolshevik), and the Polish Committee of the Comintern chaired personally by Stalin discussed about the crisis confronting the Polish Communist Party, which discussed to the attitude of Walesky. This conference also criticized Maria Koszutska, another leader of the Polish Communist Party, for his "moderate approach" to Walecki. Stalin commented: "The method of struggle recommended by Koszutska is the revival of social democratic opportunism and it carries the danger of division within the party."[20]

The Fifth Congress of the Communist International made an evaluation about the Polish party: "The Central Committee of the Polish Communist Party politically led by the group of Adolf Warski, Henryk Walecki, Maria Koszutskatalks about revolution, but in fact it has been unable to perform lines of the Comintern."[21] Therefore, the Executive Committee of the

20 Collected Works of Stalin, 1st Chinese version, vol. 6, p.234.
21 Bela Kun, The Compilation of Documents of the Communist International (II), p.100,

Comintern appointed Comintern cadres to rectify the Polish Communist Party and held an emergency meeting to restructure this party's leading organ. Those behaviors of the Comintern aggravated the factional struggles within communist parties in other countries and severely weakened their combat effectiveness.

In the late 1930s, based on the evaluation that class struggles are becoming increasingly sharp, Stalin launched a large-scale elimination of counterrevolutionaries, arrested, trialed and executed various opposition factions represented by Trotsky (spared from death because of being in exile), Zinoviev, Buharin. This was a domestic affair in the Soviet Union. However, Stalin and CPSU (Bolshevik) expanded this struggle to the Communist International and communist parties of other countries, and implicated many important leaders of fraternal parties. For example, Bela Kun , the founder of Communist Party of Hungary, the leader of Hungarian Soviet Republic in 1919 was one of them. Bela Kun, in the period from 1918 to 1920 when the Soviet Union was fighting against foreign military interventions, had made made contribution for defense of the first proletariat regime, and had earned Order of Lenin. Since the Third Congress of Communist International, Bela Kun had always been a member of the Presidium of the Executive Committee of Communist International, also served as a member of Communist International Organization Committee and as the secretary in charge of Balkans. In 1937, Bela Kun was suddenly arrested. After being trialed in a brief secret judicial proceeding by the Communist International, he was immediately executed in 1939. Another example was Milan Gorkić, general secretary of the Communist Party of Yugoslavia. He was recalled to Moscow with a urgency in the summer of 1937. His Polish wife who was working in Moscow was accused of spying and arrested. Gorkić was removed from the General Secretary position, arrested and executed as being a British spy. Communist International was planning to dissolve the Communist Party of Yugoslavia. Thanks to Tito and Dimitrov's insistence, the Communist Party of Yugoslavia had survived and the party leadership was re-arranged by Tito. The most damage faced was the Communist Party of Poland. With the excuse that some spies and moles had infiltrated into the leading organ, Communist International decided to dissolve the Communist Party of Poland. Some leaders of the Party were arrested and executed.

Stalin's great-party chauvinism and his practice of intervening domestic affairs of other parties not only caused negative consequences at that time, but also adverse effects on post-war communist movements. For example, suggested by a group of leaders including Tito, Cominform (the Information Bureau of communist parties) was established. Although according to its

441

Beijing: Joint Publishing Press, 1965.

rules the Cominform was a regional international organization whose aim was to exchange information and share experiences. But Stalin still continued to follow the methods of the Third International, continued to practice great-party chauvinism attitude and great-nation chauvinism and national egoism through Cominform, punished fraternal parties which did not obey his commands, expelled the Communist Party of Yugoslavia from the Intelligence Agency. This was an abominable example.

History has proved that when Stalin served as the leader of the Soviet Union and the Communist Party of Soviet Union, many of his approaches in handling the relationships between the Communist International center and the parties of other countries, especially in handling the relationships between the Communist Party of Soviet Union and the parties of other countries were one-sided, even mistaken. Without doubt, the Soviet Union was the first country which won the victory of proletarian revolution. The Bolsheviks had created abundant experiences during their revolutionary struggles. Under those historical conditions, the labor movements in other countries needed to learn from the experiences of the Russian Revolution. However, according to Marxism, the success of the revolution in a country, fundamentally speaking, depends on the maturity of its conditions, and depends on the efforts of its own working class. Because countries differ from each other economically, politically, and culturally, class relations and class forces are quite different, this includes the people's consciousness levels. Therefore, it is impossible to carry out revolutions according to a certain fixed pattern. Revolution cannot be imported or exported. The tasks, revolutionary road, strategy and tactics that fit the situation and characteristic of a specific country can only be found, created and decided by its own proletariat and its own party. But Stalin not only hailed the experience of the Soviet Union as sacred and absolute, but also imposed the Soviet pattern to the parties of other countries through the Bolshevization movement, thereby causing damages of different degrees to the revolutionary cause of other countries. In fact, during the process of the Bolshevization movement, many people have questioned whether the experience of the Russian Revolution could be universal or not.

The proletariat of all countries should co-operate and unite closely. This was clearly underlined by Marx and Engels. But Marx and Engels stressed that such cooperation and unity should be built on the basis that all countries are independent and mutually equal. Accordingly, the international central organizations of proletariat should not become an international command center that coarsely and strictly controls the proletarian struggles of other countries. It is especially inappropriate that a certain big party acts as th leader in international organizations that gives commands to the leaders of other parties in other countries. In the international communist movement, whether a big party or a small one, whether a ruling party or a party in opposition, there should not exist the questions such as who leads who and who directs who. Considering itself as the biggest party and demanding to command other parties contradict the principle of proletariat internationalism. Deng Xiaoping had commented on this point:

"Domestic principles (policies) and routes of political parties of different countries, the right or wrong of others' practices; these should be judged by their own parties and their own people", "we couldn't blame them for exploring in line with their reality, and also mistakes should be summarized by themselves independently so as to make new explorations. Party-to-party relations should be "new, healthy and friendly"; two, each party should handle its internal affairs in an independent and self-determined way, not subject to the decision, interests or wishes of others. No party should give orders to others"

"We oppose 'patriarchal party' and this is quite right. We disagreed with the existence of any 'center', but we also made the mistake of pointing fingers at others."

"Don't act as other's leader and give commands. We oppose people who dictate to us; so we shall never act so to others. This should be an important principle."[22]

In this aspect, Stalin has left extremely painful lessons to next generations.   443

III. Erroneous understanding of the united front policy and implementation of the "left"-leaning closed-door-ism and sectarianism

In order to win over and unite the overwhelming majority of the proletarian masses and promote the process of world revolution, correctly handling the relationship between communist parties and other factions and parties of the labor movement bears a crucial importance. However, what we see is, for quite a long time, when dealing with other labor parties, especially the social democratic parties, Stalin has been taking the "left-leaned" closed-door (sectarian) attitude. Therefore, he not only failed to isolate the social democratic parties and win over the majority of working class masses, but made the communist party isolated. As we all know, when Lenin was alive, later he experienced a strategic transformation in handling the relationships with the social democratic party.

Most of the social democratic parties supported their own governments during the First World War. Therefore, when Communist International was

---

22   Deng Xiaoping's Selected Works, vol. 2, version 2, p.319, Beijing: People's Press, 1994.

first founded, Lenin chastised these Social Democratic Parties' behavior as betrayal, and as "traitors" to the socialist revolutions, "servants" of imperialism, "hangers" of bourgeoisies, "agents" of bourgeoisies in the labor movement, and "social pillars" that kept capitalism from collapsing, etc. In addition, Lenin basing himself on the experience CPSU had accumulated when fighting with opportunism, was keen to break with opportunism thoroughly in three fields—thinking, organization and practice. Folllowing Lenin's ideas Communist International of the 20ies certainly asserted that the struggle with social democratic parties "was not a factional struggle inside the proletariat revolution, not a factional struggle within a united camp of the proletarian class, but a struggle between classes." Besides, it was asserted that: "since the rightists have been isolated, now the centrists are the primary enemy. Thus, the documents of the first and second congress of Communist International wrote: "The major enemy is the centrists," "the centrists are the most dangerous enemies." The "21 Terms of Admission to Comintern" promugaleted in the Second Congress was aimed at the centrists. Because of this communist cognition of the epoch, there was no theory or concept of united front.

However, I think that the reasons why Lenin made such struggle strategy were not only the betrayal of the social democratic parties in the First World War, but his overestimation of the revolutionary situation. After several socialist revolutions failed in Europe, Lenin timely corrected the over-optimistic view about revolutionary situation and made a more objective assessment about the consciousness level of the masses and the strength of the communist parties. He recognized that the European working class influenced by traditional Western democracy was inclined to reformism. The Social Democratic Parties still held the control of the overwhelming majority of working masses, while "the Communist Party did not win over the majority (of the working class) in any place. Not only did the communist party leadership failed fail to win the majority's support (organizationally), but also failed to assimilate the principles of communism."[23] Based on this new analysis, Lenin rejected the "left-leaning" political line, and prompted the transformation of the strategy of Communist International. Held in 1921, the Third Congress of the Communist International which was directly led by Lenin in a general manner formed the policy or concept of united front. Later the Fourth Congress of the Communist International decided and defined the strategy of building a united front of workers, and proposed the slogan "workers' government" and that "in some cases, the Communists should be ready to work with non-Communist labor parties and labor organizations together to establish labor government," thereby making a step forward to realize the strategy of united front.Fourth Congress report said:

444

23 Collected Works of Lenin, vol. 42, Chinese version 2, p.12.

The slogan of a workers' government (or a workers' and peasants' government) can be used practically everywhere as a general agitational slogan. However, as a central political slogan, the workers' government is most important in countries where the position of bourgeois society is particularly unstable and where the balance of forces between the workers' parties and the bourgeoisie brings the question of government on the order of the day as a practical problem requiring immediate solution. In these countries the workers' government slogan follows inevitably from the entire united front tactic."

After Stalin assumed the party and state leadership of the Soviet Union, he returned to the strategy that broke with and which targeted the Social Democratic parties. The united front policy was replaced by the "left-leaned" sectarian policies. Before German communists attempted the October Revolution in 1923, Stalin suggested a tactic accelerating the break-up (separation) between the leftists and rightists within the Social Democrats, namely a strategy aimed to split Democrats and this strategy also included to discredit the left wing of the Social Democrats, thereby rendering workers leaving the leftists of the leaders of the Social Democratic Party. With this struggle trick in his mind Stalin adviced the German communists to call the Social Democrat left wing to establish a united workers' government with communists.

Stalin's dual idea was as follows: if the leftists agreed, the communists would win, because the Social Democratic Party would split. If the leftists did not agree, the communists would still win, because the leftists' reformist nature would be revealed: the workers would see that the left wing social democrats were servile followers of the rightists. In either case, the hesitant working class would be won over by the communists. In a meeting of the Presidium of the Executive Committee of the Communist International, Stalin proposed the following tasks for the Communist Party of Germany when dealing with the left wing of the social democrats: (1) Task was aimed at accelerating the split of the leftists and rightists with the leftist leaders completely discredited, because these leaders were unreliable and their influence could be fatal in crucial moments. (2) At an appropriate time, the Communist Party should send an open letter to the leftists of the Social Democratic Party and keep fighting for a government united by workers and farmers. It was aimed to make workers leave the leftist leaders of Social Democratic Party. And after the failure of the German October Revolution, Stalin shifted all the blame onto the Social Democratic Party and plus the opportunists in the Communist Party. In January 1924, in the plenary session of the Russian Communist Party (Bolshevik) Central Committee, when discussing the the lessons of the united front strategy in the German revolution, Stalin argued that the petty-bourgeois social-democracy had shifted to the counter-revolutionary side, to the fascist camp. Stalin thus concluded: Do not ally with the Social Democratic Party; we should take it as the backbone of the current fascist regime and fight with it till death.

Later, in the speech "On the Foundations of Leninism" delivered by Stalin in 1924, he theoretically proposed the need to combat against the Social Democratic Party. He said we are now in the third stage: "In the third stage which began after the October Revolution. Objective should be: to consolidate the dictatorship of the proletariat in a single country, using it as a base for the defeat of imperialism in all countries. The revolution spreads beyond the confines of a single country; the epoch of world revolution has begun. The main force of the revolution: the dictatorship of the proletariat in a single country, the revolutionary movement of the proletariat in all countries. Main reserves: the semi-proletarian and small-peasant masses in the developed countries, the liberation movement of the colonies and dependent countries. Direction of the main blow: isolation of the petty-bourgeois democrats, isolation of the parties of the Second International (Ed. social democracy) which constitute the main support of the policy of compromise with imperialism. Plan for the disposition of forces: alliance of the proletarian revolution with the liberation movement in the colonies and the dependent countries." Later, in "The October Revolution and the Tactics of the Russian Communists" published in 1924, Stalin reaffirmed the above strategy towards the Social Democratic Party, and pointed out the leadership of Bolsheviks over the Russian revolution had followed the line of isolating the compromising parties, which are the most dangerous groupings in the period of the outbreak of the revolution, the line of isolating the Socialist-Revolutionaries and Mensheviks.

He said: "What is the fundamental strategic rule of Leninism?

It is the recognition of the following:

1) the compromising parties are the most dangerous social support of the enemies of the revolution in the period of the approaching revolutionary outbreak;

2) it is impossible to overthrow the enemy (tsarism or the bourgeoisie) unless these parties are isolated;

3) the main weapons in the period of preparation for the revolution must therefore be directed towards isolating these parties, towards winning the broad masses of the working people away from them."[24]

That is to say, Stalin saw petty-bourgeoisie and reformists as the main subject to combat. Stalin and the Communist Party of Russia included this conclusion in the resolution of Communist International, and demanded

24   Collected Works of Stalin, vol. 6, Chinese version 1, p.333.

that the communist parties of other countries to treat the Social Democratic Parties as the main subject to combat, and argued that only by doing this can the working masses shake off the influence of the Social Democratic Party among working masses and win them to the communist parties.

This "left-leaned" sectarian line became the thought guideline of the Fifth Congress of the Communist International. Besides that, after the failure of the German Revolution in1923, with fascists becoming increasingly rampant in Germany and Italy, Stalin and Communist International sharpened their evaluation about the Social Democratic Party. The outline on "Strategic Issues" passed in the Fifth Congress of Communist International in June 1924 asserted that "the Social Democratic Party was the third party of bourgeois," "was one of the pillars of capitalism," and further pointed out that "all capitalist political parties especially the Social Democratic Party posseses varying degrees of Fascism…Fascism and the Social Democratic Parties are the two blades on the weapon of monopolistic dictatorship. Therefore, the Social Democratic Parties can never be a reliable ally in proletarian struggle against Fascism."[25] In the article "On the International Situation" published in September 1924, Stalin even similarized the Social Democratic Party to fascism. He said, "Fascism is a fighting organization that relies on the active support of the Social Democratic Party. In fact, the Social Democratic Party is objectively the moderate wing faction of fascism… These two do not reject each other. Instead, they appeal to each other. They are not antipodes, but twins. Fascism is the invisible organization of these two major political alliances. It is the outcome of the post-war imperialist crisis. It aims to fight against the proletarian revolution."[26] Without doubt, the ideas of Communist International on the nature of the Social Democratic Party were largely inspired from Stalin.

In November 1927, Stalin stated in the "International Nature of the October Revolution: "Present-day Social-Democratism is an ideological support of capitalism."…"It is impossible to put an end to capitalism without putting an end to Social-Democratism in the labour movement. That is why the era of dying capitalism is also the era of dying Social-Democratism in the labour movement."[27] Stalin regarded any other faction in the labor movement except the communist faction as pro-fascist or fascist wing. He said, any other factions, including anarchism, anarcho-syndicalism, guild socialism, etc. were actually social democracy in disguise. Only Leninists were the only true leftists in the labor movement.

It was because of Stalin's incorrect judgments about the nature of the Social Democratic Party, till the Fifth Congress of the Communist International, the united front strategy supported by Lenin was in fact could not be enriched.

25 Bela Kun, Compilation of the Communist International, Russian version, p.448.
26 Collected Works of Stalin, vol. 6, Chinese version 1, p.246.
27 Collected Works of Stalin, vol. 10, Chinese version 1, pp.211-212.

The possibility of establishing a workers' government with the Social Democratic Party was excluded completely. Till the Sixth Congress of the Communist International in 1928, "left-leaning" sectarian policy grew more and more. The Communist International believed that the whole development process of the Social Democratic Party was a process that kept turning towards fascism. The Social Democratic Party had lost all its characteristics of a labor party and turned into a fascist one. It was a "twin brother" with fascist party. Since then, the Social Democratic Party became the main target of struggle. The guiding principle accepted during the Sixth Congress pointed out that "during its development, the Social Democratic Party showed a tendency to fascism," "was an imperialist pillar in the working class." Its right wing was "open counter-revolutionaries" while its left wing was "the most dangerous faction of the Social Democratic Party." In the tenth plenary meeting of Communist International plenary meeting held in July 1929, All these preparations for new imperialist wars are being carried out with the active co-operation and full participation of the 'socialist parties', the 'left' wing of which play the most despicable part of screening these preparations with pacifist phrases." "The leading cadres of social-democracy and of the reformist trade unions, fulfilling the orders of the bourgeoisie, are now, through the mouth of Wels, threatening the German working class with open fascist dictatorship."…"This is the road of the coalition policy of the social-democracy leading to social fascism. These are the results of the governing activities of the biggest party of the Second International. (Germany)."

Thus the concept of "social fascism" was formally incorporated into this plenary meeting resolution.

Even in January 1933 when Hitler came to power, the Presidium of the Executive Committee of the Communist International issued a statement saying: "The establishment of fascist dictatorship in Germany, in the final analysis results from that: throughout the political existence of Weimar Republic the Social Democratic Party has been always working with the bourgeoise... the Communist Party has evaluated the Social Democratic Party as fascists, which is right."

However, just as famous Marxist historian W. Bartel said, "The (communist) party should focus the direction of its attack to the fascist danger. Though the Party should concentrate on establishing a united anti-fascist front in fighting the terrorist dictatorship with workers of the Social Democratic Party, it did not change its main direction of attack in time, and failed to strongly defense the united front strategy as a major part of the proletarian policies."[28]

Regarding the Social Democratic Party as the main target to combat greatly impeded the implementation of the united front strategy, and brought

448

---

28   Walter Bartel, Germany under the Dictatorship of Fascism (1933-1945), p.106, Beijing: China Social Sciences Press, 1980.

remarkable losses to the international communist movement. Especially under the circumstances where the capitalist crisis was becoming worse day by day and fascism was more and more rampant, the communist parties followed the "left-leaned" sectarian and exclusionist line towards the group of social democratic parties, which led to their isolation. On January 30, 1933, i.e. the day when Hitler came to power, when the German Communist Party Central Committee called for a general strike, the workers influenced by the Social Democratic Party was aloof. Only few responded. The two political parties of the laborers—for a long time—were in a hostile state, which greatly weakened the overallstrength of the labor movement, naturally failed to unite and stop Hitler coming to power. The fascist forces of other countries took this as an opportunity to oppress the communist parties and the social democratic parties and any other progressive forces. Soon after he came to power, Hitler closed down the office of the German Communist Party in Berlin, provoked the "Reichstag fire" on February 27, and arrested more than ten thousand members of the Communist Party the same night. On March 3, he arrested Ernst Thälmann, the leader of the German Communist Party, and arrested G. Dimitrov, the leader of the International Bureau of Western Europe of Comintern on March 9. Then on June 22, he banned the activities of the Social Democratic Party, demise the senatorship of the Social Democratic Party. Some senators were sent to fascist prison camp. Therefore, persecuted by fascism, the biggest political party of the labor in capitalist countries disappeared from the political stage of Germany. In Italy, fascism that came to power even earlier suppressed the working class in a more terrorist manner. Thus the fascists of France, Spain, and Austria speeded up their activities. Even the fascist forces in the UK and US started to gain certain basis. Faced by the bloody fascist policies in various countries, not only the communist parties ran into a dead end, but also the social democratic parties labeled as "social fascism" by Stalin and the Communist International were the victims of fascist aggression.

449

The painful lessons of fascist forces in Germany and Italy coming to power and cruelly suppressing the Communist Parties and the Social Democratic Parties highlighted the failure of the "left-leaned" sectarian line that Stalin and the Communist International had advocated, also rendered the leaders of the Communist International and leaders of communist parties to reexamine their long-term past strategy. Stalin's attitudes then changed. In 1934, after his famous brave defense against fascist judges he was released and G. Dimitrov visited Stalin and other leaders of the Political Bureau of CPSU (Bolshevik), he proposed that the strategy of the Communist International should be changed. He argued: "why at the decisive moment, millions of people did not follow the communists, but followed the Social Democratic Party? For example, as in Germany, they followed the Social

Democratic Party?"…"The main reason lies in our publicity/propaganda system, lies in the incorrect evaluation of the European working class." He suggested that Comintern should form a new attitude towards the workers behind the Social Democratic Party. Stalin greatly agreed with Dimitrov's view on establishing a broader united front, and suggested that Dimitrov should lead the work of the Communist International. He also promised that CPSU would provide the necessary support. Later in the strategy debates within the Communist International, Stalin stood on the opposite side of the ultra-left groups. This attitude of Stalin played an important role in the shifting of strategy which was agreed in the Seventh Congress of the Communist International. Obviously, under the circumstances then, this shift would be difficult to achieve without Stalin's support.

Chapter XIII

Studies by Foreign Scholars on
Stalin's Thoughts

The studies on the thought of Stalin have continued without interruption since 1930s. The research work and articles on Stalin are voluminous. In the West, a field of Stalin studies was formed which focuses on the ideas and practices of Stalin.

Whether it is in the West or East, as time passes, the evaluations on Stalin vary at different periods. In the Soviet Union during Stalin's rule, only one voice could be heard by people, i.e., the praises and worship of Stalin, but in the West, it was prevalent to regard Stalin rule as totalitarianism. After the 20th Congress of the Soviet Party in 1956, with the revelations of Stalin's personal cult, the Soviet academy had greatly changed its attitude regarding the study on Stalin. The condemnations overweighed the praises and the mainstream Western views advocated by some scholars were accepted by the Soviet Union.

On the other side, in the West, there were some scholars who changed the Cold War way of thought, reduced the ideological prejudices and attempted to study Stalin's thoughts, his merits and demerits in a fairer and objective way. If I make a general evaluation, after since the 20th Congress of the Soviet Communist Party, although the Western and the Soviet scholars have made different evaluations on Stalin due to different ideological atmosphere (mainstream), their class stand, and other aspects, the purport of their studies have somewhat similar characteristics. Since Gorbachev assumed power, along with some classified documents and material which were opened to public and with the dramatic changes in the ideological climate, the studies on Stalin have upsurged again. The researchers carried out multi-faceted and multi-angle debates and studies including subjects such the origins of the "Stalinism", the nature and characteristics of the Stalinist model, thus numerous articles and books were published. Below we will offer a brief review on the studies of Stalin by the Soviet and Western researchers.

I. On "Stalinism"

The term "Stalinism" is not very definitely expounded. The term is sometimes used to refer to a movement, sometimes an institution or refers to a system; sometimes a theoretical system, and sometimes a form of political practice; sometimes a specific historical period and sometimes a bureaucratic ruling style, and so on. In short, it is a rather vague concept, lacking scientific accurateness. Originally, the term "Stalinism" was mainly widespread in the West, but rarely used by the Soviet scholars. When Stalin was alive, he did not agree the usage of the term Stalinism,he defined himself as the "student of Lenin." But in the era of Gorbachev, the Soviet scholars began to widely use the term "Stalinism", and have mostly followed the Western pejorative usage.

In addition to the term of "Stalinism", the concepts of "Stalinism Phenomenon" and "Stalin Model" are also widely used. The History of the Stalinist Phenomenon written byFrench communist Jean Elleinstein in France has systematically studied the source and nature of the "Stalinist Phenomenon". The author mainly advocates that the direct root of the "Stalinism Phenomenon" lies in "the debates of the 1920s and the social environment of the 1930s". The breeding basis for the "Stalinism Phenomenon" includes the historical environment and personal factors related to ancient and sacred Russian traditions, related to economic structures, social and political structures. Jean Elleinstein also evaluated Stalin's role and the failure of the opposition and so on related to Stalinism. The author has argued that the nature of the "Stalinist Phenomenon" includes "bureaucratic leadership, individual autocracy, and the individual will" and the "totalitarianism". The "Stalinism Phenomenon" has for a period promoted the development of the Soviet Union, but later became an obstacle for the Soviet Union to achieve new progress home and abroad in the post-war era. Besides Elleinstein's book, there are a large number of books with the title of the "Stalinist Phenomenon" published in the West.

The "Stalin Model" is another widely used term, which has been one of the terms often used by the Soviet and the Eastern European theorists in the period of Gorbachev as well as the Western researchers since 1960's and 1970's. The term mainly refers to the socialist system and model formed during the Stalinist period. These studies have focused on the characteristics, the causes, the historic effects and the disadvantages of the Stalinist regime (rule).

The meanings and concepts of the terms "Stalinism" "Stalinism Phenomenon" and "Stalin Model" are intertwined, but comparatively, the meaning of "Stalinism" is more general. It basically covers the contents of the term "Stalinism Phenomenon" and the "Stalin Model". The interpretations of "Stalinism" concept vary in different places at different times, which also reflect the depth and breadth of the studies on Stalin. Edited by A. Ivanov, published in 1993, the book "Stalinism Phenomenon" summarizes the stages and interpretations of the studies on "Stalinism" as follows:

1. Ivanov's book describes the five interpretations of Stalinism

The first interpretation is the classic interpretation in the Soviet Union period. According to this interpretation, "Stalinism" refers to the "establishment of socialism in the Soviet Union" (though the Soviet Union at that time refused to employ the term "Stalinism") which was marked by the new Constitution of the Soviet Union in 1936. This version of the explanation basically puts economic evaluation in the first place, and other phenomena is evaluated taking economy as the center, though this explanation also stresses the party's leadership and the importance of the mentality of the leaders.

The second is the classical Western interpretation. According to this interpretation, "Stalinism" refers to totalitarianism. After World War II, this interpretation has been dominant in the West. In contrast with the classical interpretation of the Soviet Union, the Western interpretation emphasizes the primacy of politics and evaluates the social structure as a secondary factor. Totalitarianism refers to a political system which emphasizes the control of society and citizens by the state and party and totalitarianism aims to maintain the system and aims to mobilize the masses through political pressure and terror.

This interpretation is imbued with the Cold War mentality and possesses strong ideological colors. It tends to compare totalitarianism of Nazi Germany and the Soviet system, and track the origin of this system, regarding it as the direct result of Marxism-Leninism, especially the Leninist theory on proletarian political party.

The third interpretation is the interpretation prevalent during the period of "de-Stalinization" in the Soviet Union after 1956. After the 20th Congress of the CPSU, with the loosening of ideological controls, the Soviet Union began re-evaluate Stalin. During the late 1950s and 1960s, the criticism of Stalin has mainly revealed Stalin's "mistakes" and his "excessive" behaviors, aiming to surpass Stalin's personal cult. When Khrushchev was forced to step down, the de-Stalinization began to cool down. During the 1970s, the overall assessment on Stalin of the Soviet Union was: Stalin's "personal cult" contrasted the Leninist principle, but the basic system he laid was healthy. Stalin's rapid industrialization policy, despite its high price was necessary and "socialist", without rapid industrialization, it was impossible neither to get rid of backwardness nor to achieve victory against fascism. The collectivization was necessary and basically a correct policy, although there were many "excessive" things in the treatment of farmers.

The fourth interpretation is the interpretation by the Western "revisionist" or post-revisionist historiagphy researchers of the 1970s and 1980s including the left-wing ones. The starting point of these Western "revisionist" scholars of this period have negated the "totalitarianism" approach and aimed to transcend the politically motivated "cold war mentality" of the old generation researchers. They also reflected on the new situation in the Soviet Union where the totalitarian model was declining. According to their view, during the periods of Khrushchev and Brejnev Soviet Russia had lost many of the characteristics of totalitarianism. Notably, Walter LaFeber, Joyce, Gabriel Kolko and Melvyn P. Leffler. were among them.

2. Ivanov's book acknowledges different schools in Stalin studies

There are a number of schools. One school focuses on criticizing the interpretation of "Stalinism" as totalitarianism. Another school can be seen as the continuation of the view during the period of "de-Stalinization" in the Soviet Union in the West in the 1960s. For example, Stephan F.Cohenand Moshe Levin havefollowed this point of view and stressed the fundamental differences between Lenin and Stalin and argued that Stalin was a deviation from Leninism. But they went further than interpreting the Soviet system, and put forward a kind of "Bukharin alternative" against "Stalinism", arguing that Bukharin's views and Lenin's ideas in his later years were similar.

Another, third school mainly focused on the Soviet society and history. They have argued that the driving force of the history of the Soviet Union as advocated by–"Stalinism" the totalitarian model school proves to contrast the facts and this mistaken approach takes the starting point as politics and thoughts. They have argued: "instead we should start from social forces and social processes, we think that Soviet system is far from being a passive result of the control on the society."

The fifth interpretation is the interpretation during the period of Gorbachev's "new thought" (Perestroika) after 1985. The studies in this period are the continuation of the "revisionism" which had stopped after Kruschev's fall in the 1960s. This trend has re-evaluated many phenomena of the "Stalinism", such as the Stalinist model, industrialization, agricultural collectivization, the "Great Purge" and the relationships between "Stalinism", the "Marxism" and "Leninism."

Ivanov argues that generally two ideas dominate the explanations of "Stalinism" in the West: the first explanation regards that the source of "Stalinism" as the one-party political system whose main characteristic is the dictatorial suppression not being restricted by any legal checks and argues that the nature of "Stalinism" is the inevitable result of Leninism. The second explanation focuses on the social forces and the Soviet society, arguing that the "Stalinism" was based on the emergence of a bureaucracy and the bureaucratic ruling class. According to this view, "Stalinism" has not gained any other social support except the new bureaucratic class. But some others in this second group argue that Stalin, apart from the support from the elite, has also gained some social support. He not only received "support from above", but also "support from below".

In the era of Gorbachev, the Soviet researchers discussed the problem of historical inevitability of "Stalinism" from a philosophical point of view. In the past, many historians in the Soviet Union held the view that history decides everything, arguing that the emergence of the "Stalinism Phenomenon" is the result of the development of historical laws. But since the late 1980s, some scholars tried get rid of this theoretical system based on deterministic explanation. One new idea proposed was the concept of "choice" without rejecting the framework of the Marxist idea—the historical laws. By applying the choice theory into the analysis of the history of the Soviet Union, the historians tried to explain the history of the Soviet Union based on a series of important choices and important decisions. They have underlined many examples, such as in 1921, the party made the decision to abandon the "war communism" economic policy and introduced the new economic policy (NEP). In the late 1920s, Stalin's choice of development defeated the "Bukharin's choice" and Soviet Union started to implement full-fledged industrialization and agricultural collectivization and so on.

The above summary of Ivanov may not be comprehensive enough, but basically reflects the status of the studies on Stalin, during different periods.

II. The relationship of "Stalinism" with Marxism and with Leninism

These two issues have always been one of the issues the Eastern and Western researchers. The premise of this question is Stalin evaluation. The various interpretations on the relationship between "Stalinism", Marxism and Leninism can be summarized as follows:

First interpretation argues that "Stalinism" completely inherits the doctrine of Marxism-Leninism, and the socialist practice of the Soviet Union is the most reasonable interpretation and application of the theory of Marxism-Leninism. In other words, "Stalinism" is the logical corollary of Marxism-Leninism. People who hold this view are divided among themselves: Those who have a positive attitude and those who have a negative attitude towards "Stalinism" and even Marxism-Leninism due to their stand points. The former tries to prove the legitimacy of "Stalinism" based on the certainty of Marxism-Leninism. The latter is seeks the "original sin" of Stalin's errors based on the denial of Marxism-Leninism. The former is mostly imbued with the nature of defense while the latter mostly with a negative nature.

Second interpretation argues neither simply affirms nor negates the relationship between "Stalinism", Marxism and Leninism, and advocates the need fora comprehensive analysis. The "Stalinism" is a complex phenomenon which is both in line with certain components of Marxism-Leninism, and which also in contradiction with certain components of Marxism-Leninism. Every component of "Stalinism" should be specifically analyzed according to specific conditions.

Next we will further evaluate the representative ideas related to above explanations.

The first is the "original sin" concept whose representative characters are Leszek Kolakowski (1927-2009) and A. S. Tsipko a philosopher from the Soviet Union. Kolakowski was a very active figure in the theoretical community during the period of "de-Stalinization" in Poland. He then taught in the British University. He published a three-volume history book titled Main Currents of Marxism from 1968 to 1976, linking Marx, Lenin and Stalin, he demonstrated the entire process of the birth, development and "collapse" of Marxism. He believed that originally Marx's theory was a humanist doctrine, but had become the original sin of Lenin's "totalitarian theory" inheriting the spirits of romanticism and Prometheus doctrine. Then, Kolakowski further argued that Leninism was the "original sin" for the mistakes of Stalin, arguing that any one of the most brutal atrocities in the terrible days of the era of Stalin could be proved to be correct according the principles of Leninism. He therefore asserted: the thought and practice of Marxism and its embodiment of communism, i.e. Leninism and Stalinism is the same. The latter is the reasonable and justified explanation of the former.

In the "Source of Marxism in Stalinism", Kolakowskifurther elaborated the same point of view. In this article he wrote: "'Stalinism' is the totalitarianism based on the state ownership of the means of production."[1] In his view, the source of Stalinist totalitarianism was Marxism. He argued that Marx envisaged establishing a society—through revolution—which would eliminate all causes of social conflicts, Marx believed that: "humanity in the future would be completely unified or harmonious. This means it was unnecessary to distinguish individuals from the whole mankind."…"it is this expectation of Marx—the unity of mankind and the myth that Marx created which argued the proletariat has a unique sense and role in history." "All these make Marx's theory eventually becoming the thought of a totalitarian movement". He argued: "Marx had always believed that human society can not be 'liberated' without achieving the unity. This unity of the society can not be achieved through other ways than the implementation of autocracy; can not be achieved without the suppression of the civil society, there is no other way to relieve the tense relationship between the civil society and the political society; without suppressing the individual, there is no other means to eliminate the conflicts between the individuals and the 'overall' body; without eliminating 'negative' freedom and 'bourgeois' freedom, there is no other road to 'advanced' and 'positive' freedom."[2] Thus, for him Stalin did not fundamentally distort Marxism. His basic ideas could be found in the theories of Marx. "Stalinism" is the logical and inevitable product of Marxism, and the "application of Marxism–Leninism into practice".

Similar to Kolakowski, A.S. Tsipko also saw the original source of "Stalinism" in Marx. In his view, in Stalin's writings, except his view that the class struggle would be more and more sharp with the development of socialism, Stalin "had never walked beyond the scope of the basic truths of Marxism." The "pure, non-commercial and non-market" socialism blueprint of Marx was the direct theoretical source of Stalin. Marx's idea that the farmers were the last capitalist class was the foundation of Stalin's implementation of agricultural collectivization. Because in Stalin's view, firstly farmers should be eliminated—the petty bourgeois class—in order to achieve a pure, non-commodity and non-market socialism. Stalinism, he contends, was not just the workings of an evil man. It was the natural result of a system based on myths and lies, all in the service of supposedly ideal

457

1　On the Stalinist Model from Scholars Abroad, p. 31-32, Beijing: Central Compilation and Translation Press, 1995.
2　Ibid., p. 48.

aims, which were to be attained by any means regardless of reason, common sense, human values or political realities. He points to the need to get at the roots of Stalinism and establish respect for human rights and traditions and humility in the face of truth. The view of point of A. S. Tsipko had a tremendous impact in the Soviet Union and the international community, arousing a heated debate on the origins of the "Stalinism."

The second view argues that "Stalinism", has nothing in common with Marxism and Leninism and "Stalinism" is a deviation from Marxism and Leninism. In this view, socialism of the Stalinist model is far from the socialist ideals and goals of Marxism, or even irrelevant. For example, Daniil Vasilevic Pivovarov from the former Central Research Institute of Marxism-Leninism of the Soviet Union has argued that the "Stalinism" was just a distortion of Marxism, and "the distortion does not mean the prototype". Therefore, it is completely wrong to try to seek the source of "Stalinism" in Marxism-Leninism. Milovan Djilas Petrović, Gajo from Yugoslavia believed that "there is no inheritance between Marxism and Stalinism, and on the contrary, the thoughts of Stalinism demonstrate that it is incompatible with Marxism and Marxist socialism". Another well-known philosopher Mihailo Markovic from Yugoslavia also held the same view. He pointed out that, "it is totally untenable to say that the thought and practice of Stalin is the contemporary Marxism or to say it is the inevitable practical conclusion of the theories of Marxism."[3] He compared the ideas of socialism by Marx and Stalin in order to illustrate this point.

1. Mihailo Markovic's comparison of Marx and Stalin

Firstly, both Marx and Stalin said, with the socialist revolution, the proletariat would become the ruling class, the production means would be socialized and the products would be distributed according to one's labor contribution. But in Marx's view, seizing power was only "the first step of revolution." The purpose of proletariat as the ruling class is to "change all the previous modes of production" thus change all previous social relations. But Stalin has equaled the state ownership of production means to the social ownership, and therefore did not aim to "change all the modes of production." In Stalin's view, there was no structural difference between the early stage of socialism "just as it emerges from capitalist society; which is thus in every respect, economically, morally and intellectually, still stamped with the birth marks of the old society from whose womb it emerges." and the communist society which "has developed on its own foundations." Marx believed that in the process of development of socialism, with the disappearance of classes divisions, the production means would be concentrated in the hands of individuals who associate together and the public power

3   Ibid., p. 4.

would lose its political character; but when Stalin analyzed the features of the relationships among people in the process of production, he did not allow workers participation in decision making, or participation in the actual management of production or the "state" affairs. About distribution, Marx has argued that the policy of "distribution according to labor contribution" was still within the narrow scope of bourgeoisie right which should be replaced with the policy of "distribution according to needs" but Stalin made a very simple and vulgar interpretation of this policy of "distribution according to labor contribution", i.e. "no labor, no food".

Secondly, critique of capitalism by Marx and Stalin had different depths. Markovic evaluated Marx as a humanist, and argued that Marx criticized capitalism form the progressive approaches and offered a multi-level critique: "Marxnot only criticized those apparent phenomena of capitalism in practice, but also criticized its essentials offering a deeper level of analysis as a special form of class society. Moreover, Marx also thoroughly criticized capitalism from another deeper level of anthropology. Comparatively, Stalin's critique of capitalism remained more at a superficial level, his critique of living labor being dominated by dead labor (capital), his critique of alienated labor and alienated politics was superficial.

Thirdly, Marx's and "Stalinist" concepts of socialism have fundamental differences. In the first place, their concepts of revolution differ. Marx's social revolution concept fundamentally includes the liberation of all mankind, whereas Marx saw political revolution only as the first phase of social revolution. This complex view of Marx was "all gone" in Stalin's concept of revolution. In the second place, their understanding on the conditions of revolution differ greatly. Marx held that the real socialist revolution would be realized only after the material prerequisites for revolution become developed in the womb of the capitalist society. Marx called primitive or crude collectivism as the "rough-hewn, purely instinctive sort of communism; still, it touched the cardinal point and was powerful enough amongst the working class to produce the Utopian communism of Mr Cabet in France." On the other side Stalin not only believed that socialism could be established in relatively backward society, but also regarded this kind of socialism as the existing form of the most developed democracy. In the third place, their understandings on negation of capitalism differ. Marx's negation aims a true sublation of capitalism. Marx thought, despite its limitations, results or achievements of the capitalist society would play an important role for human progress and should be selectively nurtured in the new communist society. But, Stalin's negation of capitalism was metaphysical. He asserted that capitalism was evil, oppressive and full of contradictions, whereas socialism was progressive, harmonious and free of non-contradictions.

2. The relationship of "Stalinism" with Leninism

When debating the relationship between "Stalinism" and Leninism, scholars abroad hold quite different views. A group of them represented by Kolakowski have argued that there was a logical development from Marxism to Leninism and then to "Stalinism". Stalinism was the Marxism-Leninist theory applied to practice." In *Conscience of Revolution*, (1960) Robert Vincent Daniels wrote "Stalin's victory is not a personal victory, but a symbol of victory. It is his personal victory that embodies both Leninist tenets and his own practices."[4] In *Leninism* published in 1957, Alfred George Meyer also wrote "Stalinism can and can only be seen as an ideology and mode of operation directly originating from Leninism. Stalin's view of the contemporary world, his avowed goal, his contradictory and conteversial decisions, his understanding on thetasks faced by the communist countries and many other features of his theories and practices all come from Leninism."[5] However, many scholars did not agree with the view that "Stalinism" and Leninism were in continuity and coherent. For example, Robert C. Tucker, M. Levin, Robert S. Cohen, A.F.K. Organsky, A. Ilyich, Milorad M. Drachkovitch, A.L. Rabinowitsch, etc. have all rejected this idea. The latter group seems to be more concerned about Stalin's "rupture" from Leninism.

460

Directed against the view that Leninism was the "seed" or "root" of "Stalinism", they argued that every historical view had an antecedent. In terms of "Stalinism", its "bud" and "roots" can be attributed to many phenomena, for example, Bolshevism, populism, the tsarist autocracy and even democratic ideas of Western Europe. However, we cannot say "Stalinism" was the inevitable result caused by one of these factors. Robert C. Tucker has argued that although Leninism was an important factor of "Stalinism", the latter "has not directly emerged from Leninism". He held that "Stalinism" was a unique historical phenomenon and was related with the legacy of Bolshevik revolutionary spirit and the old Russian tradition and Stalin's his own ideas and unique personality. For example, "Stalinism" "is the revolution from the above", and it has the colors of the political and cultural background of the Russian tsarist society/state which has existed as a mode of social life in the history of Russia.

Many scholars have argued that Lenin's ideas have encountered major changes. That is to say, Lenin in the period of War Communism (economic policies) was different from Lenin's ideas in the period of the New Economic Policy. And this is one field on which they discuss the continuity or non-continuity relationship between "Stalinism" and Leninism. For example, Robert C. Tucker has claimed that "socialism from above"

---

4   Robert Vincent Daniels, Conscience of Revolution, the English version, p.403, 1960.
5   A. Meyer, Leninism, the English version, pp.282-283, 1957.

advocated by "Stalinism" was "based on Lenin and Lenin's ideas during the November 1917 to 1921 Civil War and the earlier period of his revolutionary career". Leninism of these periods was used as a basis and defense for Stalin's practice of forced collectivization, grain collection system which has exploited peasants and oppression against them. This was "Leninism of Stalinism" but Lenin's theories of socialism has undergone a significant change from 1921 to 1923, which demonstrated itself as abandonment of War Communism policies and initiating the New Economic Policy. Soviet scholar Anotoli Pavlovich Butenko has asserted that according to Lenin, the purpose of the New Economic Policy was to "create the premises of civilization" and then move towards socialism, and the latter could be accomplished only after the former was achieved. However, Stalin has suspended the New Economic Policy, and obliterated socialism and boundaries towards socialism. He went beyond the certain stage of historical development and forced the implementation of "socialism" by state administrative means rather than economic means, which obviously contradicted Lenin's ideas.

Another Soviet scholar Gavril Popov expressed the same view from a slightly different angle. He has argued that Stalin's thoughts on socialism were based on the second party program adopted by the Eighth Congress of the Russian Communist Party (Bolshevik) in 1919. This implies that Stalin's socialist thought was based on Lenin's ideas before the New Economic Policy. The problem is, when Lenin had initiated the New Economic Policy, his views on how to realize socialism had changed remarkably, and this change should "logically", lead to the revision of this program. However, Stalin never deemed it necessary to discuss or doubt about this program, let alone to change it. Yugoslavian scholar G. Lekovic also wrote "during transition to the New Economic Policy, Lenin has openly proposed that the overall socialist views should be fundamentally changed, but Stalin actually stayed in the stage of 'War Communism' both in theory and practice. Lenin concluded that Russia would experience a long transition period and this period will probably include various intermediary stages; Stalin worked hard to shorten this transition period and followed such a road which forced the history to proceed beyond the intermediate stages. This is obviously reflected in the practice of the accelerated process of industrialization and forced collectivization of agriculture."[6]

When discussing about the continuity and dis-continuity between "Stalinism" and Leninism, G. Lekovic has presented a unique view: "in the studies on the relationship between the two, we should not only study Stalin's position towards Lenin, but we should also study the nature and

6   Comments of Foreign Scholars on the Stalinist Model, p.917, Central Compilation and Translation Press.

structure of Lenin's theory. In the latter case, there are "two-Lenins" Lenin's ideas and practice in the specific environment and Lenin's nature. Lenin's nature means, he studied issues based on Marxist tenets and requirements of the time. On the other side, Lenin in the specific environment of Russia and world was an activist who was affected by extreme conditions of his time and focused his efforts to find a prompt way out of troubles.

Besides the two Lenins were linked and intertwined. However, what Stalin frequently quoted was assertions or ideas proposed in the specific environment rather than Lenin's true, general nature. Lekovic in his comparison, argued that Lenin had a different understanding and practice from Stalin in a series of important issues, such as Marxist philosophy, industrialization, agricultural issues, Russian classes and the state, organization, the main motive forces of the socialist revolution/socialist construction, handling opposition elements within the party. On the issue of agricultural collectivization, Lenin held that promoting peasants' cooperatives was a necessary and appropriate step, on the other side, for Lenin to deprive peasants from their lands by collectivization would be wrong. Stalin acting with his own ideas forced peasants by exploiting rich farmers and physically eliminated all other figures—who were likely to oppose his plan—in the party in order to achieve collectivization. Another example: Lenin believed in the need for the existence of the state for a certain historical period, but he did not think that the strengthening of the state is appropriate for socialism in the long run. Stalin not only greatly increased the role of state in the Soviet political system, but also believed that the state should be strengthened, state would gradually disappear in the later process of strengthening. Lekovic added: "in a word, "Stalinism" was a break with Leninism in many aspects."

Thus Lekovic concluded : (1) Stalin was mainly the successor of the specific Lenin, Stalin continued Lenin's specific views in the specific environment. Stalin's attitude towards Lenin's legacy—especially in the most fundamental issues—was the non-continuity. (2) "Stalinism" was also to some extent related to the legacy of Lenin, but Lenin's theory cannot be equated with "Stalinism", their differences were much more than similarities. (3) Generally, "Stalinism" has deviated from Leninism, Lenin or Leninism was not responsible for what Stalin did .[7]

In the article published in the 10th issue of the Journal of Eastern Europe in 1991, East German scholar Wolfang Leonhard also asserted that Lenin and Stalin had many diametrically opposed views in theory and practice, the continuity between Leninism and "Stalinism" did not match the facts. However, Wolfang Leonhard has argued: "But Stalin has inherited Lenin's

---

7   Ibid., p.929.

idea of proletarian dictatorship and led its practice, here we see the continuity between Leninism and "Stalinism", We can even say Lenin should bear some partial responsibility for "Stalinism"."

III. On "Stalin Model"

The "Stalin Model" is another hotly debated issue which many foreign scholars have debated. What is the "Stalin Model"? What is its nature and main characteristics? How was it formed? Foreign scholars have proposed various views and different interpretations on this issue.

Generally speaking, the "Stalin Model" is closely related with "Stalinism". The former is the reflection of the latter in practice, which mainly refers to political, economic and cultural systems formed after Stalin in 1936, announced that "socialism was established" in the Soviet Union. Was the socialism of the "Stalin Model" the genuine socialism, that is, the socialism envisaged by classical writers of Marxism (Marx and Engels)? This is one of the key issues foreign scholars have explored. Most scholars have argued a negative view about this question. They have asserted that Marxist socialism is a socialism that sets the free development of men as the goal, whereas the socialism of the "Stalin Model" is "the barracks-style socialism", "the primitive socialism", and "the socialism maintained with executive orders", etc. For example, Robert C. Tucker has argued: "What Stalin has established was a "powerful, highly centralized, bureaucratic and military-wise industrialized Soviet Russia." Although he called it "advanced socialism", his socialism was manly a "poor based socialism" instead of possessing higher socialist qualities: a socialism which possesses obvious class divisions instead of a relatively undivided society; mainly a socialism in which people feel horrified and distressed instead of a socialism in which people felt ease of mind and breathed freedom. Also this socialism possessed nationalism and chauvinism instead of solidarity and fraternity among people; Stalin's socialism contained a state power which was abnormally enhanced.[8] R.C. Tucker claimed that this "socialism" was totally different from the socialism of Marx—with withering class differences—as described in Marx's *Civil War in France* and socialism and state discussed by Lenin in his *State and Revolution*.

463

---

8 Comments of Foreign Scholars on the Stalin Model, pp.138-139,Beijing: Central Compilation & Translation Press, 1995.

1. B. B. Riabov's description of the "Stalin Model" by Iv. L. Filippov V. P. Naumov

Soviet scholar B. B. Riabov made the following description of the "Stalin model". "The Stalin model was a relatively stable social and political structure formed under the joint effect of all the specific historical conditions (subjective and objective conditions) of Russia and Soviet Union combined with the world situation. This structure is based on the dominant position of state ownership which was alienated from real indivuduals, that is, producers. It is also based on the ideological monopoly of bureaucrats belonging party and the state which was closely combined or intertwined. (which also included the totalitarian intent that unifies all the aspects of people's material and mental/intellectual activities, and which attempted s arbitrarily adjust social relations, inter-ethnic relations and other relations in the society)."[9]

Soviet scholar G. Lisichkin has argued that Stalin's socialist model was a departure or deviation from Marxism and he carefully compared Stalin's socialist view and socialist views of Marx and Engels, and Lenin. Firstly, Marx and Engels explicitly distinguished between economic socialization and legal (executive-order-style) socialization. Lenin had wisely noticed that the practice of public ownership after the Russian Revolution was essentially different from the nature public ownership mentioned by Marx and Engels, and Lenin had advocated "raising the productive forces of labor and socialization of production process" giving due consideration to real social and economic life and people's consciousness. However, Stalin had implemented the socialization of production process by administrative means and "his measure of socialism was the nationalization of production means", thereby "he had greatly simplified" the task of building socialism. Secondly, Marx had admitted that private ownership was morally unjust, but he had argued that the eradication of social injustice required the eradication of private ownership by economic means rather than political means. Lenin also condemned private ownership from the moral perspective, but he was not keen to eliminate it by administrative and compulsory means; instead, Lenin explored the ways in which private ownership could be transformed to socialist ownership in a normal process. Briefly, Lenin envisioned eradicating private ownership by economic means rather than administrative means. However, "Stalin's attitude towards private ownership was completely different from that of Marx, Engels and Lenin. He held that private ownership was a scourge and something worse than the scourge. He believed that any form of public ownership was better and stronger than private ownership."[10] Lisichkin held that Stalin's attitude toward private ownership "was not inherited from Marxism, but from "false socialists""

---

9   Ibid., pp.769-770.
10   Ibid., p.243.

criticized by Marxism. Finally, these different views have led to a series of differences of Stalin and Lenin in economic policies."(Here Marx meant Proudhon and others)

Lisichkin has written that scientific socialism of Marxism has the following characteristics: "(1) it can ensure higher labor's productive forces plus all other productive forces more comprehensive than that in the capitalist system; (2) it can eliminate the differences between urban and rural regions; (3) it could eliminate the exploitation of men by men. (4) it can promote social warmness and philanthropy; (5) it can promote comprehensive development of political freedom, much broader than the most democratic bourgeois country. If we compare Stalin's socialism with Marxist scientific socialism, we can see that the two concepts are not only dissimilar, but also diametrically opposed."

Other scholars have offered different views on features of the "Stalin Model".

Soviet scholar A. Bovin called socialism of the "Stalin Model" as "early and immature socialism". He summarized the features of this immature socialism as follows: (1) On the basis of extensive production and complete public ownership, political and economic power was rigidly centralized to the maximum. (2) Social practice was country-wide unified without any consideration given to the diversity of local conditions, this includes ignorance of varying interests of the people and ignorance of the inevitable diversity in spiritual, intellectual fields, all of which demoted a lively development. (3) In the economic process, Stalin implemented the executive-order-style (top to down) management and ignored the law of value, and focused on the extensive mode of economic growth which ignored the production standards that were detrimental to quality. (4) Democratic criteria in the life of the party and in the society country were formalized and bureaucratic instead of being open and institutionalized, major decisions were made and implemented without the participation of "grassroots" party members and the masses; generally those individuals or groups who were suspected of being against "leaders" and the political system were physically eliminated. (5) There existed cultural poverty, social science studies were paralyzed, recessed self-awareness and self-criticism of historical realities, defense for the reality, myth fabricated in the ideology, and there was a contrast between words and deeds which poisoned social life.[11]

In his book *How Many Socialist Models Did Soviet Union Have?*, V. Kisilev also summarized the characteristics of the "Stalin Model": (1) Stalin administered all spheres of social life in an over centralized way

---

11 Yuri. Afanasyev, ed., There Is No Other Way, pp.724-725, Shenyang: Liaoning Publishing House, 1989.

and combined the top to down executive-order style and state terror, and even organized the mass repression and established labor camps. (2) He led an extensive economic model with a high rate of waste, in this economic model criteria of evaluating economic results according to social benefits was ignored. (3) He denied the value of the former forms of democracy or democratization, of the world civilization, Stalin undermined the policy of administering the state affairs (country) by people and building democratic systems and denied the idea of autonomous initiative of people. The Soviet system was sanctified and cult of personality became rampant. (4) Democratization of social life was ignored, plus the party and state leading organs were overly intertwined. Administrative government organs controlled and monitored people's elected organs, government organs were not put under the rule of law and isolated from the people. Kiselev asserted: all these demonstrated the arbitrary, irrational style of administration and distorted "barrack-style socialism" which were incompatible with the idea of autonomous socialism and the ideal of social emancipation advocated by Marx, Engels and Lenin.[12]

When talking about the socialist features of the "Stalin Model", V.G. Kremen believed that this "Stalin Model" of socialism was closely linked with the idea of crude collectivism, which contrasted genuine socialist collectivism. Stalin employed this idea to economic and political spheres and to all kind of social relations... In the economic sphere for example, when we look into collective farms—they did not have socialist nature, they did not even have cooperative nature. For long years, the collective farm system had a top to down mandatory feature in their operations. In the political sphere, for example, the Soviet state regime seemed to be a collective regime of elected deputies, but in fact it automatically endorsed the will of ther party will and had a bureaucratic nature. Similarly, the collective nature of party life did not work, the working style to pool and promote the collective wisdom of the party was undermined. In the party, the principle of unity of will and action was absolutized, this principle of unity was forcefully extended to the sphere of ideas and views. This meant that the party work was over-centralized, leading to the fact that the top leaders of the party undertook and led all the functions of the party work, and high level leaders and leading party departments undertook the responsibilities and gave decisions, this meant party organizations of lower all levels became passive subordinates. V.G. Kremen further pointed out that since the top to bottom executive-order administrative system was prevalent in the society, in the Stalin period the party became a social organization that combined features of the political leadership, the organ of state power and the leading organ of economic administration. There was no separation between the

466

---

12 Ibid., 492.

party work and the government work, and the party replaced the functions of the government. In social relations, relationships among the members of the working class, among the members of the collective farms and inter-ethnic relations, the genuine collective relations were not established. After his careful analysis V.G. Kremen offered a final judgment: barrack-style social relations established in the Stalin period, to a large extent, were caused by this deformed understanding of collectivism.

2. The causes for the formation of the "Stalin Model" of socialism

Researchers have discussed this issue considering several aspects of social life.

A. Bovin has argued that the formation of the "Stalin Model" of socialism was caused by two important factors: First, the socio-economic situation of the country, namely the material production and civilization, was backward in general. Russia and Soviet Union lacked democratic traditions. The masses, especially peasants, were under the effect of "tsar syndrome". Second, Soviet Union as the first socialist country was lonely, isolated and and faced with foreign hostility, and it besieged by capitalism which constantly threatened this country with war and intervention.

V.G. Kremen has argued that the Soviet socialism was a deformed socialism. We can examine its causes from the subjective and objective aspects. As for the objective causes: first, "in the final analysis deformed socialism was caused by the level of social development, historical traditions of the country and other specific historical realities of the epoch. Some causes emerged from the backwardness of Russian economy, i.e. Russia was not ready to directly enter the socialism, yet. It could not transit to socialism through the so-called classic way, according to the founders of Marxism socialism should be based on a highly developed capitalism and advanced productive forces."[13] V.G. Kremen wrote: "Under the circumstances where the advanced productive forces are absent or they are immature, the construction of socialism may contain certain risks, namely the policies which aims to establish socialist social relations may contain the risk of deformation of these social relations. Secondly, several political and historical factors have caused socialism face a series of deformations. Among them was Russian Tsarism that lasted for centuries and the deeply rooted feudalism of Russian society which effected future generations living in the Soviet Union. Moreover, the external political environment, especially the tension caused by the hostile attitude of the capitalist world, added a sectarian color to the socialist ideal." When analyzing the subjective reasons, V.G. Kremen

---

13   Foreign Scholars on Stalin Model, 702.

emphasized the causes related to the party. The organizational principles, forms and style of the party work underwent serious deformations. The most important one was that the party had lost its democratic tradition and its collective nature.

IV. On "Second Revolution"

Foreign scholars generally believed that the beginning of "Stalinist" epoch in the Soviet Union was marked with the suspension of "the new economic policy," the implementation of large-scale collectivization of agriculture, and acceleration of industrial development especially of heavy industry and massive investments in the military industry in the late 1920s. "Stalin model" formed gradually through these "big steps of changes."

Many scholars such as R.C. Tucker, Joel C. Moses and Stephen F. Cohen have evaluated these changes by Stalin as a "top-down" revolution, which forced the country into the "socialist economic track."

R.C. Tucker has argued that, Lenin's conception envisaged the conditions and the efforts to surpass the (NEP) new economic policy would occur in the course of implementing the new economic policy. The changes forward in the course of NEP should opt for reforms rather than revolutions. But "Stalin did not use reforms to surpass the new economic policy. Instead, he used ordinances and revolutionary ways even violence to eliminate the new economic policy. He did not take a gradual approach namely seek to persuade people when making advances in building socialism. Instead he advanced forward employing a risky high speed and used state power eliminates people's resistance, this style caused many damages and risks. This style of advancement destroyed a group of people who grew up in the first stage of revolution ten years ago. Soviet Union was deprived from the intellectual capacity of these people and their efforts."[14] Joel C. Moses has argued that this "top-down" revolution was a "movement specifically aimed against capitalism." Its aim was to eliminate individual small peasant farming, to ruin relatively rich farmers, abolish private business and trade, private industry and handicrafts business.

Scholars have examined the reasons why Stalin had launched this "top-down" revolution from above. Basically two different opinions are proposed: the first group argues that Stalin had launched this "revolution" basing himself on certain realistic options. His steps were both necessary and inevitable. Researchers such as Eric Van Ree, Isaac Deutscher and Alec Nove all held this opinion. They have explored the causes mainly from the objective environment. The other opinion group argues that Stalin launched

468

14 Foreign Scholars on Stalin Model, p.123.

the "revolution" with subjective calculations. They have also argued, that Stalin used political solution methods to handle economic problems, thus he went against the requirements and trends of objective laws, which brought extremely seriously disasters to the Soviet Union.

Below, we will deliver their views A. N. Kisyelov believed that the cancellation of new economic policy (NEP) by Stalin and the group of leaders around him was caused by the severe situation then. Faced with the threat of war, the Soviet Union did not have enough time to develop socialist construction according to the economic laws. Thus it could only adopt political methods to develop socialism. New economic policy, theoretically speaking, was a safer, more convenient, and tempting choice. But in practice, it was an unrealistic choice which could lead to softening and corroding and could restrain the possibility of accelerated development. Though, socialist construction was led by highly political methods, there was no other practical option. Moreover, judging from external international conditions, imperialist countries had absolute advantages in terms of economic and military power. To avoid being eliminated by them, the Soviet Union had to become an industrially developed country as soon as possible. All in all, "whether judging from domestic conditions or international conditions, there was only one way to develop socialism. That was the nature of the general policy Soviet Union followed after abandoning new economic policy… It was a general policy line that focused on accelerating industrialization and collectivization of agriculture and strengthening national defense."[15]

469

Western scholar A.S. Tsipko also held the same opinion. When he criticized Moshe Lewin and Stephen F. Cohen who saw Buharin's proposal in 1920s as a true Leninist policy, and who regarded the "new economic policy" (NEP) as a long-term feasible option for the Bolsheviks, he noted the following: "although Buharin's proposal was economically feasible but politically non-feasible." A.S. Tsipko asserted that any Bolshevik leader would enforce similar collectivization policy of Stalin at the end of 1920s.

Isaac Deutscher used his "severe social crisis" hypothesis to explain Stalin's policies. He quoted statistics to illustrate his ideas, especially mentioning the January 1928, grain purchase crisis in SU, which directly affected the food supply to the cities. That required a "revolutionary solution." He said: "Stalin who had hesitated how to react against this crisis till the last moment, took action "under this overwhelming" situation and "launched the Second Revolution" in an unexpected way. The long-term threat caused by the famine in 1928 and 1929 made him "suddenly begin collectivization movement."[16] Western scholars E.H. Carr and R.W. Davies

---

15 Book, Foreign Scholars on Stalin Model, p.437.
16 Isaac Deutscher, Political Biography of Stalin, version 2, pp.318-322, Chengdu: Sichuan People's Publishing House, 1982.

also held the same opinion. They pointed out: "The sudden decision made in 1929 was not planned beforehand," but triggered by the grain purchase crisis. Alekseevich Nikolai Kisyelov evaluated this economic crisis in that period as "an unprecedented political crisis." He asserted that at that time the economic crisis had threatened the existence of the Soviet regime. It was under the pressure of this threat that Stalin's thoughts encountered a fundamental change, making him begin the gambling decision of the first five-year plan (1928-1932).

R.C. Tucker rejects the approach that uses objective conditions to explain Stalin's policies. According to R.C. Tucker, judging from either domestic situation or abroad, there was no reason adequate or forceful enough to explain the enforced collectivization movement. When, evaluating the domestic situation, he wrote: "even at the end of 1920s when grain market lacked grain supply due to peasants' discontent with Soviet government policies peasants did not show any dangerous sign of political rebellions. "On the contrary, no matter, how angry the peasants were, they wanted to have more income so they did not let grains go into market, except economic policies farmers generally accepted the new Soviet regime. Evaluating the international situation, R.C. Tucker argued: "Though external threats did exist, they were quite exaggerated. R.C. Tucker quoted Dana G. Dalrymple's article titled, the 1932-1934 Famine of the Soviet Union: "The danger of war actually were created and exaggerated clumsily by the Soviet politicians in 1927."[17] R.C. Tucker concluded: "We should point out that the Soviet worries about the relationship with Europe was not groundless, although this "worry" in the Soviet Union political media was not because of a true fear that there was a formation of a war alliance against the Soviet Union. However, the possibility of war was possibly used to build up Stalin's domestic policies."[18] R.C. Tucker, also argued that: "Stalin had a dogmatic view about the international situation, he saw the international developments during the second half of the 1930s, as a combined revival of 1914 and of 1918 (imperialist intervention to Soviet Union), he took this evaluation as the basis to design the relations between Soviet Union and the capitalist world.

R.C. Tucker has argued that Stalin's "top-down" revolution—the overallcollectivization—was not supported by the masses, which was also written in the book *CPSU (Bolshevik) Concise Guide to History*. In fact, not only rich farmers, but also middle farmers, even a part of poor farmers were opposed to new rural policies. They joined the collective farms out of coercion or fear.

---

17   Dana G. Dalrymple, The 1932-1934 Famine of the Soviet Union, reprinted in Studies of the Soviet Union, 1964 (1), p. 261.
18   Foreign Scholars on Stalin Model, p.129.

The Soviet scholar Y.P. Sitkovsky held an opinion different from the two contrasting one. On the one hand, he admitted that objective factors have played their role in the formation of Stalin's policy. On the other, he argued that: "objective factors alone cannot be used to explain Stalin's behavior, though the pressure from objective factors has provided good foundation for Stalin's policies. We cannot ignore the possibility that there could be other options and other decisions Stalin and his group could choose, the pressure from objective factors provided so little room for a "milder" model. Meanwhile, Y.P. Sitkovsky insisted that objective factors could not explain everything for Stalin's policies: "on the one hand, the war which broke out two years later could not destroy us, since we had overcome Russia's backwardness as rapid as possible, and built the foundations of modern industry. To achieve this goal, tremendous efforts, sacrifices and mistakes were inevitable. On the other hand, some behaviors of Stalin, such as eliminating a large group of revolutionaries that were faithful to Leninism, using threatening, other servile behaviors were definitely not caused by the objective conditions, these were not inevitable and not necessary."

Although some part of the scholars have more or less admitted the achievements of industrialization, claiming that the industrialization drive had remarkably strengthened the power of the Soviet Union. The economy based on industrialization "indicated its extraordinary vividness and its obvious of rapid development." "Industrialization built the solid foundation for the victory of anti-fascist war."[19] But the majority of the researchers held a negative attitude towards the way of industrialization and its high costs. Their main arguments includes: first, sacrificing agriculture so as to develop industry has caused the imbalance of the overall economic structure in the Soviet Union. Agricultural economy and consumer goods industries have lagged seriously. The Soviet Union accumulated investment funds through price scissors policy, which led to the growing income and development gap between rural areas and urban areas, as well as between working classes and farmers. Second, overemphasis on the priority of developing heavy industry, had greatly damaged the development of light industry. Therefore, the shortage of consumer goods was serious which directly detoriated people's living standard. Finally, the process of industrialization strengthened the status of the party and state bureaucracy. In this epoch the working style when leading industrial production, bureaucratic top to down style gradually dominated the democratic style which suppressed the enthusiasm of producers.

Some scholars have rebuked Stalin's views and defense for agricultural

19 On the Issues of Stalin, vol. 2, compiled by Hangzhou University Press, 1980, pp.175-176.

collectivization and have argued that accelerating industrialization was the pretext to impose "tributes and taxes" on farmers or steal funds from peasants. R.C. Tucker has argued: "According to Stalin's ideas, the collective farm system could make it easier to collect surplus agricultural products and funds, thereby provide necessary funds for industrialization. However, if NEP policies related to agriculture had remained, the development of light industry would be the basis for the general industrialization of the Soviet Union including heavy industry."[20] Soviet scholar N.G. Basov also denied the significant role of the agriculture for the industrialization of Soviet Union. He pointed out that, in the period of the first five-year plan, the Soviet agriculture did not contribute to industrialization in any sense. Western scholar J. Arch Getty also said that the real impact that the Soviet agriculture brought to industrialization was negative. His conclusion was that: agricultural collectivization Stalin implemented was far from being a necessity for theindustrialization drive. During the rapid development of industry in the period of the first five-year plan (1928-32) agricultural sector did not provide any accumulation fund. What the agricultural collectivism brought about was disaster and no one benefited from it. The same problem applies for the rapid development of industrialization.[21]

Some other group of scholars have argued that although the decision of industrialization and collectivization of agriculture was correct, its methods were wrong. Therefore, they did not represent the true socialism. Just as Wayne H. Bowen pointed out, industrialization was necessary but its way of enhancing productive forces and its way of establishing modern industry was not socialist. Planned economy, production relations, and the managing style of the national economy should be socialist, in terms of their nature, direction and their expected results, but this problem was not addressed properly.

When evaluataing the collectivization of agriculture, Wayne H. Bowen believed, collectivization was necessary and collectivization was exactly a socialist step. But the voluntary way that Lenin advocated was lacked, andcoercion was applied on farmers. Therefore, collectivization did not become a socialist reform, instead it became a forced way to transfer resources from rural areas to urban areas. Bowen, has argued that either industrialization or collectivization were the necessary minimum, but these two could not solve the main task of socialism—main task of socialism is to guarantee that socialism can create higher productivity and productive forces than capitalism, i.e. the new system is better than the old one.[22]

Some scholars pointed out that if the Soviet Union continued implementing

---

20   Foreign Scholars on Stalin Model, p.124.
21   Stalin and Stalinism, p.133.
22   Book from Y. Afanasyév, There Is No Other Way, pp. 729-730.

Lenin's (NEP) new economic policy or the balanced industrialization policy—based on the new economy policy—as suggested by Buharin and did not implement Stalin's ideas, it would be possible to have the same speed of industrialization but with smaller cost. R.C. Tucker for example, believed that Buharin's article "An Economist's Reading notes" published in the journal "The Truth" on September 30, 1928 proposing the plan of implementing industrialization policy while keeping the new economic policy was basically a realistic economic plan. R.C.Tucker wrote: "the non-revolutionary Soviet industrialization policy that Buharin suggested at the end of the 1920s was greatly inspired by Lenin's thinking from 1921 to 1923. His option was feasible. If Soviet Union had implemented this policy, it would have played its role properly. Even if it did not work out well, the costs that the Soviet economy would pay would not be as much as those exorbitant ones which resulted from Stalinist resolutions."[23]

Scholars such as R.C. Tucker and Stephen Cohen have argued that the policy Stalin implemented made the Soviet people pay a high price. Stalin realized "socialism" against the cost of forced immigration for millions of people, sent many to concentration camps and other suppressions. In the rural areas, due to large-scale and hasty collectivization movement, many farmers lost their land, livestock, houses, and even their lives. All this resulted in a sharp decline in agricultural productivity. In urban areas, concentrating most of the available resources in heavy industry, suppression of private business, poor management system, waste of sources caused by and poor training of laborers, all these made the Soviet face long-term problems that were difficult to overcome.

473

V. Brief commentary

What we introduced above is just views on some of the key issues studied by the foreign scholars related to Stalin. There are also some other issues that foreign scholars have deeply studied, such as Stalin's suppression of the "opposition" in 1930s. Due to space limitations, we did not include them here. If we evaluate the history of foreign studies related Stalin, they are seeing an ever-deepening process from revelation to discussion. Admittedly, in this history of study both the study approach and opinions, we see that there are some points worth of recognition and some inspiring points. Therefore, all these studies help us to promote our researches of this complicated phenomenon. It shall be noted that due to different historical conditions, scholars' stances and the volume of materials have varied a lot. Some scholars have preferred analyzing and researching objectively, while some judged things with a strong ideological tone. But still we should analyze them seriously.

---

23 Foreign Scholars on Stalin Model, p.130.

As for methodologies, without doubt a historical evaluation methodology should be adopted in the research of Stalin, namely analyze the whole Stalin period in context of the overall development of the Soviet society, and study the dominant socialist view of era in the context of the whole socialist ideology history and socialist political history.

We should not discuss things abstractly without considering the historical environment and conditions. In this regard, some words from Soviet scholar B.P. Nikitin makes great sense. He said: "Stalin was created by a very violent era with sharp social and political struggles. The process of these sharp struggles has pushed him to the key position, onto the center of Soviet politics and world politics. If we evaluate an event that happens today, our standpoint will be shaped according to a completely different era, an era in which social classes and world nations begins to conciliate with each other, and where people begin to refuse the abyss of self-destruction and where people can begin a normal socialist construction. That era of Stalin was hard to understand but we must understand. Otherwise, we will not have a complete concept about history, a flowing river filled with events."[24]

474 We can see that many scholars have paid close attention to reveal the historical environment and objective conditions of Stalin period, so as to be able to relatively objectively evaluate the policies that Stalin has formed and implemented. But some scholars adopted a completely non-historical method when studying Stalin. They have started from certain abstract conceptions such as human nature and did not consider historical conditions of Stalin's political career.

As a result, these scholars indulge into empty discussions and moral judgments. Nikitin described the criticism of Stalin by the Soviet academia in 1980s: "Now the society is suffering the second moral wave caused by Stalin's lawless behaviors and cruelty. In the last two years, due to large amount of revelation of facts, the abhor towards Stalin is further strengthened, and the academic society tends to neglect the achievements of the heroic generation who accomplished the great historical mission."[25]

It was because moral judgments have replaced scientific analysis, namely according to some people, Stalin was nothing but an entire "tyrant," a "slaughter" and a politician who used manipulations. The great achievements which Soviet socialism had accomplished, and the historical heroism the Soviet Union performed in the anti-fascist war was all gone. People even doubted the efforts the Soviet Union made for the rapid development of industrialization.

---

24 Book, Foreign Scholars on Stalin Model, p. 434.
25 Ibid., p.457.

Without doubt, the Soviet Union of Stalin's period went through many setbacks and made many serious mistakes when evaluated from today's point of view, including implementing collectivization of agriculture by coercion and by suppressing farmers massively. However, we cannot ignore Stalin's contributions to the Soviet Union and to the historical progress of human kind.

About the debates on Stalin, Mao Zedong once said, there may not be a final conclusion in this century (referring to the 20th century). History has proved his view. "Stalinism" as a historical phenomenon, will not disappear in the river of history, and it will profoundly influence the world now and in the future. The studies on the historical role of Stalin will continue throughout the world.

Appendix

Studies by the Chinese Academy on Stalin's Thought

Stalin is a historical figure having a significant impact on the development of human society of the 20th century. Mao Zedong once pointed out in 1963: "the issue of Stalin is a major problem worldwide, causing a repercussion of all the classes around the world. It has been discussed nowadays. It is estimated that within the 20th century, this problem will not reach a final evaluation." For decades, scholars in China have conducted an in-depth study on Stalin's thoughts, but because of the different historical backgrounds, different personal starting point for research, the ideas on the merits and demerits of Stalin and the evaluation are also very different.

I. Study on Stalin's thoughts from the late 70s to the late 80s

At the end of the "Cultural Revolution", in the process of systematical study of China's history since the foundation (1978-81)[1], Deng Xiaoping conducted scientific analysis on Stalin's thought and the "Soviet Model" established under this thought. Thus Deng Xiaoping proposed the idea of building socialism with Chinese characteristics, which was a breakthrough in China's socialist development.[2]

In 1978, after the 3rd Plenary Session of 11th Central Committee, Deng Xiaoping focused on solving the practical problems of contemporary China and systematically summarized Stalin thought and the Soviet Model established under this thought in the following areas:

In the aspect of politics, Deng Xiaoping pointed out in the talk with the meeting with the first Central Secretary of the Polish United Workers' Party, President of the State Committee Jaruzelsky on September 29, 1986.

1 Pls see. CPC document: Resolution on certain questions in the history of our party since the founding of the People's Republic of China.
2 Adopted by the Sixth Plenary Session of the Eleventh Central Committee of the Communist Party of China on June 27, 1981), Marxist Internet Archive.

"We are indeed lacking of experiences and we might just start to seriously explore a better road now."[3]

This can be seen as Deng Xiaoping's general summary of the Soviet political model during the period of Stalin.

Although this conclusion was made when Deng Xiaoping was focusing in his thinking on how to develop economic reforms in order to meet the requirements of economic reform (during 1986s), this does not mean Deng Xiaoping only studied or focused on the problems of the Soviet model from the aspect of political system at that time.

In fact, before this time and even earlier, Deng Xiaoping had noticed and pointed out to many problems arising due to China's copying the political system of Soviet model. In the 1980s, our party CPC had proposed approach of the "long-term coexistence, mutual consultation" with various eight parties in the country and promoted academic freedom in the academic research and literature creation works. Deng Xiaoping supported this whole heartedly and led the CPC to learn from the lessons of the mistakes of Stalin: He said "Stalin made mistakes on it. He wasn't sophisticated and too simple.In the Soviet Union, Marxism research recessed in the period of him."[4]

478   After the "Cultural Revolution", Deng Xiaoping became the core of second generation leadership collective of the CPC. In his speech of enlarged meeting of the Political Bureau of CPC Central Committee in August 1980, Deng Xiaoping listed the main shortcomings of the leadership system and the cadre system of state and the party and discussed the significance of the reform of the leadership system of the party and state.

When discussing the over-excessive concentration of power in the hands of a individual person or small number of people, he said the current system deprived the majority from their rights of decision and the rights few people had were too excessive, Deng Xiaoping pointed out "this phenomenon has the relation with the impact of remnants of feudal despotism in our country, and is related with the tradition of excessive concentration of power of in the hands of the leaders (individuals) in all parties, which was implemented during the communist international."[5]

The tradition of all the parties during the period of communist international is primarily the tradition of the Soviet Party related to practices in the period of Stalin. When discussing that the leadership system, organizational system and working system of the party and state were more important,

3   Selected Works of Deng Xiaoping, Edition 2, Vol.2, pp.250-251.
4   Deng Xiaoping's Selected Works vol. 1, Version 2, p.272, Beijing: People's Publishing House, 1994.
5   Deng Xiaoping's Selected Works vol. 2, Version 2, p. 329.

fundamental, comprehensive, stable and long-term than the thought and style of the leaders, Deng Xiaoping evaluated Stalin's error, saying: "Stalin seriously damaged the socialist legal system in SU.

Comrade Mao Zedong once had said such incidents like in SU could not happen in the Western countries like Britain, France and the United States."[6] The roots of Stalin's errors were not mainly because of his own ideas and his own style, but rather the inadequate leadership system, organizational system and working system of his party. These above were Deng Xiaoping's understanding of the Soviet political model.

In the aspect of economy, back in November 1979, when proposing that socialism could also practice market economy, Deng Xiaoping put forward the problems of the impact of the Soviet economic system on China and stated: "Some of our economic systems, especially business management and enterprise organization, have been greatly impacted by the Soviet Union."[7]

To the mid-1980s, reforms in China's rural areas was successful and the economic reforms in the urbanized areas was started in full swing. The development of these practices had made Deng Xiaoping further understand another aspect:

The "Soviet model"obviously refers to the model of the Soviet's pure planned economy model with single public ownership which had started at the late 1920s when the Stalin-led CPSU (Bolshevik) had abandoned the New Economic Policy. For the pure planned economy of the Soviet model, Deng Xiaoping clearly criticized it. In February 1987, when talking with several central responsible comrades, he said that the market economy is not equal to capitalism.

The socialism is not only equal to the planned economy. Both the market and the planned economy were the ways and mechanisms to develop productive forces.

In the aspect of foreign relations, Deng Xiaoping was against that the Soviet Party claimed to be the center of the international communist movements and the Soviet Party being the top spokesman for the movement to make orders to other foreign parties and making open judgments on the issues of other parties and countries. In April 1983, Deng Xiaoping pointed out that:

During the period of Stalin, the Chinese party in some of the key issues did not listen to his words but be able to achieve the victory of the Chinese revolution."[8]

---

6   Ibid., p.333.

7   Ibid., p.235.

8   Deng Xiaoping's Selected Works vol. 3, Version 1, p.27.

About the Soviet Union's great power of chauvinism during the period of Stalin, and Stalin's standing on the side of the Chinese people and the Chinese Communist Party, Deng Xiaoping clearly expressed some criticism. He pointed out that,

Since the late 1970s, with the establishment of the party's ideological research line of "liberating our thoughts, seeking truth from facts", China's academy have started new researches on Stalin thought under quite new historical conditions and achieved new conclusions with the distinctive features of the times. These studies have focused on the following aspects:

The first is the study on the stages and theory of human social development.

Stalin, in his *History of the All-Union Communist Party (Bolsheviks), Short Course* published in 1928 pointed out that there were only five basic relations of production in the history of development of mankind, which were primitive communal system, slavery system, feudal system, capitalist system, and socialist system.

Some says: "According to Marxism the major production modes and relations of production of human society should be six instead of five including communism ... Dakun wrote: When I studied this issue in the early 1950s, my thoughts were trapped in Stalin's frame. After continuous studies, I found that Stalin's 'theory of five kinds of production modes' was neither consistent with Marx's intention nor conform to the actual development of human history."[9]

The second is the issue of the relationship between theory and methodology.

Stalin, in *Dialectical and Historical Materialism*, evaluated the historical materialism as the secondary and discussed its two major elements of Dialectical materialism and Historical Materialism separately. He argued that the "methodology is dialectical" and the "theory is materialistic". Some people think that Stalin's view has separated the approach and theory, which inevitably led to the separation of the unity of materialism and dialectics.[10]

Some people think that Stalin's statement here is inaccurate. Marx's theory of historical materialism and its method, dialectics, have always been closely together. This does not mean the significance of the dialectics can not be explained only from the aspect of methodological approach in some

480

9   Dakun Wu, Marx and the Third World, Preface, Chinese Version, pp.3-4, Beijing: Business Publishing House, 1981
10   Yihua Xue, Shuzhong Li, Correct Evaluation of Stalin's 'Dialectical Materialism and Historical Materialism', in Collected Works of Discussion of Stalin's Philosophical Thoughts, Beijing: China Social and Scientific Press, 1982.

cases. Engels and Lenin have also done this, but they have never compared theory and methodology, like what Stalin did in his book, thus Stalin's expression is inappropriate and misleading.

However, it is too much to say that he only took dialectics as methodology and materialism as theory, it is too unfair to say that he separated the dialectics and materialism and even gave an idealistic nature to dialectics when applying it. In fact, in his specific argument later related to the basic characteristics of dialectics and materialism, he analyzed the theory and methodology as a whole. Nansen Huang wrote: How can the dialectics and materialism be constituted as a unified organic whole problem, it is still a question worth further study and discussion.[11]

The third is on the features of the dialectics.

Stalin outlined four basic features of dialectics in his book *Dialectical and Historical Materialism*. Was it a progress forward or a step backwards if we compare his ideas with the dialectics thoughts of Marx, Engels and Lenin? There are two kinds of evaluations.

Some people think that Stalin's theory on the four basic features of dialectics neither inherited nor developed Lenin's dialectical thought, nor took the height of Lenin as a starting point, and even nor developed the scientific system of dialectical materialism according to Lenin's in a correct way. He simplified rich content of dialectics, not fully expressing the content of the basic law of dialectics.[12]

481

Some people think that Stalin's four basic laws of the dialectics are fundamentally in line with Marxism-Leninism. He developed Engels and Lenin's thoughts on some certain issues and made new attempts on establishing a complete theoretical system of dialectics. The evaluation of "Stalin's step backwards" is incorrect. Stalin has indeed made a contribution to dialectics.[13]

The fourth is the economic law that the relations of production must necessarily conform with the character of the productive forces. Some people think: "Stalin's statement on this law is one-sided. He only gave emphasis to the changes in the relations of production, but put the productive forces at a secondary position, defined them as something to be "conformed with." He did not discuss the determinant role of the productive force on the production relations, did not evaluate their progressive role."

11 Nansen Huang, Several Issues of Stalin's'the Dialectical Materialism and Historical Materialism', in Collected Works of Discussion of Stalin's Philosophical Thought.
12 Chaobo Chi et al., How to Evaluate Stalin's Four Features of the Dialectical Materialism, in Collected Works of Discussion of Stalin's Philosophical Thought.
13 Kuiliang Zhang, Correct Understanding of Stalin's Four Features of the Dialectics, in Collected Works of Discussion of Stalin's Philosophical Thought.

Therefore, this law should be correctly formulated as "the productive forces determine the relations of production while the relations of production must conform with the development of productive forces". When the productive forces are put at the first status, it will make this law both adapt to two situations: When the situation in which transformation of production relations are our focus and when the situation in which development of the productive forces is our priority or most important need, and this new formulation will break the limitations of the original old formulation.[14]

Some people think: "Stalin's statement is justified because it accurately reflects and captures the actual relations that exist between the productive forces and the production relationships: Both when their relationships are harmonious and inharmonious."[15]

There are also some people who suggest that: "From Stalin's life-long theoretical summarizations on the issue of the productive force and the productive relationship, his focus was to emphasize the decisive role of the productive forces compared to productive relationships", which is not one-sided. "Stalin used 'must conform' in order to reveal the most basic and most important relationship between production relations and the productive forces, I think this is more 'concise'.

What he emphasized is the objective necessity of 'conforming', i.e. He emphasized the decisive function of the productive force and the dependent nature of the production relations." "Stalin's expression fully reflects the dialectical relationship between the productive forces and the production relations with the emphasis on the ultimate role of decisive function of the productive forces compared to the production relations."[16]

The fifth is on the basic economic law of the socialism. Stalin said: "The essential features and requirements of the basic law of socialism might be formulated roughly in this way: securing of the maximum satisfaction of the constantly rising material and cultural requirements of the whole of society through the continuous expansion and perfection of socialist production on the basis of higher techniques. Consequently, instead of maximum profits–maximum satisfaction and realization of the material and cultural requirements of society."

In the early 1980s, China's national economy entered another period of adjustment, the academic community also made further discussion on the issues of Stalin's formulation on basic economic law of socialism.

14   Mengjue Guan, Studies on Socialist Politics and Economics (Beijing, Shanghai People's Publishing House, 1985), p. 18.
15   Yayu Yuan, "Question the Proposition 'The Productive Force Determines the Productive Relationship'," Journal of Sichuan University 2 (1983).
16   Shaobo Yu, Several Issues of the Law that the Productive Force must fit the Productive Relationship, in An Insight into the Historical Materialism, pp.18-19, 19.

Some scholars expressed different points of view on the content of Stalin's basic economic law of socialism. They argues that Stalin's theory of "meeting the needs" embodies "the essential characteristics of the socialist economic system, which can be said correct from the basic spirit, but too vague and general in the way of its form of expression". "For example, Stalin only took the production of use values as the production aim of socialism, which was bound to be too general and vague, to use the expression of "socialist production" was too general.""[17]

Some people argue that the basic principles and main spirit of Stalin's statement on the basic economic law was right, but not perfect, and needs to be supplemented and enriched. In Stalin's formula, the concept of "the needs of the whole society" as the purpose is too general, which easily leads to different interpretations, and is not clear. It was also inaccurate for Stalin to frequently argue that "constantly rising" needs is the criterion to distinguish between socialism and capitalism.

In fact, as a historical process, the needs of the society are always in constantly rising state. . In the strict sense, "meeting the growing needs of the whole society" only explains one part of the aim when we are realizing socialist production or certain conditions of socialist production. Our mission is "to meet social needs". It is sufficient, but to put it more completely but we should also add our ultimate goal as: "to ensure the welfare of all members of society and all-round development of their mental and physical capabilities."[18]

Some people think that Stalin's expression on the law of socialist economy lacks scientificalness, and it was not yet established completely and needs to re-examined." The law expressed by Stalin has nothing to do with objective process of production and objective economic sphere, which is not in accordance with nature of economic laws, thus it only expresses our subjective will or desire.

The laws of Marxist economics are always the reflection within a certain economic sphere and they take their form within a certain process of production. The aim of socialist production and approaches advocated by Stalin does not reflect any (objective) economic sphere, this means his formulation has no qualitative relation with a certain socialist production process and socialist aim of production."[19]

483

17   Jue Wang et al., The Theory of Necessary Values , 1988, p. 90, Beijing: People's Publishing House.
18   Refer to Zhaobin Chen, Socialist Production and the Law of Time-saving in On the Goal of Socialist Production-the National Symposium Proceedings of the Purpose of Socialist Production, pp.113-115, Changchun: Jilin People's Publishing House, 1981.
19   Shiyin Guangdi Liu, Several Views on the Purpose of Socialist Production in On the Goal of Socialist Production-the National Symposium Proceedings of the Purpose of Socialist Production, p.194,Changchun: Jilin People's Publishing House, 1981.

Some people think: "Stalin's definition is neither complete nor accurate and is seriously metaphysical and too absolute." This is reflected in: firstly, Stalin does not express that the fundamental characteristics that the masses are the masters of socialist economy; secondly, he does not emphasize that all economic sectors should develop according to plans and develop proportionally, but this will very likely cause a serious imbalances; thirdly, it is metaphysical for Stalin to put the profit requirement as opposite to securing or satisfying social needs; fourthly, he does not point out the close relationship between the development of socialist production and the need to increase the benefits of producers (working people).[20]

Majority opinion is that Stalin's statement on the basic economic law of socialism is a scientific generalization. "It can be discussed if someone thinks whether Stalin's expression is perfect, but I think the basic content of this statement is in accordance with the opinions of Marx, Engels, Lenin and other important Marxist writers." The expression of Stalin is "a scientific summarization of the basic economic law of socialism. Firstly, his definition includes the aim and means of social production.

Taking the aim of social production as the main element of the basic economic law of socialism can reflect the essential characteristics of certain relations of production, and in turn the means by which to achieve this aim goal can also reflect the nature of the relations of production and also can reflect the basic requirement (production on the basis of higher technology) of socialist production. Stalin's summary clearly mentions the basic rules and direction of development for us to scientifically organize socialist economic construction".[21]

The sixth thema is the study subject of political economics.

Stalin in *Economic Problems of Socialism in the USSR*, Stalin wrote: the province political economy is the production, (relations) the economic, relations of men. It includes: a) the forms of ownership of the means of production; b) the status of the various social groups in production and their interrelations that follow from these forms, or what Marx calls: "they exchange their activities"; c) the forms of distribution of products, which are entirely determined by them. (Here c is added by the author of this book to clearly understand Stalin's ideas.)

All these together constitute the province of political economy. This definition does not contain the word "exchange," which is included in Engels' definition. I omit it because "exchange" is usually understood by many to mean exchange of commodities, which is characteristic not of all social

---

20   Shiyin Shi,"Thoughts of Stalin's Basic Economic Laws of Socialism," Academy Monthly (9) 1980.
21   Huanzhong Zhang, "On the Purpose and the Axis of the Productive System of the Socialist Production,"Academy Monthly (1) 1980.

formations, but only of some social formations, (He means capitalist and precapitalist social formations) and this sometimes gives rise to misunderstanding, even though the word "exchange" with Engels did not mean only commodity exchange. As will be seen, however, that which Engels meant by the word "exchange" has been included, as a component part, in (my) above definition. Hence, this definition of the province of political economy fully coincides in content with Engels' definition.

All of these constitute the study subjects of political economics together. Stalin said his definition was different from Engels', but he said he has also included the views of Engels.[22]

Marx wrote in *Wage Labour and Capital*: In the process of production, human beings work not only upon nature, but also upon one another (man to man reciprocal exchanges). They produce only by working together in a specified manner and reciprocally exchanging their activities. Secondly, in order to produce, they enter into definite connections and relations to one another, and only within these social connections and relations does their influence upon nature operate—i.e., does production take place.These social relations between the producers, and the conditions under which they exchange their activities and share in the total act of production, will naturally vary according to the character of the means of production. (The word secondly above is added by the editor.)[23]

485

In 1979, Zhang Wentian's paper "On the Issue of Dual Nature of the Relations of Production" which was written in 1963 was re-published. He put forward five views on Stalin's definition explaining the study subject of Marxist political economy. Zhang Wentian believed that Stalin's definition excluded the aspect of relations of production which reflects productive forces instead his definition only included the ownership relations issue, which means he neglected other parts included in the contents of production relations. And this had led the simple and one-sided understanding on the rich contents of production relations.

Furthermore, this definition did not accept that the relationship of ownership was the sum of all the relationships of production, and only considered the sum of the relationships of only ownership of production means, distribution, exchange and consumption. This narrowed the concept of relationship of ownership, thus narrowed the meaning of socio-economic structure (ger. *ökonomischen Gesellschaftsformation*). His definition also mixed together the two type of exchanges which was explained by Marx and Engels, in *Economic and Philosophical Manuscripts of 1844* first one is "exchanges of human activities within the production itself" that is, the

22   The Selected Works of Stalin, vol. 2, pp.594-595.
23   Wage Labour and Capital, p.19.

exchanges and cooperation with others in man's labor process and this corresponds to the division of labor within a single enterprise, secondly "the mutual exchange of human's products," which refers to the exchange of labor products (commodities) among men and this corresponds to the social division of labor in the whole society, and we may call it social interaction."[24]

A Chinese scholar advocates that "Property concept can be classified into narrow sense and broad sense. The former sense refers to possession of means of production and the latter is related with the sum of all social relations of a production system. Property right institution includes the following components: How are the property rights designed, how are property rights realized in practice? In which forms are property rights realized? It also includes the division of responsibilities and interests among different economic agents and also includes institutional arrangements related to operating rules (operating of different productive assets). Rights, responsibilities and interests related to property—these three components- have connections as well as differences. Their differences means that all these three components have different connotations, roles and positions in an economic system, (enterprise, country, economy, agricultural production system, etc)."

On the other side their connections (links) of the three demonstrates that there is one single property rightinstitution (a system) which embodies all of these components and their relations And in actual practice, property relations and economic elements and economic relations are regulated and realized by this property right institution system. The dialectical unity of the three component parts above means that we cannot build anownership theorywithout having a proper property rights institution theory, or we cannot understand property issue without a property institution theory.

The classical Marxist research including Stalin and Mao had mainly focused on the narrow meaning of property theory, which was quite one-sided, therefore today we should make a deeperstudy onproperty rights institution theory."

In the early 1970s, many scholars in China have proposed new ideas on property issue and discussed the content of state (toplumsal) property in China. For example Professor Sun Yefang said: Understanding and analysis of social relations of a production system cannot be limited toproduction relations, the economic relations, forms of property, distribution relations in a separately and independent manner, on the contrary this analysis should include the analysis the sum, the wholity of its economic content, all social relations of any production system.

---

24 Wentian Zhang, "On the Issue of Dual Nature of the Relations of Production", in Economy Studies10 (1979).

Sun Yefang also pointed out: We can not simply base our analysis on the definition advocated in our university textbooks. For example, if we think different from our textbook definition, then production form (social character of production) or property form (state property) cannot alone determine that state property has social nature, in the same way it does not necessarily mean that we have established socialist public ownership. If we really aim to reach and understand socialist public ownership we should start from the detailed analysis of all social relations related to production, exchange and distribution.

Those who hold this above views mainly base themselves on Marx's text *The Poverty of Philosophy*, Marx wrote: "In each historical epoch property is differently developed and it is developed in a series of social relations entirely different. Thus defining bourgoise property is nothing other than to explain all the social relations of bourgeois production. To pretend to give a definition of property as of an independent relation, as a separate category, as an abstract and eternal idea, can only be an illusion of metaphysics or of jurisprudence".[25]

Therefore, when describing and understanding ownership (it is always a relation), Marxist economics must examine the sum of relations of production. "The studies on the relationship of ownership have no direct relation with the study of four links of the social production process. These four links are important component parts of Marx's social reproduction theory which includes as (1) production, (2) distribution, (3) exchange (circulation) and (4) consumption. Ownership can only be realized through the above four links of the social reproduction process. If there is no the social reproduction process there would be no ownership relation. Therefore, "in one sentence, the ownership should be defined as relationship between man and man throughout the four links embodied in the general process of social reproduction".[26]

Xuemo Jiang[27] also has also pointed out that there are two drawbacks in Stalin's definition: Firstly, he only notices the influence of the first aspect to the second, and the determinant effect of the first and the second aspects to the third aspect. On the other side he ignores the influence from the latter ones to the former ones. Secondly, he misleads people that the forms of distribution only depend on the former two aspects of the relations of production, but ignores the role and status of the development of the productive forces which also effect the distribution form".[28]

487

25   Section IV - Property and Rent
26   Guangyuan Yu, On the Issue of Socialist Public Ownership and Distribution according to Labor Contribution, pp. 11-12, Beijing: People's Publishing House, 1978.
27   Yefang Sun, "On the Relations of Production as the Object of Political Economics," Economy Studies, p. 8 (1979).
28   Refer to Xuemo Jiang, Twenty Items on Political Economics (Taiyuan: Shanxi People's Publishing House, 1983), p. 22.

The seventh is the difference between the definitions and understanding of the relations of production by Stalin and Marx-Engels in the issue of relations of production.

Some scholars base themselves on the definition of political economy given by Engels, in *Anti-Dühring* as follows: "Political economy, in the widest sense, is the science of the laws governing the production and exchange of the material means of subsistence in human society."…"Political economy, however, as the science of the conditions and forms under which the various human societies have produced and exchanged and on this basis have distributed their products." Here Engels includes three spheres: Production, exchange, distribution.

The changes Stalin made in the definition about the content of the relations of production were incorrect. It does not develop Engels' definition, but runs to the opposite direction. This definition of Stalin "is wrong in explaining both the historical issues and current practical issues, and brings a negative effect to our practice of both socialist revolution and socialist construction."[29] Therefore, Engels' definition should be restored again. This is the root of the problem.

488

Stalin said: "Let us examine Engels' formula. Engels' formula cannot be considered fully clear and precise, because it does not indicate whether it is referring to the seizure by society of all or only part of the means of production, that is, whether all or only part of the means of production are converted into public property. Hence, this formula of Engels' may be understood either way."

Some people think that Stalin's definition on the relations of production lack several contents when compared with the statements of Marx in *Preface of "Critique of Political Economy"*: firstly, it does not include production; secondly, it does not include exchange; thirdly, it does not have consumption; fourthly, distribution by Stalin only mentions the distribution of products and only restricted to the distribution of personal consumer goods, but does not mention on the distribution of income or distribution of production factors. Stalin's definition emphasizes unilaterally: He first mentions the form of ownership of production means; followed by "status of various social groups and their mutual interrelations". What this definition lacks is so vital that it should never be ignored, but what it has emphasized not properly expressed. Therefore, this definition lags far behind Marx's. Thus Yuanpeng Hong advocates the restoration of the theory of four links in the relations of production, study socialist relations of production from the aspect of four links; namely production, exchange, distribution and consumption.[30]

29 Yefang Sun, "On the Relations of Production as the Object of Political Economics," Economy Studies, p. 8 (1979).
30 Yuanpeng Hong, "Marx's definition should be restored—On the Relations of Production as the study subject of Political Economics," Economy Studies, p. 12 (1979).

People who are in favor of Stalin's definition believe that his view is in the same direction with the view of Marx, Engels, and Lenin. Xuemo Jiang wrote: say, "The definition of production relations including 'three aspects' made by Stalin is correct, which we cannot deny simply". "The definitions of 'three aspects' and 'four links" are complementary, they are not mutually exclusive. The concept of 'three aspects' explains the nature of the relations of production while the concept of 'four links' explains that we should not study the production relations statically in isolation, but study them within the process of production and also study the link of production, distribution, exchange and consumption which constitute the process of production. These two definitions are both Marxist and correct".[31]

Marx wrote: The conclusion which follows from this is, not that production, distribution, exchange and consumption are identical, but that they are links of a single whole, different aspects of one unit. Production is the decisive phase, both with regard to the contradictory aspects of production and with regard to the other phases. The process always starts afresh with production. That exchange and consumption cannot be the decisive elements, is obvious; and the same applies to distribution in the sense of distribution of products. Distribution of the factors of production, on the other hand, is itself a phase of production. A distinct mode of production thus determines the specific mode of consumption, distribution, exchange and the specific relations of these different phases to one another. Production in the narrow sense, however, is in its turn also determined by the other aspects.[32]

Mo Zuo brings another view: "Stalin's summary which includes the three elements of production relations deepens our understanding related to study sphere of political economics. We should move forward on this basis rather than move backward in theory to blur again the issues which were clear in the past. Based on this understanding, I insist that the issue of ownership of production should be studied as a separate issue."[33]

Some others argue that, the concepts of "three aspects" and "four links" are all wrong. The concept of "three aspects" is wrong and the "four links" of production, exchange, distribution and consumption is also step backwards. Because the "four links" concept not only repeats the error that all economic problems are simply attributed to the problem of ownership and this concept also denies the correct explanation given by the "three aspects" concept. By this I mean the "four links" concept puts the ownership within the relations of production but on the other side it combines production with distribution,

31 Xuemo Jiang, "The Nature of the Scope of the Relations of Production," Essays of the Masses 8 (1980).
32 A Contribution to the Critique of Political Economy, translated from German by S. W. Ryazanskaya, Lawrence & Wishart 1971; Part Appendix I.
33 Mo Zuo, "Several Issues of the Ownership, World of Management,", p. 3 (1988).

and also combines production with exchange and consumption, this is a step backwards. But Stalin's definition based on the concept of "three aspects" ignores one of the basic laws of historical materialism that production belirler decides distribution, exchange and consumption. Stalin wrote: the province (sphere) political economy is the production relations, the economic relations of men. It includes: a) the forms of ownership of the means of production; b) the status of the various social groups in production and their interrelations that follow from these forms, or what Marx calls: "they exchange their activities"; the forms of distribution of products, which are entirely determined by them.

All these together constitute the province of political economy. This definition does not contain the word "exchange," which is included in Engels' definition. I omit it because "exchange" is usually understood by many to mean exchange of commodities, which is characteristic not of all social formations, but only of some social formations, and this sometimes gives rise to misunderstanding, even though the word "exchange" with Engels did not mean only commodity exchange. As will be seen, however, that which Engels meant by the word "exchange" has been included, as a component part, in (my) above definition. Hence, this definition of the province of political economy fully coincides in content with Engels' definition.

490   In the process of production, human beings work not only upon nature, but also upon one another. They produce only by working together in a specified manner and reciprocally exchange their activities.

In order to produce, they enter into definite connections and relations to one another, and only within these social connections and relations does their influence upon nature operate—i.e. does production take place.

These social relations between the producers, and the conditions under which they exchange their activities and share in the total act of production, will naturally vary according to the character of the means of production.

The central content of the Marxism the theory of income distribution is a distribution according to labor. Mao Zedong emphasizes carrying out Theory of distribution according to labor, while resolutely opposes equalitarianism. Deng Xiaoping sticks to the standard of productive forces,brings out the theory of "earlier prosperity" "latter prosperity" and "common prosperity". Under market economy condition, Jiang Zemin put forward the diversified distribution system with distribution based on work as the main form.In the Report of the Seventeenth National Congress of the Communist Party of China,Hu Jintao pointed for the first time the new ideas that "the labor compensation will be enhanced in the proportion of initial distribution" and "creating conditions so that more people own property income".Those gradually enriched and developed the theory of distribution according to labor,and showed the theory quality of Marxism of progressing with times."[34]

The Eighth discussion is on the means to achieve the aim of socialist production

Stalin expressed in his book *Economic Problems of Socialism in the USSR*, "it is an approach used on the basis of high technology to make the socialism continuously progress and perfect itself." There are different views on the understanding of proper means to achieve the aim of socialist production.

Some people think that Stalin's statement is correct. "It objectively requires us to develop production basing ourselves on high technology to satisfy the needs of the people living in society to the largest extent." "Of course, in some countries where the economy is undereveloped, all production can not be immediately changed into an economy with high technology just in one night after the victory of the revolution. Socialism has a process of development and this applies also to the modernization of technology, it is also a process to develop technology, In order to meet the objective requirements of this law, after the victory of socialist revolution, the focus of work must be shifted to the construction of economy. We will go against the requirements of the basic socialist economic law if we do not fully understand the requirement of this objective law, (the construction of economy) and not actively develop production or use modern scientific technology to improve productive forces, on the other side we will go to a direction opposite which will contradict to the aim of socialist production."[35]

491

Some people advocate that Stalin's statement about the means to be used to achieve the aim of socialist production was not realistic. "Because it was in some backward countries (including Russia) where socialist revolution first succeeded. In the early period of the establishment of socialism in these countries, the foundations of socialism were weak and the basis for 'high technology' did not exist", so "it is better to say that the way to improve social production needs further socialization of production."[36]

---

34 Biao Zhan, "Making Clear What are the Relations of Production," Essays of Masses, p. 2 (1980).

35 Yongtang Shan, "Understandings of the Basic Socialist Economic Law," Guangming Daily (1979).

36 Xunhua Zhang, On the Basic Economic Law of Socialism, paper in On the Aim of Socialist Production—Proceedings of the National Symposium on the Purpose of Socialist Production, p.35.

Some people thought that Stalin's statement about means to achieve the aim of socialist production was not perfect and comprehensive enough. "The continuous growth and improvement of socialist production do not merely require high technological foundation, but rather requires advanced socialist relations of production, and on the other side only in the socialist system can this be realized." Therefore, means to reach the aim should be: "On the one hand, we should make full and wide use of advanced science and technology, promote technical innovation, and also greatly develop productive forces to improve the productive forces of labor; on the other side we should constantly adjust relations of production and the superstructure to make both of them more perfect by consciously adapting them to the objective requirements of socialist economic development."[37]

Some people believed that although Stalin put forward the means to achieve the aim of socialist production as "high technological foundation", he did not elaborate its specific content and especially he did not pay attention to the issue of giving play to producers' initiative and labor enthusiasm. Marx wrote: "Elements of production are men and natural nesneler objects. In order to develop productive forces, we need to make full use of the role of natural objects by scientific and technical means and give full play to the role of men. Under socialist conditions, only by highly technical means alone but without arousing people's enthusiasm, the aim of developing productive forces and meeting people's demands cannot be realized."[38]

The ninth is on the pace of industrialization.

For a long time, Chinese scholars have affirmed the policy of high-speed industrial development in the Soviet Union during the Stalin period. However, in the 1980s, some scholars believed that the policy of accelerated industrialization was very fast and this was a mistake. Establishing a large industry in the Soviet Union itself was beyond any imagination. The problem was too fast pace and using simple methods and isolation from the national realities in Russia, that is the dominance of small-scale peasant economy in Russia was not considered properly. Soviet leaders only stressed the need of accelerating the establishment of large industries and transforming the small-scale peasant economy, with little discussion if it was possible to have an accelerated development of heavy industry in such a country with small-peasant economy dominant. This had two consequences: The accelerated development of heavy industry would inevitably increase the burden on the economy and the people mainly cause a heavy burden on peasants; because the heavy industrial production tends to serve only for

37 Qisheng Qi, "On Contents and Presentation of the Basic Economic Law of Socialism,"Academic Monthly, p. 6 (1961).
38 Peigen Fei, "The Basic Economic Law of Socialism Should Include Economic Means,"Jianghan Forum, p. 1(1980).

itself, and it could not immediately serve for people's life, especially not serve peasants and agricultural production. Thus, interests of agriculture and peasants were undermined.[39]

Some scholars did not agree with the above statement, holding that there were some realistic causes for Stalin's high-speed industrial development: (1) the Soviet Union economically lagged behind developed capitalist countries about 50 to 100 years, and in order to reduce this gap, Russia could not move forward at a normal speed and needed rapid development of the industry. (2) Imperialist countries could possibly attack the Soviet Union at any time by making use of its technical and economic weaknesses, so it needed make full use of time to rapidly realize industrialization; (3) the imminent danger of the world war also required the rapid realization of industrialization. People holding this view also believed that Stalin's idea about high-speed industrial development was a strategic issue. Stalini when formulating plans for the industrial development, was cautious and did not always push high speed without regarding conditions and possibilities. Under his leadership, five-year plans of the Soviet Union had always left some leeway, which were often fulfilled in advance and exceeded.[40]

Some scholars claimed that the speed of socialist industrialization in the Soviet Union during the Stalin period should be analyzed specifically. Stalin was cautious about the pace of industrial development before 1927 and led Soviet Union in making remarkable achievements in production and construction. However, after 1927 Stalin repeatedly requested to improve the growth rate of socialist industry, and ordered to raise production targets and expand infrastructure and industrial investments, which made all sectors of the national economy imbalanced, and this caused that raw materials and building materials in a serious shortage and "price scissors" between industrial and agricultural products grew worse. In fact, the pace of development of heavy industry slowed down. Stalin could not realize that Soviet Union should follow a slower growth rate starting with the Second Five-Year Plan.[41]

---

39   Junrui Qian, Talking about Capitalism and Socialism, p. 270, Beijing: World Affairs Press, 1983.
40   Seven Eastern Provinces and Cities, ed., The History of Socialist Thoughts, p.430, Fuzhou: Fujian People's Publishing House, 1985.
41   Peixian Liu, ed., History of Scientific Socialism, p.507, Beijing: China Renmin University Press, 1984.

The tenth is on collectivization of agriculture.

China's academic community has long affirmed great achievements made by the Soviet Union in its accelerated collectivization of agriculture, and on the other side it is believed that in the overall process of this collectivization, some regions ignored the central government's instructions about the speed and time limit of collectivization and made "left" mistakes demanding immediate completion of collectivization without considering the real conditions.

However, in the 1980s, some people claimed that the collectivization of agriculture in the Soviet Union during the Stalin period was "a big disaster". The high-speed collectivization of agriculture caused a large number of livestock to be slaughtered; a large number of farmers resisted to collectivizationand left the collective farms; and food production fell; ties between the party and the masses was damaged; development of the socialist cause was harmed.[42]

When analyzing causes for mistakes of premature beginning to the collectivization of agriculture in the Soviet Union during the Stalin period, some people said, conditions for starting the economic campaign of collectivization were not ripe at that time, so Stalin, in order to reach the preconceived purpose, had to adopt the tool of political movement campaign, which forced the accelerated implementation by means of superstructure and tried to increase the pace of objective economic movement in this way.[43]

494

Chinese scholars have long believed that the policy of eliminating kulaks in the collectivization of agriculture in the Soviet Union during the Stalin period was necessary and correct, because kulaks had never stopped activities against the Soviet regime. However, in the 1980s, some scholars held that that policy had resulted in serious consequences at that time, because: (1) conditions of elimination of kulaks in the Soviet Union were premature; (2) too rapid change in state policies was disadvantegous for the campaign of collectivization and the development of agricultural production; (3) targets of the blows were enlarged and the collectivization and the elimination of kulaks were simultaneously, and also middle peasants who did not want to join the collective farms were all labeled as rich peasants, thus their interests was violated; (4) forms of struggle adopted to eliminate kulaks were not flexible enough to actually offer them a way out.[44]

---

42   Peng Yao, Zhengliang Hu and Ning Fang, Reform, Explore and Choose, pp.42-43,Beijing: People's Publishing House, 1987.
43   Baojiang Chen, "Brief Analysis of the Immaturity ofConditions of Collectivization of Agriculture," Research and References 1 (1985).
44   Shandong Normal Universityetc., ed., History of International Communist Movements (II), p.183, Jinan: Shandong People's Publishing House, 1983.

II. Studies on Stalin's thoughts from the late 80s to the late 90s

The disintegration of socialist countries—the Soviet Union and Eastern Europe since the late 1980s to the early 1990s had become the most serious setback for the socialist development in the 20th century. This tragedy of history was both appalling and thought-provoking. People tried to sum up lessons learned from this event from different angles, thus Stalin's thinking and the "Stalin Model" once again becomes important topic of discussion.

Since the late 1980s, China has adhered to the approach of academic freedom in studies and thoughts in the academia have been active, which is reflected in various ideas and innovative research tools and methods. With the gradual deepening of China's opening up strategy, ideas from foreign countries has inevitably affected China's academic circle. In the new historical conditions, new academic views spring up.

The first is on the origin of theory and practice of industrialization.

China's scholars have long believed that Stalin's road of industrialization by giving the priority to the development of heavy industry and his rejecting "the normal road of industrialization" was correct and necessary. In 1990s, most scholars basically affirmed achievements of Stalin's industrialization, but explanations about their reasons for Stalin's priority of heavy industry in the Soviet Union were different. Some people claimed that this was the inheritance of the unique historical experience of economic development in the modern history of Tsarist Russia. Like Peter the Great, Stalin took the road of giving priority to the development of heavy industry and defense industry (from above), and the means realizing this goal were sacrificing agricultural interests and inhibiting the improvement of living standards of members of the society by highly centralized decision making system.[45]

495

Some scholars thought that in the late 1920s, the economic development in the Soviet Union was in a critical moment. The decision was needed to be made between Stalin's "catching-up other countries strategy" by giving priority to heavy industry and Bukharin's "balanced-development strategy". The Soviet Union finally chose Stalin's "catch-up strategy" rather than Bukharin's ideas, this was not a historical accident. If we compare these two strategies, Stalin's "catch-up strategy" was more in line with Russian history (top-down development) and more easily accepted by the Soviet Party and the people, thus "catch-up strategy" had a greater feasability in practice. Bukharin's "balanced-development strategy for economic development" was more a problem proposal and analysis from a purely

---

45 Changbin Jiang, "On the Road of the October Revolution and the Stalinist Model,"Research and References 3 (1988).

economic point of view and lacked the consideration of socio-historic realities thus lacked feasibility.[46]

Some scholars claimed that Stalin's idea and practice of industrialization had in fact originated from Marx's expanded reproduction theories. The core theory of socialist industrialization of the Soviet Union during the Stalin period was giving priority to the production of means of production, especially heavy industry and its core was—developing the machine manufacturing industry. This thinking of Stalin "was mainly based on the principle of expanded reproduction model of Marx and Lenin."[47]

Some scholars argued that Stalin's industrialization attack was not the real beginning of industrialization in the Soviet Union, but it was "the remedial teaching for the industrializon task" of the past Russia. Stalin's statement about the beginning of industrialization in the Soviet Union was misleading. The book *History of the All-Union Communist Party (Bolsheviks), Short Course* only mentioned that the 14th Congress of the Party had decided the policy of all round industrialization in December 1925 and does not explicitly say when the period of industrialization started" in Russia. In fact, the Soviet Union inherited the experience of Tsarist Russia, Tsarist Russia had begun industrialization. The all round industrialization proposed by Stalin only meant that the country concentrated on industrial development for only a certain period and aimed to complete the task of industrialization which was already started. This choice was certainly correct. However, the saying that this marked the beginning of industrialization in the Soviet Union was only a propaganda purpose and was not correct.[48]

The second is on the evaluation of industrialization.

For a long time, as for how to evaluate the theory and practice of Stalin's industrialization, scholars has pointed out its shortcomings but mainly affirmed its historical achievements. Even in the early 1980s, scholars had still insisted on this view. For example, some scholars said that it was necessary to give priority to the development of heavy industry and the realization of socialist industrialization. Because this prepared the material basis for the victory of the anti-fascist war, and should be affirmed. However, the practice of giving priority to heavy industry was not a complete success. Evaluating theoretically, this idea of Stalin was one-sided. In Stalin's view, whether to give priority to heavy industry was seen as mark for dividing industrialization roads with two

46   Sujian Guo, "The Choice of History: Bukharin's Balanced Strategy and Stalin's Catch-up Strategy of Giving Priority to Heavy Industry," Issues in the Soviet Union and East Europe, p. 5 (1988).
47   Zhichao Lu, Re-understanding on Issues of Stalin, p.22, Beijing: Social Sciences Academic Press, 1994.
48   Zongyu Li, The Studies of the Stalinist Model, pp.109-114, Beijing: Central Compilation and Translation Press, 1999.

different natures: Socialist industrialization and the capitalist industrialization, this idea of him was not correct. In practice, the one-sided priority given to the development of heavy industry led to serious consequences: This strategy hindered agricultural development; caused serious backwardness of the light industry; and suspended improvement of people's living standards.[49]

In the 1990s, scholars studied again the theories and practice of Stalin's industrialization. Some people emphasized that this strategy had its own peculiar conditions and could not be generalized for all other socialist countries. The Soviet Union's socialist industrialization had a specific meaning. The path of the Soviet industrialization was determined by its special historical conditions, and its focus on heavy industry was realistic. Just within a decade, the Soviet Union had achieved the socialist industrialization, made remarkable achievements and basically completed the socialist transformation of national economy, which had established the material basis for socialism. However, this path of socialist industrialization was full of twists and turns. "It was realized in a specific domestic and international environment at the expense of huge sacrifices paid by the people. Thus, we cannot dogmatically affirm and generalize this road of industrialization."[50]

Some people claimed that traditional views, especially the assessment of *History of the All-Union Communist Party (Bolsheviks), Short Course* about the achievements of the Soviet industrialization during the Stalin period were not correct. "Beautified statements about the Soviet industrialization all came from Stalin himself." Soviet people believed Stalin's evaluations and repeated them. They evaluated Stalin according to Stalin's words and could not escape the mind-set of Stalin. Therefore, there appeared a fixed one sided assessment of the Soviet industrialization. In fact, Stalin's ultimate goal of pursuing high speed was not realized, and the Soviet Union did not achieve complete and all-round industrialization even after Stalin's death. "Out of political needs or expecting some political advantages, Stalin advocated high speed and had to exaggerate achievements caused by this high speed, and he even covered up the truth with false statistics when Soviet Union could not reach the defined goals. He convinced people with his political prestige and incited people's political enthusiasm with a fictive distant goal. If we fairly evaluate these facts above then what sad is that Soviet people often talked about the topic to complete the five-year plan within four years, and continued to repeat the lies of the propaganda machine and thus help Stalin cheat others, but in fact the reality of industrialization was one with many failures and the results were not perfect."[51]

497

49　Junrui Qian, ed., Talks on Capitalism and Socialism, p.288.
50　Zongliang Huang et al., History and Theory of the World Socialism, p.144, Beijing: Central Compilation and Translation Press, 1995.
51　Zongyu Li, The Study of the Stalinist Model, pp.108-139.

The third is the understanding on the necessity of the Soviet agricultural collectivization.

Chinese scholars have long believed that the Soviet collectivization of agriculture was necessary and timely. In the 1980s, some scholars began to challenge this idea. Back in the mid-1980s, some scholars indirectly rejected the necessity of the overall collectivization of agriculture in the Soviet Union after studying Soviet Union's problem of grain in the 1920s. For example, some people believed that it was not accurate for Stalin to mainly attribute the cause of the crisis of grain purchase to the low commodity (grain output) production rate of scattered small-peasant economy. While emphasizing objective factors, he ignored subjective factors in the policy of State's grain purchase, namely he ignored the severe shortage of industrial products in rural areas and disproportionate prices between grain and other agricultural products which had caused a reaction among peasants. Because of these subjective factors, grain commodity market controlled by the state had reduced by nearly 50%, on the other side the Gross Marketable Volume of grain had dropped by 25%. In other words, the above subjective factors in the policy of grain purchase was the main reason for the occurance of crisis in grain purchase, and it was wrong to simply accuse the low productive forces of small-peasant economy.[52]

In the late 1980s, some scholars claimed that objective and subjective conditions for the collectivization of agriculture were not prepared. Looking from the perspective of the development of productive forces, namely the mechanization of production and the mental preparation (consciousness of men as of the productive forces) of farmers we can say that the conditions of agricultural collectivization were not ripe, and there were also more potential and room for the development individual peasants economy and lower level peasant cooperatives. Agricultural collectivization decision was resulted from Stalin's subjective intention to start the rapid growth of industry and on the other side complete the transformation of ownership system in a rapid manner.[53]

In the late 1990s, some people thought that Stalin's theory of agricultural collectivization was seriously mistaken. Because After 1928, Stalin totally denied the vital status and positive role of agriculture in the socialist construction, and expelled individual peasants and small producers which resisted out of the collective farms by classifying them as capitalist elements. He labeled them as the aim hedefi of revolution and therefore they should be eliminated as a class. They were regarded as "the root of old capitalism" which should

---

52   Bo Xu, "Stalin was Inaccurate—On How to Determine the GMV of Grain in the Soviet Union in the 1920s," Research Trends of the World History, p. 12 (1985).

53   Zhongjie Li, et al, The History of Socialist Reforms and Revolutions, pp.95-96, Beijing: Spring Press, 1988.

be completely "dig up", and "a major theoretical mistake which contradicted the ideas of Lenin in his later years and his practice was in many ways parallel with Trotsky's idea of denial of peasants revolutionary role". Moreover, Stalin made many mistakes in theory and policies concerning peasants, caused by a mistaken understanding and practice of socialism, which led to isolation from national conditions of the Soviet Union, and it was type of voluntarism. Owing to these mistakes, "Stalin could not offer a proper solution on the problem of peasants' role in the socialist construction and could not create new forms of agricultural economic organizations; what is worse, the issue of peasants' role in socialism became more complicated and acute like the Achilles heel of the Soviet Union."[54]

The fourth is on the idea of "socialism in a single country".

For a long time, Chinese scholars have always maintained that Stalin's idea of "socialism in a single country" is identical with Lenin's ideas, not something that Stalin had "added" to Leninism. However, in the 1980s, this issue was put forward again by scholars in western countries even including the Soviet Union, who criticized the idea of socialism in a single country, holding that that was not Lenin's thinking. Some Japanese scholars have argued that the idea that socialism could not be established in a single country remained the basic theory of the Bolshevik Party and Lenin. Some foreign scholars also argued that there was no socialist country in the world, and wrote that the road of October Revolution have not and will not lead to any socialist society in the near future. Triggered by these new ideas, in the 1990s, Chinese scholars started a new research on Stalin's idea of "socialism in a single country."

499

Some people have argued that Stalin's "socialism in a single country" was contrary to Lenin's related theory. After the death of Lenin, in the debate with the opposition groups in the Party, Stalin distorted Lenin's two theories of "victory of socialism in a single country" and the "establishment of socialism in a single country" and put forward his theory of complete socialist society being established in a single country. Then Stalin extended his theory futher and argued that the communist society could be established in a single country, thus pushed Lenin's theory of victory of socialism in a single country to the extreme. Stalin's theory of "socialism in a single country" had obvious flaws, more specifically Stalin's ideas were vague and even contained some contradictory ideas about what socialism really was and what kind of socialism should be established in Soviet Union. Therefore, "Lenin did have the idea of 'the establishment of socialism in a single country', but it was significantly different from Stalin's idea and there was even no fundamental similarity between the two."[55]

54 Zongyu Li, The Study of the Stalinist Model, pp. 71,107.
55 Xinhua Li, "Comparison of Lenin's Idea of 'Establishment of Socialism in A Single

Some Chinese scholars fully affirmed Stalin's theory of "socialism in a single country". and wrote that "Stalin's thinking that distinguished victory of socialism 'in a single country' and 'final victory of socialism' had inherited and developed Lenin's ideas of building socialism. This clear idea of Stalin had strengthened political beliefs in the Soviet Party and people encouraged them to in building socialism and was of great theoretical and practical significance."[56]

The fifth is on the operational mechanism of socialist economy

Some scholars have argued that main content of Stalin's iktisat economic thought was "product-commodity" theory. "Stalin's ideas in his Problems of Socialist Economy in the Soviet Union had expounded the theoretical basis for the traditional socialist planned economic system." The book mainly contained the idea of product economy, this mistaken view was directly related with the failure of the Stalinist model in the former Soviet Union and this idea still poses a huge challenge when we are establishing a socialist market economic system in China. Li Xinhua wrote, still today rigid ideas about transition from capitalism to socialism and also today's various 'left' ideas hindering our reforms have their roots in this book. Therefore, its negative effects on the economic reform debates cannot be ignored."[57]

However, others scholars have argued that in this book Stalin formulated the proportional planned allocation tahsis of social labor as the law of socialist economy, and he put forward the law of planned development of economy. After this Stalin defined the relationships among the three laws: The law of planned development, the basic economic law of socialism and economic planning as the economic mehanism. Therefore, these scholars argued: "Stalin's thought of planned economy and his practice of economic planning are the enrichment and development of his idea about the form of planned economy in the future society." Stalin had also explained the necessity of commodity economy and necessity to consider the law of value under socialism, which constitutes the basic content of Stalin's theory of markets in socialism. Generally speaking, "although Stalin's exploration on the issue of relations between plan and market could not solve this long-standing historical problem of Marxist socialist economics, we can comfortably say that this exploration by Stalin, has played an important role in promoting further discussions about this relationship."[58]

Country' and Stalin's Theory of 'Socialism in A Single Country'," Trends in Theory, p. 1 (2001).
56   Zongliang Huang et al., History and Theory of the World Socialism, 138. Beijing University Press.
57   Da-jun Zhang, Political Economics in Transition (Beijing: Party School Press of the CPC Central Committee, 1995), 62.
58   Yifeng Wu, Gu Hailiang, Zhang Leisheng and Huang Taiyan, The Formation and Development of Marxist EconomicsTheory, pp.519, 526, Beijing: China Renmin University Press, 1998.

The sixth is about discussions on the "Stalin Model."

In general, China's academic community had long believed that the highly centralized political and economic system in the Stalin period was formed in the special historical circumstances of the Soviet Union, which had won the first victory of building a realistic socialist society in a single country in the ocean of capitalism, therefore the system he built was the inevitable result of many historical and real phenomena. And we generally thought that this system was in line with socialist principles and brought huge benefits for the historical development of the Soviet Union, and had offered a model for the formation of political and economic systems in later socialist countries. But in recent years, with the deepening of the socialist political and economic reforms, China's scholars have put forward some new views.

Some scholars have argued that there were many factors which had effected the formation of the political and economic system during the Stalin period. Thehistorical factors that exerted great impacts were in the following six spheres: (1) the Soviet Union was the first socialist country in the world and there was no ready socialist model for reference; (2) the Soviet Union had long been besieged by capitalism and the international environment for SU was very unfavorable, which to a large extent affected the Soviet system; (3) the basic national situation of the Soviet Union was that it marched directly into the road of socialism from an economically and culturally backward country, which was the most important condition which affected and determined the nature of the Soviet socialist system; (4) it was under the guidance of Stalin's non-scientific thinking; (5) it was negatively impacted by the successive severe inner-party struggles; (6) Problem of Stalin's personal style could not be ignored in the mistakes.[59]

501

Some people paid a special emphasis on the impact of severe inner-party struggles within the party throughout their researches. Although the formation of the Stalinist Model originated from international and domestic, theoretical, historical, social political, economic, cultural facts and facts related to other spheres. Besides all these effects the effects of acute inner-party struggles in the Soviet Union during 1920s on the formation of Stalinist Model cannot be underestimated. In this respect at least two points are worth noting: (1) the Stalinist Model when assumed its final form had actually absorbed some theories of the Trotsky and his followers' and of the New Opposition; (2) the so-called ultimate defeat of the "rightist" group had marked the end of Lenin's New Economic Policy. So the results of these two points also constitute basic features of the Stalin Model.[60]

---

59   Zhongjie Li et al., The History of Socialist Reform, p. 99.
60   Houshang Zhi, "A Brief Discussion on the Inner-party Struggle in the 1920s of CPSU"Issues in the Soviet Union and Eastern Europe 4 (1988).

Some scholars analyzed causes for the formation of Stalin's socialism model from perspectives of historical conditions and from the aspect of its thinking roots. Although the Stalin Model was also evidently characterized by Stalin's personality, it was primarily the product of the historical era of Russia and world. The establishment of the Stalin Model was consistent with the trend of historical development, and it was the result of the motion of certain "historical forces" that caused its birth and formation. "The social and historical circumstances in that era can be summarized as follows: The domestic crisis of Russia which demonstrated itself as turmoil, the unpredictable international situation and the imminent imperialist aggressive war." At the same time, the cause behind the formation of the Stalin Model had a profound ideological root. "The ideological roots mainly originated from three aspects: first, Stalin's understanding and application of Marxist-Leninist theories were both correct, rational but on the other hand dogmatic, one-sided; second, it is impacted by the Russian national-historical spirit which 'has nightmarishly covered people alive just as those dead former traditions have' as written by Marx when he evaluated the events of 1848-50 revolution in France; thirdly it was caused by the metaphysical way of thinking of Stalin himself."[61]

A scholar who has studied the Stalin Model has commented that it was the "dislocation of history." "In fact in reality the Stalinist model had caused a serious distortion in the scientific orientation of socialism which was fully revived and reproduced by Lenin in the beginning of 1920s" and it was "a flawed model based on the mistaken historical situating." Therefore, the Stalin model and imitations which were practiced by all the socialist countries of the 20th century were "mistakes of model choosing." And "this mistake had caused very serious consequences... it will not be an exaggeration to say that this historical situating and mistake of model choosing have already laid the roots of the big twists and turns in the world socialist movement."[62]

A researcher has argued that this model had played a major role in the history of Soviet Union but had certain obvious shortcomings. "It had secured the political stability of Soviet Union amids the fierce class struggles home and abroad and under the complicated historical conditions of the 1930s. This model had secured the mobilization and concentration of humanly, financial and material resources and promoted the unity of will and action of the party and Soviet state to achieve the rapid development of heavy industry.

502

61 Huiming Jin, Gu Hailiang et al., History, Theory and Reality of Socialism, pp. 280, 286, Hefei: Anhui People's Publishing House, 2000.
62 Liyan Mao, The Historic Position and Choice of Model in the History of Socialism, The Studies of Marxism, p. 3 (1999).

Thus it enabled the realization of socialist industrialization and establis-hed a relatively sound economic foundation; it secured material prerequisi-tes for the victory over fascism." However, it also demonstrated significant shortcomings which brought about huge losses to the social progress and development of the Soviet Union.[63]

The seventh is on the relationship between Stalin's thought and Marxism-Leninism.

Stalin himself though he was a student of Marx and Engels, and the only true heir of Lenin. Chinese communists had also long believed that Stalin adhered to Marxism. However, in recent years, especially since the disin-tegration of the Soviet Union, scholars have achieved new findings related to this question.

Some scholars agree that Stalin believed he firmly followed the basic Marxist principles, but in practice his full career contained two aspects, on the one hand he maintained and developed Marxism, on the other he "devia-ted" from it and applied dogmatism. "It is certain that the generation of 'old Bolsheviks', like Stalin, all had a firm faith in Communism." "Stalin and his supporters, in all the cases when they formed their important decisions, all sincerely considered adhering to Marxism and Leninism. And the results of their actions were indeed the practical results of Marxism-Leninism, but there were also a lot of elements which demonstrated dogmatic distortions of Marxism-Leninism."[64]

503

Other group of scholars have argued that, among Stalin's concepts of socialism, "there are some concepts which adhered and developed the basic principles of Marxist socialism of the 19th century plus Lenin's exploration on the questions of building socialism. But on the other side some of his socialism concepts had distorted and deviated from the basic principles of Marxism, especially his concepts deviated from certain concepts of socia-lism which Lenin had formed in his late years."

What differed from Marxism-Leninism in Stalin's concepts of socialism were: the ignorance of the necessity that socialism should have higher le-vel of development performance in the sphere of productive forces than that of capitalism; his concept unilaterally aimed to reach a higher level of public ownership forms while on the other side undermined the current development level of productive forces; another flaw of his concept stipu-lated that the socialist production relations should fully fit the productive forces, which led to a conservative understanding thus blocked the road to reforming those aspects of production relations which hindered the full de-velopment of productive forces; his another concept argued for two parallel

63   Zongliang Huang et al., The History and Theory of the World Socialism, p.147.
64   Huiming Jin, Hailiang Gu et al., The History, Theory and Practice of Socialism, p.287.

world markets which caused the closed-door policy for socialist countries in the economic development; his planning concept contained mandatory plans and administrative directives. His socialist market concept aimed to replace "non-regulatedmarkets" with "regulated markets." His production concept had a flawed understanding which evaluated commodity producti- on as a transitory compromise given to non-pure socialist (less developed) economic elements of the socialist society, this concept strictly rejected means of production being marketed as commodities. His concept of buil- ding socialism advocated class struggles becoming more and acute in so- cialist society and stressed eliminating classes through revolutionary class struggles. His administration concept included a weaker civil society and government body serving people but opted for overly strengthened use of state power.[65]

Some scholars have argued the thought of Stalin in his late years (especi- ally his economic thoughts) was inherited from Lenin's "war communism" and also abandoned the thought of new economic policy. However, "under the historical conditions in the second half of 40ies and 50ies objectively it would be less logical for Stalin to agree to Lenin's early thoughts, and more logical to follow Lenin's later thoughts which were more feasible and mature. If we should evaluate Stalin's personal responsibility for the oc- curance of mistaken thoughts and practices we can comfortably say Stalin is primarily responsible for them but the incomplete ideas and obvious shortcomings of Lenin's theories should also bear some responsibilities. Therefore, we can say that the potential problem spheres of theoretical cog- nition which had remained unsolved and which were one important reason leading to the evolution of the Eastern Europe and the disintegration of the former Soviet Union (to capitalist direction) after decades had their deep roots in the beginning days of the October Revolution. The evil seed of negating socialist commodity economy was deeply carved in the cognition of socialism of that epoch. Through decades of germination and growth, this flawed cognition has finally poisoned the healthy body of the socia- list countries as a cancer cell. These lessons can offer valuable inspirations and important lessons for the Chinese people who are striving for socialist reforms."[66]

Some scholars have argued that Stalin's thought was quite distant from Marx's thought. Despite Stalin's socialist model can be associated with Marxism, especially Leninism, "Stalin neither can be par with the theorists as Marx and Engels who were the founders of scientific socialism, nor can be par with Lenin who had made great contributions to Marxism and who

504

---

65   Liu Jiang, Chongwen Xu, Several Issues of the Modern Socialism, pp.168-173, Chongqing: Chongqing Press, 1997.
66   Da Jun Zhang, The Political Economics of the Transition Period, p.23.

had demonstrated a significant innovative spirit." Many theories of Stalin contradicted Marxism-Leninism. "Stalin's understandings of Marxism and the scientific socialism were very superficial and narrow." "The tragedy of Stalin lies in that his understandings of the lofty ideals on socialism of Marx and Engels were vulgar, simplistic and distorted. He has unjustly lowered the standards of socialism."[67]

III. The new progress in the studies of Stalin's thought in the new century

Since the new century, China's reform and opening up has left back three decades and achieved abundant experiences and in the meantime our academic community has also surpassed the "Left" thoughts to some extent. The researchers can make independent scientific exploration in a free academic atmosphere thus accomplished deeper studies on Stalin's thought.

If we evaluate the recent research literature and publications on Stalin's thought by the academy in the new century, we can say that the studies on Stalin's thought have made new progress in the following aspects:

Firstly, Stalin's thought was evaluated from a comparative point of view

This is a salient feature of the studies on Stalin's thought of the academic community in the new century. In general, scholars have two main comparative perspectives: Firstly, they have compared Stalin's thought with related views of Lenin; secondly, they have compared Stalin's thought with related thought of Mao Zedong.

For this purpose we accept the assumption that besides the true or false in any proposition there is also a third value which is neither true nor false. In other words, instead of two we accept three truth-values which any statement may have, and thus we replace the current and intuitive true-false dichotomy by the trichotomy of true, false, and tertium.

Firstly, when comparing Stalin's thought and the related view of Lenin, some scholars believe that, although Lenin was once opposed to and belittled the "trichotomy" philosophy , but he later changed his attitude and used the "trichotomy" in a large number. Although Stalin did not openly, directly or clearly put forward the "trichotomy", he also used the "trichotomy" in some of his discourses. For a long time, people have always absolute the rule that "one is divided into two" and absoluted the rule of "dichotomy" and fundamentally denied the rule that "one is divided into three" and the "trichotomy" method used by Lenin and Stalin. Zongyu wrote: "This is

505

---

67   Zongyu Li et al., The Studies of Stalin Model, pp.455, 458, 460.

wrong. We should study better, inherit and use the "trichotomy" method of Lenin and Stalin.[68]

Some scholars compare the differences between Stalin's and Lenin's understandings of socialism. Over the years, people have often long believed that Stalin and Lenin were in accordance on the two questions: what is socialism and how to build socialism?. Stalin held high the banner of Leninism. In fact, there is a big difference between the understandings of socialism of Stalin and Lenin, which are reflected in the following areas: how to look at the "new economic policy"; how to look at the small-scale peasant economy; how to treat the non-public economic sectors of the economy and the capitalist economic sectors; how to treat the different forms in which we can realize public ownership of production; how to look at the planned economy; how to solve the problem of the accumulate construction (investment) funds for socialist industrialization; how to look at the party's role in the socialist countries and the issue of multi-party political system; how to look at Russia's experience in socialist construction. I can say socialism built under Stalinist model in Soviet Union has a lot of drawbacks, which have finally caused the collapse of the USSR.[69]

Some scholars believe that the theoretical understandings of Stalin and Lenin on the question of nations and colonies were different. Around the 2nd Congress of the Communist International, Lenin published the Draft Outline of National and Colonial Issues and so on, scientifically developed the theory of nation and colonies established by Marx. However, Stalin had deviant understandings of this theory and mixed it with a strong color of self-interest, seriously damaging the national feelings and interests of the colonial and semi-colonial people.[70]

Secondly, when comparing Stalin's thought and the view of Mao Zedongsome scholars believe that after the establishment of the socialist system, Stalin based himself on books in a dogmatic way, and believed that socialism brought harmony between politics and morality, the relations of production should perfectly suit to the nature of the productive forces, and proposed the theory that there will be no contradictions or conflicts in the socialist society. Mao Zedong put forward his own theory of contradictions in socialist society starting from the reality and the real facts, thereby deepening the awareness and understandings of the problem of the contradictions of socialist society.[71]

68   Zhengliang Lei, "The 'Trichotomy' of Stalin-Lenin", Academic Forum, p. 2 (2004).
69   Ling Yang et al., "The Differences of the Stalin's and Lenin's Understandings of Socialism,"Insights of Theory, p. 4 (2005).
70   Kan Wang, "The Differences of the Stalin's and Lenin's Understandings of the Theory of Races and Colony,"Leading Edge, p. 8 (2005).
71   Baohong Huang, "Mao Zedong's Surpassing and Development of Stalin's Theory of the Contradictions of the Socialism,"Editorial Board Journal of Tibet Institute for Nationalities, p. 3 (2002).

Some scholars compared the thought of Stalin and Mao Zedong in the aspect of socialist transformation of agriculture. Stalin and Mao Zedong have similarities and differences in the aspect of socialist transformation of agriculture. The similarities include: The purpose is to guide farmers into the socialist road, improve the lives of farmers and solve the problem of food needed in industrialization (cities); carrying out co-operation as the first step and then second step to apply mechanization and industrialization; adopting a gradual transition approach step by step, but their approach became impetuous in their late years. Both leaders have falsely exaggerated the different views and normal arguments within the party as the struggles of lines; and understanding socialism in a dogmatic way and being too eager to transit to socialism.

The differences between Stalin and Mao Zedong include: firstly, the agricultural co-operation in the Soviet Union has caused severe damages to the productive forces and productivity. While China's agricultural co-operation did not cause any serious damage to the productive forces. Two and three years after the reform, there was an important increase agriculture output. But during the agricultural reform, China imitated the agricultural system of the Soviet Union, which seriously hampered the development of China's agriculture. Secondly, the Soviet Union had spent 17 years on the agricultural reform. While China's agricultural reform had only took 4 years. Thirdly, there is a difference between the collective farms in the Soviet Union and the system of advanced collective farms in China.

507

Fourthly, Stalin emphasized that the collective farm movement should be based on the working class, allied by the poor peasants and middle peasants in order to eliminate the kulaks (rich peasants). And the policy proposed by Mao Zedong was to rely on poor peasants, ally poor peasants with the lower peasants in the new middle peasants (including the mid-middle peasants) and thirdly ally with the old middle peasants, and go against the rich part of middle peasants and rich peasant elements.[72]

In addition, there are also some scholars who compared Stalin's thought and the related thoughts of Deng Xiaoping, for example, some people think that the economic theory of Stalin and the economic theory of Deng Xiaoping differ significantly in five aspects: study objects, theoretical content, direction, standards of testing the effectiveness of economic policies and the practical effects of economic policies.[73] There are also some scholars who compared Stalin's thoughts with the related thoughts of the Western Marxists. For example, some scholars compared Stalin's ontology

---

72 Beigen Zhang, "The Comparison of the Reform Agricultural Socialism of Stalin and Mao Zedong,"Editorial Board of Journal of Yunan Political Institute, p. 5 (2005).
73 Nengguo Cao, "Comparison of Stalin's Economic Theory with Deng Xiaoping's Economic Theory,"Editorial Board of Journal of Huangang Technical Institute, p. 4 (2002).

of Marxist philosophy thought with Lukàcs' ontology of Marxist philosophy, regarding that Lukàcs' was in the beginning against Stalin but got back to Stalin finally. Yang Geng wrote: Lukàcs had stringently criticized the philosophical though of Stalin, and indeed he was different from Stalin while specifically elaborating Marxist philosophy and its thought of ontology, and even reached a new state concerning the ontology of social being. However, he happened to have the same view with Stalin when it came to the relationship respectively between historical materialism and dialectical materialism and between dialectical materialism and natural materialism; the opinions of them are strikingly similar–Lukàcs conceived the ontology of dialectical materialism as the theoretical basis of historical materialism in the end, and made the ontology of dialectical materialism natural ontology-based. In this way, natural ontology criticized by Marx went so far as to become the premise and foundation of the ontology of Marxist philosophy. Lukàcs transcended Stalin, but ultimately returned to Stalin. In this sense, both reached the same end. This is really a tragedy, a theoretical tragedy that seemingly should not happen but really happened to Lukàcs. From the angle of epistemology, the fundamental cause of this tragedy was that there was a shadow lingeringin his mind, namely the investigation method in line with "time priority", i.e. the method of reductionism. On that methodological basis, Lukàcs "conceives the order of priority" of the three major modes of being – inorganic nature, organic nature and human society – "in the irreversible process of world as the core of self-thinking on ontology."[74] From this it is not difficult for us to understand why Lukàcs finally set natural ontology as the premise and foundation for the ontology of social being.

Secondly, the studies on the national theory of Stalin

Some scholars believe that Stalin's writings and speeches on the issue of nation are very rich, thus received praises from Lenin, but in practice, Stalin and Lenin had severe differences on this issue. Stalin committed serious errors on the national question during his rule and caused far-reaching negative effects. These errors made the peoples of the different nations in the Soviet Union suspect the socialist system and were easily be used to ignite the fire of nationalism which easily could shake the foundation of united state (USSR) formed by many nations.[75]

Some scholars believe that Stalin's proposal of using four characteristics when defining nations in 1913 is his contribution. Here he made his definiton of nation and the characteristics of national groups basing his analysis

74   Geng Yang, "Surpass and Return: The Comparison of Stalin's and Lukàcs' Thoughts," *Studies of Philosophy*, p. 12 (2003).
75   Changbin Jiang, Fengrong Zuo, *Understanding Stalin* (Chengdu: Sichuan People's Publishing House, 2001), p. 227, 236.

on the material conditions of social existence. Later, Stalin in the article of "The National Question and Leninism" in 1929 discussed the definition of nation for the second time. We can say, this article has hindered the development of researches on the nation theory. The approach in that new article became the shackles of the development of scientific studies.

In the initial phase of Stalin's rule, his achievements on the issue of nation were widely recognized, such as: on the establishment of a series of autonomous republics and regions, the development of the economy in non-Russian regions and the promotion of culture and education in each nation. In the first 10 years of Stalin's rule significant achievements on the solution national issues were obtained, and thus can be classified as the period of ethnic regional autonomy. However, during the collectivization of agriculture in the early 1930s, there were famine, starvation and other events in many non-Russian ethnic areas; during the collectivisation movements during first half of 1930s, many non-Russian ethnic cadres and intellectuals encountered "ethnic cleansing" and repression, especially in the events of relocation or deportation of certain nations during World War II and the doctors of the Kremlin events in the early 1950s. All these occurances had seriously violated the interests of the non-Russian ethnic peoples.[76]

Some scholars related the effects Stalin's nation theory on the later disintegration of the Soviet Union. "Although Stalin put forward a lot of valuable thoughts on the national issue which helped Soviet Union to the deal with the national issues in the Soviet Union. However, in dealing with the national issue, Stalin had some obvious theoretical limitations and made many mistakes when dealing with certain specific national issues: Great Russian nationalism was deeply rooted in his mind which caused him partialitly, thus he advocated the highly centralized unitary system of the joint organization way of the socialist Soviet state and rejected federalism which finally led to the deformation of federalism. He applied the theory of class struggle into the dealing with the ethnic issues, namely confused the contradictions among classes and contradictions among nations. He followed a baseless optimistic approach on the national issue and ignored the long-term character and complexity of the national issues. I think, all these were the seeds of the disintegration of the Soviet Union.[77]

Some scholars have also analyzed the reasons for the mistakes Stalin made on the national issue, they have argued that it is not enough to attribute the mistakes to "environmental" or "psychological" factors when analyzing Stalin's Great Russian sentiments. In fact, Stalin's mistakes on

76 Xinzhi Hua, Dongen Chen, Stalin and the Issue of Races, pp.98, 123, 144, 145, Beijing: The Central University of Nationalities, 2002.
77 Xiancong Li, "The Impact of the Stalin's Faults of the Racial Issue on the Disintegration of the Soviet," Editorial Board of Journal of Nanjing Medical University, p. 1 (2004).

the national issue were caused by many other factors: 1) the general social environment of Russia as the main factor and the precipitated and profound cultural atmosphere of the Great Russia; 2) Stalin's own ethnic identity and the practical needs of getting the support of the Russian population; the complex situation of the domestic ethnic relations and the ethnic issues, the long-term siege by imperialism and its impacts on the domestic ethnic relations in the Soviet Union; Stalin's personal level of cognition awareness and his specific personality. Stalin, theoretically confused the laws of the development of the society and the development of ethnic groups; he exaggerated the "mindset" of "class analysis" when handling national issues and he always wanted to relate the issue of "capitalist" restoration or the risk of strengthening of capitalism with national issues, because Soviet Union was surrounded by capitalism, and so on. I think one-sided analysis will not be helpful for the evaluation of the thoughts and policies of Stalin.[78]

Thirdly, Stalin's thought on the New Economic Policy.

Some scholars believe that the debate on the New Economic Policy of the Soviet Union after the death of Lenin is the debate on the ways of socialist construction and its prospects of socialist development. After the death of Lenin this discussion was made from a higher level point of view. Lenin's New Economic Policy was the development plan for a country whose majority of the population was small-scale farmers and their economic sector was dominant and a country with a severely damaged economy by the wars, Lenin, thus aimed to form an indirect path to transit to the socialist society. There were basically three explanations about the New Economic Policy within the party in the Soviet Union. Ultimately, finally the explanation of Stalin faction won. Agriculture in the Soviet Union was sokuldu entered to a period of overall collectivization and the New Economic Policy totally left the stage of history. As to why the route advocated by the faction of Stalin could win and why the New Economic Policy was abolished, these were closely related with the situation of the leaders' minds, the organizational principles dominant in the party, the changes in the composition of the party and the impact of Stalin himself at that time.[79]

Some scholars believe the reasons why Stalin did not insist to stick to the New Economic Policy were: Stalin did not take the New Economic Policy as the only way for Russia with its economic and cultural backwardness to transit and build socialism, but considered it a kind of expedient strategy; thus he theoretically refused to admit that Lenin's socialist thought in his late years was one of the important parts and contents

510

78   Xiaomin Wang, "The Root of Stalin's Faults of the National Issue,"Editorial Board of Journal of Henan Normal University, p. 5 (2001).
79   Zhichao Lu, Zhengquan Wang, Stalin and Socialism—the Analysis of the First Socialist Model of the World, pp.22, 148,153, Beijing: Social Sciences Academic Press, 2002.

of Leninism; Stalin practically distorted Lenin's thoughts developed by Lenin in his late years of the New Economic Policy in accordance with his own wishes.[80]

Some scholars believe that the New Economic Policy not only lacked the self-regulating capacity and inability to deal with unexpected social crises, but also could not resist the political demands which advocated the stopping of the implementation of the New Economic Policy. When Stalin initiated the "revolution from above", and decided to stop the implementation of New Economic Policy, Bukharin and others who advocated continuing the implementation of the New Economic Policy could not do anything. The abolishment of the New Economic Policy was a successfully completed innovation in the system dominated by the ruling party and the central government , it was a series of bold reforms by the Stalin-led CPSU (Bolshevik) Central and created the Stalinist Model. The whole process where the Stalinist Model replaced the New Economic Policy fully demonstrated the powerful energy of the ruling party and the central government when implementing the innovation of the NEP system, of course innovation was implemented forcedly.[81]

Fourthly, the inspirations of Stalin's thought on building socialism with the Chinese characteristics in the new century.

Some scholars believe that Stalin in building socialism have both positive and negative experiences which can inspire us in the socialist construction of the 21st century: firstly, the Soviet Union when Stalin was in power adhered to the socialist construction with no vacillation, but the building of socialism led by him was conducted in a rush and with a low standard.

The nature of long-term character of socialist construction was ignored and it was not right to claim that socialism was already built in a single country, the Soviet Union. Socialism to be built in the 21st century should have higher standards and should be superior to capitalism. Secondly, the Soviet Union when Stalin was in power adhered to the socialist industrialization and modernization with no vacillation, but had absolute the system of planned economy, the strategy of the priority of the development of the heavy industry and the extensive development strategy that were formed during this special path for industrialization and which was implemented forcefully in the period of World War II, had led to the rigid model of economic construction in the Soviet Union.

---

80   Rong Chen, "Why the "New Economic Policy" didn't Go Far?", Editorial Board of Journal of Central Party School of Yunnan Province, p. 2 (2002).
81   Zongwu Shen, Modern Reflex of the Stalinist Model, pp.65, 66, 67, Kunming: Nunnan People's Publishing House, 2004.

Building socialism in the 21st century in the countries with backward economy and backward culture requires flexible use of both planned and also market-based methods of the economic development to make the economic system dynamic and to achieve industrialization and modernization soonest possible. Thirdly, Stalin adhered to the Communist Party's leadership and the dictatorship of the proletariat with no vacillation. However, the over-concentration of the power, the personal authotorian leadership style of various leaders in the party. Also the failure of carrying out democracy and the damaging the law system gave harm to the image of socialism. The construction of socialism in the 21st century should adhere to the Communist Party's leadership and the proletariat with no vacillation, and adhere to the unity in the party, strengthen the publicity for people's democracy and the strictly abide with the law system at the same time, in order to have combined development of democracy with the development of socialism.[82]

Some scholars have summed up the lessons learned from the Stalinist Model, as follows: "the first is we should correctly grasp the mutually impacting relationship between politics and economy and correctly handle the relationship between political reform and economic reform; the second is that in socialism building the governments should correctly handle the relationship between centralization and decentralization of their own domestic power; the third is the government should emphasize ruling the country with erdem virtue while on the other side paying attention to rule the country with law; the forth is we should correctly grasp and handle the relationship between socialism and capitalism; the fifth is we should correctly handle the relationship between the reform of the current system and the consolidation of the system; the sixth is we should continuously strengthen and improve the leadership of the party during the historical process of reform and opening up; the seventh is we should have a full understanding of the long-term character, complexity and difficulties in the reform process of the socialism; the eighth is we should correctly handle the relationship between equity and efficiency in the entire process of socialist reforms.[83]

Some scholars believe that Stalin, in the practice of leading the socialist construction of the Soviet Union, has left us both successful lessons and on the other side he left us the closed and rigid socialist model due to his dogmatic understandings of Marxism. The inspirations from Stalin's model to us are: firstly, we should combine the basic principles of Marxism with the realistic facts of the country and the characteristics of the times when

---

82   Youzhong Cheng, The Construction of Socialism in the 21st Century still Needs the Historic Experience of the "Stalinist Model," Studies of Socialism, p. 5 (2000).
83   Jianjun Liu, "How to Understand Reform of Socialism," Teaching and Research, p. 10 (2001).

developing socialist construction secondly, we should take reform practices as the driving force of social development and take reform practices as the means to consolidate and improve the relationship between socialism and capitalism through adhering to the road to reform; thirdly, we should strengthen and improve the leadership of the Communist Party and to build the Communist Party as the strong core of the socialist cause; fourthly, we should correctly understand and deal with the relationship between socialism and capitalism and carry out the opening-up on the basis of adhering to independence, and self-reliance in order to absorb and learn from all the results of civilization created by the human society.[84]

Some scholars believe that the issue of nation is a global problem. The proper handling of it will enhance the cohesion of the nation-state; the improper handling of it will cause the disintegration of the nation and state. The errors in Stalin's national theory and policy have led to a series of ethnic problems which constituted as the fuse of the disintegration of the Soviet Union. Therefore, the ruling party and government should attach great importance to the national issue; continuously adjust the ethnic policies and peacefully resolve the ethnic conflicts. This is an important lesson we should carefully learn from Stalin's national theory and policy.[85]

Stalin in *Economic Problems of Socialism in the USSR* enunciated the basic economic law of capitalism as follows: "Most appropriate to the concept of a basic economic law of capitalism is the law of surplus value, the law of the origin and growth of capitalist profit. It really does determine the basic features of capitalist production. But the law of surplus value is too general a law; it does not cover the highest rate of profit, the securing of which is a condition for the development of monopoly capitalism. In order to fill this hiatus, the law of surplus value must be made more concrete and developed further in adaptation to the conditions of monopoly capitalism, at the same time bearing in mind that monopoly capitalism demands not any sort of profit, but precisely the maximum profit. That will be the basic economic law of modern capitalism."

Stalin, in denouncing Yaroshenko's erroneous view, said: "When speaking of the basic economic law of some particular social formation, the presumption usually is that the latter cannot have several basic economic laws, that it can have only some one basic economic law, which precisely for that reason is basic law. Otherwise we should have several basic economic laws for each social formation, which would be contrary to the very concept of a basic law. But Comrade Yaroshenko does not agree with this

---

84 Yihong Sun, "Inspiration of the Defects of the Stalinist Model," Jiangxi Social Proceedings, p. 5 (2002).
85 Ling Yang, "Malposition of Stalinist Theory and Measures of Race," Modern World and Socialism, p. 2 (2005).

idea. He thinks that it is possible to have not one, but several basic economic laws of socialism. It is incredible ..."[86] Is it creating the confusion that a particular social formation can have more than one basic economic law or a clear rebuttal of that erroneous concept? These 'theorists', the writers of the article in question, would do well to improve and perfect their study of Stalin before coming out in the open to denounce him.

According to the formulation of the latest Programme of the Communist Party of the Soviet Union, the basic economic law of socialism is "the aim of socialism."

Let us examine what Stalin had said about the brake on productive forces. And the honest way of doing it is to present his view on it. "When Marxists speak of the retarding role of the relations of production, it is not all relations of production they have in mind, but only the old relations of production, which no longer conform to the growth of the productive forces and, consequently, retard their development. But, as we know, besides the old, there are also new relations of production which supersede the old. Can it be said that the role of the new relations of production is that of a brake on the productive forces? No, it cannot. On the contrary, the new relations of production are the chief and decisive force, the one which in fact determines the further and, moreover, powerful development of the productive forces, and without which the latter would be doomed to stagnation, as is the case today in the capitalist countries... Of course, new relations of production cannot, and do not, remain new for ever, they begin to grow old and to run counter to the further development of the productive forces; they begin to lose their role of principal mainspring of the productive forces, and become a brake on them. At this point, in place of these production relations which have become antiquated, new production relations appear whose role it is to be the principal mainspring spurring the further development of the productive forces. This peculiar development of the relations of production from the role of a brake on the productive forces to that of the principal mainspring impelling them forward, and from the role of principal mainspring to that of brake on the productive forces constitutes one of the chief elements of the Marxist materialist dialectics."[87]

Stalin concluded: "Of course, our present relations of production are in a period when they fully conform to the growth of the productive forces and help to advance them at seven-league strides. But it would be wrong to rest easy at that and to think that there are no contradictions between our productive forces and the relations of production. There certainly are, and will be contradictions, seeing that the development of the relations of production lags, and will lag behind the development of productive forces. Given

86 Economic Problems of Socialism in the USSR, p. 82.
87 Ibid, pp. 68-70.

a correct policy on the part of the directing organs, these contradictions cannot grow into antagonisms, and there is no chance of matters coming to a conflict between the relations of production and productive forces of society.

"The task of the directing bodies is therefore promptly to discern incipient contradictions, and to take timely measures to resolve them by adapting the relations of production to the growth of the productive forces. This, above all, concerns such economic factors as group, or collective-farm property and commodity circulation. At present, of course, these factors are being successfully utilized by us for the promotion of the socialist economy, and they are of undeniable benefit to our society. It is undeniable, too, that they will be of benefit also in the near future. But it will be unpardonable blindness not to see at the same time that these factors are already beginning to hamper the powerful development of our productive forces, since they create obstacles to the full extension of government planning to the whole of national economy, especially agriculture."[88]

But so long as this in not the case, so long as the two basic production sectors remain, commodity production and commodity circulation must remain in force, as a necessary and very useful element in our system of national economy.... Consequently, our commodity production is not of the ordinary type, but is a special kind of commodity production... which together with its money economy is designed to serve the development and consolidation of socialist production."[89]

515

Marx said: "In production men not only act on nature but also on one another. They produce only by co-operating in a certain way and mutually exchanging their activities. In order to produce, they enter into definite connections and relations with one another and only within these social connections and relations does their action on nature, does production take place."[90]

The laws of economic development—whether in the period of capitalism or in the period of socialism—are independent of the will of man, who "may discover these laws, get to know them and, relying upon them, utilize them in the interests of society, impart a different direction to the destructive action, and allow fuller scope to other laws that are forcing their ways to the forefront; but he cannot destroy them or create new economic laws". (Economic Problems of Socialism in the USSR).

---

88   Ibid., pp. 75-76.
89   Economic Problems of Socialism in the USSR, pp. 20-21.
90   Marx and Engels, Vol.5, p.429.

Stalin in his *Economic Problems of Socialism in the USSR* concluded: "It is evident that, after the world market has split and the sphere of exploitation of the world's resources by the major capitalist countries (USA, Britain, and France) has begun to contract, the cyclical character of the development of capitalism—expansion and contraction of production—must continue to operate. However, expansion of production in these countries will proceed on a narrower basis, since the volume of production in these countries will diminish."[91]

516

---

91 Economic Problems of Socialism in the USSR,p. 63.

Postscript

A Historical and Realistic Study on Stalin's Socialism Thought is the final result of the National Social Science Fund Project The Theoretical and Practical Study of Stalin on the Socialist Construction (Grant No. 96AKS 006). The participants of this research are mainly from the Marxism School, attached to China Renmin University.

As the person in charge of the research project The Theoretical and Practical Study of Stalin on the Socialist Construction and the main editor of *A Historical and Realistic Study on Stalin's Socialism Thought*, I proposed the theme and the basic structure of the whole book. With the co-operation of the scholars in the group, we completed the result of the project in the early 2005. The result of this project got through all the good results in the expert review organized by Management Office of the National Social Science Fund Project. Meanwhile, the experts also gave some suggestions for revisions. The suggestions of revisions proposed by the experts were widely absorbed in the final version of the manuscript of the book. Here, I would like to express my sincere thanks to all the experts.

The authors of each chapter of the book are:

Foreword: Gu Hailiang (Professor, Wuhan University);

Chapter One: Gu Hailiang and Zheng Jiwei
(Vice Professor, China Renmin University);

Chapter Six and Appendix Two: Zheng Jiwei;

Chapter Two and Ten: Zhang Xin
(Professor, China Renmin University)

Chapter Three and Twelve:Zhang Leisheng
(Professor, China Renmin University)

Chapter Four and Five: Fang Zhulan
(Professor, China Renmin University)

Chapter Seven, Eight and Nine: Qin Xuan
(Professor, China Renmin University)

Chapter Eleven: Liu Jianjun (Professor, China Renmin University)

Chapter Thirteen and Appendix One: Huang Jifeng
(Professor, China Renmin University)

Zhang Shaoyong collected part of the data for Chapter Seven, Eight and Nine of this book and Ma Qinglin attended parts of addition and amendment of Chapter Eleven of this book.

Wei Wei (PhD, School of Marxism, China Renmin University) revised the Introduction of this book.

I uniformly revised and finalized the all the manuscripts of this book.

This book was funded by the Foundation Fund of Beijing Social Science Theoretical Writings, received the contributions of Tian Shuxiang and other editors of China Renmin University Press. I would like to give my sincere thanks to them.

The study the socialist thought of Stalin is a quite broad and controversial issue. What we have made in this book can only be regarded as a preliminary study. I sincerely hope that the readers can indicate and criticize the shortcomings of this book.

Gu Hailiang

December 1, 2008